Lecture Notes of the Institute for Computer Sciences, Social Informatics and Telecommunications Engineering 683

The LNICST series publishes ICST's conferences, symposia and workshops.

LNICST reports state-of-the-art results in areas related to the scope of the Institute.

The type of material published includes

- Proceedings (published in time for the respective event)
- Other edited monographs (such as project reports or invited volumes)

LNICST topics span the following areas:

- General Computer Science
- E-Economy
- E-Medicine
- Knowledge Management
- Multimedia
- Operations, Management and Policy
- Social Informatics
- Systems

Lei Zhang · Kim-Kwang Raymond Choo
Editors

Mobile and Ubiquitous Systems

Computing, Networking and Services

22nd EAI International Conference, MobiQuitous 2025
Shanghai, China, November 7–9, 2025
Proceedings, Part I

Springer

Editors
Lei Zhang
East China Normal University
Shanghai, China

Kim-Kwang Raymond Choo
University of Texas at San Antonio
San Antonio, TX, USA

ISSN 1867-8211 ISSN 1867-822X (electronic)
Lecture Notes of the Institute for Computer Sciences, Social Informatics
and Telecommunications Engineering
ISBN 978-3-032-22499-6 ISBN 978-3-032-22500-9 (eBook)
https://doi.org/10.1007/978-3-032-22500-9

This Springer imprint is published by the registered company Springer Nature Switzerland AG
The registered company address is: Gewerbestrasse 11, 6330 Cham, Switzerland

Preface

We are delighted to present the proceedings of the 22nd European Alliance for Innovation (EAI) International Conference on Mobile and Ubiquitous Systems (MobiQuitous 2025). Hosted by East China Normal University, China, the conference was held from November 7–9, 2025. The conference brought together researchers, developers, and practitioners from around the world who advance research and development in security, efficiency, architectures, and algorithms within intelligent systems and information technologies. The theme of MobiQuitous 2025 was "Mobile and Ubiquitous Systems: Computing, Networking and Services."

The technical program of MobiQuitous 2025 featured 50 full papers and 1 poster paper. The conference tracks were organized into four sessions: Session 1 – Federated Learning and Large Language Models; Session 2 – Secure, Reliable, and Efficient Intelligent Systems; Session 3 – Architectures and Algorithms for IoT; and Session 4 – Cryptographic Schemes. These papers were selected from 144 submissions through a rigorous double-blind review process, with each paper receiving at least three reviews. In addition to high-quality technical paper presentations, the program included two keynote speeches, which were delivered by Dusit Niyato from Nanyang Technological University and Jungong Han from Tsinghua University.

The success of this conference would not have been possible without the coordination and support of the steering committee chairs—Tao Gu, Takahiro Hara, and Max Mühlhäuser. We sincerely appreciate their continuous guidance and encouragement. It has also been a great pleasure to work with an outstanding organizing committee whose dedicated efforts were instrumental in planning and supporting the conference. Special thanks go to the General Chairs, Weizhi Meng and Josep Domingo-Ferrer, who successfully guided the conference organization. Our appreciation also goes to Workshop Chairs: Wenjuan Li and Wei-Yang Chiu; Publicity Chairs: Ningjing Wan, Rishikesh Sahay, and Meikang Qiu; Publication Chair: Liantao Wu; and Web Chair: Xinyu Meng. Also thanks to all Program Committee Members, who helped the peer-review process and contributed to a high-quality technical program. We are also grateful to conference manager Natasha Onofrei for her valuable support, as well as to all authors who submitted their work to MobiQuitous 2025.

We firmly believe that the MobiQuitous conference provides an excellent forum for researchers, developers, and practitioners to discuss all aspects of science and technology related to security, efficiency, architectures, and algorithms in intelligent systems and information technologies. We also look forward to future editions of MobiQuitous being as successful and inspiring as the contributions collected in this volume.

Lei Zhang
Kim-Kwang Raymond Choo

Organization

Steering Committee

Tao Gu	Macquarie University, Australia
Takahiro Hara	Osaka University, Japan
Max Mühlhäuser	Technical University of Darmstadt, Germany

Organizing Committee

General Chair

Weizhi Meng	Lancaster University, UK

General Co-chair

Josep Domingo-Ferrer	University of Rovira i Virgili, Spain

TPC Chairs and Co-chairs

Lei Zhang	East China Normal University, China
Kim-Kwang Raymond Choo	University of Texas at San Antonio, USA

Sponsorship and Exhibit Chair

Xiang Zhou	East China Normal University, China

Local Chair

Dehui Du	East China Normal University, China

Workshops Chairs

Wei-Yang Chiu	Technical University of Denmark, Denmark
Wenjuan Li	Education University of Hong Kong, China

Publicity and Social Media Chairs

Ningjing Wan	East China Normal University, China
Rishikesh Sahay	University of Illinois Springfield, USA
Meikang Qiu	Augusta University, USA

Publications Chair

Liantao Wu	East China Normal University, China

Web Chair

Xinyu Meng	Shanghai Maritime University, China

Technical Program Committee

Abhishek Kumar	University of Oulu, Finland
Akif Quddus Khan	OsloMet, Norway
Arda Goknil	SINTEF, Norway
Bo Qin	Renmin University of China, China
Branislav Kusy	CSIRO Data61, Australia
Brent Lagesse	University of Washington at Bothell, USA
Chao Qian	University of Duisburg-Essen, Germany
Chunhua Su	University of Aizu, Japan
Cornelia Győrödi	University of Oradea, Romania
Cristian Borcea	New Jersey Institute of Technology, USA
Dimitris Kavallieros	Informatics and Telematics Institute, Greece
Fusang Zhang	Institute of Software, Chinese Academy of Sciences, China
Gyu Myoung Lee	Liverpool John Moores University, UK
Hao Wang	Shandong Normal University, China
Hu Xiong	University of Electronic Science and Technology of China, China
Hua Deng	Changsha University of Science & Technology, China
Huaqun Wang	Nanjing University of Posts and Telecommunications, China
Huber Flores	University of Tartu, Estonia
Ivan Miguel Pires	Instituto de Telecomunicações/University of Aveiro, Portugal
Jianchang Lai	Southeast University, China

Jingao Xu	University of Hong Kong, China
Jinguang Han	Southeast University, China
Josep Domingo-Ferrer	Universitat Rovira i Virgili, Spain
Jun Shao	East China University of Science and Technology, China
Kai Zhang	Shanghai University of Electric Power, China
Kim-Kwang Raymond Choo	University of Texas at San Antonio, USA
Kun He	Wuhan University, China
Lei Yang	Hong Kong Polytechnic University, China
Lei Zhang	East China Normal University, China
Liantao Wu	East China Normal University, China
Lifei Wei	Shanghai Maritime University, China
Nan Jiang	Harbin Institute of Technology (Shenzhen), China
Nuno Garcia	Universidade da Beira Interior, Portugal
Oladayo Bello	New Mexico State University, USA
Peter Zdankin	University of Duisburg-Essen, Germany
Qiong Huang	South China Agricultural University, China
Rongmao Chen	National University of Defense Technology, China
Rui Zhang	Southwestern University of Finance and Economics, China
Sanjay Madria	Missouri University of Science and Technology, USA
Shihang Lu	Southern University of Science and Technology, China
Shuangyang Li	Technische Universität Berlin, Germany
Tao Chen	University of Pittsburgh, USA
Weizhi Meng	Lancaster University, UK
Xinyu Li	Southeast University, China
Xiujin Shi	Donghua University, China
Ye Dong	National University of Singapore, Singapore

Contents

Federated Learning and Large Language Models

Tiny Models, Tough Limits: Benchmarking and Optimizing Small Language Models for Edge Deployment

Alex Pissinou Makki[1(✉)], Luis Lago Enamorado[2], Claudia Saleem[2], Mostafa Elshabasy[3], and Niki Pissinou[2]

[1] Duke University, Durham, NC, USA
alexpissinoumakki@berkeley.edu
[2] Florida International University, Miami, FL, USA
[3] The George Washington University, Washington, DC, USA

Abstract. Emerging applications—disaster response drones, in-vehicle assistants, and field medical devices—require on-device language intelligence when cloud links are unreliable, privacy is mandatory, and sub-second latency is nonnegotiable. We benchmark seven SLMs (DistilBERT, MobileBERT, ALBERT, MiniLM, Phi-3 Mini, MobileLLaMA and TinyLLaMA) across four mission-aligned use cases (Watchlist Screening, Threat Detection, Document Triage, Multilingual Routing) on five border-relevant datasets (e.g., GTD, FLORES-200). Under controlled edge-like constraints (mobile-class CPU, 1–8 GB shared memory, intermittent networking), we report task quality (accuracy/F1 or ROUGE), batch-1 inference latency, and peak memory, and we introduce a reproducible, edge-budgeted evaluation protocol for security-critical scenarios. We also outline a path to multimodal edge workloads by pairing compact audio/vision encoders with SLM back ends.

Keywords: Small Language Models · Edge AI · On-Device Inference · Quantization · Low-Latency NLP · Security-Critical NLP

1 Introduction

Today, border security operates on what may be called *ten-watt frontier*. At 07:42 on an otherwise ordinary weekday, a lone officer, equipped with nothing more than a battery-powered tablet, must decide within milliseconds whether a weather-worn passport is counterfeit, reassure travelers whose language she does not share, and flag a cargo manifest that may conceal contraband. Scaled across the ∼1.08 million passengers and pedestrians processed on a typical day [38], each additional second inflates queues that already snake across checkpoint tarmac; every false positive strands legitimate travelers, while every false negative endangers lives. The computing platforms entrusted with such triage: fanless

C. Saleem and M. Elshabasy—Supported by NSF grant CNS-2244283.

L. Zhang and K.-K. R. Choo (Eds.): MobiQuitous 2025, LNICST 683, pp. 3–22, 2026.
https://doi.org/10.1007/978-3-032-22500-9_1

kiosks in pre-clearance halls, compact drones patrolling borderlands, and Raspberry Pi-class devices attached to solar panels must operate under single-digit power budgets, 4–6 GB of shared LPDDR4X, intermittent or classified-data-restricted connectivity, and privacy regimes that forbid the routing of raw documents to the cloud. In these circumstances, the celebrated 70 billion-parameter language models that dominate academic leaderboards are a nonstarter: even a 77 billion-parameter network has $\geq$ 150 GB of FP16 weights alone, far beyond edge budgets, with activations adding further overhead, and typically exceeds desktop-GPU power envelopes.

Transformer foundation models such as GPT-3 (175B), PaLM (540B), and LLaMA 2 (7–70B) achieve state-of-the-art language understanding, reasoning, and code synthesis, with performance that follows empirical scaling laws in model size, data, and compute [6,9,21,37]. Those same regimes, however, assume datacenter-class resources: FP16 weights alone for 70–540B models require on the order of 140–1,080 GB, with hundreds of GB/s of memory bandwidth and hundreds of watts of power—far beyond edge budgets. *Small language models* (SLMs) therefore offer a pragmatic path: encoder-only models (e.g., DistilBERT/MobileBERT/MiniLM) in the ~10–70M range and compact decoder models in the ~1–4B range can be adapted to edge constraints by combining structured pruning, knowledge distillation, parameter-efficient fine-tuning (LoRA/QLoRA), and post-training INT8/INT4 quantization. Recent reports show that compact models—e.g., TinyLLaMA (~1–1.5B), Phi-3 Mini (~3–4B), Gemma 1.1B, and DistilBERT-class encoders, approach larger baselines on standard NLP benchmarks while fitting within a few hundred MiB to a couple of GiB and sustaining batch-1, low-latency inference [7,11,32,35]. However, results obtained in the lab rarely reveal whether these gains persist under multilingual OCR noise from passport scans, the bandwidth/latency constraints of retrieval-augmented generation (RAG), or thermal throttling on ARM SoCs operating in direct sunlight.

Prior mobile-AI efforts primarily target generic benchmarks, smartphone SoCs, or cloud-assisted fallback designs [23,26,27,31,39]. To our knowledge, none jointly evaluates on-device retrieval-augmented generation (RAG), multilingual OCR corruption, cold-start I/O costs, and strict 4–8 GB memory ceilings in a security-critical setting. Likewise, existing work does not provide an open, reproducible test suite that runs end-to-end on commodity edge boards; open suites focus on TinyML or edge-LLM inference in isolation rather than this combined workload [4,29,47].

Prior evaluations emphasize accuracy on generic NLP benchmarks and often assume smartphone SoCs or cloud fallback, with limited attention to edge-realistic constraints such as batch-1 latency, tight memory ceilings, and energy per query [3,18,23,25,28]. Reproducible protocols that report all four axes—*quality, latency, memory, and energy*—under a consistent edge budget remain scarce. The key trade-offs across compression and acceleration approaches are summarized in Table 1.

To bridge this gap, we present a reproducible, edge-budgeted evaluation of state-of-the-art small language models (SLMs) for border-security decision support. We distill four mission-driven case studies—passport/visa verification, threat detection, document triage, and multilingual routing—from practitioner interviews and implement them with public or synthetic datasets that mirror field inputs. Seven SLMs are LoRA-tuned and INT4-quantized, then cross-compiled for Raspberry Pi 5 and Jetson Orin Nano targets with 4–8 GB RAM budgets. Our experiments report task quality (F1, BLEU, ROUGE/*perplexity* as appropriate), cold-start latency, and peak resident set size; per-query energy is estimated from measured latency combined with device-class power envelopes (no on-device sensors).

Before outlining our contributions, we summarize the compression and adaptation methods that enable on-device SLMs and the trade-offs they entail. Recent SLM progress is driven by compression and efficiency methods: knowledge distillation and parameter sharing reduce parameters and FLOPs; pruning removes redundant heads/weights; and post-training quantization (INT8/INT4) lowers memory and speeds inference. Adapter-based tuning (LoRA/QLoRA) enables task adaptation with small trainable deltas, and ONNX runtimes provide portable, kernel-optimized execution. Each method trades model quality against deployability: extreme sparsity often fails to accelerate on real hardware; aggressive low-bit formats can degrade robustness; and some approaches depend on specialized kernels or costly retraining. Motivated by these constraints and opportunities, our work contributes as follows:

- A reproducible, edge-budgeted protocol that reports quality, latency, memory, and energy under batch-1 constraints;
- A four-use-case evaluation with public/synthetic datasets reflecting border-relevant inputs;
- A comparison of LoRA-tuned, INT4-quantized SLMs on Raspberry Pi 5 and Jetson Orin Nano targets;
- Release of EdgeTinyBench (datasets, scripts, and kernels) to enable replication and extension.

The remainder of this paper is organized as follows. Section 2 reviews related work. Section 3 details our methodology, model selection, and ONNX-centric optimization pipeline. Section 4 describes the datasets and tasks. Section 5 presents the experimental setup and metrics. Section 6 presents results and analysis, with detailed findings for UC-1 (Watchlist Screening), UC-2 (Threat Detection), and UC-3 (Document Triage); UC-4 (Multilingual Routing) is summarized, with full charts provided in the extended version.

2 Related Work

Small language models (SLMs) for edge devices trace their origins to early knowledge distillation efforts. Distillation is a process where a large teacher model transfers its knowledge to a compact student model. DistilBERT demonstrated that matching teacher logs and internal representations, combined with a masked language modeling objective, could shrink BERT by 40% while losing under 3% in GLUE - although it still requires days of multi-GPU pretraining and offers limited out-of-domain robustness. TinyBERT built on this by introducing layer-wise and embedding-level distillation with data augmentation, yielding roughly 4 × compression at a 1.5% accuracy penalty. However, its multistage pipeline adds substantial engineering overhead and complicates reproducibility. Subsequent extensions, DistilRoBERTa and DistilGPT2, confirmed the generality of distillation across architectures but inherited the exact high compute and dataset curation costs, making pure distillation pipelines ill-suited for rapid iteration on niche, safety-critical edge tasks.

The parameter-sharing paradigm, while a powerful axis of compression, is not without its trade-offs. ALBERT, for instance, factored large embeddings into low-rank matrices and tied weights across layers, achieving a nearly tenfold reduction in memory while retaining the performance of the BERT base. MiniLM, on the other hand, distilled attention distributions rather than logits, allowing a six-layer student to capture much of the teacher's representational power with minimal architectural changes. However, when pushed below 100 M parameters, standard in edge settings, the rigid sharing schemes in ALBERT and MiniLM begin to bottleneck representational capacity, leading to sharp drops on specialized tasks unless fine-tuned with extensive data. These trade-offs highlight the challenges in achieving high compression without sacrificing performance.

Structured and unstructured pruning methods offer a promising avenue for post hoc removal of redundant weights and attention heads. Michel et al. demonstrated that more than 80% of Transformer heads can be pruned with negligible impact on the GLUE benchmark. Movement pruning further learns which weights to remove by gradient-based criteria, reaching over 90% sparsity at less than 1% performance loss. Although unstructured sparsity may not always translate to real-world speedups on commodity CPUs or NPUs, as irregular memory accesses often thwart hardware optimizations, block-sparse pruning shows potential in alleviating these issues on GPUs. The future of hardware optimization for mobile NPUs and embedded accelerators looks hopeful, thanks to advances in pruning methods. The most significant trade-offs between these compression and acceleration approaches are distilled in Table 1.

Quantization has become the most widely adopted strategy for reducing both the memory footprint and the arithmetic intensity of SLM once distillation and pruning have been applied. Quantization-aware training (QAT) keeps low-precision operators in the forward pass so that gradient updates compensate for rounding error; Q8BERT showed that an 8 bit BERT can match full-precision accuracy, but at roughly double the training cost and with a custom kernel stack that is hard to replicate across NPUs [45]. Post-training quantization (PTQ) avoids retraining by solving a local optimization problem for each weight block; GPTQ preserves generative coherence at 4 bits after only a few hours of calibration on a single GPU [15]. SmoothQuant (a 4-/8-bit PTQ hybrid) and BitRound (2-bit activations with 4-bit weights) push further, yet both rely on custom operators that are still absent from most edge compilers [42]. More recently, QLoRA demonstrated that adapter-based fine tuning can coexist with 4-bit base weights, enabling complete task adaptation on a single 48 GB GPU [11]; however, its efficacy has only been validated on 65 B-parameter LLMs rather than sub-1 B SLMs, and the method assumes that uniform 4-bit quantization is optimal for every layer, an assumption that breaks down in tiny models where the information density per layer varies sharply.

Table 1. High-level comparison of compression/acceleration themes for SLMs on edge devices.

Theme	Representative Methods (Year)	Typical Footprint	Primary Gains	Key Limitation
Distillation	DistilBERT (2019); TinyBERT (2020)	60–150M params	Size ↓2–4×; ≈97% accuracy	High pre-training cost; domain-shift sensitivity
Param. sharing	ALBERT (2020); MiniLM (2020)	30–80M params	Params ↓10×; FLOPs ↓3×	Rigid sharing hurts sub-100M models
Pruning	Head Pruning (2019); Movement (2021)	80–300M params	Params ↓ up to 90%	Sparse patterns rarely accelerate edge hardware
Quantization	PTQ 8/4-bit (2018–23); GPTQ (2023)	50–200M params	Memory ↓2–8×; < 1% accuracy loss	Calibration; custom low-bit kernels
Efficient arch.	Linformer (2020); Performer (2021)	50–500M params	Attention complexity $O(n)$	Stability/long-context trade-offs
Dynamic inference	DeeBERT (2020); TR-BERT (2021)	Adaptive	Avg. compute ↓30–60%	Unpredictable worst-case latency
MoE/Modular	Switch (2021); Modular-Prompt (2023)	100–1000M params	Quality ↑; multi-task flexibility	Expert storage + routing complexity
Benchmarking	GLUE/SuperGLUE (2018–19); MLPerf-Tiny (2023)	—	Standard accuracy yardsticks	No latency/energy protocols

A complementary line of work redesigns the Transformer architecture itself to lower asymptotic or constant factor costs. Linformer projects the sequence length dimension into a fixed low-rank subspace, converting the $O(n^2)$ attention cost to $O(n)$ for inputs shorter than 512 tokens. However, its low-rank assumption degrades in longer contexts every day in document-level edge workloads [40]. The performer replaces the softmax kernel with random feature maps to achieve linear time and memory; despite an elegant theory, it requires careful tuning of the feature dimension to avoid stability issues [8]. Sparse-pattern models such as BigBird and Longformer interleave local windows with global tokens. However, the scheduling logic that makes them efficient on GPUs can stall on mobile NPUs that lack fast irregular-index hardware support [5,46]. At the end of specialization, MobileGPT fuses depth-wise convolutions and token pooling with a GPT-style decoder to achieve sub-200 ms generation on a flagship smartphone NPU. However, the evaluation is limited to the prediction of the next token and does not address the full NLU pipelines or bilingual tasks [24]. The diversity of designs underscores the absence of a unified architectural recipe for SLMs that is concurrently computationally, memory, and compiler-friendly across heterogeneous edge hardware.

Even when the static model is highly compressed, dynamic inference mechanisms can trim computation on a per-input basis. DeeBERT and PABEE exit early when confidence thresholds are met, saving 20 to 50% of average FLOPs with negligible loss of GLUE [33,43]. Token-level approaches such as TR-BERT prune non-informative tokens in intermediate layers, generating additional speed-ups [44]. LayerDrop randomly removes layers during training, ensuring that the model remains robust even if layers are skipped at the test time [13]. The common drawback is unpredictable worst-case latency, a serious concern for safety-critical edge deployments where tail latencies, not averages, bound user experience.

Attempts to shrink beyond single-backbone models have explored the mixture-of-experts (MoE) and modular prompt-tuning approaches. Switch Transformers routes each token through a sparse subset of experts, achieving state-of-the-art quality with only 10% of parameters active per example. However, dormant experts still occupy flash and DRAM, making design impractical on devices with 2–4 GB of memory [14]. Modular prompt-tuning instead attaches tiny domain-specific 'expert' prompts to a shared frozen backbone; memory savings are impressive, yet an accurate and efficient router has not been demonstrated on the device [48]. Consequently, MoE remains a cloud-centric technique whose principles have yet to trickle down to edge constraints.

Taken together, the existing literature compresses and accelerates SLMs along isolated axes: distillation, sharing, pruning, quantization, or dynamic inference, but no prior framework jointly optimizes these techniques while accounting for the idiosyncrasies of real-edge accelerators. Our study tackles these gaps by (i) co-designing structured pruning and adaptive mixed-precision quantization in a single pipeline, (ii) integrating low-rank adapters for task adaptation without model bloat, and (iii) validating the resulting models on an open, end-to-end benchmark suite that reports accuracy, latency, energy, and memory on real hardware. In doing so, we move SLM research from piecemeal compression tricks to deployable language intelligence on the edge.

3 Methodology

For our research, we carefully selected a combination of public and task-specific datasets to address common challenges such as data imbalance, input noise, and the need for custom labeling tailored to each use case. We employed a mix of encoder-based architectures, such as DistilBERT, MobileBERT, and ALBERT, as well as decoder-based architectures, including Phi-3 Mini, TinyLLaMA, and MobileLLaMA. These models were chosen based on their suitability for classification or generation tasks, considering factors such as their performance on benchmark datasets and their ability to handle the specific challenges we aimed to address. We fine-tuned them using PyTorch and Hugging Face Transformers.

Due to its larger size and training complexity, we optimized Phi-3 Mini separately using QLoRA with 4-bit quantization. After training, we exported all models to the ONNX format, enabling efficient inference via ONNX Runtime. To simulate real-world edge environments such as Raspberry Pi 5; Jetson Orin Nano, we evaluated the models using key metrics, including latency, accuracy, memory usage, model size, and their ability to handle noisy or multilingual inputs. This approach provided a robust framework for comparing lightweight transformers in resource-constrained settings.

3.1 Model Selection and Optimization

Selecting language models suitable for fully on-device operation required balancing model expressivity with stringent compute, memory, and latency constraints. We curated a set of encoder-only and decoder-only architectures with parameter counts ranging from 60M to 3.8B, chosen for their support of quantization, open licensing, and prior demonstration in resource-constrained settings. The final selection includes DistilBERT [?], ALBERT [22], Phi3 [28], MobileBERT [34], TinyLLaMA-1.1B [25], MobileLLaMA [20], and MiniLM_ONNX [41]. Each model offers complementary advantages in throughput, latency, and task specialization. Their adaptability to various tasks, from low-latency classification to response generation, instills confidence in their applicability to a wide range of edge AI deployment scenarios.

We shortlisted models based on four primary criteria: (1) feasibility of full deployment on Raspberry Pi 4B (4 GB RAM) without cloud offloading or accelerators; (2) availability of pre-trained open weights and tokenizers; (3) compatibility with post-training quantization (e.g., INT8, INT4) and adapter-based tuning methods such as LoRA [16]; and (4) support for generative output to enable naturalistic vehicle-passenger dialogue. Decoder-style models, such as Phi-3 Mini and TinyLLaMA, were prioritized for response generation, while we evaluated compact encoders like MobileBERT for low-latency classification tasks. We explicitly excluded models that failed these criteria, including LLaMA [37], GPT-3 [6], and PaLM [9], all of which exceeded RAM or compute thresholds by orders of magnitude. Furthermore, lightweight encoders such as TinyBERT-4L-312H [19] and MiniLM-L12-H384 [41] were removed from consideration due to their inability to generate free-form responses, which limited their applicability in interactive settings.

This constraint-driven evaluation was not just comprehensive but yielding a diverse set of benchmarks to evaluate the trade-offs between task accuracy, inference latency, and memory usage in embedded systems. By fine-tuning each model on domain-specific corpora and subjecting them to post-training quantization and runtime profiling, we ensured a robust and reproducible pipeline for edge-native deployment. As summarized in Table 2, we evaluate seven SLMs under an edge-budgeted protocol. These models vary in architecture (encoder- vs. decoder-only), size, and efficiency. By balancing model size and inference speed with support for quantization and transferability, we narrowed our selection to the following: DistilBERT [32], ALBERT [22], MobileBERT [34], TinyLLaMA [25], MobileLLaMA [20], Phi-3 Mini [28].

Table 2. Final model set and configurations used in our edge-budgeted evaluation.

Model	Family	Params	Arch.	Quant.	UCs
DistilBERT_ONNX	BERT	~66M	Encoder	INT8/INT4	UC-1; UC-2
MobileBERT_ONNX	BERT	~25M	Encoder	INT8/INT4	UC-1; UC-2
ALBERT_ONNX	BERT†	~12M	Encoder	INT8/INT4	UC-1; UC-2
MiniLM_ONNX	BERT	~22M	Encoder	INT8/INT4	UC-1; UC-2
Phi-3 Mini_ONNX	LLaMA	3.8B	Decoder	INT8/INT4	UC-3; UC-4
TinyLLaMA_ONNX	LLaMA	1.1B/1.5B	Decoder	INT8/INT4	UC-3; UC-4
MobileLLaMA_ONNX	LLaMA	~1.4B	Decoder	INT8/INT4	UC-3; UC-4

UCs: UC-1 = Watchlist Screening; UC-2 = Threat Detection; UC-3 = Document Triage; UC-4 = Multilingual Routing.
†ALBERT uses cross-layer parameter sharing ("shared").

All selected models underwent an optimization pipeline tailored for real-time inference under severe hardware constraints. For larger decoder models such as Phi-3 Mini, we applied QLoRA [11] for memory-efficient fine-tuning, followed by post-training quantization to INT4 and INT8 formats using GPTQ [15] and SmoothQuant [42]. We exported the quantized models to ONNX to ensure cross-platform compatibility and accelerated inference using ARM-optimized runtimes. For smaller models such as DistilBERT, ALBERT, and MobileBERT, we employed standard fine-tuning on task-specific datasets, attached LoRA adapters to select projection layers to reduce adaptation overhead, and applied INT8 quantization where compatible. We tested sparsity-aware pruning, selectively applying it based on observed latency trade-offs. This multi-stage optimization pipeline ensured that all models met real-time response constraints (<1 s per turn), memory limits (<2 GB RSS), and interpretability requirements necessary for safe in-cabin deployment.

4 Datasets and Task Description

Data Availability. Modern border control operations rely on the rapid and accurate processing of information to support field agents. Agents must verify traveler documents, assess risk factors, communicate in multiple languages, and generate field reports, often in battery-powered off-line environments. Although large language models (LLMs) have demonstrated impressive reasoning and understanding capabilities, their size and computational demands make it impossible to use them on typical field devices, such as tablets, drones, or Raspberry Pi-class boards. To address this gap, this research analyzes the use of small language

Table 3. Corpora used in the border-control study (all datasets are public [1,10,12, 17,36]).

Use-case	Source & privacy	Core fields	Size/split	Main augmentations
UC-1: Doc. verif.	Synthetic passports/visas (Faker)	MRZ, issuer, expiry, tamper	120k; 80/10/10%	OCR noise; JPEG/PDF artifacts
UC-2: Multilang. triage	OpenSubtitles-18 + officer prompts	Utterance, lang-tag, intent (7)	90k turns; 1.3M tok	Code-switch; 10% ASR WER
UC-3a: Risk score	GTD 2000–2017	Country, date, casualties, severity w_s	56k events; 193 ctry-yrs	Time-decay ($t_{1/2}=2$ yr); pop. norm.
UC-3b: Risk NLP layer	GTD-derived tiers	Traveller sent.; tier label	300k sentences; balanced	Descriptors; typos; mixed noise
UC-4: Customs reports	Harmonized Tariff + synth. qty/$	Item, qty, value, notes	65k forms + 10k reports	Unit/FX random.; 150–250-token reports

models (SLM) tailored for four representative border control use cases: on-the-spot document verification, threat detection, document triage, and multilingual routing. Each use case encompasses the creation of task-specific datasets, the design of training and fine-tuning processes, and the evaluation of model performance under practical edge deployment conditions, including latency, memory usage, and offline capability (Table 3).

Use Case 1: On-the-Spot Verification of Identity Documents: Use case 1 is designed to efficiently verify identity documents, such as passports, IDs, and visas, on the spot using our Small Language Models (SLM) deployed on mobile devices. Agents can scan documents with confidence, knowing that the SLMs will process them to check format consistency, extract key fields (e.g., name, SSN, license ID), and identify anomalies such as expired dates or mismatched information.

To train the models, we created a fully synthetic data set that simulates realistic document data while protecting personal privacy. This data set captures common fields and their typical formats, preparing the models for real-world verification scenarios. Specifically, we utilized the publicly available PII-NER dataset [12], which is designed to recognize synthetic Personally Identifiable Information (PII) and includes richly annotated examples of sensitive document fields.

Our dataset cleaning and reformatting process was thorough, ensuring that it was perfectly suited for our seven models. We remove unnecessary columns and emphasize the critical fields needed for an accurate evaluation. This meticulous approach prepared the models for real-world verification scenarios, enhancing their overall robustness in verification tasks. We further enhanced the dataset by introducing logical cross-referencing between fields. For example, we systematically compared the country indicated by the phone number to the country encoded in the license ID. In real-world document verification workflows, discrepancies between these two fields often signal anomalies. Passengers may present documents from one country while using phone numbers with international codes from another, potentially indicating attempts to obscure their true identity.

We fine-tuned the SLMs using examples of both valid and inconsistent documents, enabling them to effectively differentiate between the two. For evaluation, we applied multiple F1 score metrics to assess the precision and robustness of each model in detecting anomalies quickly and reliably. This solution enables agents to perform rapid and accurate document verification in the field, helping to prevent fraud and support informed decision-making.

Use Case 2 focuses on entity and threat detection. The system processes traveler-related attributes, including country of origin, country of last visit within the past six months, and country of citizenship. We tasked the Small Language Model (SLM) with identifying suspicious travel patterns and flagging travelers for secondary inspection. This decision-making process is guided by a combination of embedded rules and learned patterns derived from historical threat data. For this use case, we selected the Global Terrorism Database (GTD) [30] as the primary data source.

Our country-level risk scoring pipeline, developed using GTD, a comprehensive database of more than 180,000 terrorist attacks worldwide from 1970 to 2017, is a testament to our commitment to accuracy. To mitigate geographic bias, we employ a range of data balancing and pre-processing techniques. We focus on recent trends, limiting the data to events from 2000 to 2017. Each attack was assigned a severity weight based on factors such as the type of attack, target, and weapon used. A time decay factor with a two-year half-life was applied to prioritize recent incidents. The scores were then aggregated by country and normalized by population to produce a per capita risk metric, allowing meaningful cross-country comparisons regardless of country size.

Our system classifies countries into three levels based on normalized country-level risk scores: High Risk (top 15%), Medium Risk (next 25%), and Low Risk (remaining 60%). These levels were then used to label a synthetic natural language processing (NLP) dataset to train the SLM. To map traveler nationalities and travel histories to the corresponding country risk levels, we applied regular expression-based pattern matching to the input text. This method allowed us to extract relevant entities and associate them with risk labels in a transparent and interpretable manner, ensuring the reliability of our system.

To simulate diverse input in the real world and enhance model generalization, we generated four types of textual variations. The syntactic variant combined traveler attributes (e.g., origin, nationality, last visited country) with cultural interests such as food, music, or history, encouraging the model to interpret broader semantic contexts instead of relying solely on country names. The noisy variant introduced typographical errors, alternate spellings, and symbols to mimic informal or error-prone input, thereby improving robustness. In the descriptor-based variant, explicit country names were replaced with generalized risk-related phrases (e.g., "conflict-prone region"). The combined variant integrated elements from all previous types to produce complex and ambiguous sentences, further testing the model's ability to extract risk-relevant signals.

We consolidated all generated samples into a single training data set, allowing a comprehensive evaluation of the SLM's capability to detect and flag patterns associated with elevated risk in traveler profiles. This diverse and augmented dataset, which exposed the model to a wide range of linguistic forms and noise conditions, is a testament to our system's adaptability and resilience in real-world deployment scenarios. Dataset/task bindings for each UC are summarized in Table 4.

Table 4. Use-cases at a glance

ID	Name	Task/Metric	Data
UC-1	Document Verification	Clf/F1	Synthetic + open
UC-2	Threat Detection Clf/F1 GTD (2000–2017)	sim	synthetic
UC-3	Document Triage	Summ/ROUGE	Incident reports
UC-4	Multilingual Routing	X-ling Clf/F1	JW300; FLoRes-200

5 Experimental Setup

To thoroughly evaluate the performance and deployment capability of small language models for border control applications, we meticulously conducted a series of experiments. These experiments simulated edge device constraints and measured key operational metrics under realistic conditions, ensuring the reliability of our findings.

Although we did not directly use physical edge hardware, the evaluation and recommendations were guided by the typical constraints of edge devices such as the Raspberry Pi 5 and Jetson Orin Nano. Limited memory, processing power, and storage capacity were considered key constraints and served as benchmarks to evaluate the suitability of each model for edge deployment. Model training was performed using PyTorch on a dedicated GPU server equipped with NVIDIA A100 80 GB PCIe GPUs (CUDA version 12.3, Driver version 545.23.08). The server supported multiple A100 units, each with up to 80 GB of memory, allowing efficient fine-tuning of lightweight and mid-sized models, including those with higher memory requirements, such as Phi-3.

Each model was meticulously trained using the Hugging Face Transformers library and followed a standardized workflow. This process involved setting up reproducible environments, loading and pre-processing labeled text data, and initializing model-specific tokenizers and architectures, ensuring the highest quality of the models.

For the anomaly detection use case, we configured training parameters using the TrainingArguments class. The learning rate was typically established between 2e–5 and 3e–5 with even a 77-billion-parameter network has greater or equal 150 GB of FP16 weights alone (activations add further overhead). Training generally ran for 8 to 10 epochs with a maximum sequence length of 512 or 1024, depending on the input format. To improve training efficiency and model generalization, we enabled mixed precision training (fp16 = TRUE), applied weight decay, and used gradient accumulation. Early stopping callbacks were used to stop training when validation performance plateaued.

On the other hand, for document verification tasks, training was configured with a 5 to 8 epoch and a learning rate of 2e–5. The batch size ranged from 7 to 8 and the maximum sequence length was set to 512 tokens. Mixed precision training was enabled with a scaling factor of 0.5 to improve efficiency. Gradient accumulation was set to simulate a larger batch size without exceeding memory limits. An early stopping threshold of 0.16 was used to prevent overfitting by terminating training when improvements in validation performance became marginal.

After training, we evaluated each model using deployment-oriented performance metrics to evaluate its practical effectiveness on edge devices. Accuracy was measured by comparing the predicted labels with the accurate labels using the model output logs on the test set. The latency was calculated as the average response time per input in multiple runs with even a 77B network stores of 1 and 8 (batch-1 is primary; bsz = 8 is secondary). We evaluated model size and memory consumption by examining disk usage and recording peak memory during inference. To assess robustness, we introduced controlled input noise, such as typos, missing words, and OCR-style substitutions, into test samples. This process simulates real-world scenarios in which the model might encounter imperfect input data. We then measured the resulting drop in precision, providing insights into the robustness of the model under adverse conditions. To estimate the energy consumption per query, we multiplied each model's average inference time (in milliseconds) by the estimated power usage (in watts) of different devices: GPU (250 W), CPU (40 W), laptop (15 W) and phone (3 W). This gave an approximate energy use in joules for running one query on each device (no on-device sensors). These metrics offer a comprehensive view of the reliability, responsiveness, and deployability of each model in resource-constrained real-world environments.

6 Results and Analysis

We provide detailed results for UC-1: Watchlist Screening, UC-2: Threat Detection, and UC-3: Document Triage; UC-4: Multilingual Routing highlights are summarized for completeness.

6.1 UC-1: Watchlist Screening

We compare baseline and ONNX variants across accuracy, latency, memory, robustness, and speed. **Key findings:** (1) DistilBERT achieves top accuracy (~78%) at low latency; (2) MobileBERT/MobileLLaMA are close (~75–76%); (3) ONNX broadly reduces latency; DistilBERT_ONNX and MobileBERT_ONNX offer the best accuracy–latency–robustness trade-off; (4) Memory: baseline TinyLLaMA and Phi-3 exceed 2 GB, but all ONNX models are

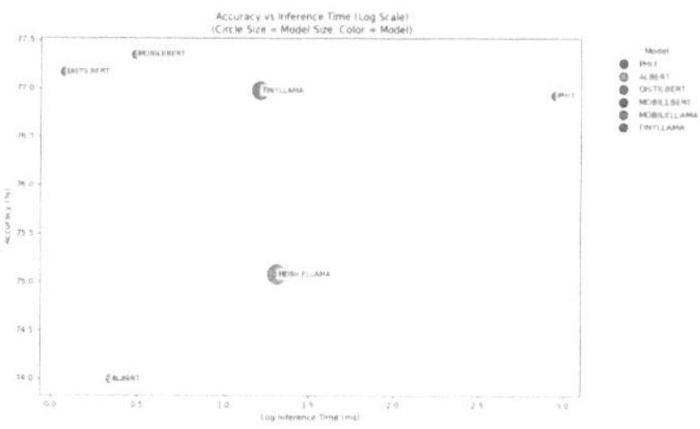

(a) Baseline: Acc. vs Latency

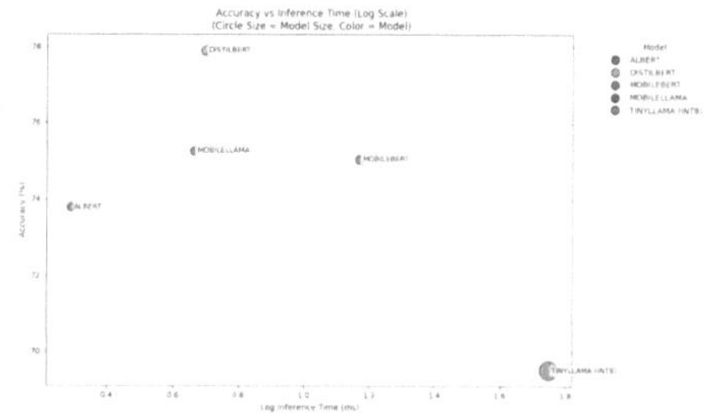

(b) ONNX: Acc. vs Latency

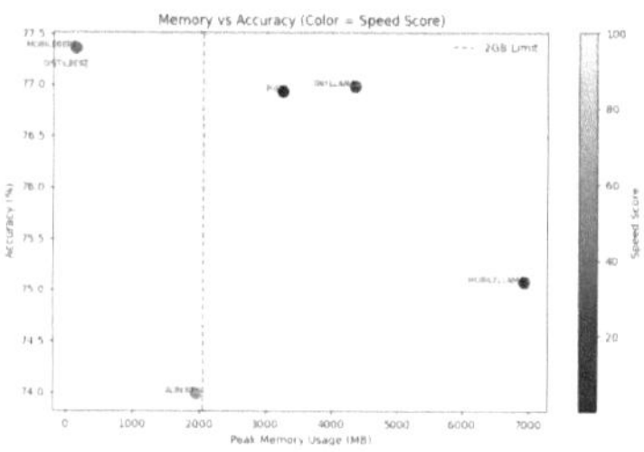

(c) Baseline: Mem. vs Acc.

(d) ONNX: Mem. vs Acc.

Fig. 1. Use Case 1—Comparative performance of baseline and ONNX-optimized models across accuracy, latency, and memory.

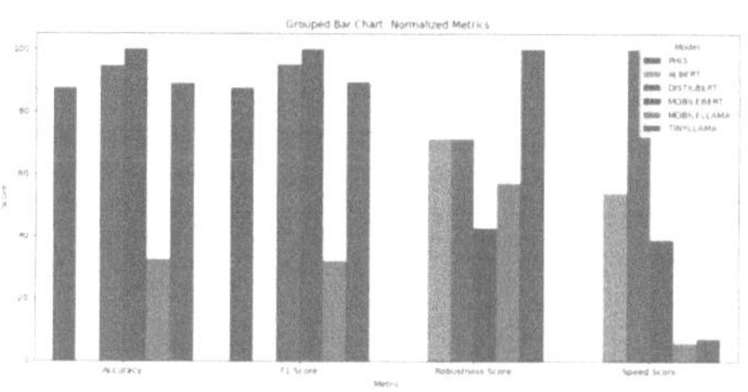

(a) Baseline: Grouped Bar

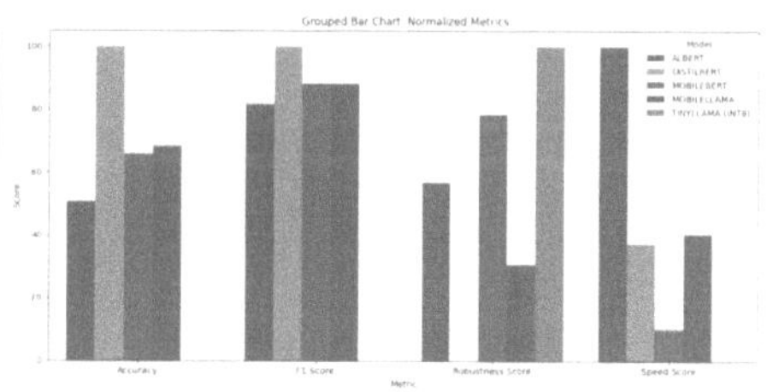

(b) ONNX: Grouped Bar

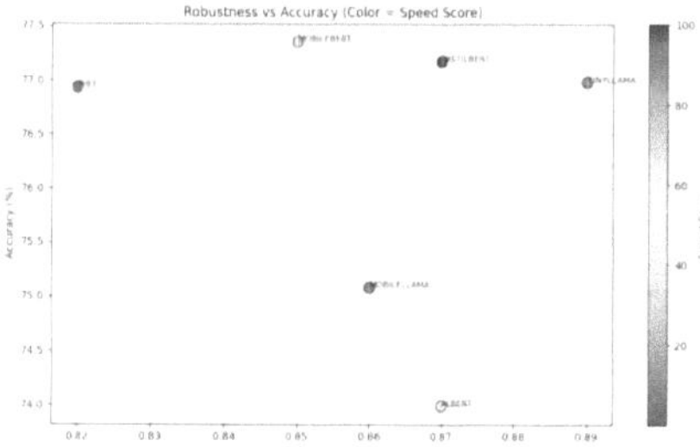

(c) Baseline: Robustness vs Acc.

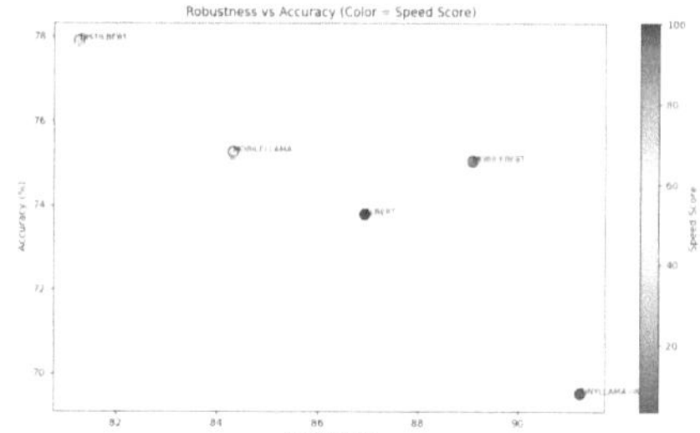

(d) ONNX: Robustness vs Acc.

Fig. 2. Use Case 1—Grouped metrics and robustness vs. accuracy.

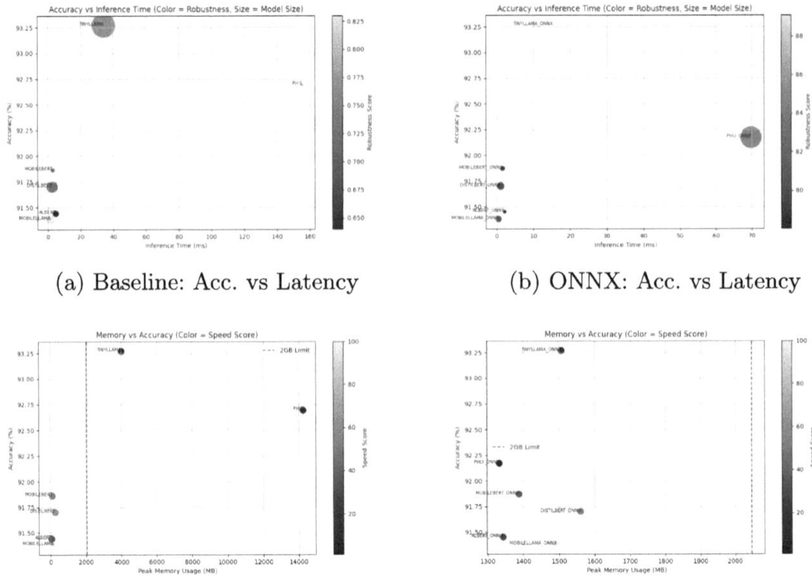

(a) Baseline: Acc. vs Latency (b) ONNX: Acc. vs Latency

(c) Baseline: Mem. vs Acc. (d) ONNX: Mem. vs Acc.

Fig. 3. Use Case 3—Comparative performance of baseline and ONNX-optimized models across accuracy, latency, and memory.

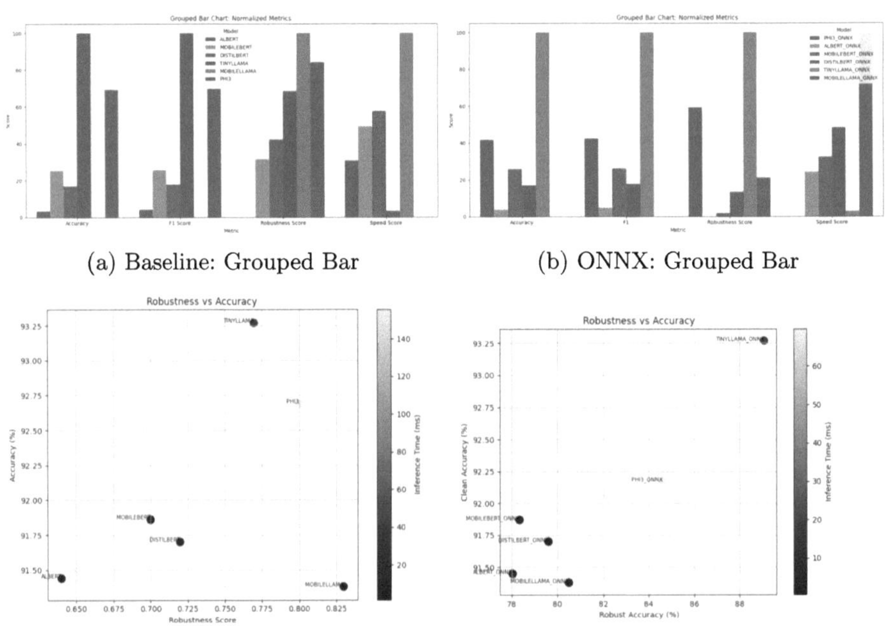

(a) Baseline: Grouped Bar (b) ONNX: Grouped Bar

(c) Baseline: Robustness vs Acc. (d) ONNX: Robustness vs Acc.

Fig. 4. Use Case 3—Grouped metrics and robustness vs. accuracy.

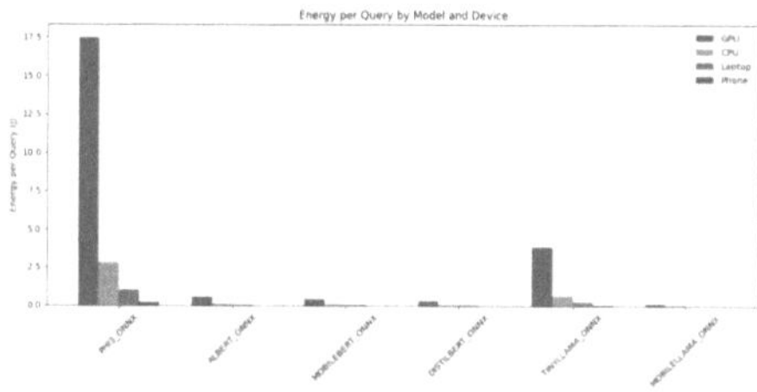

(a) Energy per Query by Device Profile

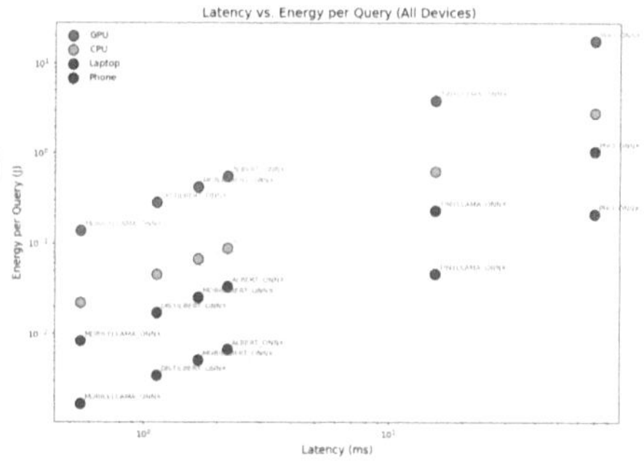

(b) Latency vs Energy (All Devices)

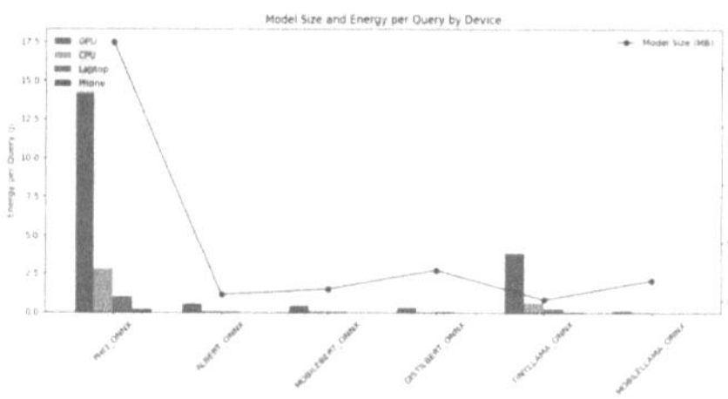

(c) Model Size vs Energy

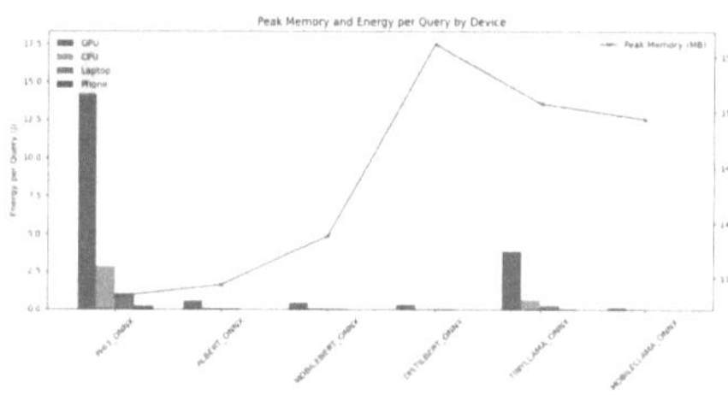

(d) Peak Memory vs Energy

Fig. 5. Use Case 3—ONNX model energy analysis across device profiles, latency, memory, and model size.

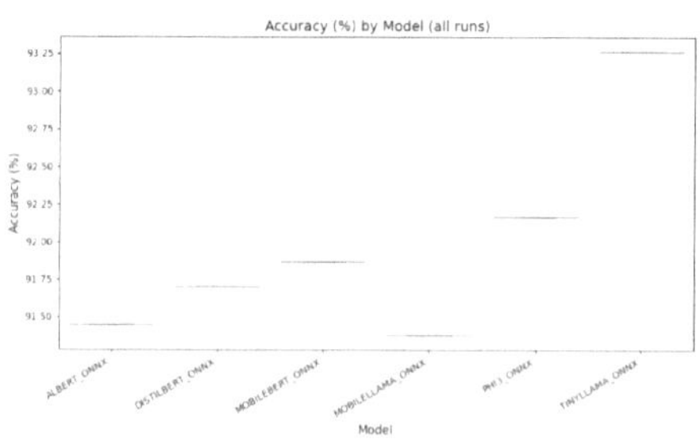

(a) Accuracy by Model

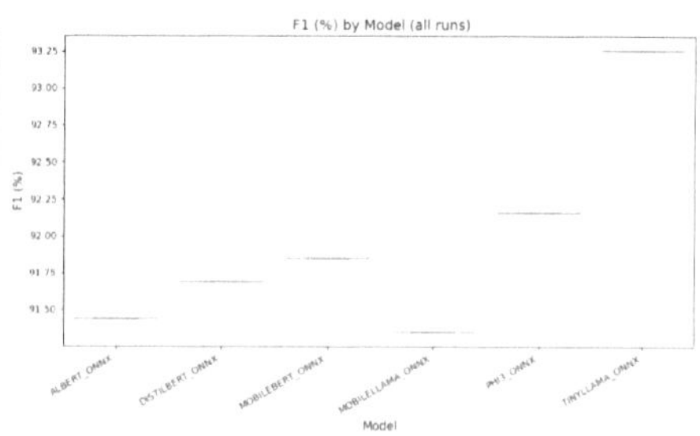

(b) F1 Score by Model

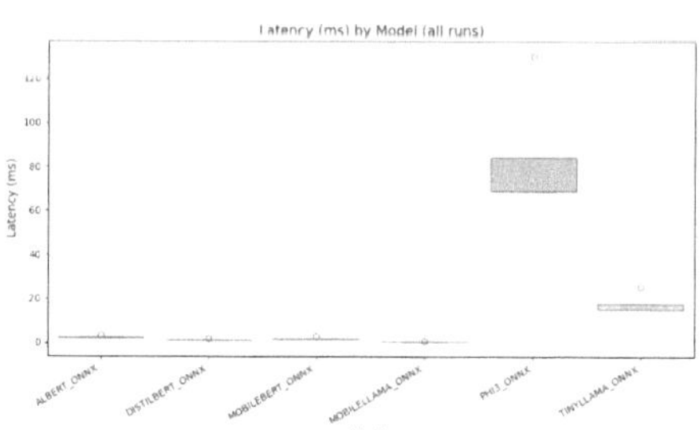

(c) Latency by Model

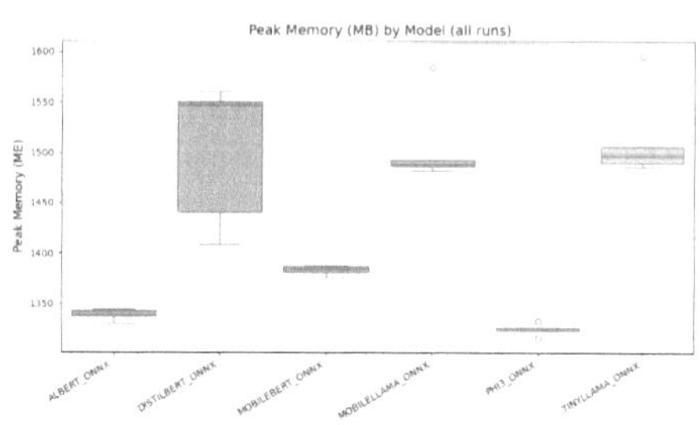

(d) Peak Memory by Model

Fig. 6. Use Case 3—Variability across five runs: Accuracy, F1, Latency, Peak Memory.

≤2 GB, with MobileBERT_ONNX and DistilBERT_ONNX especially lean. Figure 1 shows accuracy–latency and memory–accuracy trade-offs (baseline vs. ONNX). Figure 2 summarizes grouped metrics and robustness vs. accuracy.

6.2 UC-2: Threat Detection

For the threat-detection workload, the baseline accuracy–latency scatter shows TinyLLaMA achieving the highest accuracy (∼93%) with moderate inference time and high robustness. Phi-3 also demonstrates high accuracy but has the longest inference time among all models. DistilBERT and MobileBERT, positioned in the lower-left of the accuracy–latency plane, offer a favorable trade-off of low latency with moderately high accuracy and robustness—attractive for time-critical use. In contrast, ALBERT and MobileLLaMA exhibit the lowest accuracy and robustness.

In UC-2, the baseline results indicate that TinyLLaMA leads in accuracy, Phi-3 achieves similarly strong accuracy at substantially higher latency, and DistilBERT/MobileBERT occupy the low-latency, moderate-accuracy regime. From a memory perspective, TinyLLaMA and Phi-3 exceed a 2 GB edge budget (with Phi-3 sometimes exceeding 14 GB), restricting deployability, while ALBERT, MobileBERT, and MobileLLaMA remain within 2,GB. After *ONNX* conversion, however, all models fall within the 2 GB envelope, broadening the range of viable edge targets.

With ONNX optimization, the qualitative ranking persists, while inference time drops markedly. TinyLLaMA_ONNX retains top accuracy with moderate latency and strong robustness. Phi-3_ONNX maintains high accuracy / robustness with substantial latency reduction. DistilBERT_ONNX and MobileBERT_ONNX remain the most attractive low-latency options with balanced accuracy and robustness; and ALBERT_ONNX and MobileLLaMA_ONNX continue to trail on accuracy/robustness.

In memory–accuracy comparisons, although TinyLLaMA and Phi-3 achieve the highest accuracy, both exceed the 2 GB threshold in baseline form, making them less suitable for edge deployment. In contrast, ALBERT, MobileBERT and MobileLLaMA remain within 2 GB and exhibit higher speed scores, although with slightly lower accuracy. Their ONNX counterparts bring the *all* evaluated models into the ≤2 GB range, demonstrating a clear improvement in memory efficiency and allowing greater coverage of the device.

In robustness–accuracy plots, TinyLLaMA leads in both accuracy and robustness with acceptable latency, suggesting wide applicability where resources permit. Phi-3, despite the higher latency, is a strong choice when accuracy/robustness is paramount. The robustness of MobileLLaMA, despite the lower accuracy, indicates potential utility in louder inputs or adverse conditions.

6.3 UC-3: Document Triage

We evaluate the summarization/routing in incident reports under edge constraints. As summarized in Fig. 3, ONNX models generally shift points downward in the accuracy–latency plane (lower latency at similar accuracies) and reduce memory at similar accuracy levels, improving deployability. TinyLLaMA_ONNX preserves strong accuracy, but remains comparatively heavier.

MobileLLaMA_ONNX
is very fast but accuracy-limited. MobileBERT_ONNX offers the best overall balance. Figure 4 contrasts the grouped performance metrics and robustness vs. accuracy: MobileBERT_ONNX and DistilBERT_ONNX are consistently strong; TinyLLaMA_ONNX retains accuracy/F1 with some robustness/speed trade-off; MobileLLaMA_ONNX is fastest yet trails in accuracy. The energy profiles (Fig. 5a-d) show Phi-3_ONNX consuming the most energy/query between devices, particularly on GPU.

Lightweight MobileBERT_ONNX and MobileLLaMA_ONNX are most efficient. The latency–energy trade-off (Fig. 5b) disfavors TinyLLaMA_ONNX and Phi-3_ONNX for tight energy budgets. The size of the model vs. energy (Fig. 5c) correlates as expected, while the maximum memory vs. energy (Fig. 5d) is not strictly linear, favoring DistilBERT_ONNX and MobileLLaMA_ONNX in memory energy efficiency. **Run-to-run variability** across accuracy, F1, latency, and peak memory is summarized in Fig. 6.

In practice for UC-3, MobileBERT_ONNX is the best overall trade-off; TinyLLaMA_ONNX leads on accuracy/robustness but costs more latency/memory, whereas MobileLLaMA_ONNX is fastest and most energy-efficient with an accuracy penalty.

6.4 UC-4: Multilingual Routing

We evaluate cross-lingual routing/classification under the same protocol as UC-1/3 using multilingual datasets (e.g., JW300; FLoRes-200). **Highlights:** (1) multilingual encoders (XLM-R, mBERT) outperform monolingual encoders on non-EN inputs; (2) ONNX reduces latency/peak memory and brings models within a $\leq$2 GB envelope; (3) best deployment trade-off: XLM-R Base (ONNX), with mBERT (ONNX) close behind.

7 Conclusion and Future Work

We introduced a reproducible edge-budgeted protocol for the evaluation of SLM in border-relevant tasks and showed that ONNX + low bit optimization reduces single-query latency and peak memory, keeping the models within an envelope $\leq$ 2 GB under batch-1 constraints. For classification, DistilBERT_ONNX and MobileBERT_ONNX provide the strongest accuracy–latency–memory trade-offs; for UC-3, energy analyses favor MobileBERT_ONNX and MobileLLaMA_ONNX for low-power deployments. The same protocol transfers to multimodal edge workloads by pairing compact audio/vision encoders with SLM back ends while reporting the same budgeted axes.

References

1. Agić, Ž., Vulić, I.: JW300: a wide-coverage parallel corpus for low-resource languages. In: Proceedings of the 57th Annual Meeting of the Association for Computational Linguistics. Association for Computational Linguistics, Florence (2019)
2. Ai4Privacy: Pii-masking-300k: Openpii-220k and finpii-80k. Hugging Face Datasets. https://doi.org/10.57967/hf/1995
3. Anil, C., et al.: Gemma: lightweight open models for the edge. arXiv preprint arXiv:2402.05629 (2024)
4. Banbury, C.R., et al.: Mlperf tiny benchmark. In: NeurIPS Datasets and Benchmarks Track (2021). https://arxiv.org/abs/2106.07597
5. Beltagy, I., Peters, M.E., Cohan, A.: Longformer: the long-document transformer. arXiv preprint arXiv:2004.05150 (2020)
6. Brown, T.B., et al.: Language models are few-shot learners. In: Advances in Neural Information Processing Systems, vol. 33, pp. 1877–1901 (2020). https://arxiv.org/abs/2005.14165
7. Bubeck, S., et al.: Phi-3 technical report (2024). https://www.microsoft.com/en-us/research/publication/phi-3-technical-report/. Microsoft Research. Accessed 02 Aug 2025
8. Choromanski, K., et al.: Rethinking attention with performers. arXiv preprint arXiv:2009.14794 (2021)
9. Chowdhery, A., et al.: Palm: scaling language modeling with pathways. arXiv preprint arXiv:2204.02311 (2022)
10. Conneau, A., et al.: Unsupervised cross-lingual representation learning at scale. In: Proceedings of the 58th Annual Meeting of the Association for Computational Linguistics, pp. 8440–8451. Association for Computational Linguistics, Online (2020). https://doi.org/10.18653/v1/2020.acl-main.747. https://aclanthology.org/2020.acl-main.747/
11. Dettmers, T., Pagnoni, A., Holtzman, A., Zettlemoyer, L.: Qlora: efficient fine-tuning of quantized llms. In: Proceedings of the 40th International Conference on Machine Learning (ICML) (2023). https://arxiv.org/abs/2305.14314
12. Faker Community: Faker: A python library for generating synthetic data (2024). https://faker.readthedocs.io/. Accessed 14 Oct 2025
13. Fan, A., Grave, E., Joulin, A.: Reducing transformer depth on demand with structured dropout. arXiv preprint arXiv:1909.11556 (2020)
14. Fedus, W., Zoph, B., Shazeer, N.: Switch transformers: scaling to trillion parameter models with simple and efficient sparsity. In: Proceedings of the 39th International Conference on Machine Learning (2021). https://arxiv.org/abs/2101.03961
15. Frantar, E., Ashkboos, S., Hoefler, T., Alistarh, D.: GPTQ: accurate post-training quantization for generative pre-trained transformers. In: International Conference on Learning Representations (2023). arXiv:2210.17323
16. Hu, E.J., Shen, Y., Wallis, P., Li, Y., Wang, L., Chen, W.: Lora: low-rank adaptation of large language models. In: Proceedings of the 10th International Conference on Learning Representations (2022). https://arxiv.org/abs/2106.09685
17. International Civil Aviation Organization: Doc 9303: Machine Readable Travel Documents. ICAO, Montréal, Canada, 8th edn. (2021). https://www.icao.int/publications/pages/publication.aspx?docnum=9303
18. Jang, S., Morabito, R.: Edge-first language model inference: models, metrics, and trade-offs. arXiv preprint arXiv:2505.16508 (2025)

19. Jiao, X., et al.: Tinybert: distilling bert for natural language understanding. In: Findings of EMNLP 2020, pp. 4163–4174 (2020)
20. Kan, K.B., Mun, H., Cao, G., Lee, Y.: Mobile-llama: instruction fine-tuning open-source llm for network analysis in 5g networks. IEEE Netw. **38**(5), 76–83 (2024). https://doi.org/10.1109/MNET.2024.3421306
21. Kaplan, J., et al.: Scaling laws for neural language models. arXiv preprint arXiv:2001.08361 (2020)
22. Lan, Z., Chen, M., Goodman, S., Gimpel, K., Sharma, P., Soricut, R.: ALBERT: a lite BERT for self-supervised learning of language representations. In: International Conference on Learning Representations (2020)
23. Laskaridis, S., Katevas, K., Minto, L., Haddadi, H.: Melting point: mobile evaluation of language transformers. arXiv preprint arXiv:2403.12844 (2024). https://doi.org/10.48550/arXiv.2403.12844
24. Lee, S., et al.: Mobilegpt: augmenting LLMs with human-like app memory for mobile task automation. In: Proceedings of ACM MobiCom 2024 (2024)
25. Li, T., et al.: TinyLLaMA: efficiently scaling down large language models. arXiv preprint arXiv:2310.06797 (2023)
26. Li, X., Zhang, Y., Chen, Z., et al.: On-device language models: a comprehensive review. arXiv preprint arXiv:2409.00088 (2024)
27. Mehrotra, A., et al.: Designing efficient LLM accelerators for edge devices. arXiv preprint arXiv:2408.00462 (2024)
28. Microsoft Research: Phi-3 Technical Report. Technical report, Microsoft Research (2024). arXiv preprint arXiv:2404.14219
29. MLCommons Association: Mlperf inference: Tiny (2021). https://mlcommons.org/benchmarks/inference-tiny/
30. National Consortium for the Study of Terrorism and Responses to Terrorism: Global terrorism database (GTD) (2017). https://www.kaggle.com/datasets/START-UMD/gtd
31. Nguyen, C.V., et al.: A survey of small language models. arXiv preprint arXiv:2410.20011 (2024)
32. Sanh, V., Debut, L., Chaumond, J., Wolf, T.: Distilbert, a distilled version of bert: smaller, faster, cheaper and lighter. In: NeurIPS Workshop on Energy Efficient Machine Learning and Cognitive Computing (2019). https://arxiv.org/abs/1910.01108
33. Schwartz, R., Stanovsky, G., Swayamdipta, S., Dodge, J., Smith, N.A.: The right tool for the job: matching model and instance complexities. In: Proceedings of ACL 2020, pp. 593–603 (2020)
34. Sun, Z., et al.: Mobilebert: a compact task-agnostic bert for resource-limited devices. In: Proceedings of ACL 2020, pp. 2158–2170 (2020)
35. Team, T.: Tinyllama: An open 1.1b llama model trained from scratch (2023). https://github.com/jzhang38/TinyLLaMA. Accessed 02 Aug 2025
36. The Learning Agency Lab: Pii data detection (removal from educational data) (2023). https://www.kaggle.com/competitions/pii-detection-removal-from-educational-data. Kaggle competition. Accessed 14 Oct 2025
37. Touvron, H., et al.: LLaMA: open and efficient foundation language models. arXiv preprint arXiv:2302.13971 (2023)
38. U.S. Customs and Border Protection: Typical day at cbp - fy2024 (2024). https://www.cbp.gov/newsroom/stats/typical-day-fy2024. Accessed 01 June 2024
39. Wang, R., et al.: Edge-efficient large language models: methods, systems, and benchmarks. J. Syst. Architect. (2025). https://doi.org/10.1016/j.sysarc.2025.103221

40. Wang, S., Li, B.Z., Khabsa, M., Fang, H., Ma, H.: Linformer: self-attention with linear complexity. arXiv preprint arXiv:2006.04768 (2020)
41. Wang, W., Wei, F., Dong, L., Bao, H., Yang, N., Zhou, M.: MiniLM: deep self-attention distillation for task-agnostic compression of pre-trained transformers. In: Advances in Neural Information Processing Systems, vol. 33 (2020)
42. Xiao, G., Lin, J., Seznec, M., Wu, H., Demouth, J., Han, S.: Smoothquant: accurate and efficient post-training quantization for large language models. In: Proceedings of ICML 2023 (2023)
43. Xin, J., Tang, R., Lee, J., Yu, Y., Lin, J.: DeeBERT: dynamic early exiting for accelerating BERT inference. In: Proceedings of ACL 2020, pp. 2246–2251 (2020)
44. Ye, D., Lin, Y., Huang, Y., Sun, M.: TR-BERT: dynamic token reduction for accelerating BERT inference. In: Proceedings of ACL 2021 (2021)
45. Zafrir, O., Boudoukh, G., Izsak, P., Wasserblat, M.: Q8BERT: quantized 8-bit BERT. In: Workshop on On-Device NLP at ICML (2019)
46. Zaheer, M., et al.: Big bird: transformers for longer sequences. In: Advances in Neural Information Processing Systems, vol. 33 (2020)
47. Zhang, J., et al.: Elib: inference performance evaluation for llms on edge devices. arXiv preprint arXiv:2508.11269 (2025)
48. Zhou, W., Le Bras, R., Choi, Y.: Modular transformers: compressing transformers into modularized layers for flexible efficient inference. In: Findings of the Association for Computational Linguistics: ACL 2023, pp. 10503–10521 (2023). https://aclanthology.org/2023.findings-acl.664/

GUIDE: A Conversational LLM Framework for Dynamic Deep Reinforcement Learning Based Building Energy Management

Jiedong Yan[1,2], Ding He[1,2], Junxiang Ji[1,2], Guofeng Luo[1,2], and Longbiao Chen[1,2](✉)

[1] Fujian Key Laboratory of Sensing and Computing for Smart Cities, Xiamen University, Xiamen, China
{yanjiedong,23020250157824,junxiangji,guofengluo}@stu.xmu.edu.cn
[2] School of Informatics, Xiamen University, Xiamen, China
longbiaochen@xmu.edu.cn

Abstract. Efficient building energy management is critical for global sustainability, as buildings are major energy consumers. A primary challenge is aligning a manager's evolving, high-level intent with the low-level control actions of HVAC systems. Although Deep Reinforcement Learning (DRL) is a powerful approach, it struggles with this alignment because its performance is dictated by static, manually coded reward functions that cannot adapt to shifting human intent. To address this, we reframe reward design as an interactive intent alignment problem. We propose GUIDE (Grounding User Intent for Dynamic Energy Management), a conversational framework where a Large Language Model (LLM) translates a manager's natural language commands into the DRL agent's reward function, making reward engineering both transparent and steerable. Initially, the LLM leverages Retrieval-Augmented Generation over a domain knowledge base to create a precise reward function. The framework then enables a rapid, interactive refinement cycle: after reviewing the agent's performance summary, the manager provides corrective feedback in natural language, which the LLM interprets to autonomously refine the reward function. Simulation experiments demonstrate that this interactive approach allows GUIDE to adapt more effectively to changing objectives, achieving a superior balance between energy cost and occupant comfort compared to static DRL baselines.

Keywords: Large Language Models · Deep Reinforcement Learning · Building Energy Management

1 Introduction

Effective energy management in modern buildings requires a complex trade-off between energy costs and occupant comfort [27]. A core challenge lies in translating a manager's dynamic intentions—such as shifting the focus from cost

L. Zhang and K.-K. R. Choo (Eds.): MobiQuitous 2025, LNICST 683, pp. 23–39, 2026.
https://doi.org/10.1007/978-3-032-22500-9_2

savings to enhancing comfort—into precise, low-level control actions required by the Heating, Ventilation and Air Conditioning (HVAC) system. This gap between human intent and the execution of the low-level system is particularly pronounced in complex environments such as university laboratories, which feature dynamic occupancy and stringent environmental requirements.

Traditional building automation methods struggle to address this challenge. Rule-Based Control (RBC) is limited by rigid logic and cannot adapt to dynamically changing needs. Model Predictive Control (MPC), on the other hand, relies on high-fidelity physical models that are costly to build and difficult to generalize [7]. In recent years, Deep Reinforcement Learning (DRL) has gained traction as a model-free alternative due to its adaptive capabilities [16,25]. However, the success of DRL hinges upon a meticulously designed reward function. The difficulty lies in quantifying a manager's dynamic and often ambiguous trade-offs between energy cost and occupant comfort into a precise, scalar reward. Furthermore, such hand-coded reward functions often fail to generalize to new scenarios.

Recently, the remarkable capabilities of Large Language Models (LLMs) in natural language understanding and code generation have offered a transformative solution to this long-standing problem of reward function design [17,26,28,30]. This technological shift allows us to reframe the difficult task of reward function design as a problem of translation and alignment: that is, translating dynamic human intent into DRL reward function code. However, achieving this goal with LLMs is not trivial and requires us to overcome three key challenges:

- **How to accurately translate a manager's ambiguous intent?** Instructions from building managers (e.g., *Make the third floor cooler.*) are often colloquial and lack the precision required for system API calls. The primary challenge is ensuring the LLM can translate this high-level intent into accurate executable code.
- **How to rapidly adapt to the dynamically changing objectives of a manager?** Building managers must balance multiple objectives, including energy costs, occupant comfort and special environmental requirements. This balance is not static. It changes with time, building activities, and emergent special needs.
- **How to create an effective and stable feedback loop?** A key challenge is to design an interactive mechanism that can translate a manager's qualitative, natural language feedback into precise and stable modifications of the reward function code, moving beyond manual trial and error.

To address these challenges, we introduce GUIDE (Grounding User Intent for Dynamic Energy Management), a human-AI interactive framework that positions an LLM as an intelligent bridge connecting the manager's high-level intent with the DRL agent's low-level policy. By doing so, GUIDE transforms reward function engineering from a static coding task into a transparent, collaborative, and interpretable human-AI dialogue. First, we employ Retrieval-Augmented Generation (RAG) to ground the LLM's understanding in a domain-specific knowledge base [14], ensuring the generation of an accurate initial reward function. The framework then enables an interactive loop. The agent trains briefly, generating a performance report, and the manager provides corrective feedback in natural language to progressively steer the agent's learning. Our main contributions are as follows:

- We design and implement GUIDE, a framework that reframes DRL reward engineering as an interactive, human-steerable dialogue. It makes the policy refinement process transparent and interpretable, allowing managers to iteratively align agent behavior with high-level goals using natural language.
- We introduce a RAG-based strategy that fuses multi-source domain knowledge, significantly improving the accuracy of translating ambiguous human intent into precise, executable reinforcement learning reward functions.
- We propose an LLM-driven optimization process that enables the agent to understand and act on a manager's shifting priorities, effectively addressing the intractable reward design problem in traditional DRL.
- Through comprehensive simulation experiments, we validate the effectiveness of our framework, demonstrating its superiority over existing baseline methods in balancing energy consumption, occupant comfort, and critical safety constraints.

2 Relate Work

2.1 Control Methods for Building Energy Management

Building Energy Management (BEM) has evolved from traditional methods like RBC [8] and PID controllers [18,21] towards learning-based frameworks. While simple and robust in stable conditions, these earlier methods lack adaptability to modern buildings' dynamic environments [3,9]. MPC offers an improvement by using building models for optimization [1], but its performance is hindered by the difficulty and cost of creating high-fidelity models that can handle uncertainties like weather changes or occupancy shifts [29].

This modeling challenge motivated a shift to model-free deep reinforcement learning methods [25], which learns control policies through direct environment interaction [2]. DRL algorithms like DQN [23] and PPO [4] have shown significant success. However, DRL's effectiveness critically depends on reward function engineering [10]. Manually crafting a reward function to translate a manager's high-level, dynamic intent into a static mathematical formula is a major bottleneck. This challenge represents the core research gap our work addresses.

2.2 Large Language Model-Assisted Reward Function Design for RL

Recent research leverages Large Language Models to automate reward design. These approaches can be categorized into two main classes. The first class treats the LLM as a programmer. For instance, Ma et al. [17] proposed Eureka, a method that uses an evolutionary algorithm driven by an LLM to generate reward code, while Sun et al. [24] introduced CARD, which uses a Coder-Evaluator loop for automated refinement without human intervention. The second class positions the LLM as a supervisor providing real-time feedback. For example, Kwon et al. [12] demonstrated that an LLM can act as a proxy reward function to directly interpret natural language, or be used to dynamically shape an intrinsic reward during online learning, as demonstrated in the ONI framework by Zheng et al. [31].

Although powerful, these methods often assume that the LLM possesses sufficient domain-specific knowledge. In a specialized field like BEM, a general-purpose LLM can fail due to lack of knowledge about specific APIs or building physics. To this end, Chen et al. [5] have shown that RAG can mitigate this issue by providing relevant context, such as API documentation, to improve code generation accuracy. Therefore, we employed a RAG-enhanced LLM.

3 Framework Overview

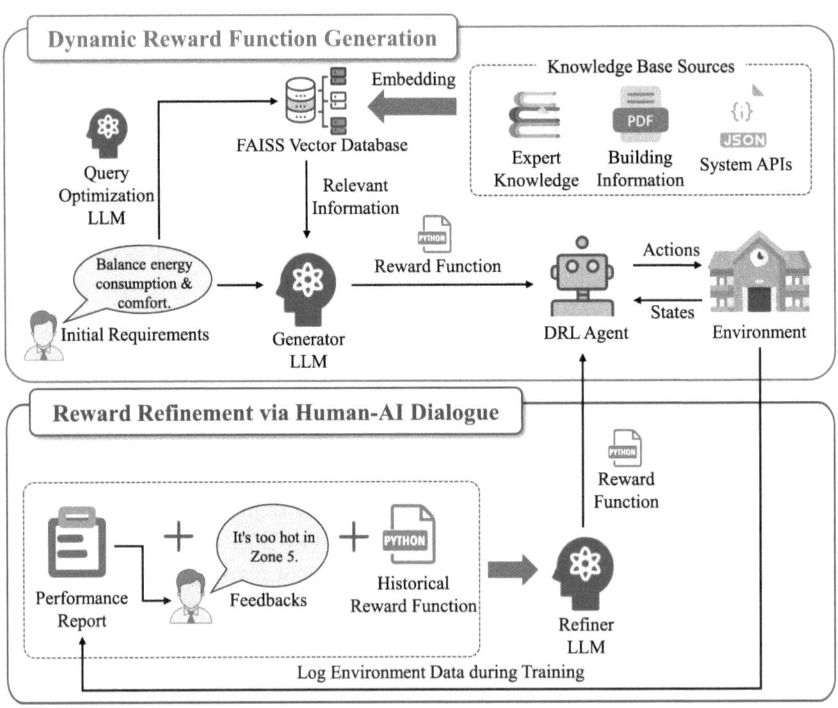

Fig. 1. The architecture of GUIDE, a framework designed to make DRL reward engineering interpretable and steerable.

To bridge the gap between managerial intent and DRL policy, we propose the GUIDE framework, as illustrated in Fig. 1. The framework reframes the reward design as a two-stage procedure. In the reward function generation stage, guided by a knowledge base of expert rules, building parameters, and system APIs, the Generator LLM translates a manager's initial natural language instructions into executable DRL reward function code. This stage aims to rapidly establish a valid and reasonable baseline policy that reflects the manager's core requirements. In the reward refinement stage, the system then enters a closed-loop refinement process. First, the DRL agent trains for a short period to quickly reveal its behavioral tendencies under the current reward function. Subsequently, the system generates a quantitative performance report with Key Performance Indicators (KPIs). After reviewing this report, the manager provides high-level, corrective feedback in natural language. Finally, the Refiner LLM interprets this feedback to pinpoint and modify the relevant sections of the reward function code. This interactive loop continues until the agent's performance aligns with the manager's stated objectives. Ultimately, this transforms the one-shot, often opaque task of reward design into a transparent, iterative, and human-steerable dialogue, where the reward function's code becomes a tangible artifact of the human-AI alignment process.

4 Dynamic Reward Function Generation with RAG and LLM

This section details how GUIDE transforms a manager's initial intent, expressed in natural language, into an executable reward function. The core of this process lies in the use of a domain-specific RAG knowledge base to enhance the code generation capabilities of an LLM, thus ensuring the accuracy and robustness of the generated reward function.

4.1 Construction and Implementation of the RAG Knowledge Base

General-purpose LLMs often lack the requisite knowledge of implicit operational rules, physical parameters, and specialized APIs for domain-specific tasks, leading to code hallucination. To mitigate this, we constructed a RAG knowledge base to ground the LLM in the specific context of our BEM environment. This knowledge base comprises three core information categories, populated from sources like HVAC operational manuals, building architectural plans, and the Sinergym API documentation. For this study, the knowledge base is static, but it is designed to be easily updatable.

Expert Knowledge: Heuristics and best practices for energy management. For example, a knowledge chunk might contain the rule: *For centralized areas like meeting rooms, linkage intelligent control is recommended. When the number of occupants is below a set threshold, the corresponding HVAC equipment should be automatically deactivated to conserve energy.* This grounds the LLM's logic in established operational strategy.

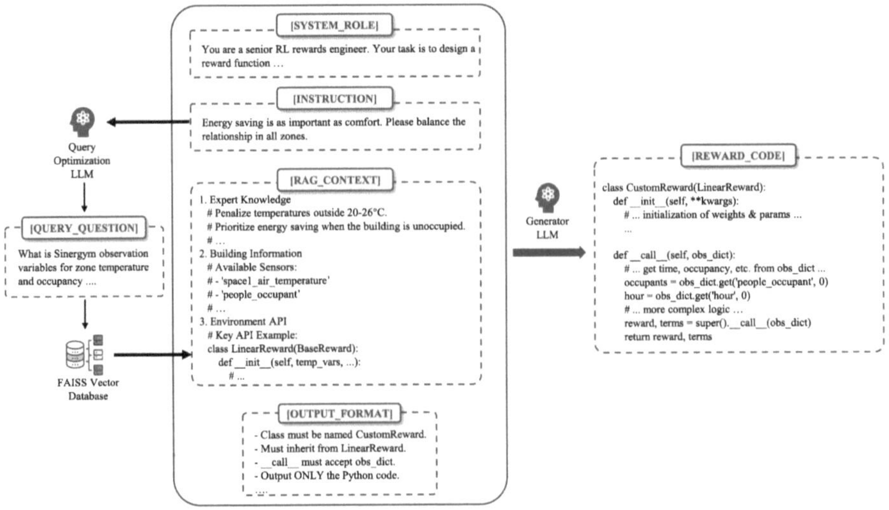

Fig. 2. The Parse-Retrieve-Generate pipeline for grounding a manager's intent in domain knowledge. A Query Optimization LLM first refines the manager's raw instruction into a precise query. The retrieved context is then injected into a structured, multi-part prompt that guides the Generator LLM to produce a syntactically correct and semantically grounded Python reward function.

Building Information: Static parameters of the building, such as the maximum occupancy for different zones, thermal properties of materials, and HVAC equipment specifications.

System APIs: Detailed documentation for the simulation environment's API, including function signatures, parameters, and expected return values, ensuring the generation of executable code.

To make the retrieval process more concrete, consider a manager's instruction: *The energy cost is too high overnight when the building is empty.* The Query Optimization LLM would generate a query like: energy saving strategy for unoccupied building at night. The RAG system might then retrieve the following key snippets: 1) from Expert Knowledge: During unoccupied hours, widen the temperature setpoint deadband to minimize HVAC activation. and 2) from System APIs: `people_occupant` observation variable returns the number of people in a zone. These retrieved items provide the Generator LLM with the precise context needed to add a time-and-occupancy-based conditional logic to the reward function code.

For the technical implementation, these diverse knowledge sources are processed and vectorized to create a rapid retrieval index. We first parse the documents into text chunks using a recursive character splitter with a chunk size of 2000 tokens and an overlap of 200 tokens to maintain semantic continuity. Each chunk is then vectorized using Google's `gemini-embedding-001` model [13]. The resulting high-dimensional vectors are stored and indexed in a local FAISS (Facebook AI Similarity Search) database [6]. This implementation combines the deep semantic understanding of an embedding model with the high-speed retrieval capabilities of FAISS, enabling the system to fetch the most relevant knowledge snippets with minimal latency during the generation process.

4.2 From Manager's Intent to Initial Reward Code

As illustrated in Fig. 2, the transformation of a manager's instruction into high-quality reward code is operationalized via a systematic parse-retrieve-generate pipeline. Upon receiving the manager's intent, a Query Optimization LLM first parses the natural language to extract key entities, objectives, and constraints, such as *Zone 5*, *reduce energy cost*, and *maintain comfort*. This structured analysis forms the basis for the next step.

These extracted components are then used to formulate a precise retrieval query for the RAG knowledge base. The system retrieves the most relevant knowledge snippets, which are subsequently integrated with the original instruction to construct a context-augmented prompt for the Generator LLM. This prompt is meticulously designed with a multi-part structure to steer the generation process effectively.

Guided by this highly specific and information-rich prompt, the Generator LLM produces the initial Python code for the reward function. This code is designed not only to be syntactically correct but also to encapsulate the manager's primary objectives, providing a robust starting point for the DRL agent's learning policy.

5 Iterative Reward Refinement via Human-AI Dialogue

Generating the initial reward function is merely the first step. To ensure the DRL agent's policy continuously aligns with a manager's evolving needs, this section details the core of GUIDE: the iterative Train-Feedback-Refine loop. We conceptualize this process as a guided human-AI dialogue, where the LLM, acting as a collaborative programmer, iteratively refines the reward function based on performance data and the manager's high-level steering commands.

5.1 DRL Agent Training and Environmental Interaction

To rapidly evaluate the practical performance of the current reward function in each iteration, we first formalize the building control problem as a Markov Decision Process [20]:

- **State Space** $\mathcal{S}$: The state $s_t \in \mathcal{S}$ is a 17-dimensional continuous vector corresponding to all observable variables provided by the energy simulation environment, including outdoor weather conditions, indoor temperatures of various zones, occupancy levels, and HVAC energy consumption.

- **Action Space $\mathcal{A}$**: The action $a_t \in \mathcal{A}$ is a 10-dimensional continuous vector representing the control setpoints for the HVAC systems in multiple zones of the building.
- **Reward Function R**: The reward at timestep t, denoted as r_t, is calculated by the current dynamic reward function f_{LLM} generated by the LLM, such that $r_t = f_{\text{LLM}}(s_t)$.
- **Transition Probability $\mathcal{P}$ and Discount Factor γ**: The state transition probability $\mathcal{P}(s_{t+1}|s_t, a_t)$ is implicitly defined by the energy simulation environment's engine. We set the discount factor γ to 0.99.

Once a new version of the dense reward function is generated, it is immediately deployed into the energy simulation environment. We employ the Proximal Policy Optimization (PPO) algorithm [22] for the DRL agent. PPO is selected for its renowned stability and data efficiency in handling continuous action spaces. The agent undergoes a short training phase of 20,000 timesteps. Through preliminary experiments, we determined that this duration is sufficient to reveal the policy's behavioral tendencies and potential deficiencies, resulting in a practical iteration time of approximately 10 min per cycle. It is important to distinguish between the refinement cycle time and the simulation timestep. The 10-min iteration time refers to the wall-clock duration of the real-world. During this phase, the system records key time-series data, which is then automatically synthesized into a quantitative performance report for the manager's review.

5.2 LLM-Driven Reward Function Refinement

The refinement stage empowers the manager to steer the policy's evolution based on empirical results. Each cycle is triggered by a natural language instruction from the manager, provided after they review the performance report. We formally express this refinement process as:

$$R_{k+1} = \mathcal{L}_{\text{LLM}}(R_k, H_k, F_k, \mathcal{K}) \tag{1}$$

where R_k is the reward function code from the k-th iteration, H_k is the quantitative performance report, F_k is the manager's natural language feedback, $\mathcal{K}$ is auxiliary RAG knowledge, and $\mathcal{L}_{\text{LLM}}$ is the LLM-driven refinement operator.

This operator is realized through a structured Refinement Prompt. The prompt provides the LLM with a comprehensive context: the previous reward function code, the summary of the agent's performance, and the manager's new directive.

For instance, after observing a performance report (H_k) indicating high energy consumption during unoccupied hours, a manager might provide the following feedback (F_k): *The energy cost is too high overnight when the building is empty. Please penalize energy use more heavily between 10 PM and 6 AM.* This qualitative instruction provides a clear, actionable target for the LLM.

The LLM is then tasked to act as an expert code optimizer: analyze the provided information, identify deficiencies in the current code, and generate a corrected, complete version of the function. The LLM's output—the refined reward

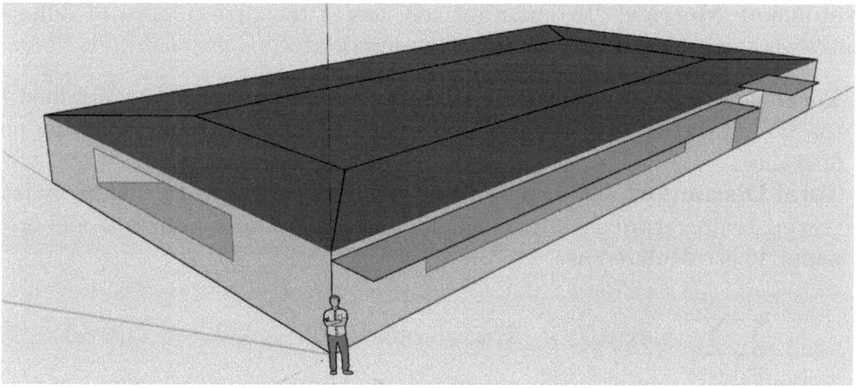

Fig. 3. The 5-zone commercial building model used as the testbed for all experiments. This single-story building model is divided into five zones consisting of one indoor and four outdoor, with a total surface area of 463.6 m^2. The HVAC system is a VAV package with both cooling and heating coils.

function R_{k+1}—is then deployed for the next training iteration. This loop continues, allowing the manager to progressively shape the agent's policy until its behavior aligns with their operational goals.

6 Evaluation

To comprehensively evaluate the effectiveness of our proposed GUIDE framework, we designed a series of experiments to validate its performance across multiple dimensions.

6.1 Experimental Setup

Simulation Environment and Dataset. All experiments were conducted in the Sinergym simulation environment [11], which is built upon the industry-standard EnergyPlus engine [19] and provides high-fidelity simulations of building thermodynamics. As depicted in Fig. 3, we selected a representative 5-zone commercial building model, driven by a Typical Meteorological Year weather file for Xiamen, China. To thoroughly assess the model's long-term performance, the simulation period was set to one full year. The system operates on a 15-min decision timestep. This corresponds to the simulation's control timestep, a discrete interval at which the DRL agent executes a control action. A 15-min resolution is standard in building energy simulation, as it offers a favorable trade-off between control fidelity and computational tractability. At each step, the agent's input is a 17-dimensional continuous state observation, which includes variables such as outdoor temperature, solar radiation, indoor temperatures of each zone, and occupancy. The agent's output is a control action defining the temperature setpoints for the five zones.

Evaluation Metrics. To quantitatively assess the performance of different control strategies, we define the following metrics:

- **Total Energy Consumption (kWh):** The total electricity consumed by the HVAC system over the evaluation period, measuring energy-saving performance.
- **Total Discomfort (°C·h·person):** Quantifies occupant discomfort by integrating temperature deviations outside the comfort zone over time and occupants. It is calculated as:

$$\sum_{t=1}^{T}\sum_{z=1}^{N_z}(\max(0, T_{z,t} - T_{c,\max}) + \max(0, T_{c,\min} - T_{z,t})) \cdot O_{z,t} \cdot \Delta t \quad (2)$$

  where $[T_{c,\min}, T_{c,\max}]$ is the comfort zone (20–26° C), $T_{z,t}$ and $O_{z,t}$ are the temperature and occupant count in zone z at timestep t, and Δt is the timestep duration. This composite metric provides a holistic assessment penalizing both prolonged minor deviations and brief significant ones more equitably [15].
- **Task Failure Rate (TFR, %):** The percentage of timesteps where the temperature in a critical zone violates its prescribed safety boundary. It is formally defined as:

$$\text{TFR} = \frac{1}{T}\sum_{t=1}^{T}\mathbb{I}(T_{c,t} \notin [T_{s,\min}, T_{s,\max}]) \times 100\% \quad (3)$$

  where T is the total number of timesteps, and $\mathbb{I}(\cdot)$ is the indicator function, which is 1 if the condition is true and 0 otherwise. This metric measures the adherence to hard constraints.
- **Constraint Violation Integral (CVI, °C·h):** Quantifies the severity of safety violations by integrating the magnitude and duration of temperature deviations outside the safety boundary, calculated as:

$$\sum_{t=1}^{T}(\max(0, T_{c,t} - T_{s,\max}) + \max(0, T_{s,\min} - T_{c,t})) \cdot \Delta t \quad (4)$$

  where $T_{c,t}$ is the temperature in the critical zone and $[T_{s,\min}, T_{s,\max}]$ is the safety boundary. Unlike TFR, CVI provides a more nuanced assessment of a policy's reliability.

Baselines. We evaluate GUIDE against four representative baselines:

- **Rule-Based Control (RBC):** A controller with predefined expert rules, serving as a fundamental benchmark for all learning-based methods.
- **Standard DRL:** A conventional DRL approach using the PPO algorithm [22] with a standard, carefully tuned linear reward function. Its goal is to represent a strong, static DRL implementation.

- **Zero-shot LLM (w/o RAG & Human Feedback):** An ablation baseline where the LLM generates the reward function in a single pass from the initial instruction, without access to the RAG knowledge base or any iterative refinement. This measures the raw, un-grounded capability of the LLM.
- **GUIDE-auto (w/o Human Feedback):** An ablation baseline where human feedback is replaced by a fixed, programmatic meta-prompt that is fed to the Refiner LLM at each iteration. This prompt is simple and goal-oriented, consisting of a fixed instruction like: *Based on the provided performance report, analyze the policy's deficiencies and suggest modifications to the reward function.*

The RBC controller required minimal setup time, involving only the definition of a few fixed rules. The Standard DRL baseline, however, demanded significant expert effort in manually designing and tuning the weights of its linear reward function through numerous trial-and-error experiments. The Zero-shot LLM baseline reduced this effort to crafting a single, effective prompt. Our proposed GUIDE framework also requires initial prompt design, but its primary overhead lies in the iterative refinement loop. This process, while requiring manager involvement, is designed to be intuitive and conversational, replacing tedious numerical tuning with high-level natural language feedback. Importantly, once a satisfactory reward function is generated and deployed, the online inference time of the GUIDE-trained agent is identical to that of the Standard DRL agent, introducing no additional latency into the real-time control loop.

6.2 Evaluation Results

Table 1. Performance comparison on the multi-objective trade-off task.

Method	Total Energy (kWh)	Total Discomfort (°C·h·person)
RBC	13014.15	562697.99
Standard DRL	13053.32	**3304.12**
Zero-shot LLM	13324.61	38376.60
GUIDE-auto	13675.98	5397.46
OURS (GUIDE)	**11131.98**	3424.72

Multi-Objective Trade-Off Between Energy and Comfort. To evaluate each policy's ability to balance the conflicting objectives of energy savings and occupant comfort, we first conducted a multi-objective trade-off analysis. The comparative results are presented in Table 1, with the corresponding Pareto front plotted in Fig. 4. As shown, GUIDE and Standard DRL jointly define the Pareto front, significantly outperforming the fully dominated RBC, Zero-shot LLM,

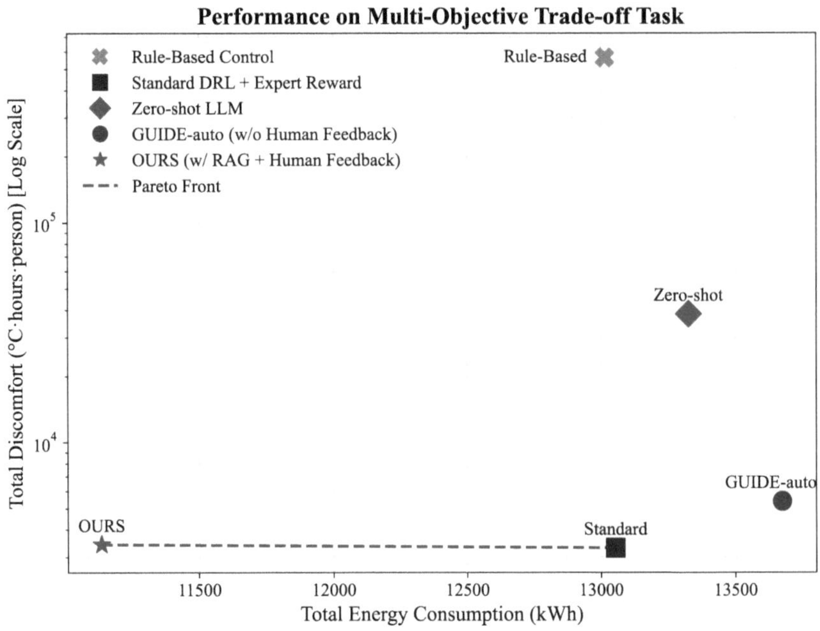

Fig. 4. Pareto front analysis of the trade-off between total energy consumption and total occupant discomfort.

and GUIDE-Auto methods. This indicates our framework's capability to identify optimal policies. More importantly, GUIDE discovers a significantly superior trade-off point compared to Standard DRL. Although Standard DRL achieves a marginally lower discomfort level, its energy consumption is nearly 2000 kWh higher. In contrast, GUIDE achieves substantial energy savings (a reduction of nearly 14.72%) at the cost of a marginal increase in discomfort (approximately 3.6%), attaining an operational state that better balances low energy consumption and high comfort. This result demonstrates that by translating a manager's qualitative feedback into reward code, GUIDE can uncover a superior policy trade-off that a static, manually-tuned DRL baseline is unlikely to find.

Adherence to Critical Safety Constraints. Next, we conducted a more demanding experiment to assess each method's ability to adhere to hard safety constraints, with the results shown in Table 2. This setup simulates scenarios with stringent environmental requirements, such as high-precision laboratories. The results demonstrate that GUIDE performs best on both key safety metrics: Task Failure Rate (TFR) and Constraint Violation Integral (CVI). Due to its rigid logic, the RBC was unable to adapt to these precise control demands, resulting in a high TFR of 49.48%. While Standard DRL reduced the TFR to 18.61%, its conservative and generalized strategy led to a significant increase in energy consumption to 15516.78 kWh. In contrast, GUIDE's ability to iteratively

Table 2. Performance comparison on the critical safety constraint task.

Method	Failure Rate	Violation Integral (°C·h)	Total Energy (kWh)
RBC	49.48%	6037.15	**13674.74**
Standard DRL	18.61%	766.23	15516.78
OURS (GUIDE)	**12.48%**	**695.91**	13981.07

```
return reward, reward_terms
```

→

```
if deviation > severe_deviation_threshold:
  excess_deviation = deviation - severe_deviation_threshold
  additional_penalty = penalty_scaler * (excess_deviation ** 2)
  severe_discomfort_penalty  = additional_penalty
...
return reward, reward_terms
```

(a) Structural Modification

```
if occupants == 0:
  current_w_energy = 0.95
```

→

```
if occupants == 0:
  current_w_energy = 0.90
```

(b) Tuning Hyperparameters

```
if occupants == 0:
  current_w_energy = self.unoccupied_energy_weight
```

→

```
if occupants == 0:
  current_w_energy = self.unoccupied_energy_weight
elif (0 < occupants <= 5) and (hour >= 22 or hour < 6):
  current_w_energy = 0.85
```

(c) Adding New Logic

Fig. 5. Three examples of code modifications made by the Refiner LLM. The LLM demonstrates the ability to (a) introduce entirely new logic like a quadratic penalty, (b) tune existing hyperparameters, and (c) add new conditional branches based on time and occupancy, all guided by the manager's natural language feedback.

incorporate human feedback allowed it to precisely target the safety violations. This resulted in the lowest TFR (12.48%) and CVI (695.91) while still maintaining lower energy consumption than the Standard DRL baseline, demonstrating the value of human-steered fine-tuning for complex, constrained tasks.

6.3 Case Studies

To more intuitively illustrate the working mechanism and intelligence of the GUIDE framework, we conducted the following case studies. These studies qualitatively demonstrate how our framework translates high-level human intent into complex control logic and how the RAG component ensures system robustness.

Evolution of the Dynamic Reward Function. To visually demonstrate how GUIDE translates high-level managerial feedback into precise, code-level optimizations, Fig. 5 tracks the evolution of a reward function across three interactive refinement operations.

Structural Modification. The manager stated: *The policy isn't working for Zone 4. We are still seeing large temperature spikes. We need to punish significant deviations from the comfort zone much more severely.* Recognizing the limitation of the existing logic, the LLM performed its most sophisticated modification: it introduced a non-linear quadratic penalty term, effectively creating a much stronger deterrent for large comfort violations.

Tuning Hyperparameters. The performance report showed the logic was too aggressive, impacting morning warm-up comfort. The manager's feedback was nuanced: *The new nighttime energy saving is good, but let's ease off a little. Slightly reduce the energy-saving weight to improve morning comfort.* Instead of changing the code's structure, the LLM correctly interpreted this as a tuning request, precisely adjusting the energy-saving weight from 0.95 to 0.90.

Adding New Logic. The agent's policy was inefficient overnight. The manager provided the feedback: *We are wasting energy at night. Please add a rule to significantly increase energy savings when the building is unoccupied, especially after midnight.* In response, the LLM introduced a new time-dependent conditional branch to the code, heavily penalizing energy use during unoccupied hours.

Avoiding API Misuse via RAG. In a comparative experiment with the RAG module removed, the LLM produced syntactically correct Python code that nonetheless caused an environment crash due to an *AttributeError* from API misuse. The root cause was the LLM's lack of knowledge regarding the specific API conventions of the Sinergym framework. In contrast, within the complete GUIDE framework, the LLM's prompt was augmented with relevant API documentation snippets retrieved by RAG. Furnished with this critical context, the LLM accurately generated fully compatible and correct code. This case clearly demonstrates that the RAG module acts as an essential guardrail, effectively preventing the LLM from making unfounded guesses in unfamiliar domains.

Digital Twin System. Finally, we developed a prototype digital twin system based on Unity, as illustrated in Fig. 6. This system not only provides a 3D visualization of the building's real-time operational status but also integrates an interactive interface. This interface allows a manager to input natural language commands, view performance reports, and converse with the GUIDE framework. This prototype serves as a proof-of-concept for how our framework could be embodied in a real-world management tool and provides a concrete vision for future work in developing and evaluating such human-AI interactive systems for complex control tasks.

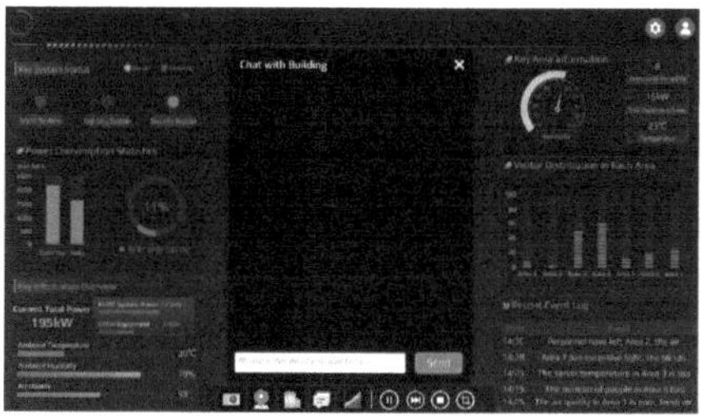

(a) System Dashboard

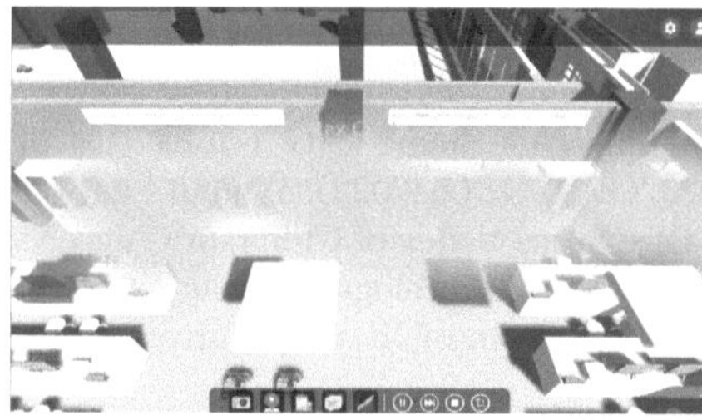

(b) Maximum Cooling Mode

(c) Energy-Saving Mode

(d) Night Shutdown

Fig. 6. The digital twin interface for the GUIDE framework and its visualized operational modes. (a) The manager interacts with the system via a dashboard and chat interface. The system visualizes the resulting dynamic control policies, such as (b) activating maximum cooling in response to high demand, (c) running a default energy-saving mode, and (d) performing a complete shutdown during unoccupied night hours.

7 Conclusion

This paper addresses the alignment challenge between human intent and DRL policies in building control by reframing reward engineering as an interactive dialogue. We introduced GUIDE, a framework that uses a RAG-enhanced LLM to translate a manager's natural language commands into reward function code. Our core contribution is a human-AI interaction cycle that makes the policy refinement process interpretable, transparent, and steerable. Experimental results validate that this interactive approach allows the agent to discover superior policies for balancing energy, comfort, and safety constraints compared to static baselines.

While this work establishes a proof-of-concept, several avenues for future research are critical. Future work will focus on bridging the significant sim-to-real gap through deployment on physical testbeds, enhancing framework stability with formal safety guarantees, and, most importantly, conducting formal HCI evaluations with real-world managers to validate the usability and effectiveness of this collaborative control paradigm.

Acknowledgements. We would like to thank the reviewers for their constructive suggestions. This research is supported by the National Key R&D Program of China

(2024YFB4504400), NSF of China No. 61802325, the Science and Technology Development Fund (SKL-IOTSC(UM)-2021-2023), the State Key Laboratory of Internet of Things for Smart City (University of Macau) (Ref. No.: SKL-IoTSC(UM)-2021-2023/ORP/GA06/2022), Wuhan East Lake High-Tech Development Zone (also known as the Optics Valley of China, or OVC) National Comprehensive Experimental Base for Governance of Intelligent Society and the Wang Deyao Outstanding Graduate Scholarship Program of Xiamen University.

References

1. Afram, A., Janabi-Sharifi, F.: Theory and applications of HVAC control systems-a review of model predictive control (MPC). Build. Environ. **72**, 343–355 (2014)
2. Aghili, S.A., Haji Mohammad Rezaei, A., Tafazzoli, M., Khanzadi, M., Rahbar, M.: Artificial intelligence approaches to energy management in hvac systems: a systematic review. Buildings (2075-5309) **15**(7) (2025)
3. Belic, F., Hocenski, Z., Sliskovic, D.: HVAC control methods-a review. In: 2015 19th International Conference on System Theory, Control and Computing (ICSTCC), pp. 679–686. IEEE (2015)
4. Chemingui, Y., Gastli, A., Ellabban, O.: Reinforcement learning-based school energy management system. Energies **13**(23), 6354 (2020)
5. Chen, J., Chen, S., Cao, J., Shen, J., Cheung, S.C.: When LLMs meet API documentation: can retrieval augmentation aid code generation just as it helps developers? arXiv preprint arXiv:2503.15231 (2025)
6. Douze, M., et al.: The faiss library. arXiv preprint arXiv:2401.08281 (2024)
7. Drgoňa, J., Arroyo, J., Figueroa, I.C., Blum, D., Arendt, K., Kim, D., et al.: All you need to know about model predictive control for buildings. Annu. Rev. Control. **50**, 190–232 (2020)
8. Fontenot, H., Dong, B.: Modeling and control of building-integrated microgrids for optimal energy management-a review. Appl. Energy **254**, 113689 (2019)
9. Hossain, J., Kadir, A.F., Hanafi, A.N., Shareef, H., Khatib, T., Baharin, K.A., et al.: A review on optimal energy management in commercial buildings. Energies **16**(4), 1609 (2023)
10. Ibrahim, S., Mostafa, M., Jnadi, A., Salloum, H., Osinenko, P.: Comprehensive overview of reward engineering and shaping in advancing reinforcement learning applications. IEEE Access (2024)
11. Jiménez-Raboso, J., Campoy-Nieves, A., Manjavacas-Lucas, A., Gómez-Romero, J., Molina-Solana, M.: Sinergym: a building simulation and control framework for training reinforcement learning agents. In: Proceedings of the 8th ACM International Conference on Systems for Energy-Efficient Buildings, Cities, and Transportation, pp. 319–323 (2021)
12. Kwon, M., Xie, S.M., Bullard, K., Sadigh, D.: Reward design with language models. arXiv preprint arXiv:2303.00001 (2023)
13. Lee, J., et al.: Gemini embedding: Generalizable embeddings from gemini. arXiv preprint arXiv:2503.07891 (2025)
14. Lewis, P., Perez, E., Piktus, A., Petroni, F., Karpukhin, V., Goyal, N., et al.: Retrieval-augmented generation for knowledge-intensive NLP tasks. Adv. Neural. Inf. Process. Syst. **33**, 9459–9474 (2020)
15. Li, H., Wang, Z., Hong, T.: Occupant-centric key performance indicators to inform building design and operations. J. Build. Perform. Simul. **14**(6), 814–842 (2021)

16. Liu, X., Wu, Y., Wu, H.: Enhancing HVAC energy management through multi-zone occupant-centric approach: a multi-agent deep reinforcement learning solution. Energy Build. **303**, 113770 (2024)
17. Ma, Y.J., et al.: Eureka: human-level reward design via coding large language models. arXiv preprint arXiv:2310.12931 (2023)
18. Mohammed, M.S., Al-Awasa, K.M., Al-Majali, H.D.: Energy management and control in microgrid with hybrid energy storage systems by using pi and flatness theory. Int. J. Eng. Trends Technol. **69**(11), 227–235 (2021)
19. Omer, A.M.: Energy, environment and sustainable development. Renew. Sustain. Energy Rev. **12**(9), 2265–2300 (2008)
20. Puterman, M.L.: Markov decision processes. Handb. Oper. Res. Manage. Sci. **2**, 331–434 (1990)
21. Sanal, A., Mohan, V., Sindhu, M., Kottayil, S.K.: Real time energy management and bus voltagedroop control in solar powered standalone dc microgrid. In: 2017 IEEE Region 10 Symposium (TENSYMP), pp. 1–6. IEEE (2017)
22. Schulman, J., Wolski, F., Dhariwal, P., Radford, A., Klimov, O.: Proximal policy optimization algorithms. arXiv preprint arXiv:1707.06347 (2017)
23. Shi, Z., Zheng, R., Zhao, J., Shen, R., Gu, L., Liu, Y., et al.: Towards various occupants with different thermal comfort requirements: a deep reinforcement learning approach combined with a dynamic pmv model for hvac control in buildings. Energy Convers. Manage. **320**, 118995 (2024)
24. Sun, S., Liu, R., Lyu, J., Yang, J.W., Zhang, L., Li, X.: A large language model-driven reward design framework via dynamic feedback for reinforcement learning. Knowl.-Based Syst. **326**, 114065 (2025)
25. Wei, T., Wang, Y., Zhu, Q.: Deep reinforcement learning for building HVAC control. In: Proceedings of the 54th Annual Design Automation Conference 2017, pp. 1–6 (2017)
26. Xie, T., et al.: Text2reward: reward shaping with language models for reinforcement learning. In: ICLR (2024)
27. Yang, R., Wang, L.: Development of multi-agent system for building energy and comfort management based on occupant behaviors. Energy Build. **56**, 1–7 (2013)
28. Yu, J., Wang, Y., Ma, W.: Large language model-enhanced reinforcement learning for generic bus holding control strategies. Transp. Res. Part E: Logistics Transp. Rev. **200**, 104142 (2025)
29. Yu, L., Qin, S., Zhang, M., Shen, C., Jiang, T., Guan, X.: A review of deep reinforcement learning for smart building energy management. IEEE Internet Things J. **8**(15), 12046–12063 (2021)
30. Yu, W., et al.: Language to rewards for robotic skill synthesis. arXiv preprint arXiv:2306.08647 (2023)
31. Zheng, Q., Henaff, M., Zhang, A., Grover, A., Amos, B.: Online intrinsic rewards for decision making agents from large language model feedback. arXiv preprint arXiv:2410.23022 (2024)

FISPA: A LLM-Based Assistance Framework for Fire Investigation

Hongjie Fu[1,2], Yunqian Li[1,2], Guofeng Luo[1,2], Ding He[1,2], and Longbiao Chen[1,2](✉)

[1] Fujian Key Laboratory of Sensing and Computing for Smart Cities, Xiamen University, Xiamen, China
{fuhongjie,liyunqian,guofengluo,23020250157824}@stu.xmu.edu.cn
[2] School of Informatics, Xiamen University, Xiamen, China
longbiaochen@xmu.edu.cn

Abstract. Traditional post-fire investigation is labor-intensive and expertise-reliant, while existing AI solutions are ill-suited for the complex, static analysis required post-incident. To address this, we propose FISPA, a two-stage "perception-reasoning" framework. Its perception stage uses an expert-guided dataset to instruction-tune multimodal models for generating structured scene descriptions. The reasoning stage employs an enhanced Retrieval-Augmented Generation (RAG) framework with query decomposition and self-reflection to fuse visual evidence with textual reports for evidence-based Q&A. Experimental results show our fine-tuned perception model significantly outperforms baselines (ROUGE-L of 0.8087), and our full reasoning framework boosts the ROUGE-L score to 0.4519 from a naive RAG baseline of 0.3401. This work offers a systematic solution for efficient and accurate fire investigation via human-machine collaboration.

Keywords: Fire Investigation · Scene Perception · Multimodal Large Language Model

1 Introduction

The high frequency of urban fires poses a persistent threat to public safety. Statistics indicate that in 2024 alone, fire departments in China responded to 908,000 fire incidents, resulting in 2,001 fatalities, 2,665 injuries, and direct economic losses amounting to 7.74 billion RMB [17]. Given the severity of fire risk and the urgent necessity to mitigate fire-related damages, fire investigation emerges as a critical undertaking. A core component of post-disaster inquiry is the environmental scene investigation, which requires investigators to meticulously analyze vast quantities of scene imagery. This process involves assessing post-fire conditions and identifying physical evidence to reconstruct the fire's progression and determine its origin and cause.

However, conventional fire investigation methodologies confront increasingly significant challenges. First, investigations are encumbered by substantial

L. Zhang and K.-K. R. Choo (Eds.): MobiQuitous 2025, LNICST 683, pp. 40–56, 2026.
https://doi.org/10.1007/978-3-032-22500-9_3

resource constraints. The sheer volume of scene imagery generated by frequent fire incidents demands meticulous, image-by-image analysis, imposing a heavy burden on human and material resources that often exceeds available capacity. Second, fire scene examination is a complex cognitive process heavily reliant on individual expertise. Investigators must simultaneously perform visual interpretation and knowledge matching, a task that demands extensive specialized knowledge in fire science and investigative techniques. This reliance on intuition and experience is difficult to replicate at scale or expedite. Training a qualified fire investigator is time-consuming, and the core competencies involve tacit knowledge that resists effective encoding and dissemination [9,18].

To alleviate these pressures, academia and industry have begun exploring AI techniques to assist in fire-related tasks. Significant progress has been made using deep learning, particularly in fire detection and early warning systems. Numerous studies employ object detection and image segmentation to identify active flames or smoke plumes in real-time video surveillance for rapid alerts [21,30,31]. Other research utilizes reinforcement learning to simulate personnel evacuation and emergency response strategies during fire scenarios [1,3,5]. However, the primary objective of these technologies is to manage ongoing fires, relying on dynamic and explicit visual signals (e.g., flame morphology). This focus fundamentally differs from the challenges of post-fire investigation. Investigation analyzes static, chaotic, and informationally compressed scenes after the event, demanding capabilities for deeper scene comprehension, evidence correlation, and logical inference. Consequently, existing fire perception technologies cannot be directly transferred to solve the core problems of scene investigation.

Concurrently, the advancement of Large Language Models (LLMs) offers new pathways for integrating extensive professional knowledge. Efforts have been made to develop domain-specific knowledge question-answering systems for fire safety, typically by fine-tuning models on professional textbooks and standards to address text-based queries [12]. While these approaches represent progress in knowledge representation, they suffer from a fundamental modality limitation. Fire investigation is intrinsically a visually-driven process, where all reasoning must be anchored to visual evidence from the scene. Text-only models cannot process or comprehend image inputs, creating an insurmountable modality gap between domain expertise and real-world visual data. Therefore, there is a compelling need for a new methodology capable of effectively integrating complex post-disaster visual scene understanding with deep domain-specific reasoning.

Fortunately, recent advancements in Multimodal Large Language Models (MLLMs) [6,11,14] offer a promising solution to this challenge. Pre-trained on vast image-text datasets, these models possess robust general-purpose scene perception capabilities. Furthermore, techniques like Retrieval-Augmented Generation (RAG) enable the fusion of real-time perceptual data derived from scenes with static professional knowledge bases [10]. This convergence makes it feasible to develop an assistive tool capable of understanding fire scene images and performing reasoning grounded in domain expertise. Motivated by this potential, we propose FISPA (Fire Investigation Scene Perception Assistant), an intelligent framework for post-fire scene examination. The core of FISPA operates on a Perception-Reasoning Two-Stage process:

- **Perception Stage:** An MLLM translates unstructured fire scene images into structured semantic descriptions, achieving an initial digitization of the scene environment.
- **Reasoning Stage:** An LLM-based, knowledge-augmented conversational reasoning engine ingests the perceptual data as factual grounding and dynamically retrieves information from a specialized fire investigation knowledge base, facilitating the transition from fundamental scene comprehension to advanced decision support for investigators.

To realize this framework, we collaborated with frontline fire investigators to design a set of structured prompt templates. Based on these templates, we annotated a specialized dataset comprising 675 authentic fire scene images, which was subsequently used to fine-tune the model for accurate generation of structured descriptions. Furthermore, we constructed a vectorized knowledge base encompassing professional textbooks and regulatory standards. We designed a reasoning workflow that integrates Retrieval-Augmented Generation with self-reflection mechanisms to ensure the professionalism and reliability of the resulting analysis.

The main contributions of this study are summarized as follows:

- We propose FISPA, the first integrated "perception-reasoning" intelligent assistant framework specifically tailored for post-fire scene investigation. This framework establishes an end-to-end workflow from raw fire scene imagery to structured analytical conclusions, providing an innovative systematic solution for efficient human-machine collaborative investigation.
- We introduce and validate an effective methodology for adapting general-purpose large models to highly specialized domains. By developing expert-guided prompt templates and curating the first instruction fine-tuning dataset for this domain, we address the visual perception challenges that general models face in unique scenarios like post-fire scenes. Concurrently, the fusion of RAG and self-reflection mechanisms significantly enhances the reliability of deep reasoning for professional tasks.

2 Related Work

2.1 Image Captioning

Image captioning has long been a fundamental task at the intersection of computer vision and natural language processing due to its wide range of applications. Early research efforts employed retrieval-based methods, searching large databases for visually similar images and outputting their corresponding textual descriptions as captions [7,19]. Evidently, this approach did not constitute genuine image comprehension by the model. The introduction of the encoder-decoder paradigm by Sutskever et al. [23] and Cho et al. [2], based on different network architectures, created possibilities for cross-modal fusion. Vinyals et al. [26] further advanced this by utilizing pre-trained CNNs as encoders to extract hierarchical and abstract visual features from images, enabling models to achieve true image understanding. Subsequently, Xu et al. [29] proposed visual attention mechanisms to improve the accuracy and interpretability of generated descriptions.

However, these methods retained the inefficiencies inherent in traditional RNNs. The development of the Transformer [25] offered a novel solution to this challenge, significantly enhancing model training efficiency. Dosovitskiy et al. [4] introduced the Vision Transformer (ViT), applying the Transformer architecture to image processing and largely supplanting the role of CNNs. To further strengthen the alignment between image and text modalities, Radford et al. [20] and Lu et al. [15] proposed a series of more sophisticated methods, greatly enhancing model capabilities and driving the emergence of current powerful MLLMs [6,14,24,27].

Despite the impressive capabilities of MLLMs, they still encounter difficulties when faced with specialized and fine-grained image comprehension tasks, often producing suboptimal results or failing to capture critical image details. Rotstein et al. [22] proposed using three expert models to perform preliminary perception of image content, embedding this pre-perceived information along with the image to improve the recognition of key objects. Li et al. [13] enhanced the model's ability to capture complex images by pre-segmenting images into patches matching the vision encoder's training process and applying separate adapters to each patch. While these studies improve model performance through image pre-processing strategies, meticulously designed prompts also possess the ability to guide large models to focus on key content. For instance, Wu et al. [28] designed comprehensive Chain-of-Thought (CoT) prompts to direct multimodal models to focus on areas of interest. Our research focuses on designing a comprehensive and professional prompt suite to enhance the understanding of post-fire scene images by MLLMs.

2.2 Vertical Large Language Models

In recent years, LLMs have achieved remarkable advancements across numerous domains of natural language processing, significantly enhancing the general-purpose problem-solving capabilities of models [6,14,24,27]. However, when applied to specialized vertical domain tasks, general-purpose LLMs often exhibit unsatisfactory performance due to a lack of relevant domain knowledge and an inability to comprehend specialized terminology.

To address this gap in expertise, "Vertical Large Language Models" have emerged. Mainstream development strategies include: 1) Domain-Adaptive Pretraining: This involves continuing the pretraining of a general model using massive volumes of in-domain text data, allowing the model to acquire the specific knowledge systems and linguistic conventions of the target field. For example, Lee et al. [8] trained models on extensive biomedical literature, significantly improving performance in the biological domain. 2) Instruction Fine-tuning:

This strategy involves fine-tuning the model on high-quality, domain-specific question-answer pairs or task data to align its behavioral patterns with professional standards.

Within the fire science domain, research has begun to explore the use of large models for related tasks. For instance, work by Luo et al. [16] enables models to formulate rational action strategies for fire progression by providing them with the necessary background knowledge and response protocols for incident assessment. Nevertheless, existing research predominantly focuses on pre-fire risk assessment or intra-fire emergency response. Research concerning the post-fire investigation phase, particularly for scenarios requiring deep reasoning integrated with visual evidence, remains largely nascent. By constructing a specialized dataset for post-fire scene examination and fine-tuning a multi-modal model, this study aims to fill this gap, creating a vertical domain model focused on post-disaster scene analysis and report generation (Fig. 1).

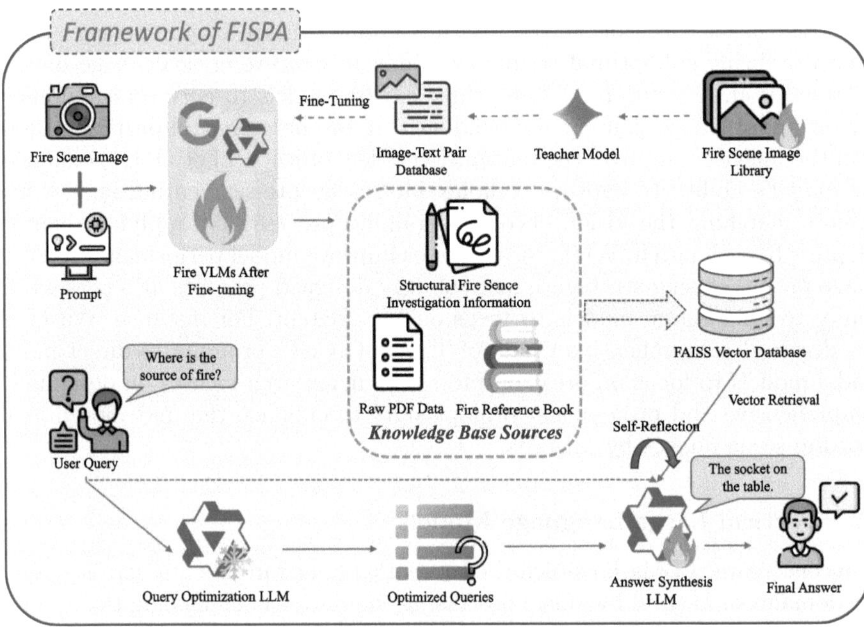

Fig. 1. The framework of FISPA.

3 Framework

To realize intelligent fire scene investigation, this study designs and implements a comprehensive assistant named FISPA. The system employs an innovative two-stage "perception-reasoning" architecture:

In the perception stage, to address the interpretation biases of general-purpose MLLMs when processing fire imagery, we first collaborated with front-line fire investigation experts. Guided by professional standards, we designed a set of structured prompt templates encompassing key dimensions such as combustion characteristics and investigative directions. Using these templates, we constructed a specialized instruction fine-tuning dataset comprising 675 real-world fire scene images. We then applied parameter-efficient fine-tuning (PEFT) to the MLLM using this dataset, enabling the model to accurately translate complex fire scene images into professional, structured textual descriptions.

In the reasoning stage, we began by compiling and vectorizing extensive resources—including fire investigation textbooks, national technical standards, and relevant party statements—to build a comprehensive professional knowledge base. Subsequently, we designed a rigorous workflow integrating Retrieval-Augmented Generation (RAG) technology with a self-reflection mechanism. This workflow utilizes the structured image descriptions generated in the perception stage as factual grounding. Upon receiving a user query, it retrieves the most relevant entries from the knowledge base to drive the LLM in generating a preliminary answer. The model then performs a logical self-consistency check and correction under specific instructions. Finally, the system provides investigators with deep, reliable conversational decision support, transforming static image analysis into an efficient human-machine collaborative investigation dialogue.

4 Methodology

This chapter elaborates on the implementation details of FISPA. Adhering to the two-stage "perception-reasoning" framework, we first introduce stage one, environmental perception generation, focusing on enabling the model to accurately comprehend complex post-disaster scenes. Subsequently, we detail stage two, event reasoning and question answering, focusing on integrating knowledge for deep analysis.

4.1 Fire Environment Perception Generation via Knowledge Transfer

A primary objective in fire investigation is extracting critical features from complex post-disaster environments. This process faces a dichotomy: on one hand, advanced MLLMs exhibit powerful general-purpose understanding capabilities, but their direct deployment incurs high costs, and they lack specific optimization for the highly specialized domain of fire investigation. On the other hand, lightweight models with fewer parameters are easier to deploy, but their perceptual capabilities are often insufficient to process the informationally dense and chaotic nature of fire scene images.

The goal of this stage is to resolve this contradiction. We propose a knowledge transfer methodology. The core idea is to first leverage the advanced capabilities of large models, combined with expert-defined knowledge paradigms, to generate analytical data. This data is then used to efficiently fine-tune lightweight models, enabling them to inherit specialized perceptual and analytical capabilities (Fig. 2).

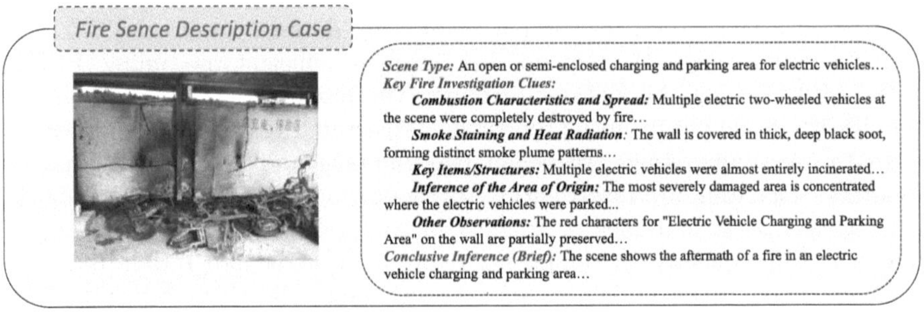

Fig. 2. An example of a fire image obtained based on a structured analysis paradigm, which illustrates the results of multi-angle analysis of the image.

Structured Analysis Paradigm for Fire Scenes. To ensure the model's analysis process aligns with actual investigative workflows, we first defined a standardized paradigm for scene information extraction. Through in-depth consultations with frontline fire investigation units, we identified and summarized the core focal points that investigators concentrate on when analyzing scene photographs, organizing them into a systematic data structure.

Let S_{pic} represent the set of scene images for a specific fire incident. For any image $Sp_i \in S_{pic}$, our analytical paradigm parses it along three dimensions: Scene Type (S_{type}), Core Investigative Clues (CI_{clue}), and Summary Conclusion (S_{con}). As shown in 1.

$$\{S_{type}, CI_{clue}, S_{con}\} = f(prompt, S_{pic}) \tag{1}$$

- **Scene Type (S_{type}):** Records the specific spatial location where the photo was taken, such as "kitchen interior," "living room sofa area," or "distribution box close-up." This provides essential context for subsequent spatial analysis.
- **Summary Conclusion (S_{con}):** Synthesizes the core findings from S_{type} and CI_{clue} to generate a concise overview, facilitating rapid retrieval and localization of key images.
- **Core Investigative Clues (CI_{clue}):** This constitutes the main body of the investigative analysis, requiring the model to delve into specific evidence within the image.

$$CI_{clue} = \sum_{i=1}^{n} \{CCS_i, SHR_i, KIS_i, ISAI_i, Others_i\} \tag{2}$$

As shown in 2, We further decompose CI_{clue} into the following five key aspects:

- **Combustion Characteristics and Spread(CCS):** Analyzing physico-chemical traces, such as the depth of carbonization on materials and V-shaped burn patterns. The objective is to reconstruct the fire's direction of development, spread path, and intensity.
- **Smoke and Heat Radiation(SHR):**Assessing the distribution and color of soot deposits, as well as material deformation caused by thermal effects (e.g., melting, warping). This helps infer the types of combustibles, fire scene temperatures, and flame propagation modes.
- **Key Items and Structures(KIS):** Identifying specific items crucial for determining the fire's cause (e.g., faulty electrical appliances, flammable material storage) or significant building components (e.g., status of fire doors, foam-core sandwich panels).
- **Ignition Source Area Inference($ISAI$):**Synthesizing all preceding clues to logically pinpoint the most probable area of origin by tracing the fire spread path in reverse, thereby narrowing the scope of the investigation.
- **Other Observations($Others$):** Recording supplementary information not covered by the above categories but possessing potential value, such as descriptions of unusual odors, signs of forced entry, or other anomalies.

Knowledge Transfer and Model Fine-Tuning for Fire Perception. To convert the aforementioned expert investigation paradigm into a format learnable by models, we constructed an image-text pair dataset for post-fire scenarios. We collected 675 high-resolution images covering diverse fire types (e.g., electrical fires, kitchen fires), various scenes, and different degrees of damage. All images were sourced from anonymized cases provided by local fire departments, ensuring data authenticity and professional relevance.

During the data annotation phase, we adopted a "teacher-student" methodology. We converted the structured analysis paradigm defined in Sect. 3.1.2 into detailed prompts for the multimodal model. We selected the Gemini 2.5 Flash model as the "teacher model" to process each image Sp_i , generating preliminary descriptions corresponding to the S_type , CI_clue, and S_con dimensions. Subsequently, fire investigation experts reviewed and refined the content generated by the "teacher model" to ensure the high quality and professional accuracy of the annotations.

To reduce practical deployment costs and transfer the analytical capabilities of the large model to a lightweight alternative, we selected lightweight multimodal models from the Qwen and Gemma series as "student models." We employed the Low-Rank Adaptation (LoRA) method, a PEFT technique. The core principle of LoRA involves keeping the pre-trained model weights (W_0) frozen while injecting small, trainable low-rank matrices $\Delta W = BA$ into key layers (such as attention layers). During training, only the parameters of A and B are updated, allowing for efficient adaptation to downstream tasks with minimal computational overhead.

The fine-tuning task was formulated as supervised image-to-text generation: fire images from the dataset served as model input, and the corresponding structured text—generated by the "teacher model" and calibrated by experts—served as the ground truth output. By minimizing the discrepancy between the generated text and the ground truth, we explicitly transferred the implicit, complex fire scene analysis capabilities of the large model to the lightweight model. The fine-tuned model can autonomously generate structured analytical reports adhering to the predefined paradigm, significantly enhancing its perceptual performance in the specific professional domain of fire investigation.

4.2 Event Reasoning and Question Answering Based on Retrieval Augmentation

In the preceding stage, by fine-tuning lightweight models, we achieved deep perception and structured description capabilities for individual fire scene images. However, a comprehensive fire investigation relies not only on discrete visual information but also requires the organic integration of this information with textual materials, such as witness statements and fire science principles, to construct complete chains of evidence and perform complex logical reasoning. Conventional methods struggle to automatically fuse heterogeneous data sources and conduct deep analysis.

Therefore, the objective of this stage is to construct a reasoning framework capable of simulating the comprehensive cognitive judgment process of human experts. We propose an event reasoning analysis framework based on RAG, designed to fuse multi-source information for deep event comprehension and auxiliary decision support.

Construction and Vectorization of the Multimodal Knowledge Base. Effective reasoning hinges on a comprehensive and retrievable knowledge base. For a specific fire incident, our knowledge base comprises the following two categories of heterogeneous data sources:

- **Textual Materials Data:** This data originates from official PDF documents, primarily including witness statements and professional textbooks and standards related to fire science. To ensure high fidelity in information extraction, we utilize Marker, an advanced layout analysis tool, to convert PDF documents into Markdown text while preserving their original structure (e.g., tables, headings, paragraph hierarchy). Compared to traditional OCR or simple text extraction, Marker more accurately retains contextual information, laying the foundation for precise subsequent retrieval.
- **Visual Perception Data:** This data consists of the outputs from Stage One. The structured analytical texts (containing S_{type}, CI_{clue}, and S_{con}) generated by the fine-tuned perception model for all scene images are treated as individual knowledge entries. This allows critical evidence derived from images to be retrieved and utilized in text format.

Upon data integration, we utilize the FAISS (Facebook AI Similarity Search) library to vectorize the entire comprehensive knowledge base. FAISS enables efficient indexing of high-dimensional text embeddings, supporting rapid similarity searches and transforming unstructured image and text knowledge into a machine-computable vector database.

Retrieval-Augmented Reasoning Framework with Self-reflection. To achieve precise and reliable conversational reasoning, we designed an enhanced RAG workflow that incorporates query preprocessing, step-wise retrieval, answer synthesis, and self-reflection validation. This workflow simulates the human expert's cognitive process: "information gathering → analysis and synthesis → reflection and verification." The entire reasoning process, which takes a user's query ($Q_u ser$) and our multi-modal knowledge base (KB) to produce a final, verified answer ($A_f inal$), can be abstractly represented as 3:

$$A_{final} = F_{RAG}(Q_{user,KB}) \tag{3}$$

The following sections detail the components of this framework. Natural language queries from users are often complex and colloquial, which can lead to inaccurate retrieval when used directly for vector search. Therefore, we introduce a query preprocessing step. When a user question ($Q_u ser$) is received (e.g., "Based on the burn patterns in the living room and the witness statements, infer the cause of the fire."), the system first employs an LLM set to a low temperature to perform two tasks:

- **Query Decomposition:** Break down complex questions into multiple atomic sub-questions.
- **Semantic Transformation:** Convert colloquial expressions into retrieval-oriented query statements that more closely match the formal language style found in the knowledge base.

This preprocessing function, $f_{preprocess}$, transforms the initial user query into a set of optimized sub-queries $Q'_1, Q'_2, \ldots, Q'_n$ that are better suited for retrieval. The decomposed sub-queries are fed into the FAISS vector database to retrieve the most relevant text chunks (C), which serve as the context. Subsequently, the original question (Q_{user}) and these retrieved contextual chunks are submitted to an LLM, denoted as the generator G_{synth}, set to a high temperature for initial answer synthesis. The high-temperature setting stimulates the model's inductive capabilities, encouraging it to fuse information from diverse sources—for instance, combining witness statements from PDF reports with evidence of smoke traces from image analysis. This process yields a preliminary, logically coherent, and comprehensive answer (A_{prelim}). To further enhance the reliability and rigor of the answers, we introduce a self-reflection stage. This final step is crucial for validating and refining the preliminary answer. After the model generates A_{prelim}, a reflective validation process, $f_{reflect}$, is initiated. The model is prompted to critically assess its own initial response, checking for logical consistency, factual grounding in the provided context, and completeness in addressing the user's query. Based on this introspective process, the model revises its output to produce a more deliberated and reliable final answer, A_{final}. This final transformation is formalized as 4:

$$A_{final} = f_{reflect}(A_{prelim}) \tag{4}$$

(a) System Main Page

(b) System Examination Page

(c) Scene Perception

(d) Dialogue Window

Fig. 3. The process begins at the main page (Fig. 3(a)), where an investigator uploads fire scene images through the 'Environmental Perception' module (Fig. 3(b)). After automated analysis, detailed reports for each image are available in a gallery view (Fig. 3(c)). Finally, the investigator proceeds to the conversational interface (Fig. 3(d)) for deep, evidence-based reasoning and Q&A.

Based on the methodology described previously, we have engineered the fire scene image perception and analysis process into an integrated system and its related window screenshots are in Fig. 3. Within this system, fire investigators can upload batches of images captured at the scene, which are then processed by the perception large model, resulting in a system-generated perception report for each image. Once all scene perception data has been generated, this content is compiled with other relevant fire-related data to create a corpus, which is used by the reasoning large model during the inferential analysis stage. This system enables investigators to efficiently process and synthesize fire information, significantly accelerating the speed of fire investigations and reducing their operational burden.

Currently, our system is in an internal testing and debugging phase. In the next stage, we plan to deploy it for a pilot program with a local fire department to further validate the effectiveness of our methodology.

5 Evaluation

This chapter aims to systematically validate the effectiveness of our proposed FISPA framework through a series of quantitative and qualitative experiments. The evaluation is divided into two core levels: first, verifying the accuracy of the perception model from Stage One, specifically its capability for fine-grained comprehension of fire scene image details; second, assessing the comprehensive performance of the reasoning framework from Stage Two, particularly the system's accuracy and reliability in fusing multi-source information for complex question answering.

5.1 Experimental Setup

Our experimental data comprises two main components to support the evaluation of the perception and reasoning stages, respectively:

- **Perception Model Fine-tuning and Testing Dataset:** This dataset contains 675 image-text pairs from real-world post-fire scenes. After initial generation by the Gemini model, these image-text pairs underwent manual review and revision to ensure quality and accuracy. We allocated 625 pairs for the training set and the remaining 50 for the test set to evaluate the performance of the perception model. To ensure comprehensive evaluation, this 50-sample test set was curated to encompass a diverse range of scenarios, including frequently occurring incidents such as electrical fires, kitchen fires, and wildfires.
- **Event Reasoning Evaluation Dataset:** This dataset is derived from 25 complete, authentic fire case files provided by a local fire department. Each file includes scene investigation photographs (40–80 images), interview records with relevant personnel, and the final fire incident investigation report (in PDF format). We selected 5 of these cases as a test set to evaluate the reasoning capabilities of the RAG framework.

The use of real-world data ensures a high degree of complexity and realism in our experiments, allowing for a thorough evaluation of our method's performance in practical scenarios. Due to the inherent difficulty in acquiring fire investigation data, our current validation is limited to the datasets described in this study. We will endeavor to obtain more extensive data in the future to further test and refine our methodology. We acknowledge this as a limitation of the present work. All experiments were conducted on a server equipped with two NVIDIA A40 GPUs (96GB total VRAM). During the inference stage, the VRAM usage of the lightweight perception model after LoRA fine-tuning was controlled to under 24GB. This demonstrates the model's potential for local deployment on consumer-grade graphics cards, highlighting its practical value.

5.2 Fire Scene Perception Capability Evaluation

This experiment aims to validate the effectiveness of our proposed knowledge transfer method (i.e., instruction fine-tuning using an expert-defined paradigm).

We used the 50 images from the test set as input for models both before (w/o SFT) and after (SFT) our supervised fine-tuning. The models compared include Gemma-4B-It, Gemma-12B-It, and Qwen2.5-VL-Instruct. We employed ROUGE and BERTScore as automatic evaluation metrics, comparing the structured text generated by the models against the ground truth produced by the teacher model (Gemini 2.5 Flash).

Table 1. Performance Comparison of Three Model With And Without Fine-tuning

Model	Rouge1-F1↑	Rouge2-F1↑	RougeL-F1↑	Bert_F1↑
Gemma3-4B-It SFT	0.7083	0.4645	0.7056	**0.7664**
Gemma3-4B-It w/o SFT	0.6782	0.4240	0.6782	0.7649
Gemma3-12B-It SFT	0.7432	0.5021	0.7432	0.7604
Gemma3-12B-It w/o SFT	0.6693	0.4542	0.6693	0.7334
Qwen2.5-VL-Instruct SFT	**0.8116**	**0.5928**	**0.8087**	0.7652
Qwen2.5-VL-Instruct w/o SFT	0.8000	0.5775	0.8001	0.7561

The results in Table 1 indicate that:

Fine-tuning is highly effective: For all tested models, there was a significant improvement across all evaluation metrics after our instruction fine-tuning (SFT versions). This proves that our proposed dataset and fine-tuning method, based on an expert knowledge paradigm, can effectively transfer specialized fire scene perception capabilities to multimodal models.

Model Performance Comparison: Among the fine-tuned models, Qwen2.5-VL-Instruct SFT achieved the highest scores on ROUGE-1, ROUGE-2, and ROUGE-L, indicating that its generated text most closely matched the ground truth in terms of content completeness and structure. Meanwhile, Gemma3-4B-It SFT obtained the highest BERTScore, suggesting the highest semantic similarity to the ground truth. This demonstrates the universality and effectiveness of our method across different model architectures.

5.3 Event Reasoning and Question Answering Capability Evaluation

This experiment employs an ablation study to validate the effectiveness of the query decomposition and self-reflection mechanisms within our enhanced RAG framework. We used 5 complete fire case files as test data. First, the perception model fine-tuned in Experiment 1 was used to process all scene images from the cases to generate structured descriptions. These descriptions were then integrated with the case's textual materials (e.g., interview transcripts) and content from fire science textbooks to construct a knowledge base. We used Gemini 2.5 Pro to automatically generate professional question-answer pairs based on this knowledge base to serve as the evaluation benchmark.

We compared three RAG strategies:

- **Naive RAG:** The basic RAG framework, which performs direct retrieval without query processing.
- **Our RAG:** Incorporates the query decomposition and semantic transformation module.
- **Our RAG + Self-reflection:** Our complete framework, including both query decomposition and self-reflection validation.

Table 2. Performance Comparison of Different RAG Strategy

Method	Rouge1-F1↑	Rouge2-F1↑	RougeL-F1↑	Bert_F1↑
Naive RAG	0.3401	0.1547	0.3401	0.6651
Our RAG	0.3935	0.1274	0.3935	**0.6702**
Our RAG + Self-reflection	**0.4519**	**0.2044**	**0.4519**	0.6693

The experimental results in Table 2 clearly demonstrate the contributions of each component in our framework. Compared to Naive RAG, "Our RAG" with the introduction of query decomposition shows improvement in both ROUGE-1/L and BERTScore. This demonstrates that breaking down complex questions into atomic queries effectively enhances the accuracy of information retrieval, which in turn improves the semantic quality of the answers. "Our RAG + Self-reflection" shows an advantage over the other two methods across all ROUGE metrics, with an increase in the ROUGE-1/L score of approximately 15%. This indicates that the self-reflection mechanism enhances the model's ability to integrate information, construct logical chains, and generate structurally complete answers, making its responses more comprehensive and closer to the standard answers written by experts. Although the BERTScore of "Our RAG + Self-reflection" is slightly lower than the intermediate version, its lead in the ROUGE scores illustrates that the primary value of the self-reflection mechanism lies in improving the completeness, logical coherence, and factual accuracy of the answers—elements that are most critical in professional domain question answering.

During our experiments, we also uncovered an interesting phenomenon. In the RAG-related experiments, the strategy incorporating self-reflection achieved ROUGE scores that were substantially higher on a different tier—than the other methods. By comparing the answers generated by the different RAG strategies, we found that content from professional textbooks constituted a disproportionately large portion of the database. This sometimes had a counterproductive effect, as the retrieval step could introduce irrelevant information into the model's context, acting as noise.

The self-reflection mechanism, however, appears to mitigate this issue. It prompts the reasoning model to critically re-evaluate the question and the retrieved context, allowing it to re-organize the salient data and formulate a more effective response. These findings are worthy of further investigation.

In summary, the experimental results robustly demonstrate the effectiveness of our proposed two-stage "perception-reasoning" framework. Through instruction fine-tuning, we successfully enhanced the model's specialized perception capabilities for fire scenes. Furthermore, by incorporating query decomposition and self-reflection mechanisms, we significantly improved the reliability and accuracy of the RAG framework in handling complex reasoning tasks.

6 Conclusion

Addressing the efficiency bottlenecks and the challenges in professional knowledge dissemination currently facing post-fire investigation, this paper proposes and implements FISPA, a two-stage "perception-reasoning" intelligent investigation assistant framework. By simulating the cognitive workflow of human experts, the framework successfully integrates the complex task of post-disaster visual scene understanding with deep domain-specific knowledge reasoning. Its primary goal is to empower fire investigators, thereby enhancing the efficiency and scientific rigor of their work.

Our main contributions are twofold: 1) We designed a comprehensive knowledge transfer methodology. By constructing a post-disaster scene dataset guided by expert knowledge and efficiently fine-tuning lightweight multimodal models, we effectively address the perceptual deficiencies of general-purpose models in this specialized domain. 2) We proposed an enhanced RAG reasoning framework integrating query decomposition and self-reflection mechanisms, which significantly improves the accuracy and logical reliability of the model when fusing heterogeneous, multi-source information for complex problem-solving. Comprehensive experimental evaluations have robustly validated the effectiveness of each component of our framework, demonstrating FISPA's significant application potential in the specialized field of fire investigation.

Despite the promising results of this study, several limitations and directions for future research remain. First, while the current perception dataset is sourced from real-world cases, its scale and scenario diversity could be expanded. Future work could include more rare types of fires and scenes of extreme damage to enhance the model's generalization capabilities. Moreover, as the capabilities of large language models continue to advance, our method could be tested and integrated with more high-performance models. Second, the fusion of additional data modalities, such as on-site 3D scan models and thermal imagery, could be explored to build a more holistic, three-dimensional understanding of the fire scene. Finally, we plan to deploy the FISPA system in the field for in-depth human-computer interaction testing with frontline investigators. We will then continuously iterate and optimize the system based on real-world feedback, with the ultimate goal of implementing this technology in the critical domain of public safety.

Acknowledgments. This research is supported by NSF of China No. 61802325, the National Key R&D Program of China (2024YFB4504400), the Science and Technology Development Fund (SKL-IOTSC(UM)-2021-2023), the State Key Laboratory of

Internet of Things for Smart City (University of Macau) (Ref. No.: SKL-IoTSC(UM)-2021-2023/ORP/GA06/2022), Wuhan East Lake High-Tech Development Zone (also known as the Optics Valley of China, or OVC) National Comprehensive Experimental Base for Governance of Intelligent Society and the Wang Deyao Outstanding Graduate Scholarship Program of Xiamen University.

References

1. Anitha, D., Kolangiammal, S., Lalitha, K., Valli, K.V.N., Ganesh, E., Muthulekshmi, M.: IoT-enabled exoskeletons for firefighters using reinforcement learning for adaptive support in emergency situations. In: 2024 Second International Conference on Intelligent Cyber Physical Systems and Internet of Things (ICoICI), pp. 455–460. IEEE (2024)
2. Cho, K., et al.: Learning phrase representations using RNN encoder-decoder for statistical machine translation. arXiv preprint: arXiv:1406.1078 (2014)
3. Ding, Z., et al.: A building information modeling-based fire emergency evacuation simulation system for large infrastructures. Reliab. Eng. Syst. Saf. **244**, 109917 (2024)
4. Dosovitskiy, A., et al.: An image is worth 16x16 words: transformers for image recognition at scale. arXiv preprint: arXiv:2010.11929 (2020)
5. Huang, P., Lin, X., Liu, C., Fu, L., Yu, L.: A real-time automatic fire emergency evacuation route selection model based on decision-making processes of pedestrians. Saf. Sci. **169**, 106332 (2024)
6. Hurst, A., et al.: GPT-4O system card. arXiv preprint: arXiv:2410.21276 (2024)
7. Kuznetsova, P., Ordonez, V., Berg, A., Berg, T., Choi, Y.: Collective generation of natural image descriptions. In: Proceedings of the 50th Annual Meeting of the Association for Computational Linguistics (Volume 1: Long Papers), pp. 359–368 (2012)
8. Lee, J., et al.: BioBERT: a pre-trained biomedical language representation model for biomedical text mining. Bioinformatics **36**(4), 1234–1240 (2020)
9. Lentini, J.J.: Scientific Protocols for Fire Investigation. CRC Press, Boca Raton (2018)
10. Lewis, P., et al.: Retrieval-augmented generation for knowledge-intensive NLP tasks In: Advances in Neural Information Processing Systems, vol. 33, 9459–9474 (2020)
11. Li, J., Li, D., Savarese, S., Hoi, S.: BLIP-2: bootstrapping language-image pre-training with frozen image encoders and large language models. In: International Conference on Machine Learning, pp. 19730–19742. PMLR (2023)
12. Li, Y., et al.: FireinvestLLM: leveraging large language models for improved fire investigation inquiries. In: 2024 IEEE Smart World Congress (SWC), pp. 983–989. IEEE (2024)
13. Li, Z., et al.: Monkey: image resolution and text label are important things for large multi-modal models. In: proceedings of the IEEE/CVF Conference on Computer Vision and Pattern Recognition, pp. 26763–26773 (2024)
14. Liu, H., Li, C., Wu, Q., Lee, Y.J.: Visual instruction tuning. In: Advances in Neural Information Processing Systems, vol. 36, pp. 34892–34916 (2023)
15. Lu, J., Batra, D., Parikh, D., Lee, S.: ViLBERT: pretraining task-agnostic visiolinguistic representations for vision-and-language tasks. In: Advances in Neural Information Processing Systems, vol. 32 (2019)

16. Luo, G., et al.: FireExpert: fire event identification and assessment leveraging cross-domain knowledge and large language model. IEEE Trans. Mob. Comput. (2025)
17. National Fire and Rescue Administration (China): Press conference (2025). https://www.119.gov.cn/qmxfxw/xwfbh/index.shtml. Accessed 23 Jan 2025
18. Nic Daeid, N.: Fire Investigation. CRC Press, Boca Raton (2004)
19. Ordonez, V., Kulkarni, G., Berg, T.: Im2Text: describing images using 1 million captioned photographs. In: Advances in Neural Information Processing Systems, vol. 24 (2011)
20. Radford, A., et al.: Learning transferable visual models from natural language supervision. In: International Conference on Machine Learning, pp. 8748–8763. PmLR (2021)
21. Ramadan, M.N., et al.: Towards early forest fire detection and prevention using ai-powered drones and the IoT. Internet Things **27**, 101248 (2024)
22. Rotstein, N., Bensaid, D., Brody, S., Ganz, R., Kimmel, R.: FuseCap: leveraging large language models for enriched fused image captions. In: Proceedings of the IEEE/CVF Winter Conference on Applications of Computer Vision, pp. 5689–5700 (2024)
23. Sutskever, I., Vinyals, O., Le, Q.V.: Sequence to sequence learning with neural networks. In: Advances in Neural Information Processing Systems, vol. 27 (2014)
24. Team, G., et al.: Gemini: a family of highly capable multimodal models. arXiv preprint: arXiv:2312.11805 (2023)
25. Vaswani, A., et al.: Attention is all you need. In: Advances in Neural Information Processing Systems, vol. 30 (2017)
26. Vinyals, O., Toshev, A., Bengio, S., Erhan, D.: Show and tell: a neural image caption generator. In: Proceedings of the IEEE Conference on Computer Vision and Pattern Recognition, pp. 3156–3164 (2015)
27. Wang, P., et al.: Qwen2-VL: enhancing vision-language model's perception of the world at any resolution. arXiv preprint: arXiv:2409.12191 (2024)
28. Wu, Y., et al.: DetToolChain: a new prompting paradigm to unleash detection ability of MLLM. In: European Conference on Computer Vision, pp. 164–182. Springer (2024)
29. Xu, K., et al.: Show, attend and tell: neural image caption generation with visual attention. In: International Conference on Machine Learning, pp. 2048–2057. PMLR (2015)
30. Zhao, H., Jin, J., Liu, Y., Guo, Y., Shen, Y.: FSDF: a high-performance fire detection framework. Expert Syst. Appl. **238**, 121665 (2024)
31. Zheng, H., Wang, G., Xiao, D., Liu, H., Hu, X.: FTA-DETR: an efficient and precise fire detection framework based on an end-to-end architecture applicable to embedded platforms. Expert Syst. Appl. **248**, 123394 (2024)

MobileLogZip: Lightweight LLM-Driven Tiered Log Compression for Mobile Computing

Yilei Zhang(✉), Jun Yuan, Linhao Yue, and Wenxin Tian

Anhui Normal University, Wuhu, China
stonezyl@gmail.com, {junyuan,ylh,tianwenxin}@mail.ahnu.edu.cn

Abstract. Mobile devices generate massive logs critical for maintenance and user experience optimization, yet their storage and transmission are severely constrained by limited resources. Existing compression methods either overlook log structure or fail to address the significant value disparity in mobile logs resulting in limited compression ratios and excessive resource consumption. This paper proposes MobileLogZip, a lightweight LLM-driven tiered compression framework tailored for mobile environments. Specifically, logs are categorized into three value tiers (high, medium, and low), and differentiated compression strategies are applied for each tier: high-value logs use lossless compression to preserve their complete structure; medium-value logs use partial lossy compression, discarding header information while retaining templates and parameters; low-value logs are subjected to deep lossy compression through semantic abstraction. Compression ratios are further enhanced by integrating dictionary encoding and using a general-purpose compressor after encoding. Evaluations across several public real-world log datasets demonstrate that MobileLogZip achieves a significant improvement in compression ratio compared to existing methods, with negligible impact on downstream tasks like anomaly detection.

Keywords: Log Compression · Lightweight LLMs · Mobile Computing

1 Introduction

Logs are structured records generated by mobile applications and devices to capture runtime events such as app status, error messages, user interactions, and hardware performance metrics. They play an indispensable role in mobile app maintenance, fault diagnosis, and user experience optimization [4,17,24]. For example, log analysis helps developers trace the root causes of app crashes [10,38], identify performance bottlenecks [20,23,24], or understand user behavior patterns [16]. However, with the widespread adoption of feature-rich mobile applications, the volume of log data on mobile devices is growing rapidly. This growth trend, coupled with the inherent limitations of mobile devices, such as limited storage capacity, restricted network bandwidth,

L. Zhang and K.-K. R. Choo (Eds.): MobiQuitous 2025, LNICST 683, pp. 57–74, 2026.
https://doi.org/10.1007/978-3-032-22500-9_4

and battery-powered operation, is placing significant pressure on device resources and data transmission efficiency. Therefore, it is urgent to develop efficient log compression technologies designed specifically for mobile environments.

Existing log compression methods can be categorized into two main types: (1) General-purpose compression tools (e.g., Gzip [3], LZMA [1]) utilize character frequency analysis but overlook the structured nature of logs, resulting in compression ratios typically below 10:1. (2) Log-specific compression methods (e.g., LogZip [25], LogShrink [22], LogReducer [36], etc.) enhance efficiency by extracting log templates (i.e., fixed structures) and separating dynamic parameters, achieving compression ratios ranging from 15:1 to 50:1. In general, these methods are primarily designed for server-side logs and have effectively reduced storage overhead in traditional server environments.

Despite their contributions, existing methods still face two primary limitations when applied to mobile log compression. First, the compression ratio is still insufficient in mobile scenarios. Mobile devices such as smartphones, wearable devices, and IoT devices have severely limited storage space. Therefore, it place extremely high demands on compression ratios. However, compressed log files generated by existing methods still occupy excessive space, rendering them impractical. Second, these methods overlook the significant value disparity inherent in mobile logs. In mobile ecosystems, log value exhibits significant variation. For instance, in IoT devices, low-value logs, such as frequent heartbeat logs that only indicate normal operation, account for a large portion, while high-value logs, such as fault logs that are critical for diagnosis, are sparse. Existing compression methods treat all logs as equally important and applies the identical compression scheme to all of them. Consequently, a substantial volume of low-value data persists in occupying a considerable portion of storage capacity even after compression, thereby inefficiently utilizing limited resources that could be allocated to storing high-value logs. This finding suggests that a generic log compression strategy is inefficient, while value-based tiered compression is both necessary and feasible.

To address these limitations, this paper proposes MobileLogZip, a tiered log compression framework that leverages lightweight LLMs for value assessment, to accommodate the resource constraints of mobile devices. MobileLogZip consists of four key components: (1) A log understanding module which extracts domain-specific knowledge from log data and establishes a comprehensive semantic understanding of log data. (2) A log value assessor based on lightweight LLMs which automatically classifies logs into high, medium, and low tiers via semantic understanding of impact, severity, and downstream relevance, eliminating manual intervention. (3) A differentiated compression strategy combining structured dictionary encoding: lossless preservation for high-value logs via structured dictionary encoding, partial lossy compression for medium-value logs by discarding non-critical header information, and semantic abstraction for low-value logs to retain only high-level patterns. (4) A secondary compression optimization mechanism using a general-purpose compressor to further enhance compression ratios. We conduct extensive experiments to evaluate MobileLogZip on public

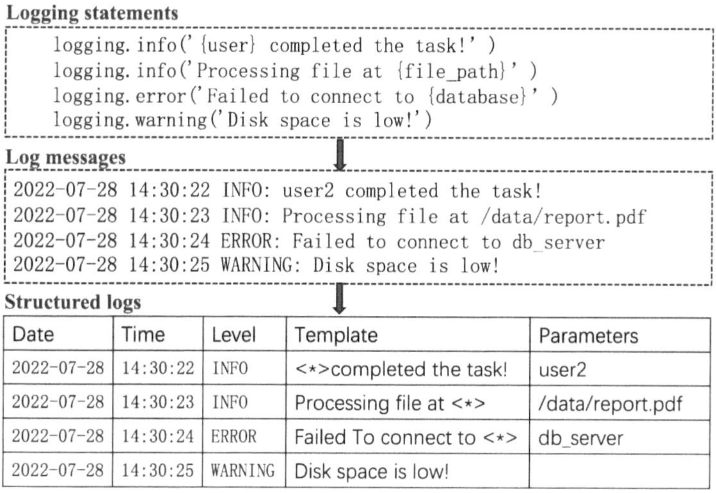

Fig. 1. The generation and parsing of log data.

real-world log datasets collected from a variety of software systems [19]. The experimental results show that MobileLogZip outperforms state-of-the-art log-specific compression methods and general-purpose compression methods in terms of compression ratio.

This work makes the following contributions:

- We propose a value-based tiered log compression framework tailored for mobile computing. By combining lossless and lossy compression strategies, it reduces storage space requirements on mobile devices while preserving critical information essential for downstream tasks.
- We develop an automated log value assessment method leveraging lightweight LLMs, eliminating the need for manual intervention and enabling efficient deployment on resource-constrained mobile environments.
- We conduct extensive evaluations of MobileLogZip across public real-world log datasets, demonstrating that it outperforms state-of-the-art methods in terms of compression ratio while mitigating accuracy degradation in downstream anomaly detection tasks.

The remainder of this paper is structured as follows: Sect. 2 reviews related work. Section 3 details the design of MobileLogZip. Section 4 describes experimental setup. Section 5 presents results and analysis. Section 6 concludes the paper.

2 Related Work

2.1 General-Purpose Compression Tools

Early approaches to log compression primarily employed generic text-oriented compression algorithms, which can be broadly categorized into dictionary-based, entropy-based, and prediction-based methods. Dictionary-based methods, such as Gzip [3] and LZMA [1], utilize LZ77/LZ78-based dictionary coding and Huffman encoding to reduce character-level redundancy. While these tools are widely adopted due to their simplicity, they overlook the structured nature of logs, including fixed templates and dynamic parameters, resulting in modest compression ratios on log datasets. Entropy-based methods (e.g., Arithmetic encoding [30]) construct probabilistic models to minimize coding size, while prediction-based techniques (e.g., PPMd [7], DeepZip [8]) use prior tokens to predict subsequent ones, adaptively encoding prediction errors. However, as Yao et al. [34] empirically demonstrated, all general-purpose compression methods process logs at the character or bit level, lacking the capability to restructure data based on log-specific characteristics such as semantic hierarchy or template-parameter duality. This fundamental limitation restricts their compression performance on log data.

2.2 Log-Specific Compression Methods

To address the inefficiencies of generic tools, researchers developed log-specific Compression methods tailored to the template-parameter structure of logs. Figure 1 illustrates the generation and parsing of log data. LogZip [25] pioneered this direction by iteratively clustering logs to extract templates, separating static text from dynamic parameters, and applying 7-Zip for secondary compression. This approach achieved compression ratios of 15:1 to 25:1 on Hadoop and Zookeeper logs but suffered from high computational overhead due to its iterative clustering. Parser-based methods [9,29,35] further developed this direction by decomposing log entries into headers, events, and variables using a log parser and processing each component separately. These techniques heuristically reduce log size by applying data type-specific encoding, such as incremental encoding of timestamps, extraction of common sub-patterns from static text, and dictionary encoding of repeated variables. They fully leverage the high redundancy of log content and timestamp patterns. Tools like CLP [26] and LogGrep [28] further expand this paradigm to enable efficient querying of compressed data: CLP parses logs into patterns and classifies variables into string-type and non-string-type, while LogGrep extracts static and runtime patterns of dictionary variables to form fine-grained encapsulations. However, they both struggle to balance high compression rates with maintaining searchability.

Subsequent research has focused on optimizing template extraction and compression efficiency. LogShrink [22] proposes a hybrid framework that uses density-based clustering algorithms for template identification and differential encoding for numerical parameters, achieving compression ratios of 20:1 to 50:1 while reducing runtime by 2.6 times compared to LogZip. DeNum [37] further optimizes numerical parameter compression through interval-based encoding, achieving a 11.8% improvement in compression ratios over LogShrink on Linux and Windows logs.

Despite these advancements, log-specific lossless methods share a critical limitation: they mandate the complete lossless preservation of all logs, regardless

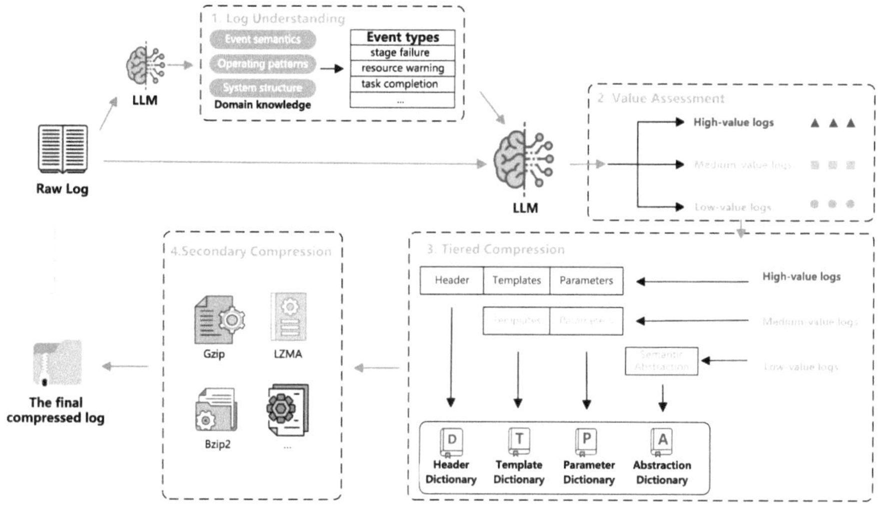

Fig. 2. The workflow of MobileLogZip framework.

of their informational value. This design inherently limits compression ratios, as even low-value logs are fully retained.

2.3 LLM-Driven Log Analysis

LLMs have revolutionized log analysis by enabling semantic log understanding. They demonstrate strong capabilities in log parsing [18,21,31,33], anomaly detection [11,12,14], and root-cause analysis [6,13,27], leveraging their pre-trained knowledge of system behaviors. LILAC [18] uses LLMs to parse log templates with 18% higher accuracy than traditional tools (e.g., Drain [15]) by leveraging semantic understanding. Similarly, LogGPT [12] fine-tunes LLMs for log anomaly detection, demonstrating superior performance on unstructured logs. It is worth noting that existing LLM-based log research focus on analysis rather than compression has not applied LLMs to the assessment of log value. Although LILAC and LogGPT utilize the structural parsing capabilities of LLMs, they do not quantify log value, which is a key gap that our framework addresses.

3 Methodology

This section provides a detailed introduction to the MobileLogZip framework. This framework leverages LLMs to perform semantic understanding of domain knowledge, aiming to balance compression efficiency and critical information retention, with a focus on preserving the utility of high-value logs for downstream tasks. Specifically, the framework consists of four modules as shown in Fig. 2: the log understanding module establishes a comprehensive semantic understanding of log data; the value assessment module classifies the value of each log based on this understanding; the tiered compression module applies tiered compression strategies to logs of different values; the secondary compression module further improves the compression rate using a general-purpose compressor.

3.1 Log Understanding

Log understanding serves as the step to extract domain-specific knowledge and semantic context directly from log datasets. This phase leverages LLMs to analyze the entire log corpus, enabling the model to autonomously infer the underlying system structure, operating patterns, and event semantics.

The process begins with a LLM conducting a comprehensive scan of the log dataset, identifying recurring components, relationships, and event types through batch processing of raw logs. For example, when analyzing HDFS logs, the LLM identifies frequent references to "Namenode," "DataNode," and "block" as core system components and infers their roles through contextual patterns: "Namenode" is consistently associated with "block management" events, while "DataNode" appears in 'heartbeat' and "replication" messages. By reviewing the log corpus, the LLM can derive operational patterns, such as distinguishing between regular status updates and abnormal events , and map these patterns to implicit system behaviors.

Building on this corpus-wide analysis, the LLM then classifies distinct events by their semantic and operational significance. This event classification involves identifying structural patterns within individual logs and grouping them into coherent categories based on inferred meaning. For instance, in a Spark log dataset, the LLM might cluster logs into "stage failure" events related to job interruptions, "resource warning" events associated with memory or disk thresholds, and regular and repetitive "task completion" events. These classifications are derived solely from log content, with the LLM leveraging its capacity to recognize contextual similarities and semantic nuances across thousands of log entries.

Finally, the preliminary tiering plan is generated based on the LLM's analysis of event frequency and semantic weight. For example, rare but critical "system crash" logs are classified as high-value events, while common "heartbeat" logs are classified as low-value events. This data-driven plan ensures that subsequent value assessment and compression strategies are based directly on the intrinsic patterns of the log dataset, rather than external assumptions.

3.2 Value Assessment

Value assessment classifies logs into high, medium, or low tiers using pre-trained LLMs via prompt engineering, enabling zero-shot inference without task-specific fine-tuning. This approach leverages the inherent semantic understanding capabilities of LLMs (e.g., Llama3.2:3B) to evaluate logs across three core dimensions: impact scope, severity, and downstream relevance. By structuring prompts to align with these dimensions, the framework ensures consistent and context-aware classification.

Impact scope is evaluated by determining whether an event affects the entire system, specific modules, or isolated components. For example, a log indicating "cluster failure" is classified as system-wide, while "executor timeout" pertains to a specific module. Severity is evaluated by the urgency of required action, ranging from critical events requiring immediate intervention (e.g., "data corruption detected") to informational updates requiring no response (e.g., "debug mode enabled"). The downstream relevance of a log is measured by its usefulness for post-compression tasks such as anomaly detection or root-cause analysis. Logs containing error stack traces or configuration mismatches are deemed highly relevant, whereas regular status messages are not.

I. Task Definition Classify logs into high/medium/low value based on impact, severity, and downstream relevance.
II. Input Content 1. Log data to be compressed: {...} 2. Semantic understandings of the dataset (if any):{...}
III. Grading Criteria 1. High-value Logs: severe incidents that may affect system ... 2. Medium-value Logs: issues that require attention ... 3. Low-value Logs: normal operation records ...
IV. Output Format Only the level corresponding to the log is returned, indicated by [number], such as ...
VI. Notes ...

Fig. 3. Key elements of the value assessment prompt.

The prompts have been carefully designed to guide LLMs consistently as shown in Fig. 3. Each prompt includes a clear task definition, explicit grading criteria and specific examples, as well as a structured output format that can be easily automated. For example: (1) Task definition: "Classify logs into high/medium/low value based on impact, severity, and downstream relevance"; (2) Grading criteria: "High value: Logs indicating system-critical events, such as "cluster initialization failed"; (3) Output format: "Output: High/Medium/Low".

This prompt-driven approach enables the LLM to infer value tiers directly from log content, even without prior knowledge of the specific system. For instance, when presented with a log from an unknown cloud service that states

'Auto Scaling Group unable to launch instances', the LLM recognizes the keyword 'failure', interprets the event in the context of the inferred system architecture 'Auto Scaling Group', and evaluates its potential impact on system availability, classifying it as a high-value log. This ability to generalize across domains and systems means the framework can be applied to a variety of log sources, ranging from traditional enterprise systems to emerging cloud architectures.

By integrating these dimensions into a unified assessment framework, the value tiering process matches compression strategies with log importance. High-value logs, identified as critical for system health or downstream analysis, are prioritized for lossless preservation, while medium and low-value logs undergo increasingly aggressive compression. This semantic-aware approach ensures that compression ratio is maximized without compromising the utility of logs for critical tasks, such as anomaly detection.

3.3 Tiered Compression

Tiered compression strategies are tailored to the value tiers identified in the assessment phase, with increasing levels of lossiness applied to logs of lower value. This tiered approach ensures that high-value logs retain full structural and semantic integrity, while medium and low-value logs undergo targeted compression to balance efficiency and critical information retention.

For high-value logs, such as those indicating system-wide errors or critical configuration anomalies, lossless compression is employed to preserve all contextual details. These logs are first parsed into three distinct components: header information including timestamps, source nodes, and metadata, fixed templates such as "Error: Block id failed to replicate", and dynamic parameters like id = "12345". In order to minimize redundancy while retaining completeness, three dictionaries are constructed: a header dictionary mapping header information to compact identifiers, a template dictionary encoding recurring structural patterns, and a parameter dictionary for dynamic values. Raw logs are then replaced with sequences of these identifiers (i.e., header ID + template ID + parameter IDs), enabling full reconstruction of the original log while reducing storage overhead through dictionary-based encoding. This ensures that high-value logs remain fully usable for downstream tasks such as root-cause analysis or anomaly detection.

Medium-value logs, including module-specific warnings and non-critical status updates, undergo partial lossy compression, focusing on retaining semantically relevant details while discarding redundant Header. Header information such as non-time-sensitive timestamps is intentionally omitted to reduce size, as these fields are considered non-critical for the Medium-value logs. The templates and parameters reuse the dictionary from high-value logs to maintain consistency.

Low-value logs, such as repetitive heartbeat messages, regular debug entries, or trivial status updates, undergo deep lossy compression through semantic abstraction, retaining only high-level event patterns. This process begins by generalizing raw logs into generic semantic templates that capture the essence of recurring events while removing variable details. For example, thousands of heartbeat logs with different timestamps such as "Node A active at 08:00," "Node A active at 08:05," are abstracted into a single template: "Node A periodic heartbeat." Similarly, general task completions such as "Task 5 finished," "Task 6 finished" are summarized as "general task completion." These semantic templates are then mapped to a semantic dictionary, with each template assigned a unique id. Raw low-value logs are replaced with these ids, significantly reducing storage requirements while preserving the ability to infer high-level system behavior (e.g., confirming that nodes remain operational via heartbeat abstractions).

These tiered strategies ensure that compression intensity scales with log value: high-value logs retain complete details, medium-value logs balance detail and compression ratio, and low-value logs achieve maximal compression through targeted abstraction. This approach maximizes overall compression ratios while ensuring the usability of critical logs for analytical tasks.

3.4 Secondary Compression

Following the tier-specific compression steps, the encoded sequences undergo a final compression step using general-purpose compressors. This secondary compression leverages the statistical redundancy inherent in the encoded ID sequences, complementing the semantic and structural redundancy reduction achieved in earlier stages.

Although the size of the encoding sequence has been significantly reduced, it still retains the repetitive ID combination patterns that are well-suited to the capabilities of general-purpose compressors. For example, high-value logs may frequently co-occur with specific header IDs and template IDs, such as the combination of the "name node" header and the "block failure" template. Low-value logs, on the other hand, often generate repetitive semantic template ID sequences, such as alternating 'heartbeat' and "normal status" IDs. Although these patterns have been pre-processed through encoding and structuring, they still contain statistical regularities, such as repetitive ID sub-sequences or skewed frequency distributions. Tools like Zstd, LZMA, or Gzip can efficiently compress them using entropy encoding and dictionary-based lookups. It is worth noting that this secondary compression preserves the integrity of the encoded IDs. This ensure that decompression can reconstruct the precise sequence required to restore specific levels of log detail, thereby maintaining compatibility with downstream tasks.

4 Experimental Setup

To validate the effectiveness of MobileLogZip, we conducted comprehensive experiments to address the following research questions (RQs):

- RQ1: How does MobileLogZip perform in terms of compression ratio and robustness compared to state-of-the-art methods?

- RQ2: How does MobileLogZip preserve the utility of logs for downstream tasks?
- RQ3: How do different lightweight LLMs affect MobileLogZip?

4.1 Datasets

Table 1. The statistics of experimental datasets

System Type	Dataset	# Logs	File Size
Mobile system	Android	1,555,005	183.37 MB
	HealthApp	253,395	22.44 MB
Operating system	Linux	25,567	2.25 MB
	Mac	117,283	16.09 MB
Distributed system	HDFS	104,815	13.57 MB
	Zookeeper	74,380	9.95 MB
Server application	Apache	56,481	4.90 MB
Supercomputer	HPC	433,489	32.00 MB
Standalone software	Proxifier	21,329	2.42 MB

We evaluate MobileLogZip on 9 public real-world log datasets from LogHub [39], spanning diverse systems to ensure generality, including mobile systems (e.g., Android, HealthApp), operating systems (e.g., Linux, Mac), distributed systems (e.g., HDFS, Zookeeper), server application (e.g., Apache), supercomputer (e.g., HPC), and standalone software (e.g., Proxifier). These datasets are chosen for their representativeness of log characteristics in mobile environments (e.g., high volume, value diversity, and structural variability). Table 1 summarizes the detailed statistics of these datasets.

4.2 Baselines

We compare MobileLogZip with six representative compression methods, covering three classic general-purpose tools (e.g., gzip, lzma, bzip2), three state-of-the-art log-specific compress methods (e.g., LogReducer, LogShrink, DeNum).

General-Purpose Compressors

- Gzip [3]: A widely used dictionary-based compressor leveraging LZ77 and Huffman coding.
- LZMA [1]: A high-ratio compressor using LZMA2 algorithm, known for strong compression but high computational cost.
- Bzip2 [2]: A block-sorting compressor utilizing Burrows-Wheeler transform and Huffman coding, balancing compression ratio and speed between Gzip and LZMA.

Log-Specific Compressors

- LogReducer [36]: Focuses on reducing log hotspots via on-the-fly compression in kernel logs.
- LogShrink [22]: A hybrid framework combining density-based clustering and differential encoding for numerical parameters.
- DeNum [37]: Optimizes numerical parameter compression via interval-based encoding.

These methods are chosen for their widespread recognition in log compression research. In order to provide a fair comparison, we downloaded the source code for all baseline models and used their default settings and hyperparameters.

4.3 Evaluation Metrics

Compression Ratio (CR) is defined as the ratio of original log size to compressed size (higher is better) to evaluate the performance of log compression:

$$\text{Compression Ratio (CR)} = \frac{\textit{original size}}{\textit{compressed size}} \tag{1}$$

F1-Score of Anomaly Detection (F1) is the harmonic mean of Precision and Recall of a log-based anomaly detector (higher is better), evaluating the downstream task utility of compressed log. Precision is the percentage of correctly detected abnormal log sequences among all detected abnormal log sequences by the model. Recall is the percentage of log sequences that are correctly identified as anomalies over all real anomalies.

$$\text{F1} = 2 \times \frac{precision \times recall}{precision + recall} \tag{2}$$

4.4 Implementation Details

MobileLogZip was implemented using Python 3.11. To ensure a fair comparison, all baseline methods were executed under identical environmental conditions, utilizing their default parameter configurations. For MobileLogZip's underlying lightweight LLM, we selected Llama3.2-3B due to its favorable balance between computational efficiency and performance capabilities. It is important to note that MobileLogZip's architecture permits seamless integration with other LLMs; in RQ3, we specifically evaluated MobileLogZip's performance when substituting Llama3.2-3B with alternative lightweight LLMs. We conduct experiments on a Linux server equipped with Intel Xeon 2.4GHz CPU, 8GB of RAM.

Table 2. Compression ratio comparison with the cutting-edge log compress methods on various datasets.

Dataset	Gzip	Lzma	Bzip2	LogReducer	LogShrink	DeNum	MobileLogZip
Android	7.742	18.857	12.787	20.776	21.857	32.494	**87.333**
HealthApp	10.957	13.431	13.843	31.694	39.072	44.472	**61.512**
Linux	11.232	16.677	14.695	25.213	29.252	30.449	**40.036**
Mac	11.733	22.159	18.074	35.252	39.860	40.789	**60.072**
HDFS	10.636	13.559	14.059	22.634	27.319	25.670	**50.369**
Zookeeper	25.979	27.667	36.156	94.562	116.981	135.251	**185.481**
Apache	21.308	25.186	29.557	43.028	55.940	58.517	**77.424**
HPC	11.263	15.076	12.756	32.070	35.878	45.275	**67.171**
Proxifier	15.716	18.982	23.619	25.502	27.029	27.288	**54.691**

Note: The highest compression ratio for each dataset is highlighted in bold.

5 Evaluation Results

In this section, we present the experimental results to answer the three research questions outlined in Sect. 4. The results are analyzed quantitatively and qualitatively to validate the effectiveness of MobileLogZip in terms of compression ratio, Robustness, downstream task utility, and adaptability to different lightweight LLMs.

5.1 RQ1: Compression Ratio and Robustness Comparison

Compression Ratio. Table 2 summarizes the CR of MobileLogZip and baselines on 9 datasets. MobileLogZip achieves the highest CR on every dataset, with particularly significant gains in mobile systems with high proportions of low-value logs. For example, on the Android dataset, MobileLogZip reaches a CR of 87.333, which is 2.7 times that of DeNum, 4 times that of LogShrink, and 11 times that of Gzip.

Robustness. Robustness is further validated by the distribution of 1/CR as shown in Fig. 4, which measures the percentage of compressed size relative to the original. MobileLogZip exhibits the smallest 1/CR values across all datasets, with a tight distribution of 0.52.5%, indicating stable performance regardless of log type. In contrast, baselines like LogReducer and LogShrink show larger variance of 0.74.6%.

Summary for RQ1: MobileLogZip outperforms all baseline methods in compression ratio across all datasets, with an average improvement of 55.4% over DeNum, a state-of-the-art log-specific compressors. It also achieves improvement of 298.7% over LZMA, a general-purpose tools. It also exhibits strong robustness across diverse log types.

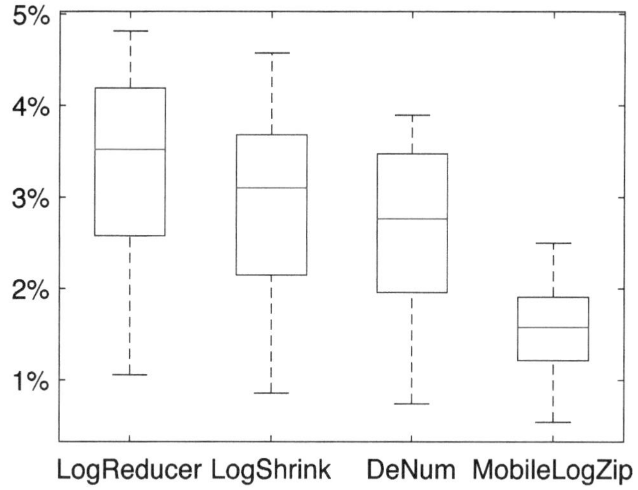

Fig. 4. Distribution of 1/CR on different datasets. 1/CR denotes the percentage of compressed log size over original log size.

5.2 RQ2: Utility Preservation for Downstream Tasks

Table 3 compares the anomaly detection performance in terms of precision, recall and F1 using raw logs and logs reconstructed from MobileLogZip's compressed files, evaluated with two representative anomaly detectors: LR [5] and LogSD [32].

The F1 of LogSD on compressed logs is 0.697 which is nearly identical to 0.699 on raw logs, with a drop of only 0.29%. Similarly, precision remains stable with 0.969 for compressed logs and 0.979 for raw logs and recall only drops from 0.544 to 0.543. This minimal degradation is attributed to MobileLogZip's lossless preservation of high-value logs, which contain the majority of anomaly-related signals.

For LR, the precision decreases slightly from 0.986 to 0.962. However, the recall drops significantly from 0.236 to 0.078, and similarly the F1 drops from 0.381 to 0.144. This is because the LR model relies on token-level features constructed from raw logs to detect anomalies, without high-level semantic features. MobileLogZip performs high-level semantic compression on a large number of low-value logs, retaining semantic information while discarding token-level details. This prevents the LR model from constructing effective features for a large number of logs. As a result, the number of anomalies detected at the specified confidence level is significantly reduced. In contrast, the LogSD model uses deep learning to analyze the semantics in the original logs for anomaly detection, while MobileLogZip retains the semantic information of the original logs in the compressed logs. Therefore, the LogSD model can still detect a large number of anomalies in the compressed logs. Notably, LogSD achieved a recall of 0.544 on compressed logs, which is slightly higher than the recall of 0.543 observed on original logs. This may be due to the fact that MobileLogZip performs semantic abstraction on the original logs, thereby assisting LogSD in better comprehending the log semantics and detecting anomalies that were previously overlooked.

Summary for RQ2: MobileLogZip retains the utility of raw logs for anomaly detection, with negligible degradation in F1-score, demonstrating that its tiered compression preserves critical information for downstream analysis.

Table 3. Anomaly detection accuracy comparison with the raw logs and reconstructed logs from compressed files.

Data	Precision		Recall		F1	
	LR	LogSD	LR	LogSD	LR	LogSD
Raw logs	0.986	0.979	0.236	0.543	0.381	0.699
Compressed logs	0.962	0.969	0.078	0.544	0.144	0.697

5.3 RQ3: Impact of Different Lightweight LLMs

In this paper, we use Llama3.2:3b as the default backbone model for MobileLogZip. To evaluate the generalization of MobileLogZip over different LLMs, we conduct experiments with two other lightweight LLMs. These LLMs are pretrained using different corpora on different architectures, making them suitable for evaluating the generalization ability of MobileLogZip. Table 4 and Table 5 compare the performance of MobileLogZip when using Llama3.2:3b, Gemma3:4b, and Qwen3:4b.

Compression Ratio. In terms of CR, the experimental results clearly demonstrate that MobileLogZip consistently outperforms all baseline models across various LLMs, regardless of the differences in their inherent semantic understanding capabilities. This indicates that MobileLogZip's core mechanism for optimizing CR is not overly reliant on the specific semantic processing strengths of a particular LLM but rather leverages a more generalized and effective compression strategy.

Notably, while MobileLogZip maintains its leading position overall, the performance of individual models exhibits variations across different datasets. For instance, Llama3.2:3b achieves the best CR among three models on the Apache datasets, whereas Qwen3:4b outperforms other models on the HealthApp datasets. These dataset-specific discrepancies can be attributed to two key factors. First, each dataset possesses unique semantic characteristics. For example, Apache logs are dominated by system-level operation records with rigid

Table 4. Compression ratio comparison with different lightweight LLMs as backbones on various datasets.

Dataset	Llama3.2:3b	Gemma3:4b	Qwen3:4b
Android	**87.333**	67.9259	65.661
HealthApp	61.512	48.391	**67.502**
Linux	40.036	45.486	**46.543**
Mac	60.072	**66.018**	64.6159
HDFS	50.369	55.027	**92.925**
Zookeeper	185.481	**194.35**	144.642
Apache	**77.424**	64.0611	65.6191
HPC	67.171	76.3377	**77.717**
Proxifier	54.691	**75.242**	35.558

Note: The highest compression ratio for each dataset is highlighted in bold.

syntax structures, while HealthApp logs contain more domain-specific medical terminologies and user behavior descriptions. Second, there are differences in semantic understanding capabilities among various LLMs. Llama3.2:3b may excel in parsing structured, rule-based log patterns, making it more effective for Apache dataset, while Qwen3:4b might demonstrate stronger proficiency in capturing domain-specific semantics, which aligns better with the characteristics of HealthApp logs. Such differences in both dataset properties and LLM capabilities directly lead to variations in the depth of understanding and semantic abstraction abilities of each model for specific datasets, thereby resulting in the observed performance divergence across datasets.

Downstream Utility. The experimental results reveal that all three LLMs maintain highly consistent downstream utility when integrated with LogSD, as evidenced by the stability of the F1 across models as shown in Table 5. Specifically, the F1 for downstream tasks ranges marginally from 0.696 to 0.697, with a maximum variance of only 0.14%. This stability can be attributed to the lossless preservation of high-value logs by all LLMs, despite minor differences in the classification of low-value logs. Since downstream tasks primarily rely on the lossless preservation of these high-value logs, overall practicality is not affected by differences in the classification of low-value logs.

Summary for RQ3: MobileLogZip is adaptable to various lightweight LLMs, with compression ratios outperform baselines and downstream utility remaining consistent.

Table 5. Anomaly detection accuracy comparison of MobileLogZip with different lightweight LLMs as backbone on various datasets.

Model	Precision		Recall		F1	
	LR	LogSD	LR	LogSD	LR	LogSD
Llama3.2:3b	0.962	0.969	0.078	0.544	0.144	0.697
Gemma3:4b	0.961	0.968	0.067	0.544	0.121	0.696
Qwen3:4b	0.969	0.969	0.091	0.544	0.149	0.697

6 Conclusion

This work presents MobileLogZip, a lightweight LLM-driven tiered compression framework designed to address the unique challenges of log management in resource-constrained mobile environments. By leveraging semantic understanding to differentiate log value and applying targeted compression strategies, MobileLogZip bridges the gap between high compression ratio and critical information preservation. Our comprehensive evaluation across 9 public real-world datasets validates the effectiveness of MobileLogZip. MobileLogZip advances log compression for mobile computing by prioritizing semantic value, offering a practical solution to the storage and transmission challenges of massive mobile logs.

Acknowledgment. The work described in this paper was supported by the National Natural Science Foundation of China (61802003), and the Anhui Provincial Merit-Based Funding Program for Overseas Returnees' Innovation Projects.

References

1. 7za tool (2025). https://linux.die.net/man/1/7za
2. The bzip2 home page (2025). https://sourceware.org/bzip2/
3. The gzip homepage (2025). https://www.gzip.org
4. Amar, A., Rigby, P.C.: Mining historical test logs to predict bugs and localize faults in the test logs. In: International Conference on Software Engineering (ICSE), pp. 140–151 (2019)
5. Bodik, P., Goldszmidt, M., Fox, A., Woodard, D.B., Andersen, H.: Fingerprinting the datacenter: automated classification of performance crises. In: European conference on Computer systems (EuroSys), pp. 111–124 (2010)
6. Chen, Y., et al.: Automatic root cause analysis via large language models for cloud incidents. In: European Conference on Computer Systems (EuroSys), pp. 674–688 (2024)
7. Cleary, J., Witten, I.: Data compression using adaptive coding and partial string matching. IEEE Trans. Commun. (TC) **32**(4), 396–402 (2003)
8. Cormack, G.V., Horspool, R.N.S.: Data compression using dynamic Markov modelling. Comput. J. **30**(6), 541–550 (1987)
9. Ding, H., Yan, S., Zhai, J., Ma, S.: Elise: a storage efficient logging system powered by redundancy reduction and representation learning. In: USENIX Security Symposium (USENIX Security), pp. 3023–3040 (2021)

10. Du, M., Li, F., Zheng, G., Srikumar, V.: Deeplog: anomaly detection and diagnosis from system logs through deep learning. In: International Conference on Computer and Communications Security (CCS), pp. 1285–1298 (2017)
11. Egersdoerfer, C., Zhang, D., Dai, D.: Early exploration of using chatgpt for log-based anomaly detection on parallel file systems logs. In: International Symposium on High-Performance Parallel and Distributed Computing, pp. 315–316 (2023)
12. Han, X., Yuan, S., Trabelsi, M.: Loggpt: Log anomaly detection via gpt. In: International Conference on Big Data (BigData), pp. 1117–1122 (2023)
13. Han, Y., Du, Q., Huang, Y., Wu, J., Tian, F., He, C.: The potential of one-shot failure root cause analysis: collaboration of the large language model and small classifier. In: International Conference on Automated Software Engineering (ASE), pp. 931–943 (2024)
14. He, M., Jia, T., Duan, C., Cai, H., Li, Y., Huang, G.: Llmelog: an approach for anomaly detection based on llm-enriched log events. In: International Symposium on Software Reliability Engineering (ISSRE), pp. 132–143 (2024)
15. He, P., Zhu, J., Zheng, Z., Lyu, M.R.: Drain: an online log parsing approach with fixed depth tree. In: International Conference on Web Services (ICWS), pp. 33–40 (2017)
16. He, S., He, P., Chen, Z., Yang, T., Su, Y., Lyu, M.R.: A survey on automated log analysis for reliability engineering. ACM Comput. Surv. (CSUR) **54**(6), 1–37 (2021)
17. He, S., Lin, Q., Lou, J.G., Zhang, H., Lyu, M.R., Zhang, D.: Identifying impactful service system problems via log analysis. In: International Conference on the Foundations of Software Engineering (FSE), pp. 60–70 (2018)
18. Jiang, Z., et al.: Lilac: Log parsing using llms with adaptive parsing cache. In: International Conference on the Foundations of Software Engineering (FSE), pp. 137–160 (2024)
19. Jiang, Z., et al.: A large-scale evaluation for log parsing techniques: how far are we? In: International Symposium on Software Testing and Analysis (ISSTA), pp. 223–234 (2024)
20. Le, V.H., Zhang, H.: Log-based anomaly detection with deep learning: how far are we? In: International Conference on Software Engineering (ICSE), pp. 1356–1367 (2022)
21. Le, V.H., Zhang, H.: Log parsing with prompt-based few-shot learning. In: International Conference on Software Engineering (ICSE), pp. 2438–2449 (2023)
22. Li, X., Zhang, H., Le, V.H., Chen, P.: Logshrink: effective log compression by leveraging commonality and variability of log data. In: International Conference on Software Engineering, pp. 1–12 (2024)
23. Li, Z., et al.: Did we miss something important? Studying and exploring variable-aware log abstraction. In: International Conference on Software Engineering (ICSE), pp. 830–842 (2023)
24. Lin, Q., Zhang, H., Lou, J.G., Zhang, Y., Chen, X.: Log clustering based problem identification for online service systems. In: International Conference on Software Engineering (ICSE), pp. 102–111 (2016)
25. Liu, J., Zhu, J., He, S., He, P., Zheng, Z., Lyu, M.R.: Logzip: extracting hidden structures via iterative clustering for log compression. In: International Conference on Automated Software Engineering (ASE), pp. 863–873 (2019)
26. Rodrigues, K., Luo, Y., Yuan, D.: CLP: efficient and scalable search on compressed text logs. In: USENIX Symposium on Operating Systems Design and Implementation (OSDI), pp. 183–198 (2021)

27. Roy, D., et al.: Exploring llm-based agents for root cause analysis. In: International Conference on the Foundations of Software Engineering (FSE), pp. 208–219 (2024)
28. Wei, J., et al.: Loggrep: fast and cheap cloud log storage by exploiting both static and runtime patterns. In: European Conference on Computer Systems (EuroSys), pp. 452–468 (2023)
29. Wei, J., et al.: On the feasibility of parser-based log compression in large-scale cloud systems. In: USENIX Conference on File and Storage Technologies (FAST), pp. 249–262 (2021)
30. Witten, I.H., Neal, R.M., Cleary, J.G.: Arithmetic coding for data compression. Commun. ACM (CACM) **30**(6), 520–540 (1987)
31. Xiao, Y., Le, V.H., Zhang, H.: Demonstration-free:: towards more practical log parsing with large language models. In: International Conference on Automated Software Engineering (ASE), pp. 153–165 (2024)
32. Xie, Y., Zhang, H., Babar, M.A.: Logsd: detecting anomalies from system logs through self-supervised learning and frequency-based masking. In: International Conference on the Foundations of Software Engineering (FSE), pp. 2098–2120 (2024)
33. Xu, J., Yang, R., Huo, Y., Zhang, C., He, P.: Divlog: log parsing with prompt enhanced in-context learning. In: International Conference on Software Engineering (ICSE), pp. 1–12 (2024)
34. Yao, K., Li, H., Shang, W., Hassan, A.E.: A study of the performance of general compressors on log files. Empir. Softw. Eng. (EMSE) **25**(5), 3043–3085 (2020)
35. Yao, K., Sayagh, M., Shang, W., Hassan, A.E.: Improving state-of-the-art compression techniques for log management tools. IEEE Trans. Softw. Eng. (TSE) **48**(8), 2748–2760 (2021)
36. Yu, G., et al.: Logreducer: identify and reduce log hotspots in kernel on the fly. In: International Conference on Software Engineering (ICSE), pp. 1763–1775 (2023)
37. Yu, S., Wu, Y., Li, Y., He, P.: Unlocking the power of numbers: log compression via numeric token parsing. In: International Conference on Automated Software Engineering (ASE), pp. 919–930 (2024)
38. Yuan, D., Mai, H., Xiong, W., Tan, L., Zhou, Y., Pasupathy, S.: Sherlog: error diagnosis by connecting clues from run-time logs. In: International Conference on Architectural Support for Programming Languages and Operating Systems (ASPLOS), pp. 143–154 (2010)
39. Zhu, J., He, S., He, P., Liu, J., Lyu, M.R.: Loghub: a large collection of system log datasets for ai-driven log analytics. In: International Symposium on Software Reliability Engineering (ISSRE), pp. 355–366 (2023)

Multi-distance Identifies Backdoors Attack in Privacy-Preserving Federated Learning

Zhihong Wang, Jiachen Shen(✉), Zhenfu Cao, and Xiaolei Dong

Shanghai Key Laboratory of Trustworthy Computing, East China Normal University, Shanghai, China
jcshen@sei.ecnu.edu.cn

Abstract. Federated learning (FL) has become a powerful distributed machine learning method that allows multiple clients to collaborate to train a global model without sharing local data, thereby protecting data privacy. However, FL is vulnerable to backdoor attacks, where malicious clients inject malicious updates into the global model, compromising its integrity. To defend against backdoor attacks under privacy-preserving conditions, we adopt a multi-distance metric approach and integrate it with secure multi-party computation (SMPC). We propose a method, called Multi-distance Federated Learning (MdFL), that effectively identifies backdoor-injected updates while preserving privacy, offering a practical solution without sacrificing model utility. We validate MdFL through extensive experiments on benchmark datasets, demonstrating its effectiveness in various backdoor attack scenarios, including both IID and non-IID data distributions. Our results demonstrate that under the condition of 50% malicious clients on the MNIST dataset, our strategy still maintains the backdoor accuracy below 20%. It not only outperforms existing defense methods but also preserves the model's accuracy and convergence speed, making it an effective solution for safeguarding FL systems against sophisticated adversaries.

Keywords: Federated Learning · Privacy Preservation · Backdoor Attack

1 Introduction

Federated learning (FL) [12,14,26] is a machine learning approach that allows multiple participants to collaboratively train a high-quality model without sharing their local data. During each training cycle, a central server distributes a global model to a selected subset of clients. These clients then update the model with their local data and return the updated parameters to the server for aggregation. FL has been effectively applied in various domains, including image processing, word prediction, medical imaging, and edge computing.

L. Zhang and K.-K. R. Choo (Eds.): MobiQuitous 2025, LNICST 683, pp. 75–94, 2026.
https://doi.org/10.1007/978-3-032-22500-9_5

Despite its advantages, FL is susceptible to privacy leakage [7,20] and various attacks, which can be categorized into untargeted and targeted types. In untargeted attacks [5,10], the adversary aims to degrade the overall model performance. In contrast, targeted attacks [1,21] seek to manipulate the model's behavior on specific inputs while preserving its performance on the main task. Among these, backdoor attacks [22,29] are particularly stealthy. In backdoor attacks, specific patterns (triggers) into a subset of training data, causing the model to misclassify triggered inputs while maintaining normal behavior on clean data. This stealthiness, combined with the minimal poisoned samples required, makes such attacks challenging to detect.

While several defenses have been developed to enhance FL's robustness, stealthy backdoors employing techniques like gradient scaling or trigger splitting can evade conventional detection methods. Cosine similarity [13,25] has been widely adopted in detection frameworks, but relying solely on this metric often yields unreliable results, especially under non-IID data distributions or adaptive attacks. To address this limitation, Huang et al. [11] proposed a multi-metric approach that incorporates additional geometric measures alongside cosine similarity. Differential privacy (DP)-based methods [16] offer another defense avenue by adding noise to updates, but often at the cost of reduced utility and slower convergence.

Privacy-preserving federated learning (PPFL) [2,4] is crucial within FL as it employs cryptographic techniques to ensure data privacy [19]. These techniques encrypt local updates and perform secure aggregations, minimizing the risk of privacy breaches. However, PPFL faces significant challenges, particularly from poisoning attacks. In these attacks, malicious clients can poison the global model by sending tampered updates. These attacks can be untargeted, aiming to degrade the overall model accuracy, or targeted, aiming to misclassifications on particular inputs. Detecting these attacks is particularly difficult because encrypted gradients obscure the malicious updates. Moreover, defense strategies in PPFL can inadvertently lead to privacy leaks if they require access to local gradients. Furthermore, the diversity of data, especially non-IID data, further complicates the detection of malicious updates, as current defense mechanisms struggle to identify anomalies in such heterogeneous data without access to the underlying distributions.

Backdoor attacks conducted under privacy-preserving settings are significantly more difficult to detect. On the one hand, since clients' data are encrypted before submission, the server cannot directly access raw inputs, making it infeasible to identify malicious behaviors from ciphertexts. On the other hand, backdoor attacks typically do not affect the model's performance on benign inputs, and their gradients are often closer to those of benign clients compared to untargeted model attacks. As a result, backdoor attacks are inherently more covert and harder to identify than general untargeted model attacks. To defend against backdoor attacks under privacy-preserving conditions, we build upon the multi-distance metric approach proposed by Huang et al. [11] and integrate it with secure multi-party computation. We propose a method that successfully defends against various backdoor attacks while preserving privacy, providing a potential solution for preventing such attacks without sacrificing model utility.

Our technical contributions are as follows:

- We present a study that enables effective defense against various backdoor attacks while preserving privacy in federated learning.
- We propose a privacy-preserving defense strategy based on secure multi-party computation and distance metrics. Our approach incorporates Byzantine fault tolerance, enabling it to support heterogeneous data scenarios, including both IID and non-IID data. Additionally, the strategy can tolerate up to 50% of malicious clients, ensuring robust defense against backdoor attacks even in the presence of a substantial number of adversaries.
- We evaluate our proposed method and several baseline approaches on the MNIST and CIFAR-10 datasets. The results demonstrate that our strategy effectively defends against backdoor attacks while maintaining high robustness and competitive performance, thereby validating the effectiveness of our approach.

2 Related Work

In this section, we will introduce defense countermeasures against poisoning attacks in Federated Learning (FL). Poisoning attacks in FL pose significant threats as malicious clients can inject carefully crafted updates that compromise the global model, often without noticeably degrading overall performance. Defense mechanisms against these attacks have evolved to enhance the robustness and security of FL systems. Generally, these defenses can be categorized into three primary approaches: those based on identifying malicious gradients, those leveraging differential privacy (DP) [16,24] techniques, and a range of other emerging methods developed in recent years.

One category of defenses aims to distinguish malicious gradients from benign gradients through classification or scoring. This approach assumes that the gradients provided by malicious clients exhibit distinct patterns that can be detected through various statistical or geometric methods. For instance, Krum and Trimmed Mean aim to reduce the impact of malicious updates by filtering outliers and only aggregating the most reliable gradients. Krum [3] selects a single update that is closest to the majority of other updates, effectively minimizing the influence of outliers. Similarly, Trimmed Mean [27] discards a percentage of the highest and lowest values before averaging, providing robustness against both untargeted and targeted attacks. Robust Federated Averaging (RFA) [17] uses the geometric median to minimize the influence of malicious updates. Another well-known method is Foolsgold [9], which exploits the consistency of malicious gradients over time, distinguishing them based on cosine similarity between historical updates. ShieldFL [13] is a recently proposed method based on homomorphic encryption can defend against encrypted model poisoning without compromising privacy in PPFL. Since it only measures the cosine distance between two gradients, it cannot effectively defend against backdoor attacks. However, these methods often rely on specific assumptions about data distribution or attack strategies, limiting their applicability. For example, Krum assumes IID data among benign clients, and FoolsGold assumes non-IID data to distinguish malicious clients that are too close to benign clients.

The other category of defenses leverages differential privacy (DP) [6,16,24] techniques. There has been research [15] proven that adding noise can to some extent defend against backdoor attacks. These methods involve clipping gradients and adding noise to obscure the influence of any single client's update. Notable examples include Weak-DP [1], which applies Gaussian noise to the global model, and FLAME, which incorporates clustering before applying DP techniques. However, the introduction of noise can significantly impair the performance and convergence of the FL model, presenting a trade-off between robustness and accuracy. Despite this drawback, DP-based methods remain among the few that provide defense against stealthy backdoor attacks without relying on specific assumptions about the attack or data distribution.

Finally, the third category encompasses other emerging strategies, which utilize distinct principles such as signal processing and statistical analysis. Wang et al. [23] proposed MM-BD, a method for post-training backdoor detection that identifies attacks with arbitrary pattern types by leveraging a maximum margin statistic. Fereidooni et al. [8] proposed FreqFed, a novel defense that transforms model updates into the frequency domain to filter out malicious contributions, demonstrating robustness against both targeted and untargeted poisoning attacks.

While the existing defenses provide valuable strategies for mitigating backdoor attacks, they are not without limitations. Gradient-based methods are susceptible to being bypassed by carefully crafted attacks that exploit the assumptions of these defenses. Similarly, DP-based methods, while effective, often degrade model performance and are not fully resilient against advanced or adaptive backdoor attacks. Furthermore, most defense strategies are ineffective when faced with encrypted data.

Therefore, preventing backdoor attacks in IID and non-IID data under data encryption is a challenge. The existing defense solutions have limited capability in distinguishing backdoors in encrypted gradients, making these strategies ineffective against encrypted backdoor attacks in privacy-preserving federated learning (PPFL). So we need a new backdoor attacks defense strategy that can be perfectly implemented under encryption conditions in PPFL.

3 Problem Statement

In this section, we will introduce system model and adversarial model of our work. Figure 1 illustrates our system model.

3.1 System Model

Key Center(KC): KC is a fully trusted party. It is responsible for distributing keys to CS and CSP.

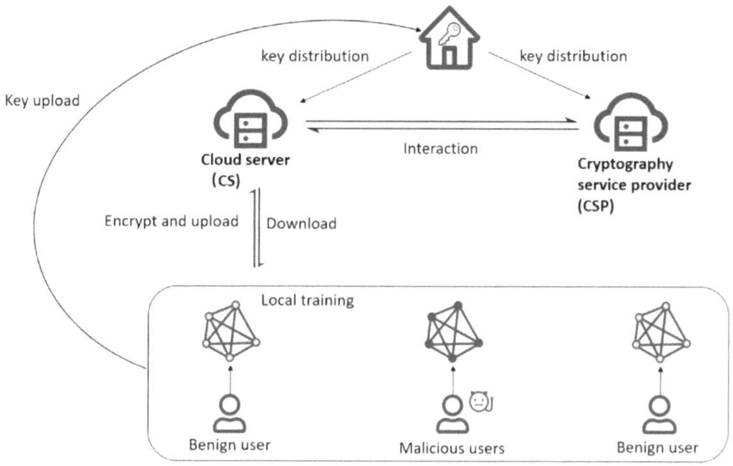

Fig. 1. System model.

Data Owner: Data owners collaboratively train a unified model under the coordination of a service provider. To ensure privacy, each client performs local training on their private data, generates a pair of keys $ek_i = (p_i, q_i)$ and $dk_i = N_i$, and encrypts their local gradient before uploading it to the cloud server. Furthermore, we assume that the data held by clients is not required to be independent and identically distributed (IID), thus allowing for non-IID distributions.

Cloud Server(CS): CS is responsible for receiving all encrypted gradients submitted by clients, and then communicating with CSP to calculate the required results. Then, the calculated results are used to detect attacks initiated by potential malicious clients.

Cryptography Service Provider(CSP): CSP is responsible for receiving data sent by CS, performing encryption and decryption operations, and communicating with CS to jointly calculate the required indicators.

3.2 Adversarial Model

CS and CSP are two honest but curious servers that honestly follow defined protocols but curiously compromise client privacy. We assume that the two servers do not collude with each other. This non-collusion assumption is widely adopted in dual-server cryptographic protocols and is crucial for ensuring privacy in our design. For clients, they are divided into benign clients and malicious clients. If one client is benign, it will honestly encrypt and submit the encrypted gradient to CS. If a client is malicious, it will launches attack by submitting encrypted malicious gradients.

The adversary $\mathcal{A}$ is assumed to have full knowledge of the aggregation and defense mechanisms. It can manipulate local training parameters, participation in every communication round, and control one or more malicious clients $\mathcal{U}^*$, provided that the number of malicious clients does not exceed 50% of the total.

4 Methodology

4.1 Efficient Multiparty Delegated Computation

We used a secure multi-party computation scheme to implement homomorphic addition, homomorphic subtraction, and homomorphic multiplication. This allows the server to perform computations without accessing clients' plaintext data, achieving privacy protection. In this paper, we adopt a recently proposed cryptographic primitive called Multiparty Delegated Computing. And the details are shown in [28].

Setup(1^λ): Given the security parameter λ. An algorithm runs a probabilistic polynomial time (PPT) trapdoor permutation generator, and outputs a pair of permutations $(f, f^{-1}))$ on $\{0,1\}^{2\lambda}$ with two pairs of public and private key pairs (cs_{pk}, cs_{sk}) and (csp_{pk}, csp_{sk}) respectively for CS and CSP. And provide two hash functions $H_1, H_2\colon \{0,1\}^* \to \{0,1\}^\lambda$. Then, it selects a big prime P_0 such that $|P_0| = |\lambda/deg_{\mathcal{F}}|$, where $deg_{\mathcal{F}}$ denotes the degree of the evaluated function. Defined the public parameter $PPR = (cs_{pk}, csp_{pk}, p_0, H_1, H_2)$.

KeyGen$(1^\lambda, PPR)$: Three big primes p_i, q_i, h_i are randomly selected by each client, ensuring that $|p_i| = |q_i| = |h_i| = \lambda$, and computes $N_i = p_i q_i$. Each client privately keeps its encryption key $ek_i = (p_i, q_i)$ and decryption key $dk_i = N_i$ and defined $PPR_i = N_i' = p_i \cdot q_i \cdot h_i$ as its public parameter. Similarly, for CSP its encryption key $ek_{csp} = (p_{csp}, q_{csp})$, decryption key $dk_{csp} = N_{csp}$, $PPR_{csp} = N'_{csp}$.

Enc$_{pk}(PPR, PPR_i, ek_i, m_{i,j}) \to CT$: PPR and PPR_i are the public parameter, ek_i is encryption key for every client, $m_{i,j}$ is the jth message which sent by ith client. Then we first compute:$B_i = p_i^{-1} p_i q_i + q_i^{-1} q_i p_i + (max(p_i, q_i))^4$, and $B_i' = k \cdot B_i, k \in_R \mathbb{Z}_{p_0}$. Then choose the random noise $r_{i,j} \in_R \mathbb{Z}_{p_0}$ and $r'_{i,j} \in_R \mathbb{Z}_{p_0}$, and compute

$$
\begin{aligned}
CT_{B_i} &= f_{cs_{pk}}(B_i), \\
CT_{N_i} &= f_{csp_{pk}}(N_i), \\
[m_{i,j}]_{ek_i} &= p_i^{-1} p_i (m_{i,j} + r_{i,j} \cdot p_0)_{q_i} \\
&\quad + q_i^{-1} q_i (m_{i,j} + r_{i,j} \cdot p_0)_{p_i} \\
&\quad + H_1(p_i \| q_i) \cdot r'_{i,j} \cdot N_i \bmod N_i', \\
CT_{i,j} &= [m_{i,j}]_{ek_i} + H_2(p_i \| q_i) B_i \bmod B_i'
\end{aligned}
$$

Where q_i^{-1}, p_i^{-1} respectively represent the inverses of q_i, p_i under $Z_{p_i}^*$ and $Z_{q_i}^*$. $(m_{i,j} + r_{i,j} \cdot p_0)_{q_i}$ denote $m_{i,j} + r_{i,j} \cdot p_0 \bmod q_i$. Finally, it sends $CT_i = (CT_{B_i} \| \cup_{j=1}^{n_i} CT_{i,j} \| CT_{N_i})$ to CS.

Eval$(PPR, cs_{sk}, csp_{sk}, ek_{csp}, dk_{csp}, \mathcal{F}, CT_i)$: Now we will define the homomorphic decryption algorithm.

Step1: CS sends CT_{N_i} to CSP.
Step2: CSP computes the decryption key $dk_i = N_i = f^{-1}_{csp_{sk}}(CT_{N_i})$.
Step3: CS calculates $B_i = f^{-1}_{cs_{sk}}(CT_{B_i})$, and $[m_{i,j}]_{ek_i} = CT_{i,j} \bmod B_i$. For any encryption $[x]_{ek_i}$ sent by CS, CSP can calculate $x = [x]_{ek_i} \bmod N_i \bmod P_0$ by using decryption key $dk_i = N_i$ and the public parameter P_0.
For any two clients, given $[m_1]_{ek_1}, [m_2]_{ek_2}$ to CS, we can calculate $[m_1+m_2]_{ek_{csp}}$, $[m_1 - m_2]_{ek_{csp}}$, $[m_1 \cdot m_2]_{ek_{csp}}$ through several rounds of communication between CS and CSP.

Algorithm 1 Setup

```
1: Input: Security parameter λ, trapdoor permutation (f, f^{-1})
2: Output: Keys cs_pk, cs_sk, csp_pk, csp_sk, PPR, PPR_i, PPR_csp
3: KC generates (cs_pk, cs_sk) ← F(λ, (f, f^{-1}))
4: KC generates (csp_pk, csp_sk) ← F(λ, (f, f^{-1}))
5: KC defines hash functions H_1, H_2 : {0,1}^* → {0,1}^λ
6: KC selects a prime p_0 such that |p_0| = ⌊λ / deg(F)⌋
7: KC broadcasts PPR = (cs_pk, csp_pk, p_0, H_1, H_2)
8: KC sends cs_sk to CS, csp_sk to CSP
9: for each client U_i, i ∈ [1, n] do
10:     U_i selects primes p_i, q_i, h_i of size λ
11:     Computes PPR_i = N'_i = p_i · q_i · h_i, and sends to KC
12:     Computes decryption key dk_i = N_i = p_i · q_i
13: end for
14: KC selects p_csp, q_csp, h_csp of size λ
15: Computes PPR_csp = N'_csp = p_csp · q_csp · h_csp
16: Computes decryption key dk_csp = N_csp = p_csp · q_csp
17: Return: Broadcast PPR_i and PPR_csp to all parties
```

4.2 Federated Learning

Federated Learning (FL) [18] is a distributed machine learning approach that enables multiple participants to collaboratively train a high-quality model without sharing their local data. One commonly used method in FL is Stochastic Gradient Descent (SGD) adapted for a federated setting.

In FL, each client i possesses a local dataset $\mathcal{D}_i$ and independently trains its local individual gradient g_i. The entire training process is divided into multiple communication rounds, with each round consisting of the following steps:

Model Initialization and Distribution
In round t, the central server distributes the global model parameters w_t to a selected subset of clients $\mathcal{U}$.

Local Gradient Computation
Each client $i \in \mathcal{U}$ computes the gradient of the local loss function $\mathcal{L}_i(w_i, \mathcal{D}_i)$ with respect to the model parameters using its local dataset $\mathcal{D}_i$:

$$g_i^{(t)} = \nabla \mathcal{L}_i(w_i, \mathcal{D}_i).$$

Here, $g_i^{(t)}$ represents the gradient computed by client i in round t.

Parameter Aggregation
After computing the local gradients, the selected clients send these gradients back to the central server. The server aggregates these gradients using a method like weighted averaging:

$$g^{(t)} = \frac{1}{|\mathcal{U}|} \sum_{i \in \mathcal{U}} g_i^{(t)}.$$

Global Model Update

The server updates the global model parameters using the aggregated gradient:

$$w_{t+1} = w_t - \eta^{(t)} g^{(t)},$$

where $\eta^{(t)}$ denotes the learning rate at round t.

Repeat the Steps
This process is repeated over multiple communication rounds until the global model converges or a predefined stopping condition is met.

Algorithm 2 Local Training

1: **Input:** Encrypted model $[\mathbf{w}^t]_{ek_{csp}}$, data D_i, PPR, PPR_i, ek_i
2: **Output:** Encrypted gradients CT_i
3: **for** each client $\mathcal{U}_i$, $i \in [1, n]$ **do**
4: **if** $\mathcal{U}_i \notin \mathcal{U}^*$ **then**
5: Train model on D_i, get g_i
6: $CT_i \leftarrow \mathsf{Enc}_{pk}(PPR, PPR_i, ek_i, g_i)$
7: **else**
8: $\mathcal{U}_i$ crafts malicious gradient g_i^*, encrypts and sends to CS
9: **end if**
10: **end for**
11: **return** CT_i or CT_i^*

---

5 Framework

5.1 Multi-distance Feature

As discussed earlier, a variety of methods have been proposed. However, most of them rely on a single metric—typically the distance between local models—as the criterion to detect malicious clients in federated learning (FL). With only one feature, adversaries can easily design strategies to bypass detection, and the effectiveness of such methods heavily depends on the specific attack strategy. In addition, due to differences in clients' data distributions, some malicious gradients may not be distinguishable by distance-based features alone. Therefore, multiple metrics are needed to jointly identify malicious clients.

In our approach, we consider three commonly used metrics: cosine similarity, Euclidean distance, and Manhattan distance. Specifically, the cosine similarity is denoted as D_{Cos}, Euclidean distance as D_{Eul}, and Manhattan distance as D_{Man}. For the ith client's gradient in each round, the metrics are defined as:

$$D_{\text{Cos}}^{(i)} = \frac{\langle g_i, g_0 \rangle}{\|g_i\| \cdot \|g_0\|}, \quad D_{\text{Eul}}^{(i)} = \|g_i - g_0\|_2, \quad D_{\text{Man}}^{(i)} = \|g_i - g_0\|_1,$$

where g_i denotes the ith client's local gradient sent to the server, and g_0 denotes the aggregated gradient from the previous round. These three metrics serve as features for detecting abnormal behaviors in client updates.

Having established the definitions of the three distinct metrics, it is important to note that their differing units lead to inconsistencies in magnitude. As a result, direct operations or comparisons across these indicators become infeasible.

To effectively integrate these metrics, an appropriate normalization technique must be employed. However, considering the interdependence among the three distance metrics, independently normalizing each metric may not yield optimal results. To address this, we propose using the sum of differences between each client's distance values and those of all other clients as a unified indicator. This approach ensures that clients whose distances are closer to the average will yield smaller values, while those farther from the average will produce larger values.

$$D'^{(i)} = \left(\sum_{j \neq i} \left| D_{Eul}^{(i)} - D_{Eul}^{(j)} \right|, \sum_{j \neq i} \left| D_{Man}^{(i)} - D_{Man}^{(j)} \right|, \sum_{j \neq i} \left| D_{Cos}^{(i)} - D_{Cos}^{(j)} \right| \right)$$

Next, we require a method to comprehensively evaluate these three indicators. To ensure that the metrics are complementary and effective across diverse data distributions, we consider applying a whitening transformation to eliminate the correlations among them:

$$\delta^{(i)} = \sqrt{\boldsymbol{D'}^{(i)\top} \boldsymbol{\Sigma}^{-1} \boldsymbol{D'}^{(i)}}.$$

$\boldsymbol{\Sigma}$ denotes the covariance matrix of $D = [D'^{(1)} D'^{(2)} \cdots D'^{(K)}]^\top$, and $\boldsymbol{\Sigma}^{-1}$ represents its inverse. Based on the above computation, dynamic weighting can be effectively applied to enhance robustness against various malicious gradients and attacks (Fig. 2).

After obtaining the anomaly score $\delta(i)$ for each gradient, we identify a subset of gradients as benign. Gradients with lower $\delta(i)$ values exhibit smaller deviations from others, indicating a higher likelihood of being benign. Therefore, it is reasonable to remove a certain proportion of gradients with higher $\delta(i)$ scores to improve model robustness [11].

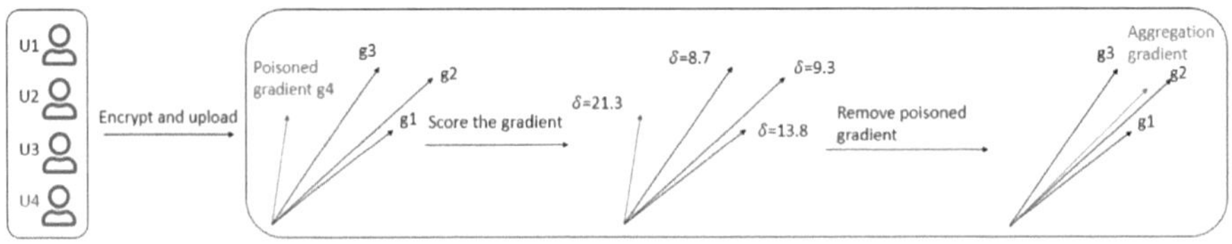

Fig. 2. Example of removing malicious gradients in MdFL

5.2 Technical Overview

In this paper, we use multi-distance to resist malicious gradients between encrypted gradients. The local model $\mathbf{w}_i$ and the global $\mathbf{w}$ are all vectors. Since the gradients submitted by clients are also vectors, we can identify outliers by calculating the similarity between each local gradient and the other gradients. Compare with the previous ShieldFL [13] method, which is limited to detecting model poisoning attacks, our approach combines three distance measures, enabling it to identify both model poisoning and backdoor attacks.

In order to prevent unfairness in key distribution by the key center, we use a secure multi-party computation method so that each participant can choose their own key. By utilizing dual servers simultaneously, privacy is preserved, ensuring that no user data is disclosed. And we allow processing of both IID and non-IID data, resolving the limitations of some methods that cannot handle non-IID data.

5.3 Algorithm Details

Following are the details of how CS and CSP collaborate to compute $D_{Eul}^{(i)}$, $D_{Man}^{(i)}$ and $D_{Cos}^{(i)}$. For each client $\mathcal{U}_i$, the local gradient g_i is encrypted as $CT_i = (CT_{B_i} \parallel \cup_{j=1}^{n_i} CT_{i,j} \parallel CT_{N_i})$ and submitted to CS.

CS: CS receives CT_i and calculates $B_i = f_{cs_{sk}}^{-1}(CT_{B_i})$ and $[x_{i,j}]_{ek_i} = CT_{i,j} \bmod B_i$ for all $j \in [1, m]$. Here, $x_{i,j}$ is each component of the gradient g_i, and

$$[g_i]_{ek_i} = ([x_{i,1}]_{ek_i}, [x_{i,2}]_{ek_i}, \ldots, [x_{im}]_{ek_i})$$

is the encrypted local gradient. $[g^{(t-1)}]_{ek_{csp}}$ is the global model for the round $t-1$.

When CS receives the gradient, a random noise $r_{i\in[1,n+1]} \leftarrow \mathbb{Z}_{p_0}$ is first selected by CS, defined as $r_i = (r_{i,1}, r_{i,2}, \ldots, r_{i,m})$ and blinds r_i to $[g_i]_{ek_i}$ and $[g(t-1)]_{ek_{csp}}$, computing:

$$[x_{i,j} + r_{i,j}]_{ek_i} = [x_{i,j}]_{ek_i} + r_{i,j},$$

$$[x_j^{(t-1)} + r_{n-1,j}]_{ek_{csp}} = [x_j^{(t-1)}]_{ek_{csp}} + r_{n-1,j},$$

$$[x_{i,j} \cdot r_{n-1,j}]_{ek_i} = [x_{i,j}]_{ek_i} \cdot r_{n-1,j},$$
$$[x_j^{(t-1)} \cdot r_{i,j}]_{ek_{csp}} = [x_j^{(t-1)}]_{ek_i} \cdot r_{i,j}.$$

Then CS sends $[x_{i,j} + r_{i,j}]_{ek_i}$, $[x_{i,j} \cdot r_{n-1,j}]_{ek_i}$, and CT_{N_i} to CSP.

CSP: CSP obtains $[x_{i,j} + r_{i,j}]_{ek_i}$, $[x_{i,j} \cdot r_{n-1,j}]_{ek_i}$, and CT_{N_i}, and computes the decryption key $dk_i = N_i = f^{-1}_{csp_{sk}}(CT_{N_i})$. CSP decrypts the blinded ciphertexts:

$$x_{i,j} + r_{i,j} = \mathrm{Dec}(N_i, [x_{i,j} + r_{i,j}]_{ek_i}),$$
$$-(x_{i,\mathrm{j}} + r_{i,\mathrm{j}}) = \mathrm{Dec}(N_i, (p_0 - 1)[x_{i,\mathrm{j}} + r_{i,\mathrm{j}}]_{ek_i}),$$
$$x_{i,j} \cdot r_{n-1,j} = \mathrm{Dec}(N_i, [x_{i,j} \cdot r_{n-1,j}]_{ek_i}).$$

Then CSP re-encrypts the blinded results:

$$[x_{i,j} + r_{i,j}]_{ek_{csp}} = \mathrm{Enc}(ek_{csp}, x_{i,j} + r_{i,j}),$$
$$[-x_{i,j} - r_{i,j}]_{ek_{csp}} = \mathrm{Enc}(ek_{csp}, -(x_{i,j} + r_{i,j})),$$
$$[x_{i,j} \cdot r_{n-1,j}]_{ek_{csp}} = \mathrm{Enc}(ek_{csp}, x_{i,j} \cdot r_{n-1,j}),$$

and sends $[x_{i,j} + r_{i,j}]_{ek_{csp}}$, $[-x_{i,j} - r_{i,j}]_{ek_{csp}}$, and $[x_{i,j} \cdot r_{n-1,j}]_{ek_{csp}}$ to CS.

CS Computes

$$\begin{aligned}[x_{i,j} \cdot x_{i,j}]_{ek_{csp}} &= [x_{i,j} + r_{i,j}]_{ek_{csp}} \cdot [x_{i,j} + r_{i,j}]_{ek_{csp}} \\ &\quad - 2[x_{i,j} + r_{i,j}]_{ek_{csp}} - r_{i,j}^2,\end{aligned}$$

$$[x_{i,j} \cdot x_j^{(t-1)}]_{ek_{csp}} = [x_{i,j} + r_{i,j}]_{ek_{csp}} \cdot [x_j^{(t-1)} + r_{n-1.j}]_{ek_{csp}},$$
$$-[x_{i,j} \cdot r_{n-1.j}]_{ek_{csp}} = [x_j^{(t-1)} \cdot r_{i,j}]_{ek_{csp}} - r_{n-1.j} \cdot r_{i,j},$$

$$\left[\langle g_i, g^{(t-1)} \rangle\right]_{ek_{csp}} = \sum_{j=1}^{m} [x_{i,j} \cdot x_j^{(t-1)}]_{ek_{csp}},$$

$$[\langle g_i \cdot g_i \rangle]_{ek_{csp}} = [\sum_{j=1}^{m} x_{i,j}^2]_{ek_{csp}} = \sum_{j=1}^{m} [x_{i,j}^2]_{ek_{csp}},$$

$$[\langle g^{(t-1)} \cdot g^{(t-1)} \rangle]_{ek_{csp}} = \sum_{j=1}^{m} [x_j^{(t-1)} \cdot x_j^{(t-1)}]_{ek_{csp}},$$

$$[x_j^{(t-1)} - x_{i,j}]_{ek_{csp}} = [x_j^{(t-1)}]_{ek_{csp}} + [-x_{i,j} - r_{i,j}]_{ek_{csp}} + r_{i,j},$$

$$\begin{aligned}[{D_{Ful}^{(i)}}^2]_{ek_{csp}} &= [\sum_{j=1}^{m} \left(x_j^{(t-1)} - x_{i,j}\right)^2]_{ek_{csp}} \\ &= \sum_{j=1}^{m} [\left(x_j^{(t-1)} - x_{i,j}\right)^2]_{ek_{csp}}.\end{aligned}$$

CS selects a positive random noise $r' \in \mathbb{Z}_{p_0}^+$:

$$[\left(x_j^{(t-1)} - x_{i,j}\right)^2 \cdot r'^2]_{ek_{csp}} = [(x_j^{(t-1)} - x_{i,j})^2]_{ek_{csp}} \cdot r'^2.$$

CS sends $[D_{Eul}^{(i)}{}^2]_{ek_{csp}}$, $\left[\langle g_i, g^{(t-1)}\rangle\right]_{ek_{csp}}$, $[\langle g_i \cdot g_i\rangle]_{ek_{csp}}$, $[\langle g^{(t-1)} \cdot g^{(t-1)}\rangle]_{ek_{csp}}$, and $[\left(x_j^{(t-1)} - x_{i,j}\right)^2 \cdot r_j'^2]_{ek_{csp}}$ to CSP.

CSP Decrypts

$$D_{Eul}^{(i)} = \left(Dec([D_{Eul}^{(i)}{}^2]_{ek_{csp}})\right)^{\frac{1}{2}},$$

$$\langle g_i, g^{(t-1)}\rangle = Dec(\left[\langle g_i, g^{(t-1)}\rangle\right]_{ek_{csp}}),$$

$$\langle g_i \cdot g_i\rangle = Dec([\langle g_i \cdot g_i\rangle]_{ek_{csp}}),$$

$$\langle g^{(t-1)} \cdot g^{(t-1)}\rangle = Dec([\langle g^{(t-1)} \cdot g^{(t-1)}\rangle]_{ek_{csp}}),$$

$$\left(x_j^{(t-1)} - x_{i,j}\right)^2 \cdot r_j'^2 = Dec([\left(x_j^{(t-1)} - x_{i,j}\right)^2 \cdot r_j'^2]_{ek_{csp}}),$$

$$D_{Man}^{(i)} \cdot r_j' = \sum_{j=1}^{m} \left[\left(x_j^{(t-1)} - x_{i,j}\right)^2 \cdot r_j'^2\right]^{\frac{1}{2}} = \sum_{j=1}^{m} \left|x_j^{(t-1)} - x_{i,j}\right| \cdot r_j'.$$

CSP sends back $D_{Eul}^{(i)}, \langle g_i, g^{(t-1)}\rangle, \langle g_i \cdot g_i\rangle, \langle g^{(t-1)} \cdot g^{(t-1)}\rangle, D_{Man}^{(i)} \cdot r_j'$ to CS.

CS Computes

$$D_{Cos}^{(i)} = \frac{\langle g_i, g^{(t-1)}\rangle}{\langle g_i \cdot g_i\rangle \cdot \langle g^{(t-1)} \cdot g^{(t-1)}\rangle},$$

and removes the random noise r' to obtain $D_{Man}^{(i)}$.

5.4 Security Analysis

Our proposed federated learning framework uses multiparty delegated computation (MPDC) to protect local model updates during secure computation. We inherit the semantic security of MPDC, which is formally proven to achieve Ind-CPA under standard cryptographic assumptions [28].

Let $\mathcal{A}$ be a probabilistic polynomial time (PPT) adversary who aims to distinguish the encryptions of two plaintexts under the MPDC algorithm with non-negligible advantage $\epsilon(\lambda)$. If the hash function H_1 is modeled as a random oracle, and the one-way trapdoor permutation f is hard to invert, then there exists a simulator $\mathcal{B}$ who can use $\mathcal{A}$ to break the one-wayness of f with the following relationship:

$$\epsilon' \geq \epsilon(\lambda) - \Pr[\mathcal{B} \text{ solves factorization of } N_i']$$

By the semantic security of MPDC, the ciphertext $[m]_{ek}$ leaks no information about m under the assumption that the adversary cannot invert f or factor N_i'. Therefore, the encrypted local model updates in our federated setting remain private, even in the presence of a semi-honest server and colluding unauthorized clients, as long as the trapdoor and H_1 remain secure.

Algorithm 3 Aggregation Algorithm

Input: Encrypted local gradients $\{CT_i\}_{i=1}^{n}$, previous global model $[g^{(t-1)}]_{ek_{csp}}$
Output: Updated global model $[g^{(t)}]_{ek_{csp}}$
for each client $\mathcal{U}_i \in \{\mathcal{U}_1, \ldots, \mathcal{U}_n\}$ **do**
  $\mathcal{U}_i$ sends CT_i to CS
end for
for each $i \in [1, n]$ **do**
  CS and CSP collaborate to compute $D_{Eul}^{(i)}$, $D_{Man}^{(i)}$, and $D_{Cos}^{(i)}$
end for
for each $i \in [1, n]$ **do**
  $D_{Eul}^{\prime(i)} \leftarrow \sum_{j \neq i} \left| D_{Eul}^{(i)} - D_{Eul}^{(j)} \right|$
  $D_{Man}^{\prime(i)} \leftarrow \sum_{j \neq i} \left| D_{Man}^{(i)} - D_{Man}^{(j)} \right|$
  $D_{Cos}^{\prime(i)} \leftarrow \sum_{j \neq i} \left| D_{Cos}^{(i)} - D_{Cos}^{(j)} \right|$
  Set $D'(i) \leftarrow (D_{Eul}^{\prime(i)}, D_{Man}^{\prime(i)}, D_{Cos}^{\prime(i)})$
end for
Construct matrix $\mathbf{D} \leftarrow [\mathbf{D}'^{(1)}; \mathbf{D}'^{(2)}; \ldots; \mathbf{D}'^{(n)}]$
Compute covariance matrix Σ of $\mathbf{D}$ and its inverse Σ^{-1}
for each $i \in [1, n]$ **do**
  Compute score $\delta^{(i)} \leftarrow \sqrt{\boldsymbol{D}'^{(i)\top} \cdot \boldsymbol{\Sigma}^{-1} \cdot \boldsymbol{D}'^{(i)}}$
end for
Select subset $\mathcal{U}'$ of clients with the lowest $p \cdot n$ scores $\delta^{(i)}$
return $g^{(t)} \leftarrow \frac{1}{|\mathcal{U}'|} \sum_{i \in \mathcal{U}'} g_i^{(t)}$

6 Experiments

In this section, we present the experimental evaluation of our proposed method. Our experiment is mainly divided into two perspectives. *i*) Evaluate the performance comparison between our method and other baseline methods under backdoor attacks. *ii*) Evaluate our method performance in different data settings including non-IID and IID data, as well as varying numbers of malicious clients.

6.1 Datasets

We evaluate our method on three benchmark datasets: MNIST and CIFAR-10.

- **MNIST**: This dataset consists of 70,000 grayscale images of handwritten digits, with 60,000 used for training and 10,000 for testing. Each image is 28×28 pixels, representing digits from 0 to 9.
- **CIFAR-10**: The CIFAR-10 dataset contains 60,000 32×32 color images across 10 categories, including airplanes, automobiles, birds, cats, deer, dogs, frogs, horses, ships, and trucks. There are 50,000 training images and 10,000 test images.

6.2 Evaluation Metrics

we use the following two metrics to evaluate our federated learning algorithm.

- **Accuracy (Acc):**Acc is the overall accuracy of the task. It is defined as the ratio of correctly predicted instances to the total number of instances in the dataset. A larger Acc indicates that the model is trained well and has high accuracy. Successful attacks will result in a decrease in Acc.
- **Backdoor Accuracy (BA):** It reflects the success of the attacker, indicating how well the model performs on the backdoor task. The attackers seek to enhance this metric, so a lower BA indicates a more effective defense. BA is defined as the success rate of backdoor tasks.

6.3 Experimental Results

In our experiments, some parameter values may vary across different settings. Unless otherwise specified, the default configuration consists of ten clients, among which one is malicious, corresponding to a 10% malicious client ratio. The hyperparameter p is typically set to 0.7 to facilitate faster convergence.

In the IID setting, the training data are evenly and randomly distributed among clients, with each client holding a representative subset of the dataset. In the non-IID setting, we use a Dirichlet distribution with concentration parameter $\alpha = 0.5$ to partition the data.

We conducted a comprehensive evaluation of the feasibility and accuracy of our proposed solution. As depicted in Fig. 3 and Table 1, our scheme was benchmarked against several baseline methods on both the MNIST and CIFAR-10 datasets. The experimental results were consistent with our theoretical expectations. On the MNIST dataset, the performance of most schemes was comparable, with no significant differences observed. However, on the CIFAR-10 dataset, our scheme exhibited a marginally slower convergence rate, which can be attributed to the exclusion of 30% of clients during the training process. Despite this slight delay in convergence, our approach ultimately achieved comparable accuracy to the baseline methods. More importantly, the superior defensive capabilities of our method against backdoor attacks well-justify the moderate sacrifice in convergence speed, making such a compromise an acceptable and valuable strategy for PPFL (Fig. 4).

Table 1. ACC and BA of various federated learning methods on MNIST and CIFAR-10

Dataset	Method	ACC	BA
CIFAR-10	FedAvg	79.03	53.5
	FedProx	78.06	34.0
	FedAvgm	78.32	39.8
	ShieldFL	79.34	18.4
	Ours	80.09	**5.5**
MNIST	FedAvg	99.27	85.2
	FedProx	99.24	82.9
	FedAvgm	99.23	83.6
	ShieldFL	99.14	34.8
	Ours	99.03	**4.9**

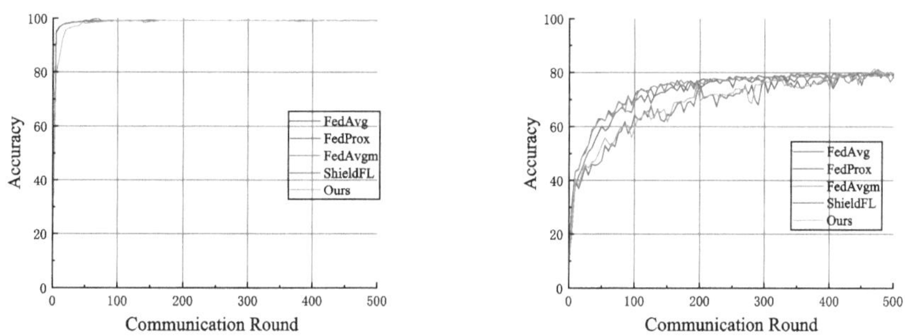

(a) MNIST (b) CIFAR-10

Fig. 3. Accuracy of various federated learning methods under backdoor attacks on MNIST and CIFAR-10

In the presence of backdoor attacks, certain classical federated learning algorithms fail to effectively mitigate the threat of malicious clients injecting backdoors, as evidenced by their significantly higher Backdoor Accuracy (BA). Furthermore, other privacy-preserving federated learning algorithms, which rely solely on cosine similarity as a detection metric, exhibit limitations in comprehensively identifying malicious clients during the detection phase. In contrast, our proposed scheme demonstrates superior robustness against backdoor attacks, achieving significantly lower BA compared to existing methods. This highlights the effectiveness of our approach in enhancing the security and reliability of federated learning systems.

In Fig. 5, we compared the BA of our proposed method with ShieldFL under varying degrees of non-IID data distributions. The results demonstrate that our method consistently outperforms ShieldFL across all non-IID settings, maintaining the BA basically below 10% with minimal fluctuations, indicating strong robustness. In contrast, ShieldFL exhibits significant variability in BA, particu-

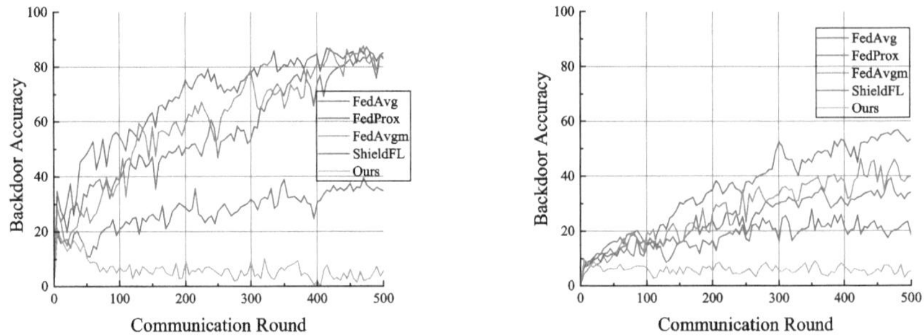

(a) MNIST (b) CIFAR-10

Fig. 4. Backdoor accuracy of various federated learning methods under backdoor attacks on MNIST and CIFAR-10

larly in highly non-IID scenarios, where its BA increases notably. These findings validate the effectiveness of our approach in mitigating backdoor attacks, especially in highly heterogeneous data environments, where it consistently achieves lower BA and demonstrates superior security and adaptability.

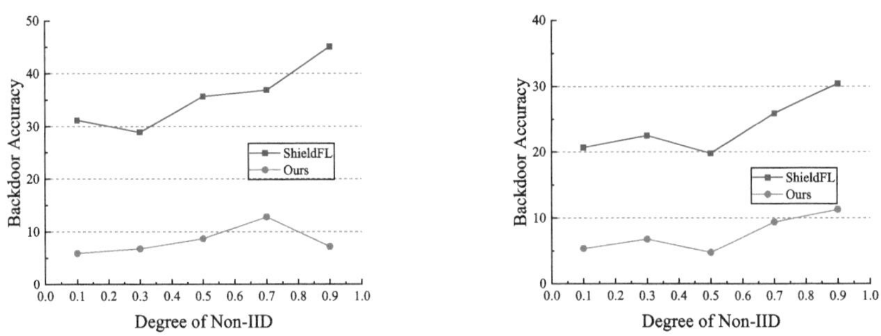

(a) MNIST (b) CIFAR10

Fig. 5. Backdoor accuracy under different degrees of non-IID on MNIST and CIFAR10

In Fig. 6, we evaluate our method under varying proportions of malicious clients. Our method consistently achieves much lower backdoor attack success rates (BA) than ShieldFL, especially when the malicious clients ratio is between 10% and 50%. In contrast, FedAvg, which lacks any defense mechanism, consistently exhibits extremely high BA across all settings. However, as the malicious clients ratio exceeds 50%, the BA of our method increases sharply, primarily because, in such extreme scenarios, the majority of clients are malicious, making it significantly more likely for benign clients to be mistakenly identified and excluded as malicious during the defense process. ShieldFL, on the other hand, demonstrates less stable behavior, with BA increasing more unpredictably at higher malicious ratios. These results highlight the robustness of our method and its reliability even under attack scenarios with up to 50% malicious clients.

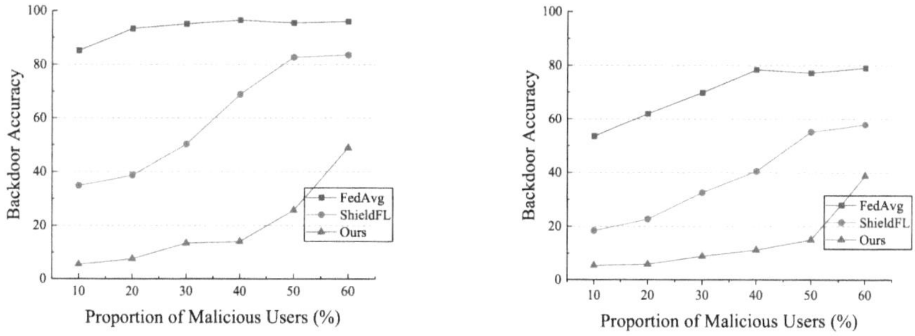

(a) MNIST (b) CIFAR-10

Fig. 6. Backdoor accuracy with different numbers of malicious clients on MNIST and CIFAR-10

6.4 Performance Evaluation

In this experiment, we comprehensively evaluated the computational and communication efficiency of the proposed method against existing federated learning frameworks, with a focus on the representative baseline ShieldFL. As illustrated in Fig. 7, our method achieves substantially superior computational efficiency and significantly reduced communication overhead compared to ShieldFL, while maintaining strong overall performance.

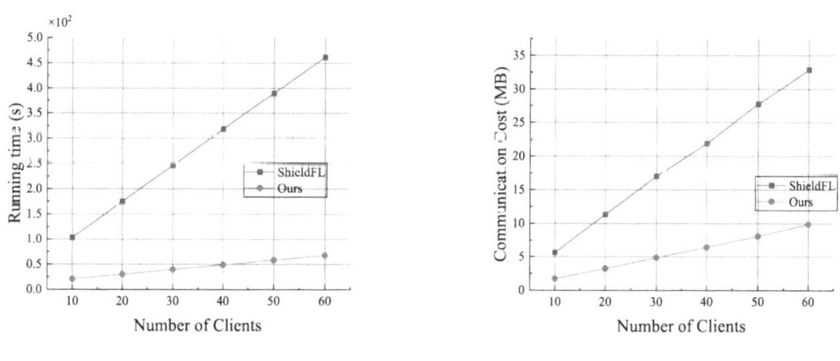

(a) Execution time under different numbers of clients

(b) Communication cost under different numbers of clients

Fig. 7. Performance Evaluation

Under the experimental configuration of $n = 10$ clients and gradient dimension $m = 250$, our method completes one training round in 104 s. In contrast, ShieldFL requires approximately 6–7 times longer execution time under identical settings. This remarkable efficiency improvement stems primarily from our novel encryption scheme, which strategically minimizes computational and communication overhead through optimized cryptographic operations.

While our approach exhibits marginally higher runtime than FedAvg (which operates on plaintext data and typically completes within 20 s), it achieves a critical balance between privacy preservation and computational practicality. This trade-off is justified given that FedAvg inherently disregards privacy safeguards, whereas our method delivers strong privacy guarantees while outperforming other privacy-preserving alternatives (e.g., ShieldFL) by orders of magnitude. These findings underscore the effectiveness of our framework in reconciling computational efficiency with rigorous privacy requirements, making it particularly suitable for large-scale distributed learning scenarios where both metrics are paramount.

In addition to computational gains, our method also achieves a 3× reduction in communication overhead compared to ShieldFL. This improvement is attributed to two key design features: (1) the elimination of normalization operations, which reduces the number of communication rounds required per aggregation; and (2) the use of compact ciphertext representations with smaller modulus sizes, significantly reducing the bit-length of each transmitted message. These optimizations collectively enhance the scalability of our framework in bandwidth-constrained federated environments.

7 Conclusion

This paper proposes a distance-based defense strategy against backdoor attacks in PPFL. Existing defense mechanisms face significant challenges in identifying and mitigating such backdoor attacks under encryption. To address the challenge of mitigating encrypted attacks, our solution identifies and filters malicious model updates by leveraging SMPC and homomorphic encryption to ensure client privacy. Extensive experiments under diverse attack scenarios demonstrate the approach's robustness in both IID and non-IID settings. Future work may focus on further improving computational efficiency and extending the defense framework to other types of adversarial threats in federated learning.

Acknowledgement. This work was supported in part by the National Key Research and Development Program of China (Grant No. 2020YFA0712300), in part by the National Natural Science Foundation of China (Grant Nos. 62132005 and 62172162), in part by Shanghai Trusted Industry Internet Software Collaborative Innovation Center, and in part by the Fundamental Research Funds for the Central Universities.

References

1. Bagdasaryan, E., Veit, A., Hua, Y., Estrin, D., Shmatikov, V.: How to backdoor federated learning. In: International Conference on Artificial Intelligence and Statistics, pp. 2938–2948. PMLR (2020)
2. Bhagoji, A.N., Chakraborty, S., Mittal, P., Calo, S.: Analyzing federated learning through an adversarial lens. In: International Conference on Machine Learning, pp. 634–643. PMLR (2019)
3. Blanchard, P., El Mhamdi, E.M., Guerraoui, R., Stainer, J.: Machine learning with adversaries: byzantine tolerant gradient descent. In: Advances in Neural Information Processing Systems, vol. 30 (2017)
4. Bonawitz, K., et al.: Practical secure aggregation for privacy-preserving machine learning. In: proceedings of the 2017 ACM SIGSAC Conference on Computer and Communications Security, pp. 1175–1191 (2017)
5. Damaskinos, G., Guerraoui, R., Patra, R., Taziki, M., et al.: Asynchronous byzantine machine learning (the case of sgd). In: International Conference on Machine Learning, pp. 1145–1154. PMLR (2018)
6. Dwork, C., Roth, A., et al.: The algorithmic foundations of differential privacy. Found. Trends® Theor. Comput. Sci. **9**(3–4), 211–407 (2014)
7. Fang, M., Cao, X., Jia, J., Gong, N.: Local model poisoning attacks to {Byzantine-Robust} federated learning. In: 29th USENIX security symposium (USENIX Security 20), pp. 1605–1622 (2020)
8. Fereidooni, H., Pegoraro, A., Rieger, P., Dmitrienko, A., Sadeghi, A.R.: Freqfed: A frequency analysis-based approach for mitigating poisoning attacks in federated learning. arXiv preprint arXiv:2312.04432 (2023)
9. Fung, C., Yoon, C.J., Beschastnikh, I.: The limitations of federated learning in sybil settings. In: 23rd International Symposium on Research in Attacks, Intrusions and Defenses (RAID 2020), pp. 301–316 (2020)
10. Guerraoui, R., Rouault, S., et al.: The hidden vulnerability of distributed learning in byzantium. In: International Conference on Machine Learning, pp. 3521–3530. PMLR (2018)
11. Huang, S., Li, Y., Chen, C., Shi, L., Gao, Y.: Multi-metrics adaptively identifies backdoors in federated learning. In: Proceedings of the IEEE/CVF International Conference on Computer Vision, pp. 4652–4662 (2023)
12. Kairouz, P., McMahan, H.B.: Advances and open problems in federated learning. Found. Trends Mach. Learn. **14**(1–2), 1–210 (2021)
13. Ma, Z., Ma, J., Miao, Y., Li, Y., Deng, R.H.: Shieldfl: mitigating model poisoning attacks in privacy-preserving federated learning. IEEE Trans. Inf. Forensics Secur. **17**, 1639–1654 (2022)
14. McMahan, B., Moore, E., Ramage, D., Hampson, S., Arcas, B.A.: Communication-efficient learning of deep networks from decentralized data. In: Artificial Intelligence and Statistics, pp. 1273–1282. PMLR (2017)
15. Nguyen, T.D., et al.: {FLAME}: taming backdoors in federated learning. In: 31st USENIX Security Symposium (USENIX Security 22), pp. 1415–1432 (2022)
16. Ozdayi, M.S., Kantarcioglu, M., Gel, Y.R.: Defending against backdoors in federated learning with robust learning rate. In: Proceedings of the AAAI Conference on Artificial Intelligence, vol. 35, pp. 9268–9276 (2021)
17. Pillutla, K., Kakade, S.M., Harchaoui, Z.: Robust aggregation for federated learning. IEEE Trans. Signal Process. **70**, 1142–1154 (2022)

18. Ruder, S.: An overview of gradient descent optimization algorithms. arXiv preprint arXiv:1609.04747 (2016)
19. Shokri, R., Shmatikov, V.: Privacy-preserving deep learning. In: Proceedings of the 22nd ACM SIGSAC Conference on Computer and Communications Security, pp. 1310–1321 (2015)
20. Shokri, R., Stronati, M., Song, C., Shmatikov, V.: Membership inference attacks against machine learning models. In: 2017 IEEE Symposium on Security and Privacy (SP), pp. 3–18. IEEE (2017)
21. Sun, Z., Kairouz, P., Suresh, A.T., McMahan, H.B.: Can you really backdoor federated learning? arXiv preprint arXiv:1911.07963 (2019)
22. Tao, G., Wang, Z., Feng, S., Shen, G., Ma, S., Zhang, X.: Distribution preserving backdoor attack in self-supervised learning. In: 2024 IEEE Symposium on Security and Privacy (SP), pp. 2029–2047. IEEE (2024)
23. Wang, H., Xiang, Z., Miller, D.J., Kesidis, G.: Mm-bd: post-training detection of backdoor attacks with arbitrary backdoor pattern types using a maximum margin statistic. In: 2024 IEEE Symposium on Security and Privacy (SP), pp. 1994–2012. IEEE (2024)
24. Xie, C., Chen, M., Chen, P.Y., Li, B.: Crfl: certifiably robust federated learning against backdoor attacks. In: International Conference on Machine Learning, pp. 11372–11382. PMLR (2021)
25. Yaldiz, D.N., Zhang, T., Avestimehr, S.: Secure federated learning against model poisoning attacks via client filtering. arXiv preprint arXiv:2304.00160 (2023)
26. Yang, Q., Liu, Y., Chen, T., Tong, Y.: Federated machine learning: concept and applications. ACM Trans. Intell. Syst. Technol. (TIST) **10**(2), 1–19 (2019)
27. Yin, D., Chen, Y., Kannan, R., Bartlett, P.: Byzantine-robust distributed learning: towards optimal statistical rates. In: International Conference on Machine Learning, pp. 5650–5659. PMLR (2018)
28. Zhou, J., Chen, S., Choo, K.K.R., Cao, Z., Dong, X.: EPNS: efficient privacy-preserving intelligent traffic navigation from multiparty delegated computation in cloud-assisted vanets. IEEE Trans. Mob. Comput. **22**(3), 1491–1506 (2021)
29. Zhuang, H., Yu, M., Wang, H., Hua, Y., Li, J., Yuan, X.: Backdoor federated learning by poisoning backdoor-critical layers. arXiv preprint arXiv:2308.04466 (2023)

A Prototype Network Assisted Training Mechanism for Edge Federated Learning Models

Xinyu Yuan[1(✉)] and Ling Shi[2]

[1] School of Data Science, The Chinese University of Hong Kong, Shenzhen 518172, China
123090778@link.cuhk.edu.cn
[2] College of Computer and Information Engineering, Henan Normal University, Xinxiang 453007, Henan, China
2108283070@stu.htu.edu.cn

Abstract. As a new computing paradigm for edge intelligence, federated learning has received extensive attention in recent years. However, the non-independent and identically distributed data and long-tail distribution seriously affect the performance of learning models. Using gradient prototypes to create an environment similar to a real balanced dataset can improve the performance of the model. Specifically, the client uses prototype contrastive loss locally to train the model, computes the local gradient prototype, and then uploads the local model, local feature prototype, and local gradient prototype to the server. Then, the cosine similarity loss between the server gradient prototype and the global gradient prototype is used to optimize the global feature prototype, and the classifier is retrained. Finally, the global feature model and the optimized global feature prototype are sent to the client. By strengthening the cooperation between clients, this method expands the feature space of each client under the premise of protecting data privacy, and effectively solves the problems of non-independent and identically distributed data and long-tail distribution. Experimental results show that the accuracy of the trained model is higher than that of classical methods.

Keywords:: prototype network · federated learning · model training · non-independent isodistribution · long-tail distribution · rate of convergence

1 Summarize

The large-scale deployment and advancement of fifth-generation (5G) mobile communication technology have not only enhanced user service quality but also laid the foundation for various emerging applications [1]. However, industries such as autonomous driving and telemedicine still face unmet demands, as they require not only ultra-high-speed data transmission but also continuous innovation in intelligence. To further elevate the development of smart cities—transitioning from the Internet of Everything (IoE) to the Intelligence of Everything—the deep integration of artificial intelligence (AI) and

L. Zhang and K.-K. R. Choo (Eds.): MobiQuitous 2025, LNICST 683, pp. 95–115, 2026.
https://doi.org/10.1007/978-3-032-22500-9_6

the Internet of Things (IoT) has become imperative. The concept of "Intelligence of Everything" entails embedding intelligence into objects, enabling them to collect and process data directly at the network edge, thereby creating an interconnected smart world where humans, objects, and intelligence seamlessly interact to meet evolving intelligent demands.

In recent years, significant improvements in the storage and computational capabilities of edge devices have empowered them to handle more complex tasks. Edge intelligence, a novel technology combining edge computing and AI, is poised to become the driving force behind realizing the Intelligence of Everything vision. In edge intelligence environments, neural network models are deployed at the edge, enabling real-time intelligent processing of data collected by edge sensing devices without the need to upload data to the cloud. Federated learning (FL), operating within the mobile edge computing (MEC) framework, serves as a distributed machine learning paradigm for achieving edge intelligence. As illustrated in Fig. 1, with the assistance of a central server, edge devices collaboratively train a global model using local data without exchanging raw data, thereby preserving user privacy and alleviating communication overhead.

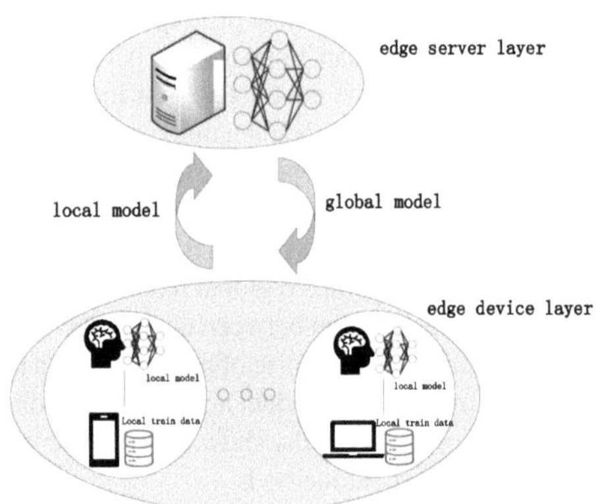

Fig. 1. Federated Learning Framework

Federated learning has found applications in numerous industries such as healthcare, industry, and finance, drawing widespread attention from researchers and enterprises. Nevertheless, due to the heterogeneity of user groups, the federated learning architecture is confronted with two inherent issues, making it challenging for neural network models to converge to the optimal solution. On one hand, the local data of clients stems from diverse sources, giving rise to a non-independent and identically distributed (non-IID) nature among these data. This heterogeneity can be further classified into inter-class heterogeneity and intra-class heterogeneity. Inter-class heterogeneity indicates that the data categories encompassed by different clients vary. Intra-class heterogeneity implies that even for the same category of data, disparities persist among different clients. On the other hand, both local data and global data (obtained by consolidating all local data) present a long-tail distribution, namely, some categories possess a considerable volume of data (head categories), while others have a meager amount (tail categories), thereby leading to poor generalization ability of the model, with a severe bias towards head categories and neglect of tail categories.

In practical applications, the data of the client side typically exhibits a situation where both non-independent and identically distributed (non-IID) and long-tail distributions coexist. Specifically, different categories of data in each client possess distinct tail classes, which renders the training of models in edge federated learning exceptionally challenging. Nevertheless, few studies have concurrently contemplated the coexistence of these two distributions. In research targeting non-IID data, the predominant approaches employed include personalized federated learning, enhancement of the local training process, and non-random selection of clients. These three methods typically assume that the data volumes of different categories are identical and are incapable of addressing the issue of long-tail distribution. In studies focused on long-tail data distribution, the principal methods utilized are rebalancing and transfer learning. These two methods commonly assume that the data categories among clients are uniform and are unable to handle the problem of non-IID data.

Inspired by prototype learning, certain research has decoupled the model into a feature extractor and a classifier. The feature extractor outputs the feature prototypes of the data, while the classifier outputs the prediction scores for each category. Through prototype comparison, data information from other clients can be acquired, facilitating the learning of superior feature representations [2]. In prototype learning, the feature prototype refers to the average of the features within the same category, demanding that the data features within each category be highly similar without intra-class heterogeneity. Evidently, this does not hold in practical applications. For instance, the category "dog" encompasses diverse breeds such as "Golden Retriever" and "Teddy", although they belong to the same prototype, they exhibit substantial disparities. The feature extractor extracts the general features of the data, while the classifier is closer to the data. Consequently, compared to the feature extractor, the classifier exerts a more significant influence on the model's performance. This has been experimentally demonstrated in Sect. 5.2.

Based on the above considerations, in order to address the issues of non-independent and non-identically distributed data (including inter-class heterogeneity and intra-class heterogeneity) and long-tail distribution faced by edge federated learning, this paper proposes an innovative method based on prototype learning to train the global model and improve recognition accuracy, following the general intuition: "A balanced global dataset training model outperforms an unbalanced local dataset training model." Throughout the federated learning process, the model is decoupled into a feature extractor and a classifier, semantic features are introduced, and the gradient prototypes of classifier parameters are used to create an environment similar to a real balanced dataset on the server. Specifically, on the client side, the model is trained using prototype contrastive loss to better utilize the data from other clients. Prototype learning processes data at the class level and can solve the problem of inter-class heterogeneity. On the server side, first, the feature prototypes are optimized using the gradient prototypes of classifier parameters to better fuse the features within each class, rather than simply aggregating them by simple averaging, which can solve the problem of intra-class heterogeneity; then, the balanced classifier is retrained using the optimized feature prototypes to make its performance similar to that of the classifier trained on a real balanced dataset, allowing the two classifiers to converge to similar optimal solutions to avoid over-biasing the head classes, thereby solving the problem of long-tail distribution. The main contributions of this paper are as follows:

- Re-design the loss function of the client. Based on the optimized global feature prototype, improve the basic loss function by adding prototype contrast loss. Under the premise of protecting user privacy security, obtain data information from other clients to expand the feature space and increase the diversity of data.
- Optimize the global feature prototype and re-train the classifier. It has been verified that re-training the classifier is important for model accuracy. Use gradient prototypes as "fake data" and create an environment in the server that is close to a real balanced dataset. By optimizing the global feature prototype, better integrate the local data of the clients and thereby solve the problem of non-independent and non-identically distributed data; solve the problem of long-tail distribution by training a balanced classifier.
- Through experiments, the effectiveness of the proposed method for long-tail and heterogeneous data has been verified. Taking animal recognition as an application case, its practicability has been clarified.

2 Related Work

This section first analyzes the existing work considering the non-independent and identically distributed (NIID) and long-tailed distribution problems faced by edge federations. Then, it introduces the application scenarios of prototype learning in federated learning.

2.1 Federated Learning with Non-iid/long-Tail Distribution

Federated learning, as a distributed machine learning method, has been widely studied and applied since its proposal [3]. However, when the data is non-iid and long-tailed, the model's accuracy will decline. Current research mainly focuses on these two distributions separately, and there are few methods that solve the problem simultaneously. Moreover, the solutions for non-iid data often only focus on inter-class heterogeneity while ignoring intra-class heterogeneity.

2.1.1 Non-iid Data

Currently, the main methods to solve the problem of non-iid data include personalized federated learning, improving the local training process, and non-randomly selecting clients. The purpose of personalized federated learning is to tailor the model for each client. Dinh et al. used Moreau envelopes as the regularization loss function and achieved personalized federated learning by designing a two-level optimization problem [4]. Alireza et al. aimed to find an initial model that can quickly adapt to local data, thereby achieving personalized federated learning [5]. Literature [6] considered both the general performance and personalized performance of the model during model training. However, these personalized models can only achieve high accuracy when recognizing local data, and often fail to achieve satisfactory results when recognizing data from other clients.

Improving the local training process usually involves adding regularization terms to the basic loss function or adjusting the learning rate. Xian et al. designed a new loss function to robustly learn common and rare classes from long-tailed data [7]. Zachary et al. improved the local training process by choosing an appropriate learning rate to enhance the model's performance [8]. Since only the client training process was improved, this method can only improve the model's performance to a limited extent.

The method of non-randomly selecting clients mainly involves choosing clients with strong communication and computing capabilities and similar data to participate in training in each round. Sawsan et al. considered factors such as CPU, memory, energy, and time of each client and selected the clients participating in federated learning in a non-random manner [9]. Jie et al. proposed a new algorithm that can ensure performance for a long time by only using the current available wireless channel information [10]. Yann et al. selected clients through clustering sampling to reduce the variance when aggregating data from different clients [11]. However, this method makes it difficult for clients with weak communication and computing capabilities and significant differences in data from other clients to participate in federated training, thus receiving unfair treatment and ultimately affecting the model's accuracy.

2.1.2 Long-Tail Distribution

The existing research methods for long-tail distribution are mainly divided into two categories: reweighting and transfer learning. Reweighting refers to keeping the training dataset balanced, which mainly includes resampling and reweighting. Tingting et al. used the SMOTE algorithm to increase the data volume of the tail class [12]. Jiangpeng et al. under-sampled the head class to eliminate redundant head class data [13]. Cao et al. improved the proportion of the tail class by reweighting [14]. Yin et al. increased the feature space of the tail class through transfer learning [15]. However, the reweighting method inevitably loses some data information, reweighting will destroy the original structure of the model, and the reweighting method can only achieve limited improvement in the performance of the model. The method of using transfer learning to solve the long-tail distribution requires knowing the global distribution of the data, which is impractical in federated learning.

2.2 Prototype Learning

Prototype learning was initially proposed for few-shot learning. By using the feature representation vectors of the average data samples of each class, a feature prototype can be learned for each class of data samples [16]. In prototype learning, the model is usually decoupled into a feature extractor and a classifier. The feature extractor converts the original data into feature representations with lower dimensions, and the classifier obtains the prediction results of the model based on the feature representations [17]. Qinbin et al. proposed a federated learning method based on model prototype comparison, using the similarity between model representations to correct the local training of individuals [18]. Yue et al. proposed a federated prototype learning framework using communication abstract class prototypes [19]. Yu et al. used multiple feature prototypes to represent a class and captured different feature representations for each class space [20].

This method uses a prototype network to train the federated learning model. By converting the original data into small-dimensional features, it can solve the problems of few data samples and heterogeneous data samples that make the extracted features not obvious and lead to low model accuracy; it also solves the problem of low training model accuracy caused by uneven data distribution through re-training. Therefore, using the prototype learning network to assist federated learning in training models is highly feasible.

The above methods for solving non-independent and identically distributed and long-tail distribution have their own limitations, and few works solve both problems simultaneously. Federated learning is similar to the scenario of few-shot learning, where clients do not have sufficient data to train high-performance models. Therefore, this paper adopts an edge federated method based on prototype learning to train a global model that can identify data with high accuracy.

3 System Overview

3.1 Scenario Setup

Standard federated learning involves a server and K clients, with the goal of collaboratively training a global model under the assistance of the server. Given a dataset $D = \{x_i, y_i\}_{i=1}^{N}$ with N samples, y_i represents the class label corresponding to the data sample x_i, $y_i \in 1, 2, \ldots, C$, and C is the total number of classes in the dataset D. Each of the K clients contains a heterogeneous data partition $D_1, D_2, \ldots, D_K$. This paper considers a more realistic scenario closer to practical applications. Dataset D follows a long-tail distribution, and the number of samples in different classes varies. Additionally, the local data $D_1, D_2, \ldots, D_K$ of the K clients also follows a long-tail distribution, and the number of samples of the same class in different clients is also different, that is, for a certain class, a small number of clients occupy the majority of the sample numbers.

3.2 Model Setup

This paper divides the neural network model into two parts: feature extractor and classifier. The model parameters are defined as $w = \{\phi, \nu\}$, where w represents the parameters of the entire neural network, ϕ represents the parameters of the feature extractor, and ν represents the parameters of the classifier. As shown in Formula (1), when inputting data x into the model, the predicted score of class C data can be obtained.

$$F(w) = F(\phi, v) = h(v; z)^{\circ} f(\phi; x) \quad (1)$$

In the feature extractor, after the local data of the input client is provided, the output is a low-dimensional feature vector [21]. In formula (2), z represents the low-dimensional feature prototype vector obtained after the processing by the feature extractor f(.), which represents the average feature value of samples belonging to the same class.

$$z = f(\phi; x) \quad (2)$$

The classifier takes low-dimensional feature vectors as input and generates prediction scores for C classes of data. Then, among these C prediction scores, the class with the maximum value is selected as the prediction result. In formula (3), q represents the prediction score for C class data obtained after the feature prototype z is processed by $h(.)$ the classifier.

$$q = h(v; z) \tag{3}$$

In the conventional federated learning paradigm, the optimization objective is formulated as minimizing the aggregated loss function over K distributed clients, as expressed in Eq. (4).

$$\min\left[\frac{1}{K}\sum_{k=1}^{K} l_k(w_k; x, y)\right] \tag{4}$$

Equation (4) is applicable when clients possess large-scale datasets. However, in federated learning settings where each client only has limited local data, solely using the loss function defined in Eq. (4) can easily lead to overfitting. Moreover, repeated local training with client-side data may cause the local model to deviate from the optimal feature prototype. To address this issue, we introduce a regularization term that leverages both local data and information from other clients to train the model, thereby aligning client models with the global model and reducing their divergence. This approach facilitates learning better feature representations. We formulate the federated learning optimization objective as Eq. (5), and theoretically prove in Sect. 3.3 that incorporating this regularization term effectively reduces generalization error and mitigates overfitting.

$$\min\left\{\frac{1}{K}\sum_{i=1}^{K}\left[l_i(w_i; x, y) + \mu l_i^{con}(w_i, w)\right]\right\} \tag{5}$$

3.3 Theoretical Proof

For client k, the ideal scenario during model training would involve computing the expected loss over the latent true distribution $P_{XY}^{(k)}$ (encompassing both known training data and unknown future data). However, obtaining such future data is inherently unattainable. Therefore, we adopt the principle of local optimality to approximate global optimality, using the empirical loss computed from the empirical distribution $\hat{P}_{XY}^{(k)}$ (i.e., the known training set) as a substitute for the expected loss.

For computational efficiency and theoretical analysis, we adopt the following linear discriminant formulation as our training model:

$$W_{Y|X}(w; y|x) = \frac{1}{C}(1 + f(x)^T h(y)) \tag{6}$$

Equation (7) defines the loss function between distributions P and W.

$$L_k^2(P, W) := \sum_{x\in X, y\in Y} \frac{(P(x, y) - W(x, y))^2}{P_X^{(k)}(x)} \tag{7}$$

$P_X^{(k)}(x)$ represents the marginal distribution over X. Under ideal conditions, the local model can be obtained by minimizing the expected loss $L_k^2(P_{XY}^{(k)}, P_X^{(k)} W_{Y|X}^{(k)})$. The loss between client k's latent true distribution $P_{XY}^{(k)}$ and the product of the marginal distribution $P_X^{(k)} W_{Y|X}^{(k)}$ and the learned model $L_k^2(P_{XY}^{(k)}, P_X^{(k)} W_{Y|X}^{(k)})$ is expressed as:

$$\begin{aligned} & L_k^2(P_{XY}^{(k)}, P_X^{(k)} W_{Y|X}^{(k)}) \\ & = L_k^2(P_{XY}^{(k)} - \hat{P}_{XY}^{(k)} + \hat{P}_{XY}^{(k)}, P_X^{(k)} W_{Y|X}^{(k)}) \\ & = \sum_{x \in X, y \in Y} \frac{(P_{XY}^{(k)}(x,y) - \hat{P}_{XY}^{(k)}(x,y) + \hat{P}_{XY}^{(k)}(x,y) - P_X^{(k)}(x)(1+f(x)^T h(y))/C)^2}{P_X^{(k)}(x)} \end{aligned} \tag{8}$$

By minimizing $L_k^2(P_{XY}^{(k)}, P_X^{(k)} W_{Y|X}^{(k)})$ in the above formulation, we reduce the divergence between the latent true distribution and the trained model, thereby obtaining the optimal model parameters. Upon simplification, the loss function $L_k^2(P_{XY}^{(k)}, P_X^{(k)} W_{Y|X}^{(k)})$ can be decomposed into a sum of three distinct components: (i) the empirical loss term quantifying the divergence between the empirical distribution (i.e., the observable training dataset) and the learned model parameters; (ii) the generalization error terms arising from the inherent unobservability of future data samples; and (iii) a constant term representing the irreducible discrepancy between the underlying true data distribution and its empirical counterpart.

Assuming the empirical marginal distribution $\hat{P}_Y^{(k)}$ coincides with the latent true marginal distribution $P_Y^{(k)}$, the second term can consequently be reformulated as:

$$\begin{aligned} & \sum_y 2P_Y^{(k)}(y)[\sum_x (P_{X|Y}^{(k)}(x|y) - \hat{P}_{X|Y}^{(k)}(x|y)) f(x)]^T h(y)/C \\ & = 2E_{P_Y^{(k)}}[E_{P_{X|Y}^{(k)}}[f(x)] - E_{\hat{P}_{X|Y}^{(k)}}[f(x)]]^T h(Y)/C \end{aligned} \tag{9}$$

The empirical conditional distribution $E_{\hat{P}_{X|Y}^{(k)}}[f(x)]$ can be derived from the available training dataset, whereas the latent true distribution E_2 remains computationally intractable. Leveraging the federated learning framework, we utilize global feature distributions aggregated from participating clients to approximate $E_{P_{X|Y}^{(k)}}[f(x)]$. Section 4.1 provides a formal specification of the loss function employed for local model training at each client.

3.4 Overall Framework

This work employs gradient prototypes of classifier parameters as "pseudo-data" to optimize global feature prototypes and subsequently retrain the global classifier. The objective is to train a model capable of effectively recognizing global data patterns while achieving comparable performance to models trained on balanced datasets. Our framework comprises two key components: client-side and server-side modules.

- On the client side, a redesigned loss function enables model aggregation through feature extraction while preserving data privacy, thereby leveraging cross-client information to train superior models. Concurrently, gradient prototypes of local classifier parameters are computed directly from raw data.

- On the server side, the global classifier's gradient prototypes – denoted as server gradient prototypes – are computed. Feature prototype optimization is achieved by minimizing the cosine similarity loss between server gradient prototypes and global gradient prototypes, followed by classifier retraining. The overall framework is illustrated in Fig. 2.

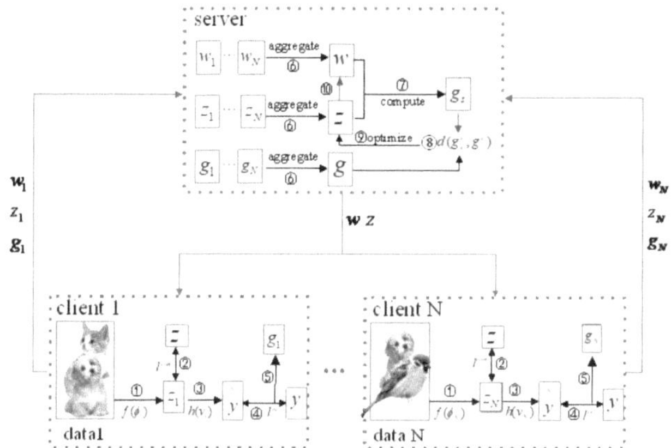

Fig. 2. Overall framework diagram

Sections 3.4.1 and 3.4.2 provide detailed specifications of the client-side and server-side training procedures, respectively.

3.4.1 Client Operation

- The feature extractor $f(.)$ processes client-side data to generate feature prototypes with significantly reduced dimensionality compared to the raw input data.
- The prototype contrast loss l^{con} is computed by comparing the client's local feature prototypes with the optimized global feature prototypes.
- The client feeds local feature prototypes into classifier $h(.)$ to obtain prediction scores $y*$.
- The client computes the cross-entropy loss l^{ce}, combines it with the prototype contrast loss l^{con} to form the total loss l^{ce}, and employs this composite loss for local model training.
- The client computes local gradient prototypes through forward propagation of the classifier.

The client uploads the local model (including both feature extractor and classifier), local feature prototypes, and local gradient prototypes to the server for global aggregation.

3.4.2 Server Operation

- The server aggregates all uploaded client models (including feature extractors and classifiers), local feature prototypes, and local gradient prototypes to form global models, global feature prototypes, and global gradient prototypes. During the first training epoch, these aggregated outputs initialize the global model. Class-wise aggregation is performed for both global feature prototypes and global gradient prototypes.
- The server computes server gradient prototypes through forward propagation of the global classifier using global feature prototypes.
- The cosine similarity loss between server gradient prototypes and global gradient prototypes is computed.
- The global feature prototypes are optimized using the cosine similarity loss calculated in step 8.
- The global classifier is retrained using optimized global feature prototypes from step 9.

Models trained on globally balanced datasets outperform those trained on locally imbalanced datasets. However, directly uploading raw data to the server incurs high communication costs and raises privacy concerns. Real-world data typically exhibits heterogeneity and long-tailed distributions, and direct model aggregation on the server may degrade performance. To address this, we propose gradient prototypes that leverage optimized global feature prototypes to retrain a balanced classifier, mitigating bias towards head classes (which inherently possess more samples) while maintaining classification equilibrium. Furthermore, each client can enhance data diversity by incorporating information from other clients' datasets.

4 Collaborative Training Between the Server and the Client

In this section, we have provided a detailed description of the proposed method.

4.1 Client-Side Model Training

Figure 3 illustrates the loss functions employed for client-side model training, comprising: (i) the empirical loss measuring the discrepancy between the classifier's predicted label scores and ground-truth labels, and (ii) the prototype contrast loss quantifying the divergence between locally extracted feature prototypes and global feature prototypes generated by the feature extractor.

Equation (10) formulates the loss function for client k as the weighted sum of empirical loss l_k^{ce} and prototype contrast loss l_k^{con} where l_k^{ce} and l_k^{con} are computed via Eqs. (11) and (12) respectively. The weighting coefficient μ balances the relative contributions of these two loss components.

$$l_k^{total} = l_k^{ce}(w_k; x, y) + \mu l_k^{con}(z_k, z) \tag{10}$$

In Eq. (11), $F_k(w_k; x)$ denotes the class-wise label scores obtained by feeding input data x into the model, which are subsequently used with the ground-truth label scores to compute the empirical loss via cross-entropy.

$$l_k^{ce} = CrossEntropyLoss(F_k(w_k; x), y) \tag{11}$$

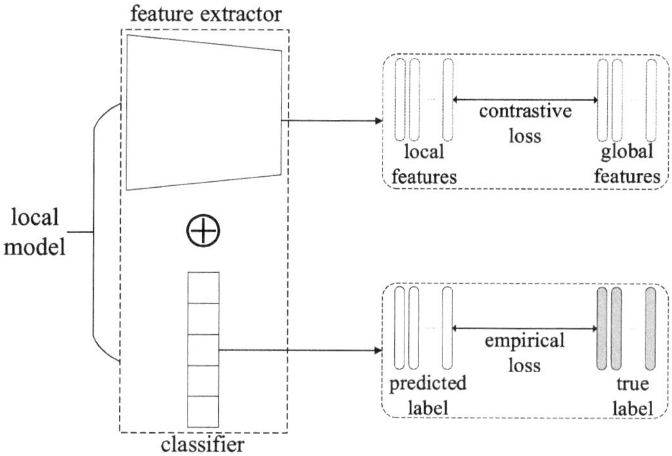

Fig. 3. Loss function of the client

In Eq. (12), $d(.)$ represents the distance metric between class- c local feature prototypes and class- c global feature prototypes, which can be quantified using quadratic distance, MSE distance, or other applicable distance measures. It should be noted that the class distribution in client k's local dataset may constitute only a subset of the global dataset. The prototype loss for client k is obtained by summing the individual prototype losses across all C_k present classes, thereby preventing deviation between local and global feature prototypes.

$$l_k^{con} = \sum_{c \in C_k} d(z_k^c, z^c) \tag{12}$$

The local feature prototypes in Eq. (12) are computed via Eq. (13), where D_k^c denotes class- c data samples from client k, and z_k^c represents the feature prototypes obtained by processing class- c samples through feature extractor $f_k(\phi_k)$. Here, z_k^c constitutes a d-dimensional feature vector, resulting in an aggregate feature dimension of $C * d$ for all C classes.

$$z_k^c = \frac{1}{|D_k^c|} \sum_{(x,y) \in D_k^c} f_k(\phi_k; x) \tag{13}$$

Upon completing local training, the client computes gradient prototypes for class- c data using Eq. (14). These gradient prototypes maintain identical dimensionality to the feature prototypes - d-dimensional per class, yielding an aggregate dimension of $C * d$ across all classes. Here, $h_k(.)$ denotes the model's classifier, while $l(h_k(z_k^c), y)$ represents the loss between predicted label scores and ground-truth labels.

$$g_k^c = \frac{1}{|D_k^c|} \sum_{(x,y) \in D_k^c} \nabla l(h_k(z_k^c), y) \tag{14}$$

Algorithm 1 describes the process by which the clientupdates the model as well as computing the gradient prototypes of the local classifier parameters. First, the server downloads the global model (including the global feature extractor and the global classifier) and the global feature prototype to the client. The client then trains a local model using the loss function shown in Eq. (10), and the local gradient prototype is computed according to Eq. (14). Finally, the client uploads the local model, local feature prototype, and local gradient prototype to the server. In the local training, each client can make full use of the data in other clients to expand the feature space of its own data, avoid over-fitting caused by its own insufficient data, and reduce generalization error.

Table 1. Algorithm 1 Client

Initialization: During local training for t_local rounds, the set of training data for class c in client k is denoted as $(x,y)\in D_k^c (c\in C_k)$

Input: global model $w(\phi,v)$ (including global feature extractor and classifier) and global feature prototypes $\{z^c \mid c\in C\}$.

Output: updated local model $w_k(\phi_k,v_k)$, local feature prototypes $\{z_k^c \mid c\in C_k\}$, and local gradient prototypes $\{g_k^c \mid c\in C_k\}$.

1: for t in t_local:

2: for batch $(x,y)\in D_k^c$:

3: calculate the cross-entropy loss: $l_k^{ce} = CrossEntropyLoss(F_k(w_k;x),y)$

4: calculate the local prototype: $z_k^c = \frac{1}{|D_k^c|}\sum_{(x,y)\in D_k^c} f_k(\phi_k;x)$

5: calculate the prototype comparison loss: $l_k^{con} = \sum_{c\in C_k} d(z_k^c, z^c)$

6: total loss function: $l_k^{total} = l_k^{ce} + \mu l_k^{con}$

7: update the local model parameters using the total loss function $w_k(\phi_k,v_k)$

8: local gradient prototype: $g_k^c = \frac{1}{|D_k^c|}\sum_{(x,y)\in D_k^c} \nabla l(h_k(z_k^c),y)$

9: return the local model, the local feature prototype and the local gradient prototype

4.2 Server

In each communication round, the server randomly selects R clients for participation. The server first aggregates local models, local feature prototypes, and local gradient prototypes according to Eqs. (15), (16), and (17), respectively. In Eqs. (16) and (17), R^C

denotes the set of clients possessing class c.

$$w = \sum_{k \in R} \frac{|D_k|}{\sum_{k \in R} |D_k|} w_k \tag{15}$$

$$z^c = \frac{1}{|R^c|} \sum_{k \in R^c} z_k^c \tag{16}$$

$$g^c = \frac{1}{|R^c|} \sum_{k \in R^c} g_k^c \tag{17}$$

The server then computes the server gradient prototypes using the global classifier obtained from Eq. (15) and the global feature prototypes derived from Eq. (16), as formalized in Eq. (18), where g_s^c denotes the gradient prototype for class-c data on server s.

$$g_s^c = \nabla l(h(z^c), y) \tag{18}$$

Subsequently, the cosine similarity loss between the global gradient prototypes from Eq. (17) and server gradient prototypes from Eq. (18) is computed via Eq. (19), where this loss metric quantifies the divergence between gradient prototypes. The gradient prototypes maintain $C \times d$ dimensionality, with $g[i]$ representing the i-th row's gradient vector.

$$D(g^c, g_s^c) = \frac{1}{C} \sum_{i=1}^{C} (1 - \frac{g^c[i] * g_s^c[i]}{\|g^c[i]\| * \|g_s^c[i]\|}) \tag{19}$$

$\frac{g^c[i] * g_s^c[i]}{\|g^c[i]\| * \|g_s^c[i]\|}$ represents cosine similarity. The closer the value is to 1, the higher the similarity. The specific calculation method is shown as formula (20).

$$\frac{g^c[i] * g_s^c[i]}{\|g^c[i]\| * \|g_s^c[i]\|} = \frac{\sum_{j=1}^{d} \left(g^c[i][j] * g_s^c[i][j]\right)}{\sqrt{\sum_{j=1}^{d} \left(g^c[i][j]\right)^2} * \sqrt{\sum_{j=1}^{r_2} \left(g_s^c[i][j]\right)^2}} \tag{20}$$

The server optimizes the global feature prototypes using the cosine similarity loss computed in Eq. (19), then retrains the global classifier with the optimized prototypes to achieve performance comparable to classifiers trained on true balanced datasets, as formalized in Eq. (21).

$$v^{update} \leftarrow v - \eta \nabla l((z, v); y) \tag{21}$$

Algorithm 2 details the server-side optimization of global feature prototypes and classifier retraining. The procedure comprises: Firstly, aggregating local models, feature prototypes, and gradient prototypes; secondly, optimizing global feature prototypes via backpropagation to minimize divergence between server and global gradient prototypes, thereby addressing intra-class heterogeneity neglected in conventional prototype contrastive learning through comprehensive fusion of same-class data across clients rather than naive averaging; thirdly, retraining a balanced global classifier to rectify performance degradation on tail-class data; finally, distributing the updated global model and feature prototypes to clients.

Table 2. Algorithm 2 Server

Initialization: Train the t_global round globally

Input: Local model of the client $w_k(\phi_k, v_k)$, local feature prototype $\{z_k^c \mid c \in C_k\}$, local gradient prototype $\{g_k^c \mid c \in C_k\}$

Output: Global model $w(\phi, v)$, global gradient prototype $\{z^c \mid c \in C\}$

1: for t in t_global:

2: Randomly select R clients

3: for k in R :

4: Aggregate local models: $w = \sum_{k \in R} \frac{|D_k|}{\sum_{k \in R} |D_k|} w_k$

5: Aggregate local feature prototypes: $z^c = \frac{1}{|R^c|} \sum_{k \in R^c} z_k^c$

6: Aggregate the local gradient prototype: $g^c = \frac{1}{|R^c|} \sum_{k \in R^c} g_k^c$

7: Calculate the server gradient: $g_s^c = \nabla l(h(z^c), y)$

8: Calculate the cosine similarity loss between the global gradient prototype and the server gradient prototype: $D(g^c, g_s^c) = \frac{1}{C} \sum_{i=1}^{C} (1 - \frac{g^c[i] * g_s^c[i]}{\|g^c[i]\| * \|g_s^c[i]\|})$

9: Use cosine similarity loss to optimize the global feature prototype

10: Retrain the classifier: $v^{update} \leftarrow v - \eta \nabla l((z, v); y)$

11: Return the global model $w(\phi, v)$ and the global gradient prototype $\{z^c \mid c \in C\}$

---

5 Experimental Results and Performance Analysis

5.1 Experimental Setup

5.1.1 Parameter Settings

The framework employs one server and 100 clients for training across 500 communication rounds. Each round randomly selects R clients for participation, with every chosen client performing 10 local training iterations.

5.1.2 Dataset Settings

The practicability of the methods proposed in this chapter is verified by using CIFAR-10 and MNIST. CIFAR-10 is a color dataset including 10 types of images, with a total of 60,000 images, among which 50,000 are training images and 10,000 are test images. MINST is a handwritten grayscale image ranging from 0 to 9, including 60,000 training images and 10,000 test images. Before starting the experiment, two heterogeneous and long-tail datasets, namely CIFAR-10-LT and MNIST-LT, need to be created. The experimental setup involves creating long-tailed and heterogeneous datasets through a two-step process: First, the imbalance ratio (IR) controls the degree of long-tail distribution by determining the ratio between the most and least frequent classes, with higher IR values resulting in more pronounced skew. Second, data heterogeneity across clients is achieved via Dirichlet distribution allocation (parameterized by α), where smaller α values produce more uneven data sharding - each client receives randomly-sized segments from each class, creating significant variation in local data distributions. Critically, the combination of large IR and small α simultaneously maximizes both long-tail characteristics (global imbalance) and client heterogeneity (local distribution mismatch), rigorously testing the method's robustness under extreme non-IID conditions. Standard benchmark values are employed (IR $\in$ {10,50,100}, $\alpha \in$ {0.1,0.5,1.0}) to systematically evaluate performance across varying difficulty levels.

5.1.3 Model Settings

The experiments employ ResNet-8 for CIFAR-10-LT and a CNN for MNIST-LT training in PyCharm. Kaiming et al. demonstrated that excessive neural network depth induces gradient vanishing/explosion, degrading model accuracy - a limitation addressed by ResNet's [22] residual architecture. The implemented CNN comprises five layers: two convolutional layers (10 and 20 channels with 5 $\times$ 5 kernels) followed by two fully-connected layers (50 and 10 channels), culminating in an output layer.

5.2 The Influence of Classifiers on Model Accuracy

This subsection analyzes layer-wise accuracy impacts using MNIST-LT and the 5-layer neural network, which is decomposed into four distinct layers plus the classifier. Each training round involves 10 randomly selected clients to demonstrate the differential contributions of each architectural component. Each client is allocated a long-tailed and heterogeneous data subset. The imbalance ratio (IR) controlling long-tail severity is set to 50, while the Dirichlet coefficient (α) governing data heterogeneity is fixed at 0.3. The FedAvg algorithm is first applied to pretrain models on heterogeneous data. Subsequently, using a balanced dataset, we selectively retrain individual model components while freezing the remaining four parts, systematically evaluating the accuracy impact of isolated module training.

Figure 4 demonstrates the accuracy variations between retraining individual layers and employing the FedAvg algorithm. Experimental results indicate that classifier retraining yields the most significant accuracy improvement, elevating model performance from 94.95% to 99.2%. As anticipated, the imbalanced classifier constitutes the primary factor limiting model accuracy. However, retraining classifiers with raw data violates federated learning's data privacy principle. To resolve this, we construct a pseudo-balanced dataset environment through gradient prototypes, subsequently optimizing global feature prototypes and retraining classifiers to achieve comparable accuracy improvements while maintaining FL compliance.

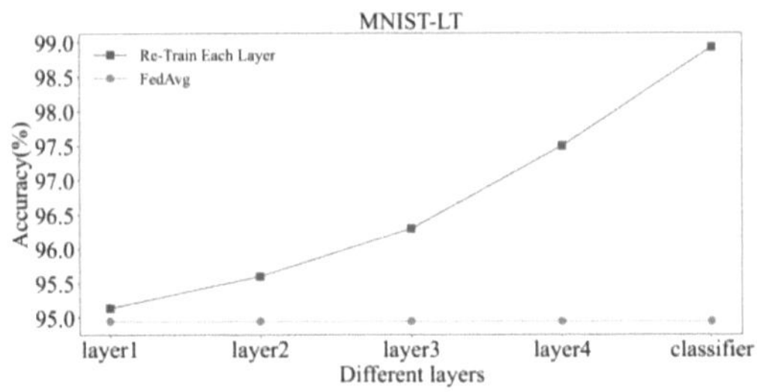

Fig. 4. Shows the accuracy variation of different layers during retraining

5.3 Accuracy Variations Under Different Values of μ

The weighting coefficient μ governs the ratio between cross-entropy loss and prototype contrast loss. To identify the optimal μ value for peak accuracy, each federated training round engages 10 clients under fixed experimental conditions ($IR = 50, \alpha = 0.3$). Meanwhile, set μ to 0.5,1,3 and 5 to test the accuracy variations of the datasets CIFAR-10-LT and MNIST-LT at different values, as shown in Fig. 5. As shown in Fig. 5. With the increase of μ, the accuracies of the two datasets show a trend of first increasing and then decreasing. When the value is 1, the accuracies reach the maximum value. The maximum accuracies of CIFAR-10 are 74.94%, and those of MNIST are 98.05%. Increasing μ enhances prototype alignment by reducing the prototype contrast loss, thereby improving accuracy as local feature prototypes converge toward global counterparts. However, excessive μ values over-constrain local model training, preventing effective utilization of client-specific data patterns and causing feature degradation that ultimately reduces model.

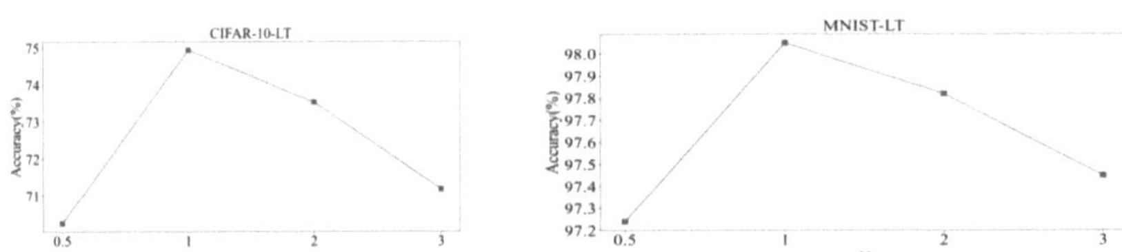

Fig. 5. Accuracy under different μ values (left: CIFAR-10-LT; right: MNIST-LT)

5.4 Comparison with Other Advanced Algorithms

This method is comparatively evaluated against four established baselines: FedAvg [3], FedProx [23], BalanceFL [7], and LDAE [24].

- FedAvg: The foundational federated learning algorithm where clients upload locally trained models to the server for weighted averaging, followed by global model redistribution to all participants.
- FedProx: An enhanced framework addressing FL heterogeneity through proximal regularization terms incorporated into local objective functions, thereby stabilizing FedAvg's training process under non-IID conditions.
- BalanceFL: A long-tail optimized FL approach that incorporates knowledge inheritance and inter-class balancing mechanisms into the loss function, effectively simulating training on balanced data distributions despite actual class imbalance.
- LDAE: A group-based multi-expert architecture that aggregates knowledge from distinct client clusters through interactive information exchange, simultaneously mitigating data heterogeneity and long-tail distribution challenges.

Comparative evaluation against these established baselines assesses the proposed algorithm's accuracy under:

- Varying client participation counts per training round
- Different degrees of non-IID data distribution and long-tail skew

5.4.1 The Number of Clients Participating in Each Round of Training

Figures 6 and 7 present the accuracy of all compared algorithms on CIFAR-10-LT and MNIST-LT. We can find that the universal accuracy improvement occurs with increased R values. The maximal gains are 77.85% and 98.86%, and the improvements are 2.91% and 0.81% in CIFAR-1-LT and MNIST-LT, respectively.

This superiority stems from enhanced feature representation learning and inter-client collaboration.

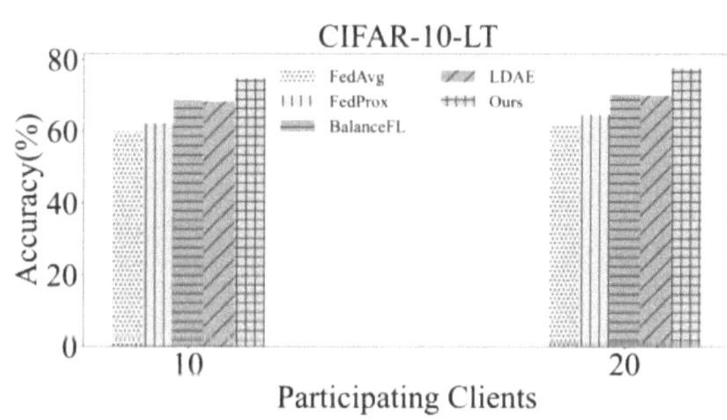

Fig. 6. The accuracy when the number of clients participating in each round of training in CIFAR-10-LT is set to 10 and 20

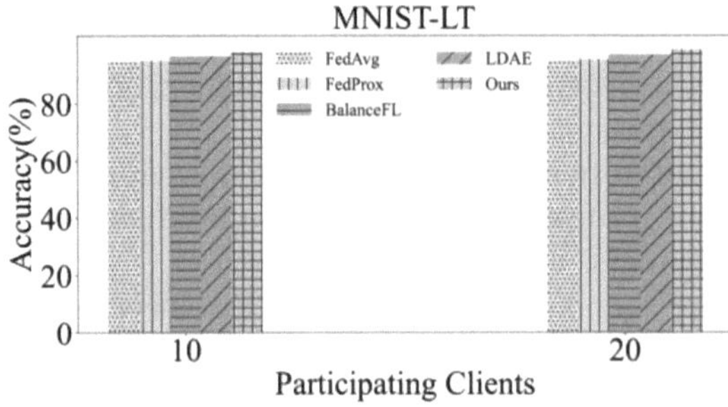

Fig. 7. The accuracy when the number of clients participating in each round of training in MNIST-LT is set to 10 and 20

5.4.2 The Degree of Heterogeneous Distribution and Long-Tail Distribution of Data

Tables 3 and 4 present the accuracy on CIFAR-10-LT and MNIST-LT for FedAvg, FedProx, BalanceFL, LDAE, and the proposed method. It is obvious to see that the accuracy improves as data heterogeneity and imbalance decrease. The proposed method consistently outperforms all baselines across configurations. On average, 6.37% and 7.08% accuracy gain are achieved with the two datasets, respectively.

Table 3. Model accuracy when Dirichlet coefficient $\alpha = 0.3$

method	CIFAR-10-LT (IR)		
	20	50	100
FedAvg	64.83	60.06	58.62
FedProx	65.92	62.33	60.49
BalanceFL	73.92	68.84	66.24
LDAE	73.87	68.35	66.16
Ours	81.31	74.94	70.52
method	MNIST-LT (IR)		
	20	50	100
FedAvg	95.86	94.95	94.07
FedProx	96.02	95.14	94.42
BalanceFL	97.64	96.72	95.94
LDAE	97.55	96.64	95.82
Ours	99.23	98.05	97.10

Table 4. Model Accuracy when Dirichlet coefficient α = 0.5

method	CIFAR-10-LT (IR)		
	20	50	100
FedAvg	65.03	62.72	61.37
FedProx	68.46	64.91	62.42
BalanceFL	79.95	72.62	70.83
LDAE	79.42	72.13	69.92
Ours	88.39	79.23	75.61
method	MNIST-LT (IR)		
	20	50	100
FedAvg	96.17	95.11	94.39
FedProx	96.58	95.71	94.67
BalanceFL	97.87	96.83	96.23
LDAE	97.65	96.75	96.16
Ours	99.93	98.66	97.48

6 Application Case: Animal Recognition System

We demonstrate practical applicability through a mobile-based animal recognition system, where user-generated wildlife images inherently exhibit heterogeneous and long-tailed distributions due to varying capture habits and environments. The implementation trains ResNet-8 on Animal-10 (a Kaggle dataset comprising 10 species including dogs, cats, and elephants with imbalanced class counts ranging from 1,000 to 5,000 samples per category).

Each federated learning round randomly selects 10 out of 50 clients for training, with each client maintaining heterogeneous long-tailed local data (IR = 50, α = 0.3). The model deployment onto an Android Studio-based recognition system [25] follows three implementation phases:

The deployment comprises three steps:

- Convert the.pth model trained in PyCharm to Android-compatible.pt format
- Integrate PyTorch dependencies into Android Studio and import both converted model and label files
- Execute model inference, achieving 97.72% accuracy on gallery image classification (Fig. 8)

Fig. 8. Local Identification System

7 Summary

This paper addresses the dual challenges of heterogeneous and long-tailed data distributions in edge federated learning by introducing gradient prototypes to simulate a balanced dataset environment, thereby enhancing model performance. We demonstrate the critical role of classifier retraining in performance improvement and theoretically justify the necessity of regularization terms. The client-side implementation incorporates a redesigned loss function that augments the base loss with prototype contrast terms, enabling secure knowledge transfer across clients to enrich feature diversity without compromising data privacy. On the server side, optimized global feature prototypes harmonize heterogeneous client data, while balanced classifier training mitigates long-tail effects. Extensive experiments validate the method's performance gains, with an animal recognition case study demonstrating practical applicability.

References

1. Zhao, X., Zhang, J., Zhang, J., Peiyan Yuan, H., Jin, X.L.: CooCo: a collaborative offloading and resource configuration algorithm in edge networks. IEEE Internet Things J. **11**(6), 10709–10721 (2024)
2. Kang, B., Rohrbach, M., et al.: Decoupling representation and classifier for long-tailed recognition. arxiv preprint: arxiv:1910.09217 (2019)
3. McMahan, B., Moore, E., Ramage, D., et al.: Communication-efficient learning of deep networks from decentralized data. In: Proc. of PMLR, pp. 1273–1282 (2017)
4. T Dinh, C., Tran, N., Nguyen, J.: Personalized federated learning with Moreau envelopes. In: Advances in Neural Information Processing Systems **33**, 21394–21405 (2020)
5. Fallah, A., Mokhtari, A., Ozdaglar, A.: Personalized federated learning with theoretical guarantees: a model-agnostic meta-learning approach. In: Advances in Neural Information Processing Systems, vol. 33, pp. 3557–3568 (2020)
6. Chen, H.Y., Chao, W.L.: On bridging generic and personalized federated learning for image classification. arxiv preprint: arxiv:2107.00778 (2021)

7. Shuai, X., Shen, Y., Jiang, S., et al.: BalanceFL: addressing class imbalance in long-tail federated learning. In: Proc. of IPSN, pp. 271–284 (2022)
8. Charles, Z., Konečný, J.: On the outsized importance of learning rates in local update methods. arxiv preprint: arxiv:2007.00878 (2020)
9. AbdulRahman, S., Tout, H., Mourad, A., et al.: FedMCCS: multicriteria client selection model for optimal IoT federated learning. IEEE Internet Things J. **8**(6), 4723–4735 (2020)
10. Xu, J., Wang, H.: Client selection and bandwidth allocation in wireless federated learning networks: a long-term perspective. IEEE Trans. Wireless Commun. **20**(2), 1188–1200 (2020)
11. Fraboni, Y., Vidal, R., Kameni, L., et al.: Clustered sampling: Low-variance and improved representativity for clients selection in federated learning. In: Proc. of PMLR, pp. 3407–3416 (2021)
12. Pan, T., Zhao, J., Wu, W., et al.: Learning imbalanced datasets based on SMOTE and Gaussian distribution. Inf. Sci. **512**, 1214–1233 (2020)
13. He, J., Lin, L., Eicher-Miller, H.A., et al.: Long-tailed food classification. Nutrients **15**(12), 2751 (2023)
14. Cao, K., Wei, C., Gaidon, A., et al.: Learning imbalanced datasets with label-distribution-aware margin loss. In: Advances in Neural Information Processing Systems, vol. 32 (2019)
15. Yin, X., Yu, X., Sohn, K., et al.: Feature transfer learning for facerecognition with under-represented data. In: Proc. of CVPR, pp. 5704–5713 (2019)
16. Snell, J., Swersky, K., Zemel, R.: Prototypical networks for few-shot learning. In: Advances in Neural Information Processing Systems, vol. 30 (2017)
17. Li, G., Jampani, V., Sevilla-Lara, L., et al.: Adaptive prototype learning and allocation for few-shot segmentation. In: Proc. of CVPR, pp. 8334–8343 (2021)
18. Li,Q., He, B., Song, D.: Model-contrastive federated learning. In: Proc. of CVPR, pp. 10713–10722 (2021)
19. Tan, Y., Long, G., Liu, L., et al.: FedProto: Federated prototype learning across heterogeneous clients. In Proc. of AAAI, pp. 8432–8440 (2022)
20. Qiao, Y., Munir, M.S., Adhikary, A., et al.: MP-FedCL: multi-prototype federated contrastive learning for edge intelligence. IEEE Internet Things J. **11**(5), 8604–8623 (2023)
21. Yang, H.M., Zhang, X.Y., Yin, F., et al.: Robust classification with convolutional prototype learning. In: Proc. of CVPR, pp. 3474–3482 (2018)
22. He, K., Zhang, X., Ren, S., et al.: Deep residual learning for image recognition. In: Proc. of CVPR, pp. 770–778 (2016)
23. Li, T., Sahu, A.K., Zaheer, M., et al.: Federated optimization in heterogeneous networks. Proc. Mach. Learn. Syst. **2**, 429–450 (2020)
24. Zeng, Y., Liu, L., Wu, B., et al.: Label-distribution-agnostic ensemble learning on federated long-tailed data (2022)
25. Yuan, P., Huang, R., Zhang, J., et al.: Accuracy rate maximization in edge federated learning with delay and energy constraints. IEEE Syst. J. **17**(2), 2053–2064 (2022)

STrustzoneFL: Secure Federated Learning Based on TrustZone

Runmeng Du[1], Chenmeng Li[1], Haotian Xu[2], Miao Wang[3(✉)], and Yuanjian Zhou[3]

[1] Xi' an Polytechnic University, Xi' an 710699, China
[2] East China Normal University, Shanghai 200062, China
[3] Jiangsu University of Technology, Changzhou 213001, China
miaowang@jsut.edu.cn

Abstract. Multiple studies have shown that during local training on the client and server, as well as the exchange of model parameters or gradients in federated learning (FL), adversaries can execute various network attacks such as data reconstruction attack (DRA) attack, property inference attack (PIA) attack, and membership inference attack (MIA) attack. These attacks enable the retrieval of sensitive information from the model parameters themselves, highlighting the importance of protecting model parameters or gradients when designing FL systems. In the context of FL, trusted execution environment (TEE) are used to safeguard data and model parameters or gradients during the training process. However, existing TEE-based FL solutions suffer from limitations such as small operating space, high overhead, and limited applicability, thereby failing to provide secure and efficient computation services that meet the requirements. In this work, we propose a federated learning system based on TrustZone, referred to as STrustZoneFL, which offers a platform for isolated execution and secure data processing in federated learning. Additionally, we enhance the system's security by using the AES symmetric encryption method to prevent attackers from intercepting and accessing data. Finally, to evaluate the framework's performance and measure the overhead of protecting federated learning, we conducted a series of experiments on a real testbed, demonstrating the feasibility of STrustZoneFL.

Keywords: Federated learning · Trusted execution environment · Advanced encryption standard · TrustZone

1 Introduction

In the context of smart environments, where data privacy and security are critical, federated learning (FL) provides a promising framework to address these

Supported by the Key Scientific Research Program of the Department of Education of Shaanxi Province for the year of 2023 (No. 23JS025), the National Key Research and Development Program of China (No. 2023YFF0905302), the Natural Science Foundation of Chongqing Municipality (No.CSTB2022NSCQ- MSX0038).

L. Zhang and K.-K. R. Choo (Eds.): MobiQuitous 2025, LNICST 683, pp. 116–130, 2026.
https://doi.org/10.1007/978-3-032-22500-9_7

challenges, enabling secure and efficient data processing across distributed systems [3,15]. The basic premise of FL involves the server distributing a global model to multiple clients, and each client trains its local model using its respective datasetm. Once all the local models are received from the clients, the server aggregates them and updates the parameters of the global model [16]. The network plays a crucial role in FL by enabling participants to communicate, share information, and collaborate on model training. Unfortunately, recent works [6,17] has demonstrated that attackers can launch various attacks to extract sensitive information from the model parameters by network. These attacks include data reconstruction attacks and inference attacks, which can be carried out on both the server-side and the client-side.

To address these security concerns in FL, several popular methods have been proposed, such as homomorphic encryption (HE) and multi-party computation (MPC). While both HE and MPC are practical for both high-end devices and mobile devices, they come with their respective challenges. HE incurs high computing costs, while MPC leads to high communication costs. As a result, there is currently no single existing solution that fully meets all the requirements, impeding the growth of FL in practical applications.

Trusted execution environment (TEE) is an emerging hardware protection technology that finds widespread use in various domains, such as TrustZone, SGX, ect. TEE offers a secure execution environment for handling sensitive tasks and information. In the context of FL, TEE can be used to protect local data and model parameters or gradients during training. However, at the present stage, TEE-based FL schemes face several challenges. These include limited runspace, high operational costs, and a lack of universal applicability. As a result, they are unable to provide secure and efficient computation services that meet the required standards. Therefore, it becomes crucial to enhance both the security and efficiency aspects of FL when leveraging TEE.

This paper presents STrustzoneFL, a novel and secure federated learning system based on TrustZone. The main objective of STrustzoneFL is to safeguard both the client and the server from the aforementioned common attacks. To achieve this, we propose several key mechanisms. Firstly, during the aggregation process, the server leverages TEE along with an aggregator for ensuring secure aggregation of model updates from multiple clients. Secondly, on the client-side, TEE is employed along with a model trainer to facilitate safe and protected training of local models. Additionally, a model coordinator is utilized to evaluate the model's performance. The specific contributions of this work can be summarized as follows:

- STrustzoneFL deploys Trustzone on both clients and the server, and proper system partitioning to enhance the security of FL through a combination of hardware and software elements. We further introduce hierarchical training and hierarchical aggregation methods. Specifically, certain layers of the model are trained and aggregated in the real-world environment, while others are processed in TEE.

- Addressing the privacy concerns associated with data transmission in FL. Since the data sent by clients are sensitive, safeguarding it from theft or unauthorized access is critical. To ensure secure data transmission, we employ the advanced encryption standard (AES) symmetric encryption method to encrypt the data output by the client. The training data is encrypted in the TEE before being transmitted to the server, and similarly, aggregated data is encrypted in the TEE before being sent to clients. This encryption mechanism significantly enhances the privacy of the system, guaranteeing its overall security.
- Conducting software implementation and feasibility testing of STrustzoneFL. Through experiments based on Raspberry Pi, we evaluate the scheme's practicality and effectiveness. By analyzing the test results of LeNet and VGG-7 models, we assess the system's operating cost, performance, and resource utilization rate. The evaluation demonstrates that STrustzoneFL is lightweight and highly efficient.

2 Related Work

In this section, we begin by introducing the prevalent TEE systems currently available. Subsequently, we delve into the related work that explores the integration of TEE with FL. The convergence of FL and TEE represents an area of active research and development within the domains of machine learning and computer security.

2.1 Trusted Execution Environment

TEE refers to a secure area within a computer or mobile device designed to safeguard sensitive data and code from unauthorized access and tampering [12]. TEE offers an isolated environment for executing code and storing data, making it well-suited for handling sensitive information like encryption keys, payment details, and personal data. Several platforms are available for implementing TEE, some of which are highlighted below:

1. TrustZone [10]: An hardware-based security platform integrated into many mobile devices, TrustZone ensures a secure environment for storing sensitive data and executing trusted code.
2. SGX [1]: Present in Intel processors, SGX is a hardware-based security feature that provides a secure execution environment for code and data. It boasts characteristics such as confidentiality, tamper-proofing, and remote authentication.
3. QSEE [10]: Integrated into Qualcomm-supported mobile devices, QSEE provides a secure environment for executing trusted code and safeguarding sensitive data.
4. Samsung Knox [4]: Found in Samsung mobile devices, Samsung Knox offers a secure platform for running trusted code and protecting sensitive data.

This paper chooses TrustZone as the execution environment for both the server and clients. Compared to other TEE options, the most significant advantage of TrustZone lies in its autonomous memory partitioning capability. The clients and server can freely allocate main memory between TEE [12] and rich execution environmentn (REE) [2] as required. Typically, hardware designs allocate 3–5 MB of main memory for securing the TEE.

2.2 Federated Learning Based on Trusted Execution Environment

Zhang *et al.*. [13] introduced a confidential FL framework based on SGX. Their proposed framework incorporated various techniques, including cryptography, game theory, and smart contracts. Through theoretical analysis and implementation-based evaluation, they demonstrated that their method is both secure and efficient, with practical applicability. Do *et al.*. [11] proposed a confidential FL framework named SecFL, leveraging TEE. To address the possibility of malicious clients colluding to steal data, SecFL implemented a transparent remote authentication mechanism capable of detecting any malicious clients. Zhang *et al.*. [14] devised a gradient-preserving FL framework, ShuffleFL, based on SGX. ShuffleFL utilized a combination of random group structures and intra-group gradient segment aggregation to defend against potential side-channel attacks. Eugene [5] introduced SecureFL, a privacy-preserving FL system utilizing SGX and TrustZone. SecureFL effectively ensured computation efficiency on both the server and client sides through well-designed partitioning and aggregation techniques. Considering the limited memory size of current TEEs, Mo *et al.*. [8] employed a greedy algorithm to train each model layer within the trusted region layer by layer based on SGX and TrustZone. Messaoud *et al.*. [7] also trained the model using SGX and TrustZone. In summary, existing advanced works [7,8] adopt SGX and TrustZone-based approaches to achieve secure federated learning training. In particular, deploying TrustZone on the client side can reduce the excessive encryption cost on clients. However, the encryption cost on the server side based on SGX has not been considered.

3 Preliminaries

3.1 Federated Learning

FL is an innovative machine learning approach that enables model training across multiple clients without centralizing raw data on a server. Instead, the learning process takes place locally on individual clients, such as smartphones or edge clients, preserving data privacy and security. A global model is initially distributed to these clients, and each device fine-tunes the model using its own data. Only model updates, not raw data, are sent back to the central server for aggregation, creating an improved global model. The key advantage of FL lies in its ability to respect user privacy, as sensitive data remains on the device. This decentralized approach also allows for efficient training in low-connectivity environments and facilitates rapid adaptation to user preferences. By revolutionizing how models are trained, FL offers a privacy-preserving, secure, and collaborative solution for machine learning applications. Next, we introduce the classical FedAVG algorithm. Here, ω_{t-1} is the aggregated average result of the $t-1$-th update at the server. The client C_i performs the local update in the t-th iteration by $\omega_t^i = \omega_{t-1} - \eta \bigtriangledown g_t^i$, where ω_t^i is the model parameter at the t-th iteration, η is the learning rate, and g_t^i is the gradient value at the t-th iteration. The server performs the global model update by $\omega_t = \sum_{i=1}^{|\{D_t\}|} \frac{\omega_t^i}{|\{D_t\}|}$, where the set $\{D_t\}$ is the selected clients by the server at the t-th iteration.

3.2 Advanced Encryption Standard

Symmetric encryption is a type of encryption that utilizes a single symmetric key to both encrypt and decrypt the plaintext. One commonly used symmetric encryption algorithm is the advanced encryption standard (AES) [9]. AES encryption involves a fixed-length cryptographic block with a block size of 128 bits, and supports key sizes of 128, 192, or 256 bits. When encrypting a plaintext message, AES encryption takes both the plaintext message and the encryption key as inputs, and generates a ciphertext as output. During the encryption process, multiple transform operations such as substitution and permutation are applied to the plaintext to produce the ciphertext. To decrypt the ciphertext and obtain the original plaintext, the same key is used in the reverse process. The security of AES encryption is dependent on the confidentiality of the key and the complexity of the encryption algorithm. It is computationally infeasible for an attacker to decrypt the ciphertext without knowledge of the key. This paper utilizes a 128-bit key for encryption, where the encryption symbol is represented by $\mathrm{Enc}(\cdot)$ and the decryption symbol is represented by $\mathrm{Dec}(\cdot)$.

3.3 Threat Model

The following are three types of privacy-related attacks in the FL system:

1. Data reconstruction attack (DRA): DRA aims to reconstruct raw input data based on the observed model or its gradient. It works by reconstructing the original data points used to generate the model's gradient through the generation of adversarial attacks (similar to the technique used in model inversion attacks).
2. Property inference attack (PIA): PIA aims to infer the value of private property in the input data. This attack is accomplished by constructing a binary classifier using gradient training of a model that has been updated with auxiliary data.
3. Membership inference attack (MIA): MIA aims to determine whether a specific data instance exists in the training dataset of the FL system. The attacker

tries to infer membership information by analyzing the outputs of the model, allowing them to ascertain whether a particular data point was part of the training set.

In the proposed threat model, we only consider external adversaries and assume that the server is trusted. Under this threat model, STrustZoneFL performs decryption and training entirely within the client-side TrustZone, and employs AES encryption for transmission, thereby preventing external attackers from accessing plaintext gradients, parameters, or the training process. As a result, DRA, PIA, and MIA can be effectively defended against.

4 System Architecture

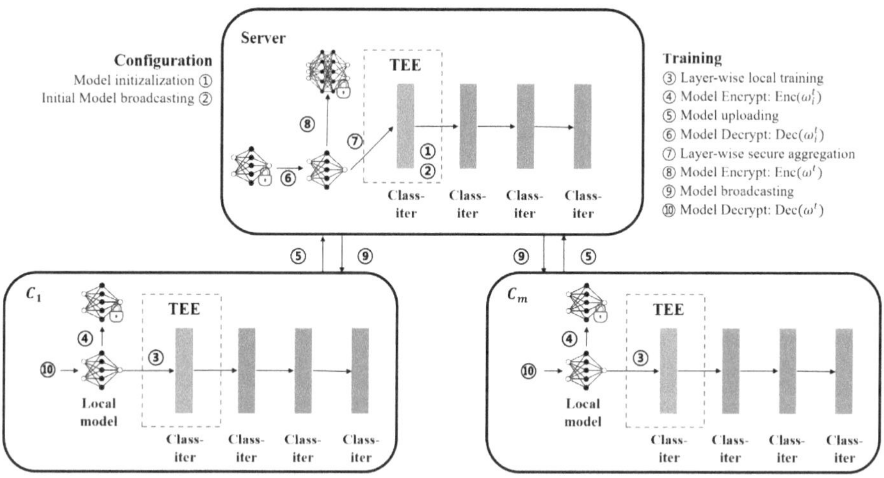

Fig. 1. The system architecture of STrustzoneFL.

STrustzoneFL adopts the utilization of TrustZone as a TEE alongside the AES encryption algorithm to ensure the secure transmission of parameters. The core components of STrustzoneFL consist of the server and client entities. The system architecture of STrustzoneFL is illustrated in Fig. 1 and summarized as follows:

1. Initialization: The FL process commences with the server initializing a global model, which is then disseminated to the client entities.
2. Client training: Within the secure confines of TrustZone's TEE, each client undertakes the FL task. The TEE provides a protected environment, safeguarding the client's local data and computations against potential software attacks.

3. Local model update: Operating within the TEE, the client performs local model updates using its own data. To maintain confidentiality during transmission, the model parameters are encrypted using the AES encryption algorithm.
4. Encrypted parameter aggregation: Subsequent to local training, the client encrypts the updated model parameters using AES before forwarding them to the server.
5. Aggregation on server: The server collects the encrypted model updates from all clients and conducts the decryption and aggregation within a secure environment.
6. Global model update: Upon successful aggregation, the server updates the global model by integrating the combined encrypted model parameters.
7. Model distribution: The updated global model is then distributed back to all participating clients, initiating further rounds of FL.

By capitalizing on TrustZone as TEE and implementing AES encryption for parameter transmission, STrustzoneFL ensures a robust security framework for FL. The hardware-based secure execution environment, along with encrypted parameter passing, bolsters the integrity and confidentiality of the learning process, making STrustzoneFL well-suited for privacy-sensitive applications.

5 Computation Component

STrustzoneFL comprises both an edge component and a cloud component. The edge component encompasses a model trainer and a coordinator, which operate on clients, as illustrated in Fig. 2(a). On the other hand, the cloud component consists of an aggregator, running on the server, as depicted in Fig. 2(b).

1. Model trainer: To selectively partition the model layers between two distinct worlds, separate model trainers are employed within TEE. Communication between the two trainers is facilitated through TrustZone's TEEC InvokeCommand method, creating a logical connection between TEE and REE. The training process starts with REE model trainer. Upon encountering a partition point that requires transfer to TEE, REE trainer sends the last layer's output before the partition to TEE trainer. Subsequently, TEE trainer continues with safety-level training for the transferred layers. After completing the security layer training, TEE trainer sends the model output back to REE for the continuation of the next training iteration.
2. Model coordinator: The model coordinator plays two key roles. First, it replicates the weights between TEE and REE. Second, it facilitates communication with the server. Once the model trainer completes several training steps, the model coordinator copies the weights of the security layer from TEE to REE. Following this, the model coordinator uploads the local model to the server for aggregation. Subsequently, the model coordinator awaits the aggregated model from the server. Upon receiving the aggregated model, the model

coordinator copies the weights from the aggregated model to TEE. It then updates both secure and non-secure layers of the local model and resumes the training process.

3. Aggregator: The aggregator is responsible for aggregating clients' local parameters and generating a shared global model. This component requires careful design to ensure secure aggregation. TrustZone's isolation feature separates REE and TEE, providing a dedicated memory area with a high level of protection accessible only by TEE processes. Access to this memory region by other entities, such as user-space processes, privileged software, or operating systems, is restricted. However, programs existing in TEE are allowed to access REE memory areas.

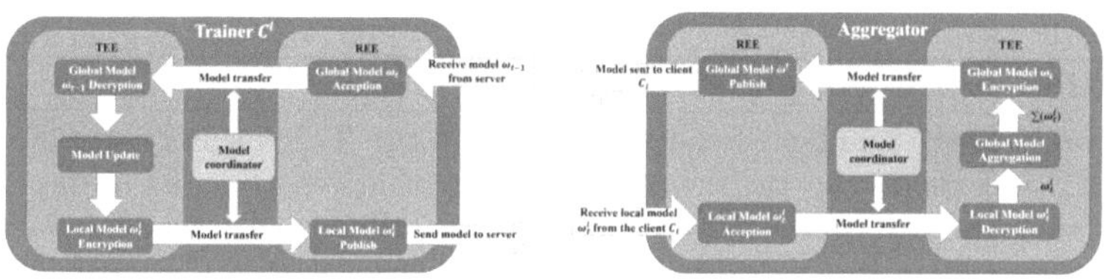

(a) The edge component. (b) The cloud component.

Fig. 2. The component.

STrustzoneFL primarily relies on the AES symmetric encryption algorithm to ensure the security of parameter transmission. However, it is essential to note that conventional AES encryption and decryption in standard environments can be susceptible to security risks, such as side-channel attacks, where attackers may extract sensitive data by analyzing system behavior and timing. To address these concerns and enhance the security of AES encryption and decryption, both processes are performed within the TEE of TrustZone.

6 Algorithm

This section primarily introduces the TrustzoneFL algorithm, which mainly includes the TEE server-side algorithm and the TEE client-side algorithm.

6.1 TrustzoneFL-TEE Server-Side Algorithm

The TrustzoneFL-TEE server-side Algorithm 1 details the operations performed by the system on the server side, assuming initial execution within the REE. First, the server initializes the global DNN model with random weights or public parameters, meaning each layer l is initialized for training (ω_t^l) and prepared for broadcasting. The server checks all available devices and constructs a set of participating clients whose TEE-allocated memory must be larger than the memory required for training.

Then it broadcasts the specific layers of the training model to these participating clients via LocalUpdate(·). Once all participating clients return their updates, the server retrieves the layer weights, performs secure layer aggregation and averaging within its TEE, and broadcasts the new version of layer l to clients for the next round of FL. This process repeats until l converges or a fixed number of rounds is completed. The layer is then considered sufficiently trained (ω_t^l), transferred to the REE, and broadcast to all clients for training the next layer. Additionally, the system allows grouping multiple layers into blocks, with each block trained within the client TEE similarly to a single layer. This option improves memory utilization within each TEE and reduces communication rounds by enabling simultaneous aggregation of multiple layers.

Algorithm 1. TrustzoneFL-TEE Server-Side

Require: N is the number of clients, S^i denotes the TEE memory size of client i, $\{S_1, ..., S_L\}$ represents the memory footprint of layers $\{1, ..., L\}$ during training (including both forward and backward propagation), and t signifies the current iteration index.

Ensure: Aggregated final parameters: Enc($\{\omega_1^t, ..., \omega_L^t\}$).

for $t \in \{1, ..., T\}$ **do**
    for $l \in \{1, ..., L\}$ **do**
        Select clients D_t with sufficient TEE memory
        for $i \in \{1, ..., |\{D_t\}|\}$ **do**
            if $S^i > S_l$ **then**
                $\{D_t\} \leftarrow \{D_t\} \cup \{i\}$
            end if
        end for
        Initialize ω^l **in TEE**
        for $i \in \{D_t\}$ **do**
            Enc($(\omega_t^i)^l$) = LocalUpdate(l, ω_{t-1}^l) (See Algorithm 2)
        end for
        Compute Dec($(\omega_t^i)^l$)
        $\omega_t^l = \frac{1}{|\{D_t\}|} \sum_{i \in \{D_t\}} (\omega_i^l)^t$ **in TEE**
        Compute Dec(ω_t^l) **in TEE**
        Store a backup of Enc(ω_t^l) =Enc($\{\omega_t^1, ..., \omega_t^L\}$)
    end for
end for
return Enc($\{\omega_t^1, ..., \omega_t^L\}$)

6.2 TrustzoneFL-TEE Client-Side Algorithm

Algorithm 2 details the operations performed by clients in this system. Each client loads the received model parameters from the server and processes target training layer l within its TEE. Prior to this, the new layer l must be connected to the previously pre-trained layers that were paused during training. Following this connection, clients attach their own classifier to layer l, consisting of fully-connected layers and a softmax output layer (the classifier).

For each training round, the process iteratively processes batches of data, executing both forward and backward propagation to update both the target layer and the classifier within the TEE. During this process, a model partitioning technique is employed, where representations from previously trained layers are transferred from REE to TEE through shared memory during forward propagation. Upon completing local training (i.e., after processing all batches and rounds), each client securely transmits the layer weights from its TEE to the server's TEE through a protected channel.

Algorithm 2. TrustzoneFL-TEE Client-Side

Require: $\text{Enc}(\omega_l^t)$ are the layer broadcast encrypted parameters, l is the target layer, E is the number of local iterations, T is the number of global iterations, $b = \{\mathbf{x}, \mathbf{y}\}$ is the local mini-batch with $\mathbf{x}$ being the feature data and $\mathbf{y}$ the label data, σ is the activation function, C is the classifier, and L is the loss function.

Ensure: $\text{Enc}((\omega_l^i)^{t+1})$ represents the updated encryption parameters of layer l for client i

for $t \in \{1, ..., T\}$ **do**
  for $e \in \{1, ..., E\}$ **do**
    for $\{\mathbf{x}, \mathbf{y}\} \in b$ **do**
      Initialize $\mathbf{T}_0 = \mathbf{x}$
      for $j \in \{1, ..., l-1\}$ **do**
        $\mathbf{T}_j = \sigma(\omega_l^t \mathbf{T}_{j-1})$
      end for
      $\mathbf{T}_l = \sigma(\omega_l^t \mathbf{T}_{l-1})$ **in TEE**
      $L_{t+1}^i \leftarrow L_{t+1}^i(C(\mathbf{T}_l), \mathbf{y})$ **in TEE**
      Compute the gradient ∇L_{t+1}^i **in TEE**
      Compute $\text{Dec}(\omega_l^t)$
      $(\omega_l^i)^{t+1} = \omega_l^t - \eta \nabla L_{t+1}^i$ **in TEE**
      Compute $\text{Enc}((\omega_l^i)^{t+1})$
    end for
  end for
end for
return $\text{Enc}((\omega_l^i)^{t+1})$

7 Experiment

To evaluate the performance of STrustzoneFL and measure the overhead of protecting FL, a series of experiments were conducted on a real test bench. The test platform consists of two main components: the server and the client. The aggregator runs on an Ubuntu 18.04 LTS server with a 3.6 GHz four-core Intel i7-7700 processor and 16 GB of RAM, supporting OP-TEE3.8. OP-TEE is a TEE designed for non-secure Linux kernels running on ARM processors and relies on TrustZone technology for hardware isolation.

The client runs on a Raspberry Pi 3B+ platform, which is a widely used IoT platform, and uses the OP-TEE3.8 operating system. For our experiments, a cluster consisting of two Raspberry Pi devices was used. To conduct experiments on a larger scale with more clients, OP-TEE and emulator QEMU version 7 could be utilized. It should be noted that although the emulator is not as representative of real client performance, it allows for the evaluation of the scalability of the aggregator. As such, we ran multiple instances of QEMU to emulate a total of 100 clients, spread across four servers.

7.1 Runtime Overhead

To determine the runtime overhead incurred by the security mechanism, we measured the impact of varying the number of model layers in the TrustZone. We evaluated the performance of the LeNet model on the MNIST dataset and the VGG-7 model on the CIFAR-10 dataset. Performance was measured by timing a round of FL, which consisted of 10 local training iterations on the client and one aggregation process on the server. We used a batch size of 50 for both models.

Figure 3(a) illustrates the training time of LeNet in TrustZone for different layer levels, ranging from 1 to 5. To establish a baseline, we measured the training time when no layers are executed in the TrustZone. Additionally, Fig. 3(a) shows the percentage of overhead in TrustZone for different scenarios. The overhead increased from 0.15% (with only one layer in TrustZone) to 25.73% (with five layers in TrustZone), with the security overhead increasing in proportion to the number of layers in TrustZone. On the client side, most of the overhead comes from updating the trust layer of the local model with the received shared model. This process involves copying from TrustZone to TrustZone, and encrypting and decrypting the protected model layer. When there is only one layer in TrustZone, the security overhead is negligible.

In Fig. 3(b), we present the training time of VGG-7 for different space division points in the model. The complexity of the VGG-7 model is reflected in the training time, which took an average of 120 s to complete 10 local training iterations, approximately one time longer than LeNet which took an average of 60 s to complete 10 local training iterations. It is worth noting that the longer training time of VGG-7 reduces the percentage of safety overhead compared to LeNet. The cost is 0.09% when there is only one layer in the TrustZone, and 7.53% when there are five layers. In contrast, putting five layers into a TrustZone using LeNet results in a cost of 25.73%.

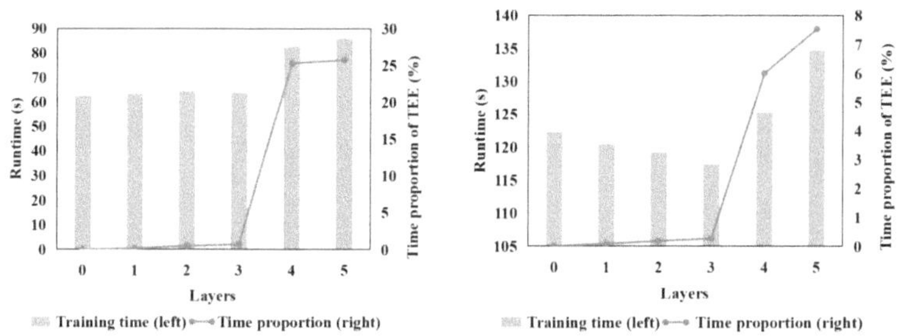

(a) LeNet. (b) VGG-7

Fig. 3. Training time with a varying number of layers executed in TrustZone, ranging from 1 to 5.

7.2 System Performance

This section provides a more in-depth analysis of the security overhead associated with each stage of the FL process. The training time for both LeNet and VGG-7 models is divided into three primary components:

1. Training time: This refers to the duration spent on training the model on the client's side.
2. Aggregation time: This denotes the time taken for aggregating the average weight values from all participating clients.
3. Communication time: This records the time required for communication between the server and the clients.

By examining these individual time components, we can better understand the security implications and potential bottlenecks of the FL approach.

Figure 4(a) illustrates the runtime breakdown of both insecure workflows (Layer 0 in TrustZone) and secure workflows (Layers 1 to 5 in TrustZone) using the LeNet model. The primary contributors to the total runtime overhead are training time and communication time. On average, traning time constitutes approximately 99.0% of the total runtime. Communication time accounts for less than 0.4%, making it negligible and can be disregarded. The aggregate time is barely noticeable in Fig. 4(a) as it represents less than 0.5% of the total runtime.

Although the aggregation time does not significantly contribute to the overall time overhead, it is worth noting that a secure workflow's aggregation time is approximately 50% slower compared to an insecure workflow. The main factor contributing to this difference is the transfer of data from REE to TEE, which adds to the secure aggregator's overhead.

In Fig. 4(b), we can observe the distinct run times of both insecure and secure workflows utilizing the VGG-7 model. Similar to LeNet, the primary contributors to the total runtime in VGG-7 are the training time and communication time. Specifically, the training time accounts for an average of 99.8% of the total runtime, which is higher compared to LeNet. This increase is attributed to the

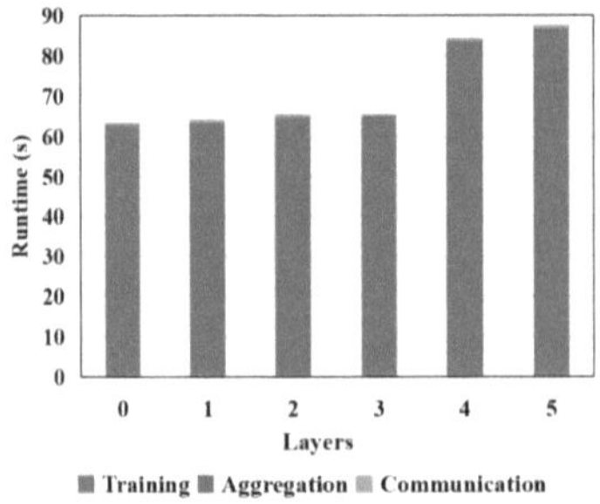

(a) LetNet runtime breakdown.

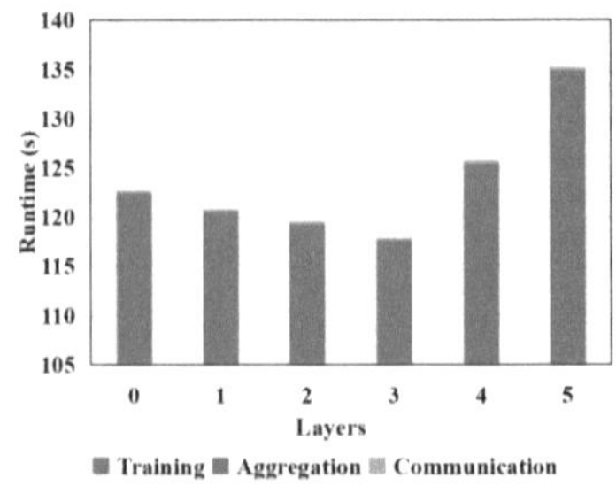

(b) VGG-7 runtime breakdown.

Fig. 4. Runtime breakdown. We broke down the training time into three major components: training time, aggregation time, and communication time.

greater complexity of the VGG-7 model in comparison to LeNet, making the training process the most significant factor contributing to the overall runtime overhead. Introducing one layer of security computing in TrustZone results in a modest overhead of 0.08%. However, when five layers are employed within TrustZone, the overhead can escalate to up to 7.53%. This indicates that the level of security measures implemented using TrustZone has a notable impact on the runtime, and the trade-off between security and computation time should be carefully considered in the VGG-7 model.

8 Conclusion

In this paper, we have introduced STrustZoneFL, a robust FL framework designed to address the issues of gradient information leakage and protect against various attacks. Our approach leverages TrustZone, a hardware-secure end-to-end FL solution. To validate the effectiveness and feasibility of STrustZoneFL, we have performed software implementation and conducted comprehensive feasibility testing. Utilizing Raspberry Pi as our experimental platform, we have assessed the practicality and efficacy of STrustZoneFL. Through extensive experimentation with LeNet and VGG-7 models, we have analyzed the system's operating cost, performance, and resource utilization rate. The evaluation reveals that our approach is not only lightweight but also highly efficient, making it a promising solution for secure FL.

In conclusion, STrustzoneFL represents a significant step forward in the field of FL by utilizing TrustZone as the foundation for a secure system design. The combination of TEE, hierarchical training, hierarchical aggregation, and encryption techniques ensures enhanced security and privacy while delivering efficient and practical FL capabilities.

References

1. Costan, V., Devadas, S.: Intel sgx explained. Cryptology ePrint Archive (2016)
2. Ekberg, J.E., Kostiainen, K., Asokan, N.: The untapped potential of trusted execution environments on mobile devices. IEEE Secur. Priv. **12**(4), 29–37 (2014)
3. Jin, Y., Zhu, H., Xu, J., Chen, Y.: Federated Learning - Fundamentals and Advances. Springer, Heidelberg (2023). https://doi.org/10.1007/978-981-19-7083-2
4. Kanonov, U., Wool, A.: Secure containers in android: the samsung knox case study. In: Proceedings of the 6th Workshop on Security and Privacy in Smartphones and Mobile Devices, pp. 3–12 (2016)
5. Kuznetsov, E.N., Chen, Y., Zhao, M.: Securefl: privacy preserving federated learning with SGX and trustzone. In: 6th IEEE/ACM Symposium on Edge Computing, SEC 2021, San Jose, CA, USA, 14–17 December 2021, pp. 55–67. IEEE (2021). https://doi.org/10.1145/3453142.3491287
6. Melis, L., Song, C., Cristofaro, E.D., Shmatikov, V.: Exploiting unintended feature leakage in collaborative learning. In: 2019 IEEE Symposium on Security and Privacy, SP 2019, San Francisco, CA, USA, 19–23 May 2019, pp. 691–706. IEEE (2019). https://doi.org/10.1109/SP.2019.00029
7. Messaoud, A.A., Mokhtar, S.B., Nitu, V., Schiavoni, V.: Shielding federated learning systems against inference attacks with ARM trustzone. In: Bellavista, P., Zhang, K., Gherbi, A., Bagchi, S., Patiño, M., Modica, G.D., Gascon-Samson, J. (eds.) Middleware '22: 23rd International Middleware Conference, Quebec, QC, Canada, 7–11 November 2022, pp. 335–348. ACM (2022). https://doi.org/10.1145/3528535.3565255
8. Mo, F., Haddadi, H., Katevas, K., Marin, E., Perino, D., Kourtellis, N.: PPFL: privacy-preserving federated learning with trusted execution environments. In: Banerjee, S., Mottola, L., Zhou, X. (eds.) MobiSys '21: The 19th Annual International Conference on Mobile Systems, Applications, and Services, Virtual Event, Wisconsin, USA, 24 June–2 July 2021, pp. 94–108. ACM (2021). https://doi.org/10.1145/3458864.3466628
9. Nechvatal, J., et al.: Report on the development of the advanced encryption standard (aes). J. Res. Nat. Inst. Stand. Technol. **106**(3), 511 (2001)
10. Pinto, S., Santos, N.: Demystifying arm trustzone: a comprehensive survey. ACM Comput. Surv. (CSUR) **51**(6), 1–36 (2019)
11. Quoc, D.L., Fetzer, C.: Secfl: confidential federated learning using tees. CoRR arxiv:2110.00981 (2021)
12. Sabt, M., Achemlal, M., Bouabdallah, A.: Trusted execution environment: what it is, and what it is not. In: 2015 IEEE Trustcom/BigDataSE/Ispa, vol. 1, pp. 57–64. IEEE (2015)
13. Zhang, W., Muhr, T.: Tee-based selective testing of local workers in federated learning systems. In: 18th International Conference on Privacy, Security and Trust, PST 2021, Auckland, New Zealand, 13–15 December 2021, pp. 1–6. IEEE (2021). https://doi.org/10.1109/PST52912.2021.9647773
14. Zhang, Y., Wang, Z., Cao, J., Hou, R., Meng, D.: Shufflefl: gradient-preserving federated learning using trusted execution environment. In: Palesi, M., Tumeo, A., Goumas, G.I., Almudéver, C.G. (eds.) CF '21: Computing Frontiers Conference, Virtual Event, Italy, 11–13 May 2021, pp. 161–168. ACM (2021). https://doi.org/10.1145/3457388.3458665

15. Zhao, P., et al.: RLL-SWE: a robust linked list steganography without embedding for intelligence networks in smart environments. J. Netw. Comput. Appl. **234**, 104053 (2025). https://doi.org/10.1016/J.JNCA.2024.104053
16. Zhou, Y., Zhao, T., Jing, Z., Zhao, Q., Zhu, Y.: A blockchain-based privacy-preserving data aggregation scheme with robustness in smart grids. J. Supercomput. **81**(7), 675 (2025). https://doi.org/10.1007/S11227-025-07156-3
17. Zhu, L., Han, S.: Deep leakage from gradients. In: Yang, Q., Fan, L., Yu, H. (eds.) Federated Learning - Privacy and Incentive, Lecture Notes in Computer Science, vol. 12500, pp. 17–31. Springer (2020). https://doi.org/10.1007/978-3-030-63076-8_2

Heterogeneous Federated Learning of Data and Models Based on Adaptive Personalized Aggregation Prototype

Kejun Zhang[1], Jun Wang[1](✉), Pengcheng Li[2], Wenbin Wang[3], Taiheng Zeng[3], Xunxi Wang[1], Bing Zou[1], and Yuhan Jin[1]

[1] Beijing Electronic Science and Technology Institute, Beijing, China
william_jun576@126.com, william_jun576@163.com
[2] University of Science and Technology of China, Hefei, China
pengchengli@mail.ustc.edu.cn
[3] Beijing University of Posts and Telecommunications, Beijing, China
{wenbin.wang,BestEndPage}@bupt.edu.cn

Abstract. Prototype learning offers promising potential for mitigating data and model heterogeneity in federated learning (FL), thereby advancing its applicability in real-world scenarios. However, existing prototype-based FL approaches typically employ a unified global prototype for aggregation, which struggles to accommodate discrepancies in feature representations caused by heterogeneous local models. This often leads to suboptimal alignment in the embedding space and exacerbates knowledge forgetting during global aggregation. To address these issues, we propose Fed-APAP, a federated learning framework based on adaptive personalized prototype aggregation. Fed-APAP introduces a trainable inter-domain similarity matrix to adaptively combine client-uploaded prototypes, generating customized global prototypes tailored to individual clients. This design alleviates the adverse effects arising from disparities in feature extraction capabilities. In addition, Fed-APAP incorporates an unlabeled-class distillation strategy that leverages historical best-performing models as teachers, enhancing the retention of private client knowledge and improving the generalization of personalized models. We conduct extensive experiments on multiple public datasets under various data distributions and model architectures. The results demonstrate that Fed-APAP consistently outperforms existing state-of-the-art federated learning methods across all evaluated settings.

Keywords: Federal learning · Data heterogeneity · Model heterogeneity · Prototype Learning

This work was supported by the Open Fund Project of the Key Laboratory of Cyberspace Security, Ministry of Education (Grant No. KLCS20240210), and by the Fundamental Research Funds for the Central Universities (Grant No. 3282025041).

L. Zhang and K.-K. R. Choo (Eds.): MobiQuitous 2025, LNICST 683, pp. 131–148, 2026.
https://doi.org/10.1007/978-3-032-22500-9_8

1 Introduction

Federated learning, introduced by Google Research in 2017 [12], is an emerging machine-learning paradigm focused on data privacy protection. The initial goal of federated learning was to enable collaborative modeling and deep learning training while preserving user privacy and data security. In practical applications, traditional federated learning models often suffer performance degradation due to statistical heterogeneity in the private data. To address this issue, various optimization algorithms, such as FedProx [10], FedAMP [4], and SCAFFOLD [6], have been proposed, primarily focusing on enhancing server-side model aggregation strategies.

Despite the attention given to data heterogeneity and its associated optimizations, most personalized federated learning algorithms still rely on model parameter aggregation for collaborative training. This approach imposes significant communication overhead on both the client and server sides. It requires all clients to maintain identical model structures and sizes, which considerably limits the application scenarios of federated learning. To address these challenges, heterogeneous federated learning methods have been developed. These methods allow clients to maintain heterogeneous models and achieve collaboration by sharing low- or high-dimensional knowledge rather than transmitting model parameters. The prevailing heterogeneous federated learning approaches rely on a public dataset to facilitate collaboration, aggregating client outputs on the public dataset and employing knowledge distillation [3] techniques to transfer knowledge from the global data domain to local clients. However, the performance of these methods depends on the choice of the public dataset. FedGen [20] introduces a generator to achieve data-free knowledge distillation, but this increases communication overhead. Prototype-based heterogeneous federated learning methods [15,18] achieve collaborative training by sharing embedded space class features (class prototypes).

Existing algorithms for generating global prototypes can be categorized into two main approaches: weighted averaging and generator-based prototype generation. The weighted averaging method aggregates prototypes based solely on data volume, making it susceptible to limitations in local heterogeneous model performance. The challenge with generator-based global prototype generation lies in the limited number of local prototypes, which makes it difficult for the generator to converge during training. Additionally, current algorithms typically generate a single prototype for the global data domain, without fully considering the distribution differences between the global data domain and private data domains.

To address the above issues, we propose a novel heterogeneous federated learning framework based on adaptive personalized aggregation prototypes, abbreviated as Fed-APAP. From the perspective of the global data domain, we analyze the distribution similarity relationships between different private data domains and establish an inter-domain distribution similarity matrix. In each iteration, this matrix is adaptively updated using gradient descent, making the generated personalized global prototypes more closely aligned with the class features in the embedded space of the private data.

We evaluated the effectiveness of Fed-APAP across multiple datasets, conducted extensive experiments under various statistical heterogeneity settings, and compared our method with five state-of-the-art heterogeneous federated learning approaches. The experimental results demonstrate that Fed-APAP outperforms other baseline algorithms in terms of accuracy, convergence speed, and stability of experimental outcomes, particularly in complex classification tasks. Our main contributions are summarized as follows:

1. We propose adaptive personalized aggregated prototypes that generate personalized global prototypes for each private data domain from the perspective of the global data domain, thereby avoiding the deviation of class-specific features in the private data embedding space caused by a single global prototype.
2. We introduce a class-agnostic distillation approach that learns posterior class relationships from the historically optimal models, preserving the privileged information of the private data domain and complementing label class learning in local supervised learning to enhance the generalization capability of local models.
3. Extensive experiments demonstrate that our proposed Fed-APAP method outperforms other heterogeneous federated learning algorithms across multiple datasets and offers advantages in communication overhead and computational costs.

2 Method

2.1 Problem Statement and Motivation

We consider a supervised learning scenario and discuss federated learning in the context of multi-class tasks with heterogeneous models and data. The objective is to enable M clients to collaboratively train using heterogeneous local models on their private and heterogeneous datasets $\{D_i := \{x_i, y_i\}\}_{i=1}^{M}$. Following the approaches of FedProto and FedTGP, we decompose the local model of client i into two modules: a feature extractor f_i and a classifier h_i. The feature extractor f_i is parameterized by θ_i and maps the input space $\mathbb{R}^D$ to the feature space $\mathbb{R}^K$. The classifier h_i, parameterized by w_i, then maps the feature space to the class space $\mathbb{R}^C$. Formally, the overall collaborative training objective can be expressed as:

$$argmin \frac{1}{M} \sum_{i=1,(x,y)\in D_i}^{M} L_i(h_i(f_i(x;\theta_i);w_i),y) \tag{1}$$

Prototype-based heterogeneous federated learning achieves knowledge communication across heterogeneous models through the sharing of class-specific features in the embedding space, known as prototypes, for collaborative training. In FedProto and FedTGP, the local prototype for each class c of client i is obtained using the following formula:

$$P_{i,c} = \mathbb{E}_{(x,c)\sim D_{i,c}} f_i(x;\theta_i) \tag{2}$$

where $P_{i,c}$ represents the local prototype for class c, and $D_{i,c}$ is a subset of client i's private data D_i, composed of all data points in D_i that belong to class c. The client then sends the generated local prototypes to the server, where they are aggregated to form global prototypes. In FedProto, the global prototype is obtained by a weighted average of the local prototypes, with the aggregation formula given as:

$$P_c^g = \sum_{i \in N_c} \frac{|D_{i,c}|}{|D_c|} P_{i,c} \tag{3}$$

Here, D_c represents the set of data for class c across all clients, P_c^g denotes the global prototype for class c generated by the server, and N_c is the set of clients that possess data for class c. In FedTGP, the global prototype is generated by a neural network model F, with the global prototype for class c given by the following formula:

$$P_c^g = F(onehot(c), \theta_F) \tag{4}$$

where onehot(c) is the one-hot encoded vector for class c, and θ_F represents the parameters of the neural network model F. FedTGP continuously optimizes and trains the neural network model F on the server to generate representative global prototypes. In both algorithms, after generating the global prototypes $P^g = \{P_c^g\}_{c=1}^C$, these prototypes are sent to each client to guide local training. The objective is to minimize the distance between the class-specific features in the embedding space generated by each client for its private data and the corresponding global prototype for class c. The local training optimization objective can be expressed as:

$$\begin{aligned} argmin\mathcal{L}_i = &\mathbb{E}_{(x,y)\sim D_i}\ell(h_i(f_i(x;\theta_i), w_i), y) \\ &+ \mu\mathbb{E}_{(x,y)\sim D_{i,c}}\phi(f_i(x;\theta_i), P_c^g) \end{aligned} \tag{5}$$

Here, ℓ denotes the supervised learning loss function used in the client's local training, μ is a hyperparameter controlling the similarity between the embedding space features of each class's data and the global prototype, and ϕ measures the Euclidean distance.

We observed from the actual data distribution that the performance of the global prototype can decline due to the distribution differences between the global data domain and the private data domains. Clients with heterogeneous local models possess different performance levels, and the size of local datasets cannot serve as a standard for assessing the class-specific features contained in the local prototypes. Although generating a single global prototype for all clients is effective in most cases, for clients whose data distributions are on the periphery of class boundaries, the global prototype generated by the server for the entire data domain may lead to data misclassification. This phenomenon is illustrated in Fig. 1. Additionally, after multiple rounds of collaborative training, the differences in private data domains may cause catastrophic forgetting as clients learn embedding space features from other private data domains.

To address these challenges, we propose Fed-APAP: (1)The server personalizes the aggregation of global prototypes based on the distribution of each client's

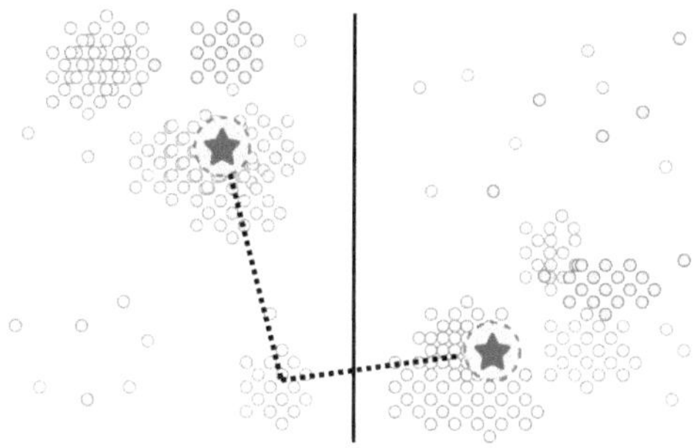

Fig. 1. The figure depicts the distribution of private data domains in the embedding spaces of four clients. A central solid black line divides the data into two categories, with colors distinguishing each client's private domain. Pentagrams mark the server-generated global prototypes, and dashed black lines indicate their distances from the private data domains.

private data domain, resulting in unique global prototypes for each client. (2)The server adaptively maintains and updates the similarity matrix of prototype distributions across domains using gradient descent, based on the distribution of class-specific features in the embedding space for each client. (3)The generated personalized global prototypes guide the training of local feature extractors and classifiers, aligning embedding space features and improving classification accuracy. (4)During the local supervised learning phase, we introduce unlabeled-class distillation by leveraging the historical best model to learn the posterior relationships between different classes, preserving the privileged information of private data domains and preventing catastrophic forgetting.

2.2 Adaptive Personalized Aggregation Prototype

Due to the differences in private data domains, generating a single global prototype for each class is insufficient to effectively represent the class-specific features in the embedding space across all clients. Therefore, an adaptive personalized aggregation is introduced. The server utilizes an inter-domain distribution similarity matrix to generate personalized global prototypes for each client, effectively leveraging the global data domain to refine the class-specific features in the embedding space of the private data domains.

We define the inter-domain distribution similarity matrix as $s \in \mathbb{R}^{M \times M}$, where M represents the total number of clients:

$$s = \begin{Bmatrix} s_{11} & \cdots & s_{1M} \\ \vdots & \ddots & \vdots \\ s_{M1} & \cdots & s_{MM} \end{Bmatrix} \tag{6}$$

Here, s_{1i} denotes the similarity coefficient between the private data domains of client 1 and client i. This value ranges between $[0, 1]$, where a higher value indicates greater similarity between the private data distributions of the two clients, while a lower value suggests a significant difference. Since private data domain similarity is non-directional, the inter-domain distribution similarity matrix s is a symmetric matrix, with the property $\sum_{m \in M} s_{im} = 1, (i \in M)$.

The personalized aggregation formula for computing the global prototype for client i is given by:

$$P^g_{i,c} = \sum_{m \in M} S_{im} P_{m,c} \tag{7}$$

Here, $P^g_{i,c}$ represents the personalized global prototype for data class c of client i. The terms $s_{i1}, \ldots, s_{iM}, (i \in M)$ denote the similarity between the private data domain of client i and those of all other clients.

To more accurately measure the differences between data domains across clients, the inter-domain distribution similarity matrix s is adaptively updated during each round of collaborative communication. The matrix s is parameterized and optimized using gradient descent. We define the optimization objective for the inter-domain distribution similarity matrix s as follows:

$$\begin{aligned} argmin\mathcal{L}(s) = &\sum_{i \in M} \mathcal{L}_s \left(\sum_{m \in M} s_{im} P_m, P_i \right) \\ &+ \|s - s_{mean}\| \end{aligned} \tag{8}$$

Here, s_{mean} represents the weighted average initial matrix of the inter-domain distribution similarity matrix s. Its value is defined as:$s_{\text{mean},im} = \frac{|D_m|}{\sum_{j \in M} |D_j|}$, $(i, m \in M)$ In Eq. (8), the term $\|s - s_{\text{mean}}\|$ acts as a regularization term to ensure that the personalized global prototypes retain a certain level of generalization ability. This prevents the corresponding coefficients from approaching zero due to significant differences in private data domains, thereby promoting collaborative communication and training among different clients.

In the t-th round of global communication and collaboration, we define the adaptive update formula for the inter-domain distribution similarity matrix s as follows:

$$\begin{aligned} s^t = &\sigma(s^{t-1} - \eta_1(\sigma(\sum_{m \in M} s^{t-1}_{im} P_m) log \frac{\sigma(\sum_{m \in M} s_{im} P_m)}{\sigma(P_i)}) \\ &- \phi(s_{t-1} - s_{mean})) \end{aligned} \tag{9}$$

In this context, s^t represents the inter-domain distribution similarity matrix updated in the t-th round, while s^{t-1} corresponds to the matrix from the previous round. The function σ denotes the softmax function, and η_1 is a hyperparameter that controls the magnitude of the adaptive update of s in each round. The adaptive update formula for s considers the distributional similarities between the private data domains of different clients, effectively enhancing collaborative training among clients with similar data distributions.

2.3 Unlabeled-Class Distillation

Traditional knowledge distillation compresses models by transferring knowledge from a larger model to a smaller one, enabling the latter to achieve comparable performance. It uses a temperature parameter to emphasize privileged information, helping the smaller model learn finer details.

In federated learning, treating the previous iteration's model as a teacher can prevent local models from forgetting private data knowledge during collaborative training, guiding optimization and improving generalization and accuracy. Advanced knowledge distillation often favors feature distillation for its richer knowledge representation. However, it demands significant computational resources, challenging client devices in federated learning. To address this, Fed-APAP adopts logit distillation, balancing efficiency and performance.

According to reference [19], the distillation loss for class c can be decoupled into two modules:

$$L_{KD} = z_c^t log\frac{z_c^t}{z_c^s} + \sum_{i=1, i\neq c}^{C} z_i^t log\frac{z_i^t}{z_i^s} \tag{10}$$

Here, z_c^t represents the softened probability for class c from the teacher model, while z_c^s denotes the softened probability for class c from the student model.The loss for labeled classes is jointly determined by the teacher and student models, and its magnitude is influenced by the performance of the teacher model. When the teacher model performs poorly in predicting labeled classes, it negatively impacts the predictive performance of the student model. During the local supervised learning phase, the one-hot labels have already guided the local model in learning knowledge of the relevant classes. The purpose of this phase is to guide the model, after collaborative training, to learn posterior class relationships and retain privileged information from the data. Therefore, in Fed-APAP, we define the distillation loss function as follows: $\mathcal{L}_{\text{UCD}} = \sum_{i=1, i\neq c}^{C} z_i^t log\frac{z_i^t}{z_i^s}$.

2.4 Fed-APAP Framework

Due to the local heterogeneity among clients, the traditional approach of collaborative training via parameter and gradient transmission is no longer applicable. Instead, Fed-APAP achieves information exchange between heterogeneous models by transmitting prototypes. The Fed-APAP process is divided into three stages: the pre-training stage, the local training stage, and the global collaborative training stage. The overall procedure of Fed-APAP is summarized in Algorithm 1, and its workflow is illustrated in Fig. 2.

During the pre-training stage, each client initializes its model and performs supervised learning using private data to thoroughly learn the local knowledge. Incorporating pre-training in a federated learning algorithm allows local models to be closer to the global optimal solution during subsequent collaborative training, thereby reducing the number of communication rounds required for model convergence. Additionally, the generated local prototypes are more aligned with the class features in the embedding space, enhancing the optimization effectiveness of collaborative training.

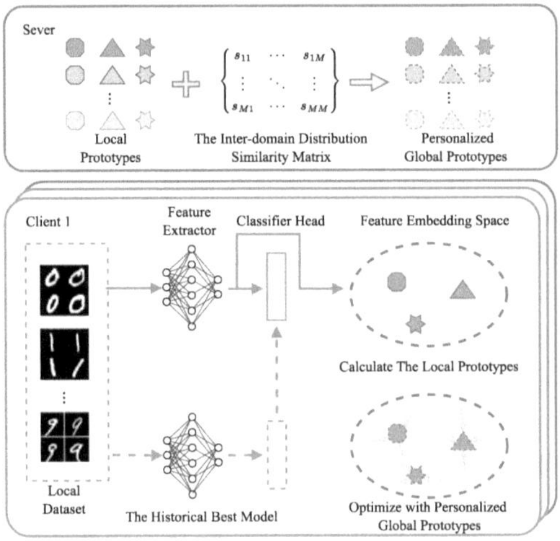

Fig. 2. The workflow of the proposed Fed-APAP framework. Each client uses a local feature extractor and classifier to compute class-wise prototypes from private data. These prototypes are sent to the server, where a trainable inter-domain similarity matrix is used to generate personalized global prototypes for each client through adaptive aggregation. The server then returns these prototypes to guide local training. Additionally, each client leverages its historical best model to perform unlabeled-class distillation, enhancing generalization and mitigating knowledge forgetting.

In the local training stage, each client engages in supervised learning based on its private data domain, where the local heterogeneous models learn the class-specific knowledge of their private data, optimizing the model's performance in accurate classification. Personalized global prototype correction learning is integrated into the supervised learning process, ensuring that the local data's embedding space class features are more closely aligned with the global prototypes. Furthermore, local class-agnostic knowledge distillation is introduced, wherein the historical best model is selected as the teacher to learn posterior class relationships, preserving the privileged information of the local data and enhancing the model's generalization ability. The historical best model is determined as the local model with the minimum value of $\ell(h_i(f_i(\mathbf{x};\theta_i), w_i), \mathbf{y})$ across different global communication rounds. Based on the local training optimization objective in (5), the loss function for the local training stage is defined as follows:

$$\mathcal{L}_i = \ell(h_i(f_i(\boldsymbol{x};\theta_i), w_i), \boldsymbol{y}) + \mu\phi(f_i(\boldsymbol{x};\theta_i), P_c^g) + \mathcal{L}_{\text{UCD}} \tag{11}$$

During the global collaborative training phase, each client first selects a local prototype from the embedded space generated by the current round of local training. The specific calculation formula for the local prototype of category c in client i is given by (2):

$$P_{i,c} = \sum_{x_j \epsilon D_{i,c}} \frac{1}{|D_{i,c}|} f_i(x_j;\theta_i) \tag{12}$$

Algorithm 1. Fed-APAP algorithm

Input: M clients with (f_i, h_i) and D_i, global communication rounds E, local training rounds LE, local collaborative training rounds CE, learning rates η, η_1, and hyperparameter μ.
Output: Well-trained client models.

```
Initialize the participants' local heterogeneous models.
for iteration t = 1, ..., E do:
    The server receives the local prototypes P_i from each client.
    The server updates s^t using (9).
    Use s^t to generate P_1^g, ..., P_M^g according to (7), and send them to the corresponding clients.
    for client i ∈ M in parallel do:
        Client i optimizes the classifier h_i using (14).
        Client i optimizes the feature extractor f_i using (15).
    for iteration lt = 1, ..., LE do:
        Update the historical best model.
        Train the local model according to (11).
        Calculate the local prototypes according to (12) and send them to the server.
return the client's local heterogeneous model.
```

After generating the local prototypes, the clients transmit them to the server. Given that the inter-domain distribution similarity matrix s has dimensions $\mathbb{R}^{M \times M}$ and that the distribution of private data domains is non-independent and identically distributed (non-IID), any missing category prototypes for a client are filled using the global average prototype. The global average prototype for category c is calculated as follows:

$$P_{c,mean}^{g} = \sum_{i \in N_C} \frac{|D_{i,c}|}{|D_C|} P_{i,c} \tag{13}$$

After filling in the missing local prototypes for certain categories, the inter-domain distribution similarity matrix s^{t-1} is adaptively updated to s^t using the private data domain distribution similarity and the characteristic information of the local prototypes, as per (9). This updated matrix s^t is then used to perform personalized aggregation of the prototypes, generating personalized global prototypes for each private data domain from the perspective of the global data domain. These personalized global prototypes are subsequently sent to the corresponding clients.

Upon receiving the personalized global prototypes, client i engages in local collaborative training. During this phase, the client optimizes both the feature extractor f_i and the classifier h_i using the personalized global prototypes. To effectively optimize the local model, multiple rounds of local collaborative training can be conducted. We define the loss function for the classifier h_i during this stage as follows:

$$\mathcal{L}_h = \sum_{c \in C} -log(\sigma(h_i(P_{i,c}^{g}; w_i))^c) \tag{14}$$

Here, $\sigma()^c$ denotes the probability value corresponding to category c in the softmax function output. The primary goal is for the classifier h_i to learn the personalized global prototype P_i^g and correctly classify it, thereby enhancing h_i's ability to recognize class features in the embedding space.

We define the loss function for the feature extractor f_i during this stage as follows:

$$\mathcal{L}_f = \sum_{c \in C} -log(\sigma(-dist_{x \in D_{i,c}}[f_i(x;\theta_i), P_i^g])^c) \tag{15}$$

where $dist_{x \in D_{i,c}}[f_i(x;\theta_i), P_i^g] \in \mathbb{R}^{1 \times C}$ represents the Euclidean distance between the embedding space features of data x in category c output by the feature extractor f_i and the personalized global prototype P_i^g. This loss function effectively enhances the feature extractor's ability to produce compact embedding space features for data of the same category while expanding the differentiation of features between different categories, thereby improving the separability of class features in the embedding space.

2.5 Communication Overhead

In conventional federated learning methods based on model parameter or gradient exchange, communication cost scales with the size of local models. For example, models in the ResNet family range from 44MB (ResNet18) to 223MB (ResNet152), resulting in per-round communication overheads between 88MB and 446MB. To improve model accuracy, larger architectures are often preferred in practice, further increasing the communication burden.

Some approaches attempt to align knowledge through public data or generative models. FedMD, for instance, utilizes a shared dataset and collects logits from clients for distillation. On CIFAR-10, this leads to roughly 24MB of data transmission per round, with each client's logits adding about 783KB. FedGen relies on distributing a generator to facilitate feature alignment, where the communication cost depends on the generator's size—typically larger than that of prototype representations.

In contrast, our proposed Fed-APAP achieves model collaboration by exchanging compact clustered prototypes, significantly reducing communication overhead. While maintaining model performance, it provides improved communication efficiency under heterogeneous client conditions.

2.6 Privacy Protection

During the global collaboration phase, similar to FedProto and FedTGP, Fed-APAP exchanges local prototypes instead of model parameters. This communication strategy does not reveal the underlying architecture of local models. Each local prototype represents the mean embedding of a class-specific data cluster, and the global prototype is generated in a personalized manner. As these exchanged representations are low-dimensional and non-invertible, the approach offers a degree of privacy protection.

3 Convergence Analysis

In this section, we analyze the convergence properties of the Fed-APAP algorithm. We define the local model parameters for client i as $\phi_i = (\theta_i, w_i)$, and denote the number of local iterations as LE, with the iteration index represented by $e \in \{0, 1, 2, \ldots, LE\}$. Let t denote the global communication round. The final local iteration in the t-th round is represented by tLE, while $tLE + 0$ corresponds to the global collaboration step at the beginning of round $t + 1$, which incorporates the personalized global prototype. The first local iteration of round $t + 1$ is denoted as $tLE + 1$. We make the following assumption:

Assumption 1 (Lipschitz Smoothness). The local objective function $\mathcal{L}_i$ with respect to model parameters $\Theta_i = (\theta_i, w_i)$ is assumed to be L_1-Lipschitz smooth, i.e., for all $t_1, t_2 > 0$ and $i \in \{0, 1, \ldots, M - 1\}$,

$$\|\nabla \mathcal{L}_i^{t_1}(\Theta_i^{t_1}) - \nabla \mathcal{L}_i^{t_2}(\Theta_i^{t_2})\|_2 \leq L_1 \|\Theta_i^{t_1} - \Theta_i^{t_2}\|_2. \tag{16}$$

This assumption further implies the following inequality:

$$\mathcal{L}_i^{t_1} - \mathcal{L}_i^{t_2} \leq \langle \nabla \mathcal{L}_i^{t_2}, \Theta_i^{t_1} - \Theta_i^{t_2} \rangle + \frac{L_1}{2} \|\Theta_i^{t_1} - \Theta_i^{t_2}\|_2^2. \tag{17}$$

Assumption 2 (Unbiased Gradient and Bounded Variance). For any client i, the local stochastic gradient $\nabla \mathcal{L}_{\text{local},i}^t(\Theta_i^t, \mathcal{B}_i^t)$ computed over a mini-batch $\mathcal{B}_i^t \subseteq D_i$ is unbiased. That is,

$$\mathbb{E}_{\mathcal{B}_i^t \subseteq D_i}[g_i^t] = \nabla \mathcal{L}_{\text{local},i}^t(\Theta_i^t), \tag{18}$$

and its variance is bounded by a non-negative constant σ^2:

$$\mathbb{E}_{\mathcal{B}_i^t \subseteq D_i}\left[\|g_i^t - \nabla \mathcal{L}_{\text{local},i}^t(\Theta_i^t)\|_2^2\right] \leq \sigma^2, \quad \forall i \in \{0, 1, \ldots, M - 1\}. \tag{19}$$

Assumption 3 (Lipschitz Continuity of Local Embedding Functions). Each local embedding function $f_i(\cdot)$ is L_2-Lipschitz continuous with respect to θ_i^t, that is,

$$\|f_i(\theta_i^{t_1}) - f_i(\theta_i^{t_2})\|_2 \leq L_2 \|\theta_i^{t_1} - \theta_i^{t_2}\|_2, \quad \forall t_1, t_2 > 0, \ i \in \{0, 1, \ldots, M - 1\}. \tag{20}$$

Assumption 4 (Bounded Local Model Shift). For each client i, the local model updated via collaborative training using the personalized global prototype at iteration $tLE + 0$ and the model after completing local training at iteration tLE are bounded in expectation. Specifically,

$$\mathbb{E}\left[\|\theta_i^{tLE+0} - \theta_i^{tLE}\|_2^2\right] \leq \varepsilon_f^2, \quad \varepsilon_f^2 \geq 0, \tag{21}$$

$$\mathbb{E}\left[\|w_i^{tLE+0} - w_i^{tLE}\|_2^2\right] \leq \varepsilon_h^2, \quad \varepsilon_h^2 \geq 0. \tag{22}$$

Assumption 5 (Bounded Variation of Personalized Global Prototype). The personalized global prototypes $P_i^{g,t}$ and $P_i^{g,t+1}$ for client i, aggregated based on the inter-domain similarity matrix during communication rounds t and $t+1$, are assumed to satisfy:

$$\mathbb{E}\left[\|P_i^{g,t+1} - P_i^{g,t}\|_2^2\right] \leq \tau^2, \quad \tau^2 \geq 0. \tag{23}$$

Theorem 1 (One-round Deviation) *Under Assumptions 1–5, for any client i, after completing one round of local updates, the expected value of the local objective satisfies the following inequality:*

$$\mathbb{E}[\mathcal{L}_i^{(t+1)LE+0}] \leq \mathcal{L}_i^{tLE+0} - \eta\left(1 - \frac{L_1\eta}{2}\right)\sum_{e=0}^{LE}\left\|\nabla\mathcal{L}_i^{tLE+e}\right\|_2^2 + \frac{L_1 LE\eta^2}{2}\sigma^2 + \eta\mu\left(L_2\varepsilon_f^2 + \tau^2\right). \tag{24}$$

Proof (Proof of Theorem 1). Based on Assumptions 1 and 2, during the $(t+1)$-th communication round, the local objective on any client i after LE local steps satisfies:

$$\mathbb{E}[\mathcal{L}_i^{(t+1)LE}] \leq \mathcal{L}_i^{tLE+0} - \eta\left(1 - \frac{L_1\eta}{2}\right)\sum_{e=0}^{LE}\left\|\nabla\mathcal{L}_i^{tLE+e}\right\|_2^2 + \frac{L_1 LE\eta^2}{2}\sigma^2. \tag{25}$$

Furthermore, based on Assumptions 3–5, the loss after client i performs collaborative training with its personalized global prototype at step $(t+1)LE+0$ can be decomposed as:

$$\begin{aligned}\mathcal{L}_i^{(t+1)LE+0} &= \mathcal{L}_i^{(t+1)LE} + \eta\Big[\ell_i^{(t+1)LE+0} - \ell_i^{(t+1)LE} + \mu(\phi(f_i(\theta_i^{(t+1)LE+0}), P_i^{g,(t+1)LE+0}) \\ &\quad - \phi(f_i(\theta_i^{(t+1)LE}), P_i^{g,(t+1)LE})) + \mathcal{L}_{\text{IKD}}^{(t+1)LE+0} - \mathcal{L}_{\text{IKD}}^{(t+1)LE}\Big].\end{aligned} \tag{26}$$

By discarding the non-negative term $\ell_i^{(t+1)LE+0} - \ell_i^{(t+1)LE} + \mathcal{L}_{\text{IKD}}^{(t+1)LE+0} - \mathcal{L}_{\text{IKD}}^{(t+1)LE}$, and applying the definition of the similarity loss ϕ, we obtain:

$$\mathcal{L}_i^{(t+1)LE+0} \leq \mathcal{L}_i^{(t+1)LE} + \eta\mu\left\|f_i(\theta_i^{(t+1)LE+0}) - P_i^{g,(t+1)LE+0}\right\|_2^2 - \eta\mu\left\|f_i(\theta_i^{(t+1)LE}) - P_i^{g,(t+1)LE}\right\|_2^2 \tag{27}$$

$$\leq \mathcal{L}_i^{(t+1)LE} + \eta\mu\left(\|f_i(\theta_i^{(t+1)LE+0}) - f_i(\theta_i^{(t+1)LE})\|_2^2 + \|P_i^{g,(t+1)LE+0} - P_i^{g,(t+1)LE}\|_2^2\right) \tag{28}$$

$$\leq \mathcal{L}_i^{(t+1)LE} + \eta\mu\left(L_2^2\|\theta_i^{(t+1)LE+0} - \theta_i^{(t+1)LE}\|_2^2 + \|P_i^{g,(t+1)LE+0} - P_i^{g,(t+1)LE}\|_2^2\right). \tag{29}$$

Taking expectations on both sides and applying Assumptions 4 and 5:

$$\mathbb{E}[\mathcal{L}_i^{(t+1)LE+0}] \leq \mathbb{E}[\mathcal{L}_i^{(t+1)LE}] + \eta\mu\left(L_2\varepsilon_f^2 + \tau^2\right). \tag{30}$$

Substituting back into the bound on $\mathbb{E}[\mathcal{L}_i^{(t+1)LE}]$ gives the final result:

$$\mathbb{E}[\mathcal{L}_i^{(t+1)LE+0}] \leq \mathcal{L}_i^{tLE+0} - \eta\left(1 - \frac{L_1\eta}{2}\right)\sum_{e=0}^{LE}\left\|\nabla\mathcal{L}_i^{tLE+e}\right\|_2^2 + \frac{L_1 LE\eta^2}{2}\sigma^2 + \eta\mu(L_2\varepsilon_f^2 + \tau^2). \tag{31}$$

Theorem 2 (Non-convex Convergence Rate of Fed-APAP). *Assume that Assumptions 1–3 hold. Based on the result of Theorem 1, for any client i and a given precision level $\epsilon > 0$, if the total number of global communication rounds E satisfies:*

$$E \geq \frac{2(\mathcal{L}^{t=0} - \mathcal{L}^*)}{\epsilon\eta(2 - L_1\eta) - L_1 LE\eta^2\sigma^2 + 2\eta\mu(L_2\varepsilon_f^2 + \tau^2)}, \tag{32}$$

then the following inequality holds:

$$\frac{1}{E}\sum_{t=0}^{E-1}\sum_{e=0}^{LE}\mathbb{E}\left[\left\|\nabla\mathcal{L}_i^{tLE+e}\right\|_2^2\right] \leq \frac{2(\mathcal{L}^{t=0} - \mathcal{L}^*)}{E\eta(2 - L_1\eta)} + \frac{L_1 LE\eta\sigma^2 + 2\mu(L_2\varepsilon_f^2 + \tau^2)}{2 - L_1\eta} \leq \epsilon, \tag{33}$$

subject to the condition:

$$\eta \leq \frac{2 + 2\mu(L_2\varepsilon_f^2 + \tau^2)}{L_1 LE\sigma^2 + L_1}. \tag{34}$$

Here, $\mathcal{L}^*$ denotes the optimal local objective value. Theorem 2 characterizes the convergence rate of the Fed-APAP algorithm and establishes that each client can achieve a convergence rate of $\epsilon = \mathcal{O}(1/E)$ in the non-convex setting. It also implies that a smaller target precision ϵ requires a larger number of global communication rounds to guarantee convergence.

Proof (Proof of Theorem 2). From the result of Theorem 1, summing over $e = 0$ to LE and applying expectation, we obtain:

$$\sum_{e=0}^{LE}\mathbb{E}\left[\left\|\nabla\mathcal{L}_i^{tLE+e}\right\|_2^2\right] \leq \frac{\mathbb{E}[\mathcal{L}_i^{tLE+0}] - \mathbb{E}[\mathcal{L}_i^{(t+1)LE+0}]}{\eta\left(1 - \frac{L_1\eta}{2}\right)} + \frac{L_1 LE\eta\sigma^2}{2\left(1 - \frac{L_1\eta}{2}\right)} + \frac{\mu\left(L_2\varepsilon_f^2 + \tau^2\right)}{1 - \frac{L_1\eta}{2}}. \tag{35}$$

Averaging over E global communication rounds yields:

$$\frac{1}{E}\sum_{t=0}^{E-1}\sum_{e=0}^{LE}\mathbb{E}\left[\left\|\nabla\mathcal{L}_i^{tLE+e}\right\|_2^2\right] \leq \frac{1}{E\eta\left(1 - \frac{L_1\eta}{2}\right)}\left(\mathcal{L}_i^{t=0} - \mathcal{L}^*\right) + \frac{L_1 LE\eta\sigma^2}{2\left(1 - \frac{L_1\eta}{2}\right)} + \frac{\mu(L_2\varepsilon_f^2 + \tau^2)}{1 - \frac{L_1\eta}{2}}. \tag{36}$$

Rewriting with a common denominator:

$$\frac{1}{E}\sum_{t=0}^{E-1}\sum_{e=0}^{LE}\mathbb{E}\left[\left\|\nabla\mathcal{L}_i^{tLE+e}\right\|_2^2\right] \leq \frac{2(\mathcal{L}^{t=0} - \mathcal{L}^*)}{E\eta(2 - L_1\eta)} + \frac{L_1 LE\eta\sigma^2 + 2\mu(L_2\varepsilon_f^2 + \tau^2)}{2 - L_1\eta}. \tag{37}$$

To guarantee convergence to an expected gradient norm smaller than ϵ, it suffices to require:

$$\frac{2(\mathcal{L}^{t=0} - \mathcal{L}^*)}{E\eta(2 - L_1\eta)} + \frac{L_1 LE\eta\sigma^2 + 2\mu(L_2\varepsilon_f^2 + \tau^2)}{2 - L_1\eta} \leq \epsilon. \tag{38}$$

Solving for E yields:

$$E \geq \frac{2(\mathcal{L}^{t=0} - \mathcal{L}^*)}{\epsilon\eta(2 - L_1\eta) - L_1 L E \eta^2 \sigma^2 + 2\eta\mu(L_2 \varepsilon_f^2 + \tau^2)}. \tag{39}$$

To ensure the denominator is non-negative, we require:

$$\epsilon\eta(2 - L_1\eta) - L_1 L E \eta^2 \sigma^2 + 2\eta\mu(L_2 \varepsilon_f^2 + \tau^2) \geq 0, \tag{40}$$

which leads to the following sufficient condition:

$$\epsilon(2 - L_1\eta) + 2\mu(L_2 \varepsilon_f^2 + \tau^2) \geq L_1 L E \eta \sigma^2. \tag{41}$$

Solving for η gives the constraint:

$$\eta \leq \frac{2 + 2\mu(L_2 \varepsilon_f^2 + \tau^2)}{L_1 L E \sigma^2 + L_1}. \tag{42}$$

4 Experiments

4.1 Setup

Datasets and Model Heterogeneity. In this study, we evaluated several popular image datasets used for multi-class classification tasks, specifically CIFAR-10 [7], CIFAR-100 [7], and Tiny ImageNet [1]. We used four different feature extractors: a 4-layer CNN [12], GoogleNet [14], MobileNet v2 ([13]), and ResNet18 [2]. At the initialization stage, each client was randomly assigned one of these four models.

Data Distribution Method. To evaluate the performance of Fed-APAP under different data distributions, we employed statistical heterogeneity settings commonly used in non-IID (non-independent and identically distributed) experiments. These settings include the pathological setting [12,15,18] and the practical setting [9,16,20]. Pathological Setting: In this setting, we assigned two classes of data from CIFAR-10, ten classes from CIFAR-100, and twenty classes from Tiny ImageNet to each client as their private data. Additionally, there is no redundancy in the data distribution. Practical Setting: In the practical setting, we sampled each data class using a Dirichlet distribution Dir(β). The default value of β is set to 0.1. All datasets are divided into training and test sets with a split of 75% for training and 25% for testing.

Baseline Methods. We selected seven popular heterogeneous federated learning algorithms as baseline comparisons: FedDistill [5], FedGen [20], FedMD [8], LG-FedAvg [11], FedGH [17], FedProto [15], and FedTGP [18]. This study compares Fed-APAP with these seven heterogeneous federated learning algorithms, leveraging diverse collaborative training strategies such as logits distillation, public dataset alignment, lightweight generator sharing, and prototype-based learning, ensuring a comprehensive performance evaluation.

Implementation Details. In the experiments, a total of 20 clients participated in federated learning, with a client participation rate of 1. For each global iteration, both the local training and local collaboration training periods were set to 5 epochs. The batch size was set to 10, the learning rate to 0.01, and the global training comprised 100 iterations. For the FedMD algorithm, the public datasets used for Cifar10 and Cifar100 were Cifar100, Cifar10, and MNIST. No corresponding public dataset was available for Tiny ImageNet, so it was not included in the experiment. The accuracy for each round of global experiments was averaged over the client test sets, with the best global accuracy taken for each experiment.

4.2 Performance

Based on the experimental results in Table 1, our Fed-APAP method outperforms other baseline algorithms across multiple datasets under both pathological and practical statistical heterogeneity settings. In our experiments, we observed that the performance of the FedMD algorithm is heavily dependent on the choice of public datasets. Under practical settings, where the variety of included data is high and the amount of data per class is low, the correlation between the public dataset and private data is weak, resulting in lower accuracy on both datasets. The FedProto algorithm is affected by model heterogeneity, as the performance of different model architectures varies. This leads to discrepancies between local prototypes and embedded space class features, making it difficult to effectively guide the optimization of local heterogeneous models through the generated global prototype. FedTGP algorithm struggles because the limited local prototypes uploaded by clients in each iteration make it extremely challenging to train the server-side prototype effectively. Consequently, the loss remains high and fails to converge, resulting in suboptimal global prototypes. In contrast, Fed-APAP adopts an adaptive update mechanism for the inter-domain distribution similarity matrix, effectively addressing the challenges posed by private data domain distribution and model heterogeneity. By generating personalized global prototypes for each private data domain, Fed-APAP improves performance. For instance, on the more challenging Tiny ImageNet dataset, Fed-APAP achieves a 5.53% higher accuracy compared to FedProto.

4.3 Impact of Different Local Epochs

In the practical settings, we conducted experiments to assess the impact of different local training rounds on model performance, with results presented in Table 2. More local rounds can accelerate model convergence on private data domains and reduce the number of global iterations needed. We observed that Fed-APAP shows minimal fluctuations in global model accuracy across different local round settings, maintaining robust performance even with varying local training configurations [12].

Table 1. Accuracy (%) of the algorithm under different statistical heterogeneity settings

Method	Practical Setting			Pathological Setting		
	CIFAR-100	CIFAR-10	Tiny-ImageNet	CIFAR-100	CIFAR-10	Tiny-ImageNet
LG-FedAvg	43.30	86.64	32.31	60.76	86.90	39.28
FedGH	37.31	85.06	30.48	59.87	86.60	38.55
FedDistill	42.66	86.76	32.43	59.13	85.84	38.97
FedGen	42.74	86.94	31.45	59.55	86.64	37.89
FedMD	42.98	83.41	–	59.35	84.30	–
FedProto	35.38	82.75	28.97	52.14	82.46	37.63
FedTGP	39.47	86.32	32.16	53.36	86.23	34.53
Fed-APAP	**44.53**	**87.99**	**33.15**	**61.31**	**87.44**	**40.94**

Table 2. Accuracy (%) of the algorithm with different local rounds settings

LE	1	5	10	20
Cifar100	44.63	44.53	**44.85**	44.40
Cifar10	87.40	**87.99**	87.12	87.62

4.4 Ablation Experiment

We conducted an ablation study on the Fed-APAP method, comparing the version with only adaptive personalized aggregation prototypes (without unlabeled-class distillation) to the complete Fed-APAP method. The experiments were performed on two datasets under practical settings, with results shown in Table 3. The results indicate that the use of unlabeled-class distillation enables the local models to learn posterior class relationships of private data domains, effectively preserving privileged information and further enhancing model accuracy and generalization capabilities.

Table 3. Accuracy (%) of the ablation experiments on the Fed-APAP method's key components on the CIFAR-100 and CIFAR-10 datasets (transposed)

Method	CIFAR-100	CIFAR-10
FedProto	35.20	82.34
Fed-APAP without UCD	44.26	87.40
Fed-APAP	**44.53**	**87.99**

4.5 More Challenging Mission Situations

To test the performance of Fed-APAP on a variety of heterogeneous models and complex classification tasks, we expanded the original four heterogeneous models to include ResNet34, ResNet50, ResNet101, and ResNet152. We then set the number of local training rounds to 5 and 1, respectively. The results are shown in Table 4. Our Fed-APAP maintained superior performance even under more extreme conditions. This is because the adaptive personalized aggregation prototype better captures the class characteristics in the embedded space of private data domains, resulting in up to a 6.1% improvement in accuracy compared to FedProto.

Table 4. Accuracy (%) of 8 heterogeneous models after 5 and 1 round of local training on the TinyImageNet dataset

		FedProto	FedTGP	Fed-APAP
LE = 5	Practical Setting	25.12	28.43	**29.70**
	Pathological Setting	32.57	33.24	**34.87**
LE = 1	Practical Setting	24.01	27.53	**30.11**
	Pathological Setting	32.78	32.29	**35.15**

5 Conclusion

We propose a data and model heterogeneous federated learning method, Fed-APAP, using adaptive personalized aggregation prototypes. This approach generates personalized global prototypes based on private data distributions, distills class features from the global domain perspective, and preserves privileged information to enhance model generalization. Experiments show that Fed-APAP outperforms baseline algorithms while maintaining lower communication overhead.

References

1. Chrabaszcz, P., Loshchilov, I., Hutter, F.: A downsampled variant of imagenet as an alternative to the cifar datasets. arXiv preprint arXiv:1707.08819 (2017)
2. He, K., Zhang, X., Ren, S., Sun, J.: Deep residual learning for image recognition. In: CVPR (2016)
3. Hinton, G., Vinyals, O., Dean, J.: Distilling the knowledge in a neural network. arXiv preprint arXiv:1503.02531 (2015)
4. Huang, Y., et al.: Personalized cross-silo federated learning on non-IID data. In: AAAI (2021)

5. Jeong, E., Oh, S., Kim, H., Park, J., Bennis, M., Kim, S.L.: Communication-efficient on-device machine learning: federated distillation and augmentation under non-iid private data. arXiv preprint arXiv:1811.11479 (2018)
6. Karimireddy, S.P., Kale, S., Mohri, M., Reddi, S., Stich, S., Suresh, A.T.: Scaffold: stochastic controlled averaging for federated learning. In: ICML (2020)
7. Krizhevsky, A., Geoffrey, H.: Learning multiple layers of features from tiny images. Technical Report (2009)
8. Li, D., Wang, J.: Fedmd: heterogenous federated learning via model distillation. arXiv preprint arXiv:1910.03581 (2019)
9. Li, Q., He, B., Song, D.: Model-contrastive federated learning. In: CVPR (2021)
10. Li, T., Sahu, A.K., Zaheer, M., Sanjabi, M., Talwalkar, A., Smith, V.: Federated optimization in heterogeneous networks. In: MLSys (2020)
11. Liang, P.P., et al.: Think locally, act globally: federated learning with local and global representations. arXiv preprint arXiv:2001.01523 (2020)
12. McMahan, B., Moore, E., Ramage, D., Hampson, S., Arcas, B.A.: Communication-efficient learning of deep networks from decentralized data. In: AISTATS (2017)
13. Sandler, M., Howard, A., Zhu, M., Zhmoginov, A., Chen, L.C.: Mobilenetv2: inverted residuals and linear bottlenecks. In: CVPR (2018)
14. Szegedy, C., et al.: Going deeper with convolutions. In: CVPR (2015)
15. Tan, Y., et al.: Fedproto: federated prototype learning across heterogeneous clients. In: AAAI (2022)
16. Tan, Y., Long, G., Ma, J., Liu, L., Zhou, T., Jiang, J.: Federated learning from pre-trained models: a contrastive learning approach. arXiv preprint arXiv:2209.10083 (2022)
17. Yi, L., Wang, G., Liu, X., Shi, Z., Yu, H.: Fedgh: heterogeneous federated learning with generalized global header. arXiv preprint arXiv:2303.13137 (2023)
18. Zhang, J., Liu, Y., Hua, Y., Cao, J.: Fedtgp: trainable global prototypes with adaptive-margin-enhanced contrastive learning for data and model heterogeneity in federated learning. In: AAAI (2024)
19. Zhao, B., Cui, Q., Song, R., Qiu, Y., Liang, J.: Decoupled knowledge distillation. In: Proceedings of the IEEE/CVF Conference on Computer Vision and Pattern Recognition, pp. 11953–11962 (2022)
20. Zhu, Z., Hong, J., Zhou, J.: Data-free knowledge distillation for heterogeneous federated learning. In: ICML (2021)

Enhancing Heterogeneous Federated Learning via Historical Dual Knowledge Distillation

Xiao Xu[1], Jinbo Xiong[1(✉)], Renwan Bi[2], Yuanyuan Zhang[1,3], and Li Lin[1]

[1] Fujian Provincial Key Laboratory of Network Security and Cryptology, College of Computer and Cyber Security, Fujian Normal University, Fuzhou, China
{jbxiong,li.lin}@fjnu.edu.cn, xuxiaodsg233@163.com, zyy837603010@163.com

[2] School of Cyber Science and Engineering, Minjiang University, Fuzhou, China
brw2806@163.com

[3] Lion Rock Labs of Cyberspace Security, Hong Kong, China

Abstract. Federated learning (FL), as a privacy-preserving distributed machine learning framework, has become a core technology for protecting user data privacy and facilitating collaborative model training. However, data heterogeneity among clients leads to model performance degradation and unstable convergence, posing a critical challenge in FL. Existing federated distillation (FD) methods often overlook the knowledge accumulation of historical global models and historical local models, limiting their effectiveness in Non-IID scenarios. To address this issue, this paper proposes FedHDKD (Federated Historical Dual Knowledge Distillation), which introduces a dual KD mechanism by integrating global knowledge distillation (GKD) and local knowledge distillation (LKD). GKD leverages a weighted aggregation of multiple historical global models, capturing and preserving global generalized knowledge, while LKD distills historical local models to maintain local personalized knowledge. Experimental results demonstrate that FedHDKD significantly outperforms baseline methods (e.g., FedAvg, FedProx) across multiple public datasets under various Non-IID settings. Moreover, FedHDKD exhibits superior stability and robustness, validating its effectiveness in heterogeneous FL.

Keywords: Federated Learning · Knowledge Distillation · Data Heterogeneity · Model Aggregation · Knowledge Transfer

1 Introduction

In the digital era, data has become a key driving force behind the advancement of artificial intelligence. However, as the scale of data continues to grow and application scenarios become increasingly complex, concerns regarding data privacy and security have become more prominent [1,2]. Against this backdrop, federated learning (FL) has emerged as a novel distributed machine learning framework

L. Zhang and K.-K. R. Choo (Eds.): MobiQuitous 2025, LNICST 683, pp. 149–166, 2026.
https://doi.org/10.1007/978-3-032-22500-9_9

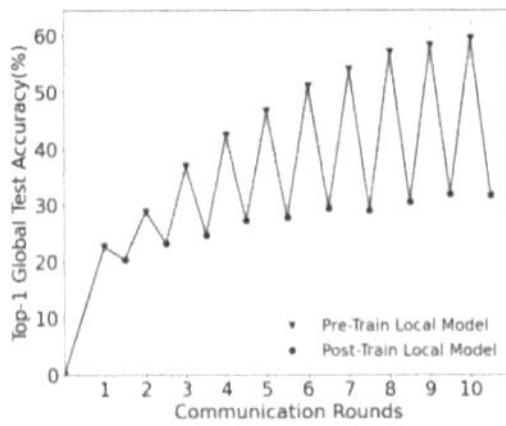

(a) Global forgetting

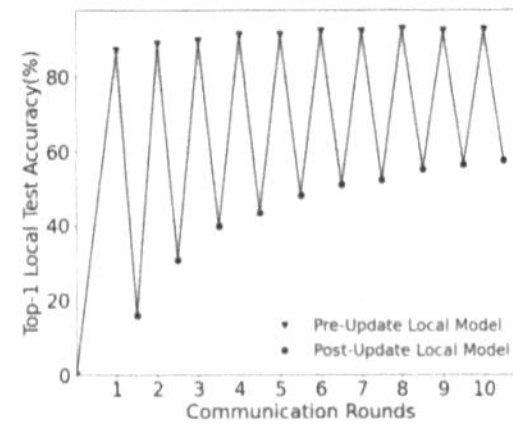

(b) Local forgetting

Fig. 1. Global generalized knowledge forgetting and local personalized knowledge forgetting in heterogeneous FL.

and is increasingly recognized as a crucial technology for safeguarding data privacy and security [3,4]. Unlike traditional centralized learning approaches, FL allows multiple clients to retain their local data while collaboratively training a global model by sharing model parameters instead of raw data [5]. This framework not only significantly reduces the risk of data privacy disclosure but also meets the stringent privacy and security requirements in domains such as healthcare, finance, and smart devices. By fully leveraging distributed data resources, FL enhances model generalization and facilitates the development of edge computing and intelligent services.

However, data heterogeneity is one of the core challenges faced by FL [6]. In real-world applications, client data often originates from diverse sources and exhibits significant distribution differences, resulting in a non-independent and identically distributed (Non-IID) nature. For instance, data on user devices may vary significantly due to differences in geographical locations, behavioral patterns, or device types, leading to highly personalized characteristics. This data heterogeneity not only causes substantial variations among client models, affecting the effective aggregation of the global model, but also causes the forgetting of both global generalized knowledge (Fig. 1(a)) and local personalized knowledge (Fig. 1(b)). As a result, it leads to performance degradation, slower convergence, and instability during the training process [7,8], thereby severely compromising the accuracy and robustness of the FL model.

Against this backdrop, federated distillation (FD) [9], an application of knowledge distillation (KD) [10] in FL, has emerged as a promising research direction for addressing data heterogeneity. Without sharing raw data, FD facilitates knowledge transfer between client models by leveraging soft-label information from the global model or other client models [11,12], thereby mitigating the impact of Non-IID data distributions. Particularly in scenarios where client data is highly heterogeneous and constrained by privacy requirements, FD can effectively enhance model generalization, accelerate convergence, and improve the stability and robustness of FL systems.

Despite various FD methods proposed to alleviate the challenges posed by data heterogeneity, several limitations remain. Firstly, existing approaches lack effective mechanisms to address the problem of global knowledge forgetting and personalized knowledge retention in highly heterogeneous settings [13–16], leading to gradual model performance degradation over multiple training rounds. Secondly, most methods rely solely on the current global model or single-round distillation processes [17–19], overlooking the potential knowledge accumulation in historical global models and historical local models. As a result, they fail to fully exploit historical information to enhance model stability and generalization.

To address these challenges and enhance the robustness and performance of FL systems in heterogeneous data environments, this paper proposes FedHDKD (Federated Historical Dual Knowledge Distillation). The core idea of FedHDKD is to fully exploit and utilize the knowledge from historical global models and historical local models by integrating a dual KD mechanism into FL for comprehensive knowledge transfer. Specifically, global knowledge distillation (GKD) utilizes the historical fused model generated by the server through a performance-based weighted aggregation strategy as the teacher model. This historical fused model integrates multiple rounds of historical global models, effectively capturing the global generalization knowledge accumulated over multiple training rounds. Meanwhile, local knowledge distillation (LKD) uses each client's previous local model as the teacher, which preserves client-specific personalized knowledge. In both distillation processes, the current local model serves as the student. By leveraging this dual KD strategy, FedHDKD effectively mitigates global knowledge forgetting and local personalized knowledge degradation, enhances adaptation to Non-IID data, and improves the overall robustness and generalization performance of FL systems.

The main contributions of this paper are as follows:

- We propose a novel FD method, FedHDKD, which leverages historical global models and historical local models to enhance the robustness of FL in heterogeneous data environments. The method introduces a dual KD mechanism, effectively transferring historical global knowledge and historical local knowledge, thereby improving model training performance and generalization capability.
- We design an effective historical model weighted aggregation method, which calculates weights based on the performance of historical global models on a public dataset to construct a historical fusion model. Additionally, we formulate both GKD and LKD to achieve the transmission of global generalization and local personalization knowledge, enhancing the model's adaptability and stability.
- Extensive experiments are conducted on multiple public image datasets and under various Non-IID settings. The results demonstrate that FedHDKD outperforms baseline methods (e.g., FedAvg and FedProx) in terms of model accuracy and adaptability to data heterogeneity, exhibiting superior performance stability and robustness.

The remainder of this paper is organized as follows: Sect. 2 reviews the foundational concepts and related work. Section 3 provides a detailed description of the FedHDKD method. Section 4 presents the experimental results and analysis

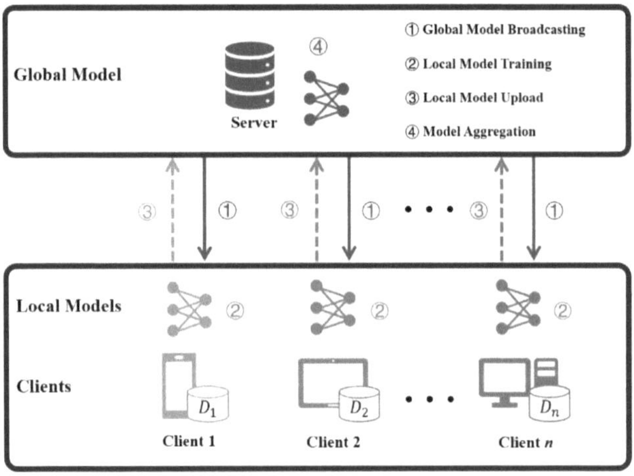

Fig. 2. The framework of FL.

to validate the effectiveness of FedHDKD. Finally, Sect. 5 concludes the paper with a summary of the work.

2 Related Work

2.1 Federated Learning

FL, as a distributed machine learning framework, aims to enable multiple clients to collaboratively train a central model while ensuring data privacy. The structure of the FL framework is shown in Fig. 2. In the standard FL framework, the most typical algorithm is FedAvg [3], whose core idea is to average the model parameter updates on the server to update the global model.

However, in practical applications, the data heterogeneity (Non-IID) problem that FL faces has become the primary challenge in improving its performance. Clients tend to overfit to their local data, which results in the degradation of the global model's generalization ability across different clients. To address the challenges brought by data heterogeneity, researchers have proposed numerous solutions. FedProx [13] introduces a proximal term in local updates to constrain model drift, thereby improving convergence stability. SCAFFOLD [15] utilizes control variates to correct local update directions, effectively reducing client drift and enhancing convergence speed. FedNova [16] tackles the issue of inconsistent model updates by using a normalized aggregation method, improving communication efficiency. MOON [14] utilizes a model-level contrastive learning mechanism to make local model representations more consistent with the global model. FedMAX [20] introduces maximum entropy regularization to effectively reduce activation discrepancies in FL. Method such as FedGen [21] enhances the diversity of data or features to help client models learn representations with better generalization capabilities.

2.2 Federated Distillation

KD, as a model compression and transfer learning technique [10], is based on the idea of transferring the rich knowledge embedded in a pre-trained teacher model to a student model. This allows the student model to achieve high generalization performance while maintaining a lower model complexity.

To address the challenges posed by data heterogeneity (Non-IID) in FL, KD has been widely applied in the FL framework, forming the FD method [9,22]. Existing research has proposed various FD algorithms to optimize model performance. For example, DS-FL [12] and FedBiKD [23] effectively mitigate the impact of data heterogeneity by utilizing public datasets for KD, improving the convergence speed and performance stability of the global model. FedBKD [24] generates synthetic data using conditional variational autoencoders for bidirectional KD, thus reducing performance loss caused by data distribution differences in traditional aggregation methods. Furthermore, methods such as LSR [25] and LSG [26] use local regularization and local self-guidance strategies, respectively, to optimize local model training through local alignment, further enhancing the model's adaptability to Non-IID data. In terms of alleviating catastrophic forgetting of knowledge caused by data heterogeneity, FedSSD [27] and FedNTD [18] strengthen global generalization knowledge in FL through different global model KD strategies, while pFedSD [19] focuses more on retaining local personalized knowledge and improving the model's adaptability to local data distributions through local model KD strategies.

3 Construction of FedHDKD

This section introduces a new FD method—FedHDKD. This method consists of two main components: GKD and LKD. The workflow of FedHDKD is illustrated in Fig. 3.

3.1 Global Knowledge Distillation

In heterogeneous FL environments, the Non-IID nature of client data can lead to the forgetting of global generalization knowledge during local training, as illustrated in Fig. 1(a), after local model training, the client's performance on the global test dataset significantly decreases. To this end, FedHDKD incorporates GKD, which helps clients distill generalized knowledge from the global model, alleviates the problem of forgetting, and enhances model robustness, ultimately enabling better generalization under heterogeneous data distributions.

However, relying solely on the current round's global model for KD may not be sufficient to fully transfer the knowledge accumulated during the FL process, especially when there are significant differences in the data distributions across clients. To better utilize the global historical information, FedHDKD adopts a weighted aggregation strategy for the historical global models, constructing a historical fused model w_{fuse} to integrate the knowledge from multiple communication rounds. This approach reduces the influence of a specific client's data

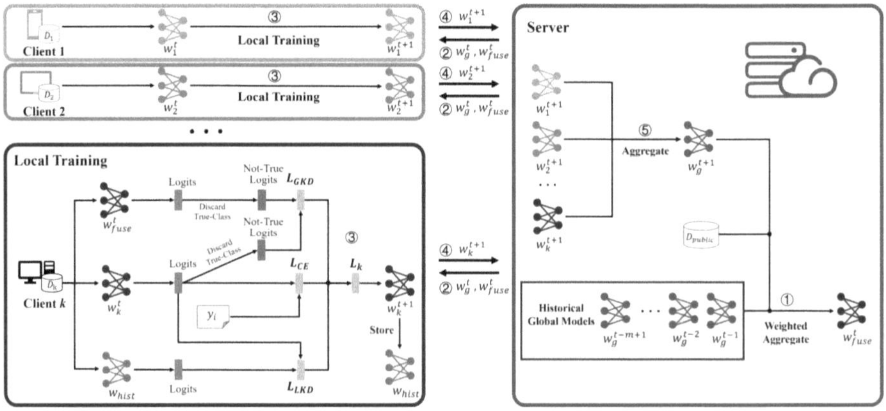

Fig. 3. The workflow of FedHDKD.

distribution on the global model in a single round, helping the client models learn more comprehensive features.

Specifically, after each round of model aggregation, the server stores the current global model and maintains a list containing the most recent m rounds of historical global models to construct the historical fused model. However, since these historical global models may differ significantly in their generalization capabilities, FedHDKD introduces a performance-based weighting method on a public dataset to fairly and effectively allocate the contribution of each historical global model during the fusion process, specifically using the cross-entropy loss as an indicator. On the public dataset, a smaller cross-entropy loss indicates better performance of the model on the global data distribution, reflecting a richer representation of global generalized knowledge. By using this loss as the basis for weight assignment, the method ensures that better-performing historical global models receive higher weights in the fusion process, effectively mitigating the adverse effects of low-quality models and enhancing the reliability of the historical fused model. The weight calculation is as follows:

$$\alpha_j = \frac{e^{-L_j/\beta}}{\sum_{k=1}^{m} e^{-L_k/\beta}} \tag{1}$$

where L_j is the validation loss of the j-th historical global model on the public dataset, and β is the hyperparameter that regulates the smoothness of the weight distribution. Based on this, the aggregation process of the historical fused model can be expressed as:

$$w_{fuse} = \sum_{j=1}^{m} \alpha_j w_j \tag{2}$$

where w_j represents the j-th historical global model. In GKD, the historical fused model w_{fuse} serves as the teacher, while the local model w_k on each client acts as the student. The knowledge is transferred through KD, and the objective function is defined as follows:

$$\mathcal{L}_{\text{GKD}} = \frac{1}{n_k} \sum_{i=1}^{n_k} KL\left(q^{\tau}\left(w_{fuse}^{t}, x_i\right) \| q^{\tau}\left(w_k^t, x_i\right)\right) \tag{3}$$

where n_k denotes the number of training samples on client k, KL represents the Kullback-Leibler divergence, and $q^{\tau}\left(w_{fuse}^{t}, x_i\right)$ and $q^{\tau}\left(w_k^t, x_i\right)$ represent the soft labels generated by the historical fused model and the local client model for sample x_i, respectively. The soft labels q^{τ} are computed by $q_c^{\tau}(w, x) = \frac{\exp(z_c(w,x)/\tau)}{\sum_j \exp(z_j(w,x)/\tau)}$ [10], where z denotes the raw logits output by the model, and τ is a temperature hyperparameter that controls the smoothness of the softmax probability distribution.

Due to the significant differences in data distributions among clients, the local client model can be directly optimized using local data for the true class. However, information regarding non-true classes is often insufficient in local data and tends to be forgotten during training. Inspired by FedNTD [18], GKD adopts a non-true class distillation strategy, where only the soft label outputs of non-true classes are distilled. This strategy constrains the local model to align its outputs on non-true classes with those of the global model, thereby preserving the memory of the global class distribution and preventing the forgetting of non-true classes knowledge during local training. Compared to conventional KD, this approach enhances the retention of global knowledge while avoiding interference with local true class tasks, thus mitigating the risk of negative transfer. The optimized objective function is defined as follows:

$$\mathcal{L}_{\text{GKD}} = \frac{1}{n_k} \sum_{i=1}^{n_k} KL_{not-true}\left(\tilde{q}^{\tau}\left(w_{fuse}^{t}, x_i\right) \| \tilde{q}^{\tau}\left(w_k^t, x_i\right)\right) \tag{4}$$

where $\tilde{q}_c^{\tau}(w, x) = \frac{\exp(z_c(w,x)/\tau)}{\sum_{j \neq y} \exp(z_j(w,x)/\tau)}$ represents the GKD applied only to the soft labels of non-true classes [18].

3.2 Local Knowledge Distillation

Although GKD can effectively enhance the adaptability of client models to global knowledge, in Non-IID data scenarios, clients may still suffer from personalized knowledge forgetting due to significant differences in data distribution. Specifically, when clients update their local models in each round, they lose historical personalized knowledge, requiring them to relearn local tasks [19]. As illustrated in Fig. 1(b), after local updates, the client's performance on its local test dataset drops significantly. Personalized knowledge is the result of optimization based on the client's local data distribution, and its forgetting can lead to a significant decline in client performance in FL [28].

Therefore, relying solely on the global model for KD is insufficient to maintain the stability and generalization ability of local models. To address this issue, FedHDKD adopts LKD, which distills knowledge from historical local models to the

Algorithm 1 FedHDKD: Federated Historical Dual Knowledge Distillation

Input: number of clients n, participation rate c, communication rounds T, local epochs E, historical model list size m, dataset D, learning rate η.
Output: The final global model w_g^T.

// D_k denotes the local dataset for client k
// D_{public} denotes the public dataset on server
procedure ServerExecute
  Initialize global model w_g^0
  Initialize historical model list $\mathcal{H} \leftarrow [\,]$
  for each communication round $t = 1, 2, \ldots, T$ **do**
    for each historical model $w_g^{t-j+1} \in \mathcal{H}$ **do**
      Compute weight $\alpha_j \leftarrow \frac{e^{-L_j/\beta}}{\sum_{k=1}^{m} e^{-L_k/\beta}}$
    end for
    Aggregate $w_{fuse}^t \leftarrow \sum_{j=1}^{m} \alpha_j w_g^{t-j+1}$
    $K \leftarrow$random sample a set of $c \cdot n$ clients
    Send w_g^t, w_{fuse}^t to clients in K
    for each client $k \in K$ in parallel **do**
      for epoch $e = 1, 2, \ldots, E$ **do**
        $w_k^{t+1} \leftarrow$ClientUpdate(D_k, w_g^t, w_{fuse}^t)
      end for
    end for
    Aggregate $w_g^{t+1} \leftarrow \sum_{k=1}^{K} \frac{|\mathcal{D}_k|}{|\mathcal{D}|} w_k^{t+1}$
    Save w_g^{t+1} in $\mathcal{H}$
    if the size of $\mathcal{H} > m$ **then**
      Remove w_g^{t-m+1} from $\mathcal{H}$
    end if
  end for
end procedure
procedure ClientUpdate(D_k, w_g^t, w_{fuse}^t)
  Update $w_k^t \leftarrow w_g^t$
  for each local data sample in D_k **do**
    $w_k^{t+1} \leftarrow w_k^t - \eta \nabla \mathcal{L}_k(D_k; w_k^t, w_{fuse}^t, w_{hist})$
  end for
  Store $w_{hist} \leftarrow w_k^{t+1}$
  return w_k^{t+1} to server
end procedure

current model. This approach mitigates the problem of personalized knowledge forgetting and enhances the model's adaptability to the local data distribution. Specifically, during the client training process, the historical local model w_{hist} (i.e., the locally updated model after the previous round of training) is used as the teacher model to perform LKD on the current round's local model w_k^t, transferring personalized knowledge. After training, the client stores the updated local model w_k^{t+1} as the new historical local model w_{hist}, which will be used for the LKD process in the next round. The objective function is defined as follows:

$$\mathcal{L}_{\text{LKD}} = \frac{1}{n_k} \sum_{i=1}^{n_k} KL\left(q^{\tau}\left(w_{hist}, x_i\right) \| q^{\tau}\left(w_k^t, x_i\right)\right) \tag{5}$$

where $q^{\tau}\left(w_{hist}^t, x_i\right)$ and $q^{\tau}\left(w_k^t, x_i\right)$ represent the soft labels generated by the historical local model and the current local model for the sample x_i, respectively.

3.3 FedHDKD Method

GKD and LKD enhance the local model's generalization ability and personalized adaptability from different perspectives. GKD provides stable global knowledge through the historical fused model, allowing the client model to learn more comprehensive features and reduce the knowledge forgetting issues caused by Non-IID data. On the other hand, LKD preserves personalized knowledge through the historical local model, enhancing the model's adaptability to local data, thereby further improving personalized performance.

To fully leverage both distillation strategies, we propose FedHDKD, which integrates GKD and LKD. During local training on the client side, both global and personalized knowledge are distilled simultaneously, promoting comprehensive knowledge transfer to build a more robust FL model. The overall objective function of FedHDKD is defined as follows:

$$\mathcal{L}_{\text{k}} = \mathcal{L}_{\text{CE}} + \lambda\mathcal{L}_{\text{GKD}} + (1-\lambda)\mathcal{L}_{\text{LKD}} \tag{6}$$

where $\mathcal{L}_{\text{CE}}$ represents the cross-entropy loss of the client, $\mathcal{L}_{\text{GKD}}$ is the GKD loss, defined as in Eq. (4), and $\mathcal{L}_{\text{LKD}}$ is the LKD loss, defined as in Eq. (5). The hyperparameter λ controls the ratio between GKD and LKD, with $\lambda \in [0, 1]$.

The overall algorithm framework of FedHDKD is shown in Algorithm 1. In each communication round, the server randomly selects a subset of clients to participate in federated training. Firstly, the server constructs a historical fusion model by weighted aggregation of the historical global models. Then, the current global model and the historical fusion model are distributed to the selected clients. After receiving the global model, the clients initialize their local models based on the current global model. During the local training process, the clients combine GKD and LKD and jointly optimize using the historical fusion model and the historical local model. This facilitates the effective transfer of both global generalization knowledge and local personalized knowledge. After training, the clients store the updated local model as the historical local model for use in the next round of training. Once the server receives the model parameters uploaded by all participating clients, it performs an averaging aggregation of the models to generate the optimized global model, which is then stored in the historical global model list for constructing the historical fusion model in subsequent communication rounds.

3.4 Complexity Analysis

Client-Side Computational Complexity. In each communication round, every client performs E local epochs, and each epoch processes a batch of size B. The standard training complexity is $\mathcal{O}(E \cdot B \cdot f)$, where f denotes the computational cost of a single forward and backward pass of the model. In FedHDKD, the client introduces GKD and LKD during local training, as defined in Eqs. (4) and (5), respectively. Both distillation operations are performed on every batch and involve a single forward pass and computation of the distillation loss. Thus, the overall client-side computational complexity remains $\mathcal{O}(E \cdot B \cdot f)$, which is of the same order as FedAvg. Although additional computations are introduced compared to FedAvg, the distillation processes only involve forward propagation and linear loss computation without introducing higher-order operations. As a result, the overall computational cost still grows linearly.

Server-Side Computational Complexity. In each communication round, in addition to performing an average aggregation of the k client models with a computational complexity of $\mathcal{O}(k \cdot d)$, the server also performs a weighted aggregation over m historical global models (as described in Equation (2)), where the model dimensionality is d. The complexity of this weighted aggregation is $\mathcal{O}(m \cdot d)$, corresponding to a weighted summation over the parameters of m models. Additionally, during the aggregation process, the server computes the loss of each historical global model on a public dataset, incurring a complexity of $\mathcal{O}(m \cdot n_{public} \cdot d)$, where n_{public} denotes the number of samples in the public dataset. Compared to FedAvg, which performs a simple model averaging with complexity $\mathcal{O}(k \cdot d)$, FedHDKD introduces higher server-side computational overhead. However, since in practice $m \ll k$ and a small-scale public dataset D_{public} is typically used (i.e., $n_{\text{public}} \ll |D_k|$), the server-side computational cost of FedHDKD remains manageable in practical settings. This additional computation brings more stable and robust global knowledge representation, which facilitates improved generalization and convergence performance under Non-IID data distributions.

Communication Overhead. In FedHDKD, during each communication round, the client must receive the current global model w_g^t and the historical fusion model w_{fuse}^t, as well as upload the current local model update w_k^t. Therefore, the communication volume per round is $\mathcal{O}(3d)$. Compared to the FedAvg, which requires a communication volume of $\mathcal{O}(2d)$ per round, the communication overhead increases by 50%. However, this additional overhead is compensated by enhanced robustness and improved model performance.

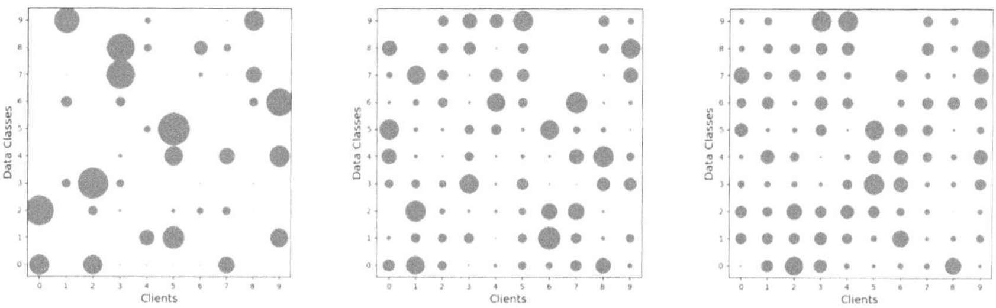

(a) Dirichlet $\alpha = 0.1$ (b) Dirichlet $\alpha = 0.5$ (c) Dirichlet $\alpha = 1.0$

Fig. 4. The data distribution across 10 clients on the CIFAR-10 dataset, where the x-axis represents client IDs, the y-axis shows class labels, and point sizes denote the number of samples per class for each client.

4 Performance Evaluation

4.1 Experimental Setup

Datasets. The experiments in this paper are based on three widely used publicly available image classification datasets: MNIST, CIFAR-10, and CIFAR-100. To simulate the Non-IID characteristics of the FL environment in real-world scenarios, the experiment employs the Dirichlet distribution $Dir(\alpha)$ for data partitioning, which controls the data heterogeneity across different clients. The experiment partitions data on the CIFAR-10 and CIFAR-100 datasets with $\alpha \in \{0.1, 0.5, 1.0\}$ to evaluate the performance of the method under varying degrees of data heterogeneity (Fig. 4). For MNIST, $\alpha = 0.1$ is used to maintain consistency with existing studies. Additionally, the server constructs a small-scale public dataset by uniformly sampling from the original datasets to assist in global model evaluation and knowledge transfer.

Model Structure. The model architecture in the experiment is similar to the 5-layer CNN used in [3], consisting of two convolutional layers followed by max-pooling layers, and two fully connected layers.

Baselines. To validate the effectiveness of the proposed method, multiple classical and recently proposed federated learning approaches are selected as baselines for comparison. These include FedAvg [3], FedProx [13], MOON [14], FedNTD [18] and pFedSD [19].

Hyperparameters. The experiments in this paper adopt a FL environment with $n = 100$ clients. The number of communication rounds is set to $T = 200$, and in each round, 10% of the clients are randomly sampled for training (i.e., $c = 0.10$). During the local training, each selected client performs $E = 5$ rounds of local updates, with a batch size set to $B = 64$. All experiments are trained

Table 1. Top-1 global test accuracy (%) of different methods on MNIST ($\alpha = 0.1$), CIFAR-10 ($\alpha = 0.1, 0.5, 1.0$), and CIFAR-100 ($\alpha = 0.1, 0.5, 1.0$) datasets.

Method	MNIST	CIFAR-10			CIFAR-100		
		$\alpha = 0.1$	$\alpha = 0.5$	$\alpha = 1.0$	$\alpha = 0.1$	$\alpha = 0.5$	$\alpha = 1.0$
FedAvg [3]	96.20	62.82	71.51	74.36	36.71	39.32	39.79
FedProx [13]	97.12	64.86	72.31	74.77	37.58	39.44	40.11
MOON [14]	95.83	60.67	71.36	74.27	36.16	38.75	39.33
pFedSD [19]	97.15	64.51	71.83	74.42	37.67	39.66	40.06
FedNTD [18]	97.52	66.77	73.45	75.29	38.85	40.39	41.14
FedHDKD	**97.68**	**67.41**	**73.91**	**75.87**	**39.47**	**41.24**	**41.43**

using the SGD optimizer, with a learning rate set to 0.01, a momentum factor of 0.90, a learning rate decay factor of 0.99, and a weight decay coefficient of 1×10^{-5}.

The baseline models are executed following the recommended settings from the corresponding papers or code implementations. For the FedProx method, the proximal term is set as $\mu \in \{0.001, 0.01, 0.1, 1\}$. For the MOON method, the contrastive loss parameter is set as $\mu \in \{0.1, 1, 5\}$. For the pFedSD method, the regularization parameter is set as $\lambda \in \{0.1, 0.5\}$. For the proposed FedHDKD method, the regularization parameter is set as $\lambda \in \{0.6, 0.7, 0.8, 0.9\}$, the temperature parameter is set as $\tau \in \{1, 3\}$, and the historical model list size is set as $m \in \{1, 3, 5, 7, 9\}$. All experiments are conducted under the same conditions and repeated multiple times, with the average results reported to mitigate bias caused by random initialization or client sampling.

4.2 Performance Analyses

Performance Comparison. Table 1 presents the Top-1 global test accuracy of the baseline methods and FedHDKD under the default settings on the MNIST, CIFAR-10, and CIFAR-100 datasets. A comparison of the performance of different methods across multiple datasets shows that, on the MNIST dataset, all methods achieve relatively high accuracy, with FedHDKD slightly outperforming the others with a performance of 97.68%, indicating its stability and effectiveness on simpler tasks. On the more challenging CIFAR-10 and CIFAR-100 datasets, FedHDKD further demonstrates its advantages. In particular, on the CIFAR-10 dataset with $\alpha = 0.1$, it outperforms the baseline methods by 4.59%, 2.55%, 6.74%, 2.90% and 0.64%, respectively, highlighting its superiority in highly heterogeneous data scenarios. On the CIFAR-100 dataset, although the task is more challenging, FedHDKD still surpasses all baseline methods, outperforming the lowest-performing baseline by a margin of 2.76% in Top-1 global test accuracy with $\alpha = 0.1$, further proving its effectiveness and robustness under high-dimensional and complex data distributions.

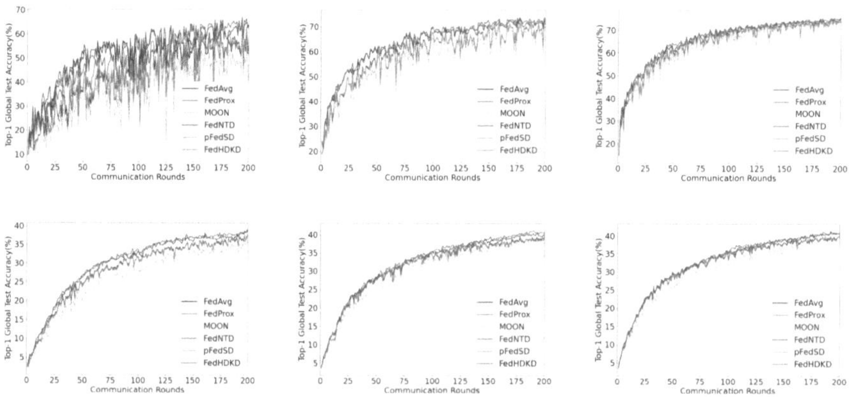

(a) $\alpha = 0.1$ (b) $\alpha = 0.5$ (c) $\alpha = 1.0$

Fig. 5. Learning curves of different methods on the CIFAR-10 and CIFAR-100 datasets under different Dirichlet parameters ($\alpha = 0.1, 0.5, 1.0$). From top to bottom, the dataset is CIFAR-10, CIFAR-100. The global test accuracy represents the performance of the global model on the test set.

The experimental results demonstrate the advantages of the dual KD method combining historical models in FedHDKD within heterogeneous data environments. This approach effectively improves the performance of the global model and overcomes the limitations of traditional algorithms under data heterogeneity. FedProx adds a proximal term to FedAvg to constrain local updates, enhancing model stability in heterogeneous data, but the results show that the proximal term's restriction suppresses the local model's adaptability to its own data, leading to slower convergence and affecting the final model performance. MOON uses model contrastive learning to mitigate the bias between the local and global models, but when data is highly imbalanced, learning feature representations is still limited, making it difficult to ensure the generalization of the global model. FedNTD retains global knowledge through KD on non-true classes to alleviate data heterogeneity, but it neglects the personalized knowledge of the local models. Compared to FedNTD, pFedSD transfers historical local knowledge through personalized distillation to improve local client training performance. However, it overlooks the generalization knowledge in the global model, leading to a gap in global test accuracy compared to FedHDKD.

Effects of Data Heterogeneity. On the CIFAR-10 and CIFAR-100 datasets, we simulate different levels of data heterogeneity by setting different Dirichlet distribution parameters $\alpha \in \{0.1, 0.5, 1.0\}$ for data partitioning. As α decreases, the data distribution becomes more imbalanced, and the data heterogeneity between clients becomes stronger. Figure 5 shows the global test accuracy trends for different methods under various α settings. From the experimental results, we observe that as data heterogeneity increases, the training curves become increasingly unstable, especially when $\alpha = 0.1$ (Fig. 5(a)), where the convergence of

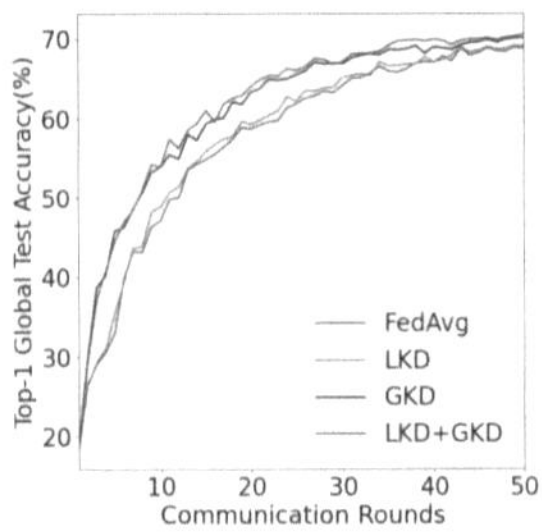

(a) Global test accuracy

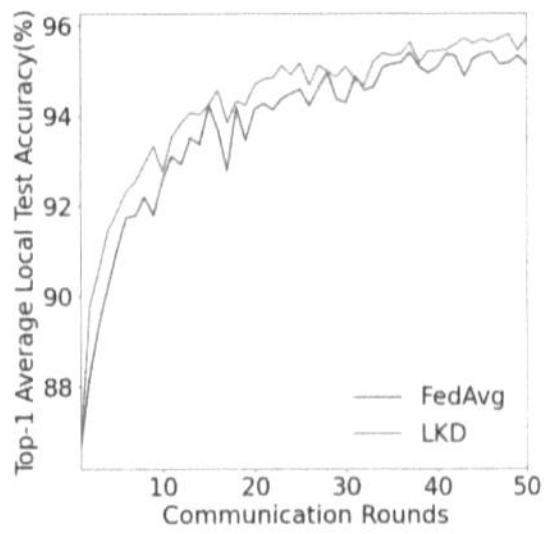

(b) Local test accuracy

Fig. 6. Performance comparison of FedHDKD and ablation variants on global and local test accuracy, conducted on the CIFAR-10 dataset.

some methods is poor, and model performance decreases significantly. The baseline methods, FedAvg and FedProx, which rely solely on simple aggregation of global models, struggle to effectively integrate global knowledge under high data heterogeneity, leading to large fluctuations in the curves. In contrast, pFedSD enhances the local model's adaptability through personalized self-distillation, but fails to significantly improve the global model's generalization ability. FedNTD and FedHDKD introduce global knowledge transfer through KD, showing better stability and higher accuracy throughout the training process. Among these, FedHDKD further combines the generalized knowledge accumulated in the historical global model with the personalized knowledge contained in the historical local models. This allows it to maintain higher test accuracy and more stable convergence under different data heterogeneity conditions, demonstrating its robustness in Non-IID scenarios.

Ablation Study. To validate the contributions of GKD and LKD in the FedHDKD framework, ablation experiments were conducted under a consistent data partitioning scheme with only $n = 10$ clients participating. The performance of models using only GKD, only LKD, and the full FedHDKD method was evaluated. GKD leverages weighted aggregation of historical global models as teachers to guide local training, enhancing long-term global knowledge transfer. Ablation results (Fig. 6(a)) show that models with only GKD outperform FedAvg significantly on the global test set, confirming its role in improving generalization under non-IID data. LKD uses the previous local model as a teacher to preserve personalized features, maintaining adaptability to each client's unique data. While its global test set improvement over FedAvg is slight (Fig. 6(a)), LKD excels in personalized performance on local test sets (Fig. 6(b)), helping alleviate the degradation of personalized knowledge. Combining GKD and LKD, FedHDKD balances global generalization and local personalization by integrating both historical knowledge types. It outperforms FedAvg and single-component models, demonstrating a synergistic effect that enhances stability and robustness in non-IID federated learning settings. These findings highlight the dual KD mechanism's effectiveness in preserving knowledge and improving model performance.

Table 2. Top-1 global test accuracy (%) of FedHDKD with different historical model list sizes under the $\alpha = 0.1$ setting.

List Size	MNIST	CIFAR-10	CIFAR-100
1	97.66	66.41	38.83
3	**97.68**	67.20	38.88
5	97.58	**67.41**	**39.47**
7	97.61	66.84	39.06
9	97.64	66.94	39.28

Effects of List Size. To find the optimal historical global model list size for the FedHDKD method, we conducted experiments with different hyperparameters for m, as shown in Table 2. The results show that on the MNIST dataset, the historical global model list size has a minimal impact on test accuracy, with the best performance achieved at $m = 3$. This is primarily because MNIST has simple grayscale digit patterns, allowing the model to converge quickly and requiring fewer historical models to capture global knowledge. Adding more historical models may introduce redundancy or unstable information from earlier training stages, harming performance. In contrast, the classification tasks in CIFAR-10 and CIFAR-100 are more complex, involving color images with higher inter-class similarity, thus a moderate number of historical global models significantly improves model performance, particularly when $m = 5$, where the global test accuracy reaches its peak (CIFAR-10: 67.41%, CIFAR-100: 39.47%). When the historical global model list is too small ($m = 1$), the model struggles to fully leverage past knowledge. Conversely, when there are too many historical global models, such as $m = 9$, outdated or redundant information may be introduced, affecting training stability. These findings suggest that, on complex datasets, carefully selecting the number of stored historical global models is crucial for the GKD effectiveness of FedHDKD.

5 Conclusion

This paper presented FedHDKD, a novel FL framework designed to address the challenges posed by data heterogeneity in heterogeneous FL environments. The method effectively combined historical models for dual KD, leveraging GKD to transfer global historical generalization knowledge, while using LKD to transmit local historical personalized knowledge. The dual KD mechanism enabled clients to retain the global model's generalization ability while maintaining the personalized adaptability of local data, thus enhancing model robustness and alleviating the challenges brought about by data heterogeneity. Experimental results showed that FedHDKD outperformed existing baseline algorithms in terms of model performance and stability under various data heterogeneity settings. While FedHDKD demonstrated significant advantages in improving model performance, the introduction of dual KD and historical model aggregation also incurred additional computational and communication costs. Future research would explore more efficient aggregation strategies and adaptive KD mechanisms to further enhance the efficiency and scalability of FL in real-world applications.

Acknowledgement. We thank the anonymous reviewers for their constructive comments. This work was supported in part by the National Natural Science Foundation of China under Grant 62272102; in part by the Natural Science Foundation of Fujian Province under Grant 2023J02014, 2024J08163; by the Foundation for Cultivated Young Talents of Fujian Province under Grant 2025350199; by the Fuzhou Municipal Science and Technology Plan Project for International Science and Technology Cooperation under Grant 2025-Y-009; by the Open Project of the Fujian Provincial University Engineering Research Center for Intelligent Systems in Manufacturing in 2025 (Project No. ZNXT26-01); by the Open Topics from the Lion Rock Labs of Cyberspace Security under Project LRL24011; by the Minjiang University Scientific Research Startup Fund for Introduced Talents under Grant MJY25019.

References

1. Li, Q., et al.: A survey on federated learning systems: vision, hype and reality for data privacy and protection. IEEE Trans. Knowl. Data Eng. **35**(4), 3347–3366 (2021)
2. Bi, R., Xiong, J., Li, Q., Liu, X., Tian, Y.: Fppnet: fast privacy-preserving neural network via three-party arithmetic secret sharing. In: International Conference on Mobile Computing, Applications, and Services, pp. 165–178. Springer, Heidelberg (2022)
3. McMahan, B., Moore, E., Ramage, D., Hampson, S., y Arcas, B.A.: Communication-efficient learning of deep networks from decentralized data. In: Artificial Intelligence and Statistics, pp. 1273–1282. PMLR (2017)
4. Li, J., Tian, Y., Zhou, Z., Xiang, A., Wang, S., Xiong, J.: Psfl: ensuring data privacy and model security for federated learning. IEEE Internet Things J. **11**(15), 26234–26252 (2024)
5. Han, Y., Zhang, X.: Robust federated learning via collaborative machine teaching. In: Proceedings of the AAAI Conference on Artificial Intelligence, vol. 34, pp. 4075–4082 (2020)
6. Zhao, Y., Li, M., Lai, L., Suda, N., Civin, D., Chandra, V.: Federated learning with non-iid data. arXiv preprint arXiv:1806.00582 (2018)
7. Kairouz, P., et al.: Advances and open problems in federated learning. Found. Trends® Mach. Learn. **14**(1–2), 1–210 (2021)
8. Shang, X., Lu, Y., Huang, G., Wang, H.: Federated learning on heterogeneous and long-tailed data via classifier re-training with federated features. arXiv preprint arXiv:2204.13399 (2022)
9. Jeong, E., Oh, S., Kim, H., Park, J., Bennis, M., Kim, S.L.: Communication-efficient on-device machine learning: federated distillation and augmentation under non-iid private data. arXiv preprint arXiv:1811.11479 (2018)
10. Hinton, G., Vinyals, O., Dean, J.: Distilling the knowledge in a neural network. arXiv preprint arXiv:1503.02531 (2015)

11. Li, D., Wang, J.: Fedmd: heterogenous federated learning via model distillation. arXiv preprint arXiv:1910.03581 (2019)
12. Itahara, S., Nishio, T., Koda, Y., Morikura, M., Yamamoto, K.: Distillation-based semi-supervised federated learning for communication-efficient collaborative training with non-iid private data. IEEE Trans. Mob. Comput. **22**(1), 191–205 (2021)
13. Li, T., Sahu, A.K., Zaheer, M., Sanjabi, M., Talwalkar, A., Smith, V.: Federated optimization in heterogeneous networks. Proc. Mach. Learn. Syst. **2**, 429–450 (2020)
14. Li, Q., He, B., Song, D.: Model-contrastive federated learning. In: Proceedings of the IEEE/CVF Conference on Computer Vision and Pattern Recognition, pp. 10713–10722 (2021)
15. Karimireddy, S.P., Kale, S., Mohri, M., Reddi, S., Stich, S., Suresh, A.T.: Scaffold: stochastic controlled averaging for federated learning. In: International Conference on Machine Learning, pp. 5132–5143. PMLR (2020)
16. Wang, J., Liu, Q., Liang, H., Joshi, G., Poor, H.V.: Tackling the objective inconsistency problem in heterogeneous federated optimization. Adv. Neural. Inf. Process. Syst. **33**, 7611–7623 (2020)
17. Dhar, P., Singh, R.V., Peng, K.C., Wu, Z., Chellappa, R.: Learning without memorizing. In: Proceedings of the IEEE/CVF Conference on Computer Vision and Pattern Recognition, pp. 5138–5146 (2019)
18. Lee, G., Jeong, M., Shin, Y., Bae, S., Yun, S.Y.: Preservation of the global knowledge by not-true distillation in federated learning. Adv. Neural. Inf. Process. Syst. **35**, 38461–38474 (2022)
19. Jin, H., et al.: Personalized edge intelligence via federated self-knowledge distillation. IEEE Trans. Parallel Distrib. Syst. **34**(2), 567–580 (2022)
20. Chen, W., Bhardwaj, K., Marculescu, R.: Fedmax: mitigating activation divergence for accurate and communication-efficient federated learning. In: Joint European Conference on Machine Learning and Knowledge Discovery in Databases, pp. 348–363. Springer, Heidelberg (2020)
21. Zhu, Z., Hong, J., Zhou, J.: Data-free knowledge distillation for heterogeneous federated learning. In: International Conference on Machine Learning, pp. 12878–12889. PMLR (2021)
22. Huang, J., Zhang, Y., Bi, R., Lin, J., Xiong, J.: Knowledge distillation enables federated learning: a data-free federated aggregation scheme. In: 2024 International Joint Conference on Neural Networks (IJCNN), pp. 1–7. IEEE (2024)
23. Shang, E., Liu, H., Yang, Z., Du, J., Ge, Y.: Fedbikd: federated bidirectional knowledge distillation for distracted driving detection. IEEE Internet Things J. **10**(13), 11643–11654 (2023)
24. Qi, P., Zhou, X., Ding, Y., Zhang, Z., Zheng, S., Li, Z.: Fedbkd: heterogenous federated learning via bidirectional knowledge distillation for modulation classification in iot-edge system. IEEE J. Selected Topics Signal Process. **17**(1), 189–204 (2022)
25. Jiang, X., Sun, S., Wang, Y., Liu, M.: Towards federated learning against noisy labels via local self-regularization. In: Proceedings of the 31st ACM International Conference on Information & Knowledge Management, pp. 862–873 (2022)
26. Bai, D., et al.: Overcoming noisy labels in federated learning through local self-guiding. In: 2023 IEEE/ACM 23rd International Symposium on Cluster, Cloud and Internet Computing (CCGrid), pp. 367–376. IEEE (2023)
27. He, Y., Chen, Y., Yang, X., Yu, H., Huang, Y.H., Gu, Y.: Learning critically: selective self-distillation in federated learning on non-iid data. IEEE Trans. Big Data **10**(6), 789–800 (2024)

28. Liu, S., Feng, X., Zheng, H.: Overcoming forgetting in local adaptation of federated learning model. In: Pacific-Asia Conference on Knowledge Discovery and Data Mining, pp. 613–625. Springer, Heidelberg (2022)

Location-Based LLM (LLLM): Trip Purpose Estimation Using Language Models of Location Data

Mizuki Miura[1(✉)], Naoto Takeda[2], and Daisuke Kamisaka[1]

[1] KDDI Research, Inc., Saitama 356-8502, Japan
mi-miura@kddi.com
[2] KDDI Corporation, Tokyo 102-8460, Japan
https://www.kddi-research.jp/english/

Abstract. Understanding human mobility is essential for addressing urban challenges such as congestion and sustainability. While smartphone location data offers a valuable source for large-scale behavioral modeling, conventional methods relying on structured annotations or rule-based inference limit scalability and generalizability. Moreover, raw GPS trajectories lack semantic context, making trip purpose inference difficult. To address these issues, we propose the Location-based Large Language Model (LLLM), an adaptation of BERT that treats sequences of discretized spatiotemporal coordinates as linguistic tokens. Focusing on trip purpose—a key semantic dimension in urban mobility—, LLLM is pre-trained on large volumes of unlabeled trip data and fine-tuned with a small set of labeled examples for classification. We evaluated LLLM using smartphone GPS data from two cities in Japan, demonstrating that incorporating contextual features such as estimated home location and workplace improves classification accuracy—particularly for mid-scale trip purposes like shopping. We also find that corpus size, rather than spatial resolution, has a greater impact on classification performance.

Keywords: Location-based LLM · Trip purpose estimation · BERT

1 Background

Understanding human mobility is essential for addressing urban challenges such as congestion and sustainability, with mobile data enabling large-scale behavioral analysis. However, prior studies have used traditional machine learning to infer travel mode or trip purpose from GPS data, typically relying on hand-crafted features or rule-based methods. These approaches depend heavily on annotated data or static heuristics, which are costly to scale and often fail to generalize across diverse populations [1–3]. Without such annotations, raw location data lack semantic context, making it difficult to capture user intent or trip purpose.

L. Zhang and K.-K. R. Choo (Eds.): MobiQuitous 2025, LNICST 683, pp. 167–177, 2026.
https://doi.org/10.1007/978-3-032-22500-9_10

To address this, recent work has begun to explore the application of natural language processing (NLP) techniques to human mobility analysis. In particular, large language models (LLMs) [4] have shown strong capabilities in learning contextual representations from large-scale sequential data. Unlike conventional models, LLMs can extract latent behavioral patterns in a context-aware, data-driven manner without relying on manually defined rules or extensive annotations. These models have attracted growing attention for their potential to uncover deeper semantic structure in human mobility.

In this study, we focus on trip purpose—a key semantic dimension in urban mobility—as a target task for evaluating LLM-based modeling. We propose the Location-based Large Language Model (LLLM), an adaptation of BERT [5] for mobility analysis. Trip purpose refers not only to large-scale routine activitis for workplace and for home, but also to mid-scale activities for shopping. LLLM treats sequences of discretized locations (grid cell IDs) as linguistic tokens and models each trip as a sentence-like unit. The model is trained in two stages: pre-training on large volumes of unlabeled trip data to learn contextual representations, followed by fine-tuning on a small set of labeled trips to classify trip purposes.

We evaluate LLLM using smartphone GPS data from two cities in Japan—Utsunomiya and Tsukuba. Results show that incorporating contextual spatial features, such as estimated home location and workplace, improves classification accuracy, particularly for mid-scale trip purposes like shopping and personal errands. We also find that corpus size, rather than spatial resolution alone, strongly affects classification performance, with intermediate vocabulary sizes yielding optimal results for certain categories. LLLM thus enables semantic inference from raw location data in a scalable and annotation-efficient manner, offering a generalizable and context-aware framework for mobility modeling in diverse urban environments.

2 Related Work

Smartphone location data has emerged as a valuable resource for modeling human mobility patterns and is widely used as a complement to conventional travel surveys [6]. Crucial information such as trip purpose or behavioral motivation is not directly observable from raw spatiotemporal traces [7]. To address this, prior studies have explored supervised learning with annotated datasets [8], rule-based inference using PoI (Point of Interest) data [9], and clustering heuristics [10]. However, these traditional machine learning methods often rely on labor-intensive annotations [1] or brittle heuristics [2], limiting scalability and generalizability across diverse urban contexts [3].

More recently, researchers have begun to treat location data as a form of language, applying NLP techniques—including both classical embedding models and LLMs—to embed locations into vector spaces that capture sequential context [7]. For example, Shoji et al. [11] applied a word2vec-style model, a classical NLP technique for learning distributed word representations, by treating

GPS points as words and trajectories as sentences. Tamura et al. [12] generated pseudo-population flows from unlabeled GPS data using fine-grained 50-meter grid cell IDs. These studies demonstrated that mobility patterns can be modeled without explicit annotations by leveraging unsupervised embedding techniques. LLM-based techniques have since expanded to broader mobility-related tasks such as movement state classification [13], demand forecasting [14], and macro-scale flow analysis [15]. Mizuno et al. [16] further applied GPT-2 to generate full-day mobility trajectories, highlighting growing interest in using LLMs to capture not just motion, but behavioral logic.

Nevertheless, many of these LLM-based models focus on replicating realistic movement sequences conditioned on check-in histories [18] or PoI categories [19], emphasizing spatial accuracy while overlooking the semantic intent behind mobility. The lack of labeled data for user intent—such as trip purpose—has left most models either pattern-oriented or reliant on static prompts. As a result, generated trajectories may appear realistic but lack cognitive depth.

3 Proposal Method

To address this, we propose the LLLM, a novel adaptation of BERT [5] for mobility modeling. Focusing on trip purpose—a key semantic dimension in urban mobility—, LLLM treats trip-level sequences of discretized regional grid cell IDs as sentence-like inputs and incorporates auxiliary features derived from raw GPS data, without requiring annotations. The model is pre-trained in a self-supervised manner to learn latent behavioral representations, then fine-tuned on a small labeled dataset for trip purpose classification. By leveraging BERT's contextual learning in a geospatial domain, LLLM bridges the gap between semantic understanding and spatial behavior, offering a scalable and interpretable framework for intent-aware mobility modeling.

In NLP, data are typically represented as sequences of "words" forming "sentences," a structure analogous to behavioral sequences such as human mobility patterns. Just as a word's meaning depends on its context, the semantic role of a location can vary depending on trip purpose—for instance, a train station might be a commute origin, a leisure destination, or a transfer point, depending on the user's intent.

BERT (Bidirectional Encoder Representations from Transformers) [5], a widely used NLP model, excels at learning contextual representations via unsupervised pre-training. This makes it particularly suitable for modeling location semantics from unlabeled smartphone GPS data. In this study, we extend the BERT framework to mobility data, enabling trip purpose inference with limited supervision.

Our approach involves pre-training on sequences of grid cell IDs representing individual trips, augmented with auxiliary features from raw GPS data. The model is then fine-tuned on a small set of labeled trips, without using explicit geographic metadata or map information. Instead, it learns semantic similarity between locations and trips purely from spatiotemporal patterns. Figure 1 illustrates the four key components of our method: preprocessing, trip encoding, pre-training, and fine-tuning, each described in the following subsections.

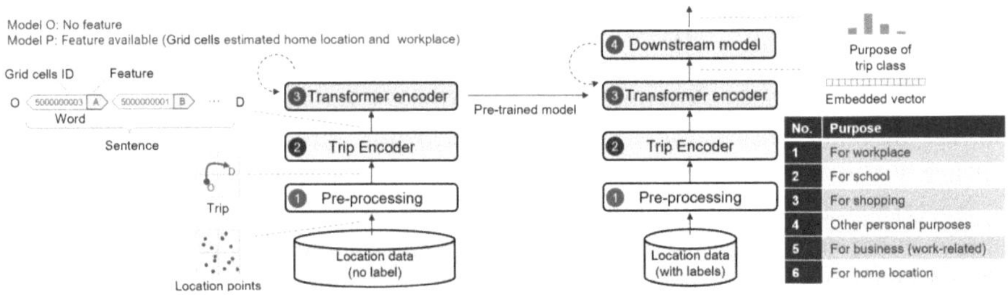

Fig. 1. System overview of the LLLM.

Preprocessing. The trip encoder extracts features and tokenizes location data into sequence-structured inputs for pre-training, analogous to words and sentences in NLP. Here, words" correspond to regional grid cell IDs and a sentence" to a single trip from an origin to a destination.

To generate these sequences, we first segment the raw GPS data into trips. A trip is defined as the trajectory between two temporally and spatially distinct stay points, which are inferred by evaluating inter-point distance and time thresholds based on the method proposed in [20]. This process identifies whether a user is moving or stationary and ensures that each trip reflects a coherent unit of mobility behavior.

Each GPS point is then mapped to a fixed-size regional grid cell ID, using Japan's quarter mesh system (approximately 250 m per side) to discretize continuous spatial coordinates. Consecutive points falling within the same grid cell are compressed into a single token to account for variable GPS sampling intervals and avoid redundancy. For instance, a sequence like A, A, A, B, C, C is encoded as A, B, C.

To incorporate contextual information such as temporal attributes or inferred user features (e.g., home/workplace estimation), we define subword tokens [21] and concatenate them to the main grid cell ID. This forms a compound token (e.g., "5000000012 5000000014") representing both spatial and contextual semantics. Tokens within a trip are separated by spaces, and a newline is used to mark trip boundaries. The resulting corpus is structured similarly to natural language text, enabling effective application of language modeling objectives.

Pre-training. For pre-training, we adopt the Masked Language Model (MLM) objective, as in standard BERT. In this self-supervised setup, some tokens (grid cell IDs) in the trip sequence are randomly masked, and the model is trained to predict them from surrounding context. Although this may seem straightforward, the model receives no explicit information about grid cell IDs systems, spatial proximity, or coordinates, and must learn semantic and spatial patterns implicitly.

Currently, grid cell IDs and subword features are not distinguished during training, so subword features may be incorrectly treated as classification targets. To prevent this, we adjust the training objective to predict only the grid cell IDs portion of each token, excluding subword features from the classification scope.

Fine-Tuning. For trip purpose estimation, we use the contextualized trip-level embeddings from the pre-trained model as input features to a classifier. We employ a three-layer Multi-Layer Perceptron (MLP) [22], trained on a separate dataset with ground truth trip purpose labels. During fine-tuning, classification errors are backpropagated to update the pre-trained model parameters, improving its performance on the classification task.

4 Evaluation Experiment

4.1 Dataset

For the pre-training phase, we used location data collected over a five-month period from March 1 to July 31, 2019, in two regional core cities in Japan: Utsunomiya City (Tochigi Prefecture) and Tsukuba City (Ibaraki Prefecture). The data consists of GPS location traces obtained with user consent from smartphone users, provided by KDDI Corporation. The total number of user IDs in the two cities used in the analysis was 61,846. To evaluate the effect of feature augmentation, we prepared two datasets to train models with/without features as follows:

Model O: No additional features—input consists only of grid cell IDs.
Model P: With features—includes estimated home location and workplace.

Home and workplace locations were inferred from raw location data based on the grid cell ID with the highest dwell frequency during nighttime and daytime hours, respectively. These features were derived solely from smartphone data, without requiring manual annotations or external surveys. We used quarter regional cells (approximately 250 m per side) as the spatial unit [23].

Trip purposes were defined according to the 2019 Person Trip Survey [25] by the Tokyo Metropolitan Area Transport Planning Council, comprising six categories: (1) For workplace, (2) For school, (3) For shopping, (4) Other personal purposes, (5) For business (work-related), and (6) For home.

We used GPS data from the "Utsunomiya MaaS Social Demonstration" [24], a two-month field experiment conducted from August 21 to October 20, 2019, involving 147 participants. A dedicated mobile app collected the GPS data. To correct for timing mismatches between user inputs and actual movements, we refined trip-purpose annotations using GPS-based stay and movement intervals. Users manually recorded trip purpose for each trip via the app interface. Each trip was thus assigned a single ground-truth label—for instance, commuting to work was labeled (1), and a visit to a hospital was labeled (4). Finally, we obtained 1,436 trips of GPS data with labels of trip purposes for the evaluation.

4.2 Evaluation Criteria

We implemented BERT using the open-source Transformers library by Hugging Face [26], following the standard architecture of 12 transformer layers, a hidden size of 768, and 12 self-attention heads [5]. To evaluate the pre-trained models (Model O and P), we measured the Top-100 accuracy on the MLM task [22], defined as the proportion of masked grid cell IDs correctly predicted within the top 100 candidates. Model O and P achieved accuracies of 93.8% and 96.3%, respectively. Further details on MLM evaluation can be found in related work [27].

For the downstream trip purpose classification, we used a MLP with 50 hidden units and cross-entropy loss, evaluated via three-fold cross-validation based on user IDs (for example, a user A appearing in the test data is not included in the training data). F1 score was used as the evaluation metric. As a baseline, we implemented LightGBM (LGBM) [28], a gradient boosting framework. We also used embeddings from our pre-trained BERT models as input features for LGBM: LGBM(O) using Model O embeddings, and LGBM(P) using Model P embeddings, which include contextual features like home location and workplace.

We hypothesized that reducing the vocabulary size through token aggregation could encourage the model to identify semantic similarities across distinct grid cells by partially unifying them under shared tokens. This compression may lead to faster learning and improved classification performance, particularly by enhancing the model's ability to generalize in sparse-data conditions. To evaluate this, we prepared four corpus configurations with vocabulary size limits of 10,000, 20,000, 100,000, and 1,000,000, to examine the trade-off between representational granularity and generalization.

4.3 Evaluation Results

The evaluation results (F1 scores) for both the proposed method and the baseline models are presented in Fig. 2 . Overall, we observed the following trends. The LGBM(O) exhibited the lowest average classification performance with a mean F1 score of 0.20. The BERT(O) followed closely with an average of 0.23. In both LGBM(P) and BERT(P) consistently outperformed LGBM(O) and BERT(O) counterparts: LGBM(P) noted an average F1 score of 0.23, while the BERT(P) noted the highest overall score with an average of 0.29.

These findings suggest important implications for modeling human mobility and trip purpose classification using location data. The consistent improvement in F1 scores from O models (without features) to P models (with features) across both LGBM and BERT demonstrates that incorporating contextual spatial features—specifically home location and workplace grid cell IDs—provides valuable information for enhancing classification performance. This is especially notable given the low dimensionality of the input (grid cell IDs alone) and the absence of explicit semantic annotations. While prior studies on transportation mode classification [13] found that home location and workplace IDs—used as proxy features—did not improve classification performance under user-based

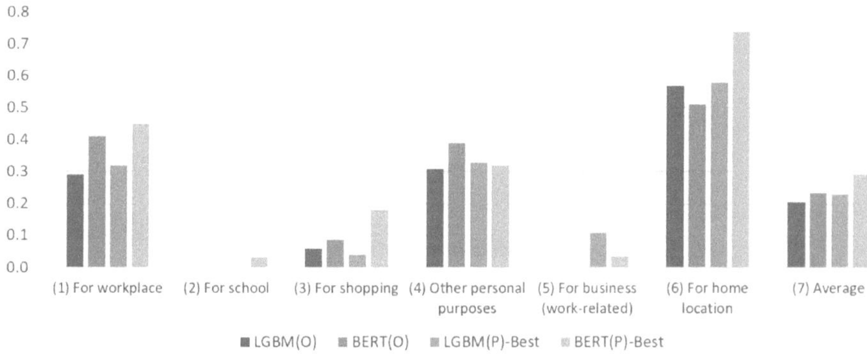

Fig. 2. Estimation results (F1 scores) by trip purpose.

cross-validation, our results show that such features are effective for trip purpose estimation. In particular, including stable location indicators helps the model better distinguish infrequent purposes.

When examining classification performance across individual trip purpose categories, substantial variation was observed. The F1 score for (2) For school was 0.00 for all models except BERT(P), and for (5) For business (work-related), both LGBM(O) and BERT(O) failed completely. These outcomes likely reflect training data biases, particularly underrepresentation of these classes in the labeled survey used for fine-tuning, which limited the models' ability to generalize.

In contrast, the models performed well on more common purposes—(6) For home exceeded an F1 score of 0.74, and (1) For workplace consistently scored above 0.45—demonstrating the framework's effectiveness when sufficient training data is available. Notably, for (3) For shopping, BERT(P) outperformed all other models, showing a clear advantage in capturing this mid-frequency, context-sensitive purpose. These results highlight the benefit of incorporating spatially stable behavioral cues. Unlike LGBM, which relies on aggregated features and may struggle with sparse or loosely structured inputs, BERT's sequence modeling captures fine-grained behavioral differences—even from symbolic representations like grid cell IDs.

We formulated the hypothesis that how tokens are segmented—specifically, whether the grid cell IDs and its associated feature are treated as a single token or split into separate tokens—could significantly influence learning dynamics. To evaluate this, we compared the model classification performance with different corpus sizes: 10,000, 20,000, 100,000 and 1,000,000. We then assessed the classification accuracy of the LGBM(P) and BERT(P)—shown earlier to yield the best classification performance—under each corpus size configuration (Fig. 3).

As a result, we found that while overall classification performance differences between LGBM and BERT were modest, their accuracy varied considerably across trip purposes depending on corpus size. (6)For home, LGBM(P) showed stable classification performance regardless of corpus size, whereas BERT(P)

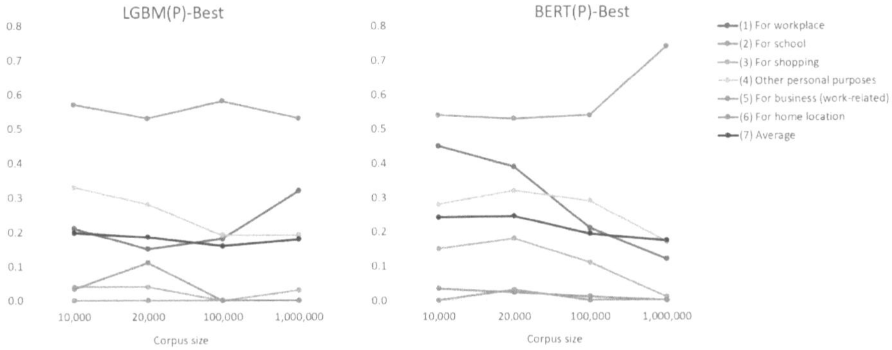

Fig. 3. Trip purpose estimation with different corpus sizes.

improved with larger corpora, reaching 0.74 at a copus size of 1,000,000. This suggests that BERT benefits from larger corpora when modeling highly regular trip patterns. In contrast, (1)For workplace, LGBM(P) improved with corpus size, increasing from 0.15 to 0.32 at the largest setting. BERT(P), however, performed best at a smaller corpus size of 10,000, achieving 0.45. This decline with larger vocabularies may be due to overfitting to infrequent or user-specific tokens, limiting generalization in user-independent settings.

These contrasting trends suggest that there is no universally optimal corpus size; rather, the ideal setting depends on both the model architecture and the specific trip purpose. BERT performs well with large vocabularies for repetitive purposes like (6) For home, but smaller vocabularies may be preferable for purposes with greater behavioral variability like (1) For workplace. Notably, for medium-frequency categories such as (3) For shopping and (4) Other personal purposes, the best classification performance was observed at a corpus size of 20,000. This highlights the need for future methods that can adapt corpus size based on the semantics of the classification target. Corpus design thus emerges as a key lever in mobility modeling, and dynamic tokenization may offer a promising direction for balancing contextual richness and generalization.

5 Conclusion

In this study, we extended the BERT framework to human mobility by applying it to the task of inferring the semantic purpose of stay locations. We developed a novel model—the Location-based Large Language Model (LLLM)—that learns high-level behavioral representations from sequential smartphone location data and predicts trip purposes using only a small amount of labeled data. Our findings reveal two key contributions: the effectiveness of incorporating contextual spatial features, such as home location and workplace, and the importance of corpus design in geospatial sequence modeling. We conclude by discussing the study's limitations and directions for future work.

Key Contributions. Incorporating contextual spatial features—specifically home location and workplace—consistently improves classification performance across both LGBM and BERT, particularly for infrequent or ambiguous trip purposes. When embedded within a language-model-based architecture, these stable location features enhance semantic inference from raw location data. The proposed LLLM thus offers a scalable, annotation-efficient solution for modeling human mobility with greater precision and interpretability.

We also show that corpus size, defined by the granularity of grid cell IDs discretization, has a substantial and non-monotonic impact on classification accuracy. Classification performance varies not only between model types (e.g., LGBM vs. BERT) but also across trip purposes. BERT benefits from fine-grained vocabularies for repetitive and localized trips, while coarser vocabularies perform better for more spatially diverse purposes. For mid-scale categories such as (3) For shopping and (4) Other personal purposes, the highest accuracy was achieved at an intermediate vocabulary size.

Limitations and Future Tasks. Classification performance varied across trip purposes, with categories like (2) For school and (5) For business scoring zero in all models except BERT(P), likely due to class imbalance and limited labeled data. This highlights the need for more balanced training and the use of few-shot learning or data augmentation for rare classes. Future work should also examine adaptive tokenization strategies—such as learning token boundaries or class-specific vocabularies—to improve generalization while preserving semantic structure.

While the study concludes that corpus size affects performance more than spatial resolution, the latter was not directly analyzed. Although corpus size reflects token granularity to some extent, a more explicit analysis—e.g., varying mesh size or grid systems—is needed to clarify the impact of spatial resolution on model behavior.

We found that an intermediate corpus size (e.g., 20,000 tokens) yielded the best results for mid-scale purposes like (3) For shopping and (4) Other personal purposes, although optimal granularity varied by trip type. This highlights the benefit of dynamic tokenization that adjusts resolution based on class semantics. Smaller vocabularies promote generalization by identifying shared spatial patterns—coarsening regions in rural areas via higher-order digits, while preserving finer detail in urban areas. However, resolution is ultimately limited by the base grid; for example, distinctions between an office and a store within a 250-meter cell remain unobservable. Future work may address this by integrating POI-level features to support finer-grained inference in dense regions.

At last, the smartphone GPS dataset used in this study cannot be made publicly available due to data governance and privacy policies. We plan to release the codebase and corpus generation scripts (excluding proprietary data) in a future version.

References

1. Nguyen, M.H., Schmöcker, J.D., Fujii, S.: Reviewing trip purpose imputation in GPS-based travel surveys. Transp. Rev. **40**(3), 369–391 (2020)
2. Saygin, Y., Duygulu, P., Gurgen, F.: Semantic annotation of GPS trajectories. In: Proceedings of the 11th International Conference on Discovery Science (DS 2008), pp. 240–254. Springer, Heidelberg (2008)
3. Gong, L., Liu, X., Wu, L., Liu, Y.: Inferring trip purposes and uncovering travel patterns from taxi trajectory data. Cartogr. Geogr. Inf. Sci. **43**(2), 103–114 (2016)
4. Brown, T.B., et al.: Language models are few-shot learners. Adv. Neural. Inf. Process. Syst. **33**, 1877–1901 (2020)
5. Devlin, J., Chang, M.-W., Lee, K., Toutanova, K.: BERT: pre-training of deep bidirectional transformers for language understanding. In: Proceedings of the 2019 Conference of the North American Chapter of the Association for Computational Linguistics: Human Language Technologies, vol. 1 (Long and Short Papers), pp. 4171–4186 (2019)
6. Uegaki, M., Amano, T., Yamaguchi, H.: Simulating urban pedestrian flows by fusing wide-area location data and spot pedestrian counts. In: Proceedings of the 21st EAI International Conference on Mobile and Ubiquitous Systems: Computing, Networking and Services (EAI MobiQuitous 2024), Oslo, Norway, pp. 1109–1116 (2024)
7. Lin, Y., Wan, H., Guo, S., Lin, Y.: Pre-training context and time aware location embeddings from spatial-temporal trajectories for user next location prediction. In: Proceedings of the AAAI Conference on Artificial Intelligence, vol. 35, no. 5, pp. 4241–4248 (2021)
8. Gao, Q., Molloy, J., Axhausen, K.W.: Trip purpose imputation using GPS trajectories with machine learning. ISPRS Int. J. Geo Inf. **10**(11), 775 (2021)
9. Sivakumar, T.Dhananjaya, D.D.: Inferring the purposes of taxi trips using GPS and POI data considering the destination context. In: 2021 IEEE International Conference on Digital Advances in Biomedical and Biological Research (ICDABI), pp. 1–6 (2021)
10. Chen, C., Liao, C., Xie, X.: Trip2Vec: a deep embedding approach for clustering and profiling taxi trip purposes. Pers. Ubiq. Comput. **23**(1–2), 53–66 (2019)
11. Shoji, Y., Takahashi, K., Dürst, M. J., Yamamoto, Y., Ohshima, H.: Location2Vec: generating distributed representation of location by using geo-tagged microblog posts. In: Proceedings of the International Conference on Social Informatics (SocInfo 2018), Lecture Notes in Computer Science (LNCS), vol. 11257, pp. 95–110. Springer, Heidelberg (2018)
12. Tamura, N., Urano, K., Aoki, S., Yonezawa, T., Kawaguchi, N. : Agent2Vec: a mobility modeling model based on unsupervised learning. In: Hara, T., Yamaguchi, H. (Eds.), Mobile and Ubiquitous Systems: Computing, Networking and Services (Lecture Notes of the Institute for Computer Sciences, Social Informatics and Telecommunications Engineering, vol. 419, pp. 553–567. Springer, Heidelberg (2022)
13. Kamisaka, D., Kobayashi, A., Takeda, N., Minamikawa, A., Morimoto, A.: BERT-based transportation mode prediction using smartphone data. In: Proceedings of the 64th Annual Conference of the Japan Society of Civil Engineers (2021)
14. Yuan, Y., Ding, J., Han, C., Jin, D., Li, Y.: UniFlow: a foundation model for unified urban spatio-temporal flow prediction. IEEE Trans. Smart Cities **2**(3), 345–359 (2020)

15. Fang, X., et al.: Foundation models for spatio-temporal data in human mobility forecasting. J. Spatio-Temporal Data Sci. **5**(1), 1–25 (2023)
16. Mizuno, T., Fujimoto, S., Ishikawa, A.: Generation of individual daily trajectories by GPT-2. Front. Phys. **10**, 102117 (2022)
17. Solatorio, A.V.: GeoFormer: predicting human mobility using generative pre-trained transformer (GPT). In: HuMob-Challenge '23, Hamburg, Germany, 13 November 2023 (2023)
18. Gong, L., et al.: Mobility-LLM: learning visiting intentions and travel preferences from human mobility data with large language models. In: Proceedings of the 38th Conference on Neural Information Processing Systems (NeurIPS 2024) (2024)
19. Wang, J., et al.: Large language models as urban residents: an LLM agent framework for personal mobility generation. In: Proceedings of the 38th Conference on Neural Information Processing Systems (NeurIPS 2024) (2024)
20. Kobayashi, N., Ishizuka, H., Minamikawa, A., Muramatsu, S., Ono, T.: A proposal of stay/move state estimation method suitable for mobile phone communication history. Trans. Inf. Process. Soc. Jpn. Databases (TOD) **10**(1), 13–23 (2017)
21. Sennrich, R., Haddow, B., Birch, A.: Neural machine translation of rare words with subword units. In: Proceedings of the 54th Annual Meeting of the Association for Computational Linguistics, Berlin, Germany, August 2016, vol. 1: Long Papers, pp. 1715–1725 (2016)
22. Murtagh, F.: Multilayer perceptrons for classification and regression. Neurocomputing **2**(5), 183–197 (1991)
23. JIS (Japan Industrial Standard) X 0410 'Grid Square Code'. https://github.com/UchidaMizuki/jpgrid/blob/main/README.en.md. Accessed 20 June 2025
24. Miyawaki, T., Tomioka, H., Takayama, K., Morimoto, A.: Study on the change in traffic behavior upon the introduction of MaaS by utilizing smartphone location information data. J. City Plan. Inst. Jpn. **55**(3), 637–644 (2020)
25. Person Trip Survey in the Tokyo Metropolitan Region. https://www.e-stat.go.jp/en/statistics/00600550. Accessed 20 June 2025
26. Hugging Face: Hugging Face Open-Source Libraries. https://github.com/huggingface. Accessed 20 June 2025
27. Kobayashi, A., Uesaka, D., Takeda, N., Minamikawa, A.: Representation learning techniques for travel demand prediction using large-scale location data. In: Proceedings of the 64th Annual Conference of the Japan Society of Civil Engineers, Planning Section, 64, ROMBUNNO.32-06 (2021)
28. Ke, G., et al.: LightGBM: a highly efficient gradient boosting decision tree. In: Proceedings of the 31st International Conference on Neural Information Processing Systems (NeurIPS 2017), pp. 3149–3157 (2017)

A Low-Resource Vision Transformer Accelerator for Edge Applications

Yunxiang Zhang[1], Xianglin Wei[1(✉)], Bin Wang[1], and Mingyi Pang[2]

[1] The Sixty-third Research Institute, National University of Defense Technology, Nanjing 210007, China
{zhangyx6153,weixianglin}@nudt.edu.cn

[2] Nanjing University of Information Science and Technology, Nanjing 210044, China

Abstract. Vision Transformer (ViT) models have recently demonstrated superior performance in computer vision tasks by effectively capturing image features. However, their complex network architecture and significant computational demands present substantial barriers to deployment on resource-constrained edge devices (limited in computational power, energy and area), while existing hardware accelerators are often not optimized for such highly constrained environments. To address these challenges, wepropose LoRViA, a <u>Lo</u>w-<u>R</u>esource <u>Vi</u>sion Transformer <u>A</u>ccelerator for edge applications. First, we design a generalized adaptive Block Double-buffered Processing Element (BD-PE) to efficiently accelerate the matrix operations prevalent in the multi-head self-attention mechanism and the fully-connected layers. This unit enables flexible adjustment of Digital Signal Processor (DSP) resource utilization through parameter configuration and further improves throughput by adopting a multi-layer double-buffering mechanism, enabling it to adapt to edge devices with scarce DSP resources. Secondly, we devise a hardware-friendly, low-resource implementation for non-linear modules such as Softmax and GELU activation functions, striking a balance between computational speed and resource consumption. We deploy LoRViA on a Xilinx Zynq-7020 platform, with experimental evaluations confirming an energy efficiency of 2.07 GOPS/W. Compared to existing FPGA-based ViT accelerators, LoRViA reduces Look Up Table (LUT) resource consumption by at least 60.37% and achieves up to 3.45× improvement in per-DSP energy efficiency.

Keywords: Vision Transformer · FPGA · Hardware Accelerator · Edge Applications

1 Introduction

Recently, Vision Transformer (ViT) architectures, including ViT [1], Swin Transformer [2], Transformer in Transformer [3], and Data-Efficient Image Trans-

This study was supported partially by the National Natural Science Foundation of China (NSFC) under Grant No. 62571539.

L. Zhang and K.-K. R. Choo (Eds.): MobiQuitous 2025, LNICST 683, pp. 178–192, 2026.
https://doi.org/10.1007/978-3-032-22500-9_11

former (DeiT) [4], have revolutionized computer vision through their powerful global feature association capabilities. These models have established new performance benchmarks across multiple tasks, surpassing traditional convolutional neural networks (CNNs). The multi-head self-attention (MSA) mechanism enhances cross-region feature interactions, significantly improving representation capacity and generalization performance in core applications like image classification and object detection [2]. However, hardware deployment of ViT faces significant challenges for resource-constrained edge devices such as autonomous vehicles and Unmanned Aerial Vehicles (UAVs). Their complex architectures exhibit high computational complexity, substantial memory requirements, and resource-intensive non-linear operations including LayerNorm, Softmax, and GELU [5]. These demanding computational characteristics necessitate intricate hardware implementations that exceed typical edge device capabilities.

Although existing research has proposed various ViT hardware accelerators for FPGA to improve inference efficiency, including model size reduction [6–8], model pruning and quantization [9–11], and algorithm optimization [12,13], most existing solutions are not adequately adapted to extreme resource constraints in edge computing environments. Typical low-end FPGA platforms such as the Zynq-7020, equipped with only 220 DSP slices and limited on-chip memory, exhibit critical limitations: restricted parallel processing capability, constrained on-chip storage, and insufficient off-chip bandwidth [14]. These resource characteristics prevent effective deployment of accelerators designed for resource-limited platforms. Consequently, developing specialized ViT accelerators capable of operating under stringent resource conditions becomes essential. To bridge this gap, this paper proposes LoRViA for edge applications, with primary contributions including:

- An adaptive Block Double-buffered Processing Element (BD-PE) is presented that covers various matrix operations in ViT inference. It employs parametric DSP allocation to dynamically adjust resources on DSP-limited edge platforms, and utilizes multi-level double-buffering to overlap computation with memory access, reducing latency and boosting resource utilization.
- For non-linear functions, including Softmax and GELU, we design hardware-friendly computing modules through pipeline optimization, algorithm simplification, and computational strategy approximation, achieving a balance between computational speed and resource consumption.
- LoRViA is implemented on a Xilinx Zynq-7020 platform to accelerate DeiT-Tiny inference, achieving 2.07 GOPS/W energy efficiency at 120MHz frequency. Compared to existing FPGA-based ViT accelerators, LoRViA reduces Look Up Table (LUT) resource consumption by at least 60.37% and achieves up to 3.45× improvement in per-DSP energy efficiency.

2 Background and Related Work

2.1 Vision Transformer

Following its great success in natural language processing (NLP) [15], Transformer architecture has rapidly been extended to computer vision. Dosovitskiy et al. proposed ViT [1], whose core advantage lies in modeling long-range spatial dependencies within input images through a global self-attention mechanism.

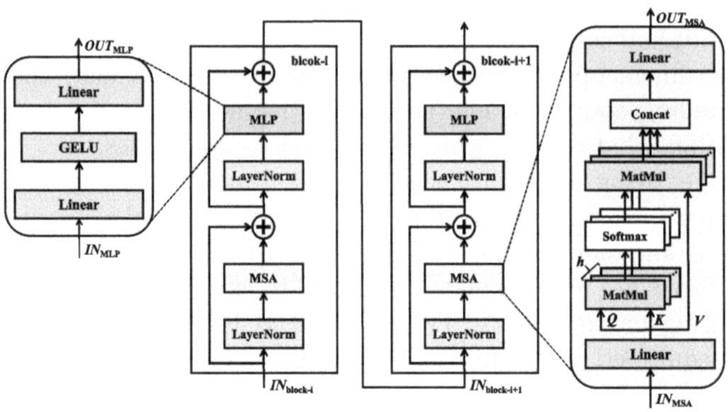

Fig. 1. Structure of the ViT block

This enables ViT to capture complex contextual relationships among distant visual features, achieving state-of-the-art performance on mainstream image classification tasks. Figure 1 illustrates the ViT block's architecture. It primarily consists of two Layer Normalization (LayerNorm) modules, an MSA module, and a Multi-layer Perceptron (MLP) module. Self-attention mechanism can be formulated as follows:

$$\text{Self-Attention}(Q, K, V) = \text{softmax}\left(\frac{QK^\top}{\sqrt{d_k}}\right)V \tag{1}$$

Here, Q, K, and V denote query, key, and value vectors. These three vectors are derived by applying distinct linear projection layers to their input embedding of dimension d_{model}, where d_k represents the dimension per attention head. Multi-head self-attention mechanism executes self-attention operations for h heads in parallel. It then concatenates outputs from these heads and projects the combined result through another linear transformation layer to produce output. Multi-head self-attention process is formally expressed as follows:

$$\text{head}_i = \text{Self-Attention}(Q_i, K_i, V_i) \tag{2}$$

$$\text{MSA}(Q, K, V) = \text{concat}(\text{head}_1, \ldots, \text{head}_h)W_{proj} \tag{3}$$

Q_i, K_i, and V_i represent projected Query, Key, and Value vectors for the i-th head, obtained by applying learnable projection matrices W_i^Q, W_i^K, and W_i^V

to the original Q, K, and V matrices respectively. These projection matrices $W_i^Q, W_i^K, W_i^V \in \mathbb{R}^{d_{\text{model}} \times d_k}$ transform inputs into head-specific representation space. $W_{proj} \in \mathbb{R}^{h \times d_k \times d_{\text{model}}}$ serves as output linear projection matrix, with h indicating the total number of heads. After MSA module processing, MLP applies non-linear transformations and feature integration to MSA output features. This module comprises two fully-connected layers with a Gaussian Error Linear Unit (GELU) activation function and an intermediate hidden dimension d_{ff}. MLP computational process is defined as follows:

$$\text{MLP}(x) = \text{GELU}(xW^H + B^H)W^L + B^L \tag{4}$$

where $W^H \in \mathbb{R}^{d_{\text{model}} \times d_{\text{ff}}}$ and $B^H \in \mathbb{R}^{d_{\text{ff}}}$ denote hidden-layer weight matrix and bias vector, while $W^L \in \mathbb{R}^{d_{\text{ff}} \times d_{\text{model}}}$ and $B^L \in \mathbb{R}^{d_{\text{model}}}$ denote output-layer weight matrix and bias vector.

2.2 Existing ViT Accelerators on FPGA

Several studies focus on hardware accelerator designs for ViT. Sarkar et al. [16] employed a streaming architecture for multi-task ViT models with Mixture-of-Experts (MoE), deploying each computational unit on FPGA and sequentially invoking them for model inference. Wang et al. [17] leveraged the residual connections in ViT/DeiT models, implementing a Half-Layer Mapping strategy to compute MSA and MLP blocks in parallel. Dong et al. [18] designed a streaming MSA unit and a reconfigurable linear computation unit. While these approaches improve accelerator throughput, they incur substantial resource overhead, rendering them unsuitable for deployment on edge devices. As noted in [12], edge devices typically possess limited parallelism (e.g., hundreds of DSP units rather than thousands) and constrained on-chip memory (e.g., hundreds of KB of block RAM (BRAM) rather than several megabytes). Marino et al. [19] integrated non-linear computations like LayerNorm and Softmax into matrix computation units, reducing memory access overhead but increasing resource consumption. Huang et al. [10] designed a general-purpose group vector systolic array, reorganizing memory data layout to enhance data reuse. However, this memory manipulation incurs additional resource costs, and such computation arrays demand significant DSP resources. Regarding model lightweighting, [9,11] devised token and weight pruning and quantization strategies to reduce model computational complexity, but this necessitates custom computation units for pruned models, imposing stricter design constraints on edge devices where such overhead should be minimized.

Most existing ViT hardware accelerators exhibit resource consumption typically exceeding 1,000 DSPs and 100,000 LUTs. In comparison, LoRViA aims to maximize computational resource utilization under stringent resource constraints. This is achieved through a generalized computation unit, parameter-controlled DSP core activation, a multi-level double-buffering hierarchy for dataflow optimization, and hardware-optimized linear computation units tailored for low-resource devices.

3 Proposed Architecture

3.1 Hardware Architecture

Figure 2 illustrates our proposed ViT accelerator architecture. This architecture primarily comprises an Input Buffer, a Matrix Multiplication module (Block Double-buffered Processing Element, BD-PE), Non-linear Processing module (LayerNorm, Softmax, GELU), and a Data Adjustment module (Add, Reshape). Within the ViT model, only LayerNorm and linear layers contain trainable parameters. Prior to model inference, input feature maps along with weight matrices and bias vectors from these parameterized layers are stored in off-chip DDR memory. Partial data tiles are loaded into on-chip BRAM via Input Buffer. Computational modules read required data from Input Buffer for processing, writing results back to DDR. Analysis of ViT model structure (Fig. 1) reveals that its computation and inference processes heavily rely on matrix multiplication. MSA module involves four linear transformations, including two linear computations, one attention score calculation, and one matrix multiplication between attention weight matrix and V. MLP module comprises two linear computations. The computations within these network layers are essentially matrix multiplications, as shown in Eq. (5):

$$Y = XW^T + b \tag{5}$$

where X is an input matrix, W represents a transformation matrix that may be either a learned weight matrix or an intermediate matrix, and b is a bias vector, with difference lying in whether weight matrix requires transposition and whether bias term requires addition.

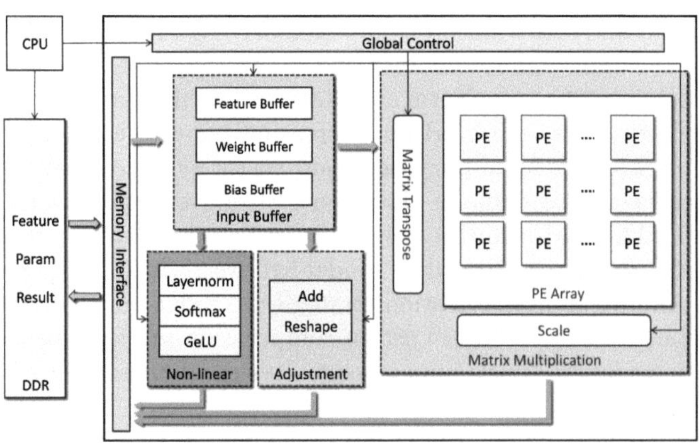

Fig. 2. Overall hardware accelerator architecture

Notably, unlike three-dimensional multi-channel convolutions in CNNs, linear layers in ViTs process two-dimensional matrices (sequence length and embedding dimension). To maximize hardware utilization and minimize complexity by leveraging a uniform computation pattern, we present BD-PE, which handles all linear layers and matrix operations specific to MSA mechanism. This unified processing strategy significantly reduces the diversity of required operators, eliminates the resource overhead associated with designing dedicated hardware units for distinct matrix multiplication forms, and simplifies control logic. Consequently, it effectively reduces the overall accelerator's resource overhead and power consumption.

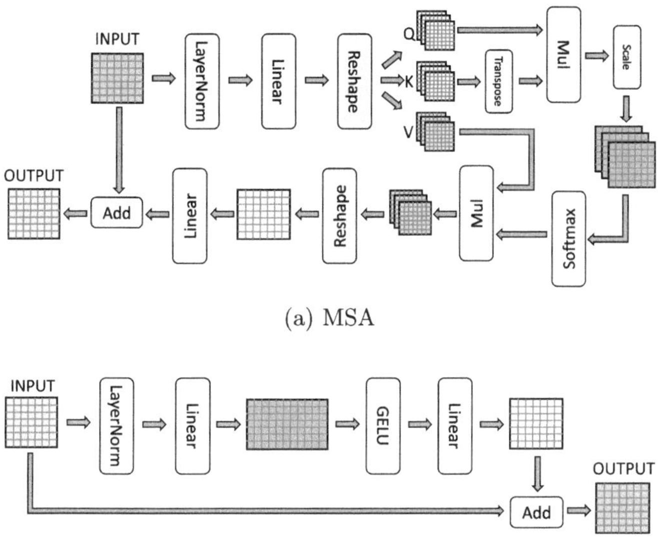

(a) MSA

(b) MLP

Fig. 3. Data analysis under the computing flow (including LayerNorm)

Figure 3a illustrates the computational flow in the first half of an encoder module. Input data first passes through LayerNorm, computing mean and variance along the embedding dimension for normalization. Normalized data then undergoes initial linear transformation to generate feature vectors. This feature set reshapes into Q, K and V matrices for multi-head self-attention. Subsequently, K matrix is transposed and multiplied with Q matrix. The resultant matrix is scaled, processed through a Softmax function to generate attention weight matrix, which is then multiplied with V matrix (as formalized in Eq. (1)). This multiplication's output undergoes another reshape operation, feeds into a subsequent linear transformation layer, and forms the MSA module output. Combining this MSA output with the module's original input via addition creates a residual connection, yielding the stage's final result. Figure 3b illustrates the computational flow in encoder module's second half. MSA output serves as input to MLP module. This input is normalized by a second LayerNorm module, then processed through that MLP's first linear layer to expand dimensionality and enrich features. A GELU activation applies non-linear transformation, followed by the second linear layer that projects features back to the original dimensionality d_{model} while aggregating representations (as formalized in Eq. (4)). MLP output adds residually to preceding MSA output, producing this block's resultant features.

3.2 Matrix Multiplication Processing Module

BD-PE is designed to maximize utilization of limited DSP resources on low-resource devices to execute the diverse matrix multiplications and associated post-processing computations required for ViT model inference. It employs a multi-level double-buffering mechanism to pipeline operations, effectively masking latency between data loading, computation, post-processing, and data storage, thereby enhancing the throughput of our design.

Substantial memory requirements of ViT hidden layers exceed BRAM capacity, necessitating partitioning of large matrices into $L \times L$ sub-blocks compliant with BRAM constraints. Crucially, the sub-block size L directly impacts data loading latency. Consider multiplying input matrix A (dimensions $M \times K$) with matrix B (dimensions $K \times N$). To compute a single output sub-block, K/L sub-blocks from A and K/L sub-blocks from B must be loaded (assuming L is a common divisor of K, M, and N). When executed in parallel, the total number of sub-block loads required for the complete $M \times N$ output matrix is $(M/L)\times(N/L)\times(K/L)$. Theoretically, if loading each $L\times L$ sub-block requires L^2 clock cycles, total matrix load cycles become $(M \times N \times K)/L$. Therefore, under BRAM capacity and ViT feature dimension constraints, increasing L reduces the clock cycles required for data loading.

Figure 4 illustrates two distinct strategies for matrix partitioning and sub-block loading: transposition-free and transposition-required.

In the transposition-free strategy, matrix A is loaded in row-major order while matrix B is loaded in column-major order. To compute the output sub-block at row i and column j, sub-block (i, k) is loaded from matrix A with row-major ordering within its sub-block, concurrently with sub-block (k, j) from matrix B

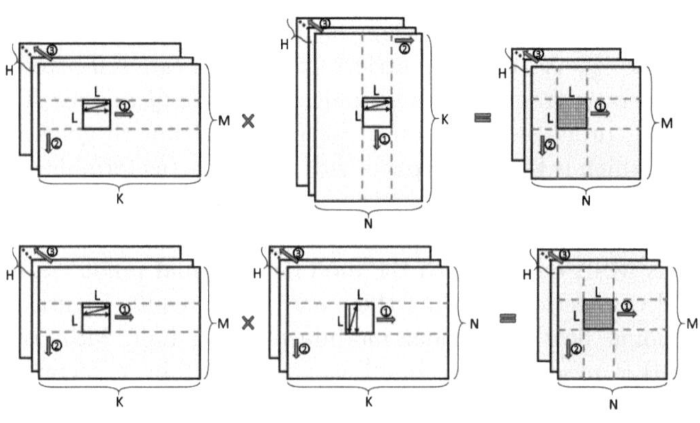

Fig. 4. Process for block matrix multiplication.

which also uses row-major ordering within its sub-block. These corresponding sub-blocks are multiplied sequentially until all output matrix sub-blocks are computed.

In the transposition-required strategy, sub-block loading for matrix A remains identical to the transposition-free method. However, matrix B must be transposed to row-major order. When loading sub-block (i, k) from matrix A, the corresponding sub-block (k, j) is loaded from the transposed matrix B. Crucially, although this sub-block from matrix B conceptually requires column-major loading to match the required data orientation, such column-major access would disrupt address continuity and break AXI burst transfers. To circumvent this limitation, we need to load the sub-block from matrix B in row-major order into a buffer that implicitly performs transposition to column-major layout. The corresponding sub-blocks are then multiplied to generate all output matrix sub-blocks.

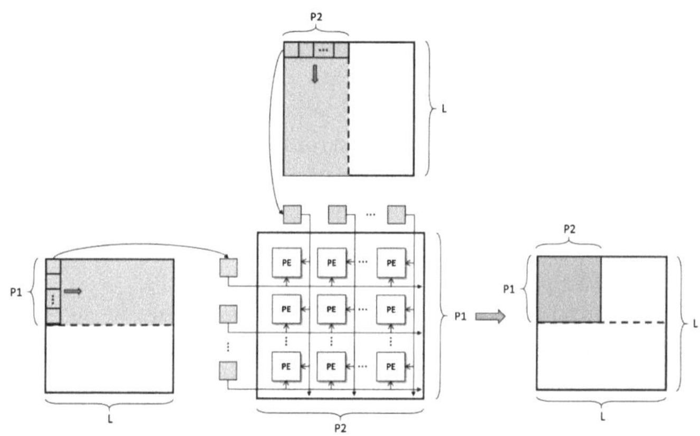

Fig. 5. PE block architecture

The multiplication of $L \times L$ sub-block matrices is performed by BD-PE array (architecture shown in Fig. 5), which features dynamic reconfigurability through configuration parameters P_1 and P_2. These parameters, required to be integer divisors of block size L, enable adjustment of the active scale (i.e., number of utilized DSP cores). The computational parallelism of BD-PE array is $P_1 \times P_2$, and for $L \times L$ sub-blocks, the cycle count for one matrix multiplication is $L^3/(P_1 \times P_2)$. For example with $L = 24$, configuration $P_1 = 6, P_2 = 8$ activates $6 \times 8 = 48$ DSP cores requiring 288 cycles, while $P_1 = 12, P_2 = 12$ activates $12 \times 12 = 144$ DSP cores requiring 96 cycles. Compared to fixed-size arrays, this scalable architecture enables flexible (P_1, P_2) selection based on computational demands, energy constraints, or resource availability. Consequently, BD-PE array maintains high computational efficiency while providing greater design flexibility and exploration space for the overall hardware design, avoiding resource underutilization

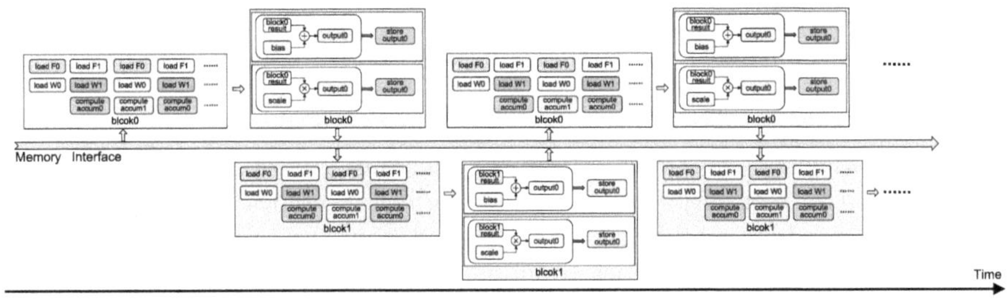

Fig. 6. Data pipeline optimization

inherent in fixed arrays, enhancing overall hardware utilization, and supporting system-level optimization.

Furthermore, BD-PE employs a multi-level double-buffering mechanism for pipeline optimization, with the data transfer process illustrated in Fig. 6.

At the single output block level, two input buffers (Buffer0 and Buffer1) are deployed. While PEs access one buffer (e.g., Buffer1) for matrix multiplication, the other buffer (Buffer0) concurrently loads the next input data batch from external memory. Upon completion of current sub-block computation and new data readiness confirmation, the PEs switch to Buffer0 for computation while Buffer1 initiates subsequent data loading. This alternating buffer mechanism effectively conceals data loading latency, maintaining continuous PEs activity after initial data load until block computation completes.

At the full output matrix level, a similar approach masks per-block computation and write-back latency. Post-processing operations (including linear layer bias addition and scaling) are merged with result write-back to external memory. When one block (e.g., Block0) completes computation, its results immediately enter post-processing and write-back. Concurrently, input data for the next block (Block1) loads and computation initiates. Upon Block1 completion, its results proceed similarly while subsequent block data loads commence. This pipeline continues until the entire output matrix is computed and stored.

The multi-level double-buffering design ensures high PE utilization throughout matrix computation while concealing latency associated with data loading, result post-processing, and storage operations.

3.3 Hardware Design for Softmax and GELU

Pipeline Optimization for Softmax. Softmax is widely used in Transformer and Vision Transformer models. A major challenge in hardware implementations is computational overflow in $\exp(x)$ evaluation, which may significantly degrade model accuracy when x exceeds the representable range. Building on [20], we use a method that subtracts each row's maximum value ($x_{\max}$) from exponential function arguments during the computation of $\frac{\exp(x_i)}{\sum_{j=1}^{N} \exp(x_j)}$. This operation effectively reduces exponent magnitudes, thereby rescaling the output ranges of $\exp(x_i)$ and $\exp(x_j)$, while maintaining mathematical equivalence without changing the Softmax results:

$$\text{Softmax}(x_i) = \frac{\exp(x_i - x_{\max})}{\sum_{j=1}^{n} \exp(x_j - x_{\max})} = \frac{\exp(x_i)}{\sum_{j=1}^{N} \exp(x_j)} \tag{6}$$

Therefore, Softmax computation can be divided into three distinct phases: loading entire rows of input data and finding their maximum values, computing Softmax values for all elements per row, and writing back results. Since each row is processed independently without data dependencies, we implement row-level dual-channel pipelining optimization for the Softmax module to reduce processing latency. As shown in Fig. 7, this scheme processes two rows of data simultaneously through optimized buffer structures including the row data buffer and row max register. When two new rows of input data are loaded for maximum lookup, the first two rows with completed maximum lookup enter the Softmax computation phase concurrently, while simultaneously, previously processed rows undergo result write-back. This pipelining mechanism achieves effective time reuse of computation units by temporally overlapping the computation phases of different data rows (assuming that each phase takes equal time), which significantly improves the overall throughput and hardware resource utilization of the module.

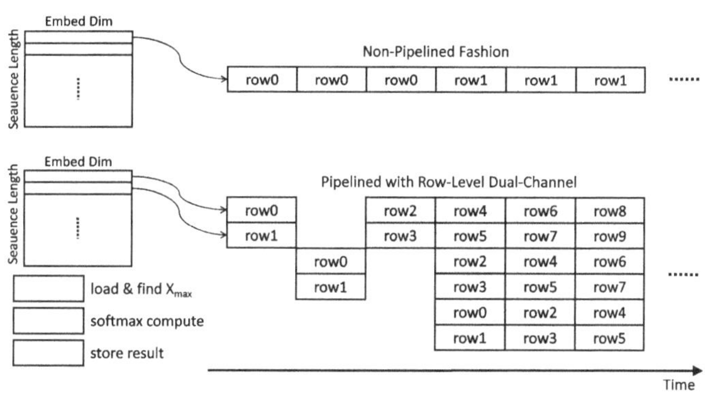

Fig. 7. Row-level dual-channel pipeline optimization for Softmax

Low-Cost GELU Approximation. The GELU activation function represents a non-linear transformation that facilitates faster and more stable convergence in neural network training. GELU(x) is computed as follows:

$$\text{GELU}(x) = x\Phi(x) = x \cdot 0.5\left(1 + \text{erf}\left(\frac{x}{\sqrt{2}}\right)\right) \tag{7}$$

where $\Phi(x)$ denotes the standard Gaussian cumulative distribution function and erf$(\cdot)$ represents the Gauss error function. As noted in [5], implementing GELU activation using Eq. (7) is extremely expensive on FPGA: it requires 160k LUTs for just a single instance using 32-bit fixed-point datatype.

Building on [16], we approximate GELU function using a lookup table in conjunction with ReLU function. ReLU is computationally simple. We approximate GELU by subtracting a calibration term $\delta(x)$ from ReLU output:

$$\mathrm{GELU}(x) \approx \mathrm{ReLU}(x) - \delta(x) \tag{8}$$

This method first calculates the absolute value $|x|$ of input x and its corresponding ReLU baseline $\mathrm{ReLU}(x) = \max(0, x)$. With the lookup table configured with a sampling step size of $\tau = 2^{-5}$ and table size $N = 128$, when $|x|$ exceeds the predefined maximum range of the lookup table, the implementation directly outputs $\mathrm{ReLU}(x)$ as GELU result. For $|x|$ within the valid lookup range, it calculates an index $\mathrm{index_f} = |x|/\tau$ and quantizes it to an integer index through nearest-neighbor approximation $\mathrm{index} = \lfloor \mathrm{index_f} + 0.5 \rfloor$. This index is then used to access a predefined GELU correction value lookup table, producing the final output result as $\mathrm{ReLU}(x) - \delta$. This approach enables a highly efficient and cost-effective hardware implementation of GELU function. Figure 8 shows the statistical results of relative errors for the GELU approximation algorithm, indicating that the majority of the computed values exhibit a relative error below 2%.

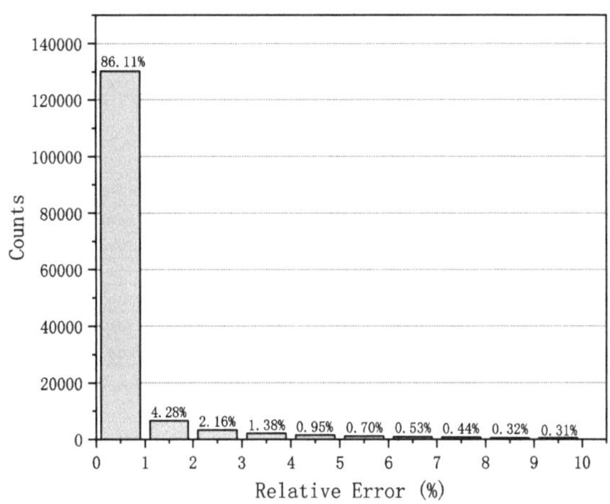

Fig. 8. Relative error analysis of GELU approximation on 197 × 768 inputs.

4 Experiments and Results Analysis

4.1 Experiments Setup

We implemented LoRViA using Xilinx Vitis HLS 2019.2. The entire project was synthesized and deployed using Vivado 2019.2. Our accelerator was deployed on a Xilinx Zynq-7020 board, a typical low-end FPGA platform equipped with only 220 DSPs, 630 KB of BRAM, 53,200 LUTs, and 106,400 FFs. We deployed DeiT-T model on LoRViA and evaluated it using ImageNet-1k dataset. Its classification results were verified to be consistent with those generated by the reference DeiT-T model implemented in PyTorch. Power consumption was obtained from the built-in power report within Vivado.

4.2 Comparison with CPU and GPU

For comparative analysis with LoRViA, we performed model inference using DeiT-T model implemented in PyTorch on both a CPU (R7-8845H) and a GPU (RTX2060). The comparative inference performance results are presented in Table 1. To estimate actual CPU power consumption, we calculated the product of CPU utilization and its Thermal Design Power (TDP). GPU power consumption during runtime was measured using nvidia-smi. Additionally, we employed efficiency, measured in GOPS/W (Giga-Operations Per Second per Watt), as a key performance-per-watt metric to enable fair comparisons across different platforms.

Table 1. Performance comparison with CPU and GPU

	CPU	GPU	Ours
Platform	R7-8845H	RTX2060	Zynq7020
Frequency (MHz)	3800	1005	120
Power (W)	45	87	2.1
Throughput (GOPS)	62.3	163.1	4.36
Efficiency (GOPS/W)	1.38	1.85	2.07

Benefiting from the low-power characteristics of FPGAs, LoRViA's power consumption was only 1/21.4 and 1/41.9 of the CPU and GPU implementations, respectively. Although constrained by clock frequency and limited computational resources, resulting in lower throughput than CPU and GPU, LoRViA attained 1.5× and 1.12× improvements in energy efficiency over CPU and GPU baselines.

4.3 Comparison with FPGA Accelerators

Table 2 details the performance comparison between LoRViA and other recent FPGA-based accelerators. As shown, LoRViA is deployed on the highly resource-constrained Zynq7020 platform. Due to the limited hardware resources and lower clock frequency, its computational throughput is lower than designs implemented on higher-performance platforms (e.g., ZCU102 or Alveo U50). This performance gap is constrained by the target platform's hardware capabilities, making direct comparisons in terms of throughput less meaningful.

Table 2. Comparison with related work

Related Work	NPE [21]	ViA [17]	SWAT [22]	UbiMoE [18]	Ours
Platform	Zynq7100	ZCU102	Alveo U50	ZCU102	Zynq7020
Model	Bert-B	Swin-T	Swin-T	M3ViT	Deit-T
Frequency (MHz)	200	300	200	300	120
DSP	2020	2420	1863	1850	194
LUT	156K	258K	271K	123.4K	48.9K
Power (W)	20	39	14.35	11.50	2.10
Throughput (GOPS)	207.9	309.6	301.9	97.04	4.36
Efficiency (GOPS/W)	10.4	7.94	21.04	8.438	2.07
Efficiency/DSP (GOPS/W)	0.0051	0.0031	0.0113	0.0045	0.0106

However, LoRViA demonstrates significant advantages in resource utilization and power consumption: it occupies only 194 DSPs and 48.9K LUTs, with an extremely low operational power consumption of 2.10 W, substantially lower than those reported in other studies. Notably, regarding the per-DSP Energy Efficiency metric, which measures hardware resource utilization efficiency, LoRViA achieves 0.0106 GOPS/W/DSP. This significantly exceeds the 0.0051 of [21], 0.0031 of [17], and 0.0045 of [18], while approaching the 0.0113 of [22]. This is because the PE arrays in prior works [17,18,21] are divided into matrix multiplications for different stages of the model, while BD-PE in our design covers all matrix calculations in model inference. The results indicate that, under extremely stringent DSP resource constraints, LoRViA achieves high hardware resource utilization efficiency.

Therefore, although LoRViA cannot compete with high-performance FPGA solutions in throughput, our optimization specifically targets highly resource-constrained edge scenarios. It remains competitive in resource utilization efficiency and maintaining usable performance at an ultra-low power, making it particularly suitable for deployment on edge devices with stringent power and resource constraints.

5 Conclusion

This paper proposes LoRViA, a low-resource ViT accelerator design for edge applications, aiming to deploy Vision Transformer models on resource-constrained edge devices. We designed a versatile BD-PE computing unit that accelerates various matrix operations in multi-head self-attention mechanisms and fully-connected layers, eliminating the resource overhead of custom computing units for different network layers. For non-linear computation modules, we developed row-level dual-channel pipeline optimization to enhance Softmax calculation speed and implemented a low-cost hardware approximation for the GELU activation function. Deployed on the Xilinx Zynq-7020 platform at 120 MHz operating frequency, LoRViA achieves 2.07 GOPS/W energy efficiency. Compared to existing FPGA-based ViT accelerators, LoRViA reduces LUT resource consumption by over 60.37% and achieves up to 3.45× improvementin per-DSP energy efficiency, making it suitable for various resource-limited edge applications.

References

1. Dosovitskiy, et al.: An image is worth 16x16 words: Transformers for image recognition at scale (2021). https://arxiv.org/abs/2010.11929
2. Liu, Z., et al.: Swin transformer: Hierarchical vision transformer using shifted windows (2021). https://arxiv.org/abs/2103.14030
3. Han, K., Xiao, A., Wu, E., Guo, J., Xu, C., Wang, Y.: Transformer in transformer (2021). https://arxiv.org/abs/2103.00112
4. Touvron, H., Cord, M., Douze, M., Massa, F., Sablayrolles, A., Jégou, H.: Training data-efficient image transformers & distillation through attention (2021). https://arxiv.org/abs/2012.12877
5. Dong, P., et aleatvit: Hardware-efficient adaptive token pruning for vision transformers. In: 2023 IEEE International Symposium on High-Performance Computer Architecture (HPCA), pp. 442–455 (2023). https://doi.org/10.1109/HPCA56546.2023.10071047
6. Mehta, S., Rastegari, M.: Mobilevit: Light-weight, general-purpose, and mobile-friendly vision transformer (2022). https://arxiv.org/abs/2110.02178
7. Huang, T., Huang, L., You, S., Wang, F., Qian, C., Xu, C.: Lightvit: Towards light-weight convolution-free vision transformers (2022). https://arxiv.org/abs/2207.05557
8. Wu, K., et alinyvit: Fast pretraining distillation for small vision transformers (2022). https://arxiv.org/abs/2207.10666
9. Dong, Q., Zhang, S., Wang, Z.: An efficient window-based vision transformer accelerator via mixed-granularity sparsity. IEEE Trans. Circuits Syst. I: Regul. Pap. 1–14 (2025). https://doi.org/10.1109/TCSI.2025.3527541
10. Huang, M., Luo, J., Ding, C., Wei, Z., Huang, S., Yu, H.: An integer-only and group-vector systolic accelerator for efficiently mapping vision transformer on edge. IEEE Trans. Circuits Syst. I Regul. Pap. **70**(12), 5289–5301 (2023). https://doi.org/10.1109/TCSI.2023.3312775
11. Parikh, D., Li, S., Zhang, B., Kannan, R., Busart, C., Prasanna, V.: Accelerating vit inference on fpga through static and dynamic pruning. In: 2024 IEEE 32nd Annual International Symposium on Field-Programmable Custom Computing Machines (FCCM), pp. 78–89 (2024). https://doi.org/10.1109/FCCM60383.2024.00018
12. Chen, C., Li, L., Sabry Aly, M.M.: Vita: a highly efficient dataflow and architecture for vision transformers. In: 2024 Design, Automation & Test in Europe Conference & Exhibition (DATE), pp. 1–6 (2024). https://doi.org/10.23919/DATE58400.2024.10546565
13. Wang, Y., Mao, W., Shi, H., Sha, J., Wang, Z.: An energy-efficient fpga accelerator for swin transformer. IEEE Trans. Very Large Scale Integ. (VLSI) Syst. **33**(6), 1774–1778 (2025). https://doi.org/10.1109/TVLSI.2025.3540844

14. Nag, S., Datta, G., Kundu, S., Chandrachoodan, N., Beerel, P.A.: Vita: A vision transformer inference accelerator for edge applications. In: 2023 IEEE International Symposium on Circuits and Systems (ISCAS). pp. 1–5. IEEE (2023). http://dx.doi.org/10.1109/ISCAS46773.2023.10181988
15. Vaswani, A., et al.: Attention is all you need (2023). https://arxiv.org/abs/1706.03762
16. Sarkar, R., Liang, H., Fan, Z., Wang, Z., Hao, C.: Edge-moe: memory-efficient multi-task vision transformer architecture with task-level sparsity via mixture-of-experts. In: 2023 IEEE/ACM International Conference on Computer Aided Design (ICCAD), pp. 01–09 (2023). https://doi.org/10.1109/ICCAD57390.2023.10323651
17. Wang, T., Gong, L., Wang, C., Yang, Y., Gao, Y., Zhou, X., Chen, H.: Via: A novel vision-transformer accelerator based on fpga. IEEE Trans. Comput. Aided Des. Integr. Circuits Syst. **41**(11), 4088–4099 (2022). https://doi.org/10.1109/TCAD.2022.3197489
18. Dong, J., et al.: Ubimoe: A ubiquitous mixture-of-experts vision transformer accelerator with hybrid computation pattern on fpga. In: 2025 IEEE International Symposium on Circuits and Systems (ISCAS), pp. 1–5 (2025). https://doi.org/10.1109/ISCAS56072.2025.11043956
19. Marino, K., Zhang, P., Prasanna, V.K.: Me- vit: A single-load memory-efficient fpga accelerator for vision transformers. In: 2023 IEEE 30th International Conference on High Performance Computing, Data, and Analytics (HiPC), pp. 213–223 (2023). https://doi.org/10.1109/HiPC58850.2023.00039
20. Wang, W., Zhou, S., Sun, W., Sun, P., Liu, Y.: Sole: Hardware-software co-design of softmax and layernorm for efficient transformer inference. In: 2023 IEEE/ACM International Conference on Computer Aided Design (ICCAD). pp. 1–9 (2023). https://doi.org/10.1109/ICCAD57390.2023.10323725
21. Khan, H., Khan, A., Khan, Z., Huang, L.B., Wang, K., He, L.: Npe: an fpga-based overlay processor for natural language processing. In: The 2021 ACM/SIGDA International Symposium on Field-Programmable Gate Arrays, pp. 227–227. FPGA '21, ACM (2021). http://dx.doi.org/10.1145/3431920.3439477
22. Dong, Q., Xie, X., Wang, Z.: Swat: an efficient swin transformer accelerator based on fpga. In: 2024 29th Asia and South Pacific Design Automation Conference (ASP-DAC), pp. 515–520 (2024). https://doi.org/10.1109/ASP-DAC58780.2024.10473931

A Multi-modality Dynamic Feature Fusion Method for Android Malware Detection

Zhen Liu[1,2](✉), Jinchun Zhang[1], Hao Chen[1], and Bitao Peng[1,2]

[1] School of Information Science and Technology, Guangdong University of Foreign Studies, Guangzhou 510006, People's Republic of China
[2] Guangdong Engineering Research Center of Data Security Governance and Privacy Computing, Guangzhou 510006, People's Republic of China
{liuzhen,pengbitao}@gdufs.edu.cn

Abstract. With the widespread adoption of smartphones and the open-source nature of the Android operating system, the number of Android malwares has increased significantly in recent years, posing serious threats to users' privacy and financial security. Traditional unimodal detection methods suffer from limited accuracy and blind spots, while many existing multimodal approaches face challenges in effective feature fusion. To address these limitations, a multi-modality dynamic feature fusion-based Android malware detection method (MMDF) is proposed. MMDF extracts three types of modality data: Behavior features, Opcode features, and Sensitive API features. It employs APIGraph for dimensionality reduction and ExtraTreesClassifier for feature selection to construct high-quality feature vectors. The vectors are fed into a two-layer dynamic fusion classifier, which uses modality-level Multi-Head Attention to capture complex relationships between individual features within and across modalities. It dynamically adjusts the contribution of each modality via TCP dynamic weight allocation, thereby enhancing detection accuracy and robustness. Extensive experiments demonstrate that MMDF achieves a classification accuracy of 97.18% and an AUC score of 98.78% on the AndroZoo dataset, indicating excellent performance.

Keywords: Android Malware Detection · Multimodal feature fusion · Mobile security

1 Introduction

With the widespread adoption of smartphones and other mobile devices, Android malware has become one of the most serious cybersecurity threats today. According to the 2024 Global Mobile Threat report by Zimperium, attackers have adopted a 'mobile-first' strategy, with 83% of phishing sites targeting mobile devices and a 200% increase in malware prevalence for apps downloaded via unofficial channels (sideloading)[1]. This trend poses significant challenges to the communications industry, and the threat is expected to persist.

[1] Source: Zimperium 2024 Report, https://www.zimperium.com/resources/2024-global-mobile-threat-report/

L. Zhang and K.-K. R. Choo (Eds.): MobiQuitous 2025, LNICST 683, pp. 193–213, 2026.
https://doi.org/10.1007/978-3-032-22500-9_12

Research on Android malware has become a hot topic in the field of cyber-security [2]. Various methods have been proposed based on unimodal feature or multi-modality fusion approaches. Xiao et al. [6] captured dynamic features from system call sequences. Vinayakumar [7] applied long short-term memory (LSTM) to the detection of Android malware. Besides, Chen et al. [11] used class call graphs (CSCG) and permission features and leveraged graph attention networks for improved detection performance.

The previous research works on Android malware detection have enhanced feature comprehensiveness through multi-feature fusion methods, thereby improving detection accuracy. However, these methods always rely on simple concatenation or weighted summation to handle different types of features. This process overlooks the relationships between features intra-modally and inter-modally, leading to fused feature representations with missing information [3]. Moreover, the fusion strategies between different modalities lack dynamic adaptability. Static fusion mechanisms are unable to dynamically adjust according to the modality importance of different samples.

To address these limitations, we proposes an Android malware detection method based on multi-modality dynamic fusion. This method integrates a multi-head attention mechanism and a dynamic weight allocation strategy, based on the True-Class Probability (TCP) mechanism [4], to achieve reliable detection of Android malware through the fusion of different modality data.

The main contributions of this paper are as follows:

- We introduce a novel Android malware detection framework that leverages multi-modality dynamic fusion. Our approach extracts 3 types of static features and employs a modality-level multi-head attention mechanism to optimize feature relations. The TCP mechanism is then utilized to dynamically fuse these features based on their information content, and the fusion features are input into a neural network classifier for binary classification.
- To enhance the fusion capability of multi-modality features and address the limitations of simple concatenation in prior work, we incorporate a multi-head attention mechanism. This mechanism effectively captures the complex relations between features from different modalities and within each modality, thereby enriching the information content.
- To address the issue of model overconfidence due to static weight allocation in traditional multi-modality fusion, we introduce a dynamic weight allocation mechanism based on the True-Class Probability, which dynamically adjusts the weights of different modalities according to the information content of each sample, ensuring that modalities with higher information content contribute more significantly to the final feature representation and reducing the impact of noisy modalities on the classification task.
- To verify the efficacy of the proposed method, we conducted 5 distinct sets of experiments. The results, supported by extensive comparative and ablation studies, indicate that our method attains a testing accuracy of 97.18% on the AndroZoo dataset and achieves a 5.53% improvement over the best-

performing method trained on the same data, thereby demonstrating robust generalization capability.

The rest of this paper is organized as follows: Sect. 2 overviews the domestic and international research status from the perspectives of single-modality and multi-modality. Section 3 elaborates on the specific implementation of our proposed MMDF framework. Section 4 introduces the datasets used in our experiments and designs multiple ablation and comparative experiments to validate the effectiveness of our method. Section 5 concludes this paper.

2 Related Works

2.1 Android Malware Detection Method Based on Unimodal Feature

Corresponding permissions are always required when malware performing malicious actions. For example, ransomware may request access to the file system to encrypt user files and postulate a ransom for decryption, or request to read or modify the user's address book and contact information. Android application package (APK) is the basic file enables Android applications to be recognized and run by the system. It contains a lot of information related to the application, especially the AndroidManifest.xml file and the classes.dex file which are key parts of static analysis and detection of Android malware. Most existing detection methods use permissions and API call relationships as reference features, which does not seem to be effective for new sophisticated samples and for a long term [5]. Xiao et al. [6] captured dynamic features using frequency vector and co-occurrence matrix, and then used machine learning (ML) algorithms to perform learning and prediction. Vinayakumar [7] pioneered the application of LSTM architecture to Android malware detection with presicison of 95.20%. Additionally, Wei et al. [8] proposed an Android malware detection method based on graph neural networks. Their approach involved extracting function call graphs from decompiled Android applications, constructing local structural features of nodes utilizing the node2vec algorithm, and integrating opcode classification with API node importance evaluation to facilitate automated feature extraction. However, the above methods all extract a certain type of features for learning and prediction, which makes it difficult to fully grasp the multi-faceted characteristics of malware.

2.2 Android Malware Detection Method Based on Multi-feature Fusion

Traditional single-modal deep learning methods rely solely on assembly language instructions, raw binary sequences, or their compressed representations as input, often overlooking critical information. This limitation impairs model performance and makes it challenging to address the diversity of Android malware variants. In contrast, multimodal learning methods can integrate different feature types or modalities, providing more comprehensive complementary information and uncovering patterns that a single modality cannot capture. Consequently, multimodal methods generally exhibit superior performance in malware classification tasks. Kim et al. [9] were the first to introduce multimodal deep learning methods in the field of Android malware detection, maximizing the learning of various feature information. Their approach demonstrates improved performance and flexibility compared to single-modal detection methods. Subsequently, Yang et al. [10] extracted binary file function call temporal features and opcode features as two distinct modalities, performing feature extraction and fusion through stacked convolutional networks. In the study by Chen et al. [11], they utilized CSCG and permission features as input data, proposing an Android malware detection method based on graph attention networks and deep fusion of multimodal features, further enhancing detection performance.

Although existing studies have demonstrated that multimodal fusion can improve detection performance to some extent, challenges remain, such as the difficulty in capturing nonlinear interactions between modalities using simple feature concatenation or weighted summation, the inability of static fusion strategies to adapt to varying modality importance across different samples, and insufficient noise suppression.

3 Methodology

3.1 Framework of Our Method

In this work, we propose a malware detection method, namely the Android malware detection model based on multimodal dynamic fusion (MMDF), that utilizes multimodal dynamic fusion to enhance the efficiency of utilizing multimodal data and improve the accuracy of Android malware detection. As shown in Fig. 1, MMDF primarily consists of three modules: Feature Extraction Module, Feature Selection and Processing Module, and Modality Dymanic Fusion and Classification Module.

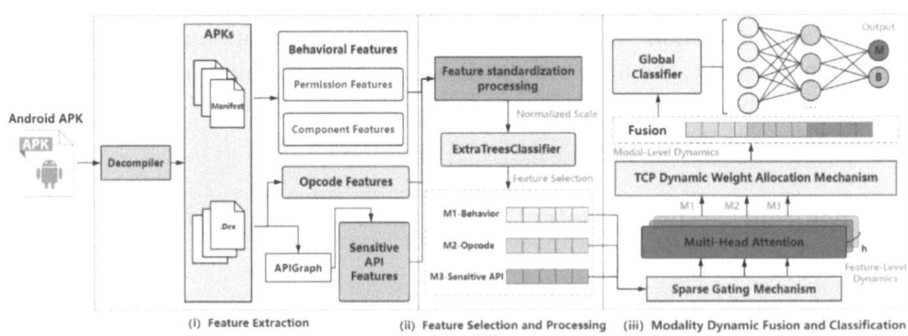

Fig. 1. Overall framework of MMDF.

3.2 Feature Extraction Module

Different types of features can reflect the characteristics of an Android application from various perspectives. Although some features, such as environmental information, may not appear to have a direct correlation with malicious behavior, they nonetheless contribute to a comprehensive depiction of the application's overall traits. The proposed MMDF framework utilizes the following three types of features: *Behavioral Features*, *Opcode Features*, *Sensitive API Features*

3.2.1 Behavioral Features Behavioral features specifically include permission and component characteristics. We employs the Androguard tool to decompile APK files from the AndroZoo dataset, ultimately extracting a total of 9,045 behavioral features from the decompiled files.

3.2.2 Opcode Features Opcode (Operation Code) features are extracted from binary DEX files and consist of two main elements: the operation code and the operand. The operation code indicates the behavior of the code, while the operand represents the target of this behavior [12].

Opcode features reflect the application's execution logic at the instruction level and are well-suited for detecting sophisticated malicious behaviors or code similarities. A typical set of opcode instructions is summarized in Table 1.

Table 1. Typical set of opcode instructions.

Instruction Category	Opcode Examples
Move instructions	move, move/16, ...
Return instructions	return-void, return, ...
Const instructions	const/4, const/16, ...
Monitor instructions	monitor-enter, monitor-exit
Object operation instructions	instance-of, new-instance
Comparison instructions	cmpl-float, cmpg-float, ...
Field operation instructions	aget, aput, ...
Call instructions	invoke-virtual, invoke-static, ...
Data transfer instructions	neg-int, neg-long, ...
Arithmetic instructions	add-int, sub-long, ...
Other instructions	Throw, nop

To decompile APK files from the AndroZoo dataset, we used Androguard, ultimately extracting a total of 227 Opcode features from the decompiled DEX bytecode files.

3.2.3 Sensitive API Features Normal permissions refer to permissions that do not pose a threat to user privacy or security. These permissions are automatically granted by the system and do not require any manual action from the user

[13]. Sensitive API features in Android applications are those that pose potential security risks, such as accessing user location or sending SMS messages. These permissions must be explicitly authorized by the user for the application to access the corresponding features, which reveal the application's intent to access system resources from a higher-level functional perspective. They are highly suitable for privacy compliance and permission abuse analysis.

To better utilize key features, we employs the APIGraph framework. It groups semantically similar APIs together [14], reducing the original set of features into different categories. The API relationship graph and its application in the extraction of sensitive API features in this study are shown in Fig. 2.

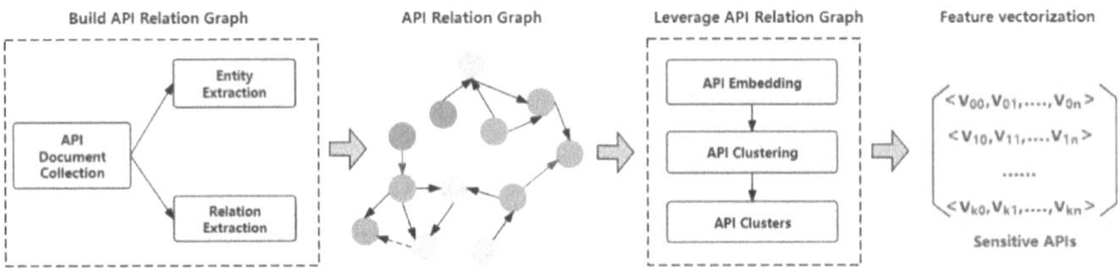

Fig. 2. APIGraph-based feature extraction method flow.

In our study, the APIGraph framework is employed to cluster over 20,000 sensitive API feature vectors into 531 categories, effectively mitigating the risk of the curse of dimensionality and improving the model training speed.

3.3 Feature Selection and Processing Module

Feature standardization is a crucial technique in data preprocessing [15]. In the last section, we constructed a vector space comprising multidimensional features. Collectively, these three modalities yield a feature space of 9,833 dimensions. These features exhibit significant differences in scale, and their high dimensionality leads to exponential increases in computational complexity, which can easily result in the curse of dimensionality. Moreover, the sparse distribution of data further amplifies noise interference, severely diminishing the model's generalization capability.

To address these issues, we employs the StandardScaler for feature standardization prior to training, as shown in Formula (1).

$$X_{scaled} = \frac{X - \mu}{\sigma} \tag{1}$$

where μ is the mean and σ is the standard deviation of the feature.

Random Forest is an ensemble learning method that constructs multiple decision trees and combines their outputs for classification or regression prediction [16]. Our method utilizes the ExtraTreesClassifier for feature selection and applies it to the original feature data using SelectFromModel, ultimately screening out features of research value.

3.4 Modality Dymanic Fusion and Classification Module

In this section, we elaborate on the proposed trustworthy multi-modality dynamic fusion framework (MMDF). At the feature level, the framework dynamically evaluates and adjusts the importance of features within and between modalities through sparse gating mechanisms (elaborated in detail in Sect. 3.4.1) and multi-head attention mechanisms (elaborated in detail in Sect. 3.4.2). At the modality-level fusion stage, the contribution of each modality is dynamically adjusted through the True-Class Probability mechanism (elaborated in detail in Sect. 3.4.3). Ultimately, the model is capable of efficiently and accurately performing binary classification predictions (Benign/Malware) for Android applications in the absence of explicit label information. The detailed architecture of the MMDF model is depicted in Fig. 3. The implementation of each component is concisely summarized in Algorithm 1, with specific details elaborated in the respective subsections.

Algorithm 1. Algorithm of MMDF

Input: $\{v^1, v^2, ..., v^m\}$: Raw multimodal feature matrices
Output: Y_{cls}: Classification results
Feature-Level Dynamics:
for each modality $i \in [1, m]$ **do**
  $p(v^i) \leftarrow \text{ProjectionLayer}(v^i)$ ▷ Project features
end for
Implementation of the Multihead Attention Mechanism:
$attn\_output, A \leftarrow \text{MultiHeadAttention}(\text{Concatenate}(p(v^1), ..., p(v^m)))$ ▷ Apply attention
Dynamic Fusion at the Modality Level:
for each modality $i \in [1, m]$ **do**
  $dynamic\_weights_i \leftarrow \text{DynamicWeightLayer}(attn\_output[:, i, :])$ ▷ Compute weights
  $feature_i \leftarrow attn\_output[:, i, :] \times dynamic\_weights_i$ ▷ Apply weights
end for
Global Classifier:
$Y_{cls} \leftarrow \text{MMClassifier}(\text{Concatenate}(feature_1, ..., feature_m))$ ▷ Final classification
return Y_{cls}

3.4.1 Feature-Level Dynamics For high-dimensional feature vectors $v_m \in \mathbb{R}^{d_m}$, there typically exists a subset of features that is closely related to class labels and effectively reflects the information they contain. In practice, the amount of information carried by different features often varies; even for the same feature, its corresponding informational value can fluctuate across different samples. This variability should be taken into account in multimodal fusion. In this regard, we have received inspiration from and improved upon the work of

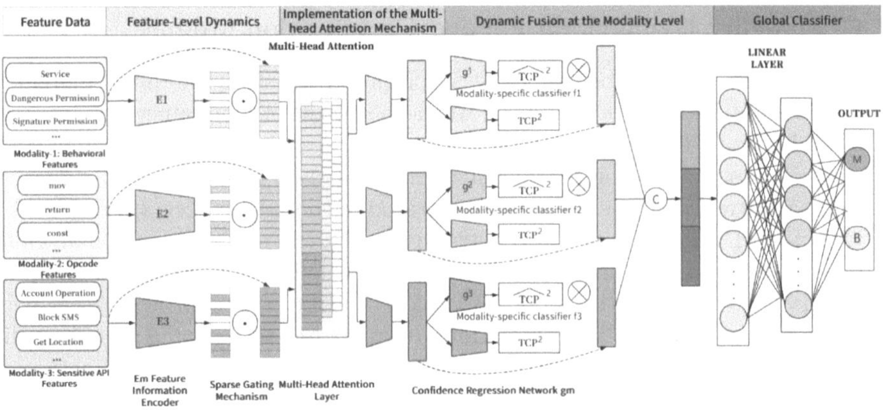

Fig. 3. Architecture of the MMDF Model. The dashed arrows in the figure indicate the flow of raw data. For each modality m ($m \in \mathbb{N}^+$), E_m denotes the Feature-Informativeness Encoder neural network, which evaluates the information value of each feature. g_m represents a regression network trained to approximate the true TCP value, with the output denoted as $\widehat{TCP}$.

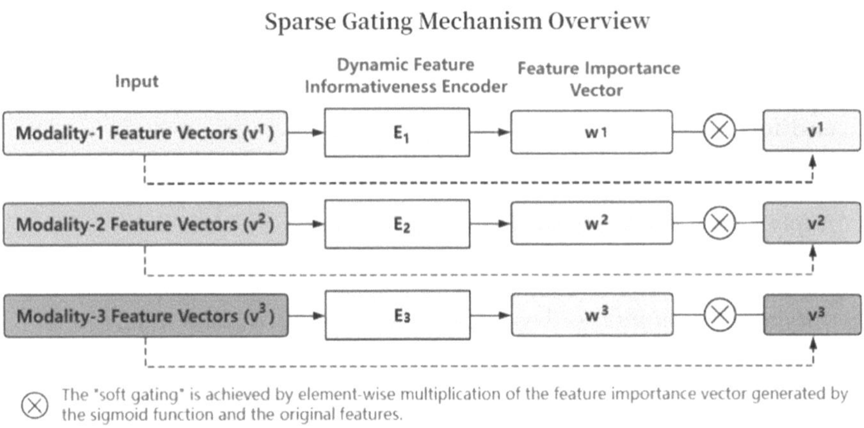

Fig. 4. Schematic diagram of the sparse gating mechanism. The on-off state of each gate is not a traditional binary state, but is continuously adjusted through the sigmoid activation function. The gate opens when the feature is informative (high weight) and closes when the feature is uninformative (low weight).

Han et al. [17] in medical diagnosis areas, employing a dynamic feature information encoder E_m and a sparse gating strategy to preserve informative features across different modalities while suppressing non-informative features (Fig. 4).

The Feature Information Encoder E_m is designed to learn the relationship between input feature vectors and output information content vectors, assessing the role of each feature in classification tasks. The output of E_m: $v^m \rightarrow w^m$, where both v^m and w^m are in $\mathbb{R}^{d_m}$ represents the feature vector and w^m is the information content vector indicating its importance to the classification task. The detailed computation process of w^m is shown in Fig. 4. Subsequently, the sparse gating mechanism dynamically weights the original feature vector with the information content vector to produce a weighted feature vector, filtering out the unimportant features. This allows the encoder to adjust the weights of features based on the information content of different samples, enabling the model to better adapt to varying input data. Formula (2) provides the specific implementation of the encoder.

$$w^m = \sigma(E_m(v^m)) = [w_1^m, \ldots, w_{d_m}^m] \tag{2}$$

where E_m denotes the Feature-Informativeness Encoder neural network, v^m represents the input feature vector for modality m, and σ is the sigmoid activation function, which compresses the encoder's output to the range of $[0, 1]$. The vector w^m represents the output information content vector, each element w_i^m indicates the information content corresponding to the input feature v_i^m.

3.4.2 Implementation of the Multi-head Attention Mechanism The proposed MMDF introduces a multi-head attention mechanism to optimize feature weights both between individual features within and across modalities, thereby enhancing feature fusion at the modality level. Specifically, the application of the multi-head attention mechanism is illustrated on line 4 of Algorithm 1.

The representation of the multi-head attention mechanism at the modality level is illustrated in Formula (3):

$$attn\_output = \text{MultiHeadAttention}(\text{Concat}[w^1 \odot p(v^1), ..., w^m \odot p(v^m)]) \tag{3}$$

where $p(v^i)$ denotes the projected features of modality i and w^i are dynamic weight vectors for them, while *attn_output* represents the output features processed through the multi-head attention mechanism.

3.4.3 Dynamic Fusion at the Modality Level

3.4.3.1 Definition of TCP Classification Confidence Quantification Traditional multimodal fusion methods typically adopt fixed modality weights, which compromises the model's robustness and reliability when encountering noisy or low-quality data. Inspired by researches conducted by [4,17], we introduce the True-Class Probability (TCP) classification confidence quantification method into the modality dimension of the MMDF model to evaluate the confidence of each modality in the classification task.

Specifically, this method assigns a modality-specific classifier f_m to each modality m, which takes the feature vector v^m of modality m as input and outputs the independent classification prediction result of that modality. Unlike traditional methods, TCP uses the Softmax output probability corresponding to the true label as the confidence measure. Given the predictive distribution $p^m(y|v^m)$ and the label y, the TCP value is calculated as follows:

$$\mathrm{TCP}^m = \sum_{k=1}^{K} y_k p_k^m \tag{4}$$

where y_k is the k-th element of the label y, and p_k^m is the k-th element of the predictive distribution. For each category k, if the sample truly belongs to that category ($y_k = 1$), the probability p_k^m that modality m predicts the sample belongs to that category is added to TCP^m; otherwise, $y_k p_k^m = 0$, which does not contribute to TCP^m.

Compared to conventional static weight assignment approaches, the TCP dynamic weight allocation mechanism enables the model to flexibly adjust modality contributions based on their individual confidence levels. This adaptive mechanism significantly enhances both the accuracy and reliability of the final classification results.

3.4.3.2 Calculation of TCP prediction value During the training phase, the model calculates the TCP value by comparing the prediction results of each modality with the true labels to quantify the classification confidence of each modality. However, in the testing phase, the test set data does not contain label information, making it impossible to directly calculate the TCP value. Therefore, this method trains a confidence regression network g_m to approximate the classification confidence value (TCP) of each modality, thereby achieving dynamic assessment of modality confidence.

In the testing phase, the confidence regression network g_m takes the feature vector v_m of modality m as input and outputs the approximate classification confidence $\widehat{\mathrm{TCP}}^m$ of that modality. By training this network, the true class probability TCP^m of each modality can be approximated. To train this network, a Sigmoid activation function is used in the final layer, and the network parameters are optimized using the mean squared error loss function:

$$\mathcal{L}^{\mathrm{conf}} = \sum_{m=1}^{M} (\widehat{\mathrm{TCP}}^m - \mathrm{TCP}^m)^2 \tag{5}$$

where $\widehat{\mathrm{TCP}}^m = g_m(v^m)$ is the output of the confidence regression network g_m.

3.4.3.3 TCP Dyanmic Feature Fusion Subsequently, we employ a modality-level gating strategy to achieve dynamic multimodal fusion based on information content. Specifically, the TCP values $\widehat{\mathrm{TCP}}^m$ estimated by the confidence regression network g_m are used as gating weights to dynamically adjust the contribution of each modality in the fusion process. The final multimodal representation h can be expressed as:

$$h = \sum_{m=1}^{M} \widehat{\mathrm{TCP}}^m h^m \tag{6}$$

where h^m is the feature representation of modality m, $\widehat{\mathrm{TCP}}^m$ is the confidence weight of modality m, and M denotes the total number of modalities.

3.4.4 Global Classifier After implementing modality dynamic fusion at both the feature level and the modality level, we define a global classifier, referred to as MMClassifier, which is responsible for the global fusion of the processed multimodal features. The global classifier consists of a sequence of neural network layers, including linear layers, ReLU activation functions, dropout layers, and a final classification layer. It is trained using a cross-entropy loss function, aiming to optimize both feature fusion and classification performance.

Cross-entropy loss is a commonly used loss function in classification tasks, primarily aimed at measuring the difference between the probability distribution predicted by the model and the true probability distribution of the labels [18]. It is defined as:

$$L = -\sum_{i=1}^{C} y_i \log(p_i) \tag{7}$$

where C represents the number of classes, y_i is the one-hot encoding of the true labels, and p_i is the probability assigned by the model to class i.

Finally, a classifier f is trained to map the multimodal representation h to the class label y:

$$y = f(h) \tag{8}$$

where y denotes the class label.

During the training process, we employs the AdamW optimizer, the learning rate is dynamically adjusted based on the gradient of the loss function to update the model parameters [19].

4 Experiments

4.1 Experimental Setup

Experimental Environment. The experiments were conducted in the experimental environment presented in Table 2.

Table 2. Experimental environment.

Name	Specific Parameters
CPU	2nd Gen Intel® Core™ i9-12900K x 24
GPU	NVIDIA GeForce RTX 3090 / PCle / SSE2
Memory	31.1TB
Operation System	Ubuntu 20.04.6 LTS (64-bit)
Python Version	3.8.16
Pytorch Version	2.2.2
CUDA Version	V10.1.243

Dataset. The dataset utilized in our study was sourced from AndroZoo [20], it aggregates APK files from Google Play, third - party app markets, and open - source communities, encompassing over 20,836,715 distinct APK files. Each APK file undergoes rigorous maliciousness annotation through analysis by dozens of antivirus products, thereby ensuring the reliability of the labels.

To construct the experimental dataset, considering that the proportion of benign applications often exceeds that of malicious applications in real-world scenarios, and to mitigate the effects of version fragmentation (ranging from Android 4.4 to 10) and concept drift, we randomly selected 17,500 APK samples from the data spanning the years 2015 to 2020. The dataset includes 10,000 benign samples (accounting for 57.14%, labeled as 1) and 7,500 malicious samples (accounting for 42.86%, labeled as 0), thereby preserving a moderate level of class imbalance.

For further processing of the dataset, we divide it into a training set (14,000 samples) and an independent test set (3,500 samples) in an 8:2 ratio using stratified random sampling to ensure consistent class distribution.

Evaluation Metrics and Experimental Details. To thoroughly assess the detection performance of the model, we mainly utilizes the following four evaluation metrics: accuracy (ACC), F1 score (F1-0 and F1-1), precision, and area under the curve (AUC). In the of binary classification problems, F1-0 generally indicates the F1 score for the Benign in unbalanced datasets, whereas F1-1 refers to the F1 score for the Malware. Both them combine precision and recall, serving to evaluate the model's predictive capability for each class, and also assist in assessing the model's performance on the majority class within imbalanced datasets. Throughout the subsequent experiments, we will rigorously reference these four metrics for the assessment and comparison of validity.

4.2 Comparison of Multi-head Attention Mechanism Configurations

In this section, an extensive series of comparative experiments were conducted to assess the necessity of incorporating the multi-head attention mechanism into the multi-modality dynamic fusion model and its specific impact on model performance at different integration points. Using the AndroZoo dataset consistently, we compared four models: the baseline model without the multi-head attention mechanism; the model with the multi-head attention mechanism introduced before TCP dynamic fusion (referred to as Early Multi-head Attention); the model with the multi-head attention mechanism introduced after TCP dynamic fusion (referred to as Late Multi-head Attention); and the dual-layer fine-grained fusion model with the multi-head attention mechanism introduced both before and after the TCP mechanism. Each model was tested multiple times, and the average values of the metrics were taken. The specific experimental results are detailed in Table 3.

As presented in Table 3, the results demonstrate that the introduction of the multi-head attention mechanism significantly enhances the model's performance

Table 3. Impact of Multi-head Attention Mechanism Introduction on Model Performance. Bold values indicate the optimal performance across all tests.

Introduction Position	ACC (%)	F1 Score (%)	AUC (%)	Precision (%)
Baseline Model	95.60	95.66	98.08	95.56
Late Multi-head Attention	96.03	96.06	97.89	97.01
Early Multi-head Attention	**97.18**	**97.62**	98.78	**97.82**
Dual-layer Attention	96.26	96.25	**99.03**	97.21

metrics compared to the baseline model. Specifically, the early introduction of the multi-head attention mechanism before TCP dynamic weight allocation achieves the highest accuracy (97.18%), F1 score (97.62%), and precision (97.82%), indicating its effectiveness in capturing complex relationships between modalities and optimizing feature weights.

However, the dual-layer attention mechanism, which incorporates additional attention layers both before and after the TCP mechanism, did not meet our expectations. Despite achieving the highest AUC value (99.03%), it underperformed in terms of accuracy and precision compared to the early multi-head attention model. This suggests that while the multi-head attention mechanism is beneficial, the dual-layer configuration may introduce unnecessary complexity.

The reasons for the suboptimal performance of the dual-layer attention mechanism may be threefold:

- Overfitting Risk: Introducing multiple attention mechanisms can lead to overfitting, where the model performs well on the training set but poorly on unseen test data.
- Computational Complexity: The dual-layer attention mechanism increases the model's computational complexity, resulting in longer training times.
- Information Redundancy: The MMDF model already effectively captures complex relationships between modalities using TCP dynamic weight allocation. Adding extra attention layers may not provide additional classification gains and could introduce redundant information.

4.3 Ablation Study

4.3.1 Ablation Study on Modality Selection and Optimal Combination This section presents the results of the ablation study, which assesses the contribution of individual modalities (behavioral, opcode, and sensitive API) to overall classification performance and compares them with the proposed multi-modality approach to investigate the impact of different multi-modality combinations on model performance. The experiments were conducted on the AndroZoo dataset. By comparing the performance of single modalities and various combinations of modalities (pairwise and all three modalities) across five key metrics—accuracy (ACC), F1-0, F1-1, precision, and area under the curve

(AUC)—the optimal multi-modality combination was determined to provide a basis for modality selection and utilization in the multi-modality dynamic fusion model. The specific experimental results are shown in Table 4.

Table 4. Multimodal Modality Ablation Experiment Results. 1: Behavioral features; 2: Sensitive API features; 3: Opcode features. Bold values indicate the optimal performance across all tests.

Modality Fusion	ACC (%)	F1-0 (%)	F1-1 (%)	AUC (%)	Precision (%)
{1}	91.20	91.55	90.82	95.77	94.67
{2}	95.58	95.61	95.54	98.38	96.22
{3}	93.61	93.62	93.60	97.74	93.99
{1,2}	96.08	96.14	96.02	98.70	97.45
{1,3}	95.07	95.14	95.00	98.47	96.69
{2,3}	95.90	95.92	95.88	98.72	96.24
{1,2,3}	**97.81**	**97.62**	**96.95**	**98.78**	**97.82**

Table 4 compares the ablation study results of different modality combinations, with grouped bar charts (see Fig. 6) providing a more intuitive comparison. In terms of individual modality contributions, sensitive API features {2} demonstrated the highest independent discriminative ability (single-modality AUC of 98.38%). When combined with Opcode features {3} the AUC performance of the {2,3} combination approached that of the full modality. Behavioral features {1}, though weaker individually (ACC of 91.20%), effectively captured dynamic behavior patterns when fused with Sensitive API features {1,2} combination, ACC of 96.08%), highlighting the intermodality associations and the comprehensive advantages of multi-modality.

The fusion strategy of the three modalities significantly enhanced malware detection performance. The full modality combination {1,2,3} achieved best performance in ACC (97.81%), AUC (98.78%), and precision (97.82%), underscoring the effectiveness of multi-modality fusion. Meanwhile, in order to illustrate the effect of the multi-head attention mechanism in more detail, we recorded the proportion of attention weights for each modality during the training process under the optimal combination, and the specific weight proportions are shown in Table 5.

The experimental results indicate that the attention weight differences among the three modalities are less than 1.2%, suggesting that the model does not significantly favor any single modality. This reflects the ability of the multi-head attention mechanism to automatically capture inter-modal dependencies, preventing the dominnce of a single modality and promoting dynamic fusion effects among the modalities (Fig. 5).

Table 5. Importance of each modality.

Modality	Attention Weight(%)	Modality type
Behaviour Feature	33.20	User behavior patterns (operation frequency)
Opcode Feature	34.00	Program instruction sequence (code logic)
Sensitive API Feature	32.80	High-risk system calls (privileged operations)

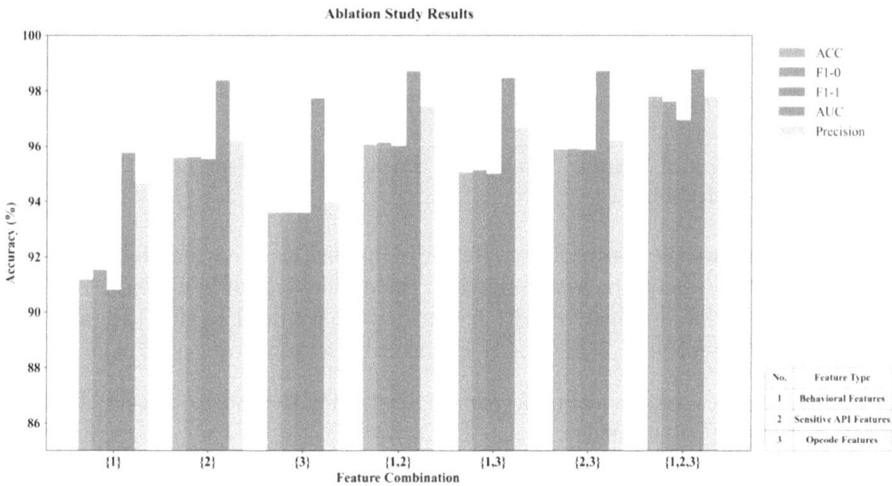

Fig. 5. Comparison of Metrics for Modality Ablation Study.

4.3.2 The Impact of Feature Selection on the Performance of the MMDF Model Multimodal learning enhances the predictive capabilities of models by integrating information from various data sources. However, irrelevant or redundant features can decrease the model's generalization ability and increase computational costs. This experiment aims to evaluate the impact of feature selection on the performance of the MMDF model in Android malware detection tasks.

We explored two approaches in our experiments. In the first approach, we directly utilized three modality feature vectors extracted from APK decompilation as inputs to the MMDF model after performing basic data cleaning. These vectors included behavioral features of 9025 dimensions, opcode features of 237 dimensions, and sensitive API features of 531 dimensions. In the second approach, we applied the *SelectFromModel* selector to the raw feature data to conduct feature selection, thereby retaining features of research value for training the MMDF model.

The experiment was conducted on the same AndroZoo public dataset, with *num_epoch* set to 1000 and *test_interval* set to 50. Each case was trained 10 times, and the average values of various model metrics and training time were recorded.

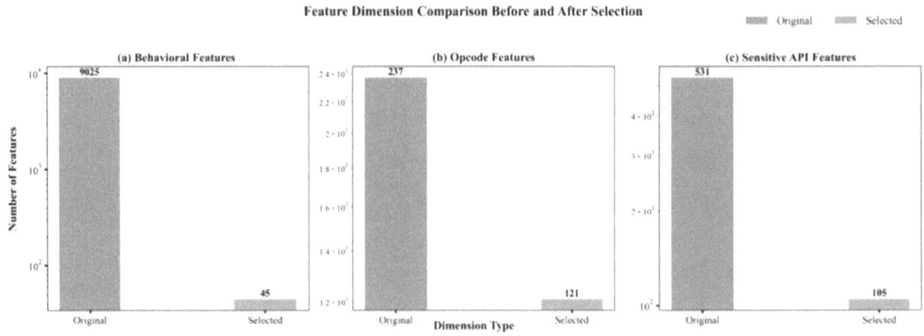

Fig. 6. Comparison of Feature Numbers for Each Modality Before and After ExtraTreesClassifier Selection.

Figure 6 shows the comparison of feature dimensions across modalities before and after feature selection. After selection, the dimensions of behavioral features, opcode features, and sensitive API features were reduced to 45, 121, and 105 dimensions, respectively, achieving a feature compression rate of 97.23%.

Table 6. Comparison of model performance, illustrating the specific impact of feature selection on model performance.

Scenario	ACC (%)	F1-0 (%)	F1-1 (%)	AUC (%)	Prec (%)	Training Time (seconds)
Original	95.29	95.34	95.25	97.50	96.05	301
Selected	97.18	97.62	96.95	98.78	97.82	35

The experimental results in Table 6 indicate that after feature selection, the model's performance improved across all evaluation metrics, particularly with the test accuracy increasing from 95.29% to 97.18%. Additionally, feature selection significantly reduced the model's training time, enhancing training efficiency by nearly 88.37%, which is crucial for real-time systems requiring rapid iteration and deployment.

4.3.3 The Effect of Dynamic TCP Weight Allocation on the Performance of the MMDF Model Within the MMDF architecture, a TCP layer is introduced subsequent to the multi-head attention mechanism. This layer is designed to compute the classification confidence of each modality's feature vector. By fusing the modal features with dynamic weights derived from the TCP values, the predictability is enhanced. The primary objective of this experiment is to evaluate the impact and necessity of the TCP dynamic weight allocation mechanism on the performance of the MMDF model in Android malware classification.

We evaluated the MMDF model in two configurations: one without the TCP mechanism and the other incorporating the TCP mechanism.

The experiment utilized the AndroZoo dataset, with *num_epoch* set to 1000 and *test_interval* set to 50. Each model was trained 10 times, and the average performance metrics were recorded, as depicted in Table 7.

Table 7. Performance comparison between models with and without TCP mechanism and with TCP mechanism.

Metric	Without_TCP	With_TCP
ACC (%)	95.70	97.18
F1-0 (%)	96.13	97.62
F1-1 (%)	95.13	96.95
AUC (%)	96.90	98.78
Precision (%)	96.10	97.82

The experimental results in Table 7 indicate that the introduction of the TCP mechanism led to improvements across all evaluation metrics. Notably, the test ACC increased from 94.63% to 97.18%, and the AUC improved from 96.50% to 98.78%. These findings demonstrate that the TCP dynamic weight allocation mechanism effectively augments the model's capacity to assess feature importance by assigning variable weights to features from different modalities, which allows our model to concentrate on modalities that contribute more significantly to the classification task.

4.4 Comparison Analysis

4.4.1 Comparison with Other State-of-the-Art Methods To further validate the framework's feasibility, we investigated and selected three representative methods for comparative experiments on the same AndroZoo dataset. The specific details are as follows:

- The model proposed by Vinayakumar et al. [7] (referred to as LSTM+CNN) is a deep learning architecture designed for evaluating known benign and malicious applications derived from static analysis.
- The model developed by Li et al. [3] (known as FGF) is a multi-modal fine-grained fusion model. Its core innovation lies in the deep integration of features from two modalities: the function call graph (FCG) and the Dex bytecode image.
- Kim et al. [9] were the first to introduce a multi-modal architecture in the field of Android malware detection, pioneering a new direction and laying a significant foundation for subsequent related research.

The specific comparative results are presented in Table 8.

Table 8. Comparison of MMDF with other state-of-the-art methods.

Model	ACC (%)	AUC (%)	F1-1 (%)	F1-0 (%)	Precision (%)
LSTM+CNN	91.45	91.44	91.43	91.44	91.40
Kim	92.71	95.23	94.12	93.99	93.30
FGF	90.88	92.08	90.12	95.22	92.54
MMDF	**97.18**	**98.78**	**96.95**	**97.62**	**97.82**

To show the comparison results more intuitively, we generates a heat map of various indicators as shown in Fig. 7:

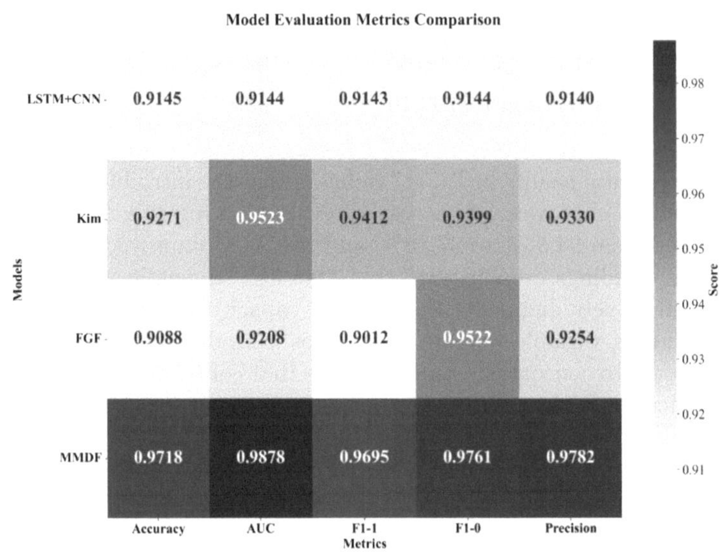

Fig. 7. Comparison of MMDF with other state-of-the-art methods.

4.4.2 Generalization Comparison Across Datasets To evaluate the model's generalization capability, performance stability, and adaptability to dataset variations, this experiment conducts training and testing on two distinct datasets. In the experiment, the CICMalDroid 2020 dataset is used for categorizing four specific types of malicious application packages—Adware, Banking, SMS malware, and Riskware—as malware with a label of 1, while benign categories are labeled as 0. Based on this classification, three types of features, totaling 17,500 data instances, are extracted in alignment with the AndroZoo dataset. Detailed performance metrics are presented in Table 9.

Table 9. Cross-dataset experiments and model generalization evaluation results.

Experimental Setup	Acc (%)	Prec (%)	AUC (%)	F1 (%)
Same-Dataset Training-Testing (AndroZoo → AndroZoo)	97.18	97.82	98.78	97.25
Same-Dataset Training-Testing (CICMalDroid2020 → CICMalDroid2020)	96.48	97.28	98.49	94.76
Cross-Dataset Training-Testing (AndroZoo → CICMalDroid2020)	91.10	90.99	93.56	91.24

Further analysis shows that the MMDF demonstrated high precision and strong fitting capability on both the AndroZoo dataset (with an accuracy of 97.18%) and the CICMalDroid2020 dataset (with an accuracy of 96.48%). This validates its stability across datasets with different distributions. In the cross-dataset evaluation, although a slight performance degradation was observed, the MMDF still achieved a high accuracy of 91.10%, demonstrating its robust generalization capability across different datasets.

5 Conclusion

In this paper, we proposed a multi-modality Android malware detection framework MMDF. It employs multi-head attention mechanisms to capture complex relationships between individual features within and across modalities. We then use TCP dynamic weight allocation to quantify modality confidence. Results show that MMDF achieved the highest accuracy, with a rate of 97.18% on the AndroZoo dataset, while maintaining a 91% feature compression rate. The framework also achieved an AUC score of 98.78%, proving its excellent accuracy and generalization capabilities.

Furthermore, we evaluated MMDF's inference performance on an Intel Core i9-12900K CPU. With 1.62M parameters, the model requires only 5.92 ms for single-sample inference (batch size = 1) and has a peak memory footprint of 382.1 MB. These results demonstrate the MMDF's high computational efficiency, characterized by low latency and moderate memory usage.

In the future, we will investigate the extraction of more discriminative static and dynamic features to enhance the feature representation capabilities by combining them through a multi-modal approach. We hope our MMDF framework can enhance the effectiveness of Android malware detection to some extent and contribute to the security of cyberspace.

Acknowledgments. We thank the anonymous reviewers for their constructive comments. This work is supported by Guangdong Basic and Applied Basic Research Foundation, China [Grant No. 2026A1515010248], Science and Technology Program of Guangzhou, China [Grant No. 2025A04J3441], Guangdong Philosophy and Social Science Foundation [Grant No. GD25YTS06], the Starting Research Fund from the Guangdong University of Foreign Studies [Grant No. 2022RC049], Humanities and Social Sciences Planning Project of the Ministry of Education [Grant No. 23YJAZH106].

References

1. Zimperium: 2024 Global Mobile Threat Report. Dallas: Zimperium (2024)
2. McLaughlin, N., Martinez del Rincon, J., Kang, B.J., et al.: Deep android malware detection. In: Proceedings of the seventh ACM on conference on data and application security and privacy, pp. 301–308 (2017)
3. Li, X., Liu, L., Liu, Y., et al.: Detecting android malware: a multimodal fusion method with fine-grained feature. Inf. Fusion **114**, 102662 (2025)
4. Corbière, C., Thome, N., Bar-Hen, A., et al.: Addressing failure prediction by learning model confidence. Adv. Neural Inf. Process. Syst. **32** (2019)
5. İbrahim, M., Issa, B., Jasser, M.B.: A method for automatic android malware detection based on static analysis and deep learning. IEEE Access **10**, 117334–117352 (2022)
6. Xiao, X., Xiao, X., Jiang, Y., et al.: Identifying android malware with system call co-occurrence matrices. Trans. Emerg. Telecommun. Technol. **27**(5), 675–684 (2016)
7. Vinayakumar, R., Soman, K.P., Poornachandran, P., et al.: Detecting Android malware using long short-term memory (LSTM). J. Intell. Fuzzy Syst. **34**(3), 1277–1288 (2018)
8. Hao-dong, W., Liang, W.: Android malware detection method based on static feature combination in graph neural networks. Computer Engineering. https://doi.org/10.19678/j.issn.1000-3428.0070073
9. Kim, T.G., Kang, B.J., Rho, M., et al.: A multimodal deep learning method for android malware detection using various features. IEEE Trans. Inf. Forensics Secur. **14**(3), 773–788 (2018)
10. Yang, X., Yang, D., Li, Y.: A hybrid attention network for malware detection based on multi-feature aligned and fusion. Electronics **12**(3), 713 (2023)
11. Chen, S., Lang, B., Liu, H., et al.: Android malware detection method based on graph attention networks and deep fusion of multimodal features. Expert Syst. Appl. **237**, 121617 (2024)
12. Darem, A., Abawajy, J., Makkar, A., et al.: Visualization and deep-learning-based malware variant detection using OpCode-level features. Futur. Gener. Comput. Syst. **125**, 314–323 (2021)
13. Calciati, P., Kuznetsov, K., Gorla, A., et al.: Automatically granted permissions in Android apps: an empirical study on their prevalence and on the potential threats for privacy. In: Proceedings of the 17th International Conference on Mining Software Repositories, pp. 114–124 (2020)
14. Zhang, X., Zhang, Y., Zhong, M., et al.: Enhancing state-of-the-art classifiers with api semantics to detect evolved android malware. In: Proceedings of the 2020 ACM SIGSAC Conference on Computer and Communications Security, pp. 757–770 (2020)
15. Bhandari, A.: Feature engineering: scaling, normalization, and standardization. Analytics Vidhya, updated 2023
16. Breiman, L.: Random forests. Machine Learn. **45**, 5–32 (2001)

17. Han, Z., Yang, F., Huang, J., et al.: Multimodal dynamics: dynamical fusion for trustworthy multimodal classification. In: Proceedings of the IEEE/CVF Conference on Computer Vision and Pattern Recognition, pp. 20707–20717 (2022)
18. Mao, A., Mohri, M., Zhong, Y.: Cross-entropy loss functions: theoretical analysis and applications. In: International Conference on Machine Learning, pp. 23803–23828 (2023)
19. Luo, L., Xiong, Y., Liu, Y., et al.: Adaptive gradient methods with dynamic bound of learning rate. arXiv preprint arXiv:1902.09843 (2019)
20. Allix, K., Bissyandé, T.F., Klein, J., et al.: Androzoo: Collecting millions of android apps for the research community. In: Proceedings of the 13th International Conference on Mining Software Repositories, pp. 468–471 (2016)

A Lightweight Federated Learning Framework with Dynamic Local Differential Privacy and Transfer Learning

Changsong Yang[1,2,3], Qiuyu Liu[1,3], Yueling Liu[1,3(✉)], Yong Ding[1,2,3], and Zhen Liu[1,3]

[1] Guangxi Key Laboratory of Cryptography and Information Security, Guilin University of Electronic Technology, Guilin 541004, China
{csyang,ylliu}@guet.edu.cn, qyliu2001@163.com, zhliu9802@163.com

[2] Lion Rock Labs of Cyberspace Security, Institute of Cyberspace Technology, HKCT Institute of Higher Education, Hong Kong, China
stone_dingy@126.com

[3] Guangxi Engineering Research Center of Industrial Internet Security and Blockchain, Guilin University of Electronic Technology, Guilin 541004, China

Abstract. Federated Learning serves as a pivotal privacy preserving technique that mitigates privacy risks from data centralization through distributed collaborative model training; however, the inherent complexity and resource intensive nature of deep learning models incur substantial communication overhead during privacy protection. To strictly safeguard client privacy while maintaining model accuracy and reducing communication costs, this paper proposes LDPTL-FL a novel FL framework integrating Local Differential Privacy and Transfer Learning. This paper proposes a parameter sharing based hierarchical algorithm for transfer learning that decomposes the backbone model into a shared encoder and a predictor. The predictor undergoes adaptive pruning. Departing from conventional federated learning, the method inspired by transfer learning updates and aggregates only the predictor, substantially reducing communication overhead. Furthermore, we develop an LDP based dynamic perturbation algorithm where each client dynamically allocates privacy budgets, injects noise into unpruned predictor segments via the Posterior Minimization mechanism, reconstructs pruned segments of the perturbed predictor, and uploads parameters to the server for aggregation, thereby ensuring privacy protection without compromising accuracy. Experimental results demonstrate that our solution achieves substantially higher average accuracy on MNIST and CIFAR10 datasets compared to FedAvg, FedDPA and FedLPS benchmarks.

This article was supported by the National Key R&D Program of China (2023YFB3107300), the Guangxi Natural Science Foundation (2024GXNSFAA010453), the National Natural Science Foundation of China (62562021, 62562019), and the Lion Rock Labs of Cyberspace Security (LRL24-1-C003).

L. Zhang and K.-K. R. Choo (Eds.): MobiQuitous 2025, LNICST 683, pp. 214–235, 2026.
https://doi.org/10.1007/978-3-032-22500-9_13

Keywords: Federated learning · Local differential privacy · Transfer learning · Perturbation mechanism · Model pruning

1 Introduction

Recent advancements in artificial intelligence have demonstrated machine learning's immense potential across diverse domains including autonomous driving, facial recognition, and data mining. However, growing data security concerns particularly regarding privacy breaches have emerged as critical bottlenecks hindering widespread adoption [20]. Traditional centralized learning paradigms require massive dataset centralization, significantly increasing leakage risks while violating data sovereignty and privacy preservation principles. To address these challenges, Google pioneered Federated Learning (FL) in 2016 [13]. This distributed framework enables collaborative training of high accuracy global models while maintaining data residency effectively enhancing client privacy protection and facilitating cross device knowledge integration. Consequently, FL improves model adaptability to heterogeneous data distributions and generalization capabilities [4].

Despite its practical successes, FL continues to present significant persistent challenges [7]. The inherent complexity and resource intensive nature of deep learning models incur substantial communication overhead in FL systems, where iterative exchanges of model updates between multiple clients and a central server during training rounds lead to prohibitive communication costs [9]. Furthermore, research indicates non-trivial privacy leakage risks during FL training [28]. Shared model updates may inadvertently expose individual data patterns, rendering them vulnerable to adversarial extraction of sensitive information including via model inversion attacks and gradient analysis when transmitted to the server without adequate safeguards [5].

To address these challenges, this paper proposes a federated learning framework integrating Transfer Learning (TL) and Local Differential Privacy (LDP) to preserve privacy while maintaining model accuracy and reducing communication overhead. For communication efficiency, we leverage TL based parameter sharing where a frozen shared encoder (excluded from aggregation) enables cross client knowledge transfer. The remaining task specific predictors undergo adaptive pruning with selective updating of modified segments. Against privacy leakage, we implement dynamic per-round privacy budget allocation followed by piecewise perturbation of updated pruned predictors. Clients locally reconstruct perturbed predictors before uploading to the central server, which aggregates models via Federated Averaging (FedAvg). Hence, the main contributions of this work are summarized as follows.

(1) We propose a privacy preserving FL framework integrating TL and LDP that maintains model accuracy while reducing communication overhead;
(2) Leveraging TL, we partition client models into a shared encoder and task specific predictors. The shared encoder generates embeddings for predictor updates, enabling global model construction through predictor aggregation.

Crucially, only the unpruned segments of predictors are updated and aggregated, significantly reducing communication costs;
(3) We introduce an LDP based privacy mechanism where clients apply a Perturbation Mechanism (PM) to updated pruned predictors. This approach prevents privacy leakage without additional communication overhead and eliminates third party dependencies;
(4) Theoretical and experimental analyses demonstrate that our solution outperforms FedAvg [13], FedDPA [22], and FedLPS [8] in privacy preservation, security, and accuracy metrics.

The remainder of this paper is organized as follows. Section 2 reviews related work on LDP and privacy preserving techniques in Federated Learning. Section 3 introduces the fundamental techniques underpinning our framework. Section 4 presents the proposed framework in detail. Rigorous privacy and security proofs of our solution are established in Sect. 5. Section 6 provides extensive experimental comparisons with state of the art approaches. Finally, Sect. 7 concludes the paper and discusses future research directions.

2 Related Work

To address the challenges posed by high communication costs and privacy leakage risks in FL, a lot of researchers have conducted extensive research efforts.

Lightweight Machine Learning Model Design. TL has emerged as a highly promising machine learning approach for knowledge transfer across domains with disparate probability distributions [15]. Tu et al. [17] pioneered a dynamic layer sharing mechanism termed FedDL, which integrates local models by leveraging weight similarities, thereby offering a novel and efficient strategy for model sharing in federated learning. Building upon this, Yu et al. [24] further proposed SPATL, a federated learning approach that reduces communication overhead, accelerates inference, and stabilizes the training process through parameter selection, model partitioning, and gradient control mechanisms. Subsequently, Tang et al. [16] proposed a privacy preserving wind power prediction framework that employs a two stage training strategy to construct accurate and personalized models without data leakage. However, existing methods still suffer from insufficient co-optimization between resource consumption and privacy protection. Although Jia et al.'s FedLPS [8] achieves efficient multi task deployment on single devices through local parameter sharing and TL while reducing resource consumption, its lack of privacy safeguards limits practical applicability. To address prolonged training times and data scarcity, Zhang et al. [26] proposed a federated lightweight network based feature extraction method for reciprocal machinery, which enables cross enterprise collaborative diagnosis and effectively mitigates data scarcity. Further advancing efficiency, Yuan et al. [25] implemented lightweight personalized models via pruning and desensitization to reduce training and communication costs. Specifically, the server distributes encoded subnetworks to clients, who then employ the Alternating Direction Method of Multipliers (ADMM) to prune unimportant parameters. Crucially, while existing works progress in model lightweighting and personalization, few simultaneously leverage TL for resource reduction while preserving privacy.

Privacy Preserving Federated Learning. In traditional FL training, privacy leakage remains a pervasive issue. To defend against adversaries attempting to steal sensitive data during training, a variety of privacy preserving techniques have been proposed to provide reliable privacy guarantees. Among them, Differential Privacy (DP) has become a widely adopted mechanism in FL due to its rigorous privacy definition and high efficiency. By injecting a controlled amount of noise into the model parameters uploaded by clients, DP obscures individual parameter details, thereby effectively mitigating membership inference attacks [6,27]. Compared to alternative approaches such as homomorphic encryption and secure multi-party computation, DP offers superior efficiency in terms of both computational and communication overhead. Dong et al. [3] proposed PADP-FedMeta, a personalized and adaptive differentially private federated meta learning mechanism that mitigates Non-IID impacts on model accuracy while accelerating convergence of adaptive privacy parameters. Building on this, Wei et al. [19] developed a gradient leakage resilient method using adaptive noise injection and trend tracking to enhance privacy in distributed SGD while optimizing accuracy and attack resilience. Subsequently, Chen et al. [2] introduced CLFLDP, an FL model integrating DP with layer wise pruning to address high communication costs and low accuracy. This approach employs adaptive privacy budget allocation to reduce privacy loss and noise magnitude, alongside layer wise top-k parameter selection. Despite these advances, current methods remain inadequate for large scale local model parameters. Yang et al. [22] addressed this via Fed-DPA, which optimizes personalized and shared parameters through adaptive differential constraints to improve convergence. However, applying noise to all local parameters introduces excessive noise that degrades accuracy and increases communication overhead. Batool et al. [1] proposed an LDP based framework for private data sharing in vehicular networks, where vehicles perturb data before sharing with roadside units (RSUs) that train model parameters updated by a central server. Further advancing this direction, Weng et al. [21] implemented a DP based FL scheme that limits LDP noise impact on convergence without compromising privacy. They introduced two strategies both modifying local objective functions to enhance convergence. Ling et al. [12] improved model accuracy under privacy constraints via a secure DP SGD protocol that calculates client specific privacy weights based on noise magnitude, incorporating directional gradient histogram features and weighted averaging with heterogeneous privacy budgets. Notably, current solutions largely neglect the communication overhead inherent in multi round FL iterations and fail to adequately address the intrinsic trade off between privacy preservation and communication efficiency.

To address this challenge, this paper proposes LDPTL-FL, a federated learning scheme integrating LDP with transfer learning. The scheme employs transfer learning to build a model architecture comprising a shared encoder and a predictor. Utilizing model pruning, it selectively updates only the parameters with high importance scores. Prior to server aggregation, dynamic privacy budgeting and piecewise perturbation mechanisms are applied to inject noise specifically into these pruned predictors. Consequently, the server aggregates only the noise perturbed predictors. This dual approach effectively minimizes both the volume of transmitted model parameters and the amount of noise introduced. LDPTL-FL thus maintains model accuracy while ensuring privacy protection and reducing communication overhead.

3 Preliminaries

3.1 FedAvg

In 2017, McMahan et al. [13] proposed the classic FedAvg algorithm. Its core idea involves clients performing multiple local updates to their model weights independently, followed by transmitting these updated weights to the server for weighted averaging. This approach effectively reduces the number of communication rounds required:

(1) **Model Initialization.** The central server broadcasts the initialized global model parameters w_0^G to all clients.

(2) **Local Model Training and Update.** During the t-th iteration, client k performs local model updates:

$$w_{t+1}^k \leftarrow w_t^G - \eta g_k, \tag{1}$$

where w_t^G denotes the global model parameters at round t, η represents the learning rate, and g_t^k is the gradient of client k at iteration t. Client k then sends the locally updated model parameters w_{t+1}^k to the central server.

(3) **Global Model Aggregation.** After receiving the locally updated models from all clients, the central server performs secure aggregation to generate the new global model w_{t+1}^G and broadcasts it back to all clients for the next iteration. The aggregation operation is as follows:

$$w_{t+1}^G \leftarrow \sum_{k=1}^{K} \frac{n_k}{n} w_{t+1}^k, \tag{2}$$

where n_k is the size of the local dataset at client k, and n represents the total size of all client datasets. Steps (2) and (3) are repeated until the federated learning global model converges or reaches the predetermined number of training rounds.

3.2 Local Differential Privacy

Differential privacy (DP) is a technique that protects individual privacy by injecting noise into data, ensuring that individual information cannot be precisely identified even during data analysis. The privacy budget ϵ represents the bound on the indistinguishability of any outputs for arbitrary pairs of data records in DP, governing the trade off between the strength of privacy protection and the accuracy of published results. Local differential privacy (LDP) is a variant of DP where random perturbation is performed by clients as opposed to the aggregator.

Algorithm A satisfies $\epsilon - \text{LDP}$ if and only if for any two adjacent datasets D and D' and any subset of possible outputs Z, the following inequality holds:

$$\Pr[A(D) = Z] \leq e^{\epsilon} \cdot \Pr[A(D') = Z], \tag{3}$$

where $\Pr[\cdot]$ denotes the probability of the enclosed random event, ϵ is the privacy budget, and a smaller ϵ corresponds to a higher security level.

3.3 Perturbation Mechanism

Wang et al. [18] proposed the Piecewise Mechanism (PM), an unbiased LDP mechanism for mean value collection, which employs the concept of piecewise randomized response to perturb data. During perturbation, if the true data value domain is $w_i \in [-r, r]$, clients should first normalize it as $\tilde{w_i} = w_i/r$ where $\tilde{w_i} \in [-1, 1]$. Then, randomly select $x \in [0, 1]$ and perturb $\tilde{w_i}$ using PM to obtain $\hat{w_i}$,

$$\hat{w_i} = \begin{cases} \text{Uniformly at random from } [\ell(\tilde{w_i}), \gamma(\tilde{w_i})], \ x < \dfrac{e^{\varepsilon/2}}{e^{\varepsilon/2} + 1} \\ \text{Uniformly at random from } [(-C, \ell(\tilde{w_i})) \cup (\gamma(\tilde{w_i}), C)], \\ \text{other} \end{cases} \tag{4}$$

The client then uploads $\hat{w_i}' = r\hat{w_i}$ to the server. After perturbation, $\hat{w_i}$ falls within the output range $[-C, C]$,

$$C = \frac{e^{\epsilon/2} + 1}{e^{\epsilon/2} - 1},$$

where, $\ell(\tilde{w_i}) = \frac{C+1}{2} \cdot \tilde{w_i} - \frac{C-1}{2}$, $\gamma(\tilde{w_i}) = \ell(\tilde{w_i}) + C - 1 = \frac{C+1}{2} \cdot \tilde{w_i} + \frac{C-1}{2}$.

The probability density function of $\hat{w_i}$ is given by the mathematical form of the function f as follows:

$$f(\hat{w_i} = x|\tilde{w_i}) = \begin{cases} p, \ if \ x \in [l(\tilde{w_i}), \gamma(\tilde{w_i})], \\ \dfrac{p}{e^{\varepsilon}}, \ if \ x \in [-C, l(\tilde{w_i})] \cup [\gamma(\tilde{w_i}), C], \end{cases} \tag{5}$$

where, $p = \frac{e^{\epsilon} - e^{\epsilon/2}}{2e^{\epsilon/2} + 2}$.

3.4 Based on Parameter Sharing Transfer Learning

Transfer learning is a key technique in machine learning that enables models to transfer and apply knowledge acquired from one task to another related task. Parameter sharing based transfer learning focuses on identifying common parameters between spatial models of source and target data, allowing knowledge transfer through further processing. In 2014, Bengio et al. [23] investigated the transferability of features across layers in deep learning, with the specific transfer learning process demonstrated in Fig. 1.

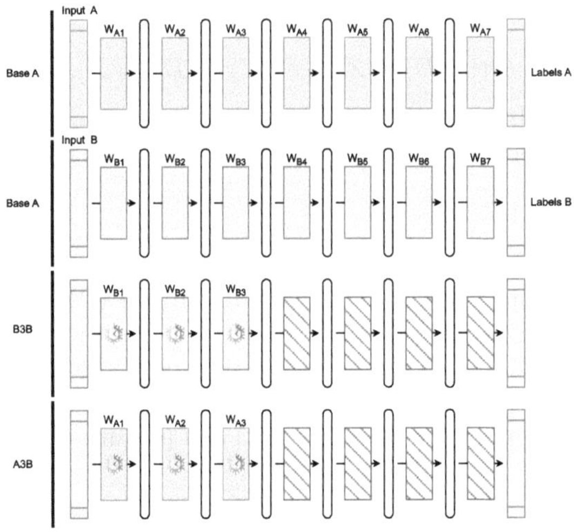

Fig. 1. Transfer learning process.

The study assumes two tasks, A and B, where each task's model comprises 7 layers denoted as $\{w_{A1}, w_{A2}, \ldots, w_{A7}\}$ and $\{w_{B1}, w_{B2}, \ldots, w_{B7}\}$ respectively. Two model architectures were designed: 1) Model $B3B$: the first 3 layers copied from task B and frozen, with 5 randomly initialized higher layers trained on dataset B; 2) Model $A3B$: the first 3 layers copied from task A and frozen, with 5 randomly initialized higher layers trained on dataset B. If $A3B$ performs as well as $B3B$, it can be concluded that the first three layers of A contain transferable features generalizable to B.

4 Design of LDPTL-FL

4.1 System Model

The system model of the proposed scheme is illustrated in Fig. 2. Within this framework, a central server interacts with N clients. Each client partitions its local model w into a shared encoder w_e and a predictor w_p, freezing the shared encoder while exclusively updating the predictor. During each federated learning communication round, clients dynamically prune their predictors and update each pruned predictor using embeddings generated by the shared encoder. Each client selects its initial dynamic privacy budget, perturbs the updated pruned predictor using the PM according to this budget, restores the pruned model parameters, and uploads the perturbed predictor to the central server. Finally, the server aggregates all perturbed predictors and broadcasts the updated model to clients for the next training round. This process iterates until clients exhaust their privacy budgets or the model undergoes sufficient training rounds.

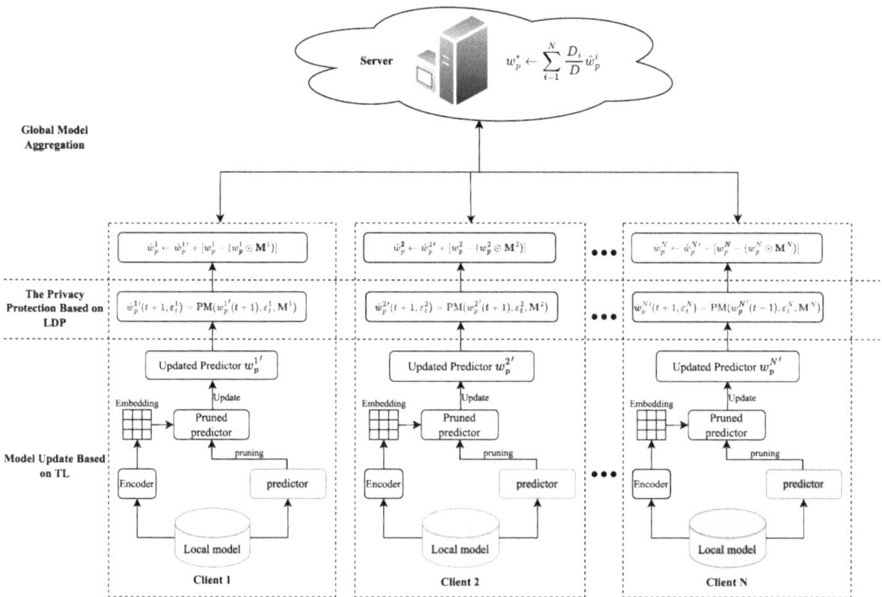

Fig. 2. System model.

As shown in Fig. 2, this proposal involves two entities:

Server. The central server initializes the global model and distributes it to all clients; receives clients' perturbed predictors; aggregates predictors using the FedAvg algorithm; and finally broadcasts the aggregated results back to all clients.

Client. The client partitions its local model into a shared encoder and a predictor, prunes the predictor, updates the pruned predictor using embeddings generated by the shared encoder, then perturbs the updated predictor with an LDP based perturbation mechanism, restores the pruned structure, and finally transmits the updated and perturbed predictor to the central server.

4.2 Threat Model

This paper involves two entities: clients and a server. The threat model is introduced as follows.

Client. All clients are assumed to be honest but curious entities that retain private data locally. They comply with the model training process without maliciously disrupting learning, but attempt to infer private information of other local participants through aggregated results or public channels. Collusion among clients is possible, where $n-2$ clients at maximum may compromise with each other using their combined information and aggregation results to infer other clients' private data. Furthermore, they may collude with the server to leverage intermediate parameters from the server for inferring private information of other clients.

Server. The server is assumed to be honest but curious, meaning it will strictly and accurately execute the federated learning protocol and return correct aggregated results to all clients after performing global aggregation on the received predictors. However, the server exhibits curiosity about participants' private information and may attempt to acquire such information by analyzing clients' intermediate parameters and their uploaded perturbed predictors.

4.3 Scheme Details

In this section, a detailed introduction will be provided to the two main stages covered by this proposal: local model training and global model aggregation.

(1) **Local Model Training**

Model Update Based on Transfer Learning. Traditional differential privacy schemes employ fixed privacy budgets with Gaussian noise mechanisms. While providing fundamental privacy preservation, they often fail to optimize the privacy utility trade off, where excessive noise impairs model accuracy and convergence rates. To address this, our solution enables dynamic privacy budget selection, achieving on demand trade offs between privacy protection and model performance. Concurrently, we introduce a PM perturbation mechanism that adaptively regulates noise magnitude based on data distributions and model characteristics, minimizing performance degradation while ensuring privacy guarantees.

The hidden layers of each client's local model w are sequentially ordered from the input layer to the output layer as the bottom layer to the top layer, and w is divided into a shared encoder w_e and a client specific predictor w_p. Here, the shared encoder w_e consists of the first n layers from the bottom of the local model, and the client specific predictor w_p consists of the remaining $N-n$ layers of the local model, where n is a tunable hyperparameter and N denotes the total number of layers in the local model. Clients input their local data into the shared encoder to generate embeddings, which are then fed into the predictor for model updating.

Figure 3 shows the update flowchart for the predictor. Assuming each predictor is a matrix, where each small cell represents the importance score of a channel within each layer, channels with low importance scores are pruned using model pruning techniques. The remaining channels are then updated, and finally, the updated pruned predictor is restored to obtain the updated predictor.

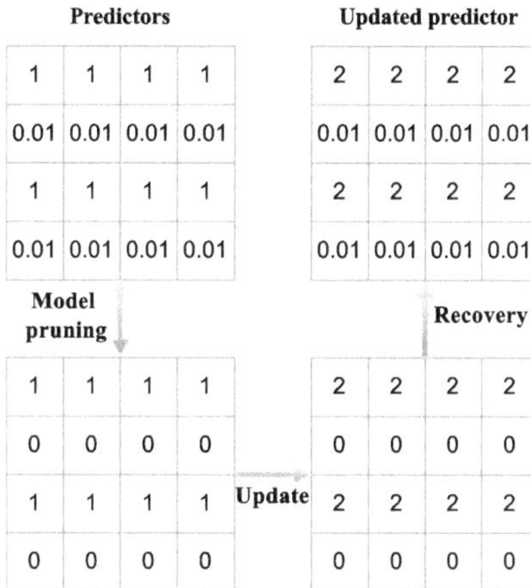

Fig. 3. The update flowchart of the predictor.

In each round of communication in FL, the client specific predictor w_p^i for client i is first pruned using the pruning ratio ρ, aiming to reduce model parameter updates and the amount of noise addition, thereby lowering training costs while ensuring model accuracy. For each client, the importance scores of channels within each layer of the predictor w_p^i are evaluated via the L1-norm, and the smallest ρ proportion of the model is removed to achieve model pruning. The pruning operation is as follows:

$$w_p^{i\prime} \leftarrow w_p^i \odot \mathbf{M}^i, \mathbf{M}^i \in \{0,1\}^{|w_p^i|}, \tag{6}$$

$\odot$ denotes element wise multiplication, and $\mathbf{M}^i$ is a binary mask matrix used to determine which channels to prune. In the mask matrix $\mathbf{M}^i$, elements with a value of 1 indicate channels to be retained, while elements with a value of 0 indicate channels to be pruned.

Then, each client performs forward propagation on the shared encoder using its local data D_i to generate embeddings $e_i = E(D_i, \sigma_e)$, where E denotes the shared encoder function and σ_e represents the global model parameters disseminated by the server. Subsequently, the embeddings e_i are used to update each pruned predictor $w_p^{i\prime}$, and the update operation is as follows:

$$w_p^{i\prime} \leftarrow w_p^{i\prime} - \eta \nabla \ell_i(w_p^{i\prime}; e_i, y_i), \tag{7}$$

η is the learning rate, $y_i$denotes the corresponding ground truth value, $\nabla \ell_i(wp^{i\prime}; e_i, y_i)$ is the local gradient of the predictor $w_p^{i\prime}$, and ℓ_i represents the Mean Squared Error (MSE) loss function for client i,

$$\ell_i(w_p^{i\prime}; e_i, y_i) = \frac{1}{n_i} \sum_{j=1}^{n_i} (f(w_p^{i\prime}; e_i^{(j)}) - y_i^{(j)}), \tag{8}$$

where, $f(w_p^{i'}; e_i^{(j)}) = softmax(\mathrm{W}e_i^{(j)} + b)$, W and b represent the weight matrix and bias vector of $w_p^{i'}$, respectively.

Algorithm 1. An LDPTL-FL update algorithm based on transfer learning

Require: The local dataset D_i of client i, $i \in 1, 2, \ldots, N$, pre-trained encoder w_e, predictor w_p^i, backbone predictor w_p, pruning ratio ρ and mask matrix $\mathbf{M}^i$

Ensure: The updated predictor $w_p^{i'}$

```
for i = 1 to N do
    w_p^i' ← w_p^i ⊙ M^i, M^i ∈ {0,1}^|w_p^i|;
    e^i ← Forward propagation on shared encode we with local data D_i;
    w_p^i' ← w_p^i' − η∇ℓ_i(w_p^i');
end for
```

Privacy Protection Based on Local Differential Privacy. Each client selects its own initial dynamic privacy budget ε_0^i. At the beginning of each training round, the client obtains the privacy budget allocated for the current round via a dynamic privacy budget allocation method. Each client dynamically adjusts its privacy budget per round based on its actual training results; when the accuracy stops improving with minimal changes, the privacy budget increases and the noise level is reduced. The global model accuracy $R_t^G = GetGlobalAccuracy(t)$ is obtained through $GetGlobalAccuracy(\cdot)$, and whether to increase the privacy budget is determined by whether the difference between the current round's global model training accuracy and the previous round's training accuracy exceeds the threshold τ. The dynamic selection mechanism for the privacy budget ε_t is as follows:

$$\varepsilon_t = \begin{cases} \lambda\varepsilon_{t-1}, & if\ |R_t^G - R_{t-1}^G| \leq \tau\ and\ \varepsilon_{min} \leq \varepsilon_{t-1} \leq \varepsilon_{\max}, \\ \varepsilon_{t-1}, & \text{else.} \end{cases} \tag{9}$$

where R_t^G denotes the global accuracy of the current round, R_{t-1}^G represents the global accuracy of the previous round, $\lambda > 1$ denotes the growth rate, ε_t indicates the privacy budget for round t, ε_{min} signifies the minimum value of the privacy budget in each training round to prevent failure in obtaining perturbed gradients due to excessively small privacy budgets, and ε_{max} represents the maximum value of the privacy budget to prevent the dynamic privacy budget method from allocating overly large privacy budgets in each round, which could lead to premature termination of training. When the model training accuracy difference is less than the threshold τ, the privacy budget increases by a factor of λ. Once the privacy budget exceeds ε_{max}, it ceases to increase until the global model converges or the preset number of training rounds is reached.

According to the selected privacy budget, the updated and restored parameters of client i in round $t+1$ are perturbed using PM, as follows:

$$\hat{w}_p^{i'}(t+1, \varepsilon_t^i) = \mathrm{PM}(w_p^{i'}(t+1), \varepsilon_t^i, \mathbf{M}^i), \quad \varepsilon_{min} \leq \varepsilon_t^i \leq \varepsilon_{\max}. \tag{10}$$

where PM(·) denotes the PM perturbation, ε_t^i represents the privacy budget for client i's update in round t, $\mathbf{M}^i$ indicates the binary mask matrix determining the channels to be pruned for client i, ε_{min} signifies the minimum value of the privacy budget in each training round, and ε_{max} denotes the maximum value of the privacy budget.

The privacy protection algorithm based on local differential privacy is depicted in Algorithm 2.

Algorithm 2. A privacy preserving algorithm based on local differential privacy

Require: The updated predictor $w_p^{i'}$, the mask matrix $\mathbf{M}^i$, the privacy budget of client i at round t ε_t^i, the learning rate η, and the scaling factor $r = 1$

Ensure: The perturbed predictor $\hat{w_p^i}'$

for $j = 1$ to $|w_p^i|$ **do**
  if $M^i[j] = 1$ **then**
    if $w_p^{i'}[j] \notin [-1, 1]$ **then**
      $r = max(w_p^{i'}[j])$;
      $\tilde{w_p^i}[j] = w_p^{i'}[j]/r$;
    end if
    Calculate the locally perturbed model parameters $\hat{w}_p^i[j]$ using PM;
    $\hat{w}_p^{i'}[j] = r\hat{w}_p^i[j]$;
  end if
end for
Send perturbed predictor $\hat{w_p^i}'$ to server.

(2) **Global Model Aggregation**

The updated and noise added client specific predictor $\hat{w}_p^{i'}$ will be sent to the central server for aggregation. Since the pruned channels have relatively low importance only from the client's perspective but their significance for the aggregation result is uncertain, the model parameters need to be restored before aggregation. The restoration operation is as follows:

$$\hat{w}_p^i \leftarrow \hat{w}_p^{i'} + [w_p^i - (w_p^i \odot \mathbf{M}^i)], \tag{11}$$

where w_p^i denotes the initial predictor, and $\mathbf{M}^i$ represents the binary mask matrix determining the channels to be pruned for client i.

Client i transmits the noise perturbed predictor $\hat{w}_p^i$ to the central server, where the central server aggregates the noise perturbed predictors $\hat{w}_p^i$ using FedAvg as follows:

$$w_p^* \leftarrow \sum_{i=1}^{N} \frac{D_i}{D} \hat{w}_p^i, \tag{12}$$

where D_i denotes the local dataset of client i, and D represents the union of all clients' datasets.

Finally, the server broadcasts the aggregation result w_p^* to all clients. The clients then proceed to the next round of training based on this aggregated result until the model accuracy converges.

The entire LDPTL-FL process and the global model aggregation algorithm are illustrated in Algorithm 3.

5 Security Analysis

In this section, an analysis of the privacy of the PM used in the scheme will be conducted. Firstly, it is demonstrated that the scheme under consideration satisfies the definition of $\epsilon - LDP$ under the given conditions.

Theorem 1. *It is demonstrated that the PM satisfies the condition of the $\epsilon - LDP$, and that the variance of the PM is*

$$Var(\hat{w}_i) = \frac{\tilde{w}_i^2}{e^{\varepsilon/2} - 1} + \frac{e^{\varepsilon/2} + 3}{3(e^{\varepsilon/2} - 1)^2}, \tag{13}$$

where, $\hat{w}_i$ is an unbiased estimate of $\tilde{w}_i$. When $|\tilde{w}_i| = 1$, PM is at its worst-case change, and the variance is determined to be:

$$Var(\hat{w}_i) = \frac{4e^{\frac{\varepsilon}{2}}}{3(e^{\frac{\varepsilon}{2}} - 1)^2}. \tag{14}$$

At this juncture, the perturbed original weight $\hat{w}_i' = r\hat{w}_i$, and its variance, are as follows:

$$Var(\hat{w}_i') = Var(r\hat{w}_i) = r^2 \frac{4e^{\frac{\varepsilon}{2}}}{3(e^{\frac{\varepsilon}{2}} - 1)^2}. \tag{15}$$

Algorithm 3. LDPTL-FL global model aggregation algorithm

Require: The local dataset D_i of client i, $i \in 1, 2, \ldots, N$, pre-trained encoder w_e, the predictor w_p^i, backbone predictor w_p, pruning ratio ρ, mask matrix $\mathbf{M}^i$, privacy budget ε_t^i of client i at round t, learning rate η

Ensure: The aggregated predictors w_p^*

1: **for** $i = 1$ to N **do**

2: $\quad w_p^i \leftarrow$ Caculate updated predictors with algorithm 1;

3: $\quad \hat{w}_p^{i\prime} \leftarrow$ Caculate perturbed predictor with algorithm 2;

4: $\quad \hat{w}_p^i \leftarrow \hat{w}_p^{i\prime} + [w_p^i - (w_p^i \odot \mathbf{M}^i)]$;

5: **end for**

6: $w_p^* \leftarrow \sum_{i=1}^{N} \frac{D_i}{D} \hat{w}_p^i$;

7: Send aggregated global model w_p^* to the client.

Proof. It has been demonstrated that, for $\forall \hat{w}_i \in [-C, C]$, and any arbitrary input value $w_i, w_i' \in [-1, 1]$, the following holds true:

$$\frac{f(\hat{w}_i = x|w_i)}{f(\hat{w}_i = x|w_i')} \leq \frac{\max\limits_{w_i} f(\hat{w}_i = x|w_i)}{\min\limits_{w_i'} f(\hat{w}_i = x|w_i')} = \frac{p}{p/e^{\varepsilon}} = e^{\varepsilon}. \tag{16}$$

Therefore, the PM satisfies $\epsilon - LDP$.

In accordance with the PM probability density function given in Equation (5), the expected value of PM can be determined through integration

$$\begin{aligned} E[\hat{w}_i] &= \int_{-C}^{l(w_i)} \frac{px}{e^{\varepsilon}}\, dx + \int_{r(w_i)}^{C} \frac{px}{e^{\varepsilon}}\, dx + \int_{l(w_i)}^{r(w_i)} px\, dx \\ &= \frac{p}{2e^{\varepsilon}}[l(w_i)^2 - r(w_i)^2] + \frac{p}{2}[r(w_i)^2 - l(w_i)^2] \\ &= \frac{p}{2}(\frac{1}{e^{\varepsilon}} - 1)[l(w_i)^2 - r(w_i)^2] \\ &= \frac{(1-e^{\varepsilon})(e^{\varepsilon/2}-1)}{4e^{\varepsilon/2}(1+e^{\varepsilon/2})}(1+C)(1-C)w_i \\ &= w_i. \end{aligned} \tag{17}$$

Thus, in the PM, $\hat{w}_i$ is an unbiased estimate of w_i.

In order to obtain the variance of the PM, it is first necessary to calculate $E[\hat{w}_i^2]$ through integration, and then using $E[\hat{w}_i] = w_i$, it can be derived that

$$\begin{aligned} Var[\hat{w}_i] &= E[\hat{w}_i^2] - E[\hat{w}_i]^2 \\ &= \int_{-C}^{l(w_i)} \frac{px^2}{e^{\varepsilon}}\, dx + \int_{r(w_i)}^{C} \frac{px^2}{e^{\varepsilon}}\, dx + \int_{l(w_i)}^{r(w_i)} px^2\, dx - w_i^2 \\ &= \frac{p}{3e^{\varepsilon}}[l(w_i)^3 - r(w_i)^3 + 2C^3] + \frac{p}{3}[r(w_i)^3 - l(w_i)^3] - w_i^2 \\ &= \frac{p}{3}[(1 - \frac{1}{e^{\varepsilon}})(r(w_i)^3 - l(w_i)^3) + \frac{2}{e^{\varepsilon}}C^3] - w_i^2 \\ &= \frac{3e^{\varepsilon}w_i^2 + 1}{3e^{\varepsilon/2}(e^{\varepsilon/2}-1)} + \frac{(e^{\varepsilon/2}+1)^2}{3e^{\varepsilon/2}(e^{\varepsilon/2}-1)^2} - w_i^2 \\ &= \frac{w_i^2}{e^{\varepsilon/2}-1} + \frac{e^{\varepsilon/2}+3}{3(e^{\varepsilon/2}-1)^2} \\ &\leq \frac{4e^{\varepsilon/2}}{3(e^{\varepsilon/2}-1)^2}. \end{aligned} \tag{18}$$

Therefore, the standard deviation of the original weights that have been subjected to perturbation is

$$Var(\hat{w}_i') = Var(r\hat{w}_i) = r^2 \frac{4e^{\varepsilon/2}}{3(e^{\varepsilon/2}-1)^2}. \tag{19}$$

Secondly, the proof provided in Proposition 1 demonstrates that the PM in Algorithm 2 provides an unbiased estimate of the average weights.

Theorem 2. *The following procedure introduces an unbiased estimate to average the weights,* $E[\bar{\hat{w}}] = \bar{w}$.

Proof. For the weights w_i of any client i, we have

$$E[\bar{\hat{w}}] = E[\frac{1}{N}\sum_{i=1}^{N}\hat{w}_i] = \frac{1}{N}\sum_{i=1}^{N}E[\hat{w}_i] = \frac{1}{N}\sum_{i=1}^{N}w_i = \bar{w}. \tag{20}$$

Finally, given the established correlation between model accuracy and the mean perturbed weights $\bar{\hat{w}}$, it is imperative to ensure that the deviation of $\bar{\hat{w}}$ from the true average weights $\bar{w}$ remains within an acceptable range. To this end, an analysis of the accuracy of the average weights will be conducted, drawing upon the previously mentioned lemma.

Theorem 3. *For any parameter* $w \in W$*, there is a probability of* $1 - \beta$ *that*

$$|\bar{\hat{w}} - \bar{w}| < O(\frac{|w|\sqrt{\ln(1/\beta)}}{\varepsilon\sqrt{N}}), \tag{21}$$

and β *is a small number close to 0.*

Proof. For each client i, there is $|\hat{w}_i' - w_i| \leq rC + r = r \cdot \frac{e^{\varepsilon/2}+1}{e^{\varepsilon/2}-1} + r = \frac{2re^{\varepsilon/2}}{e^{\varepsilon/2}-1}$, and $Var[\hat{w}_i'] = Var[\hat{w}_i' - w_i] = E[(\hat{w}_i' - w_i)^2] - E[\hat{w}_i' - w_i]^2 = E[(\hat{w}_i' - w_i)^2]$.

It is known through the Bernstein inequality that,

$$\begin{aligned}
\Pr[|\bar{\hat{w}} - \bar{w}| \geq \lambda] &= \Pr[|\sum_{i=1}^{N}(\hat{w}_i' - w_i)| \geq n\lambda] \\
&\leq 2 \cdot \exp\left\{\frac{-\frac{1}{2}n^2\lambda^2}{\sum_{i=1}^{N} E\left[(\hat{w}_i' - w_i)^2\right] + \frac{2\lambda nre^{\varepsilon/2}}{3(e^{\varepsilon/2}-1)}}\right\} \\
&= 2 \cdot \exp\left\{\frac{-n\lambda^2}{2E\left[(\hat{w}_i' - w_i)^2\right] + \frac{4\lambda re^{\varepsilon/2}}{3(e^{\varepsilon/2}-1)}}\right\} \\
&= 2 \cdot \exp\left\{\frac{-n\lambda^2}{\frac{8r^2e^{\varepsilon/2}}{3(e^{\varepsilon/2}-1)^2} + \frac{4\lambda re^{\varepsilon/2}}{3(e^{\varepsilon/2}-1)}}\right\} \\
&= 2 \cdot \exp\left\{\frac{-n\lambda^2}{r^2O(\varepsilon^{-2}) + \lambda rO(\varepsilon^{-1})}\right\}.
\end{aligned} \tag{22}$$

In accordance with the stipulated joint constraint, it is to be posited that $\lambda = O\left(\frac{r\sqrt{\ln 1/\beta}}{\varepsilon\sqrt{N}}\right)$ is such that $|\bar{\hat{w}} - \bar{w}| < \lambda$ is hold with a probability of at least $1 - \beta$.

6 Experimental Analysis

In this section, the proposed LDPTL-FL scheme is implemented on the real federated learning platform FedML, and its performance is validated and evaluated through a series of experimental analyses. First, simulation experiments are conducted to explore the specific impact of the local parameter sharing mechanism on model accuracy. Subsequently, the LDPTL-FL scheme is comprehensively compared with existing FL schemes according to their functionalities respectively, demonstrating the superiority of the proposed approach.

6.1 Experimental Setup

In the experiments, 10 clients are simulated. All clients are selected for FL training. The experiments are conducted on a GV100 GPU server, and each experiment is executed three times to calculate the average metrics.

In the experiments of this paper, two widely recognized datasets are adopted: MNIST [11] and CIFAR10 [10]. Under the IID setting, the datasets are uniformly distributed to each client. Under the non-IID setting, the Latent Dirichlet Allocation (LDA) method is used to construct non-IID data. In LDA, the concentration parameter α is employed to control data heterogeneity. This paper uses the conventional setting of $\alpha = 0.5$ in the experiments to construct non-IID data. For the LDP privacy budget settings, the minimum privacy budget per client is set to $\epsilon_0 = 0.5$ and the maximum privacy budget to $\epsilon_{max} = 2$. The central server pre-trained the initial model on ImageNet before distributing it to every client [14].

6.2 The Impact of Local Parameter Sharing

In this section, the impact of three key hyperparameters in the LDPTL-FL scheme the number of layers n in the shared encoder, the model pruning ratio ρ, and the privacy budget ϵ-on model accuracy is primarily analyzed.

The Influence of n. In LDPTL-FL, a larger number of layers n allocated to the shared encoder yields greater training cost savings. Simultaneously, reducing the number of layers involved in training may cause parameters significantly influencing the global model to be shared rather than updated, thereby decreasing model accuracy. This experiment investigates the impact of the shared encoder's layer count n on training costs and model accuracy. The layer count n is set to $\lceil 0.25N \rceil$, $\lceil 0.5N \rceil$, and $\lceil 0.75N \rceil$ respectively. Figure 4 displays the model accuracy under different shared encoder layer counts n for the MNIST and CIFAR10 datasets.

As shown in Fig. 4, a larger number of layers n in the shared encoder corresponds to lower model accuracy. To reduce communication overhead while maintaining accuracy at a satisfactory level, this experiment selects $n = 0.25N$ as the number of layers for the shared encoder.

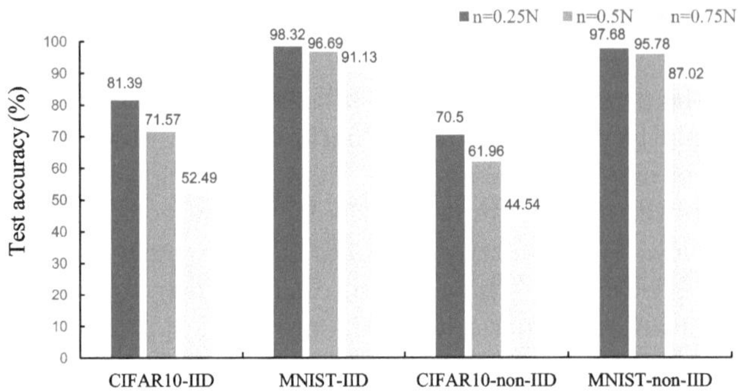

Fig. 4. The model accuracy on the MNIST and CIFAR10 datasets under different numbers of shared encoder layers n.

The Influence of ρ. The pruning ratio ρ dynamically determines the proportion of parameters updated and perturbed via clipping. Higher ρ retains fewer parameters for gradient updates and privacy protection, yielding dual effects: clipping reduces injected noise to improve accuracy, yet excessive pruning diminishes updatable parameters, potentially impairing learning capacity. Thus, identifying the optimal ρ that minimizes accuracy loss within privacy constraints requires experimental validation. This paper investigates the impact of pruning ratios $\rho = \{0,\ 0.2,\ 0.4,\ 0.6,\ 0.8\}$ on model accuracy in LDPTL-FL under two different distributions of the MNIST and CIFAR10 datasets, as shown in Fig. 5.

As shown in Fig. 5, as ρ increases, the model accuracy continuously declines with an increasingly sharp decline trend. When $\rho = 0.2$, it effectively reduces the model training overhead while maintaining model accuracy with minimal difference compared to $\rho = 0$. Therefore, this paper selects the pruning ratio $\rho = 0.2$.

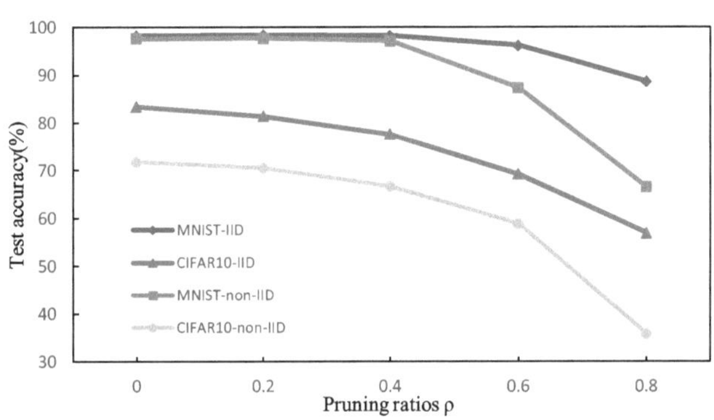

Fig. 5. Model accuracy (%) varies with the change of the pruning ratio ρ.

The Influence of ϵ. The privacy budget ϵ dictates the privacy accuracy trade off: larger ϵ reduces noise injection for higher accuracy but weakens privacy protection. Our dynamic strategy enables clients to adapt ϵ per round based on local model states, with only ϵ_0 predefined as a hyperparameter. Thus, we primarily investigate ϵ_0's impact on final accuracy. Experimental results show that under the IID distribution of the MNIST dataset, when $\epsilon_0 = \{0.1,\ 0.2,\ 0.5,\ 1,\ 5\}$, the model accuracies are $\{88.02,\ 94.79,\ 98.49,\ 98.96,\ 99.1\}$ respectively. It can be concluded that a too small ϵ_0 results in lower model accuracy, whereas a too large ϵ_0 leads to weaker privacy protection performance; therefore, this paper selects $\epsilon_0 = 0.5$.

Based on the above three analyses, after determining the shared encoder layer count $n = 0.25N$, model pruning ratio $\rho = 0.2$, and initial privacy budget $\epsilon_0 = 0.5$, the change in model accuracy of LDPTL-FL as the number of training rounds increases is shown in Fig. 6.

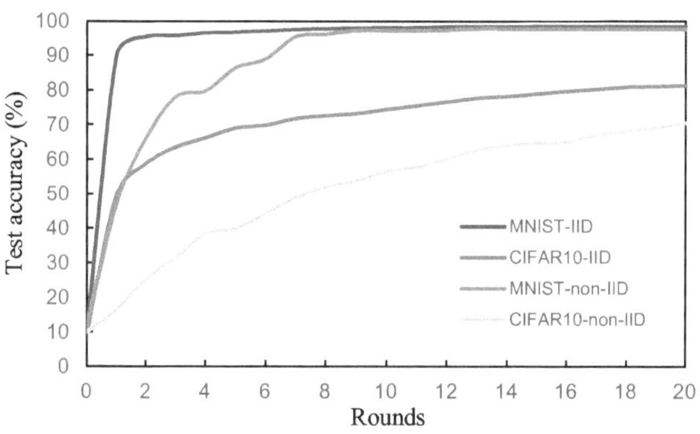

Fig. 6. When the number of shared encoder layers n is set to $0.25N$, the accuracy of LDPTL-FL changes with the number of training rounds.

6.3 Comparative Experiments

This paper compares the model accuracy of the proposed LDPTL-FL scheme with FedAvg [13], FedDPA [22], and FedLPS [8] on both IID and non-IID data. FedAvg is a traditional federated learning aggregation framework without employing any lightweight or privacy preserving techniques; FedDPA is a personalized federated learning approach with adaptive differential privacy but lacks any lightweight mechanisms; FedLPS is a federated learning framework based on local parameter sharing transfer learning for lightweight federated learning, without incorporating any privacy protection techniques. To ensure a fair comparison, identical training hyperparameters are used for LDPTL-FL and the comparative frameworks in the experiments.

In this experiment, the number of layers in the shared encoder of LDPTL-FL is set to $n = 0.25N$, that is, the first 25% of layers within the local model are used to construct the shared encoder. Table 1 details the performance of the proposed LDPTL-FL framework and three comparative methods FedAvg, FedDPA, and FedLPS on the MNIST and CIFAR10 datasets.

Table 1. Model Accuracy (%) Comparison on IID and Non-IID Data.

Data partition	FL frameworks	MNIST	CIFAR10	Average
IID partition	FedAvg [13]	98.9	73.15	86.03
	FedDPA [22]	96.42	45.6	71.01
	FedLPS [8]	98.5	82.49	90.49
	LDPTL-FL(Ours)	98.49	81.39	89.94
non-IID partition	FedAvg [13]	89.34	42.41	65.88
	FedDPA [22]	87.11	42.61	64.86
	FedLPS [8]	98.05	72.3	85.17
	LDPTL-FL(Ours)	97.68	70.5	84.09

From the experimental results in Table 1, it can be observed that the accuracy of the LDPTL-FL scheme is nearly all higher than that of the other three comparative schemes under both distributions of the MNIST and CIFAR10 datasets.

Assume the communication overhead for a client uploading one piece of original data and differentially private noise perturbed data to the central server is T_1 and T_1' respectively, while the overhead for the central server distributing one piece of aggregated original data and noise perturbed data to clients is T_2 and T_2' respectively. This paper employs differential privacy techniques to perturb data, which maintains similar size to the original data; thus T_1' and T_2' are slightly greater than T_1 and T_2. With d_{max} denoting the maximum data volume among clients, the maximum data volume uploaded and distributed in this scheme is $0.75d_{max}$. The per-round training communication overhead of LDPTL-FL is experimentally compared with three baseline methods as shown in Table 2.

Table 2. Communication overhead comparison.

FL frameworks	Communication overhead
FedAvg [13]	$d'_{\max}(T_1 + T_2)$
FedDPA [22]	$d'_{\max}(T_1{}' + T_2{}')$
FedLPS [8]	$0.75d'_{\max}(T_1 + T_2)$
LDPTL-FL (Ours)	$0.75d'_{\max}(T_1{}' + T_2{}')$

Given inconsistent fundamental parameters across studies (e.g., gradients vs. bits), we standardize communication overhead calculation via data volume. As Table 2 shows, LDPTL-FL incurs significantly lower overhead than FedAvg and FedDPA, though slightly higher than FedLPS. Crucially, our scheme achieves privacy preserving lightweight design, ultimately outperforming FedLPS in overall performance. This confirms LDPTL-FL effectively reduces training communication overhead while ensuring privacy protection.

6.4 Runtime Overhead

To evaluate the scalability of the proposed system, we measured the time cost required for the model to reach convergence under different numbers of clients, namely $N = \{10, 20, 50\}$, while keeping all other experimental conditions consistent. The detailed convergence times are summarized in Table 3.

Table 3. The computational runtime overhead under varying numbers of clients.

Number of clients	Dataset			
	Mnist-IID	CIFAR10-IID	Mnist-non-IID	CIFAR10-non-IID
10	46 m56 s	1 h34 m22 s	1h12 m15 s	2 h16 m48 s
20	1 h33 m24 s	3 h30 s	2 h56 m31 s	5 h45 m36 s
50	7 h45 m37 s	23 h45 m2 s	12 h28 m	36 h7 m12 s

As shown in Table 3, as the number of clients increases from 10 to 50, the training time exhibits an approximately linear growth trend, with no significant nonlinear acceleration or sharp escalation. Even with 50 clients, the total training time remains within approximately 20 h, which is within an acceptable range. These results demonstrate that the proposed federated learning framework exhibits favorable scalability, efficiently adapting to environments with varying client scales, and shows promising potential for practical deployment.

7 Conclusions and Future Work

This paper proposes LDPTL-FL, a federated learning scheme based on local differential privacy and transfer learning techniques. LDPTL-FL significantly reduces communication overhead by dividing each client's local model into a shared encoder and a predictor, with only the predictor being updated and aggregated. Furthermore, a dynamic perturbation scheme based on local differential privacy is introduced, which applies noise to the updated portions of the predictor using a segmented perturbation mechanism, providing privacy protection for clients while maintaining accuracy. Through theoretical analysis and extensive experimental validation, LDPTL-FL achieves guaranteed model accuracy and significantly reduced training communication overhead while ensuring client privacy.

In the future, we will conduct further research under heterogeneous client and adversarial attack scenarios to extend the applicability and robustness of the LDPTL-FL framework. Specifically, future work will focus on the following three aspects: 1) designing an asynchronous aggregation mechanism to mitigate computational delays caused by differences in client computational capabilities and network conditions, thereby enhancing training efficiency and ensuring convergence consistency; 2) further investigating decoupling and coordinated optimization among transfer learning, dynamic local differential privacy, and adaptive model pruning to reduce system complexity and coordination costs; 3) introducing robust aggregation methods to effectively mitigate potential adversarial attacks and ensure the robustness of the global model.

References

1. Batool, H., Anjum, A., Khan, A., Izzo, S., Mazzocca, C., Jeon, G.: A secure and privacy preserved infrastructure for VANETs based on federated learning with local differential privacy. Inf. Sci. **652**, 119717 (2024)
2. Chen, S., Yang, J., Wang, G., Wang, Z., Yin, H., Feng, Y.: CLFLDP: communication-efficient layer clipping federated learning with local differential privacy. J. Syst. Architect. **148**, 103067 (2024)
3. Dong, F., et al.: PADP-FedMeta: a personalized and adaptive differentially private federated meta learning mechanism for AIoT. J. Syst. Architect. **134**, 102754 (2023)
4. Ezzeldin, Y.H., Yan, S., He, C., Ferrara, E., Avestimehr, A.S.: Fairfed: enabling group fairness in federated learning. In: Proceedings of the AAAI Conference on Artificial Intelligence, vol. 37, pp. 7494–7502 (2023)
5. Ge, L., Li, H., Wang, X., Wang, Z.: A review of secure federated learning: privacy leakage threats, protection technologies, challenges and future directions. Neurocomputing 126897 (2023)
6. Gu, Y., Bai, Y., Xu, S.: CS-MIA: membership inference attack based on prediction confidence series in federated learning. J. Inf. Secur. Appl. **67**, 103201 (2022)
7. Guendouzi, B.S., Ouchani, S., Assaad, H.E., Zaher, M.E.: A systematic review of federated learning: challenges, aggregation methods, and development tools. J. Netw. Comput. Appl. 103714 (2023)
8. Jia, Y., Zhang, X., Beheshti, A., Dou, W.: FedLPS: heterogeneous federated learning for multiple tasks with local parameter sharing. In: Proceedings of the AAAI Conference on Artificial Intelligence, vol. 38, pp. 12848–12856 (2024)
9. Kairouz, P., et al.: Advances and open problems in federated learning. Found. Trends® Mach. Learn. **14**(1–2), 1–210 (2021)
10. Krizhevsky, A., Hinton, G., et al.: Learning multiple layers of features from tiny images (2009)
11. LeCun, Y., Bottou, L., Bengio, Y., Haffner, P.: Gradient-based learning applied to document recognition. Proc. IEEE **86**(11), 2278–2324 (1998)
12. Ling, J., Zheng, J., Chen, J.: Efficient federated learning privacy preservation method with heterogeneous differential privacy. Comput. Secur. **139**, 103715 (2024)
13. McMahan, B., Moore, E., Ramage, D., Hampson, S., y Arcas, B.A.: Communication-efficient learning of deep networks from decentralized data. In: Artificial Intelligence and Statistics, pp. 1273–1282. PMLR (2017)

14. Russakovsky, O., et al.: Imagenet large scale visual recognition challenge. Int. J. Comput. Vis. **115**(3), 211–252 (2015)
15. Tan, Y., Liu, Y., Long, G., Jiang, J., Lu, Q., Zhang, C.: Federated learning on non-IID graphs via structural knowledge sharing. In: Proceedings of the AAAI Conference on Artificial Intelligence, vol. 37, pp. 9953–9961 (2023)
16. Tang, Y., Zhang, S., Zhang, Z.: A privacy-preserving framework integrating federated learning and transfer learning for wind power forecasting. Energy **286**, 129639 (2024)
17. Tu, L., Ouyang, X., Zhou, J., He, Y., Xing, G.: FedDL: federated learning via dynamic layer sharing for human activity recognition. In: Proceedings of the 19th ACM Conference on Embedded Networked Sensor Systems, pp. 15–28 (2021)
18. Wang, N., et al.: Collecting and analyzing multidimensional data with local differential privacy. In: 2019 IEEE 35th International Conference on Data Engineering (ICDE), pp. 638–649. IEEE (2019)
19. Wei, W., Liu, L., Zhou, J., Chow, K.H., Wu, Y.: Securing distributed SGD against gradient leakage threats. IEEE Trans. Parallel Distrib. Syst. **34**(7), 2040–2054 (2023)
20. Wen, J., Zhang, Z., Lan, Y., Cui, Z., Cai, J., Zhang, W.: A survey on federated learning: challenges and applications. Int. J. Mach. Learn. Cybern. **14**(2), 513–535 (2023)
21. Weng, S., Zhang, L., Zhang, X., Imran, M.A.: Faster convergence on differential privacy based federated learning. IEEE Internet Things J. **11**, 22578–22589 (2024)
22. Yang, X., Huang, W., Ye, M.: Dynamic personalized federated learning with adaptive differential privacy. Adv. Neural. Inf. Process. Syst. **36**, 72181–72192 (2023)
23. Yosinski, J., Clune, J., Bengio, Y., Lipson, H.: How transferable are features in deep neural networks? In: Advances in Neural Information Processing Systems, vol. 27 (2014)
24. Yu, S., Nguyen, P., Abebe, W., Qian, W., Anwar, A., Jannesari, A.: SPATL: salient parameter aggregation and transfer learning for heterogeneous federated learning. In: 2022 SC22: International Conference for High Performance Computing, Networking, Storage and Analysis (SC), pp. 495–508. IEEE Computer Society (2022)
25. Yuan, P., Shi, L., Zhao, X., Zhang, J.: A lightweight and personalized edge federated learning model. Complex Intell. Syst. 1–16 (2024)
26. Zhang, J., Duan, L., Li, K., Luo, S.: Improved lightweight federated learning network for fault feature extraction of reciprocating machinery. Meas. Sci. Technol. **35**(4), 045115 (2024)
27. Zhang, Z., Cao, X., Jia, J., Gong, N.Z.: Fldetector: defending federated learning against model poisoning attacks via detecting malicious clients. In: Proceedings of the 28th ACM SIGKDD Conference on Knowledge Discovery and Data Mining, pp. 2545–2555 (2022)
28. Zhu, L., Liu, Z., Han, S.: Deep leakage from gradients. In: Advances in Neural Information Processing Systems, vol. 32 (2019)

Secure, Reliable, and Efficient Intelligent Systems

Application of Dual-Segment Non-integer Byte CRC in High-Reliability Satellite-To-Ground TDM Communication Verification

Shurong Xing[1,2](✉), Qiting Zhang[1,2], Hongyuan Shu[1,2], Yiwei Lv[1,2], and Shouyao Zhang[1,2]

[1] Shanghai Aerospace Electronic Technology Institute, Shanghai 201109, China
1124579620@qq.com

[2] Shanghai Key Laboratory of Collaborative Computing in Spacial Heterogeneous Networks (CCSN), Shanghai, China

Abstract. Aiming at the limitations of traditional cyclic redundancy check (CRC) in verifying time-division multiplexing (TDM) structured data in modern satellite-ground communication systems under bandwidth-constrained and harsh space environments, such as byte alignment dependency, lack of dynamic customizable model support, absence of batch processing, and weak error detection capability, this paper proposes and implements an enhanced CRC verification scheme.

Firstly, a dynamically configurable CRC calculation system based on Qt/C++ is implemented, which supports the processing of data streams with arbitrary bit widths. By combining dynamic shift registers and parallel batch processing of data streams, the CRC32 throughput can reach 2.18 Gbps on the Intel Core i7-12700K platform, and the deployment cost is much lower than that of FPGA solutions. This system is also encapsulated into a general-purpose library with a unified interface, which presets multiple CRC models for satellite communication protocols and supports dynamic parameter configuration.

Secondly, a dual-segment non-integer byte CRC verification mechanism is proposed. The optimized frame structure adopts segmented verification for synchronous slots and business slots, eliminating padding redundancy and improving the joint detection capability for burst and random errors. Simulation and satellite-ground link field test results show that the detection rate of synchronous slots is increased from 85% to 98%, the detection rate of payload data is increased from 88% to 97%, and the frame-level false negative rate is reduced to below 0.1%. Moreover, the processing delay of a single frame only increases by approximately 1.2 ms, which does not affect the real-time performance of the system.

Keywords: Non-integer Byte Cyclic Redundancy Check · Satellite-ground Communication · TDM Frame Structure Optimization

1 Introduction

In modern satellite ground communication systems, ensuring the accuracy of data transmission under bandwidth-constrained and harsh space environments is of critical importance. Factors such as space radiation interference, Doppler frequency shift effects, and

L. Zhang and K.-K. R. Choo (Eds.): MobiQuitous 2025, LNICST 683, pp. 239–256, 2026.
https://doi.org/10.1007/978-3-032-22500-9_14

atmospheric attenuation can easily introduce random bit errors and burst errors during data transmission, particularly in satellite-to-ground transmission systems employing time-division multiplexing (TDM) structures.

Cyclic Redundancy Check (CRC), a widely used error detection technique in the field of communications, plays a critical role in verifying the integrity of satellite-to-ground communication data [1]. However, traditional CRC verification tools often have limitations when dealing with non-integer byte data structures and multiple verification requirements, such as byte alignment dependency, lack of dynamic customizable model support, and absence of batch processing capabilities. When processing non-standard structured data, traditional verification tools often require additional padding operations to accommodate the verification unit due to their byte alignment dependency, which not only increases implementation complexity but may also compromise the structural integrity of the original data. Different satellite communication protocols or specific telemetry, telecommand, and payload data downlink task scenarios may require the use of different CRC models. Existing FPGA or software implementations typically hardcode parameters such as the generator polynomial, initial register values, and output XOR values during compilation, making it difficult to meet the dynamic customization requirements for adjusting verification strength based on link status across different task phases. Satellite-to-ground communication systems typically need to process massive, continuous telemetry data streams or batch instruction sets. Existing tools lack batch processing capabilities, becoming a bottleneck for system throughput.

Under the limited bandwidth conditions of satellite-to-ground communication links, satellites must perform multiple tasks such as transmitting telemetry, telecommand, high-speed payload data, and formation coordination. These tasks have a wide range of data rates and varying requirements for real-time performance and reliability. Therefore, satellite-to-ground communication systems generally adopt a TDM frame structure, where the physical channel is divided into periodic frames, each containing a synchronous slot and multiple variable-length business slots. The length of the business slots can be dynamically adjusted according to real-time requirements, ensuring that low-speed, high-priority businesses such as telemetry and telecommand always occupy fixed slots, while the remaining bandwidth is flexibly allocated to high-speed payloads. However, conventional error detection schemes only append a single CRC check code at the end of the frame, and when errors span field boundaries, their error detection capabilities are weakened.

This paper proposes an enhanced CRC check scheme aimed at overcoming the inherent limitations of traditional check tools and mechanisms in TDM satellite-to-ground communications. Distinguished from hardware-oriented CRC approaches and compiler-optimized solutions, the core system-level innovations of this scheme lie in the synergistic integration of four key capabilities: direct processing of non-integer byte data to eliminate byte alignment dependency; dynamic CRC model customization for adaptive compatibility with diverse satellite communication protocols; efficient batch processing mechanism optimized for massive data streams; and a dual-segment non-integer byte CRC mechanism with optimized frame structure to enhance error detection performance. The novelty of this work does not lie in proposing an entirely new core algorithm, but rather in the system-level integration of these technologies and application-oriented optimization to solve a specific key problem in satellite-ground communication. Under the channel conditions with real satellite link impairments, this scheme significantly improves the error detection rate of synchronous and business slots, which proves its practical effectiveness. It should be noted that the software-based implementation, while offering high flexibility and low cost, has inherent limitations: its throughput is dependent on CPU performance and may face scalability challenges in resource-constrained embedded satellite on-board systems. For such scenarios, hardware-software co-design or dedicated FPGA acceleration could be considered as complementary solutions.

2 Related Work

In 1961, Peterson and Brown proposed the CRC technique, which involves dividing the transmitted data polynomial by a predefined generator polynomial and appending the resulting remainder as a check code to the original data. Upon receiving the data, the receiver repeats this division operation and compares the calculated remainder with the appended check code to determine whether an error occurred during transmission [2].

In modern satellite ground communication systems, as constellation scales expand, TDM frame structures become increasingly complex, and non-integer byte control words or signaling segments frequently appear. Traditional byte-aligned CRC verification implementation methods can no longer meet the high-throughput, low-redundancy requirements of satellite-ground links. Zhang et al. (2024) proposed a FPGA-based bit width normalization parallel CRC (PSV-WN-CRC) method, which unifies the frame tail of arbitrary length to a fixed width by pre-calculating the "original seed," achieving a throughput of 392 Gbps on a 1024-bit bus using only 5981 LUTs, providing a hardware example for large-scale parallel processing on satellites [3]. Cai et al. (2024) further introduced a "zero-padding&alignment" mechanism into the Stride-x algorithm. Experiments showed that the Stride-1 scheme achieves an 8.5% increase in throughput and a 4.5% reduction in LUT consumption compared to traditional parallel CRC under a 256-bit bus condition, providing a feasible path for software-defined on-board processing units [4]. Arutunian et al. (2024) implemented automatic CRC identification and replacement in the GCC compiler, achieving performance improvements of 91% and 93% on x86–64 and RISC-V, respectively, validating the necessity of algorithm-hardware co-optimization in high-throughput scenarios [5]. Saleh & Mohammed (2024) proposed a CRC + Checksum hybrid verification framework, dynamically generating polynomials from IP addresses in IPv4 data streams to achieve dual verification while occupying only 72 bits of memory and incurring a 1 ms verification delay, providing insights for low-latency batch verification in resource-constrained on-board environments [6]. The aforementioned studies all indicate that eliminating byte alignment dependency, supporting dynamic polynomial configuration, and enabling batch processing parallelization have become key directions for enhancing CRC reliability and throughput in high-bandwidth satellite-ground links. They also lay the theoretical and engineering foundation for the "dual-segment non-integer byte CRC mechanism" proposed in this paper.

On the other hand, the application of CRC has extended beyond the traditional link layer. Mozaffari-Kermani et al. integrated CRC into a finite field inversion computation module and used it as a fault-tolerance detection mechanism to improve the operational reliability in the hardware implementation of post-quantum cryptography [7]. Wei et al. utilized CRC to assist in sequence reconstruction in an asynchronous time-division QR code system, so as to resist the impacts of frame loss and out-of-order transmission and achieve robust packet recovery [8]. In the interaction scenarios between the Internet of Things (IoT) and satellites, CRC has also been attempted to be combined with lightweight channel codes for quickly inferring error bit indices and enhancing the anti-interference capability of low-Earth orbit (LEO) constellations [9]. These cross-domain applications show that CRC has gradually evolved into a universal lightweight error detection method, rather than being limited to traditional link-layer verification.

Nevertheless, most existing studies focus on optimization in a single dimension, such as parallel computing efficiency [10] or functional expansion of specific protocols. In the research on comprehensive verification schemes for TDM frame structures in satellite-ground communication, especially regarding how to combine non-byte-aligned processing with the characteristics of frame structures to improve the error detection capability for key control fields and large-capacity payloads within frames in a targeted manner while ensuring high throughput, it remains a direction that has not been fully explored.

3 Implementation of a Dynamically Configurable CRC Calculation System for Non-integer Byte Data Processing

The core principle of cyclic redundancy check (CRC) is to use a predefined generator polynomial for binary division operations, relying on the iterative structure of linear feedback shift registers (LFSR) (see Fig. 1).

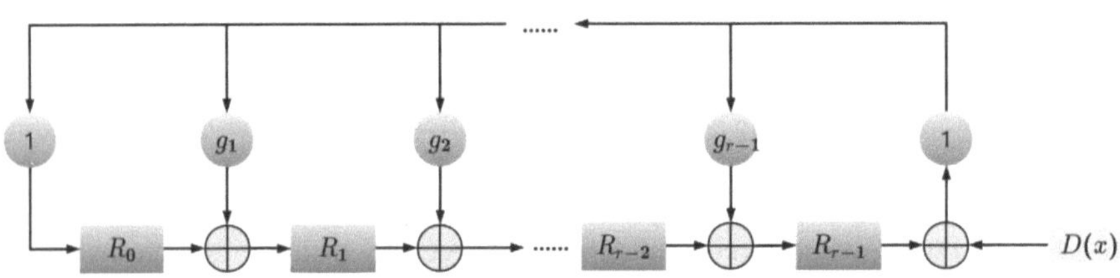

Fig. 1. CRC linear feedback shift register

At the sending end, the selected generator polynomial is used to perform polynomial division on the original data to be transmitted through shift and XOR operations. The remainder obtained from the division operation is the calculated CRC value.

Let the input data bit string be:

$$d = d_{n-1}d_{n-2}\ldots d_0(d_i \in 0, 1) \tag{1}$$

This can be expressed as:

$$D(x) = \sum_{i=0}^{n=1} d_i x^i \tag{2}$$

Select the generating polynomial of degree r:

$$G(x) = g_r x^r + g_{r-1} x^{r-1} + \cdots + g_1 x + 1, \quad g_r = g_0 = 1 \tag{3}$$

The coefficient of the first and last terms is set to 1, to ensure that the $G(x)$ first and last terms are not zero.

Shift the original data bit string $D(x)$ to the left by r bits, i.e., append r zeros to the end of the data to reserve bits for the remainder:

$$D'(x) = D(x)x^r \tag{4}$$

Perform modulo 2 division on $D'(x)$ to find the remainder:

$$D'(x) = Q(x)G(x) + R(x), \quad deg\ R(x) < r \tag{5}$$

The remainder is the CRC check code:

$$R(x) = \sum_{i=0}^{r-1} r_i x^i \tag{6}$$

Concatenate the obtained CRC checksum R(x) with the data to form the frame to be sent:

$$T(x) = D(x)x^r + R(x) \tag{7}$$

The receiving end uses the same generating polynomial $G(x)$ for the complete frame $T(x)$ and performs another modulo 2 division to obtain the remainder.

$$T(x) = Q'(x)G(x) + R'(x) \tag{8}$$

If the remainder $R'(x)$ is 0, it means that the data has not been corrupted during transmission or storage; if it is not 0, it can be determined that there is an error.

The traditional implementation, as shown in Table 1, is based on byte alignment and cannot directly interface with non-integer byte data streams, resulting in a large number of telemetry frames still needing to be filled in frame by frame during batch verification, which becomes a bottleneck for system throughput.

This solution uses a bitstream-based processing framework to process data sequences of any length through optimized algorithms, avoiding padding or truncation operations. Specifically, input data is parsed as a continuous bitstream rather than fixed byte blocks, and dynamic CRC calculation is achieved using shift registers and a configurable parameter engine. The calculation formula can be expressed as:

$$\begin{aligned} &CRC[0] = CRC_{init} \\ &CRC[i+1] = \begin{cases} (CRC[i] \ll 1) \oplus Poly, & if\ (Data[i] \oplus CRC[i][0]) = 1 \\ CRC[i] \ll 1, & otherwise \end{cases} \\ &CRC_{final} = (CRC[end] \oplus XOR_{out}) \end{aligned} \tag{9}$$

The figure shows an example of the calculation process (see Fig. 2). The input is "111101111000", which is "F78" in hexadecimal, with a length of 1.5 bytes. Using

Table 1. Traditional CRC implementation

```
Implementation 1: ByteCRC8_Update
Input : d                              // 8-bit data
        c_in                           // Current CRC value
Output : c_out                         // Updated CRC value
Constant : POLY ← 0x07                 // CRC-8 generator polynomial, representing x^8+x^2+x^1+1

c ← c_in XOR d                         // Merge the data into the register
for k ← 0 to 7 do                      // Shift out bits one by one (8 times in total)
    if (c AND 0x80) ≠ 0 then           // Is the most high bit 1
        c ← (c << 1) XOR POLY
    else
        c ← c << 1
    end if
end for
return c                               //   c is c_out
```

Table 2. Improved CRC implementation methods

```
Implementation 2: BitAligned_DynCRC
Input : {b0 … b_{n−1}}         // Arbitrary length n-bit data stream
        r                      // CRC width
        G[r−1:0]               // Generator polynomial, with the highest bit removed, is a constant of r bits
        S0[r−1:0]              // Initial value, default is all 0
        xor_out[r−1:0]         // Result XOR constant, optional
        ω                      // Step size (8/16/64), used for processing P ≤ ω bits at one time, configurable
Output : CRC[r−1:0]

S ← S0                                  // Register length r
i ← 0
while i < n do
    P ← min(ω, n − i)                   // Actual parallel bit number for this cycle
    D ← get_bits(b_i … b_{i+P−1})       // Take P bits to be processed
    for p ← 0 to P−1 do
        γ ← MSB(S) XOR D[p]             // XOR as feedback
        S ← (S << 1)                    // Left shift
        if γ = 1 then
            S ← S XOR G                 // XOR with the generator polynomial
        end if
    end for
    i ← i + P
end while
CRC ← S XOR xor_out                     // Reversal / XOR the result on-demand
return CRC
```

the CRC-7/MMC x^7+x^3+1 model with a bit width of 7, the generator polynomial is "0001001", which is '9' in hexadecimal. The initial value is 0, the input is not inverted, and the output is not inverted. The resulting XOR value is 0. The final output result is "1101110", which is "6E" in hexadecimal (see Table 2).

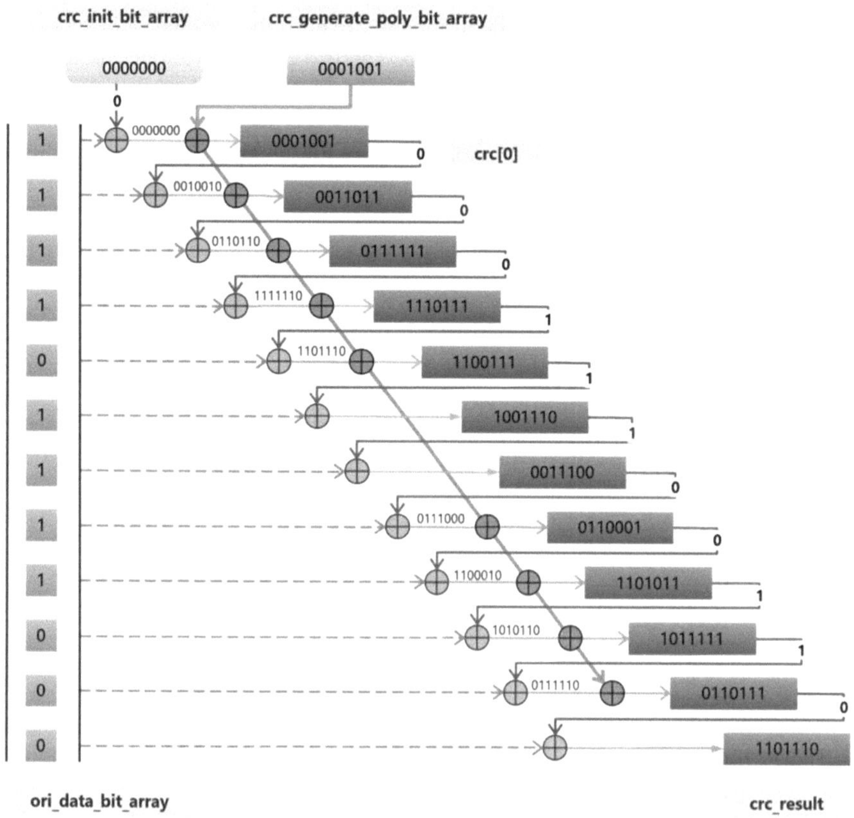

Fig. 2. Example of CRC bit flow alignment calculation process

This paper presents a fully software-based, configurable CRC calculation system implemented in the Qt/C++ environment, utilizing a two-tier architecture comprising a basic CRC calculation module and a batch file verification module. Unlike traditional calculators that only support integer-byte input and fixed polynomials, this system can perform CRC modulo calculations under any bit width and data length conditions. It also uses a custom rule engine to verify massive frame streams in a single pass, addressing the shortcomings of existing CRC calculation tools in terms of multi-mode compatibility, non-integer-byte data processing, computational efficiency, and batch verification.

Upon system startup, users can select one of the 21 built-in standard CRC models from the drop-down menu in the visual interface, or check the "Custom" option to manually enter the six parameters: bit width, generator polynomial, initial value, input/output inversion flag, and result XOR value (see Fig. 3). After the model is loaded, the parameters are serialized into a CRC Model constant class, which is instantiated at compile time using a template to create a dedicated bitwise divider. Therefore, even if the model is switched multiple times during runtime, no additional branch prediction overhead is introduced.

Subsequently, users can directly input the bit stream to be verified in hexadecimal or binary format on the "CRC Calculator" tab. The text box incorporates an anomaly data isolation mechanism: it filters out non-0 to 9 and A to F characters in real-time for hexadecimal inputs, and filters out non-0/1 characters for binary inputs. If invalid characters are detected, the interface immediately highlights them and prevents further calculations. All valid characters are parsed into continuous byte or bit arrays and then processed by a non-integer byte processing unit for intelligent truncation and padding. When the input bit count is less than the target bit width, zeros are padded at the high end; if the input is too long, it is truncated from the high end. This process follows the formula:

$$\text{Original bitstream}: \ d = d_{n-1}d_{n-2}\ldots d_0(d_i \in 0, 1) \tag{10}$$

Index bit vectors from the most significant bit (MSB) to the least significant bit (LSB), where d_{n-1} is the MSB. r represents the target CRC bit width, which can be set by the user.

$\tilde{d} = (\tilde{d}_{r-1}, \ldots, \tilde{d}_0)$: The truncated bitstream has a fixed length, where $\tilde{d}_{r-1}$ is the MSB..

$$\tilde{d}_i = \begin{cases} 0, & n < r \ and \ 0 \le i < r - n, \\ d_{i-(r-n)}, & n < r \ and \ r - n \le i < r, \\ d_{i+(r-n)}, & n \ge r \ and \ 0 \le i < r. \end{cases} \tag{11}$$

Compared to the traditional method, which can only be called in byte granularity and requires filling up the entire byte before calculation, this solution directly aligns at the bit level, avoiding unnecessary 0–7 bit padding.

After completion of the bit-level truncation or padding, the bit stream is fed into a high-performance bit-level operation engine. At the core of this engine is a dynamic shift register: the program constructs an r-bit Boolean vector S on the heap according to the user-defined bit width r, and employs a double-buffering strategy. While the main register performs the actual shift operation, the shadow register pre-reads the next batch of bit streams, thereby distributing the cost of CPU cache misses outside the pipeline.

If the user switches to the "Batch Verification" tab (see Fig. 4), the interface allows loading multiple large binary files up to several GB at once and configuring multiple sets of "verification rules" for each file: including payload start offset, bit length, original CRC position, and which CRC model to use. The rule set is serialized into JSON and passed to the verification engine, which enables OpenMP parallel for loops based on the number of CPU physical cores, completing all verifications using a two-level pipeline read/write approach combining file-level parallelism and frame-level parallelism. Threads directly reuse the basic CRC calculation module, so there is no need to reconstruct register objects regardless of changes in single-frame data length.

The dynamically configurable CRC calculation system proposed in this paper was subjected to performance testing on a standard desktop platform. The hardware configuration of the test platform is as follows: Intel Core i7-12700K CPU (8 performance cores + 4 efficiency cores), 32GB DDR4-3600 memory, and Samsung 980 Pro NVMe SSD. The operating system adopted was 64-bit Windows 11, and the software was compiled using the MSVC 2022 compiler with O2 optimization enabled.

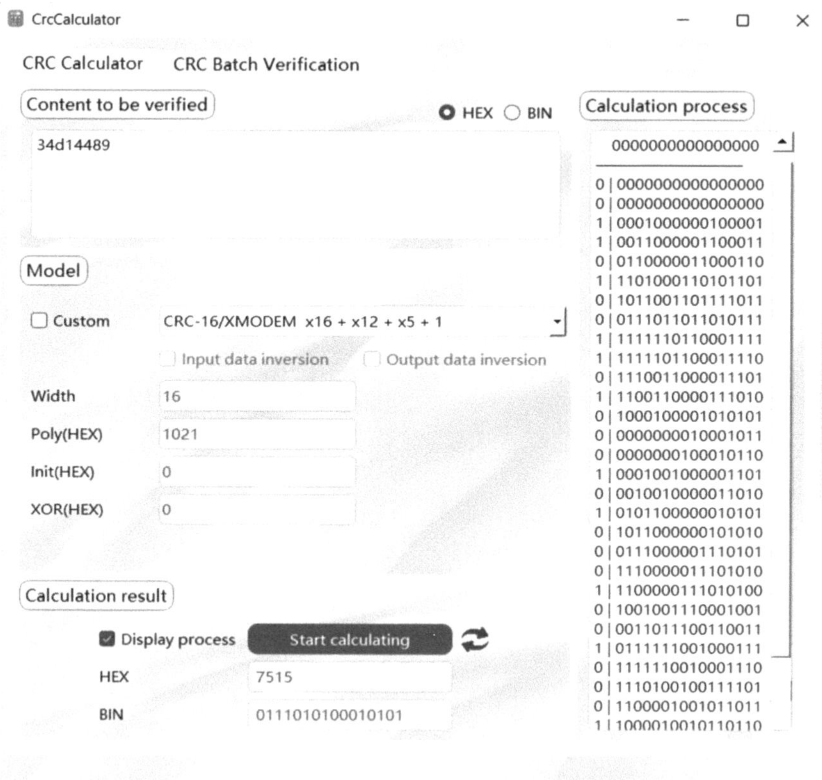

Fig. 3. Visualization interface of CRC calculation software tool

For the test, a 6GB randomly generated binary dataset conforming to the hybrid frame structure proposed in this paper was used. Excluding the file reading time limited by hardware, the system could complete full verification of the 6GB data within 22 s. Corresponding to the CRC32 scenario, the throughput reached 2.18 Gbps, demonstrating significant advantages compared with similar schemes.

In terms of functional flexibility, the system proposed in this paper supports dynamic models and non-byte-aligned processing features that most existing schemes struggle to achieve simultaneously. Regarding batch processing and parallel capabilities: the performance of the scheme by Arutunian et al. [5] is highly dependent on compiler optimization effects; the FPGA-based schemes by Zhang et al. [3] and Cai et al. [4] achieve higher parallel efficiency by virtue of hardware parallel architectures, but they incur high hardware deployment costs.

Although the throughput of the system in this paper is only one order of magnitude lower than that of hardware-based CRC implementations, it avoids the high-cost issue of FPGA schemes. It is particularly suitable for general-purpose computing scenarios that require both functional flexibility and cost control (Table 3).

In addition to the independently deployable CRC calculation tool, this paper encapsulates the core CRC calculation part that has been implemented into a general-purpose

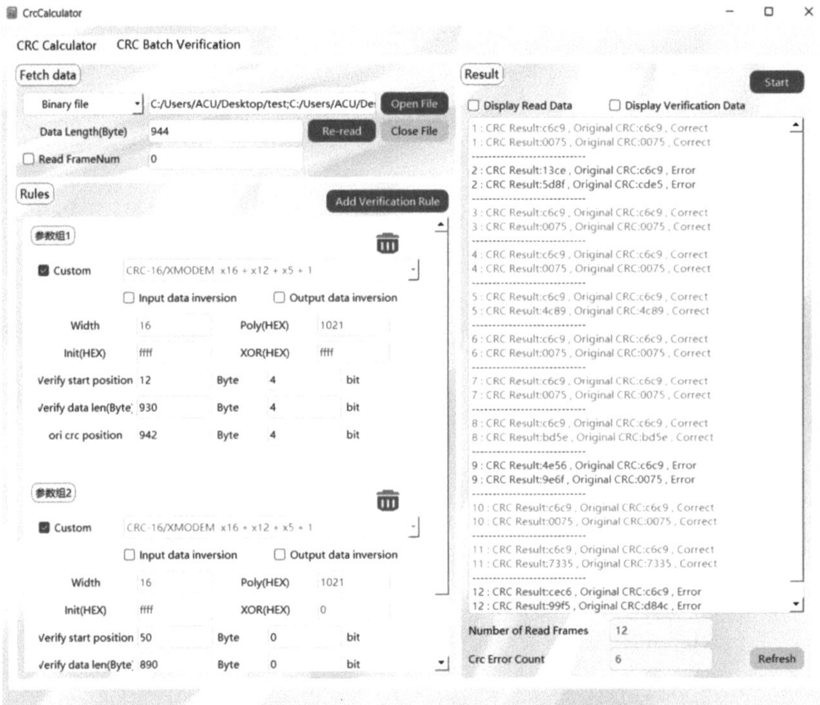

Fig. 4. Batch verification interface of CRC calculation software tool

library with standard interfaces for portability and reuse. The design of this general-purpose library will follow the principle of modularity, providing highly abstract, clear, and easy-to-use API interfaces that is not limited to pre-set models. The library adopts a layered architecture design and contains three core structures (Table 4):

(1) Unified Application Interface Layer: As the top layer of the library, it provides standardized C/C++ language function interfaces. Developers can call the library's functions through this layer's simple and clear API without worrying about the underlying implementation details. This layer is responsible for parameter validation, context management, and calling the underlying core algorithms.
(2) Protocol and Configuration Layer: This layer pre-configures standard CRC models for common satellite communication protocols such as CCSDS, AOS, and CADU, and provides a parameterized configuration mechanism to support custom or proprietary protocols. Designers can dynamically specify any CRC polynomial, initial value, result XOR value, and input/output reversal rules via the API.
(3) Efficient Algorithm Engine Layer: The core computational layer of the library, integrating the aforementioned bitstream CRC computation methods, enabling high-throughput computation on general-purpose CPUs.

Table 3. Comparison of Performance and Characteristics of Different CRC Verification Schemes

Application Scheme	Platform	Dynamic Model	Non-byte Alignment Support	Batch Processing & Parallel Capability	Throughput	Deployment Cost
This Paper	General-Purpose CPU (Software Implementation: Qt/C++)	Supported	Supported	Batch processing supported; OpenMP parallelization	2.18 Gbps	Extremely Low
Zhang et al. [3]	FPGA (Hardware Implementation)	No (Static Model)	No	No data stream batch processing; Based on hardware parallel architecture	392 Gbps	High
Cai et al. [4]	FPGA (Hardware Implementation)	No (Static Model)	No	No data stream batch processing; Based on hardware parallel architecture	11.07 Gbps	High
Arutunian et al. [5]	ARM64 Architecture CPU (Software Implementation)	No (Standard Fixed Model)	No	No data stream batch processing; Parallelization dependent on compiler optimization	19 Gbps	Low
Saleh et al. [6]	General-Purpose CPU (Software Implementation: Python)	Limited Support (Dynamic Adjustment Only Based on IP Address)	No	No data stream batch processing; No parallel capability	Single-channel 64 kbps	Extremely Low

Table 4. Standard interface specifications

Interface Functions	Parameter Declaration	Return Value	Generality
crc_init()	model: model structure	contextual handles	supports 21 predefined protocols and custom configurations

(*continued*)

Table 4. (*continued*)

Interface Functions	Parameter Declaration	Return Value	Generality
crc_compute()	handle: contextual handles data: input data pointer bit_length: data bit length	CRC results	processes data of any bit length
crc_batch()	handle: contextual handles file_list: list of file paths config: frame configuration	verification report	supports batch file processing
crc_get_info()	handle: contextual handles	performance indicators	obtains runtime data such as throughput and latency

4 Dual-Segment Non-integer Byte Optimized Verification Mechanism

In satellite-ground communication, to ensure data integrity, traditional TDM frames generally adopt a simple and intuitive verification strategy: after the end of variable-length payload data, a single CRC code is appended to the entire frame. Although this method is easy to implement, its inherent overall checksum feature tends to expose two key flaws when facing complex channels: error detection blind spots and coarse error localization granularity.

A single CRC code is designed to verify the integrity of the entire data block. When errors are distributed exactly at the boundaries of different logical segments within the frame, the error effects may cancel each other out during polynomial division operations, leading to false negatives—this is fatal for TDM frames that carry multiple types of businesses. Even if an error is detected, the receiver can only determine that "the entire frame is faulty"; it cannot distinguish whether the error occurs in critical control information or high-speed payload data. The lack of such discrimination capability forces the system to adopt the most conservative "full-frame retransmission" strategy [11], which means enormous bandwidth waste and latency for satellite links where bandwidth is extremely precious.

Addressing the pain point that TDM-based data frames are prone to errors caused by noise, attenuation, and other factors in high-speed or interference-prone channels, while conventional error detection schemes have weak error detection capabilities, this paper designs a dual-segment non-integer byte CRC mechanism and its optimized frame structure, aiming to improve the system's error detection efficiency and flexibility.

The core of this scheme lies in replacing the traditional single CRC check for the entire frame with independent dual-segment, bit-level checks for synchronous slots and business slots, thereby achieving sensitive detection of short burst errors and efficient coverage of overall errors in long frames (see Fig. 5). At the frame structure level, the TDM cycle frame begins with a fixed synchronous slot to ensure deterministic delay guarantees for low-speed, high-priority telemetry and telecontrol businesses. The subsequent multiple variable-length business slots dynamically allocate bandwidth based on link status and business requirements to carry high-speed payloads or formation coordination data.

Within the synchronous slot (112 bits), redundant bits are no longer filled in byte-aligned manner, but instead directly include a 32-bit synchronous header, a 12-bit source address, a 12-bit destination address, and a 36-bit control word, with a 20-bit CRC field appended at the end. This CRC field is divided into a 4-bit "control word-specific CRC" and a 16-bit "full-slot CRC". The role division is rationally designed based on the differentiated reliability requirements of subfields: the 36-bit control word carries real-time scheduling information, where even short burst errors (1–4 bits) can cause business misalignment, so the 4-bit dedicated CRC is designed for low-latency detection of such errors; the full-slot CRC covers all 112 bits to prevent cross-domain errors that may be missed by the dedicated CRC, ensuring overall slot integrity.

Each business slot adopts a variable-length format of "96-bit preamble control zone + N × 8-bit payload data zone," with a 32-bit dual-segment CRC appended at the tail. The 16-bit "payload data CRC" is specifically designed for precise verification of N-byte high-speed data, while the 16-bit full-slot "CRC" covers the entire slot range from the control zone to the data zone. This segmented verification strategy ensures a high detection rate for random or burst errors in large-capacity data while also enabling rapid localization and isolation of errors via the "payload data CRC" when data is damaged across boundaries, thereby preventing a single fault from causing the entire frame to be retransmitted.

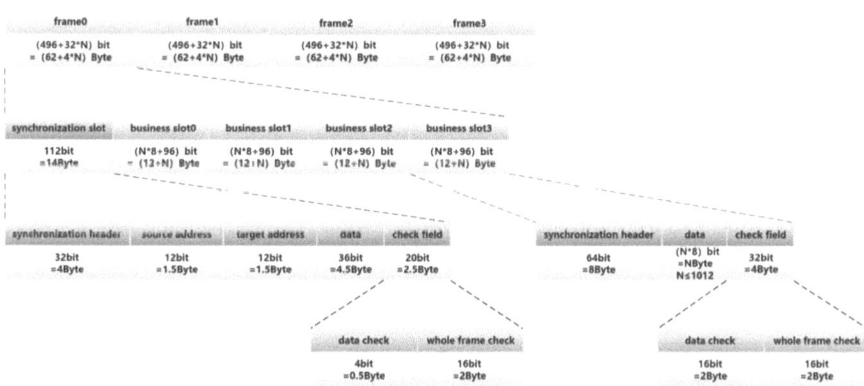

Fig. 5. Dual-segment non-integer byte CRC frame structure

It is extremely complex and ethically concerning to inject bit errors for testing directly on active satellite links. Therefore, in response to the random bit errors and burst bit errors commonly found in satellite-to-ground communication channels, this study uses the Bernoulli model and the Gilbert–Elliott channel model to model the random bit error process, and conducts testing based on the efficient batch verification tool implemented in Sect. 3. Through this experimental design, the error detection performance of the dual-segment non-integer byte CRC mechanism in the TDM frame structure of satellite-to-ground communications is verified.

During testing, the bit error rate(BER) is set within the range of $10^{-6} \sim 10^{-2}$, and bit errors are simulated using the Gilbert-Elliott model or fixed-length burst of $L_b \in \{1, 4, 8, 16, 32\}$ consecutive bit flips. The test sample set contained $N = 10^5$ frame data randomly generated according to an optimized TDM frame structure, with each frame containing a fixed 112-bit synchronous slot and an average of three business slots (the length of the business slots follows a uniform distribution between 128 and 1024 bits). After error injection, dual-segment CRC checks are performed on each frame of data.

$$P_{burst} = \frac{Number\ of\ burst\ error\ frames\ detected\ by\ control\ field\ CRC}{Number\ of\ frames\ injected\ with\ burst\ errors}$$
$$P_{sync} = \frac{Number\ of\ synchronous\ slot\ error\ frames\ detected\ by\ full-slot\ CRC}{Number\ of\ bursts\ containing\ synchronous\ slot\ errors}$$
$$P_{payload} = \frac{Number\ of\ error\ frames\ detected\ in\ the\ data\ area\ by\ payload\ data\ CRC}{Number\ of\ frames\ containing\ errors\ in\ the\ payload\ data\ area}$$
$$P_{frame} = 1 - \frac{Number\ of\ undetected\ error\ frames}{N}$$

Simulation and link test results show that when combined with a dynamic frame length adjustment strategy, this dual-segment non-integer byte CRC mechanism has a 100% detection rate for burst errors with lengths not exceeding the CRC bit width. For burst errors exceeding the CRC bit width, the combined application of the control field CRC and the full-slot CRC significantly improves the burst error detection rate from 62% in the traditional scheme to 94%; the overall detection rate for the synchronous slot and the payload data detection rate are improved from 85% and 88% to 98% and 97%, respectively; The overall error detection rate for the entire frame has increased from 90% to 99%, meaning the probability of missed detection has dropped below 0.1% (see Fig. 6).

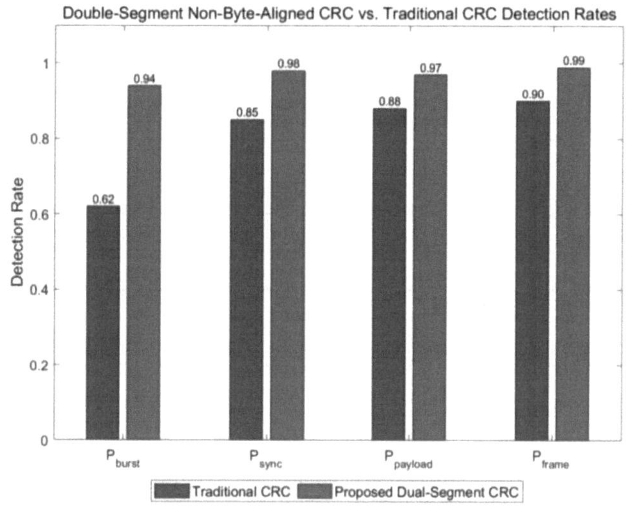

Fig. 6. Detection rate test results

To fully verify the performance and reliability of the dual-segment non-integer byte CRC mechanism in real satellite-ground links, this paper organized multiple rounds of special tests based on a real satellite downlink. The experimental system uses an on-orbit satellite as the signal source. The signal is received by a ground gateway station, processed through power amplifiers and up-down converter units, then demodulated by a modem and decrypted by encryption equipment before the data is transmitted to a business content analysis server (see Fig. 7). The data processing program in the server is integrated with the CRC verification module encapsulated and implemented in Sect. 3 of this paper, enabling rapid data screening to eliminate erroneous frames and send correct data to subsequent processing modules. Meanwhile, testers can use the visualized CRC verification tool described in Sect. 3 on the debugging host computer to perform batch re-verification and in-depth analysis of cached data. Observing the temporal distribution of erroneous frames and the positions of error bits within the frames is of great help for evaluating link stability and identifying potential causes of channel degradation.

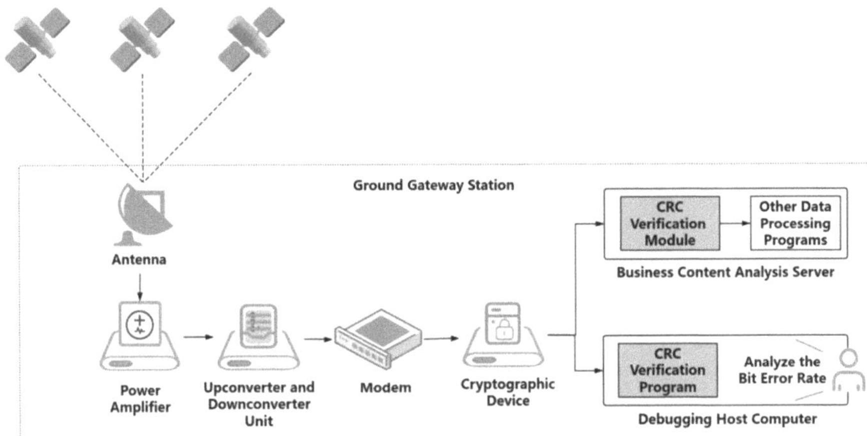

Fig. 7. Satellite Downlink Test Environment

During the test, the satellite downlink rate remained stable at 64 Mbps. A total of 15 independent test tasks were conducted, with each task continuously receiving data for 1 min. The satellite channel was divided into multiple slots for use by different ground stations, and approximately 65,000 valid data frames were actually processed in each task. Through precise comparison and analysis of the downlink data, it was confirmed that the links in the 15 tests generated a total of 239 error frames under different atmospheric conditions, and all bit errors manifested as random discrete errors spanning several bytes. After processing by the CRC verification program proposed in this paper, all 239 error frames were accurately detected, resulting in a bit error false negative rate of 0%(see Fig. 8). This proves the extremely high detection reliability of the proposed scheme for typical scattered byte errors in actual channels. Although the proposed scheme introduces more complex dual-segment verification calculations, the average single-frame processing delay only increases by approximately 1.2 ms. Under the parallel batch processing mechanism, this overhead is far lower than the inherent transmission and propagation delays of the satellite channel, such that the additionally introduced processing time has almost no impact on the real-time performance of the system.

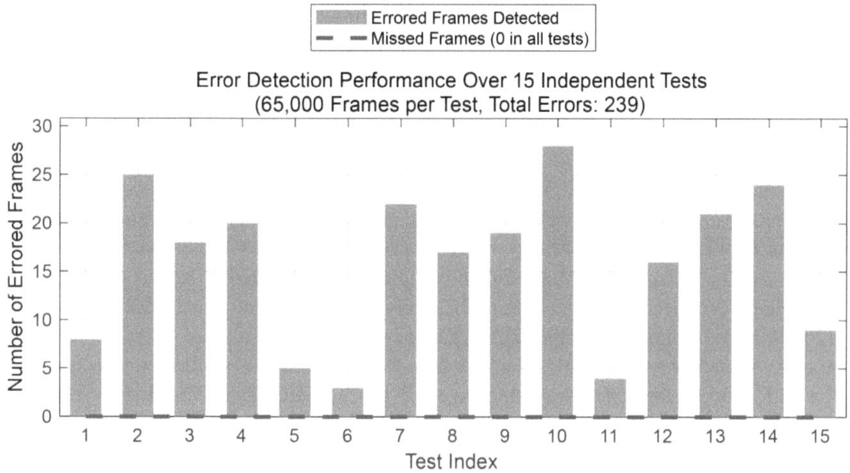

Fig. 8. Distribution of Error Frames and Their Detection Status in 15 Test Tasks

5 Conclusion

This paper proposes and implements a highly flexible software-based CRC calculation system, innovatively addressing the key bottlenecks of traditional CRC tools in multi-mode compatibility, non-integer byte data processing efficiency, and batch verification capability. Through the collaborative design of a basic calculation module and a batch verification module, the non-integer byte dynamically configurable CRC calculation tool supports bit-level CRC remainder operations for data of any bit width. Additionally, it introduces dynamic shift registers and a dual-buffer strategy to optimize calculation throughput. Aiming at the bit error characteristics of satellite-ground communication links, the dual-segment non-integer byte CRC mechanism proposed in this paper realizes accurate capture of short burst errors and efficient coverage of overall errors in long frames through a layered verification architecture that separates synchronous slots and business slots. Despite the significant improvements achieved in this study, there are still some limitations. The current software implementation prioritizes flexibility and reliability over processing speed. Future work will include the development of a dedicated FPGA IP core to leverage the inherent parallelism of the algorithm and achieve hardware-level throughput. Secondly, the dual-segment mechanism introduces a slight overhead in terms of check bits per frame. For different communication tasks, conducting a theoretical analysis to find the optimal trade-off between overhead and reliability remains an unsolved problem.

References

1. Pei, T.-B., Zukowski, C.: High-speed parallel CRC circuits in VLSI. IEEE Trans. Commun. **40**, 653–657 (1992). https://doi.org/10.1109/26.141415
2. Peterson, W.W., Brown, D.T.: Cyclic codes for error detection. Proc. IRE **49**(1), 228–235 (1961). https://doi.org/10.1109/JRPROC.1961.287814

3. Zhang, L., et al.: An efficient parallel CRC computing method for high bandwidth networks and FPGA implementation. Electronics **13**(22), 4399 (2024)
4. Cai, F., Nie, Y., Zhang, K., Luo, H., Li, Y.: A high-speed CRC-32 implementation on FPGA. In: 2024 4th International Conference on Neural Networks, Information and Communication Engineering (NNICE), Guangzhou, China, pp. 1665–1668 (2024). https://doi.org/10.1109/NNICE61279.2024.10499172
5. Arutunian, M., Sargsyan, S., Mehrabyan, M., Bareghamyan, L., Aslanyan, H.: Automatic recognition and replacement of cyclic redundancy checks for program optimization. IEEE Access **12**, 192146–192158 (2024). https://doi.org/10.1109/ACCESS.2024.3518953
6. Saleh, A.H., Mohammed, M.S.: Enhancing data security through hybrid error detection: combining cyclic redundancy check (CRC) and checksum techniques. IJEER **12**(3), 813-826 (2024). https://doi.org/10.37391/IJEER.120312
7. Canto, A.C., Kermani, M.M., Azarderakhsh, R.: CRC-based error detection constructions for FLT and ITA finite field inversions over GF (2 m). IEEE Trans. Very Large Scale Integr. (VLSI) Syst. **29**(5), 1033–1037 (2021)
8. Kang, M., Park, D.: Robust reconstruction of QR-embedded software using CRC-based sequence extraction of asynchronous time-multiplexed QR code. In: 2021 IEEE International Conference on Consumer Electronics-Asia (ICCE-Asia), pp. 1–2. IEEE (2021)
9. Zhao W, Zhang H, Zou J, et al. Effective Chirp Modulation Communication System Design for LEO Satellite IoT[J]. IEEE Internet of Things Journal, 2025
10. Cheng, C., Parhi, K.K.: High-speed parallel CRC implementation based on unfolding, pipelining, and retiming. IEEE Trans. Circuits Syst. II Express Briefs **53**(10), 1017–1021 (2006)
11. Giambene, G., Gomez, I., De Cola, T., et al.: Satellite forward VDES channel modeling and impact on higher-layer performance. Int. J. Satell. Commun. Network. **41**(2), 102–121 (2023)

Formal Verification of DMA-Enabled Memory Isolation in MPU-Based Embedded Systems

Heng Xu[1,2], Maodongbin Wang[1,2], Zhiwen Pan[1,2](✉), Zhicheng Zhang[1,2], Kaixiang Liu[1,2], and Limin Sun[1,2]

[1] Institute of Information Engineering, Chinese Academy of Sciences, Beijing, China
{xuheng,wangmaodongbin,panzhiwen,zhangzhicheng,liukaixiang, sunlimin}@iie.ac.cn

[2] School of Cyber Security, University of Chinese Academy of Sciences, Beijing, China

Abstract. Microcontrollers are widely used in embedded systems and IoT devices, relying on Memory Protection Units (MPUs) to enforce process-level memory isolation. However, MPUs can be completely bypassed by Direct Memory Access (DMA), and their effectiveness hinges on correct kernel configuration, creating serious security risks. Most existing formal verification methods for memory isolation focus on systems with a Memory Management Unit (MMU). In non-MMU settings, prior work either treats DMA as a trusted peripheral or fails to model and verify the advanced DMA behaviors found in modern microcontrollers. As a result, these methods are limited for embedded environments that rely heavily on DMA and provide only a MPU. We develop a comprehensive system-level hardware–software state model. For the first time, this model unifies CPU execution, MPU enforcement, and the dynamic behavior of a multi-channel DMA controller with advanced features such as scatter–gather and burst transfers—thereby eliminating the trusted-DMA assumption. Building on this model, we define the system's core security invariants and design a lightweight two-layer defense mechanism that preserves system security. Finally, we integrate weakest-precondition (WP) calculus into each primitive operation, enabling continuous verification of security properties, and we rigorously prove—by mathematical induction—that the security invariants hold across all legal system state transitions. We implement the core mechanisms as a portable C library and integrate them into three popular real-time operating systems: Zephyr, RT-Thread, and FreeRTOS. Experiments on real hardware—the ST Nucleo-H743ZI and TI EK-TM4C1294XL—show that our approach completely defeats a suite of sophisticated DMA attacks while imposing minimal overhead—average throughput decreases by only 3.7%—and significantly improves real-time stability under high concurrency. This work provides the first formally proven, DMA-enabled memory isolation solution for MPU-based embedded systems.

Keywords: IoT · Formal Verification · Memory Protection Unit · Direct Memory Access · Memory Isolation

L. Zhang and K.-K. R. Choo (Eds.): MobiQuitous 2025, LNICST 683, pp. 257–277, 2026.
https://doi.org/10.1007/978-3-032-22500-9_15

1 Introduction

With the rise of the Internet of Things (IoT) and embedded systems, microcontroller unit (MCU)-based devices have permeated critical domains such as industrial control, smart homes, healthcare, and automotive electronics [1]. To ensure the security of these devices, the Memory Protection Unit (MPU) has become a standard MCU feature [2,3]. By enforcing access permissions in hardware, the MPU provides basic memory isolation for software components (e.g., tasks or processes), preventing memory corruption and unauthorized access [4].

To maximize data-transfer efficiency, modern embedded systems widely rely on Direct Memory Access (DMA) controllers [5–7]. DMA enables peripherals to exchange data with memory without CPU intervention, substantially improving system throughput. However, this CPU-bypassing capability poses a serious security challenge: DMA transfers typically fall outside the MPU's purview [8]. Consequently, once a DMA controller is maliciously configured—whether via a compromised user task, a kernel-level confused-deputy vulnerability, or an arbitrary read/write exploit—an attacker can use DMA to circumvent carefully crafted MPU protections and read or write any memory region, ultimately undermining system security. It is also important to note that the MPU itself does not guarantee isolation; its effectiveness depends entirely on the kernel's correct configuration, switching, and maintenance of region descriptors [9]. Bugs in the kernel's memory manager can therefore lead to severe security issues. Designing a defense that preserves DMA's performance benefits while providing verifiable security guarantees remains an open challenge in embedded security.

Over the past decade, substantial research has focused on formally verifiable isolation, particularly in the domain of microkernel security. For example, approaches such as seL4 [11,12] and CertiKOS [13,14] provide formal proofs for access control. However, these approaches typically rely on MMU-based virtual memory and trusted DMA, making them ill-suited to embedded systems that lack MMU support and depend heavily on DMA. Other approaches (e.g., PISTIS [10] and D-Box [9]) partially address DMA security, but are difficult to deploy on MPU-only MCUs and do not model or verify complex DMA modes such as multi-channel, scatter–gather, and burst transfers. To date, the only formally verified memory-isolation work targeting MPU-based systems is Pip-MPU [16]. Yet this model likewise treats DMA as a trusted peripheral. Furthermore, Pip-MPU assumes that all interrupts are disabled during kernel service execution to avoid preemption, which constrains its ability to handle nested interrupts or task preemption—both of which may violate system invariants. Finally, the model checks invariants only at service entry and exit points, yielding coarse granularity that fails to capture security violations in intermediate states and thereby limits verification precision.

To fill these gaps, we propose a formally verified memory-isolation method for MPU-based systems with DMA support. The approach first constructs an accurate software–hardware state model that encompasses the CPU, MPU, and an advanced DMA controller (supporting multi-channel, scatter–gather and burst transfers), as well as operating-system kernel data structures, thereby eliminating the need for the trusted DMA assumption. We then model Stacked Contexts, define the system's core security invariant, and, based on this, design a lightweight dual-layer defense: a user mode DMA Guard that blocks unauthorized accesses to DMA registers, and a kernel mode Access Guard that validates all DMA transfer parameters to keep the system secure even under deeply nested interrupts and other complex scenarios. Unlike conventional methods, we integrate weakest-precondition (WP) calculus into every primitive operation, enabling continuous verification of security properties rather than checking only at service boundaries. Finally, using mathematical induction together with WP calculus, we rigorously prove that the security invariant holds under all legal system state transitions. We implement the mechanism as a portable C library and conduct empirical evaluations on three real-world RTOSes—Zephyr, RT-Thread, and FreeRTOS. The results show that our method effectively thwarts a wide range of sophisticated DMA attacks while incurring minimal overhead, with an average throughput loss of only 3.7%.

Contributions. Our main contribution is the first formally proved, DMA-enabled microkernel-style memory-isolation model for MPU-based embedded systems. More concretely, it consists of:

- **Precise formal model.** We develop a comprehensive system-state model that, for the first time, unifies the dynamic behaviors of CPU execution, MPU protection, and a multi-channel, multi-mode DMA controller.
- **Provable security invariants.** We formally define system security invariants and design a two-layer DMA guard that preserves isolation while accommodating advanced DMA features. Moreover, we provide a compositional proof strategy that covers compound operations.
- **Extensive experimental evaluation.** On real hardware, we demonstrate strong portability, robustness, security, and low overhead—achieving complete resistance to complex DMA attacks with an average throughput overhead of only 3.7%.

The remainder of this paper is organized as follows: Sect. 2 reviews related work; Sect. 3 introduces the background; Sect. 4 presents the threat model and assumptions; Sect. 5 provides an overview of the proposed method; Sect. 6 formalizes the system state model; Sect. 7 defines the security invariants; Sect. 8 presents the security proofs; Sect. 9 reports the experimental evaluation; and Sect. 10 concludes and outlines future work. Our open-source code is available at https://anonymous.4open.science/r/TEST-FB65/README.md.

2 Related Work

Formal Verification of Microkernels. seL4 [11,12] pioneered formal verification of access control for a kernel; CertiKOS [14] used compositional refinement to verify a preemptive kernel; ProvenCore [17] delivers a lightweight, certified ARM kernel; VSOS [15] verifies transportation systems by modeling them as automata in Isabelle/HOL; ExpressOS [18] verifies system security on a real ARM smartphone; Chen et al. [19] and Guo [20] extended reasoning to cover interruptible and preemptive execution; Dejon et al. introduced Pip-MPU [16], the first formally verified MPU kernel for embedded devices. However, these systems either rely on an MMU, assume interrupts are disabled, or treat DMA as trusted; thus they do not address MPU-only environments with concurrent, nested interrupts in the presence of untrusted DMA. We formally model the concurrency of nested interrupts and DMA under an MPU. Moreover, unlike large-scale efforts that aim to fully verify an entire kernel (e.g., Pip-MPU [16]), we do not rebuild a brand-new, fully verified OS. Instead, we propose a verifiable security methodology that targets the pervasive DMA risks in existing MPU-based RTOSes.

MPU-Based Memory Protection. In practice, mainstream RTOSes [5–7] provide MPU examples or APIs, but security largely hinges on correct kernel configuration and context-switch timing, with no machine-checkable guarantees of global invariants. In academia, software defenses such as EPOXY [1], SHIELD [23], CTOMP [24], among others [4,25–27]-emphasize permission orchestration or inter-domain communication hardening, yet they do not provably eliminate the root cause that allows DMA to bypass the MPU. Our work directly addresses this challenge and remedies the limitations of traditional MPU schemes in DMA.

DMA Isolation Techniques. Haglund and Guanciale formally modeled NICs and their DMA-controller interactions in HOL4 [29]; subsequent work by Haglund abstracted DMA transfers and provided reusable theorems [31]; PISTIS [10] formally secures the use of DMA and interrupts on MCUs without an MPU; D-Box [9] offered capability-based DMA isolation atop FreeRTOS-MPU, but provides no formal verification; and Tao et al. [30] extended SeKVM's verification to the ARM SMMU, leveraging dedicated hardware to block malicious DMA. These efforts either target systems with an IOMMU, model a narrower DMA feature set than what we consider (e.g., omitting scatter–gather modes common on modern MCUs), or introduce hardware changes beyond general-purpose scenarios. By contrast, we provide a more comprehensive, provably sound assurance path for non-IOMMU MCUs, aligned with practical DMA usage patterns.

3 Background

In this section, we introduce key concepts that make our system design easier to understand. We adopt ARMv7-M as our reference architecture, which covers the widely used Cortex-M3, -M4, and -M7 microcontrollers. Other architectures exhibit similar properties or impose looser requirements on protected memory regions, which simplify their use [32,33].

3.1 Memory Protection Unit (MPU)

All Cortex-M processors based on the ARMv7 architecture (including later versions) provide an MPU [4,26,28]. Unlike a full computer MMU, the MPU does not perform address translation to support virtual memory. The MPU operates as illustrated in Fig. 1a. Each MPU descriptor specifies a physical memory interval, the access permissions (distinguishing kernel vs. user mode and read/write/execute privileges), and whether the region is enabled [1]. Before each memory access, the MPU validates the target against enabled regions and permissions; absent a match or sufficient rights, a `MemManageFault` is raised and control synchronously traps to the kernel [2,3].

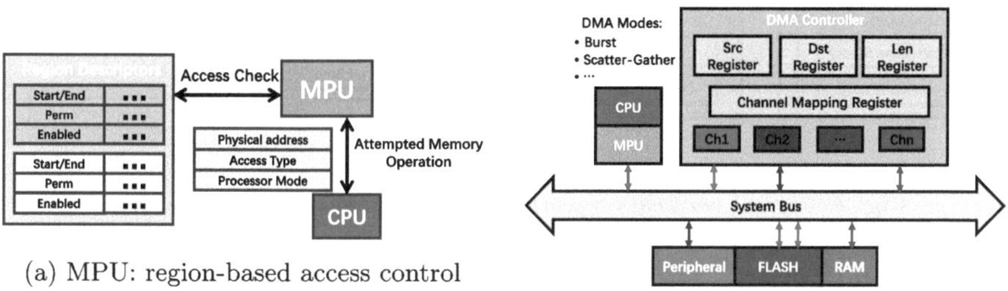

(a) MPU: region-based access control

(b) DMA: CPU-bypassing data transfer

Fig. 1. MPU and DMA controller overview.

3.2 DMA Controller

The DMA controller is an on-chip bus-master peripheral optimized for moving data from a source to a destination [9]. As shown in Fig. 1b, the DMA controller can program its internal source address register, destination address register, and data length register to communicate with slaves (peripherals, RAM, and flash) without intervention from the core processor and without any involvement from the MPU. The DMA controller also provides channel-mapping registers, enabling it to manage multiple transfer channels concurrently, which substantially increases system data-handling throughput [31]. In addition, the DMA supports multiple transfer modes—such as burst mode and scatter–gather mode—to accommodate diverse application requirements [30].

4 Threat Model and Assumptions

We assume that attackers have found a memory corruption vulnerability in any of the underlying software stack layers, and they are capable of launching a memory corruption exploit. Once the attackers have successfully launched such an exploit, they can either inject code or reuse existing code in the target MCU to achieve their goal. For example, abuse of DMA by a malicious task, a confused-deputy flaw in the DMA controller, or arbitrary read/write primitives can enable task reconfiguration, stealth peripheral control, and arbitrary memory access—culminating in full system compromise. We assume the firmware enforces memory and privilege separation but neglects DMA isolation. Furthermore, we assume the DMA controller hardware itself operates correctly as specified. We rule out all physical and hardware-focused attacks. We consider that protection against physical attacks is an orthogonal problem and can be achieved, for instance, by deploying the device inside a tamper-proof protection shield [34].

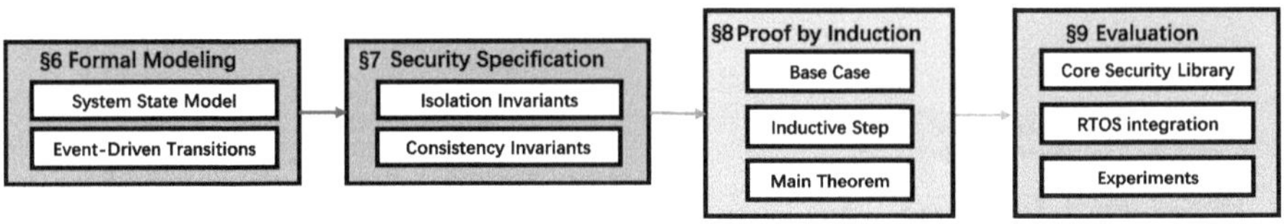

Fig. 2. Formal verification workflow for embedded-system security.

5 Methodology Overview

As shown in Fig. 2, a formal verification methodology for embedded system security is proposed. A precise state model covering both hardware and software is constructed, and instruction execution, interrupt handling, and fault processing are formalized as event-driven state transitions (see Sect. 6). Based on this model, security objectives are specified as system invariants, including $isolation\_mpu$ and $consistent\_mpu$ (see Sect. 7). Using mathematical induction together with WP calculus, it is proved that if the system is initialized in a secure state and each transition preserves the invariants, then all reachable states are secure (see Sect. 8). Finally, the security checks are realized as a portable library, integrated with several mainstream RTOSes, and empirically evaluated on real hardware (see Sect. 9).

6 Formal Modeling of System State

This section presents the formal state model we construct for the target system. We abstract the system's instantaneous state as s and partition the model into hardware state and software state. For each part, we focus only on the components relevant to the property under verification—memory isolation.

6.1 Hardware State

The following information about hardware devices is necessary to reason about memory isolation.

Program Counter (pc) $pc \in \mathbb{N}$ denotes the address of the next instruction to be executed by the CPU.

Kernel Mode Flag (*kernel_mode*) $kernel\_mode \in \mathbb{B}$, where $\mathbb{B} = \{\texttt{true}, \texttt{false}\}$. The value `true` indicates kernel (privileged) mode, and `false` indicates user mode.

Physical Memory (*data*)] $data \in \mathbb{N}^*$. We abstract physical memory as a finite sequence of natural numbers.

MPU Configuration (M_{cfg})] This models the hardware configuration of the MPU as the set of currently loaded region descriptors.
First, define the set of access permissions Π. A permission descriptor $p \in \Pi$ is a 6-tuple capturing user mode read/write/execute and privileged-mode read/write/execute permissions (ur, uw, ux, pr, pw, px):

$$p \in \Pi \triangleq \mathbb{B}^6.$$

An MPU region descriptor d belongs to the set D_{MPU} and is formalized as a quadruple containing base address, end address, permission descriptor, and an enable flag:

$$d \in D_{\text{MPU}} \triangleq \mathbb{N} \times \mathbb{N} \times \Pi \times \mathbb{B}.$$

The MPU configuration M_{cfg} is a finite subset of D_{MPU}, i.e., $M_{\text{cfg}} \subseteq D_{\text{MPU}}$.

DMA Controller State (D_{state}) We provide a model of a multi-channel DMA controller as a finite sequence, where each element represents the state of an independent DMA channel. The model is readily extensible; here we include, as found in modern MCUs, burst mode and scatter–gather mode.

We first define the basic sets that constitute the DMA state:

Channel Activity States (T_{DMA}) The channel's current activity state:

$$T_{\text{DMA}} \triangleq \{\mathit{Idle},\ \mathit{Pending},\ \mathit{Running}\}.$$

Scatter–Gather Descriptors (D_{SG}) Each descriptor specifies a single transfer block by source, destination, and length:

$$D_{\text{SG}} \triangleq \mathbb{N} \times \mathbb{N} \times \mathbb{N}.$$

Burst Size Set (B_{size}) The data width per burst transfer:

$$B_{\text{size}} \triangleq \{\mathit{BSize1},\ \mathit{BSize4},\ \mathit{BSize8}\}.$$

Based on the above, we define a single channel's configuration. A channel configuration c_{dma} belongs to the set C_{DMA} and consists of a sequence of scatter–gather descriptors, a burst size, and a burst length. Let D^*_{SG} denote the set of all finite sequences over D_{SG}. Then:

$$c_{\text{dma}} \in C_{\text{DMA}} \triangleq D^*_{\text{SG}} \times B_{\text{size}} \times \mathbb{N}.$$

Accordingly, a single DMA channel's complete state s_{dma} belongs to the set S_{DMA}, pairing the channel activity state with its configuration:

$$s_{\text{dma}} \in S_{\text{DMA}} \triangleq T_{\text{DMA}} \times C_{\text{DMA}}.$$

Finally, the entire DMA controller state D_{state} is a finite sequence of elements of S_{DMA}, formally $D_{\text{state}} \in S^*_{\text{DMA}}$.

Physical channel count (N_{dma}) The controller has a fixed number of physical DMA channels, denoted by $N_{\text{dma}} \in \mathbb{N}$.

DMA register address space (R_{dma}) Each physical DMA channel *ch* owns a dedicated register region, denoted R_{ch}. The controller's overall DMA register address space R_{dma} is defined as the union of these per-channel regions:

$$R_{\text{dma}} \triangleq \bigcup_{ch \in C} R_{ch},$$

where $\mathcal{C}$ is the set of all physical DMA channels (e.g., $\mathcal{C} = \{1, \ldots, N_{\text{dma}}\}$).

Interrupt Stream (I_{stream}) This field models asynchronous interrupt signals from external hardware as an infinite stream.

6.2 Software State

Software State refers to the kernel-maintained data structures used to manage system resources and control flow. In the following, we provide some details concerning the most important fields:

Process List (P_s) The core kernel structure that tracks all created processes.

Kernel Stack (S_k) The kernel stack used to save context upon interrupts or exceptions. It is a finite sequence of tuples, each storing the pre-interrupt *kernel_mode* flag and program counter *pc*, with type $S_k \in (\mathbb{B} \times \mathbb{N})^*$.

Free-Memory Region List (F_s) The kernel memory manager's structure for tracking unallocated physical memory blocks.

Code Segment (C) The entire system's executable code (kernel and all user programs) is modeled as a single instruction sequence.

Interrupt Vector Table (*Vtbl*) A software-configured structure mapping interrupt numbers to the entry addresses of their service routines.

6.3 Dynamic Evolution of System State

Building on the static model, we give an operational semantics for an event-driven state-transition system that uniformly accounts for instruction execution, traps, faults, and interrupts.

System Events. We abstract the trigger of each atomic transition as an `event`:

$\texttt{Ev\_Exec}(i : \texttt{instr}) \mid \texttt{Ev\_SysCall}(\mathit{svc\_num} : \texttt{nat}) \mid \texttt{Ev\_Fault}(f : \texttt{fault\_kind})$
$\mid \texttt{Ev\_IRQ}(\mathit{irq\_num} : \texttt{nat}) \mid \texttt{Ev\_DMA\_DONE}.$

Single-Step Transition Relation (`step`). Intuitively, `step` s ev s' reads: If the system is in state s and receives event ev, it transitions atomically to a new state s'. Note that the high-level semantic rules delegate concrete state updates to a set of predefined core operations. Representative rules include:

Execution of Nop: Executing `Nop` only increments the program counter.

$$\frac{s.\texttt{code}[s.\texttt{pc}] = \texttt{Nop}}{\texttt{step}\ s\ (\texttt{Ev\_Exec Nop})\ s'\ \text{ with }\ s' = s[\texttt{pc} \leftarrow s.\texttt{pc} + 1]}$$

Execution of Write: Executing `Write v a` invokes the core operation `write_physical(wpy)` to encapsulate MPU checks and the memory write.

$$\frac{s.\texttt{code}[s.\texttt{pc}] = \texttt{Write}\ v\ a \quad \texttt{wpy}\ (v\ a\ s) = (\texttt{res},\ s_{\text{intermediate}})}{\texttt{step}\ s\ (\texttt{Ev\_Exec}\ (\texttt{Write}\ v\ a))\ s'\ \text{ with }\ s' = s_{\text{intermediate}}[\texttt{pc} \leftarrow s.\texttt{pc} + 1]}$$

Handling a Hardware Interrupt: Upon `Ev_IRQ(irqnum)`, the system defers to the core operation `handle_interrupt` to save context and switch modes.

$$\frac{\texttt{handle\_interrupt}\ s\ \texttt{irqnum} = (\texttt{res},\ s_{\text{new}})}{\texttt{step}\ s\ (\texttt{Ev\_IRQ irqnum})\ s_{\text{new}}}$$

On an `Ev_IRQ(irqnum)`, the system pushes the current context to the Kernel Stack (S_k), thus forming Stacked Contexts; additional `Ev_IRQ(irqnum)` events remain admissible and drive further state transitions, which accurately models nested interrupts. Other events are handled analogously and are therefore omitted for brevity.

Multi-Step Transition Relation (`multi_step`). To model whole executions, we take the reflexive–transitive closure of `step` over event lists:

Base: $\texttt{multi\_step}\ s\ [\,]\ s.$ **Inductive:** $\dfrac{\texttt{step}\ s\ e\ s' \quad \texttt{multi\_step}\ s'\ es\ s_{\text{fin}}}{\texttt{multi\_step}\ s\ (e :: es)\ s_{\text{fin}}}.$

Together, `event`, `step`, and `multi_step` constitute a precise and unified semantics for the system state's dynamic evolution.

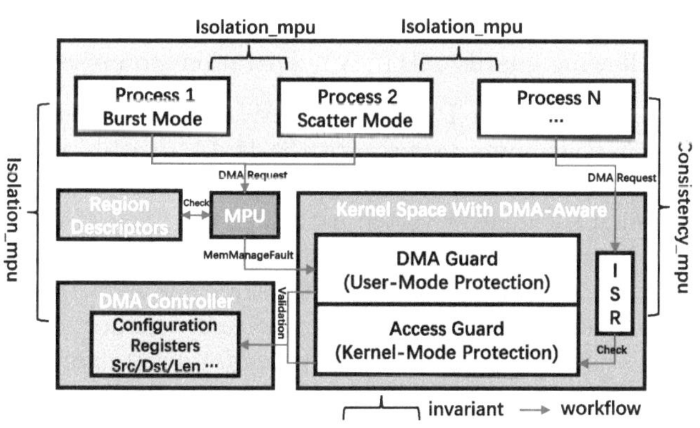

Fig. 3. Architecture and invariants for our approach.

7 Invariant Specification

To prove system security, we first formalize secure states via two invariants (as shown in Fig. 3): the memory-isolation invariant *isolation_mpu*, which protects processes' memory from adversarial access, and the system-consistency invariant *consistent_mpu*, which enforces well-formed and mutually consistent internal structures. Finally, they constitute the system security invariant *system_invariant*.

7.1 Memory-Isolation Invariant

Memory isolation ensures that distinct execution entities (e.g., processes) and critical hardware peripherals (e.g., the DMA controller) have disjoint memory spaces, thereby preventing unauthorized cross-access. In our model, this property is formalized as the predicate *isolation_mpu*.

Definition 1 (Memory-Isolation Invariant). *For a given system state s, we say $isolation\_mpu(s)$ holds iff both of the following conditions are satisfied:*

Inter-Process Isolation. *For any two distinct processes p_1 and p_2 in the process list P_s of state s, the sets of enabled MPU regions in their respective configurations are spatially disjoint. Formally, let M_p be process p's MPU configuration and $R(M_p)$ the set of enabled memory regions. Write $A \perp B$ when the address ranges covered by region sets A and B are disjoint. Then*

$$\forall p_1, p_2 \in P_s,\ p_1 \neq p_2 \Rightarrow R(M_{\mathrm{p}_1}) \perp R(M_{\mathrm{p}_2}).$$

Process–DMA Isolation. *For any process $p \in P_s$, the enabled regions in its MPU configuration must not overlap the MMIO space of the DMA controller. Then*

$$\forall p \in P_s \Rightarrow R(M_p) \perp R_{\mathrm{dma}}.$$

The static isolation invariant defines the secure memory layout; at runtime, we enforce the following guards within core operations to preserve it.

DMA Guard (User Mode Protection). When the CPU is in user mode, any instruction that attempts to write to the DMA register address ranges is deemed illegal; the attempt is immediately blocked and raises a *MemManage Fault*. Only through the guard's vetted path (i.e., the *MemManageFault* handler) can DMA transfers proceed, ensuring that source/destination addresses conform to the current process's MPU permissions and that transfers preserve isolation. Formally, let K_s be a Boolean indicating whether state s is in kernel mode (so $\neg K_s$ denotes user mode), let $W(addr)$ denote an attempted write to address $addr$, and let $\mathfrak{F}_{\mathrm{mem}}$ denote a *MemManageFault*. The DMA Guard applies uniformly across all channels. Then, for any state s and address $addr$,

$$(\neg K_s \wedge addr \in R_{\mathrm{dma}} \wedge W(addr)) \Rightarrow \mathfrak{F}_{\mathrm{mem}}.$$

Access Guard (Kernel Mode Protection). On a hardware interrupt, the processor switches to kernel mode to run the ISR, which introduces the risk that an ISR serving a user process might be tricked into launching a malicious DMA transfer. To preserve the isolation invariant—including for complex DMA modes such as scatter–gather and burst—the Access Guard requires that, before the kernel writes DMA registers to start a transfer, it invoke a validation predicate that checks every parameter of the transfer. Formally, let $\kappa(p, C_{\text{dma}})$ denote the kernel action of configuring DMA (with configuration C_{dma}) on behalf of process p, and let $\mathcal{V}(p, C_{\text{dma}})$ assert that this configuration is valid. We write $\vdash \alpha$ to denote that action α is permitted. Let $\text{Desc}(C_{\text{dma}})$ be the descriptor list, write $d \models M_p$ for descriptor d complies with process p's MPU policy M_p, and let $\mathcal{A}(d, B)$ asserts proper alignment under burst size B. Then it is defined by

$$\mathcal{V}(p, C_{\text{dma}}) \Leftrightarrow \forall d \in \text{Desc}(C_{\text{dma}}).\big((d \models M_p) \wedge \mathcal{A}(d, B(C_{\text{dma}}))\big).$$

and permission to configure DMA in kernel mode is governed by

$$K_s \Rightarrow \big(\vdash \kappa(p, C_{\text{dma}}) \;\Leftrightarrow\; \mathcal{V}(p, C_{\text{dma}})\big).$$

Note that by parameterizing both the validation predicate $\mathcal{V}$ and the set of DMA channels, our guard-based isolation enforcement is readily extensible.

7.2 System-Consistency Invariant

The invariant *consistent_mpu* ensures consistency between software data structures and hardware state, as well as internal coherence among software structures. This invariant underwrites reliable enforcement of isolation.

Definition 2 (System-Consistency Invariant). *For a given state s, we say consistent_mpu(s) holds iff all of the following groups of conditions hold:*

FreeRegionsValid: *For any free block r in the free-region list F_s, its geometry must be valid and it must not overlap the DMA register region. Let $|r|$ be the size of r, $\mathcal{B}(r)$ assert that r lies within legal physical-memory bounds, and let* II *denote overlap between two regions. Formally:*

$$\forall r \in F_s \Rightarrow |r| > 0 \wedge \mathcal{B}(r) \wedge \neg(r \,\text{II}\, R_{\text{dma}}).$$

UsedRegionsValid: *For any region r in any process p's MPU configuration, its geometry must be valid. Formally:*

$$\forall p \in P_s,\ \forall r \in R(M_p) \Rightarrow |r| > 0 \wedge \mathcal{B}(r).$$

FreeRegionsNoOverlap: *Any two distinct free blocks do not overlap. Formally:*

$$\forall r_1, r_2 \in F_s,\ r_1 \neq r_2 \Rightarrow \neg(r_1 \,\text{II}\, r_2).$$

FreeRegionsDisjointFromUsed: *Any free block is disjoint from every allocated process region. Formally:*

$$\forall r_f \in F_s,\ \forall p \in P_s,\ \forall r_u \in R(M_p) \Rightarrow \neg(r_f \amalg r_u).$$

ProcessMPUConfigValid: *Within any single process's MPU configuration, any two distinct regions do not overlap. Formally:*

$$\forall p \in P_s,\ \forall r_1, r_2 \in R(M_p),\ r_1 \neq r_2 \Rightarrow \neg(r_1 \amalg r_2).$$

CurrentMustBeInProcessList: *In any valid state, the recorded current process must be a member of the system's process list. Let* S_{valid} *be the set of valid system states and* $p_c(s)$ *the current process of state* s*. Formally:*

$$\forall s \in S_{valid} \Rightarrow p_c(s) \in P_s.$$

MPULoadedMatches: *The configuration currently loaded in the hardware MPU must exactly equal the configuration for the currently running process. Let* $M_{p_c(s)}$ *denote the MPU configuration in the currently running process. Formally:*

$$\forall s \in S_{valid} \Rightarrow M_{\text{cfg}}(s) = M_{p_c(s)}.$$

DMAChannelsLengthValid: *In any valid state, the software-maintained list of DMA channels must have length equal to the known number of physical channels. Formally:*

$$\forall s \in S_{valid} \Rightarrow |D_{\text{state}}| = N_{\text{dma}}.$$

8 Proof of the System Security Invariant

In this section we abbreviate the `system_invariant` as $\mathcal{I}$. Our central objective is to prove the **Main Security Theorem**: starting from a verified secure initial state, after any event-driven sequence of state transitions, every reachable state of the system satisfies the invariant $\mathcal{I}$ we defined.

8.1 Proof Strategy

Our proof proceeds by classical induction in two phases. In the **Base Case**, it is shown that the formal initial state already satisfies the invariant I. This state strictly adheres to the constraints: a single initial process is present, so isolation holds trivially; the free-memory list is empty, so the related consistency constraints are likewise trivially met. After each obligation is constructed and discharged, a theorem is obtained that the system starts from a well-formed state. For the **Inductive Step**, any single-step transition is proved to preserve I, i.e., $\forall s, ev, s'.\ step(s, ev, s') \wedge I(s) \Rightarrow I(s')$. The argument proceeds by case analysis over all *step* rules; for each event class (e.g., Ev_Exec, Ev_IRQ), we show that if s satisfies I, then s' does as well. When complex updates are involved—such as memory writes or DMA initiation—preservation is justified by correctness Hoare triples pre-established for low-level primitives (e.g., write_physical). Collecting these results and applying the induction principle yields the **Main Security Theorem**: $\forall s_0, s_{\text{final}}, tr.\ system\_init(s_0) \wedge multi\_step(s_0, tr, s_{\text{final}}) \Rightarrow I(s_{\text{final}})$.

8.2 Proving Compound Operations

Many core operations are not atomic but are implemented as sequences of primitives. To prove their preservation properties, we introduce an intermediate property R.

Challenge (How to determine the property R). Consider `write_physical` (abbrev. as `w_p`), whose success path is a sequential composition of a permission check `check_mpu_access` (abbrev. as `c_m`) followed by a state update `update_memory` (abbrev. as `u_m`). By the sequencing rule of Hoare logic, the postcondition of `c_m` must entail the precondition of `u_m`. However, showing that `c_m` merely preserves $\mathcal{I}$ is insufficient: the write `u_m` requires additional preconditions regarding the legality of the current access itself, which are more specific and stricter than $\mathcal{I}$. The core challenge is therefore to identify a suitable R and to prove the respective Hoare triple lemmas for `c_m` and `u_m` concerning this property.

Solution (Deriving R Backwards from the Write). We proceed backwards from the security requirement that `u_m` must preserve $\mathcal{I}$. To ensure that `u_m` does not violate the system state, it must be justified that the attempted write has been sufficiently authorized. This leads to the intermediate assertion R: it states that the MPU check has succeeded and that the target physical address lies within a legal memory boundary. With this, we decompose the overall proof into two lemmas:

Lemma 1 (Check preserves $\mathcal{I}$ and establishes R).

$$\{\mathcal{I}\}\ \texttt{c\_m}\ \{\lambda\texttt{res}, s'.\ \mathcal{I}(s') \wedge R(\texttt{res}, s')\}.$$

Rationale: `c_m` is read-only, hence $\mathcal{I}$ is preserved; R follows by case analysis on its result.

Lemma 2 (Update preserves $\mathcal{I}$ under R).

$$\{\lambda s.\ \mathcal{I}(s)\ \wedge\ R(\texttt{inl}(\texttt{tt}), s)\}\ \texttt{u\_m}\ \{\lambda\_, s'.\ \mathcal{I}(s')\}.$$

Rationale: address legitimacy is provided by R; `u_m` changes only the *contents* of *s.data*, not its structure, and therefore does not affect $\mathcal{I}$.

By composing lemmas, we prove that `w_p` preserves $\mathcal{I}$. Note that the same pattern applies to other core operations.

9 Evaluation

In this section, we conduct a comprehensive experimental evaluation of the formally verified security model. The evaluation is designed to answer the following Research Questions (RQs):

RQ1: What is the feasibility and portability of the approach?
RQ2: Can the approach stay robust and secure under high-concurrency DMA?
RQ3: What is the performance overhead of the security guarantees?

9.1 Experimental Setup

Our hardware platforms include an ST Nucleo-H743ZI (ARM Cortex-M7) running Zephyr RTOS, and a TI EK-TM4C1294XL LaunchPad (ARM Cortex-M4F) running RT-Thread and FreeRTOS. Software versions are Zephyr v3.2.0, RT-Thread v5.0.0, and FreeRTOS v10.5.1. The **Baseline** for comparison is each RTOS's native MPU and DMA drivers; **Ours** augments these with security checks synthesized from the formal verification approach. All performance metrics are collected with on-board high-precision timers, reported in microseconds (μs) or CPU cycles, with all nonessential services and debug logs disabled.

9.2 Formal Verification Effort and Portability Assessment

To address **RQ1**, we first model and prove the logic in Coq. The logic is then implemented as a portable C library and instantiated on Zephyr, RT-Thread, and FreeRTOS. Engineering effort is quantified in lines of code (LoC) (Table 1).

Table 1. Formal Verification and C Implementation Effort.

(a) Formal-Verification Effort

Cat.	Comp.	Coq LoC
F. Verif.	Spec.	2,550
	Proof	2,850

(b) C Implementation and Porting Effort

Module	Zephyr	RT-Thread	FreeRTOS
Sec. Lib.	180	180	180
Adapt.	135	160	120
Total	315	340	300
M&D (ref.)	∼2,100	∼1,850	∼1,500

The overall verification comprises 5,400 lines (2,550 specification and 2,850 proofs), indicating that a tractable level of effort sufficed for meaningful formal assurance. By decoupling the security-checked core logic from RTOS calls, the core library is just 180 LoC, the adaptation layer adds 120–160 LoC per RTOS, and total new code is 300–340 LoC—far below native MPU/DMA drivers (∼1,500–2,100 LoC), thereby enabling low-cost portability and minimizing the increase to the trusted computing base (TCB).

Table 2. Robustness and security under high-concurrency test

RTOS	Mode	Ops (K)	Ovhd.	Errs	p99 Lat. (μs)	Jitter (μs)	Atk. Succ.	Bypass %
Zephyr	Baseline	∼18.5	–	71	180.6	55.1	142	23.7%
	Ours	∼17.9	3.2%	0	189.2	32.7	0	0%
RT-Thread	Baseline	∼9.2	–	33	390.4	110.8	96	16.0%
	Ours	∼8.9	3.8%	0	401.5	65.3	0	0%
FreeRTOS	Baseline	∼9.5	–	53	375.8	102.4	117	19.5%
	Ours	∼9.1	4.2%	0	388.1	58.9	0	0%

9.3 Evaluation of Robustness and Security

To address **RQ2**, we apply a high-concurrency DMA workload and adversarial traffic within the same 10-second window to quantify and compare the stability and attack resistance of Baseline versus Ours. Our methodology emulates 10 benign tasks continuously issuing highly concurrent DMA requests during the 10-second window, while 3 malicious tasks concurrently inject 600 carefully crafted attacks. These attacks cover three representative threats: (A1) user mode direct MMIO writes, attempting to illicitly control DMA registers; (A2) a kernel mode confused deputy, where the ISR submits cross-process malicious requests; and (A3) reprogramming the DMA controller via an arbitrary-write vulnerability to exfiltrate high-privilege memory.

As shown in Table 2, the Baseline exhibits security fragility across all platforms, with an average attack bypass rate of 19.7%. By contrast, under 20 repeated trials, our approach achieves an attack success rate of 0%. All attacks are blocked by our two-layer guard mechanism: approximately 58% of user mode attacks (A1) are intercepted in hardware by the DMA Guard, while the remaining kernel mode attacks (A2/A3) are rejected by the Access Guard via exhaustive checks against formally specified invariants. Moreover, results show an average throughput overhead of only 3.7%, while p99 latency jitter is reduced by ≈42%, indicating that the guard logic increases execution-path determinism and thereby enhances real-time stability. In summary, our design delivers strong security without sacrificing system robustness.

Beyond qualitative analysis of related work, we introduce Comprehensive Security Feature Coverage (CSFC) to quantify the two most relevant systems—PISTIS and D-Box—across six key features F1–F6 (see Table 3). We define

$$\mathrm{CSFC} = \left(\frac{\sum_i S_i}{N_{\text{applicable}}} \right) \times 100\%,$$

where $S_i \in \{0, 1\}$ indicates whether feature i is supported and $N_{\text{applicable}}$ is the number of features applicable under a given architecture.

To assess F3, we construct and reproduce a cross-mode splicing attack: a user mode process submits an SG list whose legitimate and out-of-bounds segments are interleaved; after the system switches to kernel mode, the gather operation is executed. D-Box lacks strong validation of SG descriptor provenance and bounds, allowing out-of-bounds segments to be spliced and executed with privileges, resulting in address-space reads/writes. In PISTIS, descriptor reuse and inconsistent length/bounds checks similarly enable cross-mode splicing. The consolidated evaluation is shown in Table 3. Our approach covers F1–F6 with CSFC = 100% (6/6); D-Box supports F1, F2, F4, and F6 but lacks F3 and F5, yielding CSFC = 66.7% (4/6); PISTIS supports F5 and F6, lacks F1, F4, and F3, and F2 is not applicable ($N_{\text{applicable}} = 5$), yielding CSFC = 40% (2/5). In summary, CSFC provides a unified and compact metric that more comprehensively characterizes each method's coverage depth and applicability boundaries.

Table 3. Comprehensive Security Feature Coverage (CSFC) Analysis

ID	Comprehensive Security Feature	Ours	D-Box	PISTIS
F1	RTOS task-based isolation	✓	✓	×
F2	MPU hardware partition granularity	✓	✓	N/A
F3	Support for advanced DMA modes	✓	×	×
F4	Explicit DMA security policies	✓	✓	×
F5	Formal verification of core security invariants	✓	×	✓
F6	Compatibility with commercial hardware	✓	✓	✓
CSFC result		**6/6 (100%)**	**4/6 (66.7%)**	**2/5 (40%)**

9.4 Performance Evaluation

To address **RQ3**, we evaluate the approach's performance from three angles: (i) macro-level system performance, (ii) micro-level overhead on core RTOS functions, and (iii) behavior when interacting with advanced hardware features.

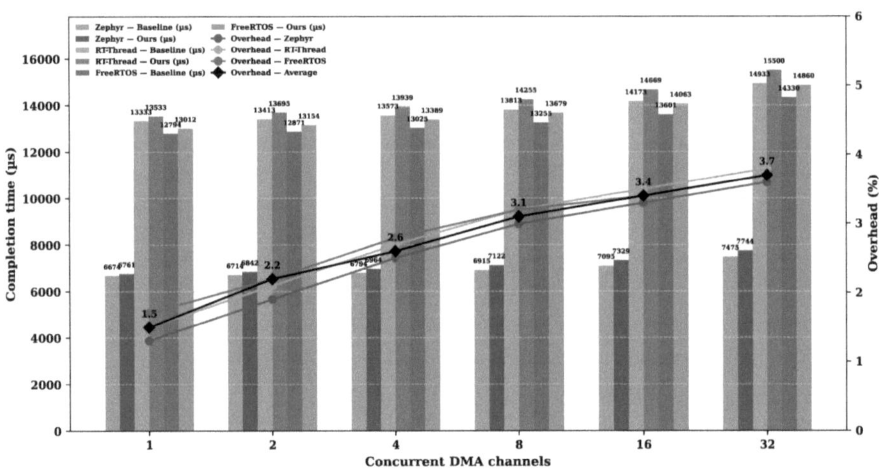

Fig. 4. Macro-benchmark of DMA transfers: to assess overhead and scalability.

Macro-Benchmark: DMA Transfer Performance. To assess the approach's impact in realistic scenarios, we design a macro-benchmark centered on DMA data transfer—the core system functionality. We measure performance in both single-channel and multi-channel settings. In the single-channel test, we record the time to transfer a contiguous 1 MB block. In the multi-channel tests, we concurrently launch 2, 4, 8, 16, and 32 DMA channels and measure total completion time to evaluate scalability under varying concurrency.

As shown in Fig. 4, the approach exhibits very high efficiency. In the single-channel case, the average overhead is only 1.5%, arising mainly from highly optimized pre-launch checks of MPU permissions and alignment for the source/destination addresses and length. Under multi-channel concurrency, overhead grows slowly with the number of channels–from +2.2% (2 channels) to +3.7% (32 channels), indicating excellent scalability: even under heavy concurrency, the impact converges to a very small steady-state value. This suggests the dominant bottlenecks at high concurrency are hardware factors (DMA controller limits, bus arbitration), rather than our security checks.

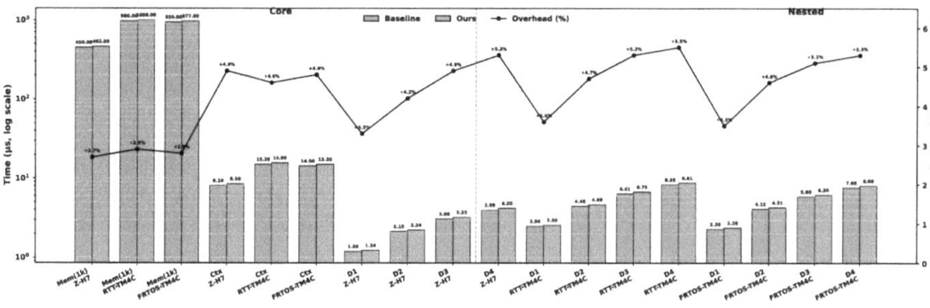

Fig. 5. Performance overhead on RTOS core functions.

Micro-Benchmark: Core Function Overhead. Beyond macro DMA performance, we conducted microbenchmarks to precisely quantify the fine-grained overhead introduced by the security approach on core OS primitives that are most fundamental and frequently invoked. These tests isolate and measure the impact on specific low-level operations. We selected three representative operations: dynamic memory allocation/free, thread/process context switching, and nested interrupt latency at varying depths.

The results in Fig. 5 indicate that our approach introduces only minimal and well-controlled overhead on RTOS core functionality. For memory management, in a 1,000-iteration allocation/free loop we observe an average overhead of ~2.8%, attributable to additional consistency checks required to maintain the *consistent_mpu* invariant. For context switching, the average increase is 4.8%, as each switch mandates strict validation and reloading of the incoming process's MPU configuration—an essential step to enforce process isolation. Finally, we measured latency from a single interrupt ($D = 1$) to four-level nesting. The data show a predictable, approximately linear, and modest growth in overhead with depth: from an average of +3.5% at $D = 1$ to only +5.4% at $D = 4$.

Application Scenario and Feature Evaluation. We now evaluate behavior when leveraging advanced DMA features.

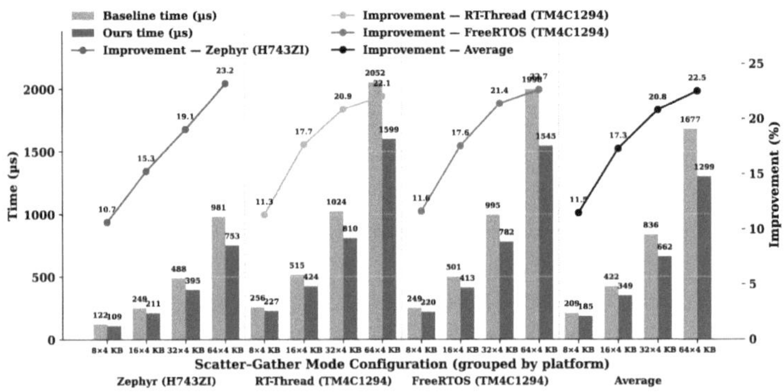

Fig. 6. Scatter–gather mode: comparison for noncontiguous transfers.

Benefit Evaluation: Scatter–Gather Mode We measure transfer performance for 8, 16, 32, and 64 noncontiguous 4 KB blocks. Since native APIs typically do not directly support secure SG configuration, we emulate Baseline by launching one DMA transfer per block (e.g., 32 blocks → 32 launches). In contrast, our method issues a single DMA request that carries a descriptor list for all blocks, which is validated once by our approach before launch.

As shown in Fig. 6, the approach delivers consistent gains across all scenarios. Average improvement grows with problem size—from 11.2% (8 blocks) to 22.7% (64 blocks). This is because Baseline requires repeated CPU interventions (start DMA, wait for interrupt, restart), incurring cumulative software overhead. Our approach pays a one-time validation cost, then leverages the hardware SG path to avoid repeated software overhead, yielding net performance benefits.

Compatibility Evaluation: Burst Mode. In this work we compare the throughput for a 1 MB transfer under different burst sizes. As shown in Fig. 7, across all burst sizes, our approach remains close to Baseline, with an average overhead under 5% that does not grow meaningfully with burst size. This indicates the security checks—especially alignment verification—are orthogonal to burst-mode benefits and do not erode its performance advantages.

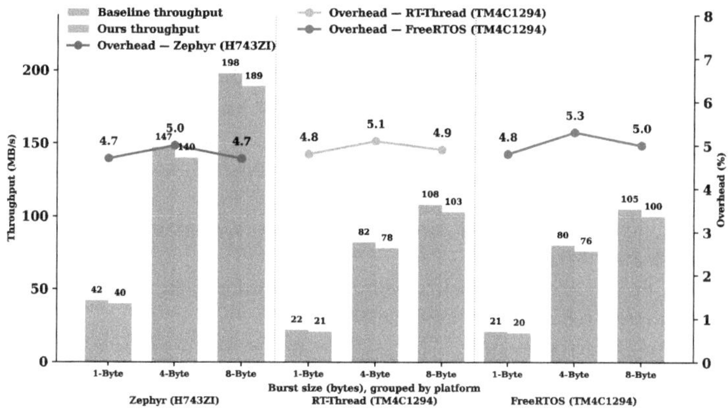

Fig. 7. Burst mode: throughput across burst sizes.

10 Conclusion and Future Work

This paper addresses the severe security threat that DMA can bypass memory protection in MPU-based embedded systems and presents the first formally verified, DMA-enabled memory isolation solution. We construct an accurate and comprehensive hardware–software state model that, for the first time, unifies the dynamic behavior of CPU execution, MPU enforcement, and a multi-channel DMA controller supporting advanced features such as scatter–gather, thereby eliminating any trusted assumptions about DMA. Building on this model, we design a lightweight two-layer defense mechanism and rigorously prove—using WP calculus and mathematical induction—that it preserves core security invariants across all legal system state transitions. Evaluation on real hardware running mainstream real-time operating systems, including Zephyr, RT-Thread, and FreeRTOS, shows that our approach fully defends against a range of sophisticated DMA attacks with an average throughput overhead of only 3.7%, while significantly improving system real-time stability. Looking ahead, we will explore developing automated tooling to generate verifiable C code directly from formal models in proof assistants such as Coq.

Acknowledgements. This work was supported by the Key Research Project of the Chinese Academy of Sciences (No. RCJJ-145-24-17), the Beijing Natural Science Foundation (Grant No. L234033), and the National Natural Science Foundation of China (Grant No. 92467201).

References

1. Clements, A.A., et al.: Protecting bare-metal embedded systems with privilege overlays. In: 2017 IEEE Symposium on Security and Privacy (SP), pp. 289–303. IEEE (2017)
2. Cortex-m3. https://developer.arm.com/Processors/Cortex-M3. Arm Developer. Accessed 24 June 2025
3. Cortex-m4. https://developer.arm.com/Processors/Cortex-M4. Arm Developer. Accessed 24 June 2025
4. Kim, C.H., et al.: Securing real-time microcontroller systems through customized memory view switching. In: NDSS (2018)
5. Freertos-mpu–freertos-security. https://www.freertos.org/zh-cn-cmn-s/Security/04-FreeRTOS-MPU-memory-protection-unit. FreeRTOS.org
6. RT-thread. https://www.rt-thread.io/. Accessed 24 June 2025
7. MPU sample code – zephyr project documentation. https://docs.zephyrproject.org/latest/samples/arch/mpu/. Zephyr Project
8. Ecker, W., Esen, V., Findenig, R., Steininger, T., Velten, M.: Model reduction techniques for the formal verification of hardware dependent software. In: 2010 IEEE International High Level Design Validation and Test Workshop (HLDVT), pp. 148–153. IEEE (2010)
9. Mera, A., Chen, Y.H., Sun, R., Kirda, E., Lu, L.: D-Box: DMA-enabled compartmentalization for embedded applications, arXiv preprint arXiv:2201.05199 (2022)
10. Grisafi, M., Ammar, M., Roveri, M., Crispo, B.: {PISTIS}: trusted computing architecture for low-end embedded systems. In: 31st USENIX Security Symposium (USENIX Security 2022), pp. 3843–3860 (2022)
11. Klein, G., et al.: SEL4: formal verification of an OS kernel. In: Proceedings of the ACM SIGOPS 22nd Symposium on Operating Systems Principles, pp. 207–220 (2009)
12. Klein, G., et al.: Comprehensive formal verification of an OS microkernel. ACM Trans. Comput. Syst. (TOCS) **32**(1), 1–70 (2014)
13. Gu, L., Vaynberg, A., Ford, B., Shao, Z., Costanzo, D.: Certikos: a certified kernel for secure cloud computing. In: Proceedings of the Second Asia-Pacific Workshop on Systems, pp. 1–5 (2011)
14. Gu, R., et al.: {CertiKOS}: an extensible architecture for building certified concurrent {OS} kernels. In: 12th USENIX Symposium on Operating Systems Design and Implementation (OSDI 2016), pp. 653–669 (2016)
15. Qian, Z., Jin, Y., Sun, G., Xing, X., Xia, K.: Formal design and verification of system task in intelligent transportation systems based on micro-kernel architecture. J. Ambient Intell. Humaniz. Comput. 1–10 (2021)
16. Dejon, N., Gaber, C., Grimaud, G.: Pip-MPU: formal verification of an MPU-based separation kernel for constrained devices. Int. J. Embed. Syst. Appl. **13**(02), 1–21 (2023)
17. Lescuyer, S.: ProvenCore: towards a verified isolation micro-kernel. In: MILS@HiPEAC (2015)
18. Mai, H., Pek, E., Xue, H., King, S.T., Madhusudan, P.: Verifying security invariants in expressos. In: Proceedings of the Eighteenth International Conference on Architectural Support for Programming Languages and Operating Systems, pp. 293–304 (2013)
19. Chen, H., Wu, X., Shao, Z., Lockerman, J., Gu, R.: Toward compositional verification of interruptible OS kernels and device drivers. In: Proceedings of the 37th

ACM SIGPLAN Conference on Programming Language Design and Implementation, pp. 431–447 (2016)
20. Guo, Y., Zhang, H.: Verifying pre-emptive kernel code with preemption control support. In: 2014 Theoretical Aspects of Software Engineering Conference, pp. 26–33. IEEE (2014)
21. Yu, M., Gligor, V., Jia, L.: An I/O separation model for formal verification of kernel implementations. In: 2021 IEEE Symposium on Security and Privacy (SP), pp. 572–589. IEEE (2021)
22. Yang, J., Hawblitzel, C.: Secure to the last instruction: automated verification of a type-secure operating system. In: Proceedings of the 31st ACM SIGPLAN Conference on Programming Language Design and Implementation, pp. 99–110 (2010)
23. Khurshid, A., Yalew, S.D., Aslam, M., Raza, S.: Shield: shielding cross-zone communication within limited-resourced IoT devices running vulnerable software stack. IEEE Trans. Dependable Secure Comput. **20**(2), 1031–1047 (2022)
24. Ma, C., Xi, N., Lu, D., Feng, Y., Ma, J.: CToMP: a cycle-task-oriented memory protection scheme for unmanned systems. SCIENCE CHINA Inf. Sci. **67**(6), 162305 (2024)
25. Khan, A., Kim, H., Lee, B., Xu, D., Bianchi, A., Tian, D.J.: {M2MON}: building an {MMIO-based} security reference monitor for unmanned vehicles. In: 30th USENIX Security Symposium (USENIX Security 2021), pp. 285–302 (2021)
26. Zhou, X., Li, J., Zhang, W., Zhou, Y., Shen, W., Ren, K.: OPEC: operation-based security isolation for bare-metal embedded systems. In: Proceedings of the Seventeenth European Conference on Computer Systems, pp. 317–333 (2022)
27. Clements, A.A., Almakhdhub, N.S., Bagchi, S., Payer, M.: {ACES}: automatic compartments for embedded systems. In: 27th USENIX Security Symposium (USENIX Security 2018), pp. 65–82 (2018)
28. Zhou, X., Bu, Y., Xu, M., Zhou, Y., Wu, L.: UBOX: a lightweight and hardware-assisted sandbox for multicore embedded systems. IEEE Trans. Dependable Secure Comput. (2024)
29. Haglund, J., Guanciale, R.: Trustworthy isolation of DMA devices. J. Bank. Financ. Technol. **4**(1), 75–94 (2020)
30. Li, S.-W., Li, X., Gu, R., Nieh, J., Hui, J.Z.: Formally verified memory protection for a commodity multiprocessor hypervisor. In: 30th USENIX Security Symposium (USENIX Security 2021), pp. 3953–3970 (2021)
31. Haglund, J., Guanciale, R.: Formally verified isolation of DMA. In: 22nd Conference on Formal Methods in Computer-Aided Design–FMCAD 2022, Trento, Italy, 17–21 October 2022 (2022)
32. Arm Limited, Armv8-M Architecture Reference Manual, ARM DDI 0553A.e (2017). https://static.docs.arm.com/ddi0553/a/DDI0553A_e_armv8m_arm.pdf. Accessed 07 Sept 2025
33. Atmel Corporation, AVR32 Architecture Document, Doc. 32000D (2011). https://www.mouser.com/ds/2/268/doc32000-1066014.pdf
34. Ravi, S., Raghunathan, A., Chakradhar, S.: Tamper resistance mechanisms for secure embedded systems. In: Proceedings of the 17th International Conference on VLSI Design, pp. 605–611. IEEE (2004)

RideStyle: Riding Style Representation from Head-Body Dynamics via Adversarial Learning

Zengyi Han[1(✉)], Yuuki Nishiyama[2], and Kaoru Sezaki[2]

[1] College of Computer Science and Technology, Jilin University, Changchun, China
hzy@ieee.org

[2] Center for Spatial Information Science, The University of Tokyo, Bunkyo City, Japan
nishiyama@csis.u-tokyo.ac.jp, sezaki@iis.u-tokyo.ac.jp

Abstract. The riding style of riders plays a vital role in micro-mobility safety. Learning representations of a rider's riding style from their dynamic behavior can not only help assess the safety level of micro-mobility operations but also provide valuable support to insurance companies. However, existing approaches often rely solely on vehicle dynamics or GPS data, which fail to accurately reflect the rider's behavior. We argue that both the rider's head and body dynamics—captured through wearable IMU sensors—are essential to understanding their riding style. To this end, we introduce RideStyle, a riding style representation learning framework that leverages head-body dynamics as its core input. RideStyle employs adversarial learning to extract robust and discriminative representations that capture diverse riding styles. Extensive evaluations on real-world traffic data from 19 participants demonstrate the effectiveness of RideStyle in modeling riding behavior.

Keywords: Mobile Computing · Intelligent Vehicles · Riding Style Representation

1 Introduction

Micro-mobility, represented by e-bikes and e-scooters, offers great advantages, including convenience, affordability, and sustainability. As the new mode of transportation, micro-mobility is perfect for short trips, reducing traffic congestion and lowering carbon emissions. Nevertheless, micro-mobility has also brought up societal issues, with traffic accidents being the most significant among them. According to the statistical data of the World Health Organization in 2023 [17], micro-mobility accounts for about 30% of all fatal traffic accidents. Research

Supported by the Fundamental Research Funds for the Central Universities (3132025240). Supported by Dalian Major Project for Key Technologies (2024JB11GX001), China.

L. Zhang and K.-K. R. Choo (Eds.): MobiQuitous 2025, LNICST 683, pp. 278–290, 2026.
https://doi.org/10.1007/978-3-032-22500-9_16

by the Centers for Disease Control and Prevention also points out that the annual medical expenses and productivity losses caused by micro-mobility-related accidents are more than $23 billion [5]. Therefore, improving micro-mobility safety is an important task that needs to be urgently addressed.

Identifying the riding style of riders accurately can significantly reduce traffic accidents [10]. Riding style refers to the habitual riding behavior of the rider, which is typically reflected in aspects such as speed control and acceleration patterns of micro-mobility. Thereby, the rider's riding style can serve as an indicator of the safety level of the micro-mobility operation. By recognizing the rider's riding style and providing feedback, it can help riders avoid unsafe driving behaviors, reduce traffic accidents, and improve overall traffic conditions. In addition, riding style representation also provides valuable support to insurance companies [6].

Most previous studies on riding (or driving) representation learning have been based solely on micro-mobility (or vehicle) body dynamics or GPS data [7,13,19,20]. Existing methods for characterizing riding style representations can only reflect the rider's operational behavior, lacking information about the rider's observations or reactions to the external environment, which is insufficient to comprehensively describe the rider (or driver).

We argue that riding style is not only about the steering habit of the rider, but also the reactions of riders to external driving contexts. Rider's head dynamic not only reflects the eye glance behavior of rider but also reflects how alert the rider is to the surrounding traffic environment [8,9]. Specifically, riding style reflects a rider's fine-grained behavioral habits of riding, safety checks, and temporal combinations of two. To this end, we use the data from helmet-mounted IMU to describe riders' reactions to the external environment. At the same time, we mounted the smartphone on the micro-mobility's handle, with the help of embedded IMU in the smartphone to capture the rider's steering dynamic.

In this paper, we introduce RideStyle, a representation learning approach that uses adversarial techniques to extract comprehensive features from both a rider's head dynamics and the steering behavior. To capture the representation of riding styles, we train a semi-supervised generative adversarial network (SGAN) using the extracted features. The learning model integrates three key components: a generator, a discriminator, and a classifier. Together, these components classify riders based on input data while also producing synthetic samples that closely resemble the training set. This helps the model learn the underlying patterns and characteristics of riding styles. The main contributions of this paper are summarized as follows:

- To the best of our knowledge, we first incorporate head dynamics into micro-mobility riding, which improves upon existing work by taking into account the rider's reaction to external riding conditions.
- We introduce RideStyle, an adversarial learning approach designed to capture riding style representations by leveraging dynamic data from both micro-mobility and the rider's head. Built on SGAN, our model effectively extracts and learns representations from the data.

- We conduct evaluation with two benchmark applications, **Rider Identification** and **Rider Number Estimation**. Experimental results demonstrate that RideStyle outperforms baseline algorithms in rider identification task. Furthermore, results show that combining steering dynamic and head dynamic can better describe riding style.

The remainder of this paper is structured as follows: In Sect. 2, we review the related work. Section 3 describe the design and technical details of *RideStyle*. Section 4 presents the evaluation process and results. Section 5 discusses the limitations of current work and the potential applications. Finally, Sect. 6 concludes the paper.

2 Related Work

Currently, vehicle as the absolute main part in the traffic, most of the research work on driving style is concentrated on the vehicle [3,16,18,22]. Various studies have attempted to characterize driver behavior in order to identify or create driver profiles, and classified according to the data used, it is mainly divided into two categories: GPS-based data and multi-sensor data-based [4].

Using GPS data as the data source is one of the mainstream in "style representation" studies. Wang et al. proposed representation learning framework for driving behavior analysis with GPS trajectory data [19]. Chen et al. proposed semi-Traj2Graph [3], a multi-task learning framework using GPS data from automobile to recognize the fine-grained driving style. Similarly, Liu et al. explored using GPS data with corresponding driving traffic condition to compute driving style representation [14,15]. However, the sampling rate of GPS data is usually relatively low (0.1 Hz), and as we discussed in the Section I, using vehicle dynamic solely cannot fully describe the driving style, since it does not contains any information of surrounding conditions. Besides, it could have potential privacy threat since above works require continuous GPS recording.

Describing the "style representation" using the data collected by various sensors that can be carried by vehicles is another mainstream approach [12,23]. For example, Fugiglando et al. propose the concept of "Driving DNA", taking a driver's individual driving behavior as a global resultant of single easy-to-measure characteristics (genes) that describe driving attitudes [7]. Specifically, they calculated driver dna using Controller Area Network (CAN) data. Similarly, Abdelrahman et al. proposed a framework for driver behavior profiling using data from On-Board Diagnostics system (OBD) [2]. Wang et al. proposed use OBD data for driving style classification [20]. They define driving style into discrete classes, including aggressive, mild and moderate styles. Zhang et al. proposed a hierarchical latent model to characterize driving style using CAN information, including speed, acceleration, steering angle, etc. [21]. Liang et al. constructing the driving style representation with the driving simulator data [11]. However, the CAN and OBD data can be difficult to get. Even it could be adopted in the micro-mobility area, the wide deployment of such systems is costly and cumbersome to maintain.

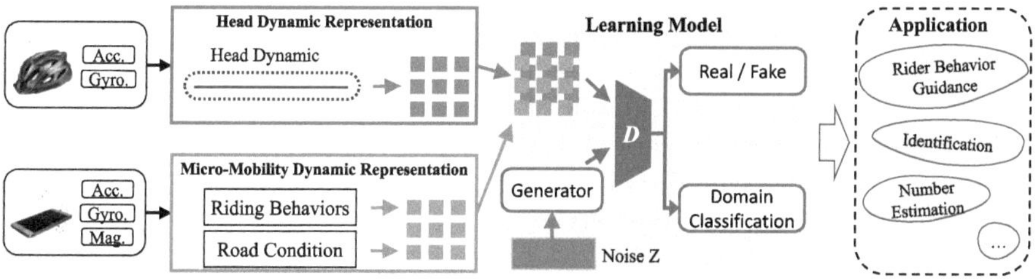

Fig. 1. The architecture of our approach, RideStyle, takes input data from bicycle handle-mounted and helmet-mounted IMU. RideStyle comprises of three key modules to compute riding style representations: micro-mobility dynamic representation, head dynamic representation, and a learning model. The output of this architecture is a set of riding style representations that can be used in various intelligent applications such as providing guidance on rider behavior and estimating the number of riders.

3 System Design and Implementation

3.1 Overview

Figure 1 illustrates the architecture of our approach RideStyle, which consists of two parts: *data segmentation* and *learning model*. RideStyle utilizes data from IMU sensors as the input, and segmentation process to truncate the data for the subsequent extraction of features that reflect an individual's personal habits during the riding process. The learning model, which is a central component of RideStyle, then processes this data to compute riding style representations. These representations can be used to support various intelligent applications such as identifying specific riders and estimating the number of riders present.

Specifically, we utilizes a sliding window to segment the continuous IMU data, which stands for micro-mobility dynamic representation and rider head dynamic representation respectively. The micro-mobility dynamic representation and rider head dynamic representation are combined to serve as input for the learning model. Specifically, we utilize a novel semi-supervised generative adversarial network (GAN) architecture to achieve this integration. GANs have proven to be effective at generating high-quality data samples and can be trained using both labeled and unlabeled data. By leveraging the power of GANs, our learning model is able to generate riding style representations that are both effective and accurate.

To process a rider's riding data, the IMU data is segmented into fixed-length intervals of L, with each segment overlapping the previous one by $L/2$. This overlap minimizes information loss between consecutive segments. Through experimental evaluation, we found that $L = 1500$ (30 s) is appropriate.

3.2 Learning Model

We use a Generative Adversarial Network (GAN) to learn riding styles. GANs are composed of two neural networks that are trained to compete with one another. The discriminator is designed to differentiate real samples from fake ones, while the generator aims to create synthetic data capable of deceiving the discriminator. Through this process of competition, GANs can generate high-quality samples that resemble real user-generated data. This enables GANs to understand the underlying distribution of the data and identify the key features that differentiate different riding styles.

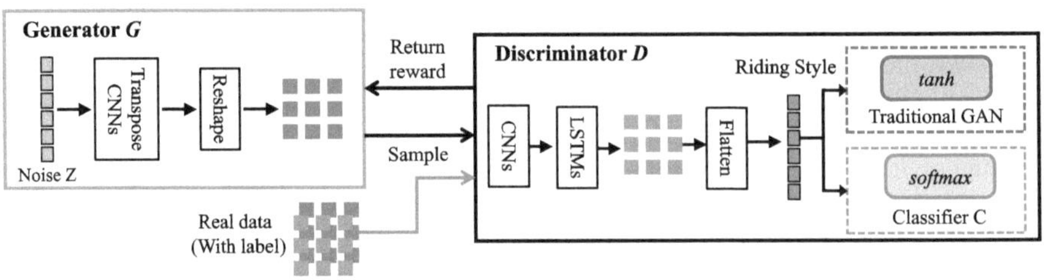

Fig. 2. The design of learning model, which consists of the generator G, the discriminator D, and the classifier C.

We have adopted a specific type of GAN architecture called semi-supervised GAN (SGAN) to construct our learning model. The model consist of two main components: a generator, G, and a discriminator, D, as depicted in the figure. In SGAN, the discriminator also acts as a classifier that assigns input samples to one of k pre-defined categories, including an additional "fake" class. The competitive interaction between the generator and discriminator, driven by rewards, enhances the quality of the resulting riding style representations. Consequently, our model not only classifies riders based on the learned riding styles but also generates synthetic riding style features that closely resemble the training samples of a specific class c.

Discriminator D (and classifier C). Discriminator D is trained in both unsupervised mode and supervised mode.

- *Unsupervised mode.* In this mode, the discriminator, D, is to discern whether a given sample is real or fake (generated by the generator, G). To accomplish this, it calculates a probability score indicating the likelihood that the sample is real. Our learning model adopts techniques similar to those used in traditional GANs, aiming to maximize the score for real samples while minimizing it for fake ones. This objective is accomplished by minimizing the discriminator's loss function, $L^{(D)}$, defined as follows.

$$L^{(D)} = -[\mathbb{E}_{x\sim p_r(x)} log D(x|\theta_d) + \mathbb{E}_{x\sim G} log(1 - D(x|\theta_d))]$$

  where $p_r(x)$ denotes the distribution of real samples from IMU data.
- *Supervised mode,* In this mode, the discriminator, D, serves as a classifier, C, to tackle a multi-class classification task. For each sample, the classifier, C,

uses its parameters to predict which of the $(k+1)$ pre-defined categories the sample belongs to. The generator, G, has the ability to produce riding style features with known labels, which allows the classifier, C, to also use the labels of fake samples during training. This can improve the model's generalization ability. In order to train the classifier, C, we strive to minimize the classifier loss, $L^{(C)}$, which is a measure of the cross-entropy loss on the true labeled samples and is calculated using the overall classifier score.

$$L^{(C)} = -\mathbb{E}_{p(x_c,c)}[logC(c|x_c, \theta_c)]$$

where x is a sample of class c, and C should correctly classify it as class c.

We have integrated the two modes discussed above into a unified framework, as illustrated in Fig. 2. The discriminator and classifier in this system share some of the layers for feature extraction but have distinct layers for output. After a series of convolutional operations, a feature tensor is produced and flattened, it then is fed into a dense layer to create a representation vector of the riding style. In a traditional GAN, this vector goes through a tanh function to determine whether it is a real or fake sample. In the case of the classifier, the vector is fed into a $softmax$ function to compute the probability of each class.

Convolutional neural network (CNN) is a type of neural network that has been widely used. It has two key features that make it well-suited for learning features from time series data, such as audio and speech: locality and weight sharing. In addition, three Long Short Term Memory (LSTM) layers are utilized to capture the temporal relevance of the CNN outputs.

Generator G. The generator, G, aims to identify a parameterized conditional distribution $G(z, c, \theta_g)$ that closely approximates the actual distribution of real samples, $p_r(x)$, and the k class labels from the real training data. The generated fake samples are dependent on network parameters θ_g, a noise vector z, and a class label c. These inputs are sampled from a prior distribution p_z and p_c, respectively.

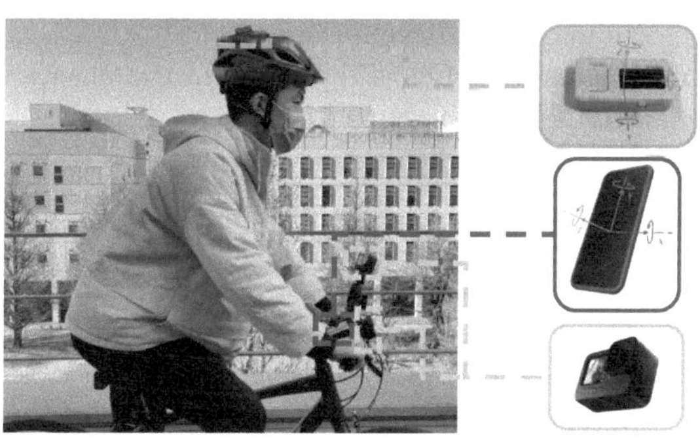

Fig. 3. Data collection equipments and setup.

As shown in Fig. 2, generator is implemented with 1D-transposed CNN layers, which transform noise vector into fake riding style features. We train G by minimizing loss $L^{(G)}$ expressed as:

$$L^{(G)} = \|\mathbb{E}_{x \sim p_r(x)} f(x, \theta_f) - \mathbb{E}_{z \sim p_z} f(G(z, c, \theta_g), \theta_f)\|_2^2$$

where $f()$ denotes activation on an intermediate layer of discriminator D, θ_f is the parameter subset of θ_d corresponding to the intermediate layer of discriminator D, and c is the class label of real sample x. The aim of the generator's training is to reduce the difference between the real and generated data distributions in the feature space.

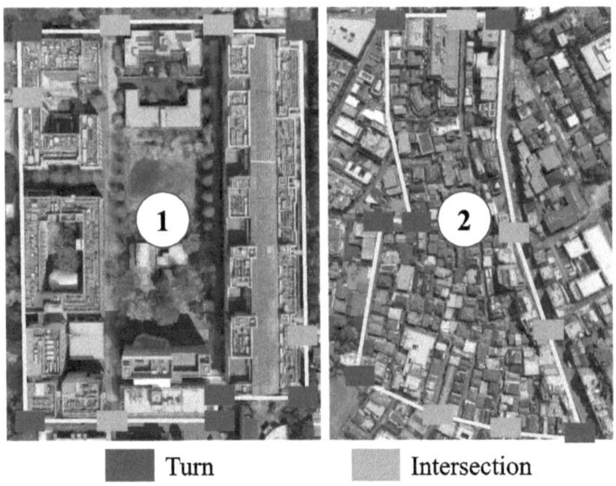

Fig. 4. Route 1, inside the campus. Route 2, outside the campus.

4 Evaluation

In this section, we conduct extensive experiments to evaluate the effectiveness of RideStyle on learning accurate riding style representations with two applications: **Rider Identification** and **Rider Number Estimation**.

4.1 Data Collection and Experiment Setup

The experimental setup for data collection is illustrated in Fig. 3. An M5StickC module (upper right in Fig. 3), a compact IoT development platform [1] equipped with a 6-axis IMU (accelerometer + gyroscope) and Bluetooth capabilities, was affixed to the rider's helmet to capture the head dynamic of the riders. A smartphone (Pixel 3a) mounted on the bicycle's handlebar record steering dynamics, with its embedded IMU detecting handlebar movements in real time. During data collection, M5StickC keeps transmitting the head dynamic data to the smartphone through Bluetooth, and the smartphone saves the data along with the self-generated IMU data. We collected the data both with a 50 Hz sampling rate. The data collection process was recorded using a GoPro camera for later analysis.

Our data was gathered from 19 volunteers, consisting of 10 males and 9 females. The data collection was designed to cover a diverse range of cycling scenarios while ensuring participant safety. To achieve this, we selected two routes: Route 1, a route within the university campus, and Route 2, a real traffic route, as depicted in Fig. 4. Our study has been approved by the Institutional Review Board (IRB).

Baseline Algorithms. To show the superior performance of our proposed method, we compare it against the following baseline algorithms: AutoEncoder (AE), CNN-GRU, Support Vector Machine (SVM), Random Forest (RF), K-Nearest Neighbor (KNN). Same to our proposed RideStyle. After obtaining the feature representations, CNN-GRU adopt the *Softmax* as the classifier for the riding style representation.

4.2 Rider Identification

The rider identification problem involves determining the rider of a given unlabeled data sample, which is a supervised multi-class classification task. We randomly select 80% of the data for training and 20% for testing. The models of all approaches are trained with labeled data, and for the testing set, the models should predict its rider identifier.

Figure 5 shows the complete confusion matrix for 19 riders' identification. As we can see, the result is rather great: the average precision we get is 92.32%, which means our model can precisely differentiate riders by their riding style extracted from their steering and head dynamic data.

Next, we examined the classification performance with baseline algorithms, and the result shows in Fig. 6. Here H+S notes that using head dynamic and steering dynamic at the same time, and S stands for using steering dynamic only. As we can see, our RideStyle has the best result here. With 80% training data, it can reach more than 85% accuracy for 19 participants' classification. Since CNN-GRU has a very similar structure to CNN-LSTM, this shows using GAN can greatly improve the performance of learning the underneath pattern, such as riding style. In the case of only using steering data, RideStyle still holds the best result among all the methods, which is 65% with 80% training data. However, it is not as great as the two data sources, which indicate that steering and head movement data together can describe a better riding style.

We further examined the performance of RideStyle with different sampling rate, and result shows in Fig. 7. We can see that high sampling rate have better classification accuracy, it is easy to understand since it can describe rider's movement more fine-grained. If we want reach 80% accuracy, we can not have sampling rate lower than 50 Hz.

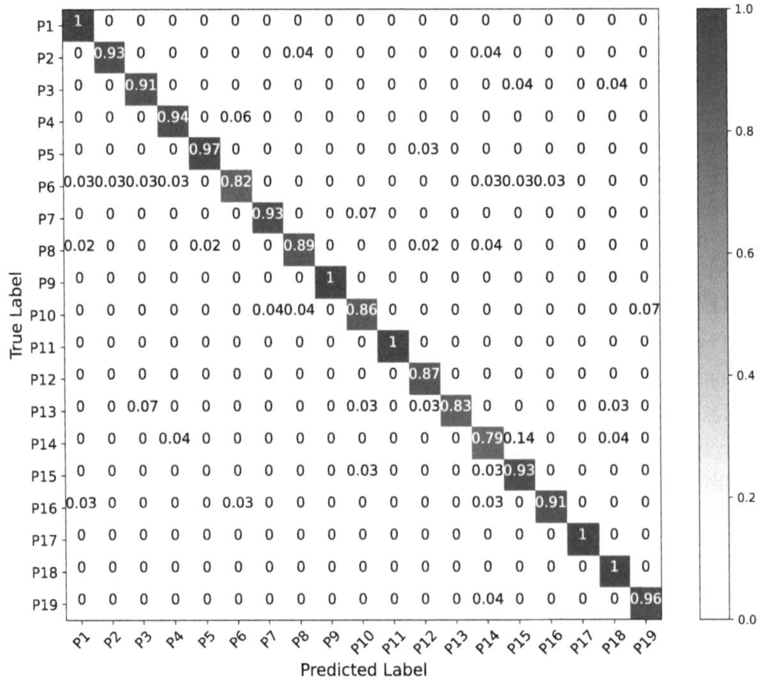

Fig. 5. Confusion matrix for rider identification.

4.3 Rider Number Estimation

To accomplish this task, we firstly train our riding style representation learning models using a set of labeled data. We then use the trained models to convert each testing data point into a riding style representation vector. After that, we apply the affinity propagation clustering algorithm to group all the representation vectors into clusters. An ideal model should be able to accurately learn the riding styles of different riders and classify the testing data generated by a specific driver into the same cluster. Finally, the number of riders is estimated by counting the total number of clusters.

To evaluate our model, we randomly select a group of 10 riders and use their data as the training set. For the testing data, we randomly select K riders from the remaining riders (who are not included in the training set) to form a group, denoted by Group K. We vary the value of K from 1 to 10. For each group, we randomly select 50 rows of data from the K riders and use this data as the testing set. We repeat this process 10 times for each value of K, and report the average results.

We evaluate different approaches using the adjusted mutual information (AMI) score, which assesses clustering quality. The AMI values range from 0 to 1, with higher values indicating better performance. Additionally, we include

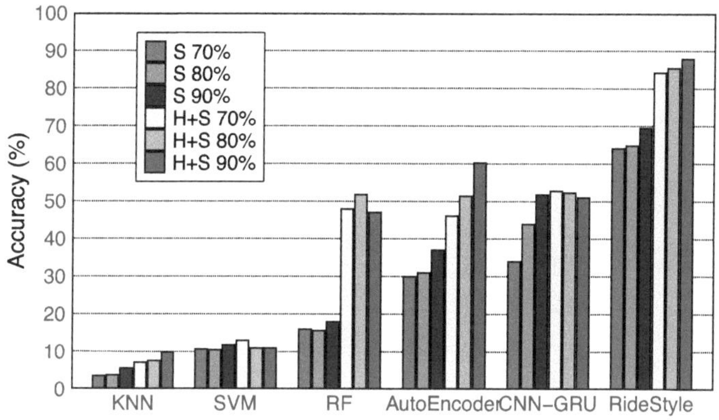

Fig. 6. Performance comparisons with baseline algorithms.

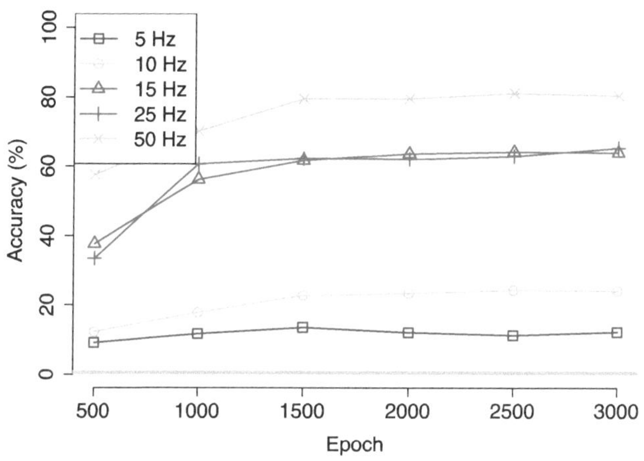

Fig. 7. Performance of RideStyle with different sampling rate.

a steering data-only group for comparison, consisting of *RS-s*, *AE-s*, and *CNN-GRU-s*.

Table 1 shows the AMI results. We see that RideStyle (RS) provides the biggest AMI among all methods. For all methods, the AMI values using both steering and head movement data are higher than them using only steering data. This once again seals what we mentioned, the data with head movement can better describe the individual riding style. In summary, better clustering quality, as reflected by higher AMI scores, correlates with greater accuracy in rider number estimation. As presented in Table 1, RideStyle successfully generates more discriminative riding style representations, thereby achieving better estimation outcomes, as evidenced by the larger AMI.

Table 1. Performance comparison on AMI for rider number estimation.

Group k	RS	AE	CNN-GRU	RS-s	AE-s	CNN-GRU-s
2	0.395	0.066	0.243	0.414	0.099	0.258
3	0.489	0.092	0.266	0.273	0.078	0.266
4	0.585	0.116	0.287	0.384	0.079	0.243
5	0.530	0.031	0.270	0.427	0.049	0.236
6	0.511	0.033	0.256	0.433	0.037	0.248
7	0.422	0.013	0.234	0.327	0.056	0.219
8	0.477	0.010	0.261	0.342	0.051	0.205
9	0.472	0.060	0.218	0.427	0.079	0.206
Average	**0.485**	0.066	0.254	**0.380**	0.053	0.235

5 Discussion

In this section, we will discuss the limitations and point out the potential applications of this study.

5.1 Limitations

1) **Limited Context:** There are many other context of micro-mobility riding that can provide insight of a rider's style, such as how closely they are paying attention to surroundings. For example, the distance a rider keeps from other objects while riding can reflect their level of caution and awareness of their surroundings. By studying these contexts, we can gain a deeper understanding of a rider's riding style and potentially identify areas for improvement to enhance safety on the road.
2) **Dataset:** Currently, the dataset used in our evaluation, which includes 19 participants, is relatively small. To ensure that RideStyle can indeed learn meaningful representations of riding styles, we plan to validate our approach on larger-scale datasets involving more riders (e.g., over a thousand) in the future.

5.2 Potential Applications

In addition to improve the traffic safety, learning riders' riding style representations from their riding data can also benefit many intelligent safety applications, e.g., riding assessment and assistance, etc. Furthermore, riding style profiling has a strong relevance in different application contexts, for example, it could be used in Usage-Based Insurance (UBI) or Pay-As-You-Ride (PAYD) schemes, to adapt the insurance premium to individual rider behavior. Another important application for rider identification is found in anti-theft systems.

6 Conclusion

We present an adversarial riding style representation learning approach RideStyle. Unlike previous works that primarily rely on GPS or vehicle-level dynamics, RideStyle leverages head-body dynamics captured by helmet-mounted and handlebar-mounted IMUs to achieve a more comprehensive and fine-grained description of riding style, while preserving rider privacy. By modeling both the rider's bodily movements and their responses to external traffic stimuli, RideStyle effectively captures the nuanced behavioral patterns of micro-mobility users. To ensure robust representation learning, we incorporate adversarial training, which enhances the model's ability to distinguish between different riding styles. Experiments on real-world datasets collected from 19 participants demonstrate that our spatio-temporal representation learning framework significantly improves the profiling of micro-mobility riders, highlighting the value of combining multimodal dynamic signals with adversarial techniques for safe and personalized riding analysis.

References

1. M5stickc (2019). https://shop.m5stack.com/products/stick-c?variant=17203451265114
2. Abdelrahman, A.E., Hassanein, H.S., Abu-Ali, N.: Robust data-driven framework for driver behavior profiling using supervised machine learning. IEEE Trans. Intell. Transp. Syst. (2020)
3. Chen, C., Liu, Q., Wang, X., Liao, C., Zhang, D.: semi-traj2graph: identifying fine-grained driving style with GPS trajectory data via multi-task learning. IEEE Trans. Big Data (2021)
4. Chu, H., et al.: A review of driving style recognition methods from short-term and long-term perspectives. IEEE Trans. Intell. Veh. **8**(11), 4599–4612 (2023). https://doi.org/10.1109/TIV.2023.3279425
5. Centers for Disease Control and Prevention et al.: Web-based injury statistics query and reporting system (WISQARS) (2022). www.cdc.gov/injury/wisqars/
6. Feraud, I.S., Naranjo, J.E.: A systematic methodology to evaluate prediction models for driving style classification. Sensors **20**(6), 1692 (2020). https://doi.org/10.3390/S20061692
7. Fugiglando, U., Santi, P., Milardo, S., Abida, K., Ratti, C.: Characterizing the "driver DNA" through can bus data analysis. In: Proceedings of the 2nd ACM International Workshop on Smart, Autonomous, and Connected Vehicular Systems and Services, pp. 37–41 (2017)
8. Han, Z., et al.: Rideguard: micro-mobility steering maneuver prediction with smartphones. In: 2024 IEEE 44th International Conference on Distributed Computing Systems (ICDCS), pp. 1039–1049 (2024). https://doi.org/10.1109/ICDCS60910.2024.00100
9. Han, Z., Xu, L., Dong, X., Nishiyama, Y., Sezaki, K.: Headmon: head dynamics enabled riding maneuver prediction. In: 2023 IEEE International Conference on Pervasive Computing and Communications (PerCom), pp. 22–31 (2023). https://doi.org/10.1109/PERCOM56429.2023.10099215

10. Jin, H., Li, H.: Alarm strategy for frontal crash warning system based on driving style. Automot. Eng. **43**(3), 405–413 (2021)
11. Liang, K., Zhao, Z., Li, W., Zhou, J., Yan, D.: Comprehensive identification of driving style based on vehicle's driving cycle recognition. IEEE Trans. Veh. Technol. **72**(1), 312–326 (2023). https://doi.org/10.1109/TVT.2022.3206951
12. Liu, S., et al.: The empathetic car: exploring emotion inference via driver behaviour and traffic context. Proc. ACM Interact. Mob. Wearable Ubiquit. Technol. **5**(3), 1–34 (2021)
13. Liu, W., et al.: Spatio-temporal pyramid-based multi-scale data completion in sparse crowdsensing. IEEE Trans. Mob. Comput. 1–16 (2025)
14. Liu, Z., Zheng, J., Gong, Z., Zhang, H., Wu, K.: Exploiting multi-source data for adversarial driving style representation learning. In: International Conference on Database Systems for Advanced Applications, pp. 491–508. Springer, Cham (2021)
15. Liu, Z., Zheng, J., Lin, J., Wang, L., Wu, K.: Radar: adversarial driving style representation learning with data augmentation. IEEE Trans. Mob. Comput. (2022)
16. Martinez, C.M., Heucke, M., Wang, F.Y., Gao, B., Cao, D.: Driving style recognition for intelligent vehicle control and advanced driver assistance: a survey. IEEE Trans. Intell. Transp. Syst. **19**(3), 666–676 (2017)
17. World Health Organization: Global Status Report on Road Safety 2023: Summary. World Health Organization (2024)
18. Wang, E., Xu, Y., Yang, Y., Jiang, Y., Yang, F., Wu, J.: Zone-enhanced spatio-temporal representation learning for urban POI recommendation. IEEE Trans. Knowl. Data Eng. **35**(9), 9628–9641 (2023). https://doi.org/10.1109/TKDE.2023.3243239
19. Wang, P., Fu, Y., Zhang, J., Wang, P., Zheng, Y., Aggarwal, C.: You are how you drive: peer and temporal-aware representation learning for driving behavior analysis. In: Proceedings of the 24th ACM SIGKDD International Conference on Knowledge Discovery & Data Mining, pp. 2457–2466 (2018)
20. Wang, W., Xi, J., Chong, A., Li, L.: Driving style classification using a semisupervised support vector machine. IEEE Trans. Hum.-Mach. Syst. **47**(5), 650–660 (2017)
21. Zhang, C., Wang, W., Chen, Z., Zhang, J., Sun, L., Xi, J.: Shareable driving style learning and analysis with a hierarchical latent model. IEEE Trans. Intell. Transp. Syst. **25**(9), 11471–11484 (2024). https://doi.org/10.1109/TITS.2024.3374771
22. Zhang, C., Wang, W., Ju, Z., Chen, Z., Venture, G., Xi, J.: An embedded driving style recognition approach: leveraging knowledge in learning. IEEE Trans. Intell. Veh. 1–14 (2024). https://doi.org/10.1109/TIV.2024.3363146
23. Zhang, C., Patel, M., Buthpitiya, S., Lyons, K., Harrison, B., Abowd, G.D.: Driver classification based on driving behaviors. In: Proceedings of the 21st International Conference on Intelligent User Interfaces, pp. 80–84 (2016)

Wave-to-Mute: In-Cabin Single Gesture Mute Control via Acoustic Sensing

Mengyao Fan[1,2(✉)], Yuqi Su[1,2], Fusang Zhang[1,2], and Beihong Jin[1,2]

[1] Institute of Software, Chinese Academy of Sciences, Beijing, China
[2] University of Chinese Academy of Sciences, Beijing, China
fmy_hnsmx@163.com

Abstract. With the development of smart cabin interaction technology, contactless gesture recognition has become an important supplement to in-cabin human-computer interaction. Addressing the inherent constraints of conventional vision-based and radar-based approaches, particularly regarding privacy concerns, implementation costs, and coverage limitations, we introduce a novel gesture-based mute control system. The proposed solution repurposes existing audio hardware components by utilizing standard speakers and microphone arrays to establish a cost-effective near-field recognition system. The system transmits high-frequency acoustic signals and extracts the channel impulse response (CIR) changes caused by hand movements to recognize mute gestures. Specifically, in order to eliminate the system delay, we first create an electrical loopback channel to extract the reference signal, which can be used to dynamically calculate the system delay for accurate CIR time alignment. Second, we develop a single-channel multidimensional feature judgment method, which is integrated with a multichannel collaborative decision-making mechanism. This approach is designed to accurately distinguish the defined gestures from various interferences, such as the movements of passengers. The experiments demonstrate that mute gesture recognition accuracy exceeds 98%, with a false alarm rate below 1.5% and system response under 0.05 s.

Keywords: In-cabin acoustic sensing · Gesture mute control · Contactless gesture recognition

1 Introduction

With the rapid advancement of smart cabin technology, the field of human-machine interaction is encountering new challenges and demands. These demands encompass ensuring driving safety, enhancing operational convenience, and increasing response speed. Traditional interaction solutions, which rely on mechanical buttons or touchscreens, necessitate drivers to engage in "eye-hand

Supported by Beijing Nova Program; National Natural Science Foundation of China (62422213, 62172394, 62072450); Beijing Natural Science Foundation (L223034).

L. Zhang and K.-K. R. Choo (Eds.): MobiQuitous 2025, LNICST 683, pp. 291–313, 2026.
https://doi.org/10.1007/978-3-032-22500-9_17

coordination" when issuing commands. This requirement poses a potential risk of distracting the driver and thereby jeopardizing driving safety. Moreover, these traditional solutions have limitations in terms of coverage. Some buttons and touchscreens are designed to support operations only in the front seats, leaving rear-seat passengers without control options and failing to meet the interaction needs of all passengers. Voice interaction involves complex, multi-stage processing, including speech recognition and semantic understanding, which demands significant computational resources and can result in response delays. These delays can compromise the fluency of interactions and degrade the overall user experience.

Contactless gesture interaction has emerged as a prominent solution in smart cabin human-machine interaction due to its unparalleled convenience and naturalness. Especially in high-frequency operation scenarios(*e.g.*, audio mute control [35]), contactless gesture interaction has demonstrated several significant advantages. It exhibits high stability in complex noise environments, demonstrates excellent adaptability to multi-user scenarios, responds rapidly to commands, and provides robust protection for driving safety. These advantages open up a new development path for the field of smart cabin human-machine interaction.

Currently, in-cabin gesture recognition solutions are mainly based on vision or radar, yet these approaches encounter several practical issues. Vision-based solutions employ cameras to capture images for gesture recognition. However, this approach not only poses risks of privacy invasion but is also highly susceptible to variations in lighting conditions. Additionally, the arrangement of car seats can obstruct the recognition range, creating blind spots. Radar-based solutions are susceptible to interference from multi-path reflections within the car, and the high hardware costs make it challenging to support full-coverage deployment. The advent of multi-modal fusion technology aims to integrate the strengths of various modalities to enhance interaction effectiveness. However, this approach faces challenges such as the difficulty of synchronizing different modalities and the high demand for computational resources. These challenges make it difficult to achieve rapid response from the system and restrict its widespread adoption in cars.

In this paper, we propose to exploit acoustic sensing for gesture interaction within the car cabin. We observe that an increasing number of cars are equipped with a large number of acoustic modules [36] (*i.e.*, speakers and microphones), which are mainly used for voice control [37] and in-car entertainment [38]. Leveraging these distributed multi-speakers and multi-microphones, we develop a gesture interaction system that supports full-coverage interaction, rapid response, and multi-user operation. This system enables natural and convenient interactions, such as the "wave to mute".

Though promising, we need to address several challenges in order to turn the idea into a fully functional system.

1) **System delay issues**. In in-cabin audio systems, the transmission of acoustic signals traverses several stages, including ADC/DAC signal conversion, audio

buffering, audio interfaces, and general operating system resource competition [39]. The random delay at each stage accumulates during signal transmission, resulting in a non-negligible system delay that is inherently uncertain. Moreover, this delay time varies randomly each time the system is initiated and cannot be measured or eliminated in advance. This system delay can induce ranging errors, which subsequently impact gesture distance alignment and feature extraction in the subsequent process.

System Delay Elimination Method Based on the Reference Signal. To address this issue, we propose a system delay elimination method based on the reference signal from the electrical loop channel[1] in the acoustic system. This method utilizes a single electrical loop channel in the acoustic system design to obtain a reference signal, thereby simulating a propagation path that only includes system delay. Specifically, by extracting the peak of the reference signal channel impulse response (CIR) as a time offset reference for system delay. Then, the Channel Impulse Response (CIR) of each microphone receiving channel is calibrated to account for time offsets. This calibration process accurately reconstructs the real propagation distance of the acoustic signal as it travels through the air. As a result, the spatial position of the gesture can be more readily determined, thereby facilitating more precise subsequent feature extraction.

2) **Complex environmental interference issues**. In real-world driving scenarios, the in-car environment is subject to multiple interfering factors. These include car vibration, passenger movement, unstable in-car audio power, and internal/external environment noise, which can severely interfere with the detection of weak gesture reflection signals.

Interference-Resistant Gesture Recognition Method. To improve the reliability of weak gesture signal recognition in environments with complex interferences, we develop an innovative gesture recognition method. This method integrates single-channel three-dimensional feature judgment with multi-channel collaborative decision-making, thereby enhancing the overall robustness and accuracy of gesture detection in challenging conditions.

First, the three-dimensional gesture feature judgment is conducted based on the Channel Impulse Response (CIR) of each individual microphone. It involves three key constraints: i) *Spatial Locality Constraint*: Focusing on near-field distances to ensure spatial precision. ii) *Energy Significance Constraint*: Detecting sudden changes in energy to identify significant gestures. iii) *Temporal Transience Constraint*: Matching short-term features to capture transient gestures accurately.

Second, leveraging the spatial partitioning of multi-microphone subarrays, we establish a multi-channel collaborative decision-making mechanism. Within

[1] In the PCB design of sound cards, the transmit signal is routed to the receiver via circuitry, which serves to provide a reference signal for audio monitoring or echo cancellation [27].

the same time-domain window, if multiple microphone channels in the target region meet the collaborative conditions, a system response can be triggered. By integrating multi-dimensional feature constraints with spatial array collaboration, this method effectively suppresses environmental interference and enhances recognition accuracy across different seating areas of the cabin.

By addressing the challenging issues, we develop a gesture mute control system on real cars. Through extensive real-car testing across various scenarios—such as those involving multiple passengers, high levels of noise, and bumpy road conditions—the system has demonstrated remarkable performance in complex environments. Specifically, it achieves an average recognition accuracy of over 98% and maintains an average false positive rate of less than 1.5%. Stable detection performance is achieved across all seating areas, with response times under 0.05 s. In summary, we have successfully implemented a real-time, full-coverage, and robust in-car gesture mute control system through acoustic sensing.

2 Related Work

2.1 Acoustic-Based Sensing

Acoustic-based sensing technology has demonstrated remarkable potential in fields such as ranging and gesture recognition by reusing built-in acoustic modules. In the application of high-precision ranging and positioning, research mainly focuses on temporal features. BeepBeep [19] and RFBeep [20] achieve centimeter-to-decimeter-level ranging accuracy through bidirectional sensing and kernel optimization, respectively. BatMapper [21] and SAMS [22] construct acoustic radar systems to complete indoor environment mapping. Guoguo [23] and ARABIS [24] achieve centimeter-level positioning via Time of Arrival/Time Difference of Arrival (ToA/TDoA).

In gesture recognition applications, research primarily relies on channel feature analysis. SoundWave [1] and AudioGest [2] recognize basic gestures by combining Doppler shift and multipath characteristics, and UltraGesture [5] introduces deep learning to improve the recognition accuracy of complex gestures to over 97% for solid medium sensing, UbiTap [25] and ForcePhone [26] use structural acoustic signals to achieve key positioning and pressure estimation, expanding interaction dimensions.

In biometric sensing and security, acoustic technology has also made breakthroughs. BreathJunior [28] and RespTracker [29] realize centimeter-level respiration monitoring, SpeakPrint [30] completes user authentication by combining voice and ultrasonic signals. The distributed acoustic sensing method proposed by Su et al. [31] achieves blind-spot-free child presence detection in the cabin through car-mounted speakers and microphone arrays, offering new ideas for complex spatial perception.

2.2 Contactless Gesture Recognition

Contactless gesture recognition technology is mainly realized through three approaches, namely acoustic, radio frequency (RF), and vision. Acoustic signal-based methods use built-in speakers and microphones of devices to recognize gestures by the characteristics of echo signals reflected by hands. SoundWave [1] and AudioGest [2] based on the Doppler effect of signals can recognize basic gestures such as swiping and clicking, but have insufficient resolution for complex finger movements. Strata [3], LLAP [4] based on channel impulse response (CIR) analysis of signals, and UltraGesture [5] introducing deep learning achieve trajectory tracking through amplitude or phase changes of CIR, improving gesture recognition accuracy, yet are limited by frequency-selective fading in complex environments. Active sonar-based solutions like FingerIO [6], despite possessing millimeter-level gesture positioning accuracy, only focus on fine fingertip motion tracking and have a detection range limited to 50×25 cm^2.

In addition, RF signal-based methods recognize gestures through devices such as WiFi, millimeter-wave radar, and Ultra-Wideband (UWB) radar. WiGest [7] and WiSee [8] achieve contactless detection using WiFi Received Signal Strength Indicator (RSSI) or Channel State Information (CSI), but due to the small bandwidth and low distance resolution of WiFi, they are susceptible to multipath interference. Radar device methods such as AllSee [9] and Rf-IDraw [10] support complex actions like air handwriting, but suffer from high hardware costs, making large-scale deployment difficult.

In contrast, vision-based methods realize gesture recognition by capturing image information through cameras. Depth camera devices such as Microsoft HoloLens [11] and Sony PlayStation VR [12] support high-precision 3D interaction, but are limited by lighting conditions and device costs methods based on ordinary cameras like DigitEyes [13] have lower costs, yet are affected by occlusion and changes in lighting conditions with insufficient robustness, and may trigger user concerns about privacy leakage, making them difficult to be widely used.

Therefore, this paper proposes an acoustic gesture interaction system based on in-cabin acoustic devices, realizing full-car coverage, rapid response, and multi-user operation without additional hardware costs.

3 System Overview

The gesture interaction system based on in-cabin acoustic devices proposed in this paper aims to build a low-cost, full-coverage near-field acoustic gesture sensing solution using distributed multi-speakers and multi-microphones already deployed in the car. The core target is to achieve real-time detection and reliable recognition of the "near-field single wave gesture" of passengers in different seats to meet the instant interaction needs of emergency mute scenarios.

3.1 Motivation and Gesture Design

The system focuses on high-frequency mute control scenarios in the in-cabin environment and defines the core interaction as a "single wave in the near field"—the user quickly waves within a specified distance (*e.g.*, 0.3 m) in front of the

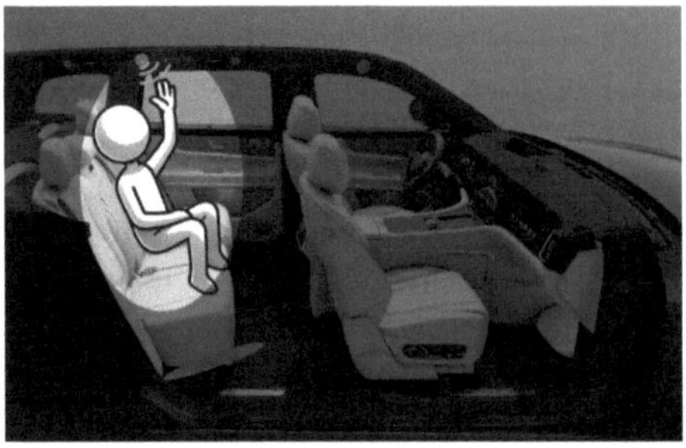

Fig. 1. Acoustic-based gesture interaction.

speaker. This gesture triggers the mute command through the change in acoustic signal reflection caused by the instantaneous movement of the hand (as shown in Fig. 1).

This gesture design has two key features. First, in signal detection, the short-term strong reflection appears as a high-energy local abrupt change in the channel impulse response (CIR), which can be easily identified by a sliding window and energy threshold. Second, in user operation, this gesture requires no precise alignment with devices or complex actions, enabling natural and simple operation that effectively adapts to passengers in different front and rear seat positions.

3.2 System Implementation

Figure 2 presents the overview of system implementation, which includes three key modules, namely signal modulation, preprocessing, and gesture recognition. We present the detailed implementation as follows.

Signal Modulation. The system first generates and modulates a high-frequency ZC-sequence signal with excellent autocorrelation characteristics. This signal is then transmitted by both the electrical loop channel and the speaker, providing input signals for the next module. The former directly provides the reference signal, while the latter sends the signal into the air, which is reflected by targets inside the car and received by the microphone array.

Preprocessing. The multi-channel microphone array receives the multi-path reflection signals and the lectrical loop channel captures the reference signal, then calculates the CIR of these signals. We first calculate the system delay based on the CIR of the reference signal, and then use this to perform time delay calibration on the CIR of the multi-microphone channels. This restores the true propagation distance of the acoustic signal in the air. This allows us to localize the gesture position precisely and lays the foundation for subsequent feature extraction.

Gesture Recognition. The gesture feature recognition module uses the CIR data calibrated by multiple channels as input to extract three-dimensional ges-

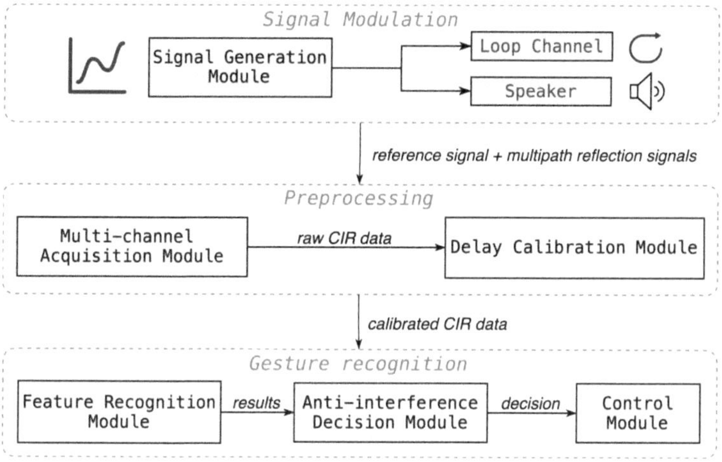

Fig. 2. System overview.

ture features that satisfy spatial locality, energy significance, and temporal transience. The feature recognition results from each channel are sent to the anti - interference decision module. This module employs a spatial array collaborative decision - making mechanism to filter single-channel noise and occasional disturbances through multiple channels. Thus, recognition reliability is enhanced in complex environments. The final decision result is used to trigger the mute command, forming a complete closed-loop process of "wave-sensing-control". The entire processing time is controlled within 0.05 s, meeting real-time requirements.

4 Detailed Modules Design and Implementation

This chapter focuses on detailed modules design and implementation. First, we discuss the modulation process of transmitted signals and the modeling process of received signals in an in-cabin environment. Then, we introduce the system delay elimination method based on reference signal. Next, we elaborate on the single-channel three-dimensional gesture feature judgment method using the CIR after delay elimination. Finally, we present the spatial collaborative decision-making mechanism based on multi-microphone channels.

4.1 Transmitted Signal Modulation and Received Signal Modeling

This section mainly introduces the design of ZC-sequence transmitted signals and the modeling of received signals in an in-cabin environment. First, we explain in detail the definition of the baseband ZC sequence and the key steps for modulating the baseband ZC sequence to the ultrasonic frequency band. Then, we introduce the process and model of signal propagation and reception in an in-cabin environment, as well as the impact of system delay on signal processing.

4.1.1 Definition and Characteristics of the ZC Sequence

To reduce the impact of multipath effects and construct a high-resolution range-time map, the transmitter uses the Zadoff-Chu(ZC) [32] sequence, which has strong autocorrelation, as the baseband signal. The signal can be represented as follows:

$$zc[n] = exp\left(-j\frac{\pi un(n+1+2q)}{N_{zc}}\right), \tag{1}$$

where u is the root parameter of the ZC sequence, determining the orthogonality and autocorrelation characteristics of the sequence. q is the phase offset, used to adjust the initial phase of the signal. $n = 0, 1, \ldots, N_{zc} - 1$, where N_{zc} is the length of the ZC sequence, determining the periodic length of the signal.

4.1.2 Modulation of Transmitted Signals

To avoid noise interference to humans during recognition, the baseband ZC signal must be modulated to the inaudible ultrasonic frequency band for transmission. The specific process is as follows.

Step 1. First, we perform a fast Fourier transform (FFT) on the ZC sequence to obtain its frequency domain representation. Then, we apply a Hamming window to suppress side lobes and reduce spectral leakage, resulting in the frequency domain baseband ZC signal.

Step 2. We shift the baseband ZC signal to the target carrier center frequency f_c, and then symmetrically shift its conjugate to $-f_c$. Finally, we convert back to the time domain via Inverse Fast Fourier Transform(IFFT) to complete the frequency spectrum shifting.

Step 3. We repeat and splice single-frame ZC signals multiple times to generate a periodic long signal of specified duration. After that, we filter the signal through an 18 kHz–20 kHz band-pass filter (matching the 19kHz center frequency) to suppress out-of-band noise and focus energy in the target ultrasonic frequency band, thus obtaining the transmitted signal.

The modulated transmitted signal exhibits concentrated energy in the ultrasonic frequency band and good side-lobe suppression, as shown in Fig. 3.

4.1.3 Modeling of Received Signals

The transmitted signal is sent by multiple speakers, propagates in the enclosed in-cabin space, and then is received by multiple microphones. The in-cabin space has a complex reflection environment, with dense static objects like seats, dashboards, and doors. Thus, the signal propagates to the microphone array along both direct and multiple reflection paths. Therefore, the received signal can be represented as the superposition of Line-of-Sight (LoS) signals, multi-path reflection signals, and background noise, as shown below:

$$y[n] = \sum_{i=1}^{P} A_i e^{-j\phi_i} \cdot zc_T[n - \tau_i f_s] + noise[n], \tag{2}$$

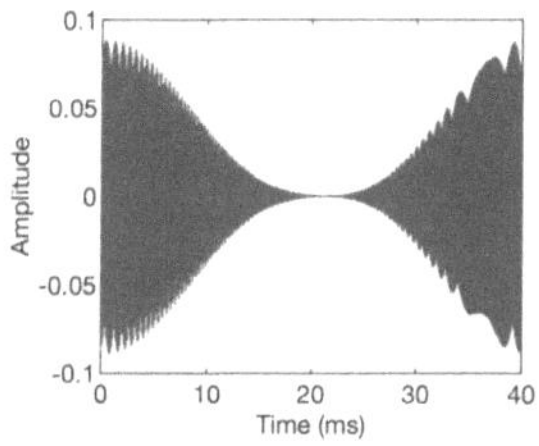

(a) Time-domain waveform of transmitted signal.

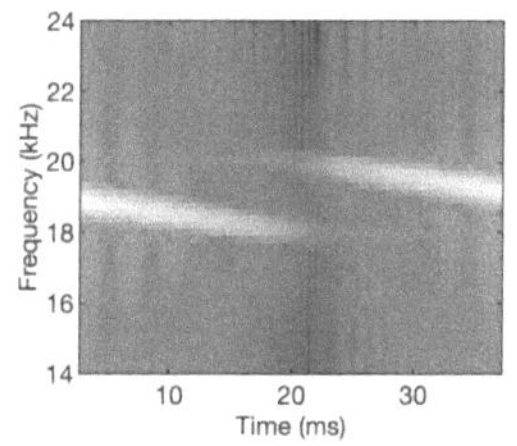

(b) Spectrum of transmitted Signal.

Fig. 3. Time-domain waveform and spectrum of transmitted signal.

where $zc_T[n]$ is the transmitted signal. $y[n]$ is the received signal. A_i is the amplitude attenuation of the i-th path, which is related to the propagation distance, the material of the reflective surface. $\phi_i = \frac{2\pi d_i}{\lambda}$ is the phase delay caused by propagation. τ_i is the total delay of the i-th path. f_s is the sampling rate noise[n] is the background noise. d_i is the path length of the i-th path. λ is the wavelength of the acoustic signal. c is the speed of sound in air.

In an in-cabin audio system, transmitting acoustic signals must pass through multiple stages, including ADC/DAC signal conversion, audio buffering, audio interfaces, and general operating system resource competition. The random delays in each stage accumulate in the propagation path, forming a system delay with uncertainty at startup (this delay cannot be determined by advance measurement). Therefore, the total delay τ_i for each path must comprehensively consider the physical delay of the propagation path and the uncertain system delay introduced by each stage of the audio system, and can be expressed as:

$$\tau_i = \frac{d_i}{c} + \tau_{\text{sys}}, \tag{3}$$

where $\frac{d_i}{c}$ represents the time taken for the acoustic signals to propagate through the air, and τ_{sys} represents the random system delay.

If system delay is not eliminated, the peak position of the channel impulse response (CIR) will shift. This shift causes distance ambiguity. It further makes it difficult to effectively distinguish between gesture features and other dynamic disturbances inside the car. For example, if the reflection path length is 0.5 m, the propagation time is approximately 1.46 ms. If the system delay $\tau_{\text{sys}} = 2.9$ ms is added, the equivalent misjudgment distance is approximately 1.5 m, which will severely affect the position estimation and feature extraction of the gesture.

4.2 System Delay Elimination Based on Reference Signal

4.2.1 Reference Signal Modeling

In order to obtain an accurate gesture position, we propose a method to eliminate the system delay by utilizing the reference signal of an electrical loopback

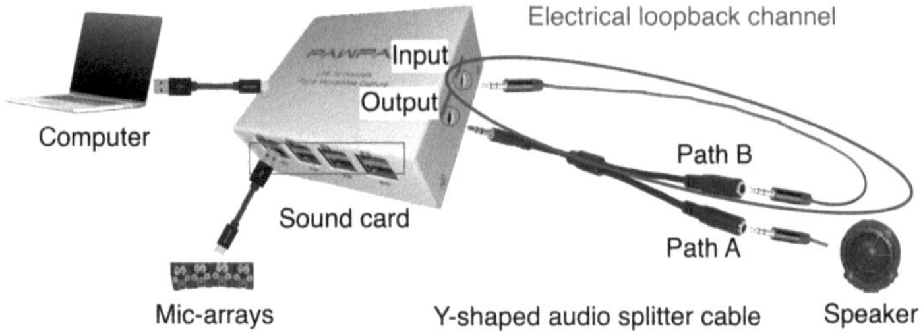

Fig. 4. Hardware connection method.

channel, which is constructed in the sound card [34]. Our hardware is connected as follows.

As shown in Fig. 4, the computer is connected to the sound card to drive the speakers for signal transmission and the microphone array for signal reception. The sound card has an output port and a input port on its right side. At the output port, we use a Y-shaped audio splitter cable to split the transmitted signal into two paths (*i.e.*, path A and path B). Path A connects to an amplifier to drive the speakers to transmit acoustic signal into the air. Path B (*i.e.*, electrical loopback channel) connects to a 3.5 mm audio cable, which returns the signal back into the input port.

This configuration establishes the electrical loopback channel, providing a reliable reference for subsequent system delay calibration and multipath signal analysis.

The reference signal contains key information about the system delay, and its expression is:

$$y_{\text{ref}}[n] = A \cdot zc_T[n - \tau_{\text{sys}} f_s], \tag{4}$$

where A denotes the amplitude attenuation during signal propagation and is approximated in the electrical loopback channel as 1. The reference signal y_{ref} can also be considered as a cyclic convolution $h_{\text{sys}}[n] \otimes zc_T[n]$. Since the propagation time of the audio cable is negligible compared to the system delay, the peak in the channel impulse response of the reference signal corresponds to the total system delay. The CIR of the reference signal can be expressed as:

$$h_{\text{sys}}[n] = \delta[n - \tau_{\text{sys}} f_s], \tag{5}$$

where $\tau_{\text{sys}} f_s$ is the index of system delay sampling points, and $\delta[n]$ is the Dirac delta function.

4.2.2 System Delay Calculation

Based on the reference signal modeling, the system delay is dynamically calculated through the following steps.

Step 1. **Reference signal framing.** The reference signal is divided into frames according to the single-period length L of the ZC signal, yielding multi-frame

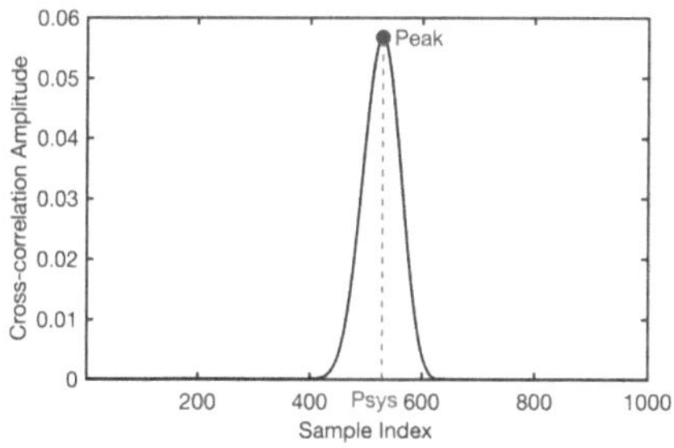

Fig. 5. Cross-correlation result of reference signal.

signals $y_{\text{ref}}[m,n]$ (where m denotes the frame index). This facilitates subsequent cross-correlation processing on a frame-by-frame basis.

***Step 2.* Cross-correlation calculation**. For each frame of the reference signal, a cross-correlation operation is performed with the transmitted signal frame zc_T to obtain the CIR frame:

$$h_{\text{sys}}[m,n] = IFFT(FFT(zc_T)^* \cdot FFT(y_{\text{ref}}[m,n])), \tag{6}$$

where $FFT(\cdot)$ denotes the fast fourier transform operation, $IFFT(\cdot)$ denotes the inverse fast fourier transform operation, and $(\cdot)^*$ denotes the conjugate of the transmitted signal zc_T after fourier transformation. By using the method of calculating the cross-correlation in the frequency domain, the computational complexity is reduced from $O(L^2)$ to $O(L\cdot logL)$, meeting real-time requirements.

We arrange the multi-frame cross-correlation results along the time dimension. The arranged results correspond to the range-time map (as shown in Fig. 6a). The CIR of received signals from microphones is calculated in the same way as above, and presented as $h[m,n]$.

***Step 3.* Peak detection and delay estimation**. As shown in Fig. 5, the position with the maximum cross-correlation amplitude is taken as the delay estimate:

$$P_{\text{sys}} = arg\max_n |h_{\text{sys}}[m,n]|, \tag{7}$$

where P_{sys} corresponds to the sample point value of the strong cross-correlation main peak, $P_{\text{sys}} = \tau_{\text{sys}} \cdot f_s$.

4.2.3 System Delay Elimination

To eliminate the impact of system delay on distance estimation of the channel impulse response in each receiving channel, dynamic calibration of the original CIR is required.

Specifically, let the original CIR be $h[m,n]$ (where $n = 0, 1, \ldots, L-1$, and L is the length of the CIR samples). We cyclically shift the CIR by P_{sys} along the sample point dimension to obtain the calibrated CIR $h_{\text{true}}[m,n]$:

$$h_{\text{true}}[m,n] = \text{circshift}(h[m,n], P_{\text{sys}}), \tag{8}$$

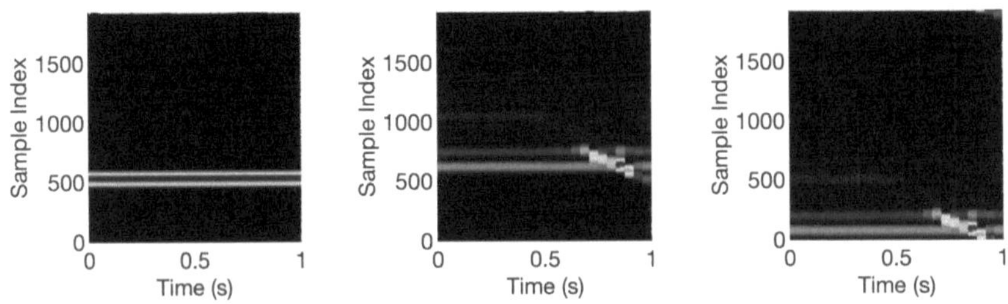

(a) Range-Time Map of reference channel.

(b) Range-Time Map before system delay elimination.

(c) Range-Time Map after system delay elimination.

Fig. 6. System delay elimination.

where circshift(·) denotes the circular shift operation. Through this operation, the sample points in the original CIR are realigned to their true positions. For example, the time-of-flight originally corresponding to sample point $n + P_{\text{sys}}$ is adjusted back to sample point n. This adjustment eliminates the influence of system delay on distance measurement. Figure 6b and Fig. 6c show a comparison of the CIR before and after signal calibration. This indicates that the correspondence between the sample point index and the actual distance has been corrected, verifying the effectiveness of this method.

4.3 Single-Channel Three-Dimensional Feature Judgment Method

To accurately extract gesture features and suppress environmental interference, this section constructs a three-dimensional feature model encompassing spatial locality, energy saliency, and temporal transience based on CIR. Effective gesture information is gradually screened through hierarchical constraints.

4.3.1 Spatial Locality Constraint

Standard gesture operations are concentrated in the near-field region of the speaker (defined as 0–0.3 m). To suppress gesture-like features from far-field introduced by environmental noise, random car bumps, or passenger movements, the analysis range must be constrained.

We define the spatial constraint function as follows, namely retaining only CIR information in the near-field region:

$$\mathcal{S}_D(\mathbf{h}) = \begin{cases} h[m,n] = h[m,n], & n \in [0, L_w - 1] \\ h[m,n] = 0, & \text{otherwise} \end{cases}, \tag{9}$$

where n is the sample point index, L_w is the sample point corresponding to the defined near-field region boundary. This function retains the original value when $n \in [0, L_w - 1]$ represents the near-field region and sets $h[m,n] = 0$ otherwise representing the far-field region.

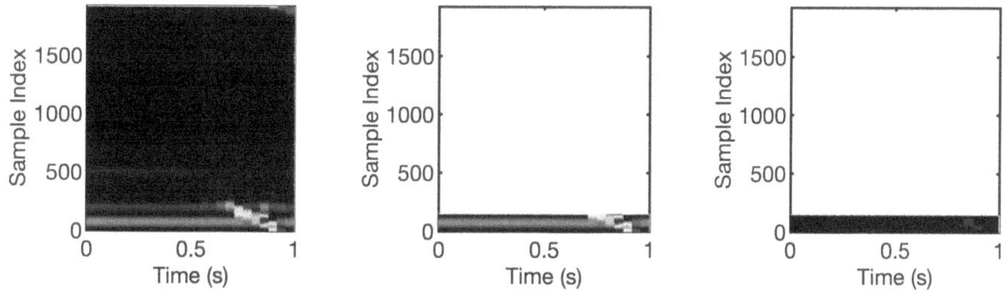

(a) Range-Time Map after system delay elimination. (b) Range-Time Map after spatial constraint. (c) Range-Time Map after energy constraint.

Fig. 7. Spatial constraint and energy constraint.

Applying this function to the CIR after system delay elimination ($h_{\text{true}}[m, n]$), the near-field constrained CIR is obtained:

$$h_D[m, n] = \mathcal{S}_D(h_{\text{true}}[m, n]). \tag{10}$$

Figure 7a and Fig. 7b illustrate the range-time map before and after spatial constraint for a single time window. This operation suppresses far-field interference and retains only CIR information in the gesture-concentrated region.

4.3.2 Energy Saliency Constraint

High-energy reflection pulses triggered by gestures are significantly different from steady-state direct and reflected paths in terms of time domain amplitude. Further screening of high-energy points is required.

First, we define a dynamic energy threshold to adapt to scene-specific energy variations:

$$\theta = \alpha \cdot \max(h_D[m, n]), \tag{11}$$

where $\alpha \in (0, 1)$ is the sensitivity coefficient, which balances detection rate and interference resistance, and $max(h_D\,[m, n])$ represents the maximum value of the matrix, which is the maximum energy of the near-field CIR. Then, the CIR is binarized through an energy constraint function:

$$\mathcal{S}_E(\mathbf{h}) = \begin{cases} h[m, n] = 1, & h[m, n] \geq \theta \\ h[m, n] = 0, & \text{otherwise} \end{cases}. \tag{12}$$

After applying the energy constraint, a binarized energy-salient matrix is obtained:

$$h_E[m, n] = \mathcal{S}_E(h_D[m, n]). \tag{13}$$

When $h_D[m, n] \geq \theta$, $h_E[m, n] = 1$, otherwise, $h_E[m, n] = 0$. This screens out high-energy points, as shown in Fig. 7b and Fig. 7c.

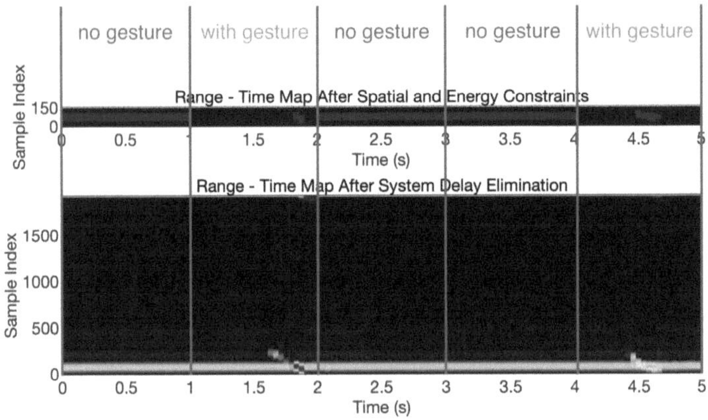

Fig. 8. Multi-window Range-Time Map.

4.3.3 Temporal Transience Constraint

The physical meaning of temporal transience is that gesture reflections exhibit transient temporal characteristics due to the suddenness of hand movements (short duration, as shown in the range-time map of a window with gestures in the upper part of Fig. 8). In contrast, static background reflections have steady-state temporal characteristics across cycles (long duration, as shown in the range-time map of a window without gestures in Fig. 8). Gesture features are extracted by leveraging this temporal dimension difference.

We define a temporal continuity measurement function to calculate the time proportion of high-energy points at the same distance:

$$\mathcal{T}(n, \mathbf{h}) = \frac{1}{M} \sum_{m=1}^{M} h[m, n], \tag{14}$$

where M is the total number of frames. This function reflects the duration of high-energy points at a fixed distance.

Set a threshold $\tau_h = 0.2$ (a robust value verified by experiments) and define the temporal constraint function:

$$\mathcal{S}_T(\mathbf{h}) = \begin{cases} 1, & \forall n, \mathcal{T}(n, \mathbf{h}) < \tau_h \\ 0, & \text{otherwise} \end{cases}. \tag{15}$$

If the time proportion of all distance units is less than τ_h, the signal is judged as a gesture feature.

4.3.4 Final Feature Judgment

Through the three-layer constraints of space → energy → time, the final feature judgment result for the i-th channel is:

$$s_g^i = \mathcal{S}_T(\mathcal{S}_E(\mathcal{S}_D(h_{\text{true}}[m, n]))). \tag{16}$$

If $s_g^i = 1$, the i-th channel detects a valid gesture, else if $s_g^i = 0$, no gesture is detected in the i-th channel.

This judgment logic is essentially a joint screening process for three-dimensional constraints. A gesture feature is valid only if it satisfies all three conditions simultaneously i) near-field feature presence, ii) energy saliency, and iii) transient temporal continuity of energy-salient points.

4.4 Multi-channel Collaborative Decision-Making Mechanism

Based on the multi-seat interaction requirements of in-cabin scenarios, this system adopts a distributed acoustic sensing unit layout with four seats in the front and rear rows. Based on research into the layout of speaker and microphone arrays in common car models, the sensing units are installed on the A/B-pillars.

Each unit contains 1 speaker and 4 microphone channels. The channel numbering is as follows, sub-array 1 (driver's seat) includes microphones 1–4, with the state vector $\mathbf{s}_1 = [s_g^1, \ldots, s_g^4]$. Sub-array 2 (front passenger seat) includes microphones 5–8, with the state vector $\mathbf{s}_2 = [s_g^5, \ldots, s_g^8]$. Sub-array 3 (rear left seat) includes channels 9–12, with the state vector $\mathbf{s}_3 = [s_g^9, \ldots, s_g^{12}]$. Sub-array 4 (rear right seat) includes channels 13–16, with the state vector $\mathbf{s}_4 = [s_g^{13}, \ldots, s_g^{16}]$. Here, $s_g^i \in \{0, 1\}$ indicates whether a gesture signal is detected in the i-th channel.

Each sub-array uses a consistent channel collaborative decision logic. Taking sub-array k as an example, define the sub-array decision function:

$$f_{\text{vote}}(\mathbf{s}_k) = \mathbb{I}\left(\|\mathbf{s}_k\|_0 \geq 3\right), \tag{17}$$

where $\|\cdot\|_0$ denotes the l_0-norm, used to quantify the number of channels in the sub-array that detect gestures. If the number of channels ≥ 3, it returns 1 (indicating that the seat sub-array detects a gesture), otherwise, it returns 0.

By analyzing the decision results of the four sub-arrays, the system determines the final feedback result. First, identify all sub-arrays with an output of 1. If only one sub-array outputs 1, the final result is the seat number corresponding to that sub-array. If multiple sub-arrays output 1 simultaneously, the result is the set of seat numbers corresponding to these sub-arrays. If no sub-array outputs 1, the final result is marked as 0.

This logical design retains the ability to accurately locate a single seat while supporting multi-seat interaction scenarios. Through this multi-channel collaborative decision-making mechanism, the system can detect and locate gestures more reliably. Channel-level collaboration ensures that multiple channels of a single array detect gestures consistently. Sub-array-level arbitration achieves spatial positioning through the logical combination of multiple arrays.

The final decision result is fed back to the car infotainment system via the bus, triggering custom commands (*e.g.*, audio mute) to achieve gesture-controlled car operations. This mechanism effectively improves the reliability of gesture detection and positioning accuracy in complex in-cabin environments while reducing the false trigger rate.

(a) Acoustic sensing unit deployment in car.

(b) Hardware description of single acoustic sensing unit.

Fig. 9. Acoustic sensing unit deployment and description of single acoustic sensing unit.

5 Evaluation

5.1 Experimental Setup

We deploy our system on the audio module of a real car. In a typical deployment scenario, there are four sets of acoustic sensing units, as shown in Fig. 9a, which are respectively installed on the A/B pillar. Each acoustic sensing unit consists of one Bose speaker [33] and a 4-element microphone array, as shown in Fig. 9b. Additionally, we deploy a camera below the rearview mirror inside the car to record hand gesture events as the ground truth.

A computer generates periodic ZC-sequence signals (with the center frequency $f_c = 19$ kHz, bandwidth $B = 2$ kHz, and signal periodic sampling length $L = 1920$). Through a sound card (PXUA216MB-DL2-M/XMOS [34]), the speaker is driven to transmit the acoustic signals. The microphone array collects reflected signals at a sampling rate of $f_s = 48$ kHz, and the signals are transmitted to the computer in real-time via the sound card for signal processing. The sliding window for processing is set to a duration of 1 s and a step size of 0.5 s to ensure real-time performance.

Based on the ground truth obtained by the camera, four types of gesture events are defined as follows. 1) True Positive (TP), namely successfully detecting a real gesture with correct direction judgment, 2) False Negative (FN), namely failing to detect a real gesture, 3) Directional False Positive (FP_1), namely detecting a gesture but with inconsistent direction judgment, 4) False Alarm (FP_2), namely outputting a gesture event when there is no real gesture.

Therefore, key metrics for system performance evaluation are defined as Accuracy Rate $= TP/(TP + FN + FP_1)$, False Alarm Rate $= FP_2/(TP + FN + FP_1)$. The average processing time for each window is also evaluated.

5.2 Overall Performance

We collect data from six volunteers[2], both doing gestures and non-doing gestures. In order to ensure that the experiment is closer to the real scenario, we

[2] We have obtained the written consent from all volunteers before experiments, and our Institutional Review Boards have approved entire research activities.

Fig. 10. Volunteer at different seats.

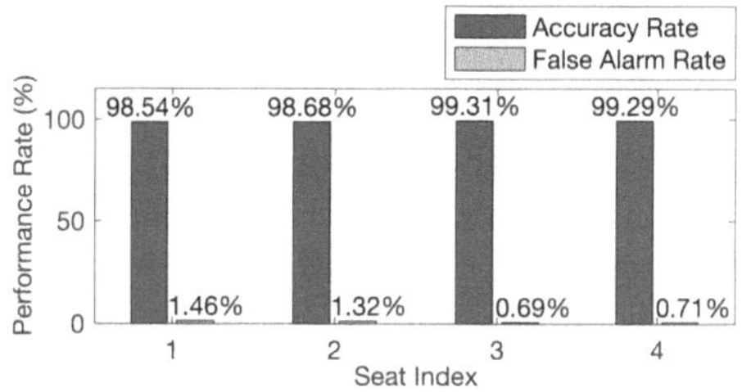

Fig. 11. Performance at different seats.

do not restrict any other activities of the volunteers, they can feel free to exhibit daily behaviors such as shaking their bodies, using phones, eating, and so on. In our experiments, we consider the effect of different seats and number of passages on the performance of the system. Since we are based on acoustic signals for gesture sensing, we also verify the effect of different environmental noise on the system performance, *e.g.*, rain noise, music, people speaking, and traffic noise In addition, we also evaluate the system performance under different road conditions *e.g.*, speed bumps, mountain roads, streets, highways. Overall, we collect a total of 10 h data under various settings and scenarios, comprising 20 datasets.

The detection results demonstrate an accuracy rate exceeding 99.05%, a miss rate below 1%, and a false alarm rate below 0.5%. The average processing time per window does not exceed 0.05 s, which is significantly lower than the sliding step threshold of 0.5 s. This fully verifies the system's recognition capability and real-time processing performance in the in-car environment.

In addition, by comparing performance across different scenarios, it is found that the system maintains high robustness even in complex acoustic environments. This is attributed to the combined effect of the single-channel three-dimensional feature judgment method and the multi-channel collaborative decision-making mechanism.

5.3 Performance at Different Seats

To test the performance at different seats, volunteers take turns sitting in seat positions 1–4 (as shown in Fig. 10), with 20 min of data collected for each position. A total of 1.3 h of data is gathered across all seats.

Experimental results in Fig. 11 show the system maintains a detection accuracy rate exceeding 98.5% for each seat, with a miss rate below 1.5%. This demonstrates the system achieves full in-car gesture detection coverage through distributed acoustic sensing units and a three-dimensional feature decision method. By leveraging delay elimination and spatial constraint functions, the system precisely partitions near-field regions, ensuring each seat's sensing unit responds only to local gesture features.

5.4 Performance in Multi-passenger Scenarios

We evaluate the system's performance in multi-passenger scenarios, controlling the total number of passengers in the car from 1 to 4, to analyze the impact of other passenger's activities on acoustic signals propagation. As the number of passengers increases, the acoustic signals propagation paths inside the car become more complex due to human body movement and reflection, potentially leading to signal attenuation or multipath effects.

As shown in Fig. 12, experimental results show that when the number of passengers increases from 1 to 4, the accuracy rate remains relatively stable between 99.45% and 98.68%. The reason for this is because our multi-channel collaborative decision-making mechanism effectively excludes the interference of other passengers by utilizing spatial locality constraint. Therefore, we conduct ablation experiments by removing this module. As shown in the green part of Fig. 12, the accuracy rate decreases gradually as the number of passengers increases (*i.e.*, dropping from 87.80% to 77.92%), which indicates the mechanism's critical role in resisting interference from passenger activities.

This indicates that the system effectively mitigates interference introduced by other passenger's activities through a multi-channel collaborative decision-making mechanism, ensuring the reliability of detection in multi-passenger scenarios.

Building on the multi-passenger scenario, we further assess the interference effects of passenger body movements on the system. Experimental results show that routine body movements, such as arm swinging, posture adjustments, or raising hands to touch the head, do not cause misjudgments. However, when taller passengers rapidly sway their bodies forward and backward, causing their heads to come too close to the speaker, the reflection of acoustic signal by the head can form gesture-like features, which may be mistakenly interpreted as valid gestures.

To mitigate this, the acoustic unit can be relocated toward the front of the car. This spatial adjustment ensures passengers' heads (in normal seating postures) rarely intrude into the speaker's near-field sensing area, directly reducing false alarms from head-induced signal reflections while balancing in-cabin ergonomics and detection reliability.

5.5 Performance in Different Noise Scenarios

Since we are based on acoustic signals for gesture sensing, the impact of ambient noise on system performance is a concern for many people. Therefore, we conduct experiments under four daily environmental noise, *i.e.*, rain noise, music, people speaking, and traffic noise.

The experimental results, as shown in Fig. 13, indicate that ambient noise has a minimal impact on the system's performance. This is because most environmental noises in daily life (e.g., rain, casual conversations, background music) are low-frequency signals (frequency $<$ 18 kHz). Meanwhile, the system's target gesture signals are transmitted using a carrier frequency band of 18–20 kHz. This

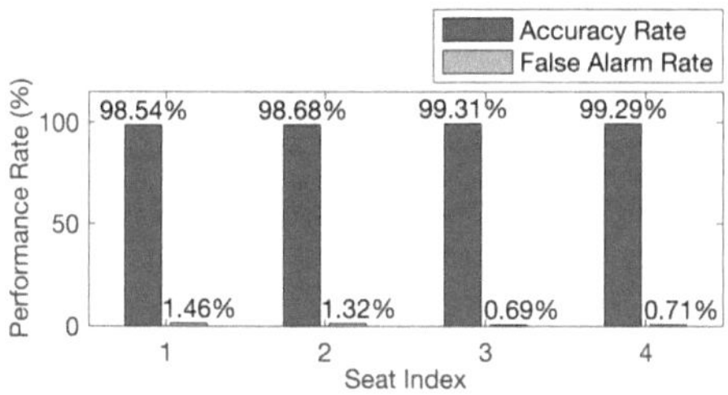

Fig. 12. Performance in Multi-passenger Scenarios.

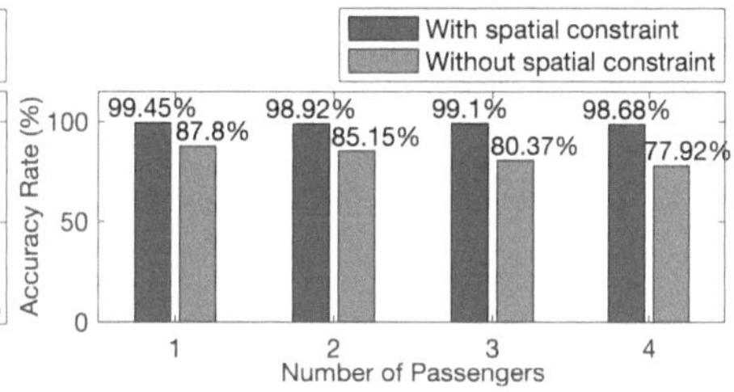

Fig. 13. Performance in different noise scenarios.

band naturally avoids the frequency ranges where noise energy concentrates. Even when confronted with full-spectrum noise interferences like car honks, the signal energy remains predominantly concentrated in non-target frequency bands. The typical time-frequency characteristics of such interferences are shown in the 0.3–0.7 s interval of Fig. 14a. In the range-time map (Fig. 14b), the noise only interferes with the low-energy regions caused by multi-path effects. Therefore, by leveraging the spatial locality constraint within the three-dimensional feature judgment method, the system effectively identifies and suppresses noise interferences that overlap with gesture features. This suppression mechanism eliminates noise impacts in non-target frequency bands and low-energy multi-path regions. In conclusion, daily environmental noises have almost no substantial impact on the system's gesture detection performance.

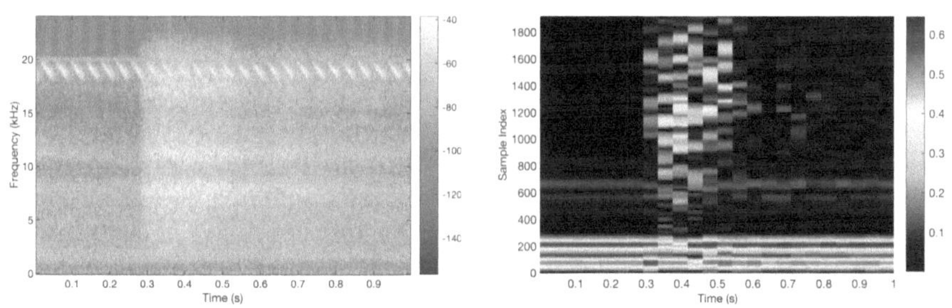

(a) Spectrogram of the received signal in high-frequency noise interference senario.

(b) Range-Time Map of the received signal in high-frequency noise interference scenario.

Fig. 14. Received signal in high-frequency noise scenarios.

5.6 Performance in Different Road Conditions

In the road condition interference experiment, we test the gesture recognition performance when the car traverses four typical road conditions, namely speed bumps, mountain roads, urban streets, and highways. We also conduct a window-open/window-closed comparison experiment to assess the interference of strong winds on the acoustic channel during high-speed driving. In the experiment, volunteers perform gesture actions from different seats, and data is simultaneously collected under mechanical vibration and wind noise conditions.

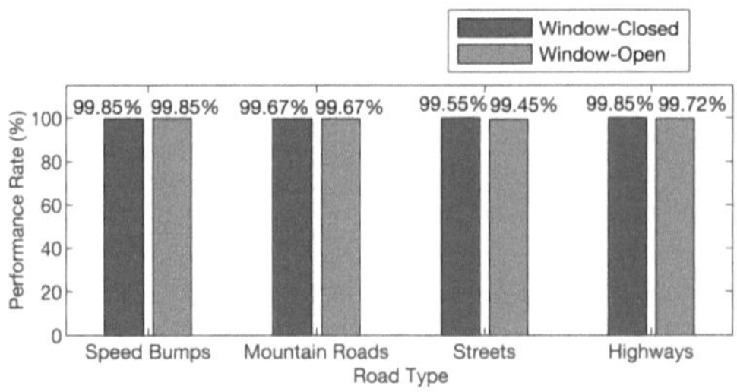

Fig. 15. Performance in different road conditions.

The experimental results, as shown in Fig. 15, indicate that, under conditions where acoustic devices are securely fixed, the impact of car mechanical vibrations on gesture detection is minor, with accuracy rate remaining at a high level across all road conditions. While strong winds at high speeds may introduce channel fluctuations, these do not meet the near-field high-energy transient characteristics required for gesture features, thus not leading to misjudgments.

6 Conclusion

This paper introduces an innovative in-cabin acoustic-based gesture mute control system, designed to address key challenges such as high costs, limited operational range, and privacy concern. By leveraging existing in-cabin speakers and microphones, we have developed a high-frequency acoustic sensing technology coupled with a self-calibrating delay mechanism. These advancements effectively overcome the cost and privacy limitations inherent in conventional solutions. The result is a lightweight, low-cost, highly responsive, and full-coverage smart cabin interaction solution that enhances user experience without compromising on functionality or security.

References

1. Gupta, S., Morris, D., Patel, S., Tan, D.: SoundWave: using the doppler effect to sense gestures. In: Proceedings of the SIGCHI Conference on Human Factors in Computing Systems (CHI 2012), pp. 1911–1914. Association for Computing Machinery, New York, NY, USA (2012). https://doi.org/10.1145/2207676.2208331

2. Ruan, W., Sheng, Q.Z., Yang, L., Gu, T., Xu, P., Shangguan, L.: AudioGest: enabling fine-grained hand gesture detection by decoding echo signal. In: Proceedings of the 2016 ACM International Joint Conference on Pervasive and Ubiquitous Computing (UbiComp 2016), pp. 474–485. Association for Computing Machinery, New York, NY, USA (2016). https://doi.org/10.1145/2971648.2971736
3. Yun, S., Chen, Y.-C., Zheng, H., Qiu, L., Mao, W.: Strata: fine-grained acoustic-based device-free tracking. In: Proceedings of the 15th Annual International Conference on Mobile Systems, Applications, and Services (MobiSys 2017), pp. 15–28. Association for Computing Machinery, New York, NY, USA (2017). https://doi.org/10.1145/3081333.3081356
4. Wang, W., Liu, A.X., Sun, K.: Device-free gesture tracking using acoustic signals. In: Proceedings of the 22nd Annual International Conference on Mobile Computing and Networking (MobiCom 2016), pp. 82–94. Association for Computing Machinery, New York, NY, USA (2016). https://doi.org/10.1145/2973750.2973764
5. Ling, K., Dai, H., Liu, Y., Liu, A.X.: UltraGesture: fine-grained gesture sensing and recognition. In: 2018 15th Annual IEEE International Conference on Sensing, Communication, and Networking (SECON), pp. 1–9. IEEE Press (2018). https://doi.org/10.1109/SAHCN.2018.8397099
6. Nandakumar, R., Iyer, V., Tan, D., Gollakota, S.: FingerIO: using active sonar for fine-grained finger tracking. In: Proceedings of the 2016 CHI Conference on Human Factors in Computing Systems (CHI 2016), pp. 1515–1525. Association for Computing Machinery, New York, NY, USA (2016). https://doi.org/10.1145/2858036.2858580
7. Abdelnasser, H., Youssef, M., Harras, K.A.: WiGest: a ubiquitous WiFi-based gesture recognition system. In: 2015 IEEE Conference on Computer Communications (INFOCOM), pp. 1472–1480. IEEE Press, Hong Kong, China (2015). https://doi.org/10.1109/INFOCOM.2015.7218525
8. Pu, Q., Gupta, S., Gollakota, S., Patel, S.: Whole-home gesture recognition using wireless signals. In: Proceedings of the 19th Annual International Conference on Mobile Computing & Networking (MobiCom 2013), pp. 27–38. Association for Computing Machinery, New York, NY, USA (2013). https://doi.org/10.1145/2500423.2500436
9. Kellogg, B., Talla, V., Gollakota, S.: Bringing gesture recognition to all devices. In: Proceedings of the 11th USENIX Conference on Networked Systems Design and Implementation (NSDI 2014), pp. 303–316. USENIX Association, USA (2014)
10. Wang, J., Vasisht, D., Katabi, D.: RF-IDraw: virtual touch screen in the air using RF signals. In: Proceedings of the 2014 ACM Conference on SIGCOMM (SIGCOMM 2014), pp. 235–246. Association for Computing Machinery, New York, NY, USA (2014). https://doi.org/10.1145/2619239.2626330
11. Microsoft: Hololens. https://www.microsoft.com. Accessed 13 June 2025
12. Sony: PlayStation VR. https://www.playstation.com. Accessed 13 June 2025
13. Rehg, J.M., Kanade, T.: Visual tracking of high DOF articulated structures: an application to human hand tracking. In: Proceedings of the Third European Conference on Computer Vision (ECCV 1994), pp. 35–46. Springer, Heidelberg (1994)
14. Nandakumar, R., Chintalapudi, K.K., Padmanabhan, V., Venkatesan, R.: Dhwani: secure peer-to-peer acoustic NFC. In: Proceedings of the ACM SIGCOMM 2013 Conference on SIGCOMM (SIGCOMM 2013), pp. 63–74. Association for Computing Machinery, New York, NY, USA (2013). https://doi.org/10.1145/2486001.2486037

15. Lopes, C.V., Aguiar, P.M.Q.: Aerial acoustic communications. In: Proceedings of the 2001 IEEE Workshop on the Applications of Signal Processing to Audio and Acoustics (ASPAA 2001), pp. 219–222. IEEE Press, New Platz, NY, USA (2001). https://doi.org/10.1109/ASPAA.2001.969582
16. Lee, H., Kim, T.H., Choi, J.W., Choi, S.: Chirp signal-based aerial acoustic communication for smart devices. In: 2015 IEEE Conference on Computer Communications (INFOCOM), pp. 2407–2415. IEEE Press, Hong Kong, China (2015). https://doi.org/10.1109/INFOCOM.2015.7218629
17. Ka, S., et al.: Near-ultrasound communication for TV's 2nd screen services. In: Proceedings of the 22nd Annual International Conference on Mobile Computing and Networking (MobiCom 2016), pp. 42–54. Association for Computing Machinery, New York, NY, USA (2016). https://doi.org/10.1145/2973750.2973774
18. Cai, C., Chen, Z., Luo, J., Pu, H., Hu, M., Zheng, R.: Boosting chirp signal based aerial acoustic communication under dynamic channel conditions. IEEE Trans. Mob. Comput. **21**(9), 3110–3121 (2022). https://doi.org/10.1109/TMC.2021.3051665
19. Peng, C., Shen, G., Zhang, Y., Li, Y., Tan, K.: BeepBeep: a high accuracy acoustic ranging system using COTS mobile devices. In: Proceedings of the 5th International Conference on Embedded Networked Sensor Systems (SenSys 2007), pp. 1–14. Association for Computing Machinery, New York, NY, USA (2007). https://doi.org/10.1145/1322263.1322265
20. Uddin, M., Nadeem, T.: RF-Beep: a light ranging scheme for smart devices. In: 2013 IEEE International Conference on Pervasive Computing and Communications (PerCom), pp. 114–122. IEEE Press, San Diego, CA, USA (2013). https://doi.org/10.1109/PerCom.2013.6526721
21. Zhou, B., Elbadry, M., Gao, R., Ye, F.: BatMapper: acoustic sensing based indoor floor plan construction using smartphones. In: Proceedings of the 15th Annual International Conference on Mobile Systems, Applications, and Services (MobiSys 2017), pp. 42–55. Association for Computing Machinery, New York, NY, USA (2017). https://doi.org/10.1145/3081333.3081363
22. Pradhan, S., Baig, G., Mao, W., Qiu, L., Chen, G., Yang, B.: Smartphone-based acoustic indoor space mapping. Proc. ACM Interact. Mob. Wearable Ubiquitous Technol. **2**(2), Article 75 (2018). https://doi.org/10.1145/3214278
23. Liu, K., Liu, X., Li, X.: Guoguo: enabling fine-grained indoor localization via smartphone. In: Proceedings of the 11th Annual International Conference on Mobile Systems, Applications, and Services (MobiSys 2013), pp. 235–248. Association for Computing Machinery, New York, NY, USA (2013). https://doi.org/10.1145/2462456.2464450
24. Wang, Y.-T., Li, J., Zheng, R., Zhao, D.: ARABIS: an asynchronous acoustic indoor positioning system for mobile devices. In: 2017 International Conference on Indoor Positioning and Indoor Navigation (IPIN), pp. 1–8. IEEE Press, Sapporo, Japan (2017). https://doi.org/10.1109/IPIN.2017.8115892
25. Kim, H., Byanjankar, A., Liu, Y., Shu, Y., Shin, I.: UbiTap: leveraging acoustic dispersion for ubiquitous touch interface on solid surfaces. In: Proceedings of the 16th ACM Conference on Embedded Networked Sensor Systems (SenSys 2018), pp. 211–223. Association for Computing Machinery, New York, NY, USA (2018). https://doi.org/10.1145/3274783.3274848

26. Tung, Y.-C., Shin, K.G.: Expansion of human-phone interface by sensing structure-borne sound propagation. In: Proceedings of the 14th Annual International Conference on Mobile Systems, Applications, and Services (MobiSys 2016), pp. 277–289. Association for Computing Machinery, New York, NY, USA (2016). https://doi.org/10.1145/2906388.2906394
27. Texas Instruments: TAS5825M Product Page. https://www.ti.com/product/TAS5825M. Accessed 13 June 2025
28. Wang, A., Sunshine, J.E., Gollakota, S.: Contactless infant monitoring using white noise. In: Proceedings of the 25th Annual International Conference on Mobile Computing and Networking (MobiCom 2019), pp. 1–16. Association for Computing Machinery, New York, NY, USA, Article 52 (2019). https://doi.org/10.1145/3300061.3345453
29. Wan, H., Shi, S., Cao, W., Wang, W., Chen, G.: RespTracker: multi-user room-scale respiration tracking with commercial acoustic devices. In: IEEE INFOCOM 2021 - IEEE Conference on Computer Communications, pp. 1–10. IEEE Press, Vancouver, BC, Canada (2021). https://doi.org/10.1109/INFOCOM42981.2021.9488881
30. Dai, H., Wang, W., Liu, A.X., Ling, K., Sun, J.: Speech based human authentication on smartphones. In: 2019 16th Annual IEEE International Conference on Sensing, Communication, and Networking (SECON), pp. 1–9. IEEE Press, Boston, MA, USA (2019). https://doi.org/10.1109/SAHCN.2019.8824958
31. Su, Y., et al.: Embracing distributed acoustic sensing in car cabin for children presence detection. Proc. ACM Interact. Mob. Wearable Ubiquitous Technol. **8**(1), Article 16 (2024). https://doi.org/10.1145/3643548
32. Popovic, B.M.: Generalized chirp-like polyphase sequences with optimum correlation properties. IEEE Trans. Inf. Theory **38**(4), 1406–1409 (1992)
33. Bose: In-Cabin Experiences. https://automotive.bose.com/road-ahead/in-cabin-experiences. Accessed 13 June 2025
34. PXUA216MB-DL2-M/XMOS. https://docs.pawpaw.ltd/. Accessed 13 June 2025
35. BMW Group. Gesture Control in the BMW 7 Series with Audio Mute Control Support. https://www.bmw.com. Accessed 13 June 2025
36. AITO. AITO M9 Panoramic Smart Flagship SUV with 25-unit acoustic design. https://aito.auto/model/m9/. Accessed 14 June 2025
37. Nissan Global. Nissan Voice Control Technology. https://www.nissan-global.com/EN/INNOVATION/TECHNOLOGY/ARCHIVE/VC/. Accessed 14 June 2025
38. Audi USA. Audi Sound Systems by Bang & Olufsen®: 3D Surround Sound Technology for In-Car Entertainment. https://www.audiusa.com/en/inside-audi/innovation/3D-sound/. Accessed 14 June 2025
39. Tung, Y.-C., Bui, D., Shin, K.G.: Cross-platform support for rapid development of mobile acoustic sensing applications. In: 16th ACM MobiSys (Annual International Conference on Mobile Systems, Applications, and Services), pp. 455–467. ACM, Munich (2018)

Improving NTP Time Synchronization Accuracy for NTS Enhancement

Yilun Liu[1], Weiping Zhu[1(✉)], Chao Ma[2(✉)], and Chuanhe Huang[1]

[1] School of Computer Science, Wuhan University, Wuhan, People's Republic of China
{liuyilun,wpzhu,huangch}@whu.edu.cn

[2] School of Cyber Science and Engineering, Wuhan University, Wuhan, People's Republic of China
chaoma@whu.edu.cn

Abstract. With growing demands for time consistency in cloud computing, finance, and distributed systems, traditional network time protocols face challenges in security and precision due to weak authentication and vulnerability to delay attacks. The IETF's NTS extension adds TLS and AEAD to NTP but remains susceptible to delay-based threats, and public NTS server distribution lacks systematic evaluation. This paper addresses these issues via four phases: large-scale measurement, dynamic selection, sample fusion, and active defense. A high-concurrency scanning framework rapidly discovers NTS-KE services across global IPv4 space, followed by a dynamic scoring model based on certificate compliance, hierarchy, synchronization distance, and availability to construct a server pool with over 600 nodes. The proposed NTS client, Tychron, implements a "polling - filtering - selection - clustering - combining" pipeline to achieve fine-grained time sample fusion across multiple servers, improving accuracy and load balance. To counter delay asymmetry, a joint offset-skew model with a Kalman filter and adaptive noise adjustment is introduced; peer reselection is triggered when filter gain and asymmetry surpass thresholds, mitigating malicious delay effects. Evaluations against Chrony and NTPsec in real and simulated environments show that Tychron significantly reduces cumulative time error and server load across normal, degraded, and attack scenarios, providing a practical, secure, and cost-effective time service solution for critical infrastructure in open networks.

Keywords: Network Time Security · Network Time Protocol · Kalman Filter

1 Introduction

Time synchronization underpins numerous networked systems, especially in financial trading, cybersecurity, scientific instrumentation, and distributed control. The Network Time Protocol (NTP), operating over UDP on port 123, has long served as the standard for synchronizing clocks to Coordinated Universal

L. Zhang and K.-K. R. Choo (Eds.): MobiQuitous 2025, LNICST 683, pp. 314–334, 2026.
https://doi.org/10.1007/978-3-032-22500-9_18

Time (UTC) by estimating and correcting round-trip delays between clients and reference servers.

Despite its simplicity and wide adoption, NTP is vulnerable to various attacks such as DoS amplification, replay, MITM, and delay attacks [5,11,13]. Delay attacks are particularly insidious, allowing adversaries to manipulate one-way delay without breaching cryptographic integrity, thereby inducing persistent timing errors—a critical threat in systems where timestamps govern ordering, anomaly detection, and compliance.

To enhance security, the IETF introduced the Network Time Security (NTS) extension, combining TLS-based key establishment (NTS-KE) with AEAD-authenticated synchronization [7]. While this design defends against replay and MITM threats without requiring stateful server tracking, it inherits a key NTP flaw: the assumption of symmetric round-trip delays. In practice, asymmetries and adversarial manipulation can subvert this assumption, leaving NTS exposed to stealthy delay attacks [6,14].

Furthermore, the global NTS ecosystem lacks transparency. Public servers are limited, heterogeneously configured, and insufficiently evaluated, forcing clients to synchronize without insight into server trustworthiness, stability, or availability. These issues complicate secure, high-precision time synchronization over the public Internet.

1.1 Motivation and Research Objectives

This study tackles two fundamental challenges in NTS-based synchronization: (1) the inability to detect and mitigate asymmetric delay attacks, and (2) the absence of systematic visibility into public NTS infrastructure. We aim to build a robust, measurement-driven, multi-server synchronization framework that improves both accuracy and resilience.

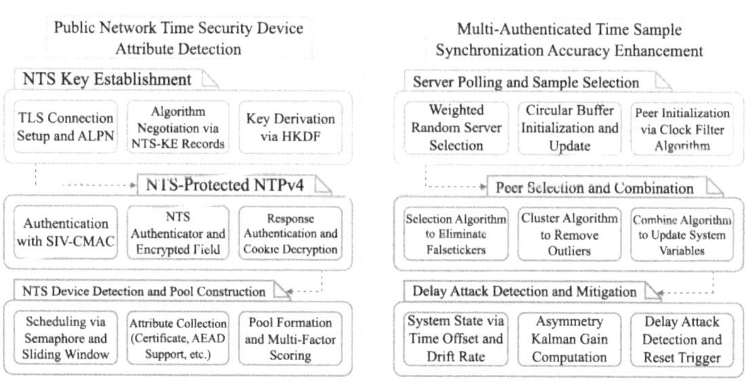

Fig. 1. Research and technical detail overview

As shown in Fig. 1, we first deploy a high-concurrency scanning framework to survey the global IPv4 space for NTS-KE services, collecting certificate validity, AEAD support, delay variance, and synchronization behavior. This enables the construction of a dynamic, high-quality server pool. Second, we design a redundant multi-server synchronization pipeline that polls multiple authenticated peers and processes time samples through filtering, selection, clustering, and combining. To combat asymmetry, we introduce a Kalman filter that jointly estimates offset and drift while adapting noise models to delay metrics, triggering peer reselection upon anomaly detection.

1.2 Main Contributions

The principal contributions of this paper are:

- **Global-scale NTS server scanning and scoring:** We develop a high-concurrency, semaphore-controlled scanner that evaluates over 600 NTS-KE servers using metrics such as certificate health, synchronization distance, and delay consistency.
- **Multi-source synchronization via Tychron client:** We implement the Tychron client, which employs a five-stage pipeline—polling, filtering, selection, clustering, and combining—to improve synchronization accuracy and balance server loads.
- **Asymmetric delay defense using Kalman filtering:** We introduce a model coupling offset and drift with delay asymmetry, using a dynamically adjusted noise profile. When anomalous gains emerge, Tychron initiates peer reselection, mitigating adversarial influence.

1.3 Organization of the Paper

Section 2 reviews related work on NTP security and synchronization. Section 3 details our measurement methods, server pool design, and Tychron client architecture. Section 4 presents experimental results under various conditions. Section 5 concludes and outlines future work.

2 Related Works

Time synchronization is essential to distributed systems, with precision and resilience being key to correctness in time-sensitive applications. Prior research spans two key areas: synchronization control mechanisms and techniques to enhance NTP accuracy under asymmetric or lossy conditions.

2.1 Time Synchronization Control and Coordination Mechanisms

Recent work has explored lightweight coordination frameworks, particularly for constrained or wireless environments. Carroll et al. [2] introduced STTP for real-time telemetry with TLS and X.509 support, achieving high throughput and compression, but lacking explicit time alignment or asymmetry handling.

In wireless sensor networks, Zhou et al. [15] proposed CFTS, a cluster-based scheme combining bi-directional exchange and passive listening. Through MLE and linear regression, it achieves robust synchronization with low power consumption, despite not targeting NTP use cases directly.

From a control-theoretic angle, Li et al. [8] developed models guaranteeing synchronization via Lyapunov-based controllers, formalizing Time Synchronization Stability (TSS) and its fixed-time variant (FTSS). Jiang et al. [4] further introduced a disturbance-aware synchronization controller with guaranteed convergence bounds. Though these models apply to continuous systems and omit packet-switching dynamics, they lay foundational ground for extension to NTP-like networks.

2.2 Accuracy-Oriented Improvements for NTP

To address network-induced delay variability, several enhancements to NTP have been proposed. Machizawa et al. [9] showed synchronization error increases exponentially with hop count, recommending hop-minimized server selection via TTL-based heuristics. However, its effectiveness degrades in dynamic or firewall-restricted networks.

Mkacher et al. [10] used external "time-box" units for direct one-way delay measurement, offering precision at the cost of high overhead and frequent recalibration in volatile topologies.

Chronos [13] employs randomized multi-server polling and cross-verification to detect delay attacks, but is hindered by DNS dependency, server-switching jitter, and unresolved upstream threats [3,11].

Kwon et al. [5] highlighted vulnerabilities in the global NTP Pool due to BGP hijacking and rogue server injection, capable of introducing long-term synchronization bias [1,12]. These systemic risks threaten global timekeeping integrity.

In summary, existing solutions either lack adaptability to network dynamics or are impractical at scale. This motivates the need for redundancy-aware, asymmetry-resilient synchronization frameworks—principles central to our Kalman-filter-based architecture.

3 Proposed Method

This section presents our proposed approach to secure and accurate time synchronization. It consists of two main components. First, we perform large-scale measurement and cryptographic profiling of publicly available NTS servers to construct a high-quality, dynamically maintained server pool (Sect. 3.1). Second, we introduce a robust synchronization pipeline based on multi-sample fusion, Kalman filter-based bias estimation, and asymmetry-aware anomaly detection within the Tychron client (Sect. 3.2).

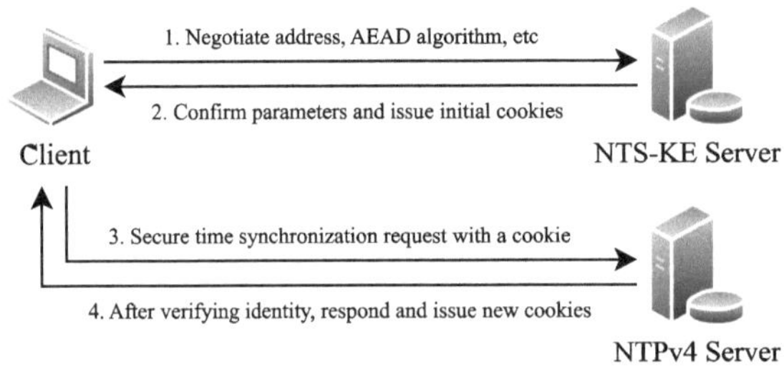

Fig. 2. Two-stage process of NTS

3.1 Measurement and Profiling of Public NTS-Capable Servers

To enable reliable and secure time synchronization, we begin with a systematic survey of publicly accessible Network Time Security (NTS) servers. This involves analyzing the protocol, constructing a scalable probing framework, and establishing a high-quality server pool based on multi-dimensional evaluation.

NTS Protocol Structure. As standardized in RFC 8915, NTS enhances the classical NTP by introducing cryptographic protections through two protocol stages (see Fig. 2):

- **NTS-KE:** The key establishment phase operates over TLS 1.2/1.3 on TCP port 4460. Clients and servers negotiate an AEAD cipher (e.g., AES-SIV-CMAC), derive session keys via HKDF, and issue encrypted cookies encapsulating session state.
- **NTS-protected NTPv4:** Using UDP port 123, clients embed cookies and authentication tags in requests. Servers decrypt the cookies to reconstruct session keys and verify authenticity, without maintaining per-client state.

This design supports scalability and robustness against message tampering and replay attacks.

High-Concurrency Measurement with Adaptive Control. Global-scale NTS scanning poses concurrency and intrusion detection challenges. We design a semaphore-controlled framework with an adaptive feedback loop:

- A counting semaphore of capacity $c_{\max}$ governs probe concurrency.
- A sliding window tracks error rate and round-trip delay over recent w samples.
- If anomalies arise (e.g., rising error rate or latency), the concurrency limit is reduced. Otherwise, it is gradually restored.

This strategy ensures efficient probing while minimizing strain on remote servers—crucial for TLS-based services.

Cryptographic Capability Probing. For each responsive endpoint on port 4460, we attempt a full NTS-KE handshake to extract:

1. TLS certificate chains and issuer metadata,
2. Supported AEAD cipher suites, particularly AES-SIV-CMAC variants,
3. Session keys and cookies,
4. Protocol metadata such as AEAD IDs and NTP endpoint hints.

This enables classification of server cryptographic posture and interoperability readiness.

Authenticated NTP Exchange and Timestamp Extraction. Using the session material, we issue authenticated NTPv4 requests. Each response is parsed for:

- Stratum level, root delay, dispersion, and identifiers,
- Timestamps T_1T_4 for delay and offset computation,
- Updated cookies, if provided, to support ongoing synchronization.

These metrics confirm full RFC 8915 compliance and inform network performance models.

Scoring-Based Server Pool Construction. We calculate a quality score for each server as:

$$\text{Score} = \max\left\{50,\ 100 \times \kappa^{10(1-\alpha)} \times \kappa^{2(\beta-1)} \times \kappa^{100\lambda} \times \kappa^{(\eta-1)/100}\right\}, \quad (1)$$

Here, α is availability, β is stratum, λ is synchronization distance, η is estimated hop count, and $\kappa = 0.95$ is a decay factor. This model penalizes low availability, high delay, and distant or high-stratum servers, while maintaining adaptability to transient fluctuations.

Ultimately, we curate a dynamic pool of over 600 NTS-compliant servers, selected for robust cryptographic support, network accessibility, and temporal accuracy. This pool forms the foundation for subsequent time synchronization across diverse network environments.

3.2 Robust Synchronization with Multiple Authenticated Samples

To improve the accuracy and robustness of time synchronization in adversarial and fluctuating environments, we propose a multi-sample strategy that leverages a pool of authenticated NTS servers. Our approach builds upon the core NTP synchronization logic, enhances the sample processing pipeline within the Tychron client, and integrates a Kalman filter-based bias estimation model to mitigate asymmetric delay and detect delay attacks.

Overview of the NTP Synchronization Pipeline. The standard NTPv4 synchronization algorithm comprises five sequential stages: polling, clock filtering, candidate selection, clustering, and final offset computation. Let T_1, T_2, T_3, T_4 represent the four timestamps exchanged between a client and server. The offset θ and delay δ are classically computed as:

$$\theta = \frac{(T_2 - T_1) + (T_3 - T_4)}{2}, \quad \delta = (T_4 - T_1) - (T_3 - T_2). \tag{2}$$

This model assumes symmetric delay between the client and server—an assumption often violated in practice. To cope with dynamic conditions, the Tychron client implements a restructured pipeline:

- **Polling:** Probes are sent to multiple NTS servers using authenticated packets. Servers are selected from the dynamic pool based on score and jitter history.
- **Filtering:** A sliding window retains the n most recent samples from each server. Samples with missing responses, excessive delay, or invalid MACs are discarded.
- **Selection and Clustering:** Servers with high stratum or high dispersion are pruned. Among remaining candidates, samples are clustered based on offset similarity.
- **Combining:** Selected samples are combined using weighted averaging. Weights incorporate root distance, jitter, and recent reliability. This yields a composite offset with reduced variance.

Kalman Filtering for Bias Estimation and Asymmetry Correction. To mitigate the impact of asymmetric network delay and dynamically estimate synchronization bias, we formulate a state-space model and apply a Kalman filter to infer the hidden timing offset and local clock drift. This allows the client to perform noise-aware fusion of multiple authenticated timestamp samples.

State Definition and System Model. Let the hidden state vector at time k be:

$$\mathbf{x}_k = \begin{bmatrix} \theta_k \\ \rho_k \end{bmatrix}, \tag{3}$$

where θ_k denotes the current timing offset (bias), and ρ_k is the instantaneous clock drift. We assume a constant drift model with additive noise, leading to the following linear time-invariant state transition:

$$\mathbf{x}_{k+1} = \mathbf{A}\mathbf{x}_k + \mathbf{w}_k, \quad \mathbf{A} = \begin{bmatrix} 1 & \Delta t \\ 0 & 1 \end{bmatrix}, \tag{4}$$

where Δt is the polling interval, and $\mathbf{w}_k \sim \mathcal{N}(\mathbf{0}, \mathbf{Q})$ is the process noise with covariance matrix $\mathbf{Q}$.

The observed measurement y_k is the estimated offset derived from authenticated NTP exchanges. The observation model is:

$$y_k = \mathbf{H}\mathbf{x}_k + v_k, \quad \mathbf{H} = \begin{bmatrix} 1 & 0 \end{bmatrix}, \quad v_k \sim \mathcal{N}(0, R_k), \tag{5}$$

where v_k represents the measurement noise, and R_k is dynamically adjusted based on observed asymmetry.

Kalman Filter Update Procedure. Given the state estimate $\hat{\mathbf{x}}_{k|k}$ and covariance matrix $\mathbf{P}_{k|k}$ at time step k, the Kalman filter performs the following computations for time step $k+1$:

Prediction Step:

$$\hat{\mathbf{x}}_{k+1|k} = \mathbf{A}\hat{\mathbf{x}}_{k|k}, \tag{6}$$

$$\mathbf{P}_{k+1|k} = \mathbf{A}\mathbf{P}_{k|k}\mathbf{A}^\top + \mathbf{Q}. \tag{7}$$

Measurement Update (Correction) Step:

$$K_{k+1} = \mathbf{P}_{k+1|k}\mathbf{H}^\top(\mathbf{H}\mathbf{P}_{k+1|k}\mathbf{H}^\top + R_{k+1})^{-1}, \tag{8}$$

$$\hat{\mathbf{x}}_{k+1|k+1} = \hat{\mathbf{x}}_{k+1|k} + K_{k+1}\left(y_{k+1} - \mathbf{H}\hat{\mathbf{x}}_{k+1|k}\right), \tag{9}$$

$$\mathbf{P}_{k+1|k+1} = (\mathbf{I} - K_{k+1}\mathbf{H})\mathbf{P}_{k+1|k}. \tag{10}$$

Here, K_{k+1} is the Kalman gain, balancing model prediction against measurement confidence. $\hat{\mathbf{x}}_{k+1|k+1}$ is the updated state estimate, and $\mathbf{P}_{k+1|k+1}$ is the updated estimation uncertainty.

Dynamic Noise Covariance Adjustment via Asymmetry. To account for network asymmetry during NTP exchanges, we define an asymmetry metric:

$$\text{Asym}_k = \left|(T_2 - T_1) - (T_4 - T_3)\right|, \tag{11}$$

where T_1 to T_4 are the four standard NTP timestamps. The measurement noise covariance R_k is then dynamically adjusted as:

$$R_k = R_0 + \lambda \cdot \text{Asym}_k^2, \tag{12}$$

where R_0 is the baseline noise level, and λ is a scaling factor that controls sensitivity to asymmetry. This dynamic adjustment reduces overconfidence in samples with high delay skew and prevents instability in the update step.

In implementation, the filter runs independently for each trusted NTS server and aggregates bias estimates using a weighted scheme. The gain evolution, innovation residual, and filtered bias trajectory are continuously monitored to detect anomalies. If the gain exhibits sudden amplification correlated with rising asymmetry, or residuals exceed a statistical threshold, a peer re-selection process is triggered to replace unstable servers.

The Kalman filter acts as an adaptive bias estimator that integrates time series samples under uncertainty. By incorporating both physical delay asymmetry and measurement consistency into the filter logic, the system achieves improved synchronization accuracy and effective suppression of delay-based attacks under adversarial network conditions.

Steady-State Monitoring and Attack Detection. Over time, the Kalman filter converges toward a steady-state bias estimate. We track the rate of change in estimated bias, innovation residuals, and the gain vector to monitor abnormal behavior. In particular:

- Sudden gain amplification or innovation spikes may signal a delay injection attack.
- Persistently skewed asymmetry metrics across multiple servers suggest coordinated manipulation.
- In such cases, the client triggers peer reselection and re-weights the sample pool, preferring servers with minimal asymmetry and stable bias contributions.

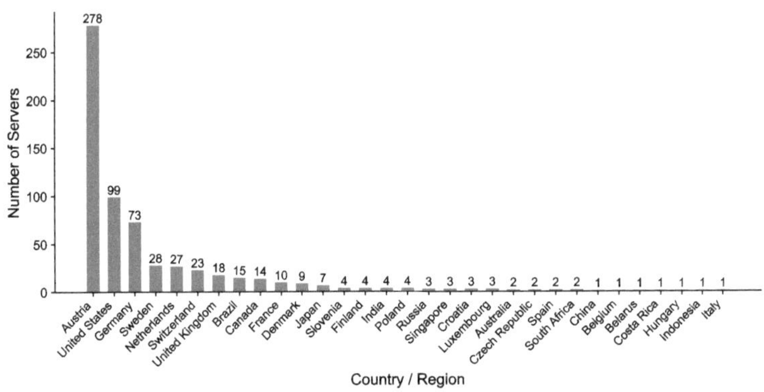

Fig. 3. NTS-KE server country/region distribution

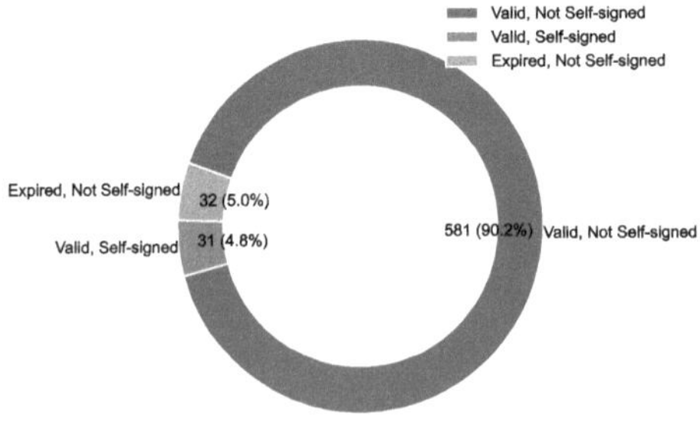

Fig. 4. NTS-KE server TLS certificate status distribution

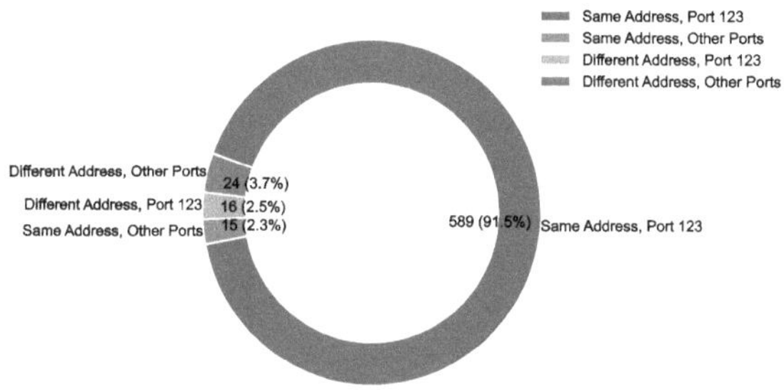

Fig. 5. Negotiated NTPv4 address distribution

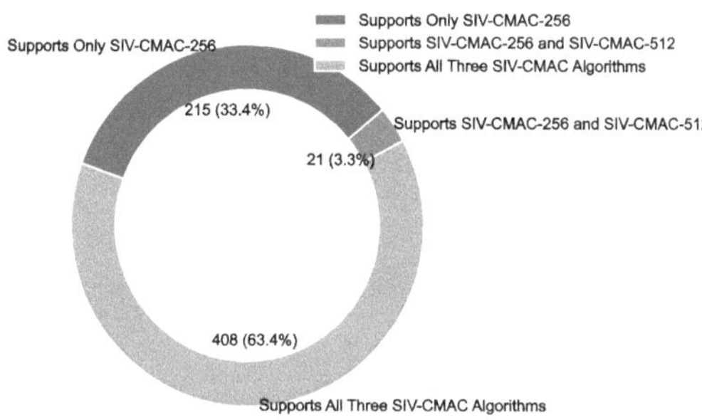

Fig. 6. AEAD algorithm support

This filter-based attack detection mechanism enables the Tychron client to proactively suppress the influence of adversarial samples without rejecting synchronization entirely.

Summary. Our multi-sample synchronization scheme enhances the traditional NTP model by introducing redundancy, intelligent filtering, and model-driven bias correction. The integration of Kalman filtering with real-time delay asymmetry tracking enables effective resistance against stealthy manipulation while maintaining high accuracy under benign conditions. This pipeline serves as the core of the Tychron client implementation and underpins our experimental evaluation in Sect. 4.

4 Experimental Evaluation

To validate the practical benefit of the proposed framework we carry out a focused experimental campaign that centers on **(i)** the current state of public NTS deployments and **(ii)** the end-to-end performance of **Tychron** in comparison with two widely-used secure NTP clients, `Chrony 4.5` and `NTPsec 1.2.3`. Only the seven experiments that are the most relevant to the delay-aware multi-sample design are reported here; all other micro-benchmarks are omitted for brevity.

1. Section 4.1 summarises the *NTS-KE server property analysis*;
2. Section 4.2 presents the *quality assessment of authenticated time sources*;
3. Section 4.3 quantifies the *effectiveness of Kalman filtering*;
4. Section 4.4 compares *server-side load* generated by different clients;

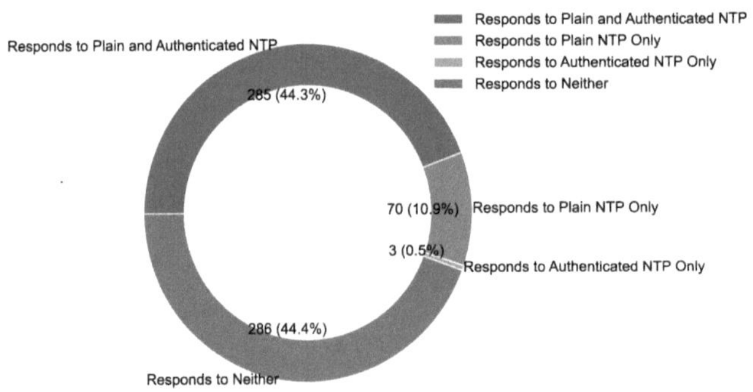

Fig. 7. Types of time synchronization service support

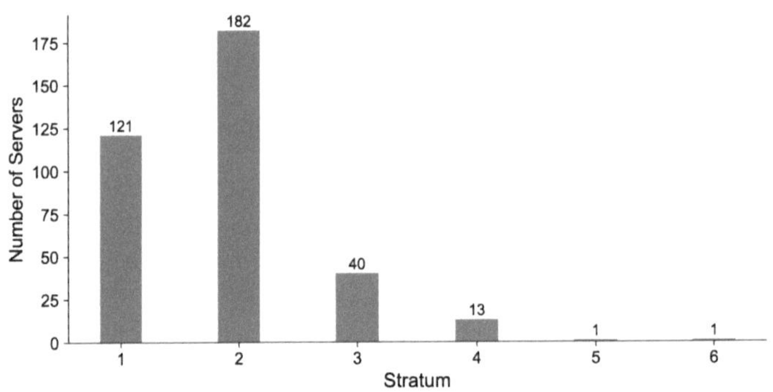

Fig. 8. NTS NTPv4 server stratum distribution

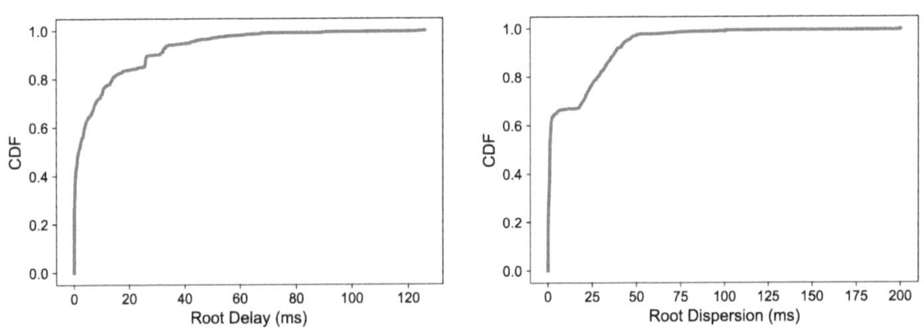

(a) CDF of root delay

(b) CDF of root dispersion

Fig. 9. NTS NTPv4 server root delay and dispersion distribution

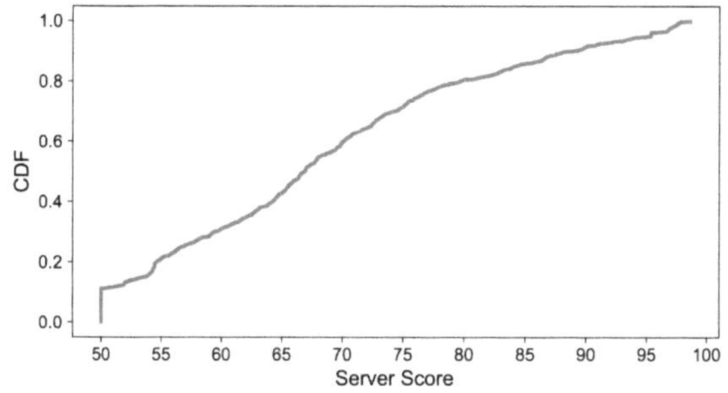

Fig. 10. NTS NTPv4 server score distribution

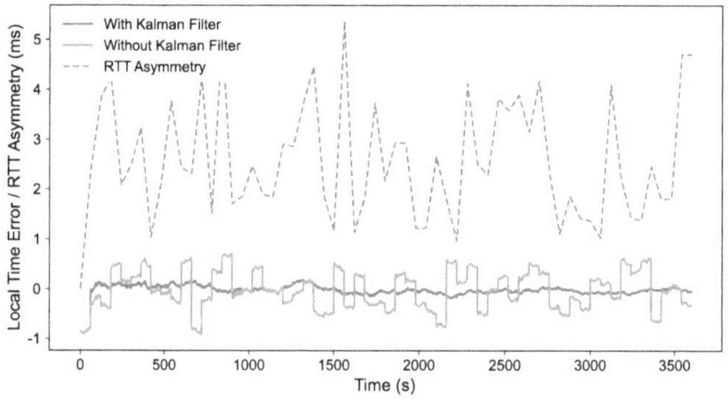

Fig. 11. Effects of Kalman filtering in time-delay disturbance environment

5. Section 4.5 contrasts their *timing accuracy*;
6. Section 4.6 evaluates *temporal smoothness*;
7. Section 4.7 studies *delay-attack resilience.*

4.1 NTS-KE Server Property Analysis

A four-stage active scan over the entire IPv4 address space reveals **644** publicly reachable NTS-KE endpoints. Country/region distribution is heavily skewed (Austria alone contributes 43.2%; Fig. 3), and only **358** of the hosts return a usable `NTPv4` address after the TLS handshake.

Figure 4 shows that more than 90% of the detected servers present a certificate that chains to a system CA, whereas 5% exhibit expired certificates and 4.8% rely on self-signed ones—both categories introduce a potential man-in-the-middle risk. Deployment diversity is further illustrated in Fig. 5: most operators co-locate NTS and NTP on port 123, while fewer than 10% adopt a split-port configuration. On the cryptographic side, Fig. 6 indicates that `AEAD_AES_SIV_CMAC_256` dominates, yet nearly 60% of servers already support the full SIV-CMAC family, suggesting a healthy trend towards multi-cipher compatibility. Finally, Fig. 7 reveals that about 44% of advertised NTP addresses are

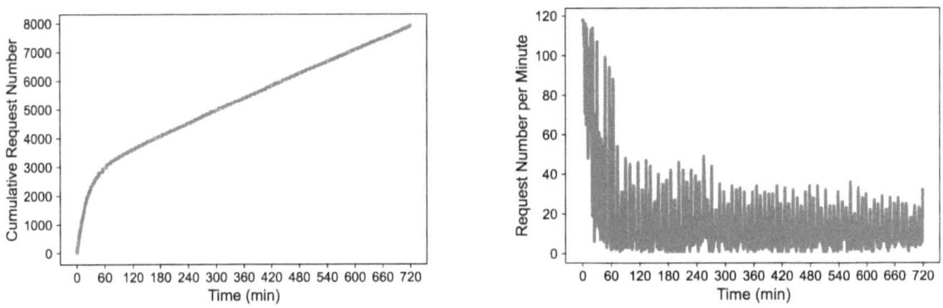

(a) Cumulative number of requests from Chrony over time

(b) Number of requests per minute from Chrony

Fig. 12. Server load situation of Chrony

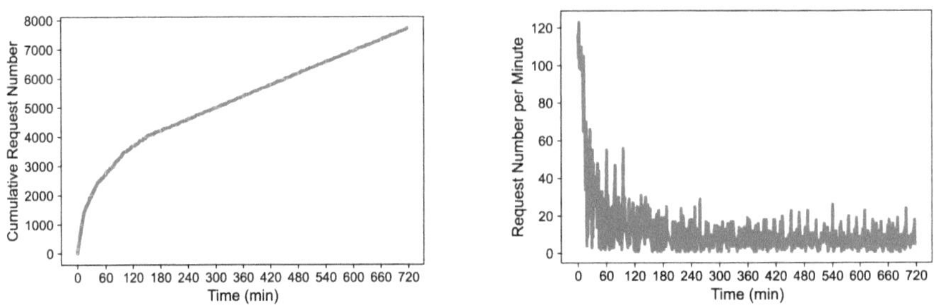

(a) Cumulative number of requests from NTPsec over time

(b) Number of requests per minute from NTPsec

Fig. 13. Server load situation of NTPsec

actually unreachable, underscoring the importance of in-band liveliness checks before a client decides to trust a peer.

4.2 Quality of Authenticated Time Sources

After discarding the inaccessible endpoints we analyse the **358** functional servers from three orthogonal angles:

Stratum Composition. Figure 8 shows that Stratum-1 and Stratum-2 nodes account for 33.8% and 50.8%, respectively, a significantly higher top-tier ratio than that of the generic NTP ecosystem.

Path Stability. The cumulative distributions of `RootDelay` and `RootDispersion` (Fig. 9a and Fig. 9b) indicate that roughly two-thirds of the hosts keep both metrics below 5 ms and 2 ms, respectively.

Composite Scoring. Using the weighting scheme of Sect. 3.1, every server obtains a score in the range [50, 100]. The CDF in Fig. 10 confirms that high and low

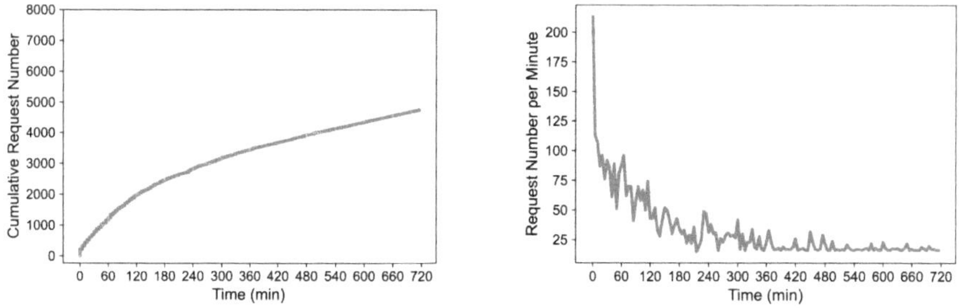

(a) Cumulative number of requests from Tychron over time

(b) Number of requests per minute from Tychron

Fig. 14. Server load situation of Tychron

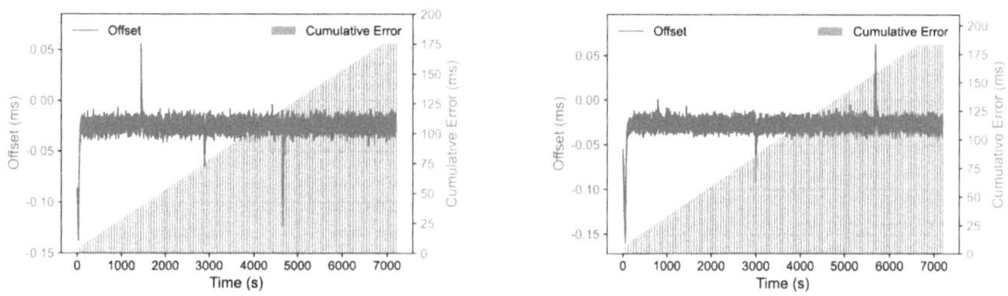

(a) Offset variation and cumulative error of Chrony

(b) Offset variation and cumulative error of NTPsec

Fig. 15. Timing error of Chrony and NTPsec in the ideal environment

performers are clearly separable, providing a solid basis for Tychron's weighted peer-selection logic.

4.3 Kalman Filter Effectiveness

We deploy two Tychron instances on the same host—one with the Kalman module enabled, the other with it disabled—and inject controlled RTT asymmetry that fluctuates between 0 ms to 8 ms. Figure 11 plots the resulting system offset. With Kalman support, the time error stays within ± 0.3 ms even when the asymmetry peaks; without it, the offset exhibits millisecond-level swings. The gain suppression triggered by the rising asymmetry (ε) ensures that contaminated samples are down-weighted in near real-time, validating the model design of Sect. 3.2.

4.4 Server-Side Load Comparison

Three clients—Chrony, NTPsec, and Tychron—are run for twelve hours against the same set of high-score NTS servers; all traffic is captured via `Wireshark`. As

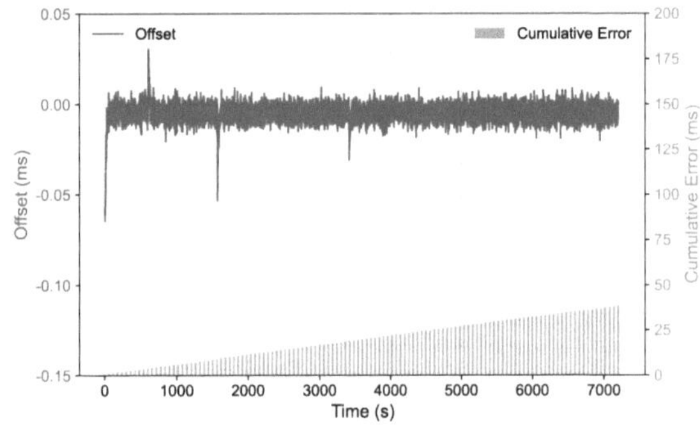

Fig. 16. Timing error of Tychron in the ideal environment

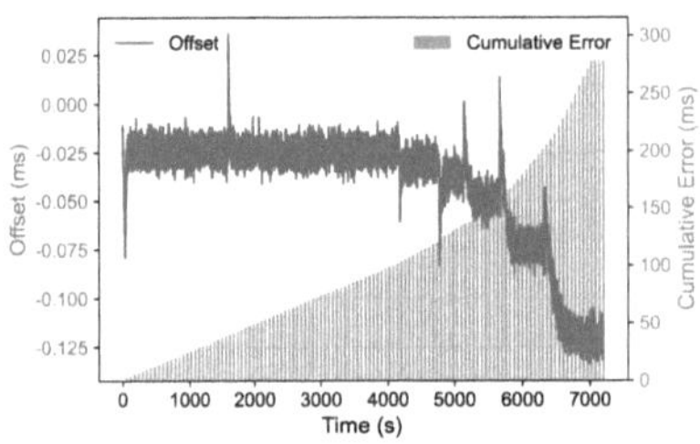

(a) Offset variation and cumulative error of Chrony

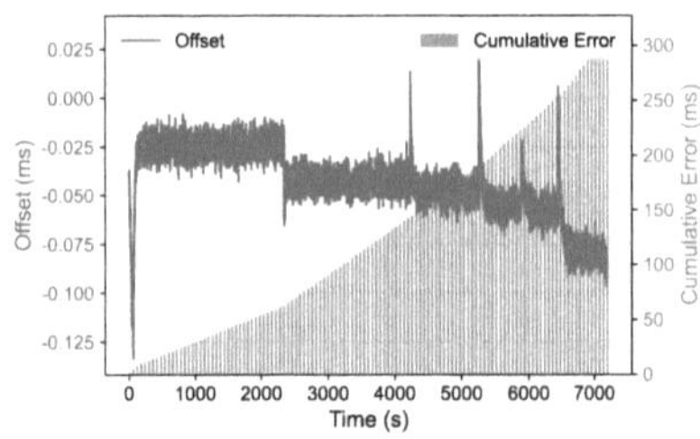

(b) Offset variation and cumulative error of NTPsec

Fig. 17. Timing error of Chrony and NTPsec in the degraded environment

depicted in Fig. 12, Fig. 13, and Fig. 14, both Chrony and NTPsec stabilise at about 11 requests/minute after an aggressive start-up probing phase. Tychron, in contrast, averages only **6.63** requests/minute thanks to its five-minute cyclical polling design, while still maintaining comparable (indeed, higher—see below) timing precision. The lower per-server footprint is particularly valuable in large-scale deployments where fairness matters.

4.5 Timing Accuracy Comparison

Accuracy is quantified by the absolute error with respect to an in-house Stratum-1 reference (S_U). Three network scenarios are considered:

- **Ideal LAN.** Tychron's cumulative error is only 42.8 ms, whereas Chrony and NTPsec accumulate 182.8 ms and 199.3 ms, respectively (Fig. 15a, Fig. 15b, and Fig. 16).
- **Degraded LAN.** When packet loss and small random delays are introduced, Tychron keeps the total error below 80 ms (Fig. 18), roughly one quarter of its competitors (Fig. 17a, Fig. 17b).

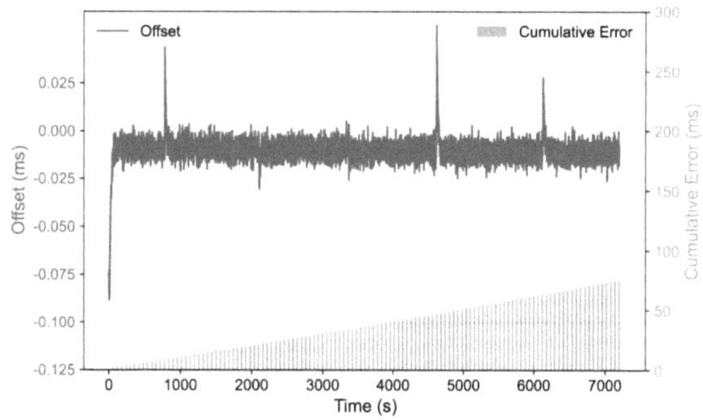

Fig. 18. Timing error of Tychron in the degraded environment

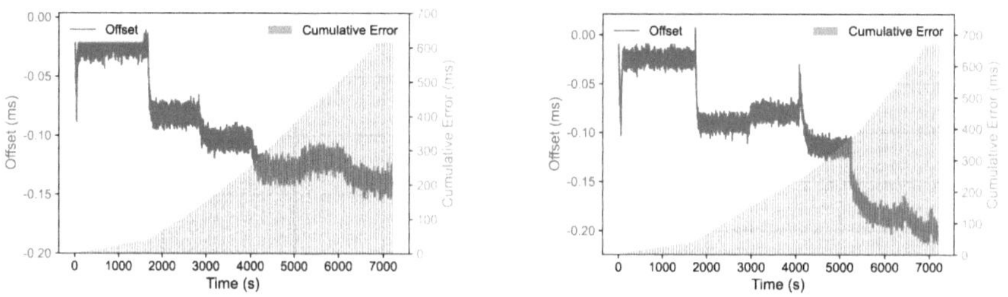

(a) Offset variation and cumulative error of Chrony

(b) Offset variation and cumulative error of NTPsec

Fig. 19. Timing error of Chrony and NTPsec in the real environment

- **Real Internet.** Over a six-hour Wi-Fi session (Wuhan, China, 100 Mbps uplink), Tychron's error sums to 152.9 ms (Fig. 20), whereas Chrony and NTPsec exceed 660 ms and 720 ms (Fig. 19).

4.6 Temporal Smoothness Comparison

Temporal smoothness is evaluated through the distribution of successive offset changes $|\Delta\theta|$. CDFs in Fig. 21 and Fig. 22 show that Tychron has the steepest ascent in every environment: more than 90% of its updates are smaller than 0.02 ms; the competing clients exhibit heavier tails, especially under real-world churn and during delay attacks.

4.7 Delay-Attack Resilience Comparison

The attack testbed involves ten adversarial servers that inject Gaussian, linear, or intermittent extra delay on the server-to-client leg. Chrony and NTPsec eventually drift by ~ -5 ms with cumulative errors above 11 s (Fig. 23). Tychron confines the peak error to below 0.4 ms and limits the cumulative offset to 1071.2 ms

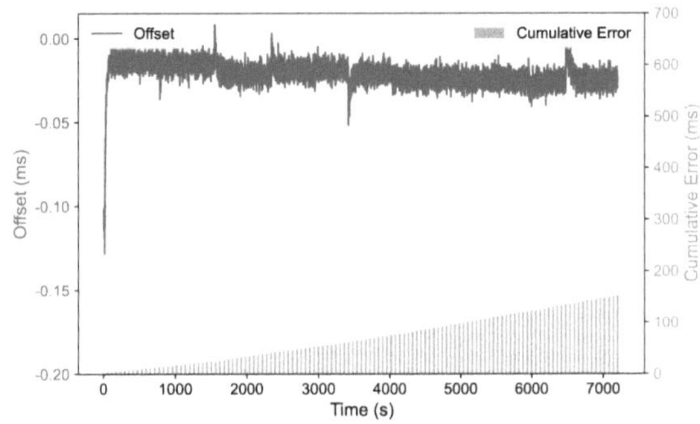

Fig. 20. Timing error of Tychron in the real environment

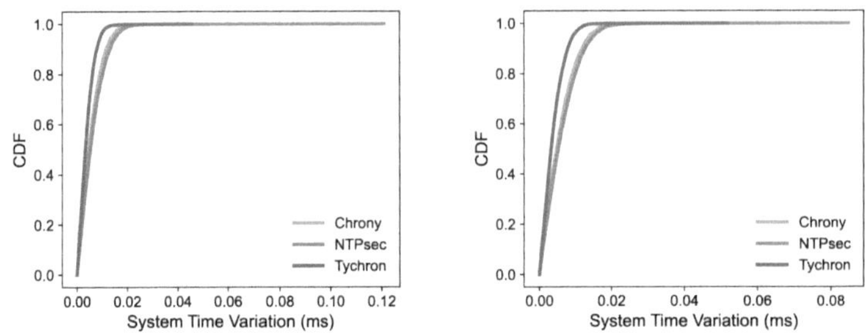

(a) Distribution of time variation in the ideal environment

(b) Distribution of time variation in the degraded environment

Fig. 21. Distribution of time variation of different NTP clients in ideal and degraded environments

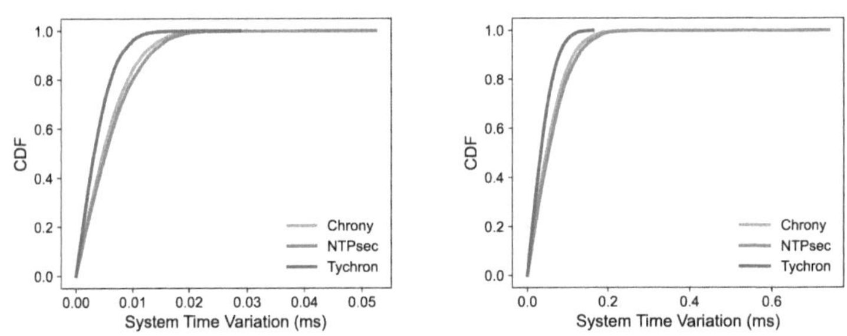

(a) Distribution of time variation in the real environment

(b) Distribution of time variation under delay attacks

Fig. 22. Distribution of time variation of different NTP clients in real and delay-attack environments

(Fig. 24). Disabling the Kalman module multiplies this error by a factor of four (Fig. 25), confirming that the asymmetry-aware state filter is critical for security.

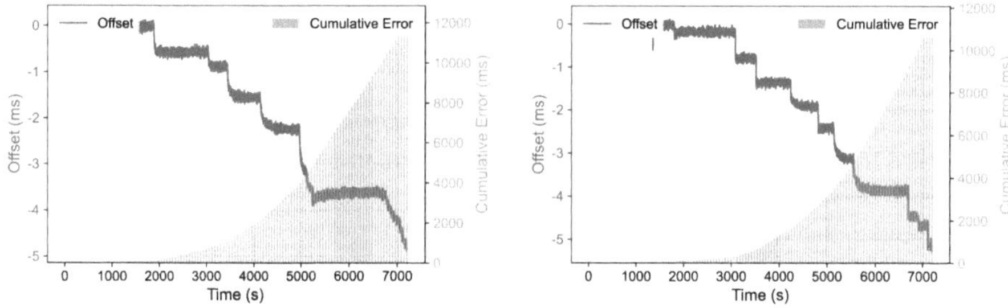

(a) Offset variation and cumulative error of Chrony

(b) Offset variation and cumulative error of NTPsec

Fig. 23. Timing error of Chrony and NTPsec under delay attacks

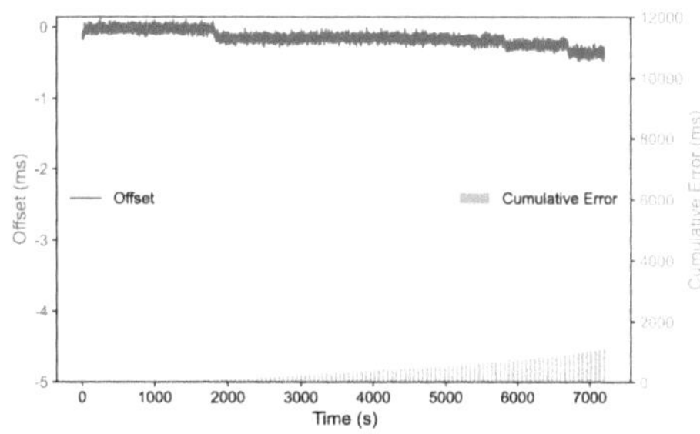

Fig. 24. Timing error of Tychron under delay attacks

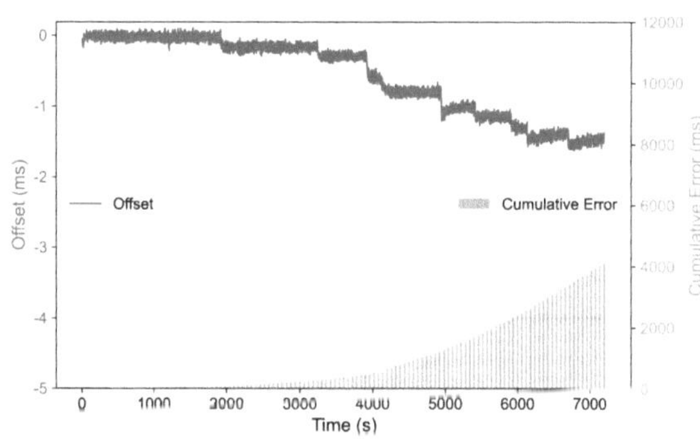

Fig. 25. Timing error of Tychron without Kalman filter under delay attacks

4.8 Summary of Findings

- *Public deployment.* Less than 400 NTS servers currently provide fully functional, certificate-backed authenticated time; yet a sizeable subset already demonstrates Stratum-1 quality and low path jitter.

- *Kalman advantage.* The adaptive filter reduces offset variance by an order of magnitude under asymmetric delay and is instrumental in mitigating delay attacks.
- *Resource friendliness.* Tychron cuts the per-server query rate nearly in half relative to Chrony/NTPsec, without compromising accuracy.
- *Overall performance.* Across all metrics—accuracy, smoothness, and attack resilience—Tychron consistently outperforms the two state-of-practice Secure-NTP clients.

5 Conclusion

This work presents a comprehensive framework to enhance the precision and security of NTP time synchronization in the presence of Network Time Security. Our contributions span from global-scale measurement and infrastructure construction to client-side algorithm design and robust delay-resilient synchronization. The major accomplishments of this research can be summarized as follows:

- We design and implement a high-concurrency NTS server discovery framework that actively scans the entire IPv4 address space. Using semaphore-based concurrency control and batched handshake parallelism, the system extracts key server attributes including certificate status, cryptographic suite support, and synchronization quality. A multidimensional scoring model incorporating availability, root distance, and stratum hierarchy is constructed to filter high-quality servers. The resulting public NTS server pool provides a solid foundation for secure time synchronization at scale.
- We develop **Tychron**, a custom NTS client that integrates a five-stage sample processing pipeline: polling, clock filtering, peer selection, sample clustering, and weighted combining. This design enables redundancy-aware fusion of authenticated timestamps from heterogeneous peers. By balancing sample quality and network load, the system improves resistance to jitter while maintaining temporal smoothness and accuracy.
- To mitigate asymmetric delay-induced bias, we introduce a Kalman filter that models both clock offset and local drift as a unified state vector. The measurement noise covariance is dynamically adjusted using real-time estimates of round-trip delay asymmetry. When abnormal gain suppression or skewed delay metrics are detected, the system proactively triggers peer reselection to suppress long-term drift. This approach significantly enhances synchronization resilience under delay attacks.
- We implement a reproducible experimental platform and conduct extensive evaluations comparing Tychron against Chrony and NTPsec. Experiments cover global NTS deployment profiling, scoring model verification, timing accuracy, temporal smoothness, and attack resilience. Results show that Tychron achieves superior accuracy and stability while maintaining lower polling overhead and stronger resistance to asymmetric manipulation.

While the proposed architecture significantly improves NTS-based time synchronization, several open problems remain and suggest directions for future work. First, a federated public NTS server pool akin to the NTP Pool could be developed, requiring lightweight registration, supervisory quality control, and DNS-based traffic steering under encrypted transport. Second, Tychron's peer evaluation may benefit from adaptive models incorporating additional features (such as `precision` or link jitter), or reinforcement and heuristic optimization strategies like genetic algorithms for dynamic scoring. Third, considering the bandwidth overhead of NTS, hybrid synchronization schemes could be introduced, using full authentication only for key samples and lightweight methods for supplementary data under acceptable threat models. Lastly, integration with Precision Time Protocol (PTP) is a promising direction: co-deployment of NTS-NTP and PTP may yield both high accuracy and strong security, especially when supported by hierarchical synchronization and mutual cross-validation in heterogeneous infrastructures.

Acknowledgements. This research is supported in part by National Natural Science Foundation of China No. 62172310, and Hubei Natural Science Foundation No. 2022CFB309.

References

1. Bhaskar, R.: A day in the life of NTP: analysis of NTPPool traffic. Master's thesis, University of Twente, Enschede (2022)
2. Carroll, J.R., Lackner, C., Robertson, F.R., Murphy, S.: Using streaming telemetry transport protocol to send time synchronized real time data at scale. In: 2024 International Conference on Smart Grid Synchronized Measurements and Analytics (SGSMA), pp. 1–6 (2024)
3. Jeitner, P., Shulman, H., Waidner, M.: Pitfalls of provably secure systems in internet the case of Chronos-NTP. In: 2020 50th Annual IEEE-IFIP International Conference on Dependable Systems and Networks-Supplemental Volume (DSN-S), pp. 49–50. IEEE (2020)
4. Jiang, W., Ge, S.S., Ji, R., Li, D.: Time-synchronized control with the least upper bound of fixed settling time. J. Autom. Intell. (2025)
5. Kwon, J., Song, J., Hur, J., Perrig, A.: Did the shark eat the watchdog in the NTP pool? Deceiving the NTP pool's monitoring system. In: 32nd USENIX Security Symposium, pp. 6151–6166 (2023)
6. Lamshöft, K., Dittmann, J.: Covert channels in network time security. In: Proceedings of the 2022 ACM Workshop on Information Hiding and Multimedia Security (IH&MMSec), pp. 69–79. Association for Computing Machinery, New York (2022)
7. Langer, M., Bermbach, R., Teichel, K., Sibold, D.: Performance comparison between network time security protocol drafts: improvements and accuracy of the latest NTS draft. In: 2019 Joint Conference of the IEEE International Frequency Control Symposium and European Frequency and Time Forum (EFTF/IFC), pp. 1–7. IEEE (2019)
8. Li, D., Yu, H., Tee, K.P., Wu, Y., Ge, S.S., Lee, T.H.: On time-synchronized stability and control. IEEE Trans. Syst. Man Cybern.: Syst. **52**(4), 2450–2463 (2022)

9. Machizawa, A., Iwama, T.: Exponential degrading of NTP synchronization with number of network hops. In: 2013 Joint European Frequency and Time Forum & International Frequency Control Symposium (EFTF/IFC), pp. 97–100. IEEE (2013)
10. Mkacher, F., Duda, A.: Calibrating NTP. In: 2019 IEEE International Symposium on Precision Clock Synchronization for Measurement, Control, and Communication (ISPCS), pp. 1–6. IEEE (2019)
11. Perry, Y., Schiff, N.R., Schapira, M.: A devil of a time: how vulnerable is NTP to malicious timeservers? In: The Network and Distributed System Security Symposium (NDSS) (2021)
12. Rytilahti, T., Tatang, D., Köpper, J., Holz, T.: Masters of time: an overview of the ntp ecosystem. In: 2018 IEEE European Symposium on Security and Privacy (EuroS&P), pp. 122–136. IEEE (2018)
13. Schiff, N.R., Schapira, M., Dolev, D., Deutsch, O.: Preventing (network) time travel with chronos. In: Proceedings of the Applied Networking Research Workshop, pp. 17–17 (2018)
14. Zhang, M., et al.: Talking with familiar strangers: an empirical study on https context confusion attacks. In: Proceedings of the 2020 ACM SIGSAC Conference on Computer and Communications Security (CCS), pp. 1939–1952. Association for Computing Machinery, New York (2020)
15. Zhou, J., Chen, R., Guan, Y.: Cluster-based fast time synchronization for wireless sensor networks. In: Proceedings of the 2024 11th International Conference on Wireless Communication and Sensor Networks (icWCSN), pp. 26–33. Association for Computing Machinery, New York (2024)

SPUAuth: Strengthening Pattern Unlock Authentication with Behavioral Biometrics Against Shoulder Surfing Attacks

Guiyuan Tang[1,2], Zhiwei Zhang[1,3(✉)], and Ning Xi[1,2]

[1] Shaanxi Key Laboratory of Network and System Security, Xidian University, Xi'an 710126, China
tanggy@stu.xidian.edu.cn, {nxi,zwzhang}@xidian.edu.cn
[2] School of Cyber Engineering, Xidian University, Xi'an 710126, Shaanxi, China
[3] School of Computer Science and Technology, Xidian University, Xi'an 710126, Shaanxi, China

Abstract. Pattern unlock is a widely adopted smartphone authentication method due to its high usability and intuitive interaction. However, its vulnerability to shoulder surfing attacks poses a critical security concern. In this paper, we propose SPUAuth, a robust authentication framework designed to defend against such attacks by leveraging fine-grained behavioral biometrics captured through built-in motion sensors. Unlike prior works that treat the unlocking sequence as a unified signal, SPUAuth introduces a sub-gesture modeling mechanism to explicitly represent the structural semantics of pattern input. By identifying turning points in user trajectories, we construct gesture graphs and extract structure-aware features. To enhance discriminability and robustness, we further develop a multimodal time-frequency feature fusion strategy and employ a triplet loss-based deep embedding learning framework. Extensive experiments conducted on both a self-collected dataset and the public H-MOG dataset demonstrate that SPUAuth achieves superior performance across multiple metrics, outperforming existing state-of-the-art methods. Moreover, simulated attack evaluations confirm its effectiveness in resisting both imitation and unseen impersonation attempts, showcasing strong anti-spoofing capabilities and practical robustness.

Keywords: User Authentication · Behavioral Biometrics · Pattern Unlock · Shoulder Surfing Attacks

1 Introduction

Pattern unlock serves as an effective smartphone authentication mechanism by combining intuitive interaction, memorable sequences, and highly customizable designs [16]. However, this graphical interaction modality is highly vulnerable to shoulder surfing attacks [24]. Unlike spoofing or malware-based techniques that demand specialized equipment and technical expertise, shoulder surfing

L. Zhang and K.-K. R. Choo (Eds.): MobiQuitous 2025, LNICST 683, pp. 335–355, 2026.
https://doi.org/10.1007/978-3-032-22500-9_19

can be performed with minimal effort [5]. Attackers may observe the unlocking process directly in crowded public settings (e.g., subways, cafes, classrooms) or record it using concealed cameras. Once the pattern is captured, they can readily reconstruct the unlock sequence and gain access to personal communications, financial accounts, and enterprise applications.

To counter these threats, a common approach is to supplement pattern unlock with physiological biometrics such as fingerprint and facial recognition. While effective in many cases, these methods have inherent limitations. They perform static, one-time verification at the point of entry. Fingerprint sensors are susceptible to moisture, dust, or worn ridges [12], while facial recognition performs poorly in low light, with occlusions, or against adversarial spoofing using photos and videos [11,23]. Critically, if an attacker has already obtained the unlock pattern through shoulder surfing, these static biometrics provide no further protection once the device is unlocked. Early studies focused on enhancing the visual interface to protect surface-level input, for example by obfuscating trajectories [21] or randomizing keypad layouts [7]. While effective to some extent, these methods often degrade user experience. More recently, researchers have shifted toward continuous authentication during the unlock process. This paradigm leverages behavioral signals from built-in motion sensors during pattern drawing to enable implicit identity verification. These methods require no additional hardware and offer high transparency during user interaction.

Despite promising advancements, current solutions still suffer from three major limitations: (1) Most approaches treat the entire unlocking sequence as a monolithic time series, lacking explicit modeling of the structural information inherent in pattern inputs, thereby failing to capture fine-grained individual behavioral differences. (2) Feature extraction is typically confined to the time domain, ignoring rhythm information in the frequency domain and the complementary relationships among multimodal sensor signals, resulting in vulnerability to noise and environmental variability. (3) Most methods are evaluated in constrained environments, which limits their generalizability to real-world, unconstrained user behavior.

To address these limitations, we propose SPUAuth, a robust authentication framework against shoulder surfing attacks. Our approach integrates structural modeling with behavioral feature representation to enhance authentication security and robustness. Specifically, we exploit motion sensor signals recorded during pattern drawing and extract multi-dimensional features encompassing temporal dynamics, frequency characteristics, and gesture structure. These features are then mapped into a unified representation space through a deep embedding learning scheme, which enables the construction of a discriminative and generalizable identity representation.

The main contributions of this paper are summarized as follows:

- We propose SPUAuth, a continuous authentication framework that leverages motion sensor signals from smartphones and requires no external hardware.
- We introduce a sub-gesture modeling mechanism tailored to the structural characteristics of pattern unlocks. By detecting turning points in the input

trajectory, we construct gesture graphs and extract structure-aware features to improve fine-grained behavior modeling.
- We design a multimodal feature fusion strategy that integrates time-frequency representations across sensors, and we adopt a triplet loss-based embedding learning framework to enhance identity discriminability and generalizability.
- We conduct extensive experiments on a self-collected dataset and the public H-MOG dataset. Results demonstrate that SPUAuth outperforms state-of-the-art methods across multiple authentication metrics, showing strong robustness and adaptability.
- We design and implement simulated attack scenarios to evaluate security under adversarial conditions. Experimental results show that SPUAuth effectively resists impersonation attempts and achieves strong anti-spoofing performance.

The rest of this paper is organized as follows: Sect. 2 reviews related work and discusses its limitations. Section 3 presents the threat model and provides an overview of the SPUAuth system architecture. Section 4 introduces the authentication framework. Section 5 presents experimental evaluations and performance analysis. Finally, Sect. 6 concludes with a summary and directions for future research.

2 Related Work

2.1 Shoulder Surfing Defense in Unlocking Systems

Pattern unlock is one of the most popular mechanisms on mobile devices, offering intuitive interaction and low cognitive load for users. However, its strong visual exposure in open environments makes it highly vulnerable to shoulder surfing attacks [29], where attackers can infer the unlock pattern through observation or video recording.

To mitigate this threat, some studies have focused on enhancing the input interface itself. For example, Shin et al. [17] proposed replacing the traditional static grid with a dynamic rotating ring layout, introducing random distortions in the input path to disrupt the observer's visual consistency. Tang et al. [21] developed the Eye-Shield system, which applies real-time blurring to screen content, making it unreadable from non-target viewing angles and thereby providing effective visual protection. However, such methods may negatively impact usability and user acceptance. To reduce user burden and improve stealthiness, Zhou et al. [29] proposed the FingerPattern system, which captures the friction sound produced by the fingertip rubbing against the screen during pattern drawing. Fingerprint-related acoustic features are extracted as an auxiliary authentication factor. Even if the pattern is successfully mimicked, it is still difficult for the attacker to replicate the frictional sound, thus enhancing defense against shoulder surfing. Similarly, Liu et al. [9] proposed SoundID, a system that introduces dynamic acoustic challenges during authentication. By leveraging acoustic propagation characteristics of the device, it constructs a secondary identity factor and improves robustness against imitation. However, such methods may face deployment challenges due to variations in hardware performance, such as microphone and speaker quality. Behavioral biometrics, in contrast, can be captured and modeled at low cost during natural user interactions with the device. Cheon et al. [4] demonstrated the effectiveness of inertial behavioral features during pattern drawing as a secondary authentication factor, achieving strong resistance to video-based shoulder surfing attacks. Cheng et al. [3] further explored the use of high-dimensional physiological signals, such as EEG and eye movement data, to build a multimodal implicit authentication system that can accurately identify attackers during shoulder surfing attempts.

While these methods offer improved resistance to shoulder surfing, many still suffer from limitations in usability or hardware support.

2.2 Behavioral Biometric Authentication on Smartphones

Behavioral biometrics offer a non-intrusive, continuous, and hard-to-replicate means of user authentication. Prior work has explored their use for both explicit and implicit authentication. Their primary advantage lies in enabling real-time identity verification without requiring explicit user input [2].

Sensor-based behavioral authentication typically relies on accelerometers, gyroscopes, and magnetometers to capture user motion dynamics [13]. For example, keystroke dynamics use inertial sensors to learn distinctive typing behaviors [20]. Li et al. [8] proposed a continuous authentication system based on a conditional adversarial autoencoder, trained on user motion captured via accelerometers and gyroscopes. Fereidooni et al. [6] extended this with magnetometer data and used a Siamese network for few-shot learning-based authentication. Touch-based authentication systems use data from touchscreen sensors to analyze user interaction patterns such as swipe velocity, finger position, and touch pressure [14,18]. Given that most modern smartphones are equipped with capacitive touchscreens [15], such methods can be seamlessly integrated into the user experience without requiring extra hardware. AaBy et al. [1] proposed a touch-based authentication scheme that is independent of swipe direction. Zhao et al. [28] developed a user authentication framework based on spatiotemporal touch trajectories, employing hidden Markov models and gradient boosting classifiers to model temporal and spatial features separately. Recognizing the limitations of unimodal sensing, multimodal continuous authentication has been proposed to enhance accuracy and robustness by fusing heterogeneous features. Zhang et al. [26] introduced TouchID, which combines touchscreen gestures and inertial sensor signals to build a multidimensional behavioral representation for user authentication. Similarly, Shen et al. [14] proposed a multimodal authentication framework that integrates diverse behavioral features (e.g., motion patterns, touch dynamics, and environmental context) using a deep one-class classifier. Stylios et al. [19] fused touch gestures and keystroke dynamics at the feature level to enable continuous authentication while balancing security and usability. Zhang et al. [25] also proposed a persistent phone protection scheme by fusing ultrasonic and inertial sensors for anti-theft and gait-based authentication when the user picks up the phone.

Despite significant progress in behavioral biometrics, existing methods have not fully explored or utilized the correlation between behavioral patterns and gesture structures in pattern unlock scenarios.

3 Threat Model and Framework Overview

3.1 Threat Model and Design Goals

This paper focuses on the shoulder surfing threat in the context of pattern unlock, where an attacker attempts to bypass the authentication system by visually observing the user's unlocking process.

We assume that the attacker has strong observational capabilities, enabling them to accurately obtain the graphical pattern through direct observation or smudge-based residue analysis, and subsequently reproduce the unlocking trajectory on the same device.

However, the attacker cannot capture the fine-grained motion behaviors naturally generated by the user during the unlocking process. These behavioral features can typically be captured only in real time by inertial sensors embedded in the device, such as the accelerometers, gyroscopes, and magnetometers. We do not consider stronger threat models such as puppet attacks (in which the attacker physically forces the user to unlock the device) or sensor side-channel attacks (where the attacker has access to historical sensor data or model parameters). Our focus is on the core challenge: given that the attacker has fully obtained the pattern trajectory, how can we reliably distinguish legitimate users from impostors by leveraging the user's unique dynamic behavioral patterns.

To address this threat model, we propose the SPUAuth framework, which is designed with the following goals: (1) it supports an implicit authentication mechanism that is seamlessly embedded into the standard pattern unlock process, requiring no additional user interaction, and (2) it can effectively extract and utilize time-domain inertial features, frequency-domain response features, and sub-gesture transition patterns from motion sensor data during pattern drawing, to distinguish legitimate users from attackers, even when the unlock pattern is precisely known and imitated.

3.2 Overview of SPUAuth

To enhance the robustness of pattern unlock authentication against shoulder surfing attacks, we propose SPUAuth, a behavior-enhanced authentication system leveraging behavioral biometrics. As illustrated in Fig. 1, the system comprises three main components: the feature extraction module, the embedding space training module, and the authentication decision module.

Feature Extraction Module. This module first collects raw motion signals from motion sensors, including accelerometer, gyroscope, and magnetometer data along the X, Y, and Z axes during the pattern unlock process. Considering the inherent structural segmentation of gesture trajectories, we identify

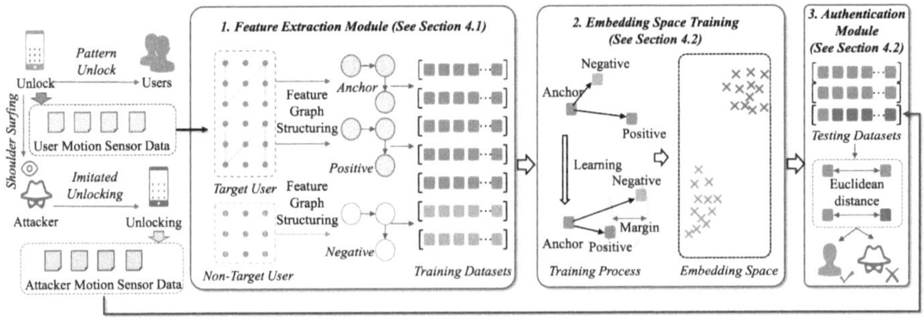

Fig. 1. The overview of SPUAuth.

turning points to divide each pattern gesture into a sequence of sub-gestures. These sub-gestures are then modeled as nodes in a directed gesture graph, where the edges represent the transitions between adjacent sub-gestures, defined by the corresponding turning points. For training, we construct triplets (anchor, positive, negative) using behavioral samples from the target user and non-target users, serving as the foundation for metric learning.

Embedding Space Training Module. This module learns a discriminative embedding space where samples from the same user are pulled together, while those from different users are pushed apart. Training is guided by a semi-hard triplet mining strategy and optimized using a triplet margin loss.

Authentication Decision Module. During authentication, each test sample is projected into the learned embedding space. The system computes its Euclidean distance to the centroid of the target user's training embeddings. A test sample is accepted as legitimate if its distance to the centroid is below a threshold. Otherwise, it is rejected as an impostor.

4 Authentication Framework

4.1 Data Processing and Gesture Representation

We first describe the procedures for data collection and subsequent denoising, followed by the temporal and frequency-domain characterization methods applied to the motion sensor data in SPUAuth.

Data Collection and Denoising. During data collection, the system continuously samples motion sensor signals at a fixed rate f_t. The motion sensor suite includes a tri-axial accelerometer, gyroscope, and magnetometer, which respectively capture the device's linear acceleration (a_x, a_y, a_z), angular velocity $(\omega_x, \omega_y, \omega_z)$, and magnetic field strength (m_x, m_y, m_z), with the smartphone's orientation described by the roll, pitch, and yaw axes shown in Fig. 2. All sensor streams are synchronously recorded during the pattern drawing process to ensure temporal alignment and data consistency.

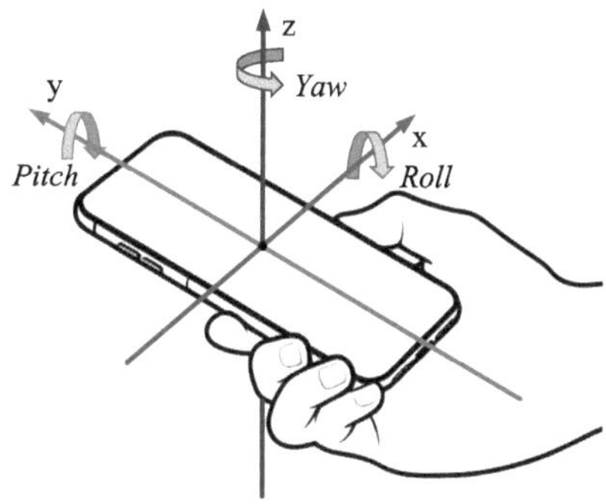

Fig. 2. Smartphone rotation axes illustrating roll, pitch, and yaw.

The system continuously samples motion sensor data during pattern input, and upon detecting a turning point, it retrieves sensor readings surrounding the event from the buffer to construct a temporal window corresponding to the sub-gesture. This strategy captures the complete micro-dynamics surrounding each sub-gesture. The collected raw data for each gesture instance is organized into a 9-dimensional time series vector as follows:

$$\mathcal{S}(t) = [a_x(t), a_y(t), a_z(t), \omega_x(t), \omega_y(t), \omega_z(t), m_x(t), m_y(t), m_z(t)]. \quad (1)$$

In practice, sensor readings are inevitably contaminated by ambient noise and device-specific interference. To mitigate this, we apply a unified wavelet-based denoising procedure to all sensor channels. This technique effectively removes high-frequency noise while preserving essential dynamic characteristics.

Motion Sensor Feature Extraction. After denoising, we augment the raw 9-axis sensor data by computing the total acceleration $a' = \sqrt{a_x^2 + a_y^2 + a_z^2}$ and total angular velocity $g' = \sqrt{\omega_x^2 + \omega_y^2 + \omega_z^2}$, resulting in an 11-dimensional sensor channel set.

For each segmented sub-gesture window, we independently extract a comprehensive set of time-domain and frequency-domain features from each sensor channel to construct a fine-grained behavioral representation. In the time domain, six statistical descriptors are computed: mean, maximum, minimum, variance, signal energy, and autocorrelation, capturing the fundamental characteristics of user motion. In the frequency domain, the power spectral density is estimated using Welch's method [10], from which six additional descriptors are derived: spectral centroid, spectral spread, spectral skewness, spectral kurtosis, mean spectral power, and spectral entropy. All features are computed on a per-channel, per-window basis, ensuring that the dynamic patterns of user interaction are captured across both temporal and spectral dimensions.

Structured Modeling of Gestures. To capture the fine-grained behavioral dynamics during the pattern unlock process, we propose a sub-gesture decomposition and graph-based modeling mechanism. In practical usage, the pattern

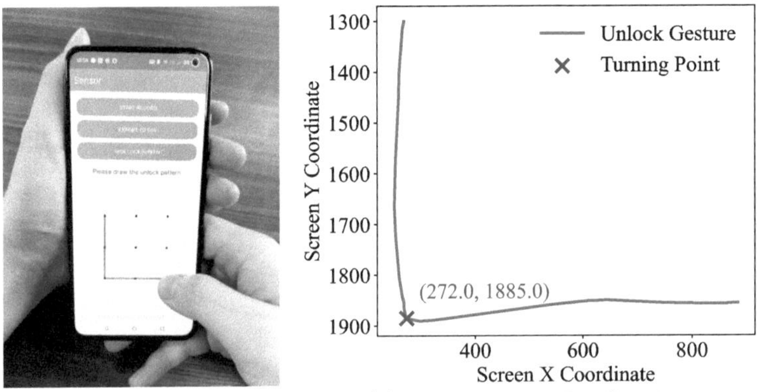

(a) Pattern drawing. (b) Turning point localization.

Fig. 3. Pattern gesture drawing and turning point detection.

unlock gesture is formed by the user's continuous finger movement across the screen, inherently passing through multiple turning points. Figure 3(a) illustrates the process of pattern drawing, while Fig. 3(b) shows the localization of turning points. We introduce a turning point detection method based on curvature extrema. Specifically, given a sequence of raw screen coordinates $\{(x_t, y_t)\}_{t=1}^{\mathcal{T}}$, we first apply a smoothing operation to suppress local jitters:

$$\tilde{x}_t = \frac{1}{w} \sum_{i=t-\lfloor w/2 \rfloor}^{t+\lfloor w/2 \rfloor} x_i, \quad \tilde{y}_t = \frac{1}{w} \sum_{i=t-\lfloor w/2 \rfloor}^{t+\lfloor w/2 \rfloor} y_i, \tag{2}$$

where w denotes the smoothing window size, and $(\tilde{x}_t, \tilde{y}_t)$ is the smoothed coordinate sequence. Based on the smoothed trajectory, for each inner point $t \in [2, \mathcal{T} - 1]$, we construct two motion vectors:

$$\mathbf{v}_t^{pre} = (\tilde{x}_t - \tilde{x}_{t-1},\ \tilde{y}_t - \tilde{y}_{t-1}), \quad \mathbf{v}_t^{post} = (\tilde{x}_{t+1} - \tilde{x}_t,\ \tilde{y}_{t+1} - \tilde{y}_t). \tag{3}$$

The angular response at point t is computed as:

$$\theta_t = \arccos \left(\frac{\langle \mathbf{v}_t^{pre}, \mathbf{v}_t^{post} \rangle}{\|\mathbf{v}_t^{pre}\| \cdot \|\mathbf{v}_t^{post}\|} \right), \tag{4}$$

where $\theta_t \in [0, \pi]$ quantifies the local turning intensity. This produces an angular sequence $\{\theta_t\}_{t=2}^{\mathcal{T}-1}$, from which we extract turning points satisfying both a local maximum condition and a threshold constraint $\theta_t > \eta$. The formal definition of turning points is given as follows:

$$\mathcal{C} = \{t \in [2, \mathcal{T} - 1] \mid \theta_t > \eta,\ \theta_t \ \textit{is a local maximum}\}. \tag{5}$$

Using the turning points as boundaries, the original gesture is segmented into a sequence of sub-gesture windows.

On this basis, we represent the gesture execution as a directed sub-gesture graph $\mathcal{G} = (\mathcal{V}, \mathcal{E})$. Here, $\mathcal{V} = \{v_1, v_2, \ldots, v_N\}$ denotes the set of graph nodes, where each node v_i corresponds to a sub-gesture segment. The edge set $\mathcal{E} = \{e_{i,i+1}\}_{i=1}^{N-1}$ explicitly models the temporal transitions between adjacent sub-gestures.

Each node v_i is associated with a feature vector $\mathcal{F}_i \in \mathbb{R}^d$ extracted from its corresponding motion sensor sequence $\mathcal{S}_i(t) \in \mathbb{R}^{\mathcal{T}\times 11}$ via a feature mapping function:

$$\mathcal{F}_i = \Phi(S_i(t)), \quad \Phi : \mathbb{R}^{\mathcal{T}\times 11} \rightarrow \mathbb{R}^d. \tag{6}$$

To further embed temporal context into each node, we define two directional difference vectors representing the behavioral change trend across adjacent sub-gestures:

$$\delta_i^{(b)} = \begin{cases} \mathbf{0}, & i = 1 \\ \mathcal{F}_{i-1} - \mathcal{F}_i, & otherwise \end{cases}. \tag{7}$$

$$\delta_i^{(a)} = \begin{cases} \mathbf{0}, & i = N \\ \mathcal{F}_i - \mathcal{F}_{i+1}, & otherwise \end{cases}. \tag{8}$$

The final context-aware node representation is constructed as a concatenation of the forward difference, the original node feature, and the backward difference:

$$\mathbf{h}_i = \left[\delta_i^{(b)} \parallel \mathcal{F}_i \parallel \delta_i^{(a)}\right] \in \mathbb{R}^{3d}. \tag{9}$$

This enriched representation not only preserves the local dynamics of each sub-gesture but also explicitly models the behavioral transitions across turning points, enabling a structurally aware understanding of user interaction patterns.

4.2 Embedding Network Architecture

The authentication system is built upon a triplet learning framework, aiming to construct a discriminative embedding space for effectively distinguishing legitimate user interactions from potential impostor behaviors. At its core lies a Residual Multi-Layer Perceptron based embedding network, which is trained using triplet inputs and optimized under a Euclidean distance criterion to facilitate implicit user verification. The system consists of three key components: feature extraction module, distance computation module, and decision-making module.

Feature Extraction. The feature extraction module adopts a weight-shared triple-branch architecture, where each branch processes one of the triplet inputs: anchor, positive, and negative samples. Each input corresponds to a behavioral feature vector derived from the user's pattern unlock activity, with an input dimensionality of d_{in}. Each branch is implemented as a Residual-MLP network. The network first projects the input feature vector into a higher-dimensional latent space via a linear transformation, followed by batch normalization and GELU activation to enhance training stability and nonlinear representation capability. To further deepen the network and improve representational expressiveness, multiple residual blocks are stacked. Each residual block consists of two fully connected layers with batch normalization and GELU activation, and incorporates skip connections to alleviate gradient vanishing. Finally, the output is projected into a fixed-dimensional embedding space and normalized using ℓ_2-norm to constrain the outputs onto a unit hypersphere, which facilitates subsequent distance-based comparisons and triplet loss optimization. Through this module, each raw input feature vector is transformed into a normalized embedding $\mathcal{F} \in \mathbb{R}^d$, characterizing the user's behavior during pattern drawing.

Distance Computation. The distance computation module evaluates the similarity between embedded feature vectors to measure behavioral consistency or divergence. We employ the Euclidean distance as the similarity metric. Specifically, given an anchor embedding $f(\mathcal{A})$, we compute the distances to a positive sample $f(\mathcal{P})$ and a negative sample $f(\mathcal{N})$ as follows:

$$d(\mathcal{A}, \mathcal{P}) = \sqrt{\sum_{i=1}^{n} (f_i(\mathcal{A}) - f_i(\mathcal{P}))^2}, \quad d(\mathcal{A}, \mathcal{N}) = \sqrt{\sum_{i=1}^{n} (f_i(\mathcal{A}) - f_i(\mathcal{N}))^2}, \tag{10}$$

where $f_i(\cdot)$ denotes the i-th element of the embedding vector, and n is the embedding dimensionality. A smaller distance indicates higher similarity in the embedding space, while a larger distance implies greater dissimilarity.

Authentication Decision. The decision module adopts a center-based distance discrimination mechanism. It determines whether an input sample belongs to the target user by measuring its proximity to the user-specific center in the embedding space. During training, we compute the center of all embedding vectors corresponding to the target user's samples, which serves as a representation of the user's behavioral distribution. During testing, the Euclidean distance between each test sample and this center is calculated. A sample is accepted as belonging to the target user if its distance to the center falls below a predefined threshold; otherwise, it is rejected as a potential impostor. This metric-based decision strategy eliminates the need for training an explicit classifier and enables seamless adaptation to new test instances.

4.3 Model Training and Implementation

We adopt an end-to-end training strategy based on Triplet Loss to optimize the authentication model. The objective during training is to encourage embeddings of behavioral samples from the same user to cluster tightly in the feature space, while pushing samples from different users farther apart, thus establishing a discriminative embedding space.

While triplets can be formed by random sampling of anchor-positive-negative tuples, such naive selection often results in poor training efficiency. In particular, easy negatives that are too far from the anchor contribute little to gradient updates, whereas hard negatives that are very close to the anchor may impede convergence and destabilize training. To address this, we employ a semi-hard negative mining strategy. In this scheme, the negative sample $\mathcal{N}^{(i)}$ is chosen such that it lies farther from the anchor $\mathcal{A}^{(i)}$ than the corresponding positive $\mathcal{P}^{(i)}$, yet remains within the margin α:

$$\|f(\mathcal{A}^{(i)}) - f(\mathcal{P}^{(i)})\|_2^2 < \|f(\mathcal{A}^{(i)}) - f(\mathcal{N}^{(i)})\|_2^2 < \|f(\mathcal{A}^{(i)}) - f(\mathcal{P}^{(i)})\|_2^2 + \alpha. \quad (11)$$

This mining strategy effectively balances training difficulty, avoiding both trivial and overly challenging sample pairs, thereby accelerating convergence and enhancing the robustness of the decision boundary. The authentication model is trained using the AdamW optimizer, combined with a cosine annealing scheduler to dynamically adjust the learning rate. During each iteration, triplet samples are organized into mini-batches and fed into the network for forward propagation and loss computation, followed by backpropagation and parameter updates.

We use the triplet margin loss as our training objective, defined as:

$$\mathcal{L}_{\text{triplet}} = \sum_{i=1}^{M} \left[\|f(x_i^a) - f(x_i^p)\|_2^2 - \|f(x_i^a) - f(x_i^n)\|_2^2 + \alpha \right]_+, \quad (12)$$

where $f(\cdot)$ denotes the embedding function, x_i^a, x_i^p, and x_i^n represent the anchor, positive, and negative samples respectively, and α is a margin hyperparameter. The operator $[\cdot]_+$ denotes the ReLU function.

To mitigate overfitting, we apply an early stopping strategy. The model is periodically evaluated on the training set, and training is terminated early if no performance improvement is observed over a fixed number of epochs.

Once training is complete, we compute the mean embedding of all target user samples in the training set to establish a user center in the embedding space. During inference, test samples from both the target user and other users are projected into the same embedding space, and their Euclidean distances to the user center are calculated. Authentication is then performed by comparing these distances against a predefined threshold. Authentication is performed by thresholding these distances. The framework combines supervised triplet-based learning with fine-grained decision boundary modeling, thereby enabling robust identity verification under diverse behavioral conditions.

5 Evaluation

5.1 Experimental Setup

We developed a dedicated Android application to collect multimodal sensor data during the pattern unlock process. The experiments were performed on a Meizu 17 smartphone, which features a 6.6-inch display and 8 GB of RAM. Motion sensor signals were sampled at 60 Hz. A total of 21 volunteers (14 males and 7 females) participated in the study, all of whom were proficient smartphone users.

During the experiment, no constraints were imposed on participants' interactions. Each user performed the pattern unlock task multiple times to simulate natural behavior in real-world usage scenarios. After data collection, the samples were organized according to a user-centric authentication setting: the target user was treated as the positive class, and the remaining users were treated as the negative class. For each user, their data was split into training and testing sets, and separate models were trained for each target user individually. We adopted a leave-one-user-in evaluation strategy, where each user was alternately treated as the legitimate subject. The average performance across all 21 users was reported as the overall evaluation result. To further assess the generalizability and adaptability of the proposed method, we conducted additional experiments on the publicly available H-MOG dataset, which contains motion sensor data during user interactions.

All experiments were implemented in Python and included stages for data preprocessing, time-frequency feature extraction, model training, and performance evaluation. The authentication models were developed using the PyTorch deep learning framework, with auxiliary tools such as NumPy, scikit-learn, and Matplotlib for scientific computing and visualization. All training and evaluation procedures were executed on a high-performance workstation equipped with a 13th-generation Intel Core i9-13900K CPU (24 cores, base frequency 3.00 GHz) and 128 GB DDR5 memory, running 64-bit Windows 10 Professional.

Table 1. Performance comparison of different authentication methods.

Dataset	Method	Performance		
		EER	FAR	FRR
Our Dataset	MMAuth	0.1013	0.1052	0.0976
	TNNAuth	0.1443	0.1694	0.0999
	GSAuth	0.1293	0.1293	0.1293
	SPUAuth	**0.0167**	**0.0168**	**0.0166**
H-MOG	MMAuth	0.1594	0.1601	0.1589
	TNNAuth	0.0921	0.0895	0.1000
	GSAuth	0.1400	0.1433	0.1433
	SPUAuth	**0.0344**	**0.0348**	**0.0340**

5.2 Performance of SPUAuth

In this subsection, we evaluate the overall authentication performance of SPUAuthon both our self-collected dataset and the public H-MOG dataset. We compare our system against three state-of-the-art baseline methods:

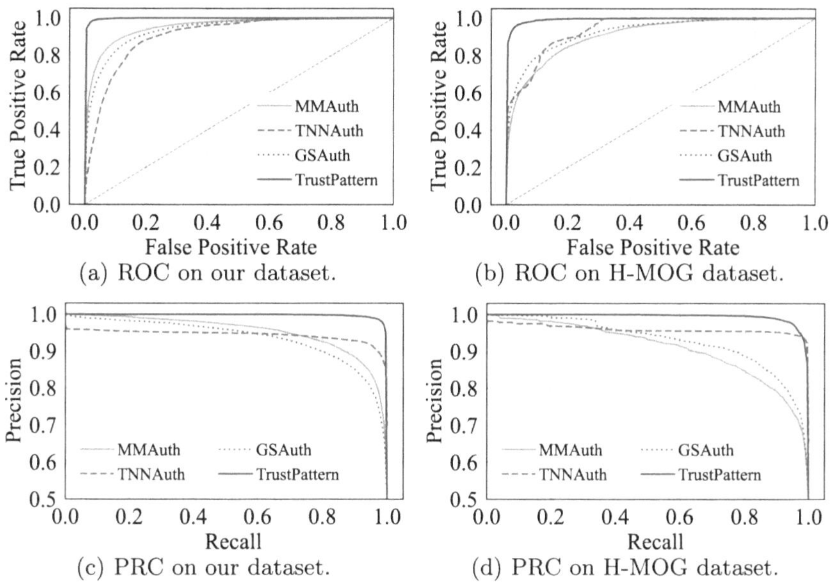

(a) ROC on our dataset. (b) ROC on H-MOG dataset.

(c) PRC on our dataset. (d) PRC on H-MOG dataset.

Fig. 4. ROC and PRC of SPUAuth and all the baselines.

MMAuth [14] leverages multi-modal behavioral features (motion, touch, and usage context) together with a deep one-class classifier to enable robust and continuous user authentication in unconstrained real-world scenarios.

GSAuth [22] proposes a gesture-sensor fusion framework that combines dynamic selection of tapping and swiping gestures with motion sensor data. It uses a one-class classifier to achieve continuous smartphone user authentication.

TNNAuth [27] introduces a smartphone-based continuous authentication system that utilizes multi-sensor behavioral data to support seamless and implicit user verification.

Table 1 reports the performance of all methods in terms of Equal Error Rate (EER), False Acceptance Rate (FAR), and False Rejection Rate (FRR). The results demonstrate that SPUAuth consistently outperforms the baselines across both datasets. In particular, it achieves the lowest EER of 1.67% on our dataset and maintains strong performance on the H-MOG dataset with an EER of 3.44%, surpassing all baseline methods.

Figure 4 illustrates the ROC and PR curves of the evaluated methods on both datasets. The curves of SPUAuth consistently dominate those of the baselines, demonstrating larger Area Under the Curve (AUC) and Average Precision (AP) values. This indicates that SPUAuth maintains high true positive rates while effectively suppressing false alarms.

To further validate the robustness and generalization of SPUAuth, we visualize the authentication accuracy for all methods on both datasets in Fig. 5. The results show that SPUAuth not only maintains high accuracy on the self-collected dataset but also demonstrates strong generalization ability on the H-MOG dataset. Additionally, its performance exhibits low variance across users, suggesting good adaptability to diverse behavioral patterns.

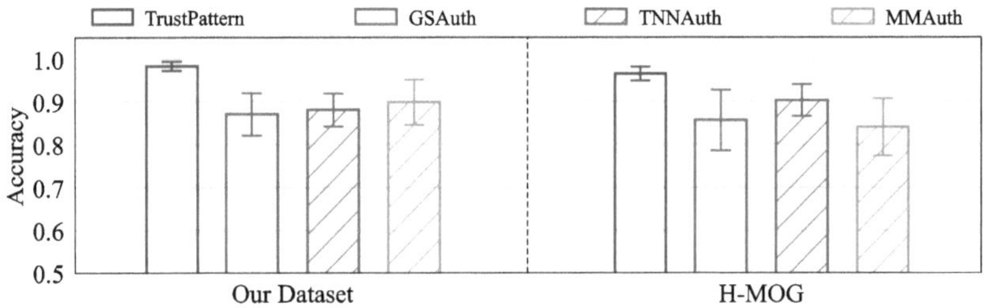

Fig. 5. Performance comparison of SPUAuth and baseline methods on our dataset and the H-MOG dataset.

In summary, SPUAuth delivers superior authentication performance and exhibits strong robustness to inter-user variability as well as unseen scenarios.

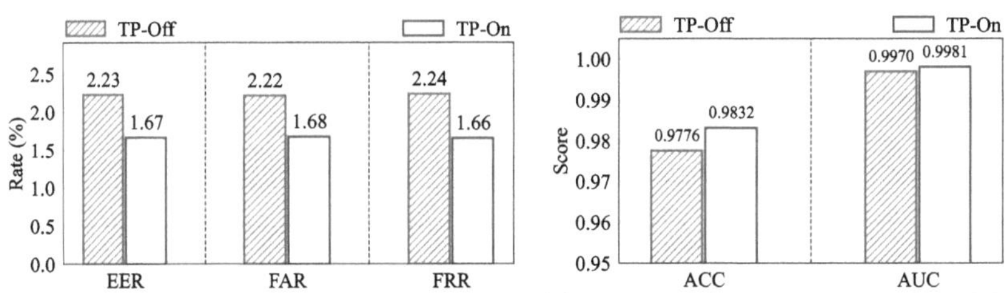

(a) Impact of turning point on EER, FAR, and FRR.

(b) Impact of turning point on ACC and AUC.

Fig. 6. Effect of turning point on authentication performance.

5.3 Component Evaluation

Effectiveness of Turning Point Integration. To evaluate the necessity of incorporating turning point (TP) features in sub-gesture modeling, we conducted a controlled experiment by comparing two settings: enabling turning point features (TP-On) versus disabling them (TP-Off), while keeping all other model structures and training procedures identical. Figure 6 presents the comparative results across five key authentication metrics: EER, FAR, FRR, ACC, and AUC.

As shown in Fig. 6(a), under the TP-Off configuration, the model exhibits noticeably degraded performance in all three error-related metrics. The average error rates are more than 0.5% higher than those under the TP-On setting.

Figure 6(b) further illustrates improvements in accuracy and area under the ROC curve, indicating that the inclusion of turning point information significantly improves the discriminability between sub-gestures and enhances the system's sensitivity to behavioral variations. Overall, turning points are not redundant components in sub-gesture modeling but serve as critical behavioral landmarks within a user's motion trajectory. By constructing differential representations between adjacent sub-gestures around each turning point, the model more effectively captures shifts in behavioral inertia, thus enhancing the accuracy and robustness of user authentication.

Table 2. Performance of different sensor modality combinations.

[0.8pt] ID	Feature Modality			Metric		
	Acc.	Gyr.	Mag.	EER	FAR	FRR
[0.8pt] **A**	√	×	×	0.0992	0.0984	0.1000
G	×	√	×	0.1444	0.1434	0.1454
M	×	×	√	0.0483	0.0487	0.0479
AG	√	√	×	0.0736	0.0723	0.0749
AM	√	×	√	0.0233	0.0235	0.0231
GM	×	√	√	0.0392	0.0389	0.0396
AGM	√	√	√	0.0167	0.0168	0.0166

Impact of Sensor Modality Combinations. To investigate the impact of different sensor modality combinations on authentication performance, we conducted a set of controlled experiments. Specifically, we evaluated the effectiveness of individual modalities—accelerometer (A), gyroscope (G), and magnetometer (M)—as well as their various pairwise and full combinations (AG, AM, GM, and AGM). All experiments were conducted under consistent model architectures and training protocols, with only the input features being varied.

As observed from Table 2 and the ROC and DET curves in Fig. 7(a)–(b), the tri-modal combination AGM consistently outperforms all other configurations across evaluation metrics, demonstrating superior discriminability and error robustness. Figure 7(c)–(d) further illustrates the trends in accuracy, equal error rate, average precision, and F1 score across different modality settings. Overall, unimodal methods show inferior performance and less stability compared with multimodal configurations.

To further examine the distribution of false acceptance and false rejection rates, boxplots for each configuration are presented in Fig. 7(e)–(f). The results indicate that the AGM configuration yields the most concentrated error distributions with the smallest variance, suggesting more reliable and stable authentication behavior across users and samples. In comparison, unimodal settings exhibit greater variance and a higher incidence of outliers.

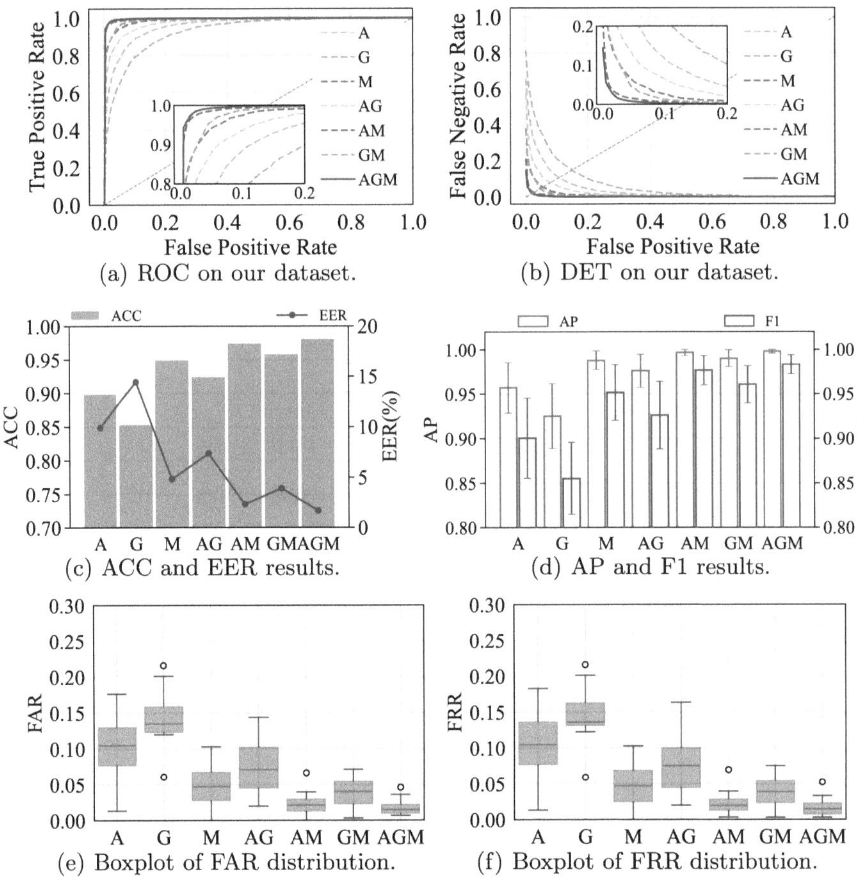

(a) ROC on our dataset.
(b) DET on our dataset.
(c) ACC and EER results.
(d) AP and F1 results.
(e) Boxplot of FAR distribution.
(f) Boxplot of FRR distribution.

Fig. 7. Performance comparison of sensor modality combinations on authentication metrics.

Overall, these results confirm the effectiveness of multimodal fusion in enhancing authentication performance. The three motion sensors capture complementary aspects of user interaction, enabling the system to model behavioral nuances across multiple physical dimensions.

Impact of Training Data Size and Number of Gestures. To investigate the impact of training sample size and the number of authentication gestures on system performance, we conducted a series of systematic experiments. During training, different quantities of samples from the target user (ranging from 100 to 500) were used. During testing, we varied the number of gesture segments from 1 to 5 and adopted a sliding-window voting strategy to aggregate sub-gesture predictions into a final authentication decision.

Figure 8(a)–(c) present the authentication performance in terms of ACC, AUC, and EER under different training and testing configurations. Overall, as

Number of Gestures \ Number of Training Gestures	100	200	300	400	500
1	0.8795	0.8813	0.9608	0.9629	0.9678
2	0.8788	0.8812	0.9621	0.9626	0.9676
3	0.954	0.9547	0.9943	0.9956	0.9968
4	0.9562	0.9557	0.9936	0.9962	0.9973
5	0.9828	0.9828	0.9983	0.9988	0.9991

(a) ACC across gesture counts and training sizes (higher is better).

Number of Gestures					
1	0.8795	0.8813	0.9608	0.9629	0.9678
2	0.9538	0.9549	0.9944	0.9949	0.9961
3	0.9799	0.9807	0.9988	0.9991	0.9994
4	0.991	0.991	0.9997	0.9998	0.9999
5	0.9959	0.9959	0.9999	0.9999	0.9999

(b) AUC across gesture counts and training sizes (higher is better).

Number of Gestures					
1	0.1204	0.1186	0.0391	0.037	0.0321
2	0.1209	0.1173	0.0377	0.0365	0.0314
3	0.0459	0.0452	0.0056	0.0043	0.0031
4	0.0431	0.0427	0.0047	0.0029	0.0019
5	0.0171	0.0171	0.0015	0.001	0.0008

(c) EER across gesture counts and training sizes (lower is better).

Fig. 8. Heatmaps of authentication performance across training and authentication gesture counts.

the number of training samples increases, the model's generalization capability improves steadily, resulting in enhanced authentication performance. Meanwhile, incorporating more gesture segments during the authentication stage significantly reduces recognition errors through temporal voting aggregation.

Furthermore, we observe that increasing the number of testing gesture segments provides more substantial performance gains under limited training conditions. In contrast, when sufficient training data are available (e.g., 500 samples), the marginal benefit from additional gesture segments diminishes.

In summary, the results demonstrate that the proposed system can effectively compensate for limited training data by increasing the number of gestures during authentication. From the perspective of gesture input, more complex unlock patterns typically result in more sub-gesture segments, thereby offering richer behavioral cues. Therefore, rather than introducing performance degradation, increased unlock complexity serves as a natural mechanism to enhance authentication reliability and security in our framework.

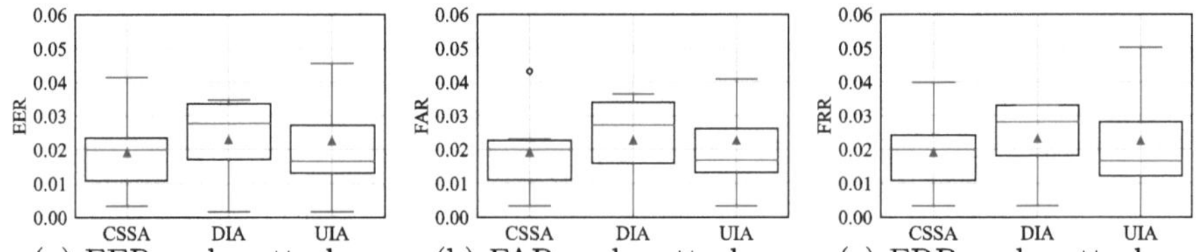

(a) EER under attacks. (b) FAR under attacks. (c) FRR under attacks.

Fig. 9. Robustness evaluation against CSSA, DIA, and UIA attacks.

5.4 Robustness Under Attacks

To systematically evaluate the robustness of SPUAuth under different adversarial conditions, we simulated three types of attacks, each reflecting a distinct level of attacker capability and intent: *Casual Shoulder Surfing Attack (CSSA)* represents a low-threat scenario in which the attacker performs imitation based solely on a rough visual observation of the unlocking process. *Deliberate Imitation Attack (DIA)* simulates a more capable attacker who repeatedly observes and deliberately practices the victim's unlock behavior, reflecting a proactive and targeted mimicry attempt. *Unseen Impersonation Attack (UIA)* assesses the system's generalization ability by introducing impostors who were never seen during the model training phase, i.e., entirely unknown to the system.

Figure 9 presents the authentication performance of SPUAuth under these three attack scenarios, measured by EER, FAR, and FRR. As shown in Fig. 9(a), under CSSA, the system maintains a low error rate (average EER of 1.9%), indicating a strong resistance to low-effort attacks. In the more challenging DIA setting, where attackers exhibit stronger imitation capabilities, SPUAuth still achieves stable results, suggesting its effectiveness in capturing personalized behavioral traits. Under the most adversarial UIA scenario, in which test samples are collected from entirely unseen users, the system demonstrates strong generalization robustness, with only minor variations in performance metrics.

In summary, SPUAuth exhibits strong robustness across a spectrum of attack scenarios, highlighting its effectiveness in resisting spoofing attempts and its potential applicability in real-world threat environments.

6 Conclusion

In this paper, we proposed SPUAuth, a behavioral biometric authentication framework designed to defend against shoulder surfing attacks during smartphone pattern unlock. By leveraging built-in motion sensors and modeling user behavior at the structural sub-gesture level, SPUAuth captures fine-grained behavioral traits that are difficult for attackers to mimic. Our approach integrates a turning-point-based gesture decomposition mechanism, a structure-aware feature extraction pipeline, and a triplet-loss-driven embedding strategy. Extensive experiments conducted on both a self-collected dataset and the public H-MOG dataset demonstrate that SPUAuth achieves strong performance across multiple evaluation metrics. Moreover, the proposed system exhibits notable robustness against various adversarial threats, including casual shoulder surfing, deliberate imitation, and unseen user impersonation attacks.

While these results are promising, we acknowledge several challenges for real-world deployment. Real-time efficiency on resource-constrained devices, robustness under highly diverse usage conditions, and privacy concerns regarding behavioral data collection must be carefully addressed. In future work, we will extend SPUAuth to broader authentication scenarios and explore lightweight and privacy-preserving techniques to enable reliable real-world adoption.

Acknowledgments. This work was supported by the National Key R&D Program of China (Grant No. 2023YFB3107500), National Natural Science Foundation of China (Grant No. 92267204, Grant No.92467201), Key R&D Program of Shandong Province (Grant No. 2024CXPT039), and funded by China Scholarship Council.

References

1. Aaby, P., Giuffrida, M.V., Buchanan, W.J., Tan, Z.: An omnidirectional approach to touch-based continuous authentication. Comput. Secur. **128**, 103146 (2023)
2. Amini, S., Noroozi, V., Pande, A., Gupte, S., Yu, P.S., Kanich, C.: Deepauth: a framework for continuous user re-authentication in mobile apps. In: Proceedings of the 27th ACM International Conference on Information and Knowledge Management, pp. 2027–2035 (2018)
3. Cheng, S., Wang, J., Sheng, D., Chen, Y.: Identification with your mind: a hybrid BCI-based authentication approach for anti-shoulder-surfing attacks using EEG and eye movement data. IEEE Trans. Instrum. Meas. **72**, 1–14 (2023)
4. Cheon, E., Oakley, I.: Securing gesture passwords against shoulder surfing using behavioral features. In: Proceedings of the Extended Abstracts of the CHI Conference on Human Factors in Computing Systems, pp. 1–8 (2025)
5. Farzand, H.: Understanding shoulder surfing and informing the design of protection mechanisms. Ph.D. thesis, University of Glasgow (2025)
6. Fereidooni, H., et al.: Authentisense: a scalable behavioral biometrics authentication scheme using few-shot learning for mobile platforms. arXiv preprint arXiv:2302.02740 (2023)
7. Kirkwood, D., et al.: Pin scrambler: assessing the impact of randomized layouts on the usability and security of pins. In: Proceedings of the 21st International Conference on Mobile and Ubiquitous Multimedia, pp. 83–88 (2022)
8. Li, Y., Ouyang, C., Huang, H.: Aeganauth: autoencoder GAN-based continuous authentication with conditional variational autoencoder generative adversarial network. IEEE Internet Things J. (2024)

9. Liu, D., et al.: Soundid: securing mobile two-factor authentication via acoustic signals. IEEE Trans. Dependable Secure Comput. **20**(2), 1687–1701 (2022)
10. Parhi, K.K., Ayinala, M.: Low-complexity welch power spectral density computation. IEEE Trans. Circuits Syst. I Regul. Pap. **61**(1), 172–182 (2013)
11. Pinto, A., Schwartz, W.R., Pedrini, H., de Rezende Rocha, A.: Using visual rhythms for detecting video-based facial spoof attacks. IEEE Trans. Inf. Forensics Secur. **10**(5), 1025–1038 (2015)
12. Qiu, L., De Luca, A., Muslukhov, I., Beznosov, K.: Towards understanding the link between age and smartphone authentication. In: Proceedings of the 2019 CHI Conference on Human Factors in Computing Systems, pp. 1–10 (2019)
13. Shen, C., Li, Y., Chen, Y., Guan, X., Maxion, R.A.: Performance analysis of multi-motion sensor behavior for active smartphone authentication. IEEE Trans. Inf. Forensics Secur. **13**(1), 48–62 (2017)
14. Shen, Z., Li, S., Zhao, X., Zou, J.: Mmauth: a continuous authentication framework on smartphones using multiple modalities. IEEE Trans. Inf. Forensics Secur. **17**, 1450–1465 (2022)
15. Shen, Z., Li, S., Zhao, X., Zou, J.: CT-auth: capacitive touchscreen-based continuous authentication on smartphones. IEEE Trans. Knowl. Data Eng. **36**(1), 90–106 (2023)
16. Shi, D., et al.: Fine-grained and context-aware behavioral biometrics for pattern lock on smartphones. Proc. ACM Interact. Mob. Wearable Ubiquitous Technol. **5**(1), 1–30 (2021)
17. Shin, H., Kim, D., Hur, J.: Secure pattern-based authentication against shoulder surfing attack in smart devices. In: 2015 Seventh International Conference on Ubiquitous and Future Networks, pp. 13–18. IEEE (2015)
18. Song, Y., Cai, Z., Zhang, Z.L.: Multi-touch authentication using hand geometry and behavioral information. In: 2017 IEEE Symposium on Security and Privacy (SP), pp. 357–372. IEEE (2017)
19. Stylios, I., Chatzis, S., Thanou, O., Kokolakis, S.: Continuous authentication with feature-level fusion of touch gestures and keystroke dynamics to solve security and usability issues. Comput. Secur. **132**, 103363 (2023)
20. Stylios, I., Skalkos, A., Kokolakis, S., Karyda, M.: Bioprivacy: development of a keystroke dynamics continuous authentication system. In: European Symposium on Research in Computer Security, pp. 158–170. Springer (2021)
21. Tang, B.J., Shin, K.G.: {Eye-Shield}: {Real-Time} protection of mobile device screen information from shoulder surfing. In: 32nd USENIX Security Symposium (USENIX Security 2023), pp. 5449–5466 (2023)
22. Tang, G., Zhao, J., Xu, Z., Wang, Y., Yang, H., Zhang, Z.: Continuous smartphone user authentication based on gesture-sensor fusion. In: 2024 International Conference on Networking and Network Applications (NaNA), pp. 516–522. IEEE (2024)
23. Xu, Y., Price, T., Frahm, J.M., Monrose, F.: Virtual u: defeating face liveness detection by building virtual models from your public photos. In: 25th USENIX Security Symposium (USENIX Security 2016), pp. 497–512 (2016)
24. Ye, G., et al.: A video-based attack for android pattern lock. ACM Trans. Privacy Secur. (TOPS) **21**(4), 1–31 (2018)
25. Zhang, J., Xie, L., He, L., Wang, Z., Chen, J.: Enhanced cell phone security: an ultrasonic and sensor fusion-based persistent cell phone protection method integrating anti-theft & identity authentication. Comput. Secur. **148**, 104176 (2025)

26. Zhang, X., Yin, Y., Xie, L., Zhang, H., Ge, Z., Lu, S.: Touchid: user authentication on mobile devices via inertial-touch gesture analysis. Proc. ACM Interact. Mob. Wearable Ubiquitous Technol. **4**(4), 1–29 (2020)
27. Zhao, C., Gao, F., Shen, Z.: Multi-motion sensor behavior based continuous authentication on smartphones using gated two-tower transformer fusion networks. Comput. Secur. **139**, 103698 (2024)
28. Zhao, G., Zhang, P., Shen, Y., Peng, L., Jiang, X.: Exploiting screen-touch trajectory for passive user authentication in industrial internet of things systems. IEEE Trans. Ind. Inform. (2024)
29. Zhou, M., et al.: Fingerpattern: securing pattern lock via fingerprint-dependent friction sound. IEEE Trans. Mob. Comput. **23**(6), 7210–7224 (2023)

Robust Reinforcement Learning for Q-Network in Worst-Case Scenarios

Xiao Sun[1(✉)], Xing Hong Ling[2], and Lanlan Gong[2]

[1] School of Computer Science and Technology, Soochow University, Suzhou 215006, China
gongrensx@gmail.com
[2] Suzhou City University, Suzhou 215104, China
lingxinghong@suda.edu.cn, Gongll@szcu.edu.cn

Abstract. Reinforcement learning faces the problem of vulnerability against perturbations on the agent's input to the extent that a small perturbation in the observation can defeat a well-trained agent. It is crucial to train an agent that can perform well under the most severe perturbations. A novel Q function introduced by WocaR-RL is used to predict the value of the worst case. However, it can hardly predict worst-case values without enhancing robustness. In this paper, we begin by defining two types of Bellman updating equations which is used to analyze the instability issue inherent in such Q network. To tackle this problem, we introduce a Q-smoothing mechanism that specifically smooth the unstable Q network. Besides, considering that the Q network can not access the accurate action set and can only rely on a superset, we identify another underestimation problem and propose a double Q mechanism. Both two mechanisms will not compromise the computational efficiency of WocaR-RL algorithm. Empirical validation on the Mujoco corroborates that our methods outperform WocaR-PPO and other SOTA algorithms in terms of robust performance and success rate in training a robust agent.

Keywords: Robust reinforcement learning · State perturbation · Worst-case Q network · Smoothing regularization

1 Introduction

Deep Reinforcement learning (DRL) aims to maximize cumulative rewards by interaction with the environment. The use of DRL makes a significant progress in addressing challenging problems across different domains. Despite its great advantages, as highlighted by Goodfellow et al. [4], DNNs can be easily misled into producing incorrect labels with minor perturbations to their inputs. The vulnerabilities of DRL agents are first demonstrated by [7,10,17] and further explored across various environments and attack scenarios [1,21]. Robust deep reinforcement learning aims at training a robust agent against strong adversarial

Supported by Organization X.

L. Zhang and K.-K. R. Choo (Eds.): MobiQuitous 2025, LNICST 683, pp. 356–374, 2026.
https://doi.org/10.1007/978-3-032-22500-9_20

attacks. Among different kinds of adversarial attacks, an attack on agent's observation is the most studied area. Zhang et al. [31] first formulate the perturbation on state observations as a modified Markov Decision Process (MDP) which is called State-Adversary MDP (SA-MDP). This lays a theoretical foundation for the subsequent research.

To robustify the DRL agent, Several works [20,24,29] are contributed to solving this weakness by regularizing the policy network to output a similar action despite the state perturbations. Nonetheless, these methods neglect the intrinsic vulnerability of policy since they only pay attention to current time step. Zhang et al. [29] and Sun et al. [25] consider train an optimal attacker which treats the victim model as a part of dynamics of environment and then turn the problem of training an attacker into training an ordinary agent. However, the training of adversary is also a RL problem and it doubles the computational burden.

A framework [16] which estimates the worst-case-aware Q values is designed to both consider the long-term robustness and computational efficiency. However, this approach is too conservative since the worst-case-aware Q network predicts the worst case of future reward. This means that the agent knows a minimum value that the agent can obtain by taking an action in the state at the current time step, assuming that the state is perturbed to the worst case scenario at each subsequent step. To accurately train such a Q-network, it is necessary to compute sets of actions that the agent would take if observed states were perturbed accordingly—a challenging task indeed. Liang proposes approximating this action set with a superset where both upper and lower bounds are greater than and smaller than those of the actual set respectively—resulting in trained Q-networks unable to precisely reflect true values for each state-action pair. Mao et al. [18] propose that tightness of Interval bound propagation bounds(IBP) improves with a sufficient network width, whcih can help make supersets tighter and more precise. However, this study is too theoretical to be directly applied to calculate a more accurate action set. In addition, Q-network is prone to have an unstable training due to the way it is updated. About this part of the reasoning we will further explain in Sect. 4.

To address the problem, our method does not directly make further constraints on the superset to increase the accuracy of the Q-network, but rather improves the stability of the Q-network through an indirect method since it's hard to make action set tighter. In view of the two weaknesses of Q network, we respectively put forward two effective methods, Q-smoothing mechanism and double Q-network mechanism. Our contributions can be summarized as below:

- We further investigate the worst-case Q function and analyze why such a Q network is unstable and conservative.
- We define two kinds of updating criteria for Bellman equations, through which we propose a Q-network smoothing term that can improve the stability of the Q network
- We utilize a special double Q mechanism to address the issue of underestimation.

- We compare our algorithm to WocaR-PPO and other SOTA algorithms in continuous action spaces. Through empirical studies on Mujoco, we validate the effectiveness of our two mechanisms, demonstrating both higher rewards under strong attacks and training stability.

The rest of the paper is organized as follows. In Sect. 2, we introduce related works, including adversary setting in DRL, Research on state perturbation, and smoothing mechanism. In Sect. 3, we briefly review the definition of worst-case Q network and its Bellman equation. The implementation of our 2 effective methods is described in Sect. 4. In Sect. 5, we further describe the experimental details and discuss experimental results. In Sect. 6, we summarize the work of this paper and provide an outlook for future work.

2 Related Work

Adversary Setting in DRL. Due to the unstable nature of reinforcement learning, an adversarial attack will have a huge impact on the performance of the agent several studies have used adversarial perturbation to increase the robustness of the agent. Pinto et al. [22] propose to train an agent and an adversary so that the adversary can change the true environments states directly. This approach is to improve the robustness against environment parameter change, such as mass, length. In SA-MDP setting, the ture state remains not changed, while the agent observes the perturbed observations. SA-MDP characterizes how the agent behaves in the presence of errors in sensor measurements. That's because when the sensor has errors, the true state of the object is not changed, but the sensor gets the wrong data. In Multi-Agent RL setting [9,27], agents are more vulnerable to adversarial attacks compared to single-agent RL, as the failure of a single agent may cause the failure of the whole team.

Besides the above adversarial settings. Another lines of work consider attacks on action space [13,14,26] and reward function [6,8,23]. In our work, we continue our study on state perturbation, and we focus on l_p-norm adversarial perturbations on agents' observations since this threat model is adopted by many existing works of adversarial training.

Research on State Perturbation. Huang et al. [7] use an FGSM based attack and show a significant drop in the performance of RL algorithms in discrete action space. Zhang et al. [29] develop a theoretically principled policy regularization and SA-MDP. With SA-MDP, they propose Alternating Training with Learned Adversaries(ATLA), which involves the training of an adversary online together with a victim agent. Orikarinen et al. [20] improve the robustness by carefully designed adversarial loss functions and propose a new evaluation method, Greedy worst-Case Reward(GWC). The GWC estimates the worst-case reward of a policy under state perturbations. Similar to GWC, Liang et al. [16] designs a function to estimate the worst-case value of a policy and propose a new framework called Worst-case-aware Robust RL(WocaR-RL). Several works also compute lower bounds of value network. However, they can't be applied to continuous control task.

Smoothing Mechanism. Adding a nearly imperceptible perturbation to an input image can completely alter the network's prediction. Randomized smoothing is a useful technique for certifying adversarial robustness to handle input perturbation [2,12,15]. Kumar et al. [11] propose a policy smoothing mainly based on randomized smoothing technique. Shen et al. [24] and Zhang et al. [29] propose that similar states should lead to similar actions for natural environments with continuous state space. Their method is different from randomized smoothing since they need to find the action with the greatest deviation in the face of disturbance. However, randomized smoothing adds an isometric Gaussian noise to the input and doesn't need to impose strict restrictions to obtain the input noise. Despite the widespread use of Policy smoothing, Q smoothing is not as effective.

3 Preliminary

3.1 Notations and Background

Like previous work, we define a Markov decision process (MDP) as (S, A, R, p, γ), where S is the state space, A is the action space, $R : S \times A \times S \rightarrow \mathbb{R}$ is the reward function, and $p : S \times A \rightarrow \mathcal{P}(S)$ is the transition probability of the environment, where $\mathcal{P}(S)$ defines the set of all possible probability measures on S. $\gamma \in [0, 1)$. Besides, we denote the policy as $\pi : S \rightarrow \mathcal{P}(A)$. The natural performance can be measured by the value function $V^{\pi}(s) = \mathbb{E}_P^{\pi}\left[\sum_{t=0}^{\infty} R(s_t, a_t) \mid s_0 = s\right]$, and the action-value function $Q^{\pi}(s,a) = \mathbb{E}_P^{\pi}\left[\sum_{t=0}^{\infty} R(s_t, a_t) \mid s_0 = s, a_0 = a\right]$. Our experiment is based on l_p norm adversarial perturbation ϵ, we define the perturbed state set as $B(s, \epsilon) \in S$ and perturbed state as $\hat{s}$.

3.2 Analysis of Q_{wst}

In an actor-critic framework, the agent needs two networks, namely the value network and the policy network. The value network will score the state actions of the agent, and the policy network will constantly adjust agent's behavior according to the score. Since traditional reinforcement learning requires learning the best strategy with maximal Q function, the following formula updates its own value network:

$$Q_{vanilla}(s,a) = \mathbb{E}_{s' \backsim P(s,a)}[R(s,a) + \gamma \max_{a' \in A} Q(s', a')] \tag{1}$$

Unlike $Q_{vanilla}$, Q_{wst} doesn't follow the maximal strategy. Since the Q_{wst} acts as an predictor directly predicting the worst-case cumulative reward instead of learning an optimal adversary. The worst case indicates that the agent's observation is perturbed into the a "worst" observation in each step. It means that agent will take an action $\hat{a}$ based on $\pi(\hat{s})$, and the cumulative reward $Q(s, \hat{a})$ is least among all perturbed states. So, the update of Q_{wst} is almost contrary to $Q_{vanilla}$, the worst-attack Bellman equation is defined as:

$$Q_{wst}(s,a) = \mathbb{E}_{s' \backsim P(s,a)}[R(s,a) + \gamma \min_{a' \in A_{adv}(s',\pi)} Q(s',a')] \tag{2}$$

$$A_{adv}(s,\pi) = \{a \in A : \exists s \in B(s,\epsilon) s.t. \pi(\hat{s}) = a\} \tag{3}$$

where A_{adv} is the set of actions that the policy π can be mislead into taking the wrong actions due to the perturbed state $\hat{s}$. The perturbed state surrounds the clean state s'. After defining the Bellman equation of Q_{wst}, the loss function of Q_{wst} is straightforward:

$$L(Q_{wst}) = \frac{1}{N}\sum_{t=1}^{N}(Q_{wst}^{target} - Q_{wst}(s_t, a_t))^2 \tag{4}$$

where $Q_{wst}^{target} = r_t + \gamma \min_{a' \in A_{adv}(s',\pi)} Q_{wst}(s', a')$, a common way to update Q functions using the Temporal Difference(TD).

However, it is hard to compute the accurate A_{adv} due to the complexity of neural network. A common approach is using convex relaxation of networks to compute the approximate set of actions. This approximate set is a superset of A_{adv}, bounded by $\overline{\pi_\theta(s)}$ and $\underline{\pi_\theta(s)}$. As in the previous study, we choose the l_∞ norm perturbations as an example. Given an l_∞ perturbation budget ϵ, we denote the output of neural network with the input s as $f_\theta(s)$, convex relaxations receive perturbed input and output $\overline{\pi_\theta(s)}$, $\underline{\pi_\theta(s)}$ such that:

$$\underline{\pi_\theta(s)} \leq \min_{||s'-s||_\infty \leq \epsilon} f_\theta(s') \leq \max_{||s'-s||_\infty \leq \epsilon} f_\theta(s') \leq \overline{\pi_\theta(s)} \tag{5}$$

4 Methdology

In this section, we first propose a robust Q_{wst} network with Q smoothing regularization term, and analyze why Q_{wst} can achieve better results after introducing Q smoothing terms. Then, we analyze another weakness of Q_{wst} and propose a different double Q mechanism. Finally, we introduce other modules in this framework and show the complete framework of the algorithm.

4.1 Unstable Update of Q_{wst} and a Q-Smoothing Mechanism

Theorem 4.1. We divide the updating methods of Q network into two categories: one can select actions from whole action set for updating, and the other can only select actions from a partial action set. We define the first one as Q_{update}^{w} and the second one as Q_{update}^{p}, and Q_{update}^{w} is more stable than Q_{update}^{p}.

Theorem 4.1 says that since the action set A_{adv} is part of the whole action set A, when there is a slight change in state s', the action set A_{adv} will also change slightly due to its being computed by state. In Fig. 1(a), we visualize Q_{update}^{p},

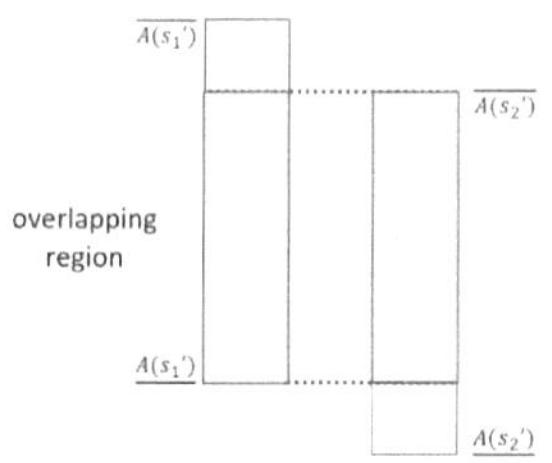

(a) visualizing Q^p_{update}

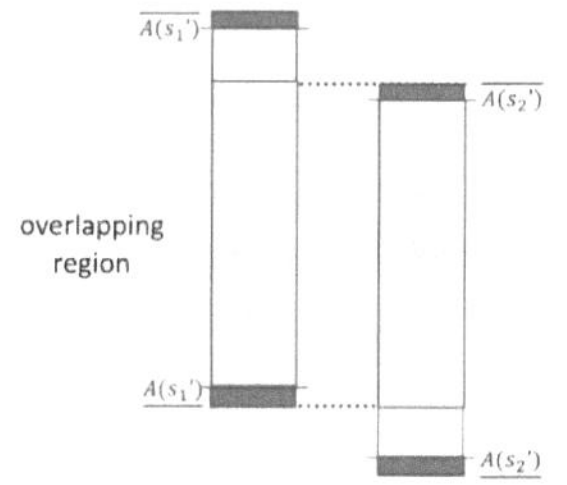

(b) visualizing Q^w_{update}

Fig. 1. Comparison of Q^p_{update} and variant of Q^p_{update}(using superset instead of a precise action set). The red rectangle represents the set of actions that the agent can select in the next time step, the blue rectangle represents the set of actions that can be selected in the next time step if the state is slightly disturbed, and the middle part of the dashed line represents the overlapping part of the action set. (Color figure online)

s_1' and s_2' represents two different states with little deviation, A denotes the action set. As we can see, if the chosen action is selected from the overlapping region, there will be no significant deviation from the Q_{target} against small state change. If the chosen action is selected from the other region, the selected action can be wildly biased, resulting in unstable updates to the Q value. Contrarily, for Q^w_{update}, the action set is the whole action set, a change in state does not affect the action set. As is discussed in Sect. 3.2, A_{adv} is an approximate action set of actual set of action. We assume that the upper and lower bounds of the superset are a fixed value above and below the actual upper and lower bounds, respectively. We color the portion of the superset that is larger than the real set in blue, as we depict in Fig. 1(b). The area of the overlapping part will increase, and the area of the non-overlapping part will remain relatively unchanged because the upper and lower sides of the two rectangles are changing, so the possibility of taking the action of the non-overlapping part still exists. We attribute the updating method of Q_{wst} to Q^p_{update}, and point out that Q_{wst} is also faced with the problem of instability. In other words, finding the worst action in the A_{adv} based on the state s' in the next time step is similar to the agent actively selecting the worst action from the set of actions that can be selected, however, similar states should result in a similar action rather than choosing a distinct action, which is mentioned in [24,29].

In our approach, we propose to use a Q-smoothing mechanism to deal with this instability, ensuring that our Q_{wst} does not produce large deviations in the case of small perturbations in the state, and we believe that such a Q_{wst} can correctly predict the worst cumulative reward for each state action pair.

Regarding the implementation of Q-smoothing, we introduce a smoothing regularization term into the loss function of Q function update, the objective function of Q function update is as follows:

$$L = L_{\text{nom}} + \lambda \max_{\hat{s}_t \sim B(s_t, \epsilon)} \left(Q(s_t, a_t) - Q(\hat{s}_t, a_t)\right)^2 \tag{6}$$

where L_{nom} denotes the nominal loss function such as Eq. (2), and λ denotes a hyperparameter controlling the strength of regularization. Since minimizing Eq. (6) involves a min-max problem, we use Interval Background Propagation (IBP), a commonly used method in proving the robustness of classifier and RL [5,19]. IBP works by propagating the input region through the Neural Network (NN). For each layer h_i in the NN, it will receive the output regionx_{i-1} of the last layer and process the region and output a new bound to the next layer h_{i+1}. Different from prior work, we note that Q smoothing is more suitable for Q^p_{update} than Q^w_{update} because Q^p_{update} updates are more unstable. What's more, in previous work [24], Q smoothing is used to help policies output similar actions against state disturbances, and in our work, this is used to improve the stability of Q_{wst} networks.

Algorithm 1. Q-Smoothing Worst Q Estimate(QSWE)

Input: Number of iterations T, perturbation radius ϵ, smoothing weight λ
Initialize policy parameter θ and Worst Q estimate ϕ
for $k = 0, 1, ..., T$ **do**
  Collect a set of trajectories $D = \tau_k$ by running policy π_θ, each trajectory τ_k contains $\tau_k = s_t, a_t, r_t, s_{t+1}$
  Use IBP methods to calculate $A_{adv} : [\underline{\pi_\theta(s_t)}, \overline{\pi_\theta(s_t)}]$
  Use gradient descent to find the worst action $\hat{a}_{t+1}$:

$$\hat{a}_{t+1} = \arg\min_{a \in A_{adv}} Q^\phi_{wst}(s_{t+1}, a)$$

  compute the target Q^ϕ_{wst}:

$$\underline{y_t} = \begin{cases} r_t + \gamma Q^\phi_{wst}(s_{t+1}, \hat{a}_{t+1}) & \text{for non-terminal } s_{t+1} \\ r_t & \text{otherwise} \end{cases}$$

  Compute the Q-smoothing regularization using convex relaxations according to Eq.(6):

$$L = L_{\text{nom}} + \lambda \max_{\hat{s_t} \sim B(s_t, \epsilon)} \left(Q(s_t, a_t) - Q(\hat{s_t}, a_t)\right)^2$$

  Update Q_{wst} using Q-smoothing regularization and TD-error term
end for

4.2 Conservative of Q_{wst} and a Double Q-Network Mechnism

In this subsection, we analyze another weakness of Q_{wst}, the predicted Q_{wst} is lower than the true Q_{wst}. Since A_{adv} is a predicted superset, the agent may take an action that should not be considered in practice when taking the worst action, for example, the real action set may be [−0.5,0.5], the worst action is 0, and the action set solved by the IBP method may be [−0.6,0.6]. The worst action is 0.55, resulting in an underestimation with every update to Q_{wst}. Therefore, we propose to use a double Q network, each time the Q network is updated, the maximium value of the two network predictions is selected as the target Q value. This method is similar to TD3 algorithm [3], TD3 algorithm is used to solve the problem of overestimation of Q value, and we take the maximum value to solve the problem of underestimation. It is worth noting that the input of TD3 algorithm into two Q networks is the same which means that the gradient descent of one of the Q networks is used to find the action input to the Q network. Through our experiments, passing the same input into two Q networks does not yield good results. It is better to select the worst action of two Q networks by gradient descent respectively. The reason for the difference is that the second case can improve the possibility of the agent choosing the action that is not underestimated. We regard the process of finding the worst action by the Q network through gradient descent as the agent actively choosing an action. If the action selected by the agent is not in the real action set but in the superset, we call it choosing a "bad action", A_b, since it will lead to the underestimation of this round of update. On the other hand, if choosing the action of the actual action set, it is a "good action", A_g, because it does not generate underestimation. Now that the agent has two networks to assist in action selection, even if the Q_1 network makes the agent choose a bad action, as long as the Q_2 network does not choose a bad action, the agent will eventually choose a good action for bellman update (Fig. 2).

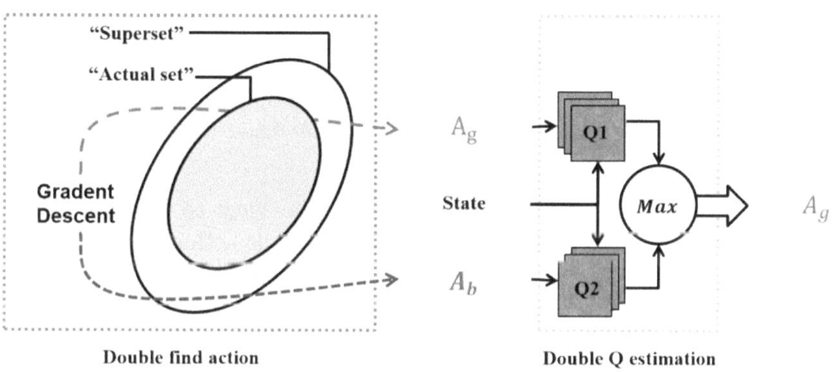

Fig. 2. Figure of double Q mechanism.

Supplementary Statement. Here we show the complete framework of the whole algorithm. Step 1: the agent interacts with the environment to sample the trained trajectory, uses the trajectory to update the value function V of the PPO

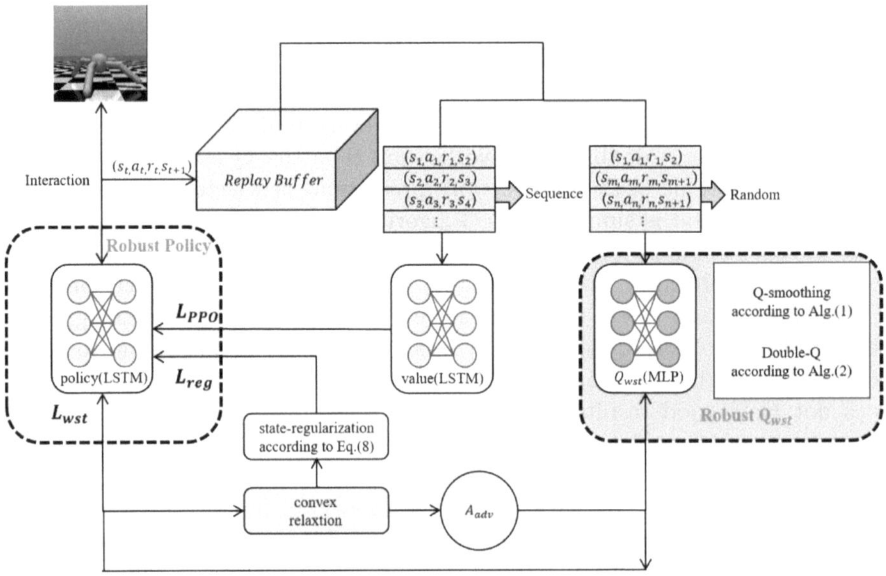

Fig. 3. The overall framework of algorithm, including the main framework for training a robust policy using Q_{wst} and our 2 methods for enhancing Q_{wst}.

algorithm, and calculates the advantage function A based on V. Step 2: Train the Q_{wst} network according to Eq. (2). In this step, we utilize our methods to help train a better Q_{wst}. Step 3: Update the policy network. The loss function of the policy network consists of the loss function term of the vanilla ppo, the prediction term of Q_{wst}, and the state regularization term. We show the prediction term of Q_{wst} and loss function of State regularization in Eq. (7) and Eq. (8):

$$L_{wst}(\pi(\theta), Q_{wst}) = -\frac{1}{N}\sum_{t=1}^{N}\sum_{a\in A}\pi_\theta(a|s_t)Q_{wst}(s_t, a) \tag{7}$$

where the prediction term of Q_{wst} is to encourage the agent to select an action with a higher worst-case Q value, avoiding the dangerous action.

$$L_{reg}(\pi_\theta) = \frac{1}{N}\sum_{t=1}^{N}\max_{\hat{s_t}\sim B(\hat{s_t},\epsilon)} D_{KL}(\pi_\theta(s_t), \pi_\theta(\hat{s_t})) \tag{8}$$

where D_{KL} is a method to compute the total variation distance for distributions. We should note that state regularization term can help the policy network output similar actions for state perturbations, and can also help us reduce the scope of the action set A_{adv}. Therefore, we continue to use this method, and we do not assign weights to each state regularization term according to the importance of the state like WocaR-PPO. Because that's not what we're studying. We show the complete training framework in Fig. 3. The loss function of policy can be

Algorithm 2. Double Finding Worst Action and Double Q Estimation(DFDQ)

Input: Number of iterations T, perturbation radius ϵ, smoothing weight λ

Initialize policy parameter θ and Worst Q estimate $\phi 1$, $\phi 2$

for $k = 0, 1, ..., T$ **do**

  Collect a set of trajectories $D = \tau_k$ by running policy π_θ, each trajectory τ_k contains $\tau_k = s_t, a_t, r_t, s_{t+1}$

  Use IBP methods to calculate $A_{adv} : [\underline{\pi_\theta(s)}, \overline{\pi_\theta(s)}]$

  Use gradient descent of $Q^{\phi 1}_{wst}$ and $Q^{\phi 2}_{wst}$ to find the worst action $\hat{a}^1_{t+1}$ and $\hat{a}^2_{t+1}$ respectively:

$$\hat{a}^1_{t+1} = \arg\min_{a \in A_{adv}} Q^{\phi 1}_{wst}(s_{t+1}, a)$$

$$\hat{a}^2_{t+1} = \arg\min_{a \in A_{adv}} Q^{\phi 2}_{wst}(s_{t+1}, a)$$

$$\underline{y_t} = r_t + \gamma \max\{Q^{\phi 1}_{wst1}(s_{t+1}, \hat{a}^1_{t+1}), Q^{\phi 2}_{wst2}(s_{t+1}, \hat{a}^2_{t+1})\}$$

  Update Q_{wst} using TD-error term

end for

defined as:

$$L_{\pi(\theta)} = L_{RL}(\pi(\theta)) + K_{wst} L_{wst}(\pi(\theta), Q_{wst}) + K_{reg} L_{reg}(\pi(\theta)) \quad (9)$$

where K_{wst} and L_{reg} are hyperparameters balancing natural rewards and robustness (Fig. 4).

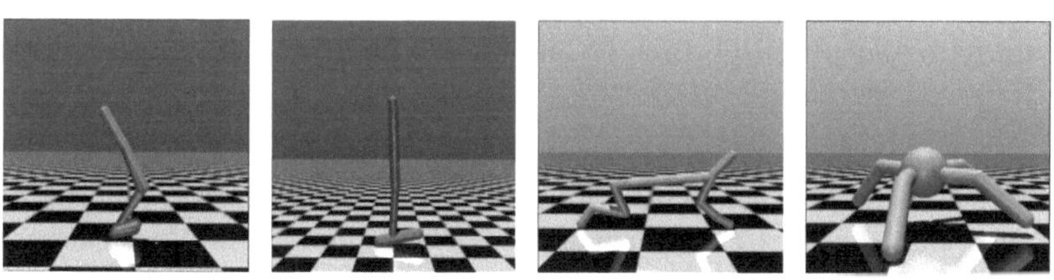

(a) Walker2D (b) Hopper (c) Halfcheetah (d) Ant

Fig. 4. Four tasks in MuJoCo platform.

5 Experiment and Analysis

In our experiment, we test our method on MuJoCo tasks with continuous action spaces. Following most prior work, We select four MuJoCo environments, including hopper, walker, halfcheetah and ant. We apply our algorithm on PPO and

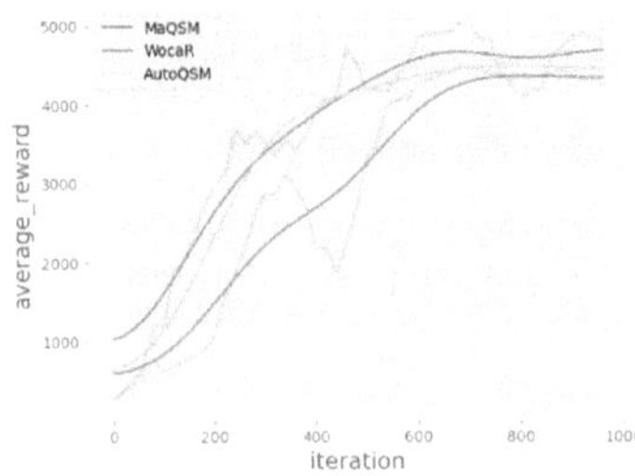

(a) Walker

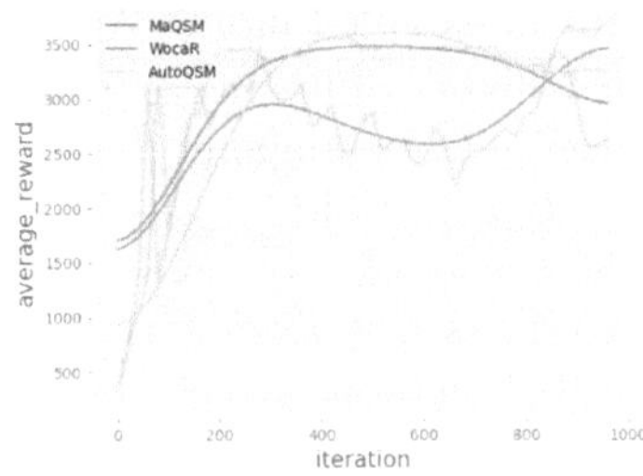

(b) Hopper

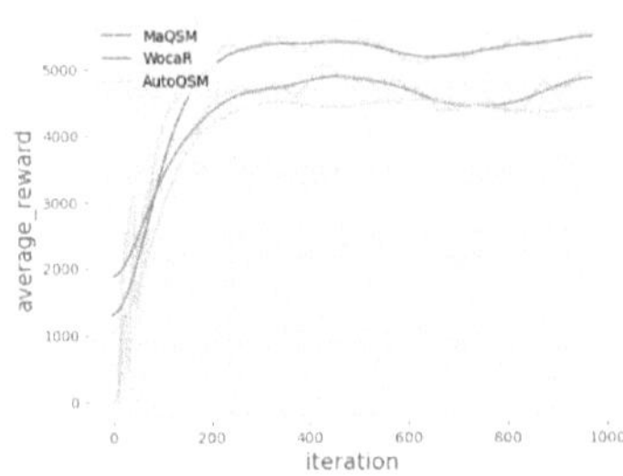

(c) Halfcheetah

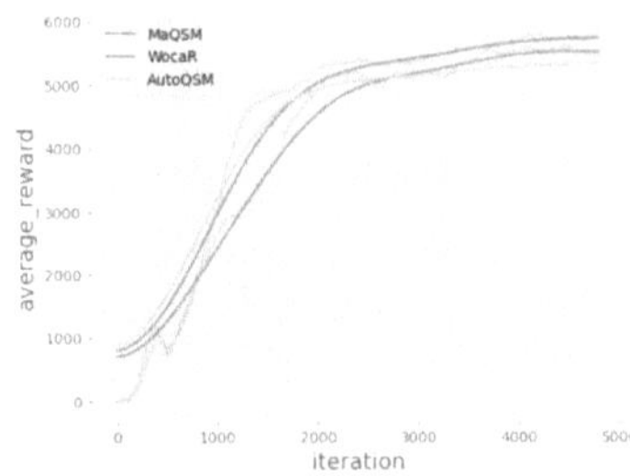

(d) Ant

Fig. 5. Learning curves of our methods and WocaR-PPO during training on four mujoco environments, we test the model every 20 iterations. We ues the same training steps as in WocaR-PPO. For Walker2D, Hopper and Halfcheetah, we ran 980 iterations. For a high-state-dimension environment halfcheetah, we run 4900 iterations. Each iteration contains 1024 steps.

compare it to WocaR-PPO directly due to our work is an improved version of it.

Evaluation Metrics. We chose three mainstream attacks to test our model, including: (1) Random attack (2) MAD attack (maximal action difference) (3) RS attack (train a robust critic to attack model). Among them, RS attack is very aggressive. For each model, we trained the robust sarsa Q netwrok by adjusting two parameters through grid search. For each model, a total of 25 groups of RS critic network composed of different parameters are trained, and the group with the best attack effect is selected as the test result of RS attack. In order to reflect the most representative results, we test each agent for 50 episodes and calculate the mean and variance of the reward value obtained over 50 episodes.

5.1 Comparison of Q-Smoothing Mechanism

In our experiments, although we directly compare WocaR-PPO with our algorithm. For a comprehensive study, we choose other state-of-the-art algorithm, SA-PPO and ATLA, for comparison.

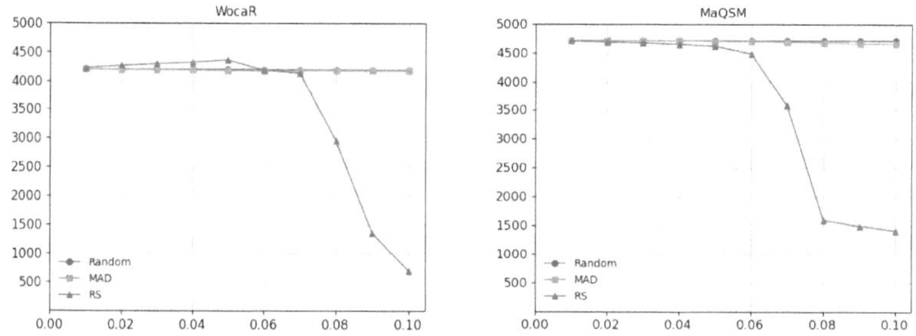

(a) Walker

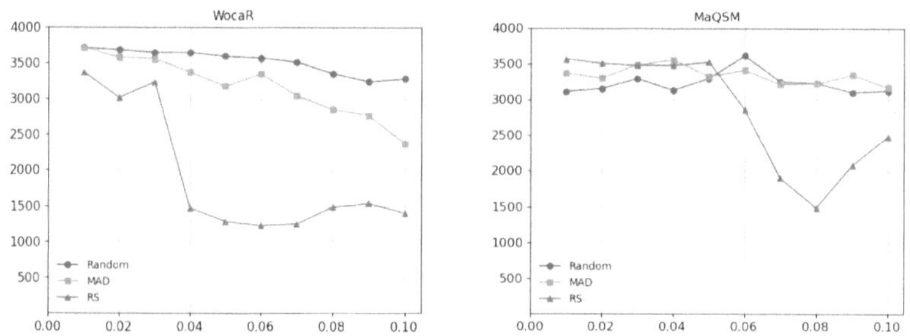

(b) Hopper

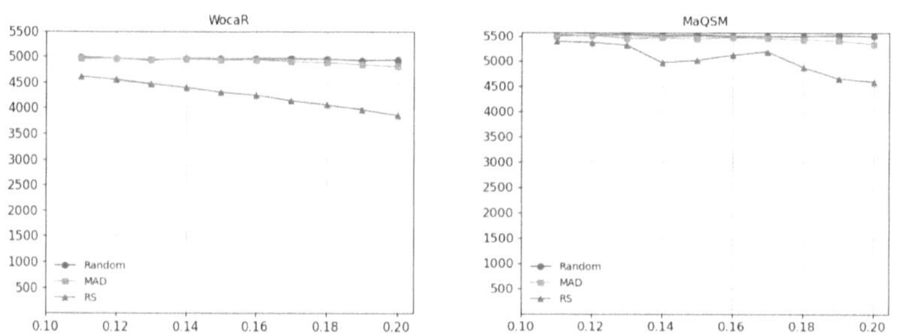

(c) Halfcheetah

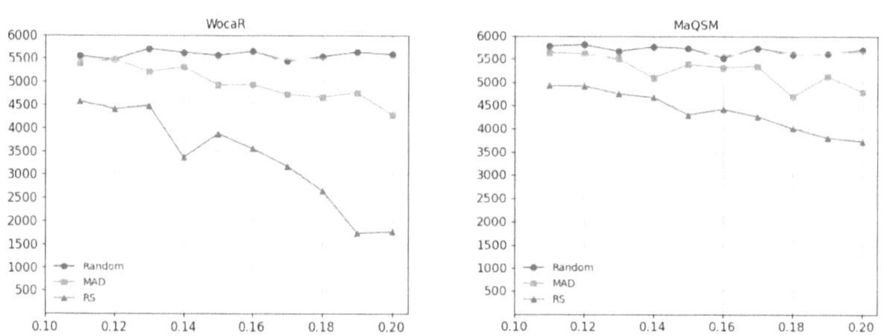

(d) Ant

Fig. 6. Comparison of agent under different attack budgets.

- PPO(vanilla): PPO with a simple 3-layer MLP network.
- SA-PPO: using state regularization with convex relaxation methods.
- ATLA: train the victim model and adversary model alternatively. The model is trained with LSTM networks and a state regularization based on SA-PPO.
- WocaR-PPO: Q_{wst} with MLP network, both policy and critic using LSTM network. Since WocaR-PPO has not released a full version implemented by the LSTM network, we reproduce WocaR-PPO ourselves based on the author's code and were able to achieve similar results to the paper. We use a 2-step Stochastic Gradient Langevin Dynamics (SGLD) gradient when implementing state-regularization, as convex relaxations of LSTMs are expensive.
- Ours: since the Q smoothing involves a min-max problem, We utilize two methods to solve the convex relaxation of Q_{wst}: a **Ma**nually designed IBP method and a well-developed toolbox, **Auto**_LiRPA [28], using IBP+CROWN scheme [30]. These two methods are referred to as MaQSM and AutoQSM respectively. Both methods are cost-effective for solving convex relaxation problems. To prove that our method is superior to WocaR-PPO, we use the parameters of WocaR-PPO.

Since we don't use the value-enhanced state regularization used in WocaR-PPO, the results may be lower than those in the paper, but the final result is within our acceptance range. We show the comparison results in Table 1. We can see that on Ant, Walker2D, Halfcheetah, the model we reproduce is robust when faced with a powerful RS attack. On Hopper, the results similar to those in the paper cannot be obtained. Nonetheless, the released model of author can only achieve 1400 when tested against RS attack, which also can't obtain the results in paper. Besides, our methods, MaQSM outperforms other robust training methods both in terms of natural reward and best attack reward except in Hopper. About our two methods implementing Q-smoothing, there is an interesting finding: MaQSM(a manually designed IBP methods) outperforms AutoQSM(using IBP+CROWN). IBP based training is effective but suffer from the stability issues. IBP+CROWN combines the efficiency of IBP and a tighter linear convex based bonuds of CROWN. However, results show that AutoQSM can't achieve the same effects as MaQSM obviously and even can't be as good as WocaR-PPO when a powerful RS attack is applied. In Fig. 5, we show the learning curves of our methods and WocaR-PPO during training on four mujoco environments and the learning curve is Gaussian smoothed. Our method(MaQSM) has a higher reward value compared to WocaR-PPO. In Fig. 6, we conduct a comprehensive investigation of the reward values obtained by agents under different attack budgets. The attack budget range is within plus or minus 0.05 of the attack budget for each environment. Our approach is not only more robust within the trained attack budget, it also performs better when faced with a larger attack budget.

We emphasize that we use the best WocaR-PPO for a fair comparison. In order to implement a high-quality WocaR-PPO, First of all, we need to improve the output of LSTM policy network for batch actions, because in the entire training framework, training Q_{wst} network not only requires each trajectory (s_t, a_t, r_t, s_{t+1}), but also requires the policy network to output action again. If a batch is randomly selected from the whole trajectories, as in MLP network structure, it will ignore the time sequence information. We divide the whole trajectories into several consecutive sequences, and update each sequence separately, so that the actions output by the LSTM policy network can make full use of the time sequence information. Then we use the hyperparameters of ATLA(implemented by LSTM network) and conduct a small scale of grid search on the learning rate of agent to find the optimal hyperparameters. We choose the entropy coefficient in [0.01, 0.0003, 0.0001], since for LSTM network we should allow a larger entropy bonus cofficient to allow sufficient exploration of the agent, which is mentioned in [29]. For the history length of LSTM cell, we choose it in [50, 100]. About the learning rate of Q_{wst}, we ues the same parameters released by the author of WocaR-PPO. After searching the above parameters, we find our best WocaR-PPO. Our method uses the same parameters as WocaR-PPO, and λ, parameter of our Q-smothing regularization, is chosen from $[0.01 \rightarrow 0.3]$.

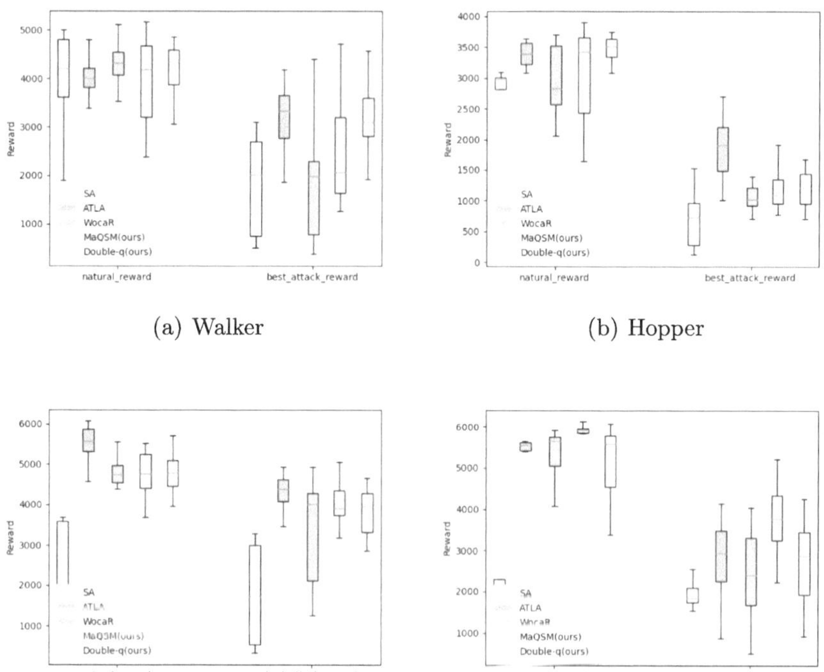

(a) Walker (b) Hopper

(c) Halfcheetah (d) Ant

Fig. 7. Box plots of natural rewards and best attack(RS) rewards. Each box is obtained from 15 agents trained with same hyperparameters. The red lines represent the median rewards, and the upper and lower sides of the boxes show 25% and 75% percentile rewards of 15 agents. The line segments outside the boxes show min or max rewards. (Color figure online)

Table 1. Average episode rewards ± standard over 50 episodes on 4 baselines and 2 our methods. We report natural rewards (no attacks) and rewards under 3 attacks. For each environment, we bold the vest results. And the row for the most robust agent is highlighted as gray.

Environment	Model	Natural Reward	Random	MAD	RS
Halfcheetah $\epsilon = 0.15$	PPO(vanilla)	**7117±98**	5486±1378	1836±866	489±758
	SA-PPO	3632±20	3619±18	3624±23	3283±20
	ATLA	6157±852	**6164±603**	**5790±174**	4806±392
	WocaR-PPO	4970±81	5000±51	4926±99	4304±127
	MaQSM(ours)	5522±57	5516±71	5434±70	**5053±220**
	AutoQSM(ours)	4416±90	4394±85	4306±93	4206±240
Walker2D $\epsilon = 0.05$	PPO(vanilla)	4472±635	3007±1200	2869±1271	1336±654
	SA-PPO	4487±61	4465±39	20±689	2071±665
	ATLA	3842±475	3927±368	3836±492	3239±294
	WocaR-PPO	4190±20	4194±17	4173±32	4187±31
	MaQSM(ours)	**4616±6**	**4712±8**	**4703±13**	**4614±9**
	AutoQSM(ours)	4414±72	4425±25	4387±189	4109±171
Hopper $\epsilon = 0.075$	PPO(vanilla)	3167±542	2101±793	1410±655	794±238
	SA-PPO	3702±3	2710±801	2652±835	1130±42
	ATLA	3282±633	3165±576	2814±725	**2244±618**
	WocaR-PPO	3590±3	3577±12	**3578±49**	1024±791
	MaQSM(ours)	**3697±25**	**3712±21**	3472±536	1333±754
	AutoQSM(ours)	3684±27	3694±21	3265±663	1506±741
Ant $\epsilon = 0.15$	PPO(vanilla)	5687±758	5261±1005	1759±828	268±227
	SA-PPO	4292±384	4986±452	4662±522	2412±1755
	ATLA	5359±153	5366±104	5240±170	4136±149
	WocaR-PPO	5729±398	**5768±120**	5333±139	4050±170
	MaQSM(ours)	**5838±122**	5732±92	5386±108	**4387±132**
	AutoQSM(ours)	5387±773	5469±124	**5456±119**	4023±216

5.2 Comparison of Double Q Mechanism

Through our experiments, we find that the double Q mechanism do not show significantly higher rewards when applying strong attacks. However, the overall performance of the agent is more stable than that of WocaR-PPO. In this subsection, we utilize a new way to reflect the stability of our method. We randomly train 15 groups of agents and compared the reward values of our methods and WocaR-PPO, ATLA-PPO and SA-PPO under the strongest attacks. We utilize boxplot to reflect the stability of our method.

In Fig. 7, we can see that in all four environments, ATLA-PPO exhibits excellent experimental results, appearing to outperform WocaR-PPO. However, during our experiments, we find that WocaR-PPO, while lacking robust stability and potentially delivering poor performance when encountering strong RS attacks, consistently achieves 3–4 instances of exceptionally good results in an average of every 15 training sessions. The unstable performance of WocaR-PPO validates inherent flaws in the algorithm, as discussed in Sect. 4.1, 4.2. About our double Q mechanism, The fluctuation value is obviously smaller than that of WocaR-PPO especially in Walker2D and Halfcheetah environment. In both environments, there is no significant difference in the natural reward, but when a strong attack is added, the model trained by our method can obtain a more stable reward value, although the median value of the two methods is similar. On Ant, the two methods show similar fluctuation value when facing RS attack. This could be because the number of steps trained in ant environment is much larger than that in other environments, so ant environment does not perform more stable. However, all indicators in the boxplot are higher than those in WocaR-PPO. Although on Hopper, our reproduced experimental results are not ideal, WocaR-PPO may not be applicable to Hopper. The effect will also be improved after the double Q mechanism is added. Except for Hopper, we find that our model tends to be more unstable when no attacks is employed, but obviously more stable when strong attack is applied.

Regarding the Q-Smoothing mechanism, although stability is not its main advantage, we still present its boxplot. Due to its superior performance compared to AutoQSM, we only plot the boxplot for MaQSM. It can be seen that MaQSM is significantly superior to WocaR-PPO, although it also faces unstable training situations, especially in the Walker environment. In the Ant environment, MaQSM achieve a very significant effect, showing strong robustness compared with all other algorithms. This is because the Ant environment has a 111-dimensional state space, and our smoothing measures are designed to keep the relative output of the Q_{wst} network unchanged when there is a small state disturbance. This phenomenon also proves the effectiveness of our Q smoothing mechanism.

In summary, the two mechanisms we designed, Q smoothing and double Q mechanism, are superior to WocaR-PPO, which can be clearly seen from the boxplot. Although compared with ATLA-PPO, our method may not be comprehensively superior in the four environments, our method has the possibility of obtaining a more stable model, that is, higher reward value when facing strongest attacks, but the defect is that such a model cannot be guaranteed to appear frequently in the training process. According to our experimental statistics, In every 15 training sessions, there are often 2–5 very ideal models, which are far more effective than ATLA-PPO. Apart from these very ideal models, the rest of the models may achieve slightly worse results. This phenomenon leads to the fact that in our boxplot, The models in the walker and halfcheetah environments are slightly inferior to ATLA-PPO.

5.3 Analysis of Time Efficiency

In this section, we compare the training time of the algorithm, since the core advantage of WocaR-PPO is to train a Q_{wst} network instead of training an optimal opponent, this algorithm has the advantage of taking less time. The comparison of algorithm training time is shown in Table 2. In the Ant environment, we find that the use of Q_{wst} network do not significantly reduce the training time compared with ATLA, because the two algorithms have the same training steps. Although ATLA needs to train an adversary, the training time of the adversary in our experiment only accounts for about 1/6 of the training time of the agent. In environments other than Ant, the training time is significantly reduced because the WocaR algorithm converges in only 2 million steps. In addition, regarding our method, Q smoothing mechanism, based on the fact that we use IBP to calculate the smoothing term, the calculation of this term increases the running time by 7.4% (implement by IBP) and 29% (implemented by IBP+CROWN). Using IBP+CROWN technique takes far more time than using IBP method. With respect to the double-Q method, since each iteration adds one more backpropagation of the network and requires an additional gradient descent to find the worst action, this increases the training time by 25%.

Table 2. Efficiency comparison of state-of-the art algorithms and our methods. The table only displays the Halfcheetah and Ant environments because Walker2D and Hopper have the same training time as Halfcheetah.

model	Halfcheetah		Ant	
	Time (h)	Step (m)	Time (h)	Step (m)
SA-PPO	0.6	2.0	3.2	10.0
ATLA-PPO	7.4	5.0	16.5	10.0
WocaR	2.7	2.0	13.9	10.0
MaQSM	2.8	2.0	15	10.0
AutoQSM	3.5	2.0	18.9	10.0
Double-Q	3.4	2.0	16	10.0

6 Conclusion

In this work, we mainly focus on the inner vulnerability of the worst-case Q estimate function. A simple Q_{wst} network cannot accurately predict the worst value, so we propose two effective methods to address the instability and over-conservative problems of Q_{wst} network itself. Experiments show that our two methods can improve the robustness of the trained model from different aspects compared with WocaR-PPO. In addition, we propose to classify two different Q network updates, Q^p_{update} and Q^w_{update}, which highlights the impact of dynamic action sets on the stability of Bellman equation updates.

However, there is room for exploration in our approach. Our work is an indirect way to improve the Q_{wst}, it is also worth studying to try to make the bounds of A_{adv} tighter which is mentioned in [16], such as improving the tightness of IBP or another way to solve convex relaxation. In addition, although our approach can maintain good results in the face of strong attacks, it is not always successful. As our experimental results show, the model is less stable than ATLA in some environments, so a robust reinforcement learning approach that can improve the success rate of model training should be paid attention to.

References

1. Behzadan, V., Munir, A.: Vulnerability of deep reinforcement learning to policy induction attacks. In: Machine Learning and Data Mining in Pattern Recognition: 13th International Conference, MLDM 2017, New York, NY, USA, 15–20 July 2017, Proceedings 13, pp. 262–275. Springer (2017)
2. Cohen, J.M., Rosenfeld, E., Kolter, J.Z.: Certified adversarial robustness via randomized smoothing (2019)
3. Fujimoto, S., Hoof, H., Meger, D.: Addressing function approximation error in actor-critic methods. In: International Conference on Machine Learning, pp. 1587–1596. PMLR (2018)
4. Goodfellow, I.J., Shlens, J., Szegedy, C.: Explaining and harnessing adversarial examples (2015)
5. Gowal, S., et al.: On the effectiveness of interval bound propagation for training verifiably robust models (2019)
6. Han, Y., et al.: Reinforcement learning for autonomous defence in software-defined networking (2018)
7. Huang, S., Papernot, N., Goodfellow, I., Duan, Y., Abbeel, P.: Adversarial attacks on neural network policies (2017)
8. Huang, Y., Zhu, Q.: Deceptive reinforcement learning under adversarial manipulations on cost signals (2019)
9. Prabuchandran, K.J., Hemanth Kumar, A.N., Bhatnagar, S.: Multi-agent reinforcement learning for traffic signal control. In: 17th International IEEE Conference on Intelligent Transportation Systems (ITSC), pp. 2529–2534 (2014). https://doi.org/10.1109/ITSC.2014.6958095
10. Kos, J., Song, D.: Delving into adversarial attacks on deep policies. arXiv preprint arXiv:1705.06452 (2017)
11. Kumar, A., Levine, A., Feizi, S.: Policy smoothing for provably robust reinforcement learning (2022)
12. Lecuyer, M., Atlidakis, V., Geambasu, R., Hsu, D., Jana, S.: Certified robustness to adversarial examples with differential privacy (2019)
13. Lee, X.Y., Esfandiari, Y., Tan, K.L., Sarkar, S.: Query-based targeted action-space adversarial policies on deep reinforcement learning agents (2021)
14. Lee, X.Y., Ghadai, S., Tan, K.L., Hegde, C., Sarkar, S.: Spatiotemporally constrained action space attacks on deep reinforcement learning agents (2019)
15. Li, B., Chen, C., Wang, W., Carin, L.: Certified adversarial robustness with additive noise (2019)

16. Liang, Y., Sun, Y., Zheng, R., Huang, F.: Efficient adversarial training without attacking: worst-case-aware robust reinforcement learning. Adv. Neural. Inf. Process. Syst. **35**, 22547–22561 (2022)
17. Lin, Y.C., Hong, Z.W., Liao, Y.H., Shih, M.L., Liu, M.Y., Sun, M.: Tactics of adversarial attack on deep reinforcement learning agents. arXiv preprint arXiv:1703.06748 (2017)
18. Mao, Y., Müller, M.N., Fischer, M., Vechev, M.: Understanding certified training with interval bound propagation (2023)
19. Mirman, M., Gehr, T., Vechev, M.: Differentiable abstract interpretation for provably robust neural networks. In: International Conference on Machine Learning, pp. 3578–3586. PMLR (2018)
20. Oikarinen, T., Zhang, W., Megretski, A., Daniel, L., Weng, T.W.: Robust deep reinforcement learning through adversarial loss. Adv. Neural. Inf. Process. Syst. **34**, 26156–26167 (2021)
21. Pan, X., et al.: Characterizing attacks on deep reinforcement learning. arXiv preprint arXiv:1907.09470 (2019)
22. Pinto, L., Davidson, J., Sukthankar, R., Gupta, A.: Robust adversarial reinforcement learning (2017)
23. Rakhsha, A., Radanovic, G., Devidze, R., Zhu, X., Singla, A.: Policy teaching via environment poisoning: training-time adversarial attacks against reinforcement learning (2020)
24. Shen, Q., Li, Y., Jiang, H., Wang, Z., Zhao, T.: Deep reinforcement learning with robust and smooth policy. In: International Conference on Machine Learning, pp. 8707–8718. PMLR (2020)
25. Sun, Y., Zheng, R., Liang, Y., Huang, F.: Who is the strongest enemy? Towards optimal and efficient evasion attacks in deep RL. arXiv preprint arXiv:2106.05087 (2021)
26. Tan, K.L., Esfandiari, Y., Lee, X.Y., Aakanksha, Sarkar, S.: Robustifying reinforcement learning agents via action space adversarial training (2020)
27. de Vrieze, C., Barratt, S., Tsai, D., Sahai, A.: Cooperative multi-agent reinforcement learning for low-level wireless communication (2018)
28. Xu, K., et al.: Automatic perturbation analysis for scalable certified robustness and beyond. Adv. Neural. Inf. Process. Syst. **33**, 1129–1141 (2020)
29. Zhang, H., Chen, H., Boning, D., Hsieh, C.J.: Robust reinforcement learning on state observations with learned optimal adversary. arXiv preprint arXiv:2101.08452 (2021)
30. Zhang, H., et al.: Towards stable and efficient training of verifiably robust neural networks (2019)
31. Zhang, H., et al.: Robust deep reinforcement learning against adversarial perturbations on state observations. Adv. Neural. Inf. Process. Syst. **33**, 21024–21037 (2020)

Gaze-Aware Voronoi-Based Key Region Optimization for Virtual Reality Text Input

Peng Du[1,2], Peng Liu[1(✉)], and Kentaro Go[2(✉)]

[1] Hangzhou Dianzi University, Hangzhou 310018, China
perryliu@hdu.edu.cn
[2] University of Yamanashi, Kofu 400-8510, Japan
go@yamanashi.ac.jp

Abstract. We present a lightweight optimization method to improve text input performance on virtual "drum-like" keyboards in immersive VR environments. By leveraging users' keypress positions, gaze behavior, and input errors, we reshape key response regions using a weighted Voronoi-based partitioning approach. Our system maintains a fixed visual layout while adapting key regions based on user interaction patterns. In a user study with 15 participants using the HMD with integrated eye tracking and controller input, both the weighted and unweighted Voronoi conditions improved typing speed compared to the baseline (mean = 24.88, 24.59, and 23.02 WPM; $p < 0.05$), without a corresponding increase in error rate. Further analysis revealed that users who benefited most from the optimization employed more frequent central or near-central visual targeting before keystrokes. These findings highlight the potential of gaze-aware spatial optimization in enhancing VR text input without additional hardware or layout modifications.

Keywords: Virtual Reality Text Input · Adaptive Interface · Eye Tracking · Geographic Partitioning

1 Introduction

Virtual keyboards have become essential input solutions across a wide spectrum of computing platforms, including smartphones, tablets, wearable devices, and immersive virtual or augmented reality environments. Despite their ubiquity, these keyboards often suffer from reduced typing speed and increased error rates compared to their physical counterparts, primarily due to the lack of tactile feedback and diverse contextual use conditions.

In immersive VR/XR environments, text input becomes even more challenging due to the lack of physical anchors and precise haptic feedback. To address these issues, researchers have explored various strategies, such as introducing external input hardware [9,14,21,25,42], reimagining input modalities [3,4], or combining modalities like hand tracking and speech [1]. However, these

L. Zhang and K.-K. R. Choo (Eds.): MobiQuitous 2025, LNICST 683, pp. 375–393, 2026.
https://doi.org/10.1007/978-3-032-22500-9_21

approaches often come with added hardware costs, lower input precision, or increased system complexity.

Among the emerging interaction paradigms, a "drum-like" virtual keyboard, where users strike floating keys in space using handheld controllers, has gained attention for its natural motion and compatibility with full-body VR setups [4,18]. Notably, these keyboards often retain a conventional 2D QWERTY layout but operate in a spatial 3D setting, introducing temporal and depth-related dynamics absent in touch-based input. Yet, few studies have examined how to adapt the input detection mechanism in such systems to account for user behavior and spatial variability.

In this work, we focus on optimizing key response regions in drum-like virtual keyboards by leveraging a behavior-driven approach. Specifically, we propose a 3D optimization framework based on Voronoi partitioning, where key response areas are dynamically adapted based on keypress locations, gaze behavior, input errors, and striking speed. This enables flexible adjustment of response boundaries while preserving a consistent visual layout—offering both adaptability and user familiarity.

Our goal is to enhance text input performance in immersive environments without altering the keyboard layout or requiring additional hardware.

Specifically, we contribute the following:

- We propose a novel 3D optimization framework that refines key response regions by combining spatial and temporal input features with gaze and error data, using Voronoi diagrams. This approach maintains a stable visual layout while improving typing efficiency, and can be extended to other spatial input modalities beyond VR.
- Through empirical analysis, we find that users who rely more on visual targeting gain the greatest benefit from the weighted Voronoi optimization. This finding emphasizes the value of incorporating gaze behavior in designing adaptive response regions for spatial input systems.

2 Related Work

2.1 Text Input Techniques in VR/XR Environments

To improve text entry performance in immersive environments, researchers have explored a wide range of techniques. One direction involves integrating external hardware, such as touch-sensitive surfaces for handwriting [9,21], motion or pressure sensors [14,25,42], designing novel dedicated input devices [15], and smartphones as auxiliary input devices [5,31,32]. While such solutions can improve input precision, they often entail higher cost and lower portability.

Another strategy leverages controller-based or hand-tracking interaction with virtual keyboards [33,35], or combines modalities like speech [1]. However, these techniques may suffer from latency, recognition errors, or ambiguous gesture interpretation. Recent studies [16,36] have shown that simple tap-based input often yields better performance in VR settings compared to gesture- or trajectory-based approaches.

Virtual keyboard layout redesign has also been explored to improve typing efficiency [22,29,37–39]. Nevertheless, empirical findings suggest that traditional 2D QWERTY layouts still provide superior speed and accuracy due to user familiarity [43].

An alternative line of research introduces novel interaction paradigms such as "drum-like" input, where users strike floating keys using handheld controllers [3,4,18]. This style has demonstrated competitive performance in immersive contexts. Notably, these works focus primarily on interaction modality rather than dynamically adapting the input response mechanism.

2.2 Virtual Keyboard Text Entry Optimization

Virtual keyboard optimization has been extensively studied in touchscreen contexts. Initial efforts explored alternative static layouts [19,20,23,30], though such designs often require users to relearn key positions, resulting in increased cognitive load.

To maintain layout familiarity while improving input, researchers have proposed dynamic key resizing or repositioning techniques, such as adjusting key regions based on touch distributions [11], or predictive models for next-character probability [2,13]. However, maintaining visual layout stability has been shown to be critical for usability [10].

More recent work has incorporated contextual and behavioral signals—such as user-specific error patterns [17], fingers interaction [7,24], detailed analysis of touch events [8,34,40], and sensor data [12,41], to create personalized or adaptive keyboards. While promising, many of these methods introduce additional hardware requirements or increase system complexity.

Advances in AI have led to the application of large language models for real-time text prediction and correction [6,26], but such methods can introduce computational overhead and latency, particularly in standalone VR/AR devices.

In contrast to these approaches, our method optimizes input performance by dynamically refining key response regions in a spatial virtual keyboard, without altering the visual layout or requiring external sensors. By leveraging gaze behavior, keypress offsets, and error patterns, we provide a lightweight, behavior-adaptive solution that improves performance while preserving usability and deployability in immersive environments.

3 Method

We present a behavior-aware input optimization framework for virtual keyboards in immersive VR environments. Our method is built upon a 3D Voronoi-based response mechanism that leverages the spatial and kinetic properties of drum-style interactions. To further adapt to individual user behavior, we introduce a multimodal weighting scheme that integrates gaze attention, character-level input frequency, and historical error patterns. This section details the core components of our approach, including the baseline Voronoi response modeling, geometric correction via displacement vectors, and behaviorally driven modulation of key selection dynamics.

3.1 Voronoi-Based Response Region Optimization

Our system adopts a drum-like virtual keyboard, where users interact with keys by striking down onto a shared trigger surface using a virtual mallet. Unlike traditional 2D keyboards, this setup allows us to leverage the *depth* (z-axis) and velocity of collisions to infer more nuanced intent during fast or imprecise input. In this context, we propose a Voronoi-based response region design that operates in 3D space and supports transparent response optimization.

Formally, let $\mathbf{p} \in \mathbb{R}^3$ denote the *3D contact point* of a mallet strike, and let $\mathbf{c}_i \in \mathbb{R}^3$ denote the center position of key i, both represented in a normalized local coordinate space to ensure device-independent scaling. Each key is initially associated with a cuboid response region. The system computes the Euclidean distance between the contact point and all key centers:

$$d_i = \|\mathbf{p} - \mathbf{c}_i\| \tag{1}$$

The key with the smallest d_i is selected as the input key. This effectively implements a *3D Voronoi tessellation*, where each key center defines a region of influence in the shared trigger volume.

To further improve input accuracy while preserving the visual layout, we collect a set of actual contact points $\{\mathbf{p}_i^{(j)}\}_{j=1}^{N_i}$ for each key i, and compute a *mean displacement vector* $\boldsymbol{\delta}_i$ between the contact points and the key center:

$$\boldsymbol{\delta}_i = \frac{1}{N_i} \sum_{j=1}^{N_i} \left(\mathbf{p}_i^{(j)} - \mathbf{c}_i\right) \tag{2}$$

Rather than altering the physical key layout, we incorporate the mean displacement vector as an offset during runtime, effectively personalizing the Voronoi sites without disrupting user familiarity.

$$\tilde{\mathbf{c}}_i = \mathbf{c}_i + \boldsymbol{\delta}_i \tag{3}$$

Adjusting selection without changing visual layout. The updated selection rule is:

$$\hat{\imath} = \arg\min_i \|\mathbf{p} - \tilde{\mathbf{c}}_i\| \tag{4}$$

This strategy preserves the visual layout and user familiarity while reducing selection error in a data-driven manner. The result is a transparent, personalized optimization process that adapts to user tendencies (e.g., consistent directional bias) without increasing cognitive or visual burden.

This design is particularly suited for drum-like input mechanisms, which naturally involve motion depth and kinetic variability. Unlike existing 2D input methods such as raycasting or gaze-based keyboards that operate solely in the xy plane, our method leverages the additional depth dimension to refine response regions. Furthermore, by projecting or reducing this 3D optimization to lower dimensions, the approach can be adapted to enhance response accuracy in conventional 2D keyboards as well.

3.2 Behavior and Attention-Driven Voronoi Field Modulation

While the previous section optimized Voronoi response regions based on aggregated 3D contact points from user strikes, this approach still relies solely on spatial information and assumes equal importance for all keys. Such geometry-driven adjustment may not fully capture user-specific behavioral patterns and cognitive cues.

To address this limitation, we propose a multimodal weighting scheme that integrates not only strike locations but also users' visual attention, character-level usage frequency, and input discrepancies. By combining these behavioral signals, the system modulates Voronoi regions in a personalized manner.

Gaze-Based Attention Estimation. We begin by analyzing the user's gaze behavior to infer the visual attention distributed across the keyboard. Using eye-tracking data, we compute the total gaze time spent on each key and derive an average gaze duration d_i per key. To obtain a normalized attention score, we scale this value to the range $[0, 1]$:

$$g_i = \frac{d_i - d_{\min}}{d_{\max} - d_{\min}} \tag{5}$$

This step prioritizes keys that were consistently monitored during the input process.

Input Error-Based Frequency Estimation. To account for actual typing behavior, we compute the per-character discrepancy between the intended text and the user's input. Let h_i denote the frequency of character i in the target sequence and u_i the frequency in the user's actual input. The difference $f_i = h_i - u_i$ reflects the underuse or overuse of each character. We normalize this to:

$$f_i' = \frac{f_i - f_{\min}}{f_{\max} - f_{\min}} \tag{6}$$

This highlights keys that are frequently confused, offering a behaviorally grounded correction signal.

Adaptive Multimodal Blending. To integrate the visual and behavioral priors, we use an adaptive weight blending strategy. Let T_{keyboard} and T_{total} denote the total gaze time on the keyboard and the entire interface, respectively. We define the gaze engagement ratio:

$$\alpha = \text{clip}\left(\frac{T_{\text{keyboard}}}{T_{\text{total}}},\ 0.2,\ 0.8\right) \tag{7}$$

To prevent extreme gaze ratios from dominating the blending weights, we constrain α within a reasonable range $[0.2, 0.8]$. This ensures that the blending mechanism remains responsive to user attention, while avoiding overly large or small values that may arise from brief or highly focused gaze patterns. Then, for each key, we blend the visual attention score and the error score into a unified weight:

$$w_i = \alpha \cdot g_i + (1 - \alpha) \cdot f_i' \tag{8}$$

To enable direct use of the weights in subsequent geometry computations, we transform the blended weights w_i into size scaling factors that represent each key's relative size. We introduce a scaling parameter $\delta \in (0, 1)$ to constrain the range of size changes, and compute the final weight as:

$$\tilde{w}_i = 1 - \delta + 2\delta \cdot \frac{w_i - w_{\min}}{w_{\max} - w_{\min}} \tag{9}$$

This produces normalized scaling factors $\tilde{w}_i \in [1-\delta,\ 1+\delta]$, where $\tilde{w}_i$ directly determines the key's geometric size. For example, $\tilde{w}_i = 0.8$ means the key is reduced to 80% of its original size, while $\tilde{w}_i = 1.2$ indicates a 20% enlargement.

We set $\delta = 0.2$ to limit key resizing within $\pm 20\%$, ensuring perceptual consistency, usability, and numerical stability for the downstream Voronoi-based distance computations. This range is empirically chosen to balance adaptive geometric feedback and key usability, while also enabling stable use in subsequent distance-based selection mechanisms.

Weighted Voronoi Distance and Response Adjustment. To integrate multimodal behavioral priors into the input process, we redefine the Voronoi distance function as a weighted form:

$$d_i = \frac{\|\mathbf{p} - \mathbf{c}_i\|}{\tilde{w}_i} \tag{10}$$

where $\mathbf{p}$ is the user's contact point and $\mathbf{c}_i$ is the original center of key i. The term $\tilde{w}_i$ represents a normalized behavioral weight for key i, derived from visual attention, target frequency, and historical input performance.

This modification causes keys with higher weights to dominate a larger share of the Voronoi space, thus becoming easier to activate even when the contact is imprecise.

In addition, we refine the Voronoi site position by combining this weight with the mean displacement vector $\boldsymbol{\delta}_i$ computed earlier:

$$\tilde{\mathbf{c}}_i = \mathbf{c}_i + \tilde{w}_i \cdot \boldsymbol{\delta}_i \tag{11}$$

Unlike purely geometric corrections, this adjustment is further modulated by behavioral weight, reinforcing keys that are not only frequently mistapped but also behaviorally important.

This weighted Voronoi site defines the new selection rule:

$$\hat{i} = \arg\min_{i} \frac{\|\mathbf{p} - \tilde{\mathbf{c}}_i\|}{\tilde{w}_i} \tag{12}$$

This strategy builds on data-driven displacement correction while seamlessly incorporating behavioral priors, all without disrupting the visual layout.

Interpretation and Benefits. The proposed weighted Voronoi optimization improves input precision by dynamically adapting key response regions based on users' behavioral signals, such as gaze patterns and input errors. Rather than changing the visual layout of the keyboard, our method refines the internal key selection logic by adjusting Voronoi regions to reflect usage intent and reliability.

Figure 1 illustrates two different methods of optimizing key response regions using Voronoi diagrams. The top subfigure shows the unweighted Voronoi optimization, where key centers are adjusted based on touch data, improving alignment with user behavior while keeping region sizes uniform. The bottom subfigure presents the weighted Voronoi optimization, which further adjusts both the positions and the sizes of the response regions according to behavioral relevance. Keys with low gaze attention and frequent incorrect activations receive smaller regions, while those with higher omission rates are allocated larger regions to improve selection accuracy.

For instance, the key "B" was down-weighted due to low gaze attention and frequent incorrect activation, whereas the key "T" received a larger region due to frequent omission despite being appropriately gazed at.

This method adjusts the internal key selection logic without changing the visible keyboard layout, preserving users' spatial familiarity while improving selection accuracy. It is device-agnostic and applicable to both 2D (e.g., touchscreen) and 3D (e.g., VR) input scenarios.

4 Experimental Design

4.1 Experiment Setup

The experiment was conducted using the HTC VIVE Focus Vision, a standalone VR headset equipped with built-in eye-tracking capabilities. Before the typing tasks, each participant reviewed and signed an informed consent form, completed a brief questionnaire regarding typing and VR experience, and received instructions on how to operate the VR headset and controller. Gaze calibration was performed using the headset's native system to ensure accurate eye-tracking.

Participants performed text input tasks using a virtual keyboard with a drum-like input style. Specifically, users held a virtual mallet and performed tapping actions onto a virtual keyboard surface, simulating rhythmic drumming

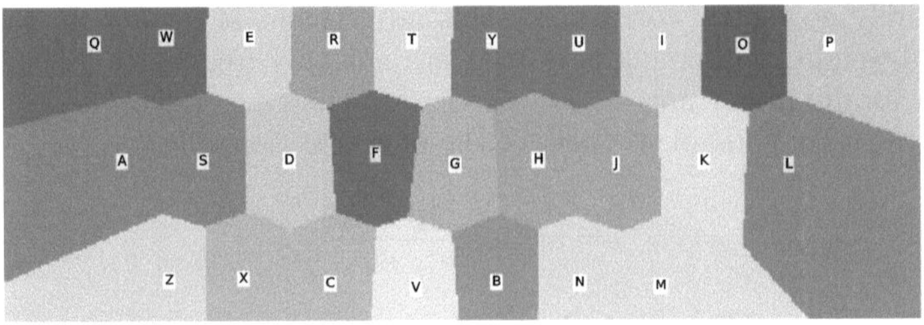

(a) Unweighted Voronoi projection after key center shifts.

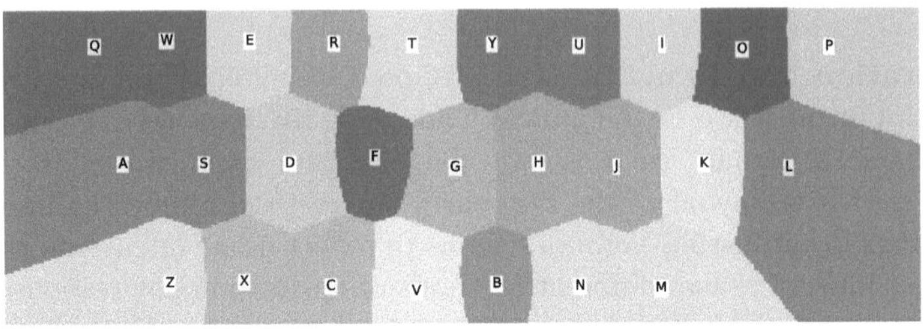

(b) Weighted Voronoi projection with adaptive region sizes based on attention and errors.

Fig. 1. Projected XY-plane diagrams of key response regions after Voronoi-based optimization. (a) Key centers are adjusted using user touch behavior, resulting in behavior-aligned Voronoi boundaries while keeping region areas equal. (b) Both key centers and response region sizes are adapted based on behavioral weights, expanding or shrinking areas to reflect attention and error-driven significance.

behavior. This interaction method enabled clear spatial targeting and emphasized rapid tapping input, differing from traditional hand-hovering or direct-touch typing in VR.

Three keyboard conditions were tested in the experiment: (A) a baseline version without any optimization, (B) a version with key response areas optimized via Voronoi partitioning (Voronoi optimization), and (C) a version with both key response positions and sizes jointly optimized using weighted Voronoi partitioning (Weighted Voronoi optimization). Notably, while the visual layout of the keyboard remained consistent across all conditions, the responsive regions varied internally based on the optimization strategy.

Each condition required participants to transcribe 35 short English sentences presented in the virtual environment. Participants were instructed to complete each transcription task as quickly and accurately as possible. The sentence stimuli were selected from a standardized phrase set specifically designed for evaluating text entry techniques [27], which ensures a balance of linguistic properties and enables comparability across studies. A practice session was provided before the formal tasks, and a ten-minute break was scheduled between keyboard conditions to reduce fatigue. To mitigate order effects such as learning or fatigue bias, the sequence of keyboard conditions was randomized for each participant.

Throughout the experiment, the system automatically recorded various behavioral signals, including gaze fixation points, keystroke positions and timestamps, and total input time per sentence. Participants were free to pause or withdraw from the study at any time.

4.2 Evaluation Metrics

To evaluate the text entry performance across different keyboard conditions, we employed three widely used metrics: *Words Per Minute* (WPM), *Corrected Error Rate* (CER), and *Uncorrected Error Rate* (UER), as standardized in prior work on text entry evaluation [28]. WPM was calculated as:

$$\text{WPM} = \frac{(|T| - 1)}{t} \times \frac{60}{5}$$

where $|T|$ is the number of transcribed characters and t is the time in seconds. The subtraction of one accounts for the fact that timing starts after the first keystroke, and a standard word is defined as five characters.

CER and UER were computed as follows:

$$\text{CER} = \frac{IF}{C + INF + IF}, \quad \text{UER} = \frac{INF}{C + INF + IF}$$

where C denotes the number of correct characters in the transcribed text, INF the number of incorrect characters that were not corrected, and IF the number of incorrect characters that were corrected via backspace. In this study, IF is approximated by the total number of deleted characters recorded during typing, since the number of backspace key presses does not necessarily equal the number of corrected errors due to varied typing behaviors.

These metrics collectively capture both the speed and accuracy of the user's input, including their error correction behavior during VR-based text entry.

5 Experimental Results

5.1 Participants

A total of 15 participants (12 males, 3 females; mean age = 27.73, SD = 8.05) took part in the experiment. All participants had prior experience typing on virtual keyboards, while only 3 participants had previous experience typing specifically in VR environments. Although none of the participants were native English speakers, which potentially affected overall typing speed and variance, the relative performance differences between keyboard conditions remain valid and interpretable. This background information was collected via a pre-experiment questionnaire.

5.2 Typing Performance Across Conditions

To evaluate typing performance under different conditions, we compared WPM, UER, and CER across three keyboard conditions: Normal, Voronoi (V), and Weighted Voronoi (WV). Each metric was analyzed across 15 participants.

Typing Speed (WPM). As shown in Fig. 2, participants achieved the highest average typing speed under the WV condition (mean = 24.88 WPM, SD = 6.29), followed by the V condition (mean = 24.59 WPM, SD = 5.78), and then the Normal condition (mean = 23.02 WPM, SD = 5.96). However, the typing speeds exhibited relatively wide interquartile ranges and several outliers. This variation is likely due to differences in sentence difficulty and participants' non-native English proficiency, which could cause certain sentences to take more or less time. Despite this variability, the optimized layouts generally yielded faster typing speeds than the Normal layout.

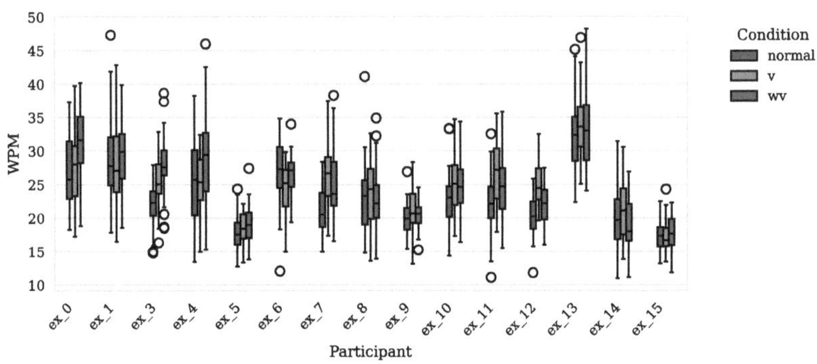

Fig. 2. WPM across the three keyboard conditions. WV demonstrates the highest typing speed with a tighter distribution across participants.

Error Rates. As shown in Figs. 3 and 4, both UER and CER remained low and comparable across all conditions. UER values were 0.0072 (SD = 0.0205) for Normal, 0.0075 (SD = 0.0183) for V, and 0.0077 (SD = 0.0220) for WV. CER values were 0.0307 (SD = 0.0492) for Normal, 0.0344 (SD = 0.0495) for V, and 0.0309 (SD = 0.0489) for WV. Variation among participants was small, and no outliers were observed.

Statistical Analysis of Typing Performance. To examine the impact of different input conditions on typing performance, we conducted a *repeated-measures ANOVA* across three key metrics: WPM, UER, and CER. Table 1 presents the results.

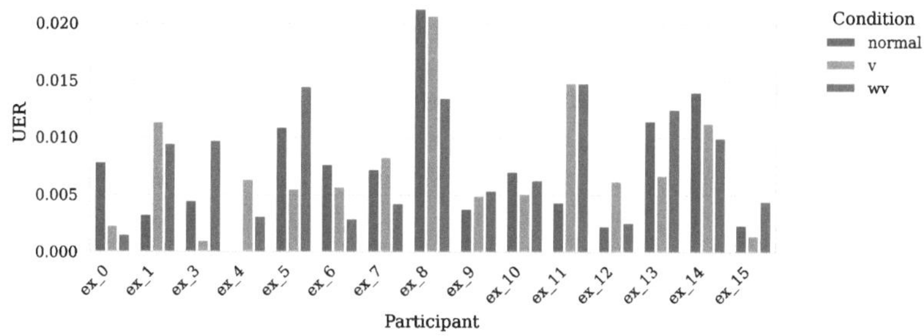

Fig. 3. UER per participant across conditions. Error rates remain low across all conditions, with no statistically significant differences.

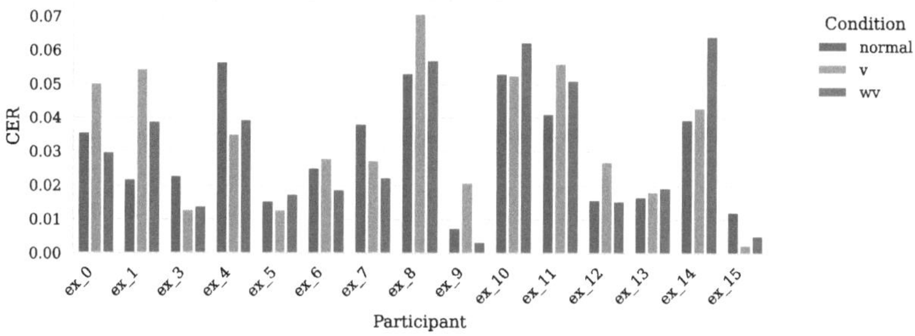

Fig. 4. CER per participant. The V condition induces more corrections, while WV mitigates this and returns CER closer to baseline.

The analysis revealed a significant main effect of input condition on WPM, $F(2, 28) = 7.12$, $p = .0032$, with a *partial* η^2 of .337, indicating a medium-to-large effect size. In contrast, no significant effects were found for UER ($F(2, 28) = 0.07$, $p = .9311$, partial $\eta^2 = .005$) or CER ($F(2, 28) = 0.91$, $p = .4126$, partial $\eta^2 = .061$), suggesting that the different input methods did not significantly influence error rates.

Table 1. Repeated-Measures ANOVA Results Across Input Conditions

Measure	F	df	p-value	partial η^2
WPM	7.12	(2, 28)	.0032	.337
UER	0.07	(2, 28)	.9311	.005
CER	0.91	(2, 28)	.4126	.061

To further explore differences between specific conditions, *pairwise comparisons* were conducted using paired t-tests. Table 2 summarizes the mean changes, percentage differences, p-values, *Cohen's d effect sizes*, and *statistical power estimates* (computed at $\alpha = 0.05$) across the three keyboard conditions.

The results indicate that both the Voronoi and Weighted Voronoi conditions significantly improved typing speed compared to the Normal condition. Specifically, WV vs. Normal yielded an 8.07% increase in WPM ($p = 0.0023$, $d = 0.96$), and V vs. Normal yielded a 7.37% increase ($p = 0.0126$, $d = 0.74$), both with high statistical power. After applying Bonferroni correction for multiple comparisons (adjusted significance level $\alpha' = 0.05/3 \approx 0.0167$), these differences remain statistically significant.

However, no significant differences were observed for either UER or CER across any condition pairs. The small effect sizes and low power in these metrics suggest that the differences in error rates are likely negligible.

Taken together, these findings suggest that our proposed optimizations significantly enhance typing speed while maintaining comparable levels of accuracy.

Table 2. Summary of pairwise comparisons between keyboard conditions (Normal, Voronoi, Weighted Voronoi). Each row shows mean difference (in % for WPM), p-value, effect size (d), and statistical power. Bold values indicate statistically significant differences ($p < 0.05$).

Metric	Comparison	Mean Change (%)	p / d / Power
WPM	WV vs Normal	**+1.85 (8.07%)**	$p = 0.0023$, $d = 0.96$, power=0.93
	V vs Normal	**+1.56 (7.37%)**	$p = 0.0126$, $d = 0.74$, power=0.76
	WV vs V	+0.29 (1.06%)	$p = 0.6050$, $d = 0.14$, power=0.08
UER	WV vs Normal	+0.0005	$p = 0.7188$, $d = 0.09$, power=0.06
	V vs Normal	+0.0003	$p = 0.8399$, $d = 0.05$, power=0.05
	WV vs V	+0.0002	$p = 0.8624$, $d = 0.05$, power=0.05
CER	WV vs Normal	+0.0003	$p = 0.9292$, $d = 0.02$, power=0.05
	V vs Normal	+0.0039	$p = 0.2999$, $d = 0.28$, power=0.17
	WV vs V	-0.0036	$p = 0.2441$, $d = -0.31$, power=0.21

Summary. Both Voronoi-based conditions increased typing speed without introducing substantial increases in error rates. The WV condition, in particular, achieved the best balance between speed and accuracy, outperforming both the baseline and unweighted Voronoi variants in speed while maintaining low error rates. While our study focused on VR-based drum-like keyboards, the benefits observed with weighted Voronoi optimization may inform future designs in other text entry contexts.

5.3 Gaze Behavior Differences Between Effective and Ineffective Users

To explore individual behavioral differences in response to the WV condition, we divided participants into two groups based on WV performance gain: Group A consists of the top three participants with the largest WPM improvement under WV compared to the Normal layout, while Group B includes the three participants who showed the least benefit from WV. We analyzed the gaze behavior of these two groups to explore how differences in visual attention patterns may underlie the variability in performance improvements observed under the WV optimization.

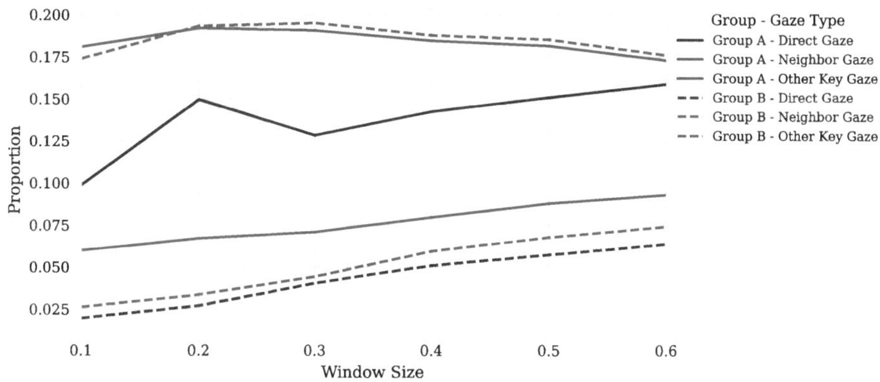

Fig. 5. Proportion of gaze types in the forward window (before keypress) for Group A and Group B across window sizes. Group A shows higher Direct and Neighbor Gaze.

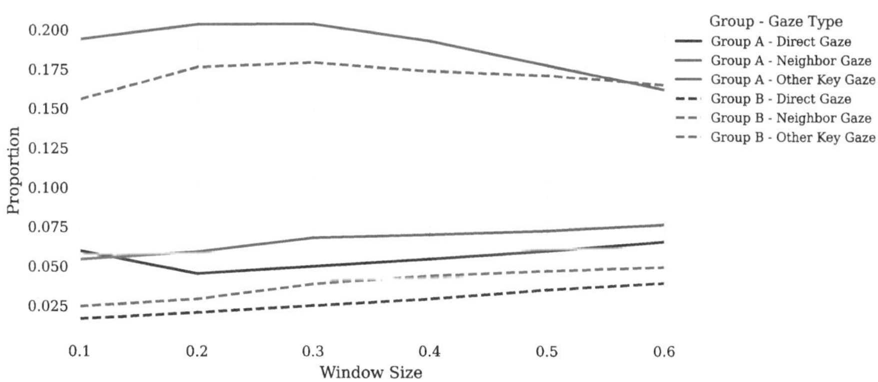

Fig. 6. Proportion of gaze types in the backward window (after keypress) for Group A and Group B. Differences are less pronounced.

Gaze Behavior Around Keystrokes. To understand how users visually targeted keys during typing, we examined gaze positions in the temporal window surrounding each keystroke. Each gaze sample was classified into one of three types: Direct Gaze (looking directly at the target key), Neighbor Gaze (looking at a key adjacent to the target), and Other Key Gaze (looking at any other key). Given that participants typed at 20–30 WPM (i.e., approximately 0.4–0.6 s per character), we analyzed gaze type proportions within windows ranging from 0.1 to 0.6 s before and after each keystroke.

Figure 5 shows gaze proportions in the forward window (before keystroke). Group A exhibited consistently higher proportions of Direct and Neighbor Gaze compared to Group B across all window sizes, while both groups had similar levels of Other Key Gaze. This suggests that Group A more frequently used central or near-central vision to locate keys prior to pressing them, whereas Group B tended to distribute their visual attention more broadly across the screen, often fixating on the overall input display rather than precisely targeting keys. Such dispersed gaze behavior may partly explain Group B's least benefit with the weighted Voronoi layout.

Figure 6 presents gaze behavior in the backward window (after keystroke). Here, both groups showed relatively stable proportions as the window size increased. Although Group A still had slightly higher Direct and Neighbor Gaze, the differences were less pronounced. Moreover, the proportion of Direct Gaze remained low overall, indicating that post-typing visual confirmation was quick and likely performed using peripheral rather than focused vision.

Gaze Heatmap Projection. To further examine visual targeting during typing, we analyzed gaze heatmaps projected onto the keyboard surface, specifically reduced to the keyboard's first row to reflect the typical visual path between input text and keyboard. Figure 7 contains three subplots: Group A's gaze distribution, Group B's distribution, and the difference map (Group A minus Group B). Notably, Group A showed lower visual fixation time over the central keys (RTYU) but higher peaks at keys E and I compared to Group B. This pattern suggests that Group A participants rely more on precise visual search targeting specific keys during typing, whereas Group B tends to keep gaze focused on the keyboard center area, using peripheral vision to locate needed keys. Such focused visual-motor coordination in Group A likely contributes to their greater typing speed improvements under the weighted Voronoi condition.

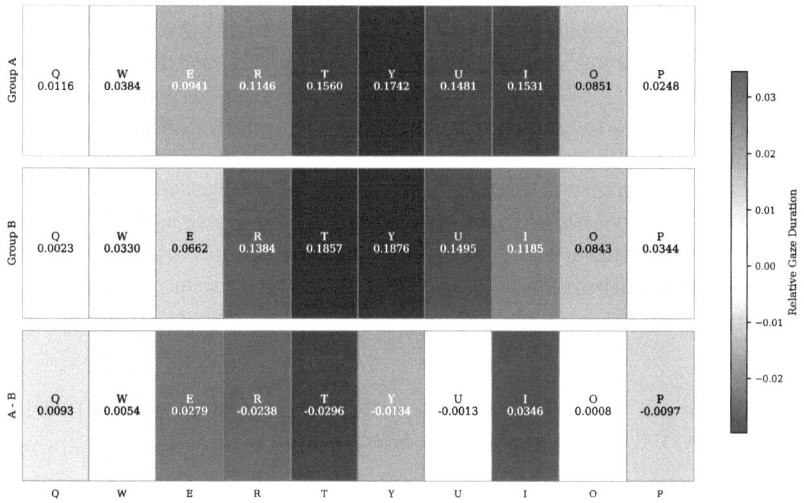

Fig. 7. Gaze heatmap projections onto the first row of the keyboard, showing visual fixation time distributions. Three subplots depict Group A, Group B, and the difference (A minus B). Group A shows lower fixation in central keys (RTYU) but higher peaks at E and I compared to Group B, indicating more targeted visual search versus Group B's reliance on broader central fixation and peripheral vision.

6 Conclusion

This study proposed a virtual keyboard optimization method based on geographic partitioning utilizing Voronoi diagrams to dynamically define key response areas, aiming to enhance typing efficiency. Experimental evaluations demonstrated that both the pure Voronoi and weighted Voronoi optimization methods improved typing speed compared to the traditional keyboard, with the WV method showing a slight but statistically non-significant advantage over the V method. Importantly, these improvements were achieved without significant increases in error rates. These results indicate that Voronoi-based spatial partitioning optimization can effectively enhance input performance, while the weighting scheme may provide incremental benefits that warrant further investigation.

Furthermore, in-depth analyses of gaze behavior revealed distinct differences between users who demonstrated clear performance improvements under the WV optimization and those whose performance changes were minimal or negative. Specifically, users benefiting from the WV method exhibited more focused visual attention on target keys, indicative of more efficient visual-motor coordination. These findings emphasize the relevance of accounting for individual differences in visual strategies when designing adaptive keyboard interfaces.

Nonetheless, this study has several limitations. The sample size was relatively small, and all participants were non-native English speakers, which may limit the generalizability of the findings. Furthermore, the eye-tracking data were collected using consumer-grade VR devices, which may lack the precision of specialized eye-tracking equipment, potentially affecting the accuracy of gaze behavior analyses.

Future work should validate these findings with larger and more diverse user groups, while considering cognitive and ergonomic factors such as load and fatigue. Further efforts will focus on enhancing the robustness of Z-axis data under motion-induced noise to ensure stable depth-aware key response modeling, and on exploring adaptive weighting based on users' visual strategies for more personalized optimization. Finally, extending the Voronoi-based framework to other input modalities, such as gesture or voice, represents a promising direction.

Acknowledgment. This research was partially supported by JSPS KAKENHI Grant Numbers JP20K11904, JP24K15633, and JP22H00549.

References

1. Adhikary, J., Vertanen, K.: Text entry in virtual environments using speech and a midair keyboard. IEEE Trans. Visual Comput. Graphics **27**(5), 2648–2658 (2021). https://doi.org/10.1109/TVCG.2021.3067776
2. Aulagner, G., François, R., Martin, B., Michel, D., Raynal, M.: Floodkey: increasing software keyboard keys by reducing needless ones without occultation. In: Proceedings of the 10th WSEAS International Conference on Applied Computer Science, pp. 412–417 (2010)
3. Boletsis, C., Kongsvik, S.: Controller-based text-input techniques for virtual reality: an empirical comparison (2019)
4. Boletsis, C., Kongsvik, S.: Text input in virtual reality: a preliminary evaluation of the drum-like VR keyboard. Technologies **7**(2), 31 (2019)
5. Boustila, S., Guégan, T., Takashima, K., Kitamura, Y.: Text typing in VR using smartphones touchscreen and HMD. In: 2019 IEEE Conference on Virtual Reality and 3D User Interfaces (VR), pp. 860–861. IEEE (2019)
6. Chen, L., et al.: Supporting text entry in virtual reality with large language models. In: 2024 IEEE Conference Virtual Reality and 3D User Interfaces (VR), pp. 524–534 (2024). https://doi.org/10.1109/VR58804.2024.00073
7. Choi, D., Cho, H., Cheong, J.: Improving virtual keyboards when all finger positions are known. In: Proceedings of the 28th Annual ACM Symposium on User Interface Software and Technology, pp. 529–538. UIST '15, Association for Computing Machinery, New York, NY, USA (2015). https://doi.org/10.1145/2807442.2807491
8. Edelmann, J., et al.: Towards the keyboard of oz: learning individual soft-keyboard models from raw optical sensor data. In: Proceedings of the 2012 ACM International Conference on Interactive Tabletops and Surfaces, pp. 163–172. ITS '12, Association for Computing Machinery, New York, NY, USA (2012). https://doi.org/10.1145/2396636.2396662
9. Fang, F., et al.: Handwriting Velcro: endowing AR glasses with personalized and posture-adaptive text input using flexible touch sensor. Proc. ACM Interact. Mob. Wearable Ubiquitous Technol. **6**(4) (2023). https://doi.org/10.1145/3569461

10. Findlater, L., Wobbrock, J.: Personalized input: improving ten-finger touchscreen typing through automatic adaptation. In: Proceedings of the SIGCHI Conference on Human Factors in Computing Systems, pp. 815–824. CHI '12, Association for Computing Machinery, New York, NY, USA (2012). https://doi.org/10.1145/2207676.2208520
11. Go, K., Endo, Y.: Catkey: customizable and adaptable touchscreen keyboard with bubble cursor-like visual feedback. In: Human-Computer Interaction–INTERACT 2007: 11th IFIP TC 13 International Conference, Rio de Janeiro, Brazil, September 10-14, 2007, Proceedings, Part I 11, pp. 493–496. Springer (2007)
12. Goel, M., Findlater, L., Wobbrock, J.: Walktype: using accelerometer data to accommodate situational impairments in mobile touch screen text entry. In: Proceedings of the SIGCHI Conference on Human Factors in Computing Systems, pp. 2687–2696. CHI '12. Association for Computing Machinery, New York, NY, USA (2012). https://doi.org/10.1145/2207676.2208662
13. Gunawardana, A., Paek, T., Meek, C.: Usability guided key-target resizing for soft keyboards. In: Proceedings of the 15th International Conference on Intelligent User Interfaces, pp. 111–118. IUI '10. Association for Computing Machinery, New York, NY, USA (2010). https://doi.org/10.1145/1719970.1719986
14. He, Z., Lutteroth, C., Perlin, K.: Tapgazer: Text entry with finger tapping and gaze-directed word selection. In: Proceedings of the 2022 CHI Conference on Human Factors in Computing Systems. CHI '22. Association for Computing Machinery, New York, NY, USA (2022). https://doi.org/10.1145/3491102.3501838
15. Jackson, B., Caraco, L.B., Spilka, Z.M.: Arc-type and tilt-type: pen-based immersive text input for room-scale VR. In: Proceedings of the 2020 ACM Symposium on Spatial User Interaction. SUI '20, Association for Computing Machinery, New York, NY, USA (2020). https://doi.org/10.1145/3385959.3418454
16. Kern, F., Niebling, F., Latoschik, M.E.: Text input for non-stationary XR workspaces: investigating tap and word-gesture keyboards in virtual and augmented reality. IEEE Trans. Visual Comput. Graphics **29**(5), 2658–2669 (2023). https://doi.org/10.1109/TVCG.2023.3247098
17. Ko, S.: A study on dynamic adaptation of soft keyboard using adjacent-typo. J. Korea Multimedia Soc. **21**(11), 1263–1270 (2018)
18. Kongsvik, S.: Text Input Techniques in Virtual Reality Environments-An empirical comparison. Master's thesis (2018)
19. Kuno, Y., Shizuki, B.: Meyboard: A qwerty-based soft keyboard for touch-typing on tablets. In: Human-Computer Interaction. Interaction Contexts: 19th International Conference, HCI International 2017, Vancouver, BC, Canada, July 9-14, 2017, Proceedings, Part II 19, pp. 193–207. Springer (2017)
20. Kuno, Y., Shizuki, B., Tanaka, J.: Long-term study of a software keyboard that places keys at positions of fingers and their surroundings. In: International Conference on Human-Computer Interaction, pp. 72–81. Springer (2013)
21. Kuś, S., Szmurło, R.: CNN-based character recognition for a contextless text input system in immersive VR. In: 2021 22nd International Conference on Computational Problems of Electrical Engineering (CPEE), pp. 1–4. IEEE (2021)
22. Leng, J., Wang, L., Liu, X., Shi, X., Wang, M.: Efficient flower text entry in virtual reality. IEEE Trans. Visual Comput. Graphics **28**(11), 3662–3672 (2022). https://doi.org/10.1109/TVCG.2022.3203101
23. Li, F.C.Y., Guy, R.T., Yatani, K., Truong, K.N.: The 1line keyboard: a qwerty layout in a single line. In: Proceedings of the 24th annual ACM symposium on User interface software and technology, pp. 461–470 (2011)

24. Li, Z., Yu, C., Gu, Y., Shi, Y.: Restype: invisible and adaptive tablet keyboard leveraging resting fingers. In: Proceedings of the 2023 CHI Conference on Human Factors in Computing Systems. CHI '23. Association for Computing Machinery, New York, NY, USA (2023). https://doi.org/10.1145/3544548.3581055
25. Lu, Y., et al.: Handpad: make your hand an on-the-go writing pad via human capacitance. In: Proceedings of the 37th Annual ACM Symposium on User Interface Software and Technology. UIST '24. Association for Computing Machinery, New York, NY, USA (2024). https://doi.org/10.1145/3654777.3676328
26. Ma, Y., Li, T., Li, Z., Bi, X.: LLM-powered text entry in virtual reality. In: 2025 IEEE Conference on Virtual Reality and 3D User Interfaces Abstracts and Workshops (VRW), pp. 1628–1629 (2025). https://doi.org/10.1109/VRW66409.2025.00459
27. MacKenzie, I.S., Soukoreff, R.W.: Phrase sets for evaluating text entry techniques. In: CHI '03 Extended Abstracts on Human Factors in Computing Systems, pp. 754–755. CHI EA '03. Association for Computing Machinery, New York, NY, USA (2003). https://doi.org/10.1145/765891.765971
28. MacKenzie, I.S., Tanaka-Ishii, K.: Text entry systems: Mobility, accessibility, universality. Elsevier (2010)
29. Nguyen, A., Bittman, S., Zank, M.: Text input methods in virtual reality using radial layouts. In: Proceedings of the 26th ACM Symposium on Virtual Reality Software and Technology, pp. 1–3 (2020)
30. Oney, S., Harrison, C., Ogan, A., Wiese, J.: Zoomboard: a diminutive qwerty soft keyboard using iterative zooming for ultra-small devices. In: Proceedings of the SIGCHI Conference on Human Factors in Computing Systems, pp. 2799–2802. CHI '13. Association for Computing Machinery, New York, NY, USA (2013). https://doi.org/10.1145/2470654.2481387
31. Pan, Z., Pan, Z., Luo, T., Zhang, M.: Exploring the use of smartphones as input devices for the mixed reality environment. In: Proceedings of the 18th ACM SIGGRAPH International Conference on Virtual-Reality Continuum and its Applications in Industry, pp. 1–7 (2022)
32. Qi, X., Weng, D., Hao, J., Li, Z.: Text input through swipe gestures based personalized AI agent. In: 2024 3rd International Conference on Automation, Robotics and Computer Engineering (ICARCE), pp. 435–439 (2024). https://doi.org/10.1109/ICARCE63054.2024.00088
33. Shen, J., Dudley, J., Kristensson, P.O.: Fast and robust mid-air gesture typing for AR headsets using 3D trajectory decoding. IEEE Trans. Visual Comput. Graphics **29**(11), 4622–4632 (2023). https://doi.org/10.1109/TVCG.2023.3320218
34. Shi, W., Yu, C., Yi, X., Li, Z., Shi, Y.: Toast: ten-finger eyes-free typing on touchable surfaces. Proc. ACM Interact. Mob. Wearable Ubiquitous Technol. **2**(1) (2018). https://doi.org/10.1145/3191765
35. Spiess, F., Weber, P., Schuldt, H.: Direct interaction word-gesture text input in virtual reality. In: 2022 IEEE International Conference on Artificial Intelligence and Virtual Reality (AIVR), pp. 140–143 (2022). https://doi.org/10.1109/AIVR56993.2022.00028
36. Wang, Y., et al.: A comparative study of the typing performance of two mid-air text input methods in virtual environments. Sensors **23**(15), 6988 (2023)
37. Whitmire, E., et al.: Digitouch: reconfigurable thumb-to-finger input and text entry on head-mounted displays. Proc. ACM Interact. Mobile Wearable Ubiquitous Technol. **1**(3), 1–21 (2017)

38. Wu, J., Wang, Z., Wang, L., Duan, Y., Li, J.: Fanpad: a fan layout touchpad keyboard for text entry in VR. In: 2024 IEEE Conference Virtual Reality and 3D User Interfaces (VR), pp. 222–232 (2024). https://doi.org/10.1109/VR58804.2024.00045
39. Yanagihara, N., Shizuki, B.: Cubic keyboard for virtual reality. In: Proceedings of the 2018 ACM Symposium on Spatial User Interaction, pp. 170–170 (2018)
40. Yanai, Y., Karashima, M.: Research on two dimensional touched position distributions of the touch screen qwerty keyboard. In: Stephanidis, C. (ed.) HCI International 2013 - Posters' Extended Abstracts, pp. 561–565. Springer, Berlin Heidelberg, Berlin, Heidelberg (2013)
41. Yi, X., Wang, C., Bi, X., Shi, Y.: Palmboard: leveraging implicit touch pressure in statistical decoding for indirect text entry. In: Proceedings of the 2020 CHI Conference on Human Factors in Computing Systems, pp. 1–13. CHI '20. Association for Computing Machinery, New York, NY, USA (2020). https://doi.org/10.1145/3313831.3376441
42. Yi, X., et al.: ATK: enabling ten-finger freehand typing in air based on 3D hand tracking data. In: Proceedings of the 28th Annual ACM Symposium on User Interface Software and Technology, pp. 539–548 (2015)
43. Yildirim, C., Osborne, E.: Text entry in virtual reality: a comparison of 2D and 3D keyboard layouts. In: International Conference on Human-computer Interaction, pp. 450–460. Springer (2020)

A Traffic Prediction Scheme for LEO Satellite Networks with Graph Neural Networks

Yong Zuo[1,2], Bo Wu[3], Zhipeng Zhang[4], Yongrui Chen[5], Nan Hao[1], and Zhenjie Yao[2,6](✉)

[1] Zhejiang Laboratory, Hangzhou, China
[2] Purple Mountain Laboratories, Nanjing, China
[3] School of Software, Nanchang Hangkong University, Nanchang, China
[4] China Mobile Research Institute, Beijing, China
[5] School of Electronic, Electrical, and Communication Engineering, University of Chinese Academy of Sciences, Beijing, China
[6] Institute of Microelectronics, Chinese Academy of Sciences, Beijing, China
yaozhenjie@ime.ac.cn

Abstract. Accurately predicting traffic flow in LEO satellite networks is crucial to enhance the system performance in terms of network congestion avoidance, routing strategy optimization and onboard processing resources allocation. However, existing prediction methods based on the statistical models usually tend to the mean value of historical data and rarely incorporate the topology information of networks. In this letter, we investigate traffic prediction problem for LEO satellite networks, considering LEO network topology changes are predictable and periodic. We utilize spatial temporal graph convolutional neural networks (STGCN) to capture both the temporal and topological information of the traffic flow in LEO satellite networks. Temporal convolution is utilized for dynamic modeling, while graph convolution is employed for topological modeling. Numerical findings on a simulated dataset spanning 35 d demonstrate that the proposed approach yields superior prediction performance by encoding both temporal and topological information in a neural representation. The MAE is reduced by 36.7% compared to traditional neural networks, and 7.7% compared to state-of-the-art graph neural networks.

Keywords: LEO satellite networks · traffic prediction · spatial temporal graph convolutional neural networks

1 Introduction

Recently, people have realized that the terrestrial Internet still cannot achieve global seamless coverage, which makes a large number of populations especially

Supported by the Fundamental Research Funds for the Central Universities (E3E41902 and E3ET1901X2), and the Jiangxi Provincial Natural Science Foundation, China (20242BAB20049).

L. Zhang and K.-K. R. Choo (Eds.): MobiQuitous 2025, LNICST 683, pp. 394–407, 2026.
https://doi.org/10.1007/978-3-032-22500-9_22

in rural areas and isolated islands unable to enjoy Internet service. To provide global seamless access services, these low-cost, low-latency, and high-throughput ambitious low earth orbit (LEO) satellites projects have been launched, such as OneWeb, SpaceX Starlink, and O3b. Moreover, inter-satellite links (ISL) has been proposed as a promising technology that can connect any two satellites within line-of-sight to each other. Based on ISL technology, LEO constellation constitutes a network system formed by organizing satellites as network nodes, which connects user terminals and ground stations [9]. In addition, LEO satellites move with higher speeds relative to the earth's surface, resulting in a highly dynamic satellite constellation topology. Meanwhile, traffic requirements of LEO satellite networks are unbalanced due to the varying population density, which is high in cities, low in rural areas, and almost zero over the oceans. Therefore, accurate and timely traffic prediction in LEO satellite networks is critical to system performance improvement, such as avoiding network congestion [11], optimizing routing algorithm design [16,23], coordinating onboard processing resources allocation [17,20].

Traffic information acquisition in LEO satellite networks mainly depends the reports on real-time queue information of each satellite through ISLs, while is rarely based on prior global traffic prediction. A link in the LEO satellite network is considered to be in a congested state once its queue length crosses a set threshold, as determined through continuous monitoring. To maintain network performance, data flow is then diverted away from these congested pathways [2]. In addition, to solve resource utilization reward maximization problem in LEO satellite networks, researchers have investigated prediction-based methods for resource allocation, yet these approaches can be limited. For instance, the method in [12] uses a human behavior model with low variability and high predictability, and statistical models generally tend to regress to the mean of past data, as seen in the video traffic prediction method of [6]. Conversely, the Long Short-Term Memory (LSTM) network presented in [22] has demonstrated promising results for forecasting satellite spectrum usage.

Meanwhile, for the terrestrial networks, a significant number of studies have been dedicated to Internet traffic prediction, with most existing work concentrating on capturing the temporal information within traffic flow series. While conventional techniques like linear time series models were widely used [1], later research introduced more complex models. For example, Cortez et al. [3] adopted a Multi-Layer Perceptron (MLP) that also accounted for network topology. Advancing this direction, Zhuo et al. [24] appended a Deep Neural Network (DNN) after an LSTM to better model the autocorrelation characteristics inherent in network traffic. Yao et al. proposed a novel model called temporal-topological graph convolutional neural network to precict internet traffic, which take network topology into consideration by graph convolutional neural networks (GCN) [19].

Inspired by the success of GCN in terrestrial communication network [13,15,19] and traffic network [7,14,21] modeling, we investigate traffic prediction problem for LEO satellite networks with enough consideration that LEO network topology changes are predictable and periodic. Accurate LEO satellite traffic forecasting requires modeling both temporal dynamics and topological information. Our work addresses this need with a Spatio-Temporal Graph Convolutional Network (STGCN), which is designed to model time-series patterns through temporal convolution and spatial relationships through graph convolution. The key contributions of this letter are as follows.

1. This study pioneers the integration of spatial-temporal graph convolutional neural networks to LEO satellite networks traffic prediction, which is designed to simultaneously capture temporal dynamics and topological relationships, thereby constructing a holistic representation of the LEO satellite network traffic time series.
2. Numerical results confirm that the proposed architecture yields significant gains by constructing a neural representation that inherently mirrors the underlying spatiotemporal structure of the traffic data.

The subsequent sections of this letter are arranged in the following manner. The discussion commences with the system model and problem statement in Sect. 2. Section 3 presents STGCN for LEO satellite network traffic forecasting. Section 4 shows a simulation-based performance comparison between the proposed approach and current strategies. Finally, Sect. 5 offers concluding observations and discusses potential avenues for future research.

2 Preliminaries

2.1 LEO Satellite Networks Architecture

Figure 1 presents the simulated LEO satellite network scenario, which is structured into a space layer and a ground layer. The space layer consists of a micro-satellite constellation where each node, despite having constrained processing power, maintains persistent ISLs with its immediate neighbors, forming a fixed inter-satellite graph. Conversely, the ground layer, containing user terminals and ground stations, interacts with the space layer through transient links. It is critical to note that while the core inter-satellite topology is held fixed for the purpose of this study, the network traffic is subject to high dynamism. This is a direct result of the continuous orbital motion and terminal mobility, which cause intermittent satellite-ground connectivity and thereby drive rapid and significant fluctuations in traffic load across the satellite backbone.

2.2 Problem Statement

The traffic prediction problem for LEO satellite networks can be formulated as a multivariate time-series prediction problem.

Figure 2 shows a simple network with star topology, and corresponding traffic data get from each link. Due to the different frequencies and processing procedures of the data transmission and reception links between two nodes, it is

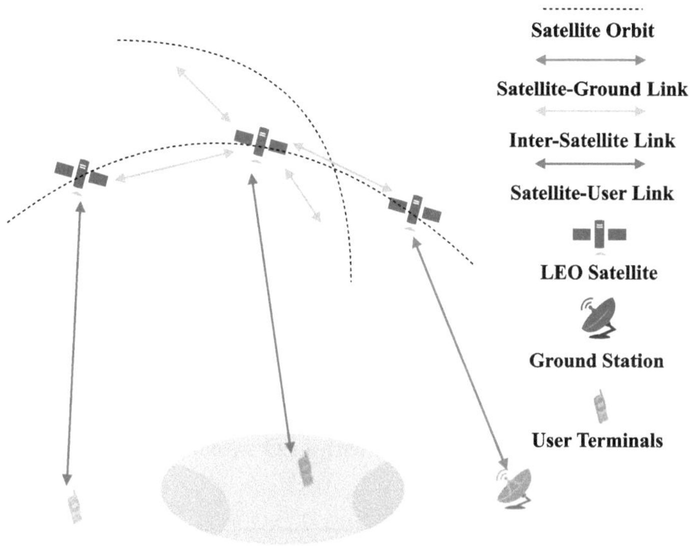

Fig. 1. LEO satellite networks.

assumed that there are two directed edges between each pair of nodes. As shown in Fig. 2a , there are 5 nodes, which are 5 satellite nodes and 1 ground station node. Structured in a star topology, ten directed communication links originate from or target to the central node S1. Figure 2b visualizes the subsequent network traffic, organizing the recorded information such that the ten distinct links are represented vertically, while a sequence of twelve observational intervals extends horizontally.

This study aims to forecast future traffic flow for each network link using historical data. As illustrated in Fig. 2b , the task is to predict the traffic volume across all links in a future window T_p, given their corresponding historical data from a preceding window T_h. In the provided snapshot, $T_h = 7$ and $T_p = 5$.

Formally, let $X \in \mathbb{R}^{N \times T}$ represent the traffic flow matrix for an LEO satellite network, where N denotes the number of links and T the total time steps. The element $x_{i,t}$ corresponds to the traffic volume on the i-th link at the t-th time step. The prediction problem is thus formulated as deriving the future matrix $X_p \in \mathbb{R}^{N \times T_p}$ from the historical input matrix $X_h \in \mathbb{R}^{N \times T_h}$.

3 STGCN for LEO Satellite Network Traffic Forecasting

In this section, we present a detailed description of the STGCN and explain how it is applied to traffic forecasting in LEO satellite networks.

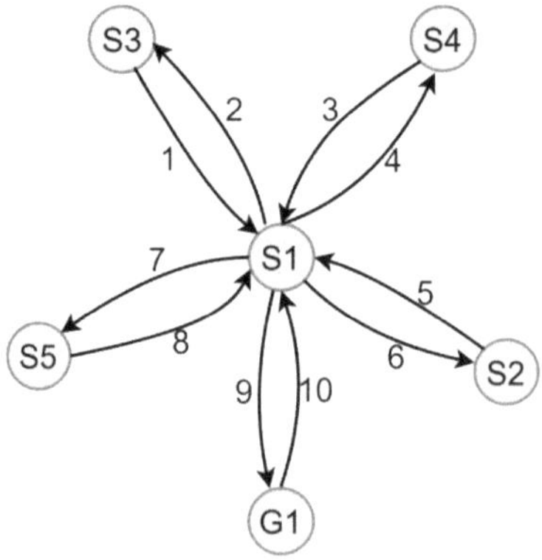

(a) A toy network with LEO satellite networks

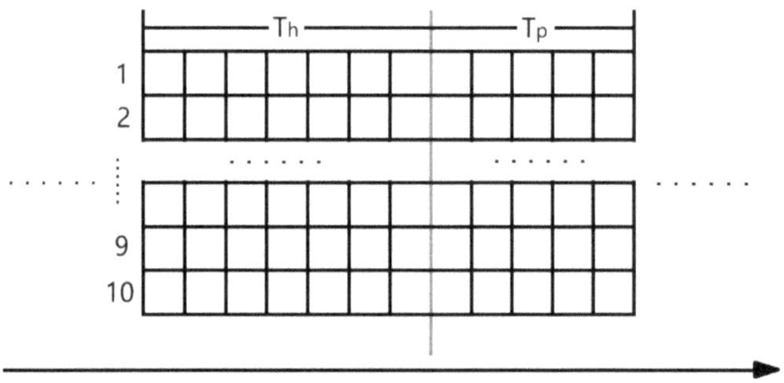

(b) Traffic flow data on the LEO satellite networks

Fig. 2. Traffic flow of a toy network with star topology.

3.1 Modeling the Topology of LEO Satellite Network

To achieve reliable traffic prediction, it is essential to incorporate the topological characteristics of the LEO satellite constellation.

In this work, the topological interconnections among all inter-satellite links (ISLs) are represented using an adjacency matrix, which quantifies the connectivity between satellites. The adjacency matrix A is formulated as follows:

$$A_{i,j} = \begin{cases} 1, & \text{if links } i \text{ and } j \text{ are connected to a common satellite,} \\ 0, & \text{otherwise,} \end{cases} \tag{1}$$

If ISLs i and j share a common satellite, then $A_{i,j} = 1$; otherwise, $A_{i,j} = 0$. This matrix captures the complete topological structure of the LEO satellite network, enabling the model to exploit spatial dependencies for more accurate traffic forecasting.

3.2 STGCN

The proposed STGCN model is composed of two successive SpatialTemporal Convolution (ST-Conv) blocks and an Output block, as illustrated in Fig. 3.

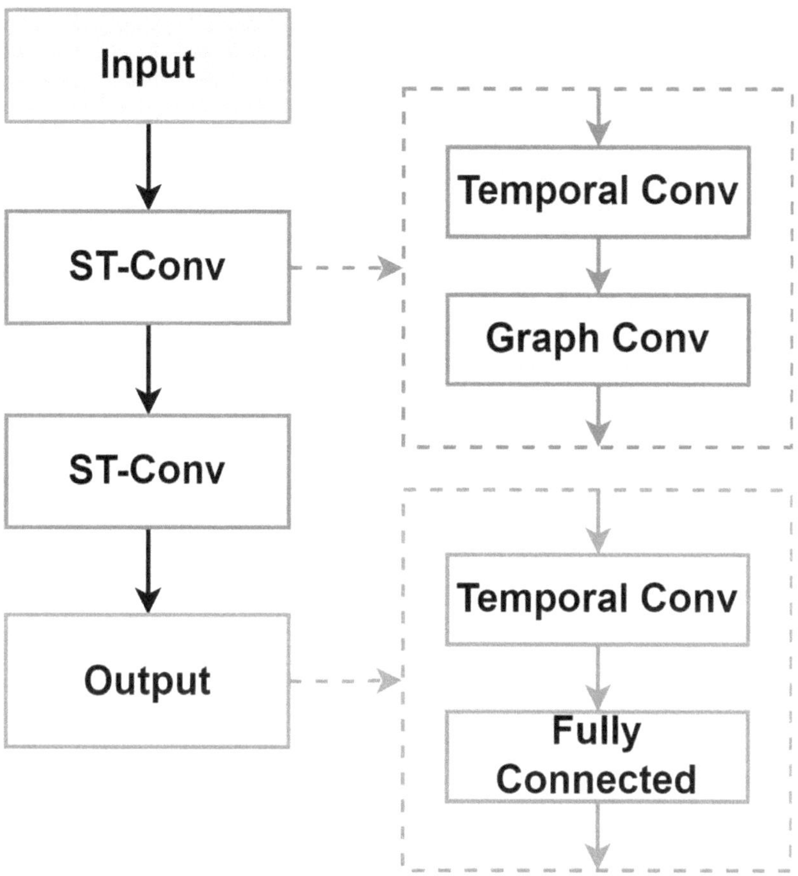

Fig. 3. Architecture of the proposed STGCN model.

ST-Conv Block. Each ST-Conv block integrates a gated temporal convolutional layer with a spatial graph convolutional layer. The temporal convolution is designed to capture sequential dependencies along the time axis, while the graph convolution is employed to extract spatial relationships between nodes.

The gated temporal convolutional layer applies a convolutional operation with a Gated Linear Unit (GLU) activation function. Unlike recurrent mechanisms such as Gated Recurrent Units (GRU) or Long Short-Term Memory (LSTM) networks, GLU enables efficient parallel computation and stable gradient propagation, simplifying model optimization. The GLU operation is expressed as:

$$Y = S \odot \sigma(T), \tag{2}$$

where $S = K * X$ and $T = K_g * X$; $\odot$ denotes the element-wise Hadamard product, $*$ represents convolution, and σ is the sigmoid activation function, defined as

$$\sigma(x) = \frac{1}{1 + e^{-x}}. \tag{3}$$

Here, X denotes the input feature sequence, while K and K_g are the convolution kernels. The output Y retains both the temporal context and the nonlinear gating effects.

Given the high complexity of LEO network topology, a graph convolutional layer is used to model inter-satellite correlations, efficiently capturing topological dependencies within the constellation.

The graph convolutional operation [4,8,10] is formulated as:

$$H^{(l+1)} = \gamma(\tilde{L} H^{(l)} W^{(l)}), \tag{4}$$

where $H^{(l)}$ is the node feature matrix of layer l, $W^{(l)}$ is the trainable weight matrix, and $\gamma(\cdot)$ denotes the activation function, specifically the Rectified Linear Unit (ReLU):

$$\gamma(x) = \max(0, x), \tag{5}$$

$\tilde{L}$ represents the normalized Laplacian matrix of the graph $\mathcal{G}$, defined as

$$\tilde{L} = \tilde{D}^{-\frac{1}{2}} \tilde{A} \tilde{D}^{-\frac{1}{2}}, \tag{6}$$

where $\tilde{A} = A + I$ denotes the adjacency matrix with self-loops, I is the identity matrix, and $\tilde{D}$ is the degree matrix of $\tilde{A}$, whose diagonal elements correspond to the degrees of nodes including self-connections.

By alternately stacking temporal and spatial convolutional layers, two consecutive ST-Conv blocks are constructed. This design allows the model to jointly capture multi-scale temporal dynamics and spatial structures, producing comprehensive representations that incorporate both temporal evolution and topological features of the LEO satellite links.

Output Block. The Output block comprises a fully connected layer following the final gated temporal convolution. After the last temporal convolutional layer, deep temporalspatial features are extracted, encapsulating the temporal dynamics and spatial dependencies learned from previous layers.

These features are then passed through a fully connected layer to generate N predicted traffic values, corresponding to the N links in the LEO network.

The multi-step forecasting process is formulated as follows:

$$y_{:,t+s} = f_s([x_{:,t-T_h+1}, x_{:,t-T_h+2}, ..., x_{:,t}]), \tag{7}$$

where $x_{:,t}$ denotes the observed traffic values at time step t, and $y_{:,t+s}$ represents the predicted values s steps ahead. The prediction function $f_s(\cdot)$ corresponds to the proposed STGCN model. Multi-step forecasting can be achieved by employing independent prediction functions for each step.

4 Experimental Results

4.1 Simulation Setup

We conduct our simulations by using MATLAB and Satellite Tool Kit (STK) to evaluate the performance of our proposed algorithm. In this simulation, Iridium constellation [5] is adopted to construct satellite networks. The detailed parameters are shown in Table 1. The traffic requirements form the user terminal to the ground station are based on differential population density [18]. To facilitate the analysis, the simulation only considers shortest path routing strategy (Dijkstra algorithm). However, our proposed algorithm is still applicable to other routing algorithms. Three ground stations are Beijing $(39.9°, 116.3°)$, Sanya$(18.2°, 109.5°)$, and Xi'an $(34.5°, 109.5°)$. In addition, each satellite has four inter-satellite buffer queues and one satellite-ground buffer queues. The number of data packets transmitted per minute on each link is recorded as the network traffic feature.

4.2 Metrics and Baselines

The Mean Absolute Error (MAE) is utilized for evaluating the predictive capabilities of various methods, which is defined as

$$\mathtt{MAE}(y, \hat{y}) = \mathtt{E}\left(|y_i - \hat{y}_i|\right) = \frac{\sum_{i=0}^{N} |y_i - \hat{y}_i|}{N}. \tag{8}$$

where $|\cdot|$ denotes taking absolute values, N is the number of predicted points. A smaller MAE value indicates superior performance.

Six traditional and state-of-the-art models serve as baseline references for performance evaluation, encompassing:

- HA (Historical Average), which predicts the future traffic flow on each ISL with the mean value of historical traffic records.
- AR (Auto-Regressive), which is a prevalent linear model for time series prediction.
- LSTM (Long Short-Term Memory), which is utilized to model traffic flow as a multivariate time series.
- GRU (Gated Recurrent Unit), which are employed to capture the temporal dynamics of traffic flow in a multivariate context.
- STTM (Spatial-Temporal Transformer Networks [14]), which models traffic flow and the topology of the network with graph transformer.
- ADSTSGN (Automated Dilated Spatio-Temporal Synchronous Graph Networks [7]), which models traffic flow and the topology of the network with customized graph neural networks (GNN).

Table 1. Parameter setting of simulation.

Parameter	Value
Number of satellites	66
Number of planes	6
Number of satellites per plane	11
Inter-plane separation	31.6°
Inter-satellite separation on the same plane	32.73°
Altitude	780 km
Inclination	86.4°
ISL latitude threshold	60°
Elevation mask	8.2°
Number of ground station	3
Number of ISL per satellite	4
The bandwidth of inter-satellite links	5Gbps
The bandwidth of satellite-ground links	10Gbps
The bandwidth of satellite-user links	2Gbps
Routing strategy	Dijkstra algorithm
Packet size	1kb
Queue size per inter-satellite link	1Gb
Queue size of satellite-ground link	1 Gb
Simulation duration	35 d
Sampling Period	1 min

HA and AR represent conventional linear models for time series prediction, while LSTM and GRU are classical nonlinear neural networks for forecasting multivariate time series, which predict through temporal features without taking topology information into consideration. STTM, ADSTSGN, and STGCN integrate both spatial and temporal information from the network to improve traffic prediction accuracy, which model network topology using graph neural networks.

4.3 Experimental Setting

The data is temporally split, with the initial 80% (28 d) allocated for training and validation, while the remaining 20% (approximately 7 d) is reserved for testing purposes. The time windows are set as $T_h = 30$ and $T_p = 5$.

The ST-Conv block comprises 64 and 128 channels respectively. The temporal convolutional kernel size for both Temporal Conv is set to 3. Training of the GNN models involves minimizing the mean squared error using the Adam optimizer for a duration of 150 epochs. The batch size is configured to 50, and the learning rate starts at 0.001.

4.4 Prediction Results

Figure 4 illustrates the MAE of all prediction algorithms on the test dataset across various time steps. As depicted, the prediction error escalates with the increase in time steps across all methods. Long-term forecasting poses greater difficulty compared to short-term forecasting.

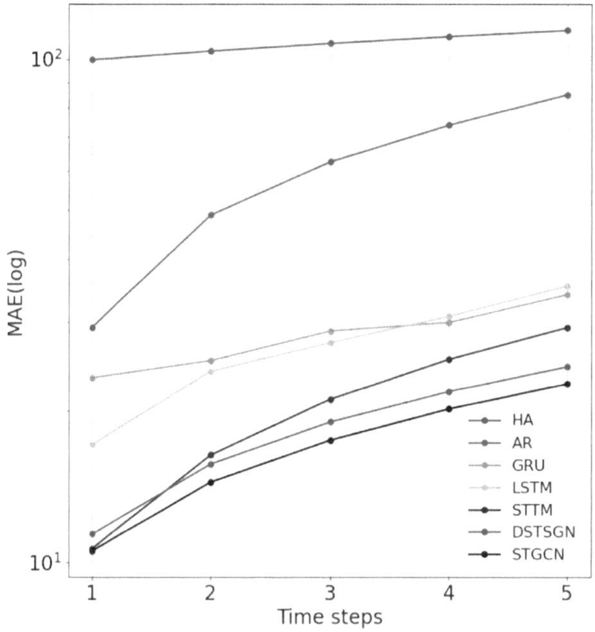

Fig. 4. MAE of different methods.

A comparison of MAE across methods reveals that the HA approach consistently yields the highest error at all time steps. While the AR model outperforms HA, it remains inferior to nonlinear alternatives. This performance disparity underscores a fundamental limitation of linear models in representing the complex, nonlinear dynamics of LEO satellite network traffic. Furthermore, a key inherent shortcoming of both HA and AR is their treatment of network links in isolation, disregarding critical spatial dependencies that more sophisticated models successfully exploit.

The error curves of GRU and LSTM models are closely aligned, and both exhibit substantially lower error rates compared to the linear models previously discussed. This performance improvement is notable because GRU and LSTM models are designed to handle multivariate time series data effectively. They excel in identifying and modeling intricate, nonlinear relationships that often characterize traffic flow in LEO satellite networks. However, GRU and LSTM models do not inherently consider the correlations between different variables or links. Their primary focus remains on temporal dependencies within the data rather than explicitly modeling the interactions between different elements of the network.

All three GNNs (STTN, ADSTSGN, and STGCN) show a significant performance improvement over the four previously mentioned models, as indicated by their markedly lower error curves. The ability of these GNNs to incorporate both temporal and spatial features enables them to model the dynamic interactions between satellites and the evolving network structure more effectively. This comprehensive approach enhances their predictive accuracy, making them more adept at handling the complexities of satellite network traffic. Among the three GNNs, STGCN stands out with the lowest error, highlighting its superior predictive performance. The advantage of Graph Convolutional Networks over Graph Transformers in this context is their direct ability to capture and model the intricate topology of satellite networks. This capability is particularly advantageous in LEO networks, where understanding and modeling the network's structure is crucial for accurate traffic forecasting.

Table 2 presents the average error across various time steps for each model to make a quantitative comparison, reflecting their predictive performance over different durations. For instance, column 2 displays the average MAE of each model over a 2-minute prediction horizon, while column 4 showcases the average error over a 4-minute horizon.

Table 2. Performance comparison of different models.

Model	1min	2 mins	3 mins	4 mins	5 mins	Average
HA	99.793	103.832	107.528	110.935	114.098	107.237
AR	29.330	49.015	62.550	73.929	85.044	59.974
GRU	23.294	25.192	28.849	29.989	34.044	28.274
LSTM	17.133	23.992	27.343	30.839	35.417	26.945
STTM [14]	10.653	16.339	21.098	25.343	29.299	20.546
ADSTSGN [7]	11.383	15.685	19.007	21.867	24.500	18.488
STGCN	**10.535**	**14.441**	**17.488**	**20.182**	**22.642**	**17.058**

Upon conducting a thorough comparison of the models' performances quantitatively, it is found that: Regardless of the prediction horizon, STGCN consistently achieves the lowest MAE among all models, underscoring its robust predictive capability. STTM and ADSTSGN have comparable performance, but there is still a gap. LSTM and GRU follow the GNNs with a significant margin. Linear models consistently exhibit the poorest performance.

For instance, considering the average MAE over a 2-minute prediction horizon, STGCN achieves an MAE of 14.441, whereas STTM, ADSTSGN, LSTM and GRU achieve 16.339, 15.685, 23.992 and 25.192, respectively. AR and HA yield significantly higher MAE values of 49.015 and 103.832, respectively.

All the neural networks significantly surpass linear models, demonstrating their advanced ability to capture the complex nonlinear dynamics present in LEO satellite network traffic data. By effectively handling the nonlinearities in the data, these neural networks can model the complex dependencies, leading to enhanced predictive performance.

Comparison between STGCN and GRU/LSTM reveals GNNs' markedly superior performance. For instance, for all the 5 time steps, STGCN achieves an average MAE of 17.058, whereas GRU and LSTM yield 28.274 and 26.945, representing reductions of 39.7% and 36.7%, respectively. This indicates that the STGCN architecture outperforms conventional neural networks models significantly, which can be attributed to the topological modeling prowess on satellite network of GCN.

Compared to STTM and ADSTSGN, STGCN improved MAE by 17.0% and 7.7% respectively. The improvement in MAE shows the enhanced performance of STGCN in capturing the dynamic nature of network traffic and intricate relationships between satellites compared to the other models.

5 Conclusion and Future Works

This paper presents the application of STGCN for traffic forecasting in LEO satellite networks, marking a pioneering use of GNN in this context. STGCN demonstrates its effectiveness in capturing both the network's topology and dynamic flow comprehensively. Evaluation using a simulated dataset spanning 35 d reveals an average MAE of 22.642 over 5-minute intervals, representing a significant improvement over traditional methods.

Looking forward, there is a strong interest in advancing the STGCN architecture for LEO satellite network traffic prediction. This includes exploring more flexible mechanisms to achieve a nuanced representation of network dynamics, with the aim of further enhancing predictive accuracy.

References

1. Box, G.E.P., Jenkins, G.M.: Time series analysis. forecasting and control. Holden-Day, Incorporated (1990)
2. Chen, C., Ekici, E.: A routing protocol for hierarchical leo/meo satellite IP networks. Wireless Netw. **11**(4), 507–521 (2005)
3. Cortez, P., Rio, M., Sousa, P., Rocha, M.: Topology aware internet traffic forecasting using neural networks. In: International Conference on Artificial Neural Networks, pp. 445–454. Springer (2007)
4. Defferrard, M., Bresson, X., Vandergheynst, P.: Convolutional neural networks on graphs with fast localized spectral filtering. Adv. Neural Inf. Process. Syst. **29** (2016)
5. Dong, C., Xu, X., Liu, A., Liang, X.: Load balancing routing algorithm based on extended link states in LEO constellation network. China Commun. **19**(2), 247–260 (2022)

6. Du, J., Jiang, C., Qian, Y., Han, Z., Ren, Y.: Resource allocation with video traffic prediction in cloud-based space systems. IEEE Trans. Multimedia **18**(5), 820–830 (2016)
7. Jin, G., Li, F., Zhang, J., Wang, M., Huang, J.: Automated dilated spatio-temporal synchronous graph modeling for traffic prediction. IEEE Trans. Intell. Transp. Syst. **24**(8), 8820–8830 (2022)
8. Kipf, T.N., Welling, M.: Semi-supervised classification with graph convolutional networks. arXiv preprint arXiv:1609.02907 (2016)
9. Kodheli, O., et al.: Satellite communications in the new space era: a survey and future challenges. IEEE Commun. Surve. Tutorials **23**(1), 70–109 (2020)
10. M, G.R., Hammond, D.K., Vandergheynst, P.: Wavelets on graphs via spectral graph theory. Appl. Comput. Harmonic Anal. **30**(2), 129–150 (2011)
11. Nishiyama, H., Kudoh, D., Kato, N., Kadowaki, N.: Load balancing and QOS provisioning based on congestion prediction for geo/leo hybrid satellite networks. Proc. IEEE **99**(11), 1998–2007 (2011)
12. Song, C., Qu, Z., Blumm, N., Barabási, A.L.: Limits of predictability in human mobility. Science **327**(5968), 1018–1021 (2010)
13. Wu, B., Xu, Q., Yao, Z.: A deep temporal graph convolutional neural network for network traffic forecasting. In: 2022 2nd International Conference on Frontiers of Electronics, Information and Computation Technologies (ICFEICT), pp. 381–386. IEEE (2022)
14. Xu, M., et al.: Spatial-temporal transformer networks for traffic flow forecasting. arXiv preprint arXiv:2001.02908 (2020)
15. Xu, Q., Yao, Z., Tu, Y., Chen, Y.: Attention-based multi-component LSTM for internet traffic prediction. In: International Conference on Neural Information Processing, pp. 770–777. Springer (2020)
16. Yan, D., Wang, L.: TPDR: traffic prediction based dynamic routing for LEO&GEO satellite networks. In: 2015 IEEE 5th International Conference on Electronics Information and Emergency Communication, pp. 104–107. IEEE (2015)
17. Yang, X., Liu, A., Liang, X.: Spectrum occupancy prediction based on LEO satellite mobile communication service. In: 2020 IEEE 6th International Conference on Computer and Communications (ICCC), pp. 712–717. IEEE (2020)
18. Yang, Y., Xu, M., Wang, D., Wang, Y.: Towards energy-efficient routing in satellite networks. IEEE J. Sel. Areas Commun. **34**(12), 3869–3886 (2016)
19. Yao, Z., Xu, Q., Chen, Y., Tu, Y., Zhang, H., Chen, Y.: Internet traffic forecasting using temporal-topological graph convolutional networks. In: 2021 International Joint Conference on Neural Networks (IJCNN), pp. 1–8. IEEE (2021)
20. Yong, Z., Mingyang, Y., Huiyuan, Y., Liantao, W., Xiaojun, Y.: Integrating communication, sensing and computing in satellite internet of things: challenges and opportunities. IEEE Wirel. Commun, 1–7 (2024), early Access
21. Yu, B., Yin, H., Zhu, Z.: Spatio-temporal graph convolutional networks: A deep learning framework for traffic forecasting. In: Twenty-Seventh International Joint Conference on Artificial Intelligence IJCAI-18 (2018)

22. Yu, L., Chen, J., Ding, G., Tu, Y., Yang, J., Sun, J.: Spectrum prediction based on taguchi method in deep learning with long short-term memory. IEEE Access **6**, 45923–45933 (2018)
23. Yunxue, H., Bohao, F., Aleteng, T., Ping, D., Shui, Y., Hongke, Z.: An efficient differentiated routing scheme for MEO/LEO-based multi-layer satellite networks. IEEE Trans. Netw. Sci. Eng. **11**(1), 1026–1041 (2024)
24. Zhuo, Q., Li, Q., Han, Y., Yong, Q.: Long short-term memory neural network for network traffic prediction. In: 2017 12th International Conference on Intelligent Systems and Knowledge Engineering (ISKE) (2017)

A Trust-Based Incentive Mechanism Combined with Behavioral Economics and Payment Member for Truth Discovery in Mobile Crowdsensing

Xiaoyu Zhu[1], Da Li[1], Yuxin Liu[1], Qinglong Tian[1](✉), Hua Deng[1], Anfeng Liu[2], and Yuntao Wu[1]

[1] Changsha University, Changsha 410022, China
{zhuxiaoyu,yuxinliu,chinatql,hdeng}@ccsu.edu.cn, lida@stu.ccsu.edu.cn

[2] Central South University, Changsha 410083, China
afengliu@mail.csu.edu.cn

Abstract. With the quick development of mobile intelligent devices and sensing abilities, mobile crowdsensing (MCS) can provide large-scale data sensing in a flexible way. In order to solve the problems of unstable data quality and insufficient participation in MCS, this paper proposes an incentive strategy that integrates trust evaluation and behavioral mechanism for truth discovery in MCS. Firstly, a payment member incentive mechanism was introduced to provide membership fee discounts to high-trust workers to motivate them to participate in high-value tasks. Secondly, the trusted worker and member worker was preferentially recruited by the platform to ensure the quality of submitted data. Finally, a trust-based truth value discovery algorithm was combined to optimize the data aggregation process, and a dynamic trust update model was designed to dynamically adjust the trust value of workers according to the quality of sensing data. Experiments show that this strategy not only improves the utility of the platform, but also significantly improves the accuracy of sensing data.

Keywords: Truth Discovery · Crowdsensing · Behavioral Economics

1 Introduction

In recent years, with the quick development of Internet of Things (IoT), mobile crowdsensing (MCS) has attracted widespread attention as an innovative data sensing paradigm [1]. The mobile intelligent devices integrate with multiple sensors can finish different kinds of sensing tasks. MCS can solve the high cost, maintain difficulty, limited scale and inflexible problems in traditional data collection scenario. The low-cost and high-efficient data collection mechanism promotes the widespread application of MCS in application scenarios such as traffic monitoring, road condition analysis, and noise monitoring, which greatly assists the applications and services in smart cities and facilitates the interconnection of IoT [2].

L. Zhang and K.-K. R. Choo (Eds.): MobiQuitous 2025, LNICST 683, pp. 408–427, 2026.
https://doi.org/10.1007/978-3-032-22500-9_23

Obtaining high-quality data to enhance service quality is a fundamental challenge in MCS. The platform can adopt a redundancy strategy by assigning the same task to different workers to ensure quality, then it integrates the data collected by these workers to obtain the truthful data value for each sensing task. However, this redundancy approach faces the challenge of noisy or conflicting data. Truth discovery is a data mining paradigm designed to address conflicts in multi-source noisy data, aiming to extract accurate results, known as truths, from conflicting data [3]. Currently, the most common strategy for improving quality is based on the CRH method, which involves recruiting workers to perform the same tasks and minimizing the loss function to estimate the true value. Due to the openness and low barriers of MCS, any worker can freely participate and submit collected data. To obtain rewards, some malicious workers may intentionally submit poor-quality or even erroneous data. As the proportion of malicious workers increases, the accuracy of the ground truth gradually decreases. When the proportion of malicious users exceeds half, their combined attacks can cause the true value generated by the CRH [4] to significantly deviate from the ground truth.

To address the shortcomings of the CRH method, the researchers proposed trust-based schemes which choose trustworthy workers to obtain high-quality data [5, 6]. The premise of these trust-based approaches is that workers who consistently submit high-quality data are generally trustworthy. Therefore, the key to improving quality is to determine the trust values of workers. However, it is difficult for the platform to identify the types of workers due to the lack of necessary references, and it is important to design a worker recruitment scheme to select high-trust workers to finish the sensing tasks. In previous scenarios, the recruited workers were considered to have the same priorities. However, workers with different levels of trust values should have different levels of priority to be recruited.

In the data collection process of MCS, the workers consume their own equipment resources, resulting in an increasing cost, and the budget of the sensing platform is limited, which will affect the worker's enthusiasm to submit data, thereby affecting the quality and stability of the sensing data. Therefore, it is necessary to design an appropriate incentive mechanism to improve the utility of the platform and motivate workers to participate in the task. The researchers proposed a variety of incentive mechanisms to motivate the MCS schemes [7, 8]. However, these incentive approaches do not consider behavioral economics. In many shopping malls, the promotions of payment members are very popular. The members of the platform can purchase goods at a low price, while ordinary customers can only buy these goods at the original price. In order to be able to enjoy the rights and interests of membership, some consumers will choose to apply for a membership card, which is conducive to increasing the profit of the mall.

Thus, the member incentive mechanism is introduced into the design of our incentive mechanism. First of all, the sensing platform sets up a member mechanism and divides the sensing tasks into high-profit member tasks and low-profit ordinary tasks. For ordinary workers who want to choose member tasks, they must submit membership fees to become platform members. When the worker selects the task, the difference between the expected income of the member task and the expected income of the ordinary task is considered as the worker's reference loss, that is the loss caused by abandoning the member task. Thus, the worker will increase the probability of participation in the member task in order to avoid this part of the loss, and the platform can improve its utility by collecting membership fees.

In this paper, we propose a trust-based incentive mechanism combined with behavioral economics and payment member for truth discovery in crowdsensing (IBTD). Specifically, in order to improve the accuracy of the sensing task, we need to first process the submitted sensing data and evaluate the accuracy of the workers' data based on some high-trust workers. Then, adjust the workers' trust according to the quality of the submitted sensing data. In addition, an incentive mechanism based on behavioral economics is proposed to motivate workers to pay membership fees to participate in member tasks. Finally, a certain discount on membership fees is given to users with high trust to enhance the enthusiasm of users with high trust to participate. In the process of worker recruitment, workers with high trust and membership have high priority to be recruited to improve the data quality of sensing tasks.

The main contribution of this paper is summarized as follows:

(1) An incentive mechanism based on behavioral economics is proposed. The workers can obtain discount member fees with high trust values, which enhances the stickiness of workers and improves the utility of the sensing platform.
(2) A worker recruitment algorithm based on member and trust is proposed. The platform evaluates the priorities of workers by evaluating the trust values and membership, which enhances the enthusiasm of workers to become members and submit high-quality data.
(3) A trust-based truth discovery algorithm is proposed. The workers' trust values are evaluated based on partially known high-trust workers, and the malicious workers are identified as the periods increase. The precision of the ground truth is improved in our proposed scheme.
(4) The experimental results show that our incentive mechanism based on trust and behavioral economics can improve the data quality and improve the utility of the platform.

The rest of this paper is organized as follows. Section 2 introduces the related work. Section 3 presents the system model and problem description. Section 4 describes the detailed process of our proposed method. Section 5 shows the performance evaluation of our work with other baseline approaches. Section 6 summarizes the whole work.

2 Related Work

Truth discovery [9] technology is usually used to solve conflicts in data mining and evaluate the source quality of tasks. In MCS, the low-quality workers may submit noisy or inaccurate data. Furthermore, the platform does not have prior information of workers' quality and the ground truth of data, it is really a difficult to guarantee the quality of sensing tasks.

In order to solve the data quality problem of truth discovery in MCS, researchers proposed many truth discovery schemes. Wang et al. [10] proposed to use UAV to solve the uncontrollable data quality problem in MCS, the sensing data collected by the UAV was used as a standard to compare with the sensing data collected by workers.

Shen et al. [11] proposed a truth discovery scheme based on blockchain in MCS, the reputation-based aggregation algorithm in the contract to reach a consensus on the ground truth, and a worker recruitment algorithm and reward strategy to are proposed to select appropriate workers to finish tasks. Li et al. [12] proposed a truth discovery scheme based on prediction and reputation, the spatio-temporal Transformer network is used to learn and predict worker's sensing data's ground truth from historical sensing data, a reputation-based truth discovery algorithm is designed to identify low-quality data and malicious workers. Yuan et al. [13] proposed a privacy-preserving truth discovery scheme in spatial crowdsensing, which used edge nodes to partition the workers into groups, and the bloom filter and mixed secret sharing technologies are used to mix the sensing objects and preserve privacy. Bai et al. [5] proposed a bilateral privacy-preserving truth discovery scheme based on matrix encryption, the trust-based worker recruitment and trust update algorithms were proposed to improve the precision of truth value. Li et al. [14] proposed a novel metric to evaluate the aggregation sensing quality to optimize Quality of Information, and a mutual aid truth discovery scheduling mechanism was designed to estimate the sensing reliability and improve the aggregate sensing quality in uncertain vehicle conditions.

Xie et al. [15] proposed a privacy-preserving data sharing mechanism in app assisted mobile crowdsensing scenario, and an auction-based and deep reinforcement-based incentive algorithms were proposed to improve the utility of workers. Wang et al. [16] proposed an incentive mechanism in truth discovery scheme to incentivize the trustworthy workers to submit high-quality data to improve the precision of ground truth. Chen et al. [6] proposed a privacy-preserve mechanism based on an anonymous third party, a trust evaluation method composed of multiple factors was used to identify more trustworthy workers, and an incentive mechanism through reasonable budgets and approximate Sharpley methods was proposed to achieve fair reward distribution. Cheng et al. [17] introduced social psychology into MCS to assign the responsibility of assessing data quality to each worker, and an auction-based incentive mechanism was proposed to ensure the mechanism can be implemented within the budget constraint. Liu et al. [18] introduced the concept of capital deposit and intertemporal choice in behavioral economics, and an addiction-based incentive mechanism was proposed to improve the participation and repetition rates. Liu et al. [19] proposed an incentive mechanism based on reference effect in behavioral economics, a participation selection algorithm was proposed to control the task selection and pricing strategy. Li et al. [20] introduced cognitive bias and reference effect in behavioral economics to explain the principle of path dependence, which improved the platform coverage.

3 System Definitions

This section mainly introduces how to design an incentive mechanism based on reference dependence for MCS. Firstly, the physical model of MCS based on reference dependence is introduced, then the idea of reference dependence is introduced, and finally the reference dependence is mapped with the physical environment of MCS to construct a logical model.

3.1 System Model

In this paper, we introduce reference dependence in behavioral economics into the MCS incentive mechanism to construct a system model based on paid members. The system model includes the platform and task workers. The platform publishes a variety of tasks, and divide all tasks into two categories: member tasks and ordinary tasks, the workers can get more profits from member tasks, the ordinary tasks' profits obtained are less. The purpose of partitioning member tasks and ordinary tasks is to establish reference dependence for workers, and to motivate ordinary users to submit membership fees to the platform in order to select member tasks, so as to improve the utility of the platform. Figure 1 shows the system model.

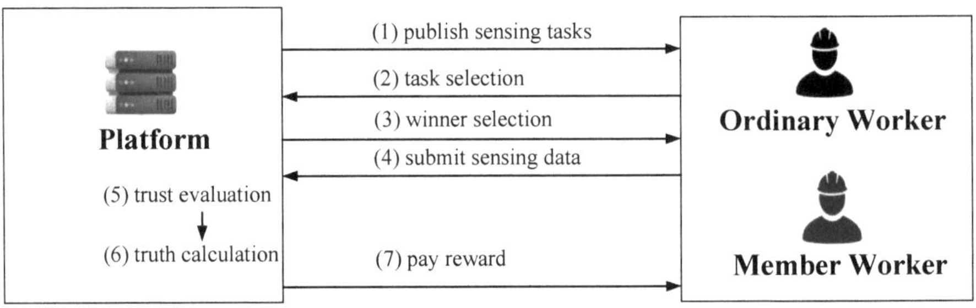

Fig. 1. System model

3.2 Reference Dependence

In many shopping malls, the promotions of payment members are very popular. The members of the platform can purchase goods at a low price, while ordinary customers can only buy these goods at the original price. In order to be able to enjoy the rights and interests of membership, some consumers will choose to apply for a membership card, which is conducive to increasing the profit of the mall.

The process of attracting consumers to join the members is illustrated as follows: when ordinary consumers buy specific goods, they find that members can be discounted and buy such goods at a lower price. Due to the existence of reference dependence, consumers have a reference point for the price, that is, the member price, and the ordinary price is higher than the member price. At this time, the consumer's utility is below the reference point, and the consumer felt the loss. The larger the difference between the member price and the ordinary price, the greater the consumer's perceived loss, the more the consumers want to become members.

Table 1. Mappings.

	Membership	MCS
Incentive object	Consumers	workers
Environmental factor	Shopping malls	Sensing tasks area

(continued)

Table 1. *(continued)*

	Membership	MCS
Reference points	Member price	Reward of member task
Membership benifits	Discounts on buying goods	Members can choose member tasks and obtain high rewards
Incentive process	If consumers want to buy member goods, they submit membership fees	If the workers choose member tasks, the workers submit membership fees
Incentive results	The marketer charges membership fees to improve profit	The platform charges membership fees and improves platform utility

When the attraction reaches a certain level, consumers choose to submit membership fees to become mall members. This paper maps this process to the MCS process, the platform uses the member task profit as a reference point, the workers want to avoid their task profit below the reference point, and submit member fees to the platform. Table 1 illustrates the mappings.

3.3 Problem Formulation

The objectives of this paper are summarized as follows:

(1) Platform utility: The platform utility is improved compared with the accuracy of schemes not combined with trust or membership.
(2) High accuracy: The accuracy of the final truth value of the sensing task is improved compared with the accuracy of schemes not combined with trust or membership.

4 Our Proposed IBTD Scheme

In this section, we introduce the reference dependence in behavioral economics into the worker's task selection module and model its selection process. The specific process is as follows: firstly, we study how the rules published on the platform affect the worker's expected profit. Then, the expected profit of member task is taken as the reference point, and then the reference loss of chosen an ordinary task is calculated. Finally, the probability of participation in the member task is obtained, and the impact of the reference loss on the participation probability is discussed. Table 2 illustrates the notations.

Table 2. Notations.

Notations	Description
$\mathbb{T}$	Set of tasks
$\mathbb{U}$	Set of workers

(continued)

Table 2. (*continued*)

Notations	Description
M	Number of tasks
N	Number of workers
U_h, U_l	Set of member workers, set of ordinary workers
T_h, T_l	Set of member tasks, set of ordinary tasks
$\mathcal{L}_h^{\tau-1}, \mathcal{L}_l^{\tau-1}$	The average reward of sensing tasks in $\tau - 1$-th period
$\theta_{i,j}^h, \theta_{i,j}^l$	The estimated profit of worker u_i for the member task and ordinary task in the τ-th period
v_j^τ	The real value of task t_j in the τ-th period
$\eta_{i,j}$	The reference loss of worker u_i for task t_j in the τ-th period
$\mathbb{T}_i$	The task set chosen by worker u_i
f	The basic membership fee
f_i	The membership fee of worker u_i
ξ_i	The participation probability of worker u_i to the member task
$p_{i,j}^\tau$	The actual reward of worker u_i finish task t_j in the τ-th period
W	The utility of the platform
R	The trust values of all workers
d_i	The sensing data of worker u_i
w_i	The weight of worker u_i
r_i	The trust value of worker u_i
X_q^j	The final ground truth of task t_j

4.1 Overview

In this subsection, we give an overview of our proposed incentive mechanism based on behavioral economics and trust evaluation.

(1) The platform initializes the task and worker trust, and the platform divides the task into member tasks and ordinary tasks, and the platform divides the workers into high-trust workers and workers with unknown trust values.

(2) The platform publishes the average profit of member tasks and ordinary tasks in the last round. Workers calculate the estimated benefits of different types of tasks based on the task information provided by the platform. Based on the estimated reward of the member task as a reference point, the worker calculates the reference loss caused by selecting an ordinary task, that is, the reward that will be lost if selecting an ordinary task. Calculate the probability of the worker's participation in the member's task under the influence of the reference loss. If the probability is greater than the threshold, the worker sends a request to the platform to apply for

member tasks and submits a discounted membership fee to the platform based on trust. If the probability is less than the threshold, the worker requests to participate in the ordinary task.

(3) The platform calculates the worker priority according to the worker's trust and worker's type, and the platform selects part of workers from the worker set as the winners to complete the task according to the worker priority.

(4) The winner selected by the platform submits the sensing data to the platform, and the platform compares the data submitted by the worker with the data of the high-trust worker, updates the worker's trust, and calculates the truth value according to the worker's trust, and the platform issues rewards to the worker, and the member tasks get member rewards, and ordinary tasks get ordinary rewards.

4.2 Initialization Process

The task and trust value initialization stage divides the task into member task and ordinary task. Then, initialize the worker's trust value. Suppose the platform sets the high-profit tasks and uses r as the proportion of the total number of high-profit tasks. Then, divide the first $r \cdot M$ tasks into high-profit areas, as member tasks T_h, and the remaining parts as low-profit areas, as ordinary tasks T_l. Assume that the platform knows that some workers are high-trust workers, ε is used as the proportion of high-trust workers in the total number of workers, and the top $\varepsilon \cdot N$ users are high-trust workers, the trust value is 1, and the high-trust workers set is denoted as U_a. The trust values of the remaining workers are unknown, the trust values are initialized to 0.5, and the unknown trust workers set is denoted as U_b. Algorithm 1 illustrates the task and trust value initialization process.

Algorithm 1: Task and trust value initialization

Inputs: $\mathbb{T}, \mathbb{U}, M, N, r, \varepsilon$.

Outputs: T_h, T_l, U_a, U_b, R.

$T_h = \emptyset, T_l = \emptyset, U_a = \emptyset, U_b = \emptyset$;

for $j = 1,2, \ldots, M$ **do**

  if $j \le r \cdot M$ **then** $T_h = T_h \cup t_j$

  else $T_l = T_l \cup t_j$

  end if

end for

for $i = 1,2, \ldots, N$ **do**

  if $i \le \varepsilon \cdot N$ **then**

    $r_i = 1$

    $U_a = U_a \cup u_i$

  else

    $r_i = 0.5$

    $U_b = U_b \cup u_i$

  end if

end for

4.3 Task Selection Process

The task selection process is based on reference dependence and trust value. In the task selection process, the probability of worker participation in the member task is calculated, and the set of workers who choose the member task is obtained.

(1) Calculate member fee for worker based on trust value

The worker's membership fee is based on the basic membership fee and trust value. The platform gives a discount to the membership fee for the worker according to the worker's trust value.

$$f_i = \kappa * \frac{f}{r_i}. \tag{4}$$

where κ is the discount factor, f is the basic membership fee, r_i is the trust value. f_i is the membership fee for worker u_i. The higher the worker's trust value, the lower the membership fee.

(2) Calculate the estimated profit for the member task and ordinary task

If the worker is an ordinary worker, the worker calculates the estimated profit for member and non-member tasks. In the τ period, the platform publishes the average reward of winners $\mathcal{L}_h^{\tau-1}$ and $\mathcal{L}_l^{\tau-1}$ for the member task area and the ordinary task area in the $\tau - 1$ period. $\mathcal{L}_h^{\tau-1}$ and $\mathcal{L}_l^{\tau-1}$ are calculated as follows.

$$\mathcal{L}_h^{\tau-1} = \frac{\sum_{u_i \in U_h^{\tau-1}} p_{i,j}^{\tau-1}}{|U_h^{\tau-1}|}. \tag{5}$$

$$\mathcal{L}_l^{\tau-1} = \frac{\sum_{u_i \in U_l^{\tau-1}} p_{i,j}^{\tau-1}}{|U_l^{\tau-1}|}. \tag{6}$$

where $U_h^{\tau-1}$ denotes the member worker in $\tau - 1$ period, $U_l^{\tau-1}$ denotes the ordinary worker in the $\tau - 1$ period.

In the τ period, the worker u_i calculates $\theta_{i,j}^h$ and $\theta_{i,j}^l$ for task t_j. $\theta_{i,j}^h$ and $\theta_{i,j}^l$ is composed of the worker's reward $p_{i,j}^{\tau-1}$ in $\tau - 1$ period and the average reward $\mathcal{L}_h^{\tau-1}$ and $\mathcal{L}_l^{\tau-1}$ in different task areas. $\theta_{i,j}^h$ and $\theta_{i,j}^l$ are calculated as follows.

$$\theta_{i,j}^h = x * p_{i,j}^{\tau-1} + y * \mathcal{L}_h^{\tau-1}, t_j \in T_h^{\tau-1} \tag{7}$$

$$\theta_{i,j}^l = x * p_{i,j}^{\tau-1} + y * \mathcal{L}_l^{\tau-1}, t_j \in T_l^{\tau-1} \tag{8}$$

where $T_h^{\tau-1}$ denotes the set of member tasks in $\tau - 1$ period, $T_l^{\tau-1}$ denotes the ordinary task in $\tau - 1$ period. $0 < x, y < 1$ and $x + y = 1$, x, y represents the proportion of reward in $\tau - 1$ period and average reward.

(3) Calculate the reference loss of choosing an ordinary task.

In our proposed scheme, due to the existence of reference dependence, the worker compares the estimated profit of the ordinary task with the membership task. The difference between them is the loss value of choosing an ordinary task, and the worker's loss value in the case of reference dependence is represented by $\eta_{i,j}$, which is denoted as the reference loss.

$$\eta_{i,j} = \left| -\lambda \left(\theta_{i,j}^{h} - \theta_{i,j}^{l} \right)^{\sigma} \right| \tag{9}$$

where $0 < \sigma < 1$, the aversion coefficient is $\lambda > 1$.

Based on the calculated reference loss, the worker's estimated utility for member tasks and ordinary tasks is calculated as follows.

$$\mathcal{O}_{i,h} = \sum_{j=1}^{n} \theta_{i,j}^{h} + \sum_{j=1}^{n} \eta_{i,j} - \sum_{j=1}^{n} \varphi_{i,j}^{h} - f_i \tag{10}$$

$$\mathcal{O}_{i,l} = \sum_{j=1}^{n} \theta_{i,j}^{l} - \sum_{j=1}^{n} \varphi_{i,j}^{l} \tag{11}$$

where $\theta_{i,j}^{h}$ and $\theta_{i,j}^{l}$ represent the estimated reward of the worker's member tasks and ordinary tasks. $\eta_{i,j}$ represents the worker's loss value under the reference dependency, $\varphi_{i,j}^{h}$ and $\varphi_{i,j}^{l}$ represent the cost of member tasks and ordinary tasks, respectively, f_i denotes the membership fee for worker u_i.

(4) Calculate the participation probability of member task.

When faced with the choice of whether to join the membership, the user will calculate the expected utility of different choices according to the reference loss. The platform will evaluate the worker's participation probability of the membership task according to the expected utility. The greater the impact of reference dependence on the worker, the higher the worker's participation probability ξ_i of the member task.

Ordinary workers have two choices: select a member task and submit a membership fee or select an ordinary task. The softmax function is often used to represent the probability that a decision maker chooses an option when faced with multiple choices. We use softmax function to represent the probability of the worker's participation in the member task.

$$\xi_i = \frac{e^{\omega * \mathcal{O}_{i,h}}}{e^{\omega * \mathcal{O}_{i,h}} + e^{\omega * \mathcal{O}_{i,l}}} \tag{12}$$

where $\mathcal{O}_{i,h}$ represents the worker's estimated utility for the selected member task, and $\mathcal{O}_{i,l}$ represents the worker's estimated utility value for the ordinary task, the utility value refers to the difference between income and expenditure. ω represents the difference sensitivity, the higher the value ω, the more sensitive the worker is to the difference between members and non-members, and $\omega \in [0,5]$. The higher the participation probability value ξ_i, the higher the likelihood that the user will choose the member task.

(5) Choose member task or ordinary task according to probability.

If the participation probability ξ_i of u_i is greater than the threshold ξ, the worker selects a member task and submits a discounted membership fee to the platform to join the set of members. Otherwise, u_i chooses an ordinary task.

Algorithm 2 illustrates the task selection process based on reference dependence and trust value. The input is the average profit $\mathcal{L}_h^{\tau-1}$ and $\mathcal{L}_l^{\tau-1}$ of the winners of the member task area and the ordinary task area in the $\tau - 1$ round. The output is the set of selected tasks $\mathbb{T}_i$, the set of member workers U_h, the set of ordinary workers U_l. Firstly, the member fee for worker based on trust value is calculated. Secondly, the worker calculates the estimated profit for the member task and ordinary task. Thirdly, the worker calculates the reference loss of choosing an ordinary task. Then, the worker calculates the participation probability of the member task. Finaly, the worker chooses the member task or ordinary task according to probability.

Algorithm 2: Task selection based on reference dependence and trust value

Inputs: $\mathcal{L}_h^{\tau-1}$, $\mathcal{L}_l^{\tau-1}$, T_h, T_l, $\mathbb{U}$, f, R.
Outputs: $\mathbb{T}_i$, U_h, U_l.
$\mathbb{T}_i = \emptyset$
for all $u_i \in U$ **do**
  $f_i = \kappa * f / r_i$
  while $u_i \notin U_h$ **do**
    $\theta_{i,j}^{h} = x * p_{i,j}^{\tau-1} + y * \mathcal{L}_h^{\tau-1}$
    $\theta_{i,j}^{l} = x * p_{i,j}^{\tau-1} + y * \mathcal{L}_l^{\tau-1}$
    $\eta_{i,j} = \left|-\lambda\left(\theta_{i,j}^{h} - \theta_{i,j}^{l}\right)^{\sigma}\right|$
    $O_{i,h} = \sum_{j=1}^{n} \theta_{i,j}^{h} + \sum_{j=1}^{n} \eta_{i,j} - \sum_{j=1}^{n} \varphi_{i,j}^{h} - f_i$
    $O_{i,l} = \sum_{j=1}^{n} \theta_{i,j}^{l} - \sum_{j=1}^{n} \varphi_{i,j}^{l}$
    $\xi_i = \frac{e^{\omega * O_{i,h}}}{e^{\omega * O_{i,h}} + e^{\omega * O_{i,l}}}$
    if $\xi_i > \xi$ **then**
      $\mathbb{T}_i = \mathbb{T}_i \cup \{\tau_j | \tau_j \in T_h\}$
      $U_h = U_h \cup u_i$
    else
      $\mathbb{T}_i = \mathbb{T}_i \cup \{\tau_j | \tau_j \in T_l\}$
  end while
end for

4.4 Winner Selection Process

According to the set of tasks $\mathbb{T}_i$ selected by worker u_i, the corresponding set of workers U_j for each task t_j can be obtained. In the winner selection process, the platform calculates the worker's priority according to the worker's trust value and whether the worker is a member, the priority is calculated as follows.

$$\delta_i = \begin{cases} \alpha * r_i + \beta \; if \; u_i \in U_h, \\ \alpha * r_i \qquad else. \end{cases} \tag{13}$$

where $\alpha, \beta > 0$. If the worker is a member, the priority is calculated as $\alpha * r_i + \beta$. If the worker is an ordinary worker, the priority is $\alpha * r_i$. The priority of member worker is higher than that of the ordinary worker, the worker with a higher trust value has a higher priority than the worker with a lower trust value.

Algorithm 3 illustrates winner selection process based on trust and member. The input is the set of workers U_j that chooses the task t_j, the output is the set of winners U_s^j of task t_j. For each task t_j in U_j, the platform calculates the priority of the workers, and sort the set of workers by priority in a decreasing order. Then, the platform chooses the first π workers and put them into U_s^j.

Algorithm 3: Winner selection based on trust and member

Inputs: $U_j,\ U_h,\ U_l,\ U, R$.
Outputs: U_s^j.

```
1: Initialize winner group U_s^j = {}
2: for each worker u_i ∈ U_j do
3:     if u_i ∈ U_h
4:         δ_i = α * r_i + β
5:     else
6:         δ_i = α * r_i
7:     end for
8:     Sort workers by δ_i for U_j in descending order
9:     U_s^j ←Select the first π workers from U_j
10: end for
```

4.5 Truth Calculation Process

In the truth calculation process, the platform calculates the truth after receiving the sensing data from the winner workers. For each task t_j, the set of winner workers is U_s^j, the data submitted by each worker is denoted as d_i. If there exist high-trust workers among the set of winner workers, the platform obtains high-trust worker's data d_h for worker in U_a and calculates the distance $dist(d_i, d_h)$ between d_i and d_h. If the distance $dist(d_i, d_h)$ is less than the threshold ϖ, the worker's trust value increases. If $dist(d_i, d_h)$ is greater than the distance threshold ϖ, the worker's trust value decreases. Then, the platform initializes the task's truth X_q^j for task t_j, and calculates the worker's weight w_i. Then, the platform calculates the truth value X_q^j, the platform calculates the truth iteratively until the distance between X_q^j and X_{q-1}^j is less than the truth threshold ε. Finally, we get the final truth value X_q^j for the task t_j. Algorithm 4 illustrates the truth calculation process based on trust.

Algorithm 4: Trust-based truth calculation

Inputs: Worker's data $\{d_i\}_{i=1}^{|U_s^j|}$, U_a.
Outputs: Final ground truth X_q^j.
Obtain high-trust worker's data d_h for worker in U_a;
for $i = 1,2,\ldots,N$ **do**
  Compute distance as $dist(d_i, d_h) = \left\|\frac{d_h - d_i}{d_h}\right\|$;
   if $dist(d_i, d_h) < \varpi$ **then**
     $r_i = r_i + \theta$;
   else
     $r_i = r_i - \theta$;
end for
Initialize the period as $q = 1$;
repeat
   Initializes the truth value as $X_q^j = \frac{\sum_{i=1}^{N} d_i}{N}$;
   for $i = 1,2,\ldots,N$ **do**
     $w_i = \log\left(\sum_{i=1}^{N} d(d_i, X_q^j)\right) - \log(d(d_i, X_q^j))$;
   end for
   $X_q^j = \frac{\sum_{i=1}^{N} d_i w_i r_i}{\sum_{i=1}^{N} w_i r_i}$;
   $q = q + 1$;
until $\left\|X_q^j - X_{q-1}^j\right\| < \varepsilon$
Return X_q^j.

After the task is completed, the platform issues rewards to the workers. The worker u_i obtains the actual reward $p_{i,j}^{\tau}$ after completing the task t_j in the τ period. The platform utility is the difference between the actual revenue of the platform and the rewards paid to the workers. If the probability of workers participating in member tasks increases, the more workers join the membership, the more membership fees the platform obtains, and the higher the platform utility. The platform publishes tasks in ψ periods, in each period τ, for each task t_j, the value of t_j is denoted as v_j^{τ}, the platform selects a set of winner workers U_s^j. For each worker u_i in U_s^j, the worker u_i completes the task t_j in τ period and obtains the actual reward $p_{i,j}^{\tau}$. In each period τ, for each task t_j, the task's value v_j^{τ} minus the total rewards paid to the workers, then plus the membership fee of members, is equal to the platform utility.

$$W = \sum\nolimits_{\tau=1}^{\psi} \sum\nolimits_{j=1}^{M} \left(v_j^{\tau} - \sum\nolimits_{u_i \in U_s^j} p_{i,j}^{\tau}\right) + \sum\nolimits_{i=1}^{|U_h|} f_i \tag{14}$$

5 Performance Analysis

In this section, we analyze and evaluate the performance of the proposed scheme, which includes the initialization algorithm, task selection algorithm, worker recruitment and trust-based truth calculation algorithm. In order to better prove the effectiveness of the proposed scheme, we conduct experiments based on Python to show the performance. The operating system is 64-bit Windows 10. Table 3 illustrates the experimental settings.

Table 3. Experimental settings.

Parameter	Value
M	[30, 40, **50**, 60, 70]
N	[40, 80, 120, 160, **200**, 240, 280, 320, 360, 400]
ψ	10
y	[0.1, 0.2, 0.3, 0.4, **0.5**, 0.6, 0.7, 0.8, 0.9]
ω	[0.5, **1.0**, 1.5, 2.0, 2.5, 3.0, 3.5, 4.0, 4.5, 5]
f	[5, 10, 15, 20, 25, **30**, 35, 40, 45, 50, 55, 60]
κ	0.7
α	0.5
β	0.5
λ	2.25
σ	0.88

5.1 Utility of Workers and Platform

Figure 2 shows the influence of y on the worker's loss utility, from the figure, we can see that the worker's loss value increases with the increase of y, and the reference loss is higher than the actual loss. The gap between the reference loss and the actual loss is also getting larger with the increase of y.

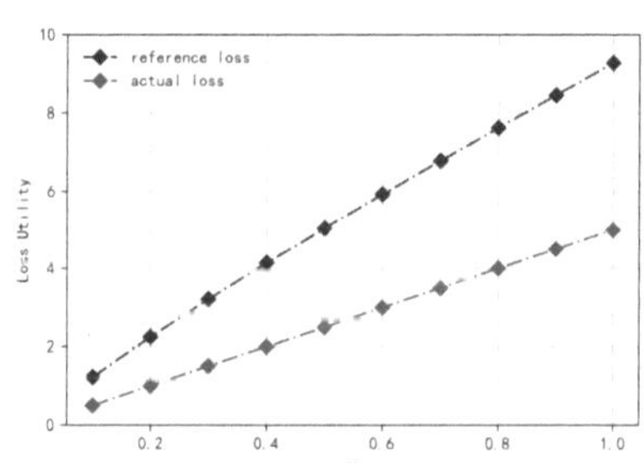

Fig. 2. Loss utility v.s.y

Figure 3 shows the impact of y and N on the number of members, when N is determined, the number of members increases with the increase of the y, because when y increases, the reference loss increases, and the worker's expected income from the member task increases, resulting in an increase in the probability of participation in the member task, so the number of members increases.

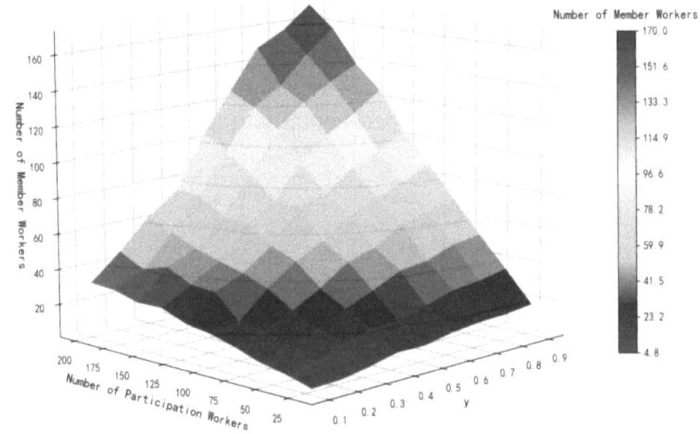

Fig. 3. Number of member workers v.s. y, N

Figure 4 shows the utility of workers, it can be seen from the figure that the utility of members is generally higher than that of ordinary workers as the members can choose high-profit member tasks.

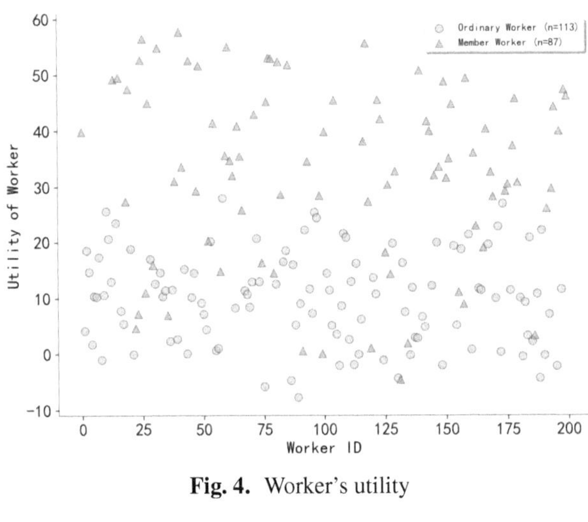

Fig. 4. Worker's utility

Figure 5 shows the impact of f, y on the platform utility, we can observe that the platform utility does not increase strictly in accordance with f. With the same N, the greater the ω, the higher the platform utility, but the impact of different ω on the platform utility does not change much. With the same N, the greater the y, the higher the platform utility.

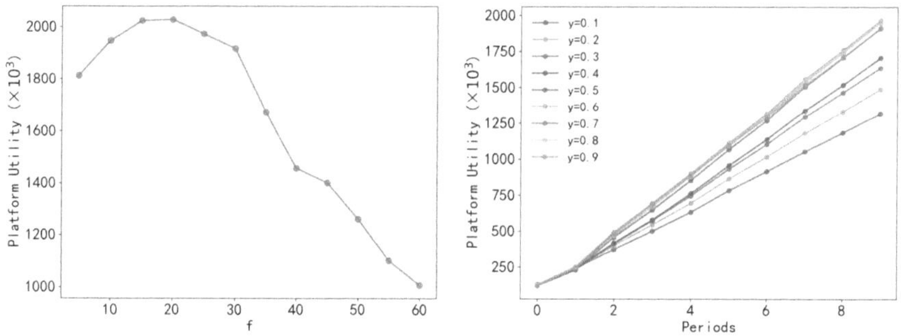

(a) f (b) y

Fig. 5. Platform utility v.s. f, y

We compare our IBTD scheme with the other two schemes, IBTD-noTrust and IBTD-noMember. Figure 6 shows that the impact of periods on the average utility of workers, and Fig. 7 shows the impact of f on the average utility of workers. The average utility of members is higher than that of ordinary users, and the member workers of IBTD scheme is higher than that of workers in the IBTD-noMember and IBTD-noTrust schemes, while the average utility of ordinary workers is not as good as that of the other schemes because they can only participate in tasks in the low-profit zone. Figure 8 shows that the impact of periods on the platform utility, the platform utility of IBTD scheme is higher than that of platform utility in the IBTD-noMember and IBTD-noTrust schemes.

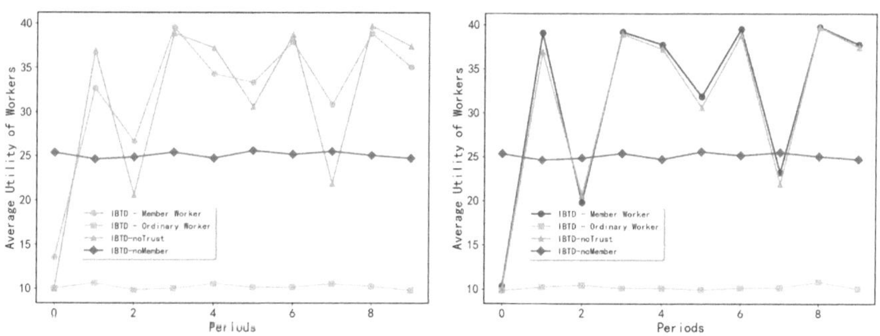

(a) $\kappa = 0.5$ (b) $\kappa = 0.7$

Fig. 6. Average utility of workers v.s. periods

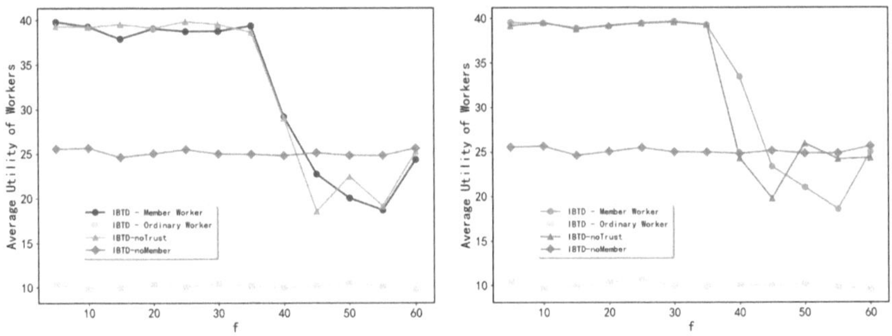

(a) $\omega = 1$ (b) $\omega = 3$

Fig. 7. Average utility of workers v.s. f

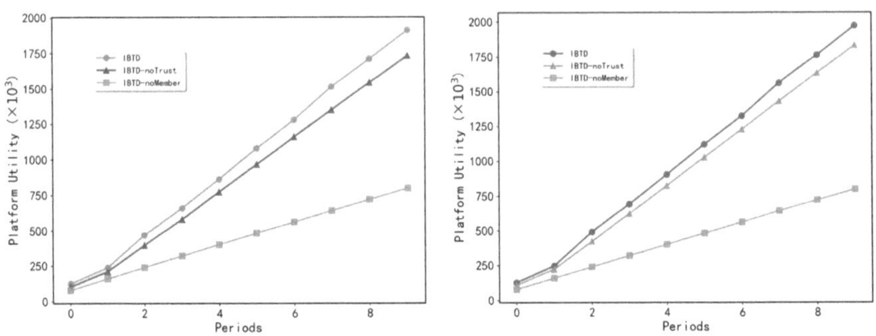

(a) $\psi = 0.5$ (b) $\psi = 0.7$

Fig. 8. Platform utility v.s. periods

5.2 Accuracy of Truth Value

We compare our IBTD scheme with the other two schemes, random and CRH [4]. Figure 9 and Fig. 10 shows the impact of M on RMSE and MAE performances of three schemes. Figure 11 and Fig. 12 shows the impact of N on RMSE and MAE performances of three schemes. The truth value's accuracy of IBTD scheme is higher than that of accuracy in the random and CRH schemes.

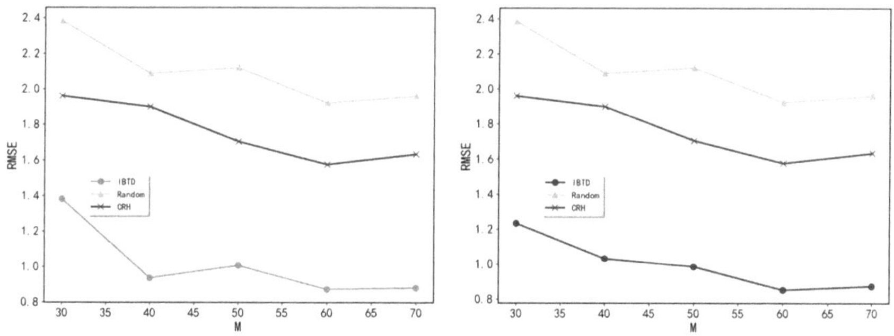

(a) $\alpha = 0.1$ (b) $\alpha = 0.5$

Fig. 9. RMSE v.s. M, α

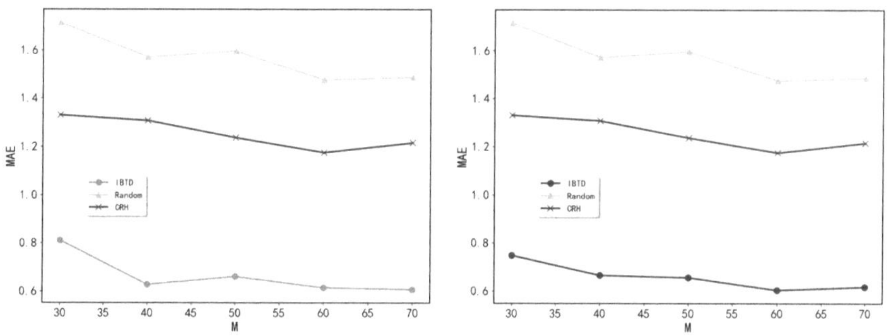

(a) $\alpha = 0.1$ (b) $\alpha = 0.5$

Fig. 10. MAE v.s. M, α

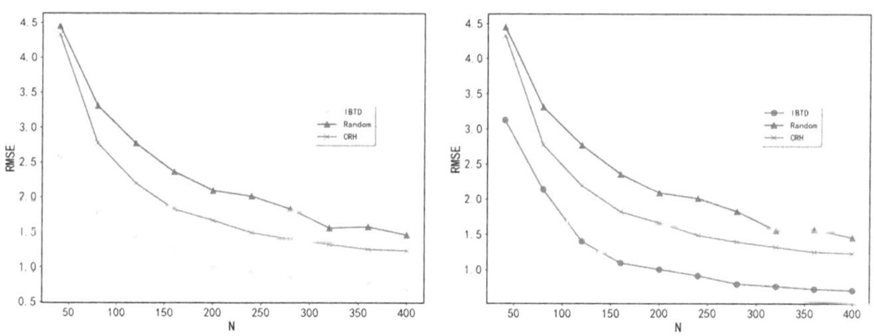

(a) $\beta = 0.1$ (b) $\beta = 0.5$

Fig. 11. RMSE v.s. N, β

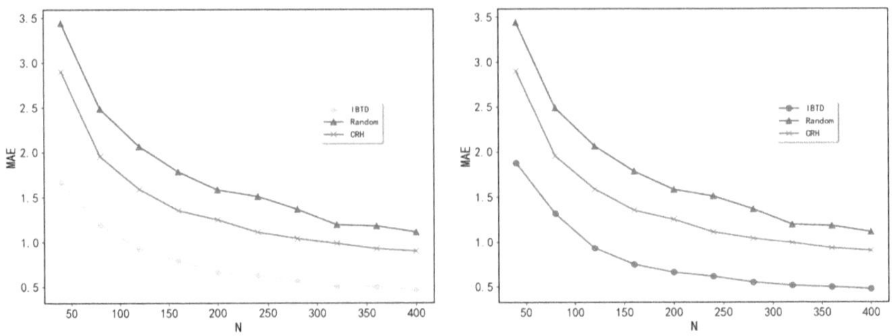

(a) $\beta = 0.1$ (b) $\beta = 0.5$

Fig. 12. MAE v.s. N, β

6 Conclusion

This paper proposes an incentive mechanism based on behavioral economics and trust in MCS, which aims to improve the quality of truth value and improve the utility of the platform. The payment member mechanism in behavioral economics is utilized in our scheme to incentive workers to participate in member tasks and pay membership fees. The tasks are divided into member tasks and ordinary tasks, the workers calculate the reference loss when choosing tasks, which can prompt them to pay membership fees and complete high-reward tasks. Furthermore, we propose a worker recruitment algorithm by calculating the priority of workers based on the membership and trust value of workers. The workers with high-trust values can also enjoy a discount on the membership fee, which can encourage workers to become members. Finally, we propose the truth discovery and trust evaluation algorithm to improve the accuracy of truth value. The experimental results show that our proposed scheme can improve the platform utility and the accuracy of truth value.

Acknowledgments. This work was supported in part by the National Natural Science Foundation of China under Grant 62302062, 62372067, in part by the Hunan Provincial Natural Science Foundation of China under Grant Number 2023JJ40081, 2025JJ50372, in part by the Scientific Research Fund of Hunan Provincial Education Department under Grant Number 23B0797.

References

1. Xu, Y., et al.: Rethinking the effect of sparse data completion on sparse mobile crowdsensing tasks. IEEE Trans. Mob. Comput. **24**, 5094–5105 (2025)
2. Zhang, J., Zhang, Y., Wu, H., Li, W.: An ordered submodularity-based budget-feasible mechanism for opportunistic mobile crowdsensing task allocation and pricing. IEEE Trans. Mob. Comput. **23**, 1278–1294 (2024)
3. Wang, S., et al.: A survey on truth discovery: concepts, methods, applications, and opportunities. IEEE Trans. Big Data **11**, 314–332 (2025)
4. Li, Y., et al.: Conflicts to harmony: a framework for resolving conflicts in heterogeneous data by truth discovery. IEEE Trans. Knowl. Data Eng. **28**, 1986–1999 (2016)

5. Bai, J., Gui, J., Wang, T., Song, H., Liu, A., Xiong, N.N.: ETBP-TD: an efficient and trusted bilateral privacy-preserving truth discovery scheme for mobile crowdsensing. IEEE Trans. Mob. Comput. **24**, 2203–2219 (2025)
6. Chen, X., et al.: An anonymous, trust and fairness based privacy preserving service construction framework in mobile crowdsourcing. IEEE Trans. Serv. Comput. 1–14 (2025)
7. Zhou, Q., Zhang, X., Yang, Z.: Unknown worker recruitment with long-term incentive in mobile crowdsensing. IEEE Trans. Mob. Comput. **24**, 999–1015 (2025)
8. Xu, Y., Xiao, M., Zhu, Y., Wu, J., Zhang, S., Zhou, J.: AoI-guaranteed incentive mechanism for mobile crowdsensing with freshness concerns. IEEE Trans. Mob. Comput. **23**, 4107–4125 (2024)
9. Wang, P., Jiao, D., Su, Z., Zhou, C., Li, M.: Truth discovery for multiple judgments with crowdsourced sparse data. IEEE Internet Things J. **12**, 5122–5136 (2025)
10. Wang, Y., et al.: A coverage-aware high-quality sensing data collection method in mobile crowd sensing. IEEE Trans. Mob. Comput. **24**, 3025–3040 (2025)
11. Shen, X., Xu, C., Zhu, L., Lu, R., Guan, Y., Zhang, X.: Blockchain-based lightweight and privacy-preserving quality assurance framework in crowdsensing systems. IEEE Internet Things J. **11**, 974–986 (2024)
12. Li, J., Gu, B., Gong, S., Su, Z., Guizani, M.: Can we enhance the quality of mobile crowdsensing data without ground truth? IEEE Trans. Mob. Comput. **24**, 4451–4465 (2025)
13. Yuan, S., et al.: Enabling accurate and efficient privacy-preserving truth discovery for sparse crowdsensing. IEEE Trans. Dependable Secure Comput. 1–16 (2025)
14. Li, Z., et al.: QUEST: quality-informed multi-agent dispatching system for optimal mobile crowdsensing. In: IEEE INFOCOM 2024 - IEEE Conference on Computer Communications, pp. 1811–1820 (2024)
15. Xie, L., Su, Z., Chen, N., Wang, Y., Liu, Y., Li, R.: A privacy-preserving incentive scheme for data sensing in app-assisted mobile edge crowdsensing. IEEE/ACM Trans. Networking **32**, 4765–4780 (2024)
16. Wang, P., Li, Z., Guo, B., Long, S., Guo, S., Cao, J.: A UAV-assisted truth discovery approach with incentive mechanism design in mobile crowd sensing. IEEE/ACM Trans. Networking **32**, 1738–1752 (2024)
17. Cheng, Z., Chen, J., Liu, J.: Utilizing social psychology solutions to enhance the quality assessment ability of unreliable data in mobile crowdsensing. IEEE Internet Things J. **12**, 3800–3815 (2025)
18. Liu, J., Huang, S., Li, D., Wen, S., Liu, H.: Addictive incentive mechanism in crowdsensing from the perspective of behavioral economics. IEEE Trans. Parallel Distrib. Syst. **33**, 1109–1127 (2022)
19. Liu, J., Yang, Y., Li, D., Deng, X., Huang, S., Liu, H.: An incentive mechanism based on behavioural economics in location-based crowdsensing considering an uneven distribution of participants. IEEE Trans. Mob. Comput. **21**, 44–62 (2022)
20. Li, D., Li, C., Deng, X., Liu, H., Liu, J.: Familiar paths are the best: incentive mechanism based on path-dependence considering space-time coverage in crowdsensing. IEEE Trans. Mob. Comput. **23**, 9304–9323 (2024)

Progressive Weight Loading: Accelerating Initial Inference and Gradually Boosting Performance on Resource-Constrained Environments

Hyunwoo Kim[1(✉)], Junha Lee[2], Mincheol Choi[2], Jeonghwan Lee[2], and Jaeshin Cho[2]

[1] Intel, Seoul, South Korea
onion.kim@intel.com
[2] Yonsei University, Seoul, South Korea
{junha4304,charmfe,hwan1997,cjs823}@yonsei.ac.kr

Abstract. Deep learning models have become increasingly large and complex, resulting in higher memory consumption and computational demands. Consequently, model loading times and initial inference latency have increased, posing significant challenges in mobile and latency-sensitive environments where frequent model loading and unloading are required, which directly impacts user experience. While Knowledge Distillation (KD) offers a solution by compressing large teacher models into smaller student ones, it often comes at the cost of reduced performance. To address this trade-off, we propose Progressive Weight Loading (PWL), a novel technique that enables fast initial inference by first deploying a lightweight student model, then incrementally replacing its layers with those of a pre-trained teacher model. To support seamless layer substitution, we introduce a training method that not only aligns intermediate feature representations between student and teacher layers, but also improves the overall output performance of the student model. Our experiments on VGG, ResNet, and ViT architectures demonstrate that models trained with PWL maintain competitive distillation performance and gradually improve accuracy as teacher layers are loaded—matching the final accuracy of the full teacher model without compromising initial inference speed. This makes PWL particularly suited for dynamic, resource-constrained deployments where both responsiveness and performance are critical.

Keywords: Progressive Weight Loading · Knowledge Distillation · Fast Initial Inference · Resource-Constrained Environments

1 Introduction

With the rapid advancement of deep learning, modern AI models have grown substantially in both size and complexity [1], leading to increased computational

L. Zhang and K.-K. R. Choo (Eds.): MobiQuitous 2025, LNICST 683, pp. 428–451, 2026.
https://doi.org/10.1007/978-3-032-22500-9_24

and memory demands [2,3]. While larger models often deliver improved performance, their size also results in longer loading times, which can become a critical bottleneck during deployment [4]. In memory-constrained environments like edge devices, these loading delays can be especially severe. A recent study reported that for multi-billion-parameter models, the time spent loading the model into GPU memory can account for over 90% of the total inference latency [5]. Fast and efficient model loading is especially important in latency sensitive applications such as autonomous driving, robotics, and interactive AI services, where delays in model initialization may adversely affect user experience or even compromise safety.

One of the simplest approaches to reducing model loading time is to make the model smaller. Knowledge distillation is a widely used technique that compresses large models into smaller ones while attempting to retain their performance [6,7]. In this process, student models are trained under the guidance of larger teacher models by mimicking the teacher's output logits [6] and intermediate features [8]. However, the performance of student models often falls short of that of their teacher models [9] and is generally constrained by the student model's size. This means that although smaller student models can achieve faster loading times, they may struggle to match the accuracy of their larger counterparts.

In this paper, we propose a novel approach called Progressive Weight Loading (PWL) to tackle the challenge of balancing model loading time and performance. As illustrated in Fig. 1, PWL achieves fast loading by initially loading a smaller student model, then progressively loading the teacher model's weights layer by layer while enhancing the student's performance. This strategy allows us to strike a balance between rapid loading and high accuracy, making it particularly suitable for resource-constrained mobile and latency-sensitive environments. Additionally, we introduce a distillation training method and a student model architecture designed to enable seamless performance improvement as layers of the student model are incrementally replaced by those of the teacher model.

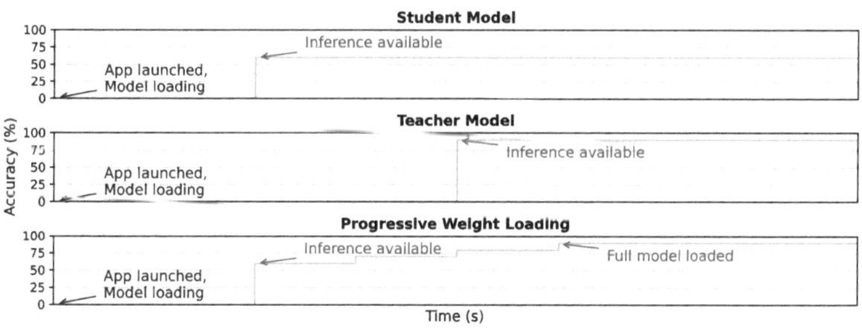

Fig. 1. Illustration of the Progressive Weight Loading (PWL) timeline. Initial inference is performed using the lightweight student model, enabling a fast response. As layers are progressively replaced with those of the teacher model, the overall performance improves gradually toward that of the full teacher.

2 Background

Deploying deep neural networks on resource-constrained edge devices—such as smartphones, IoT systems, and AR/VR headsets—poses significant challenges due to limited compute, memory, and power resources compared to cloud environments [10,11]. These constraints often necessitate model loading and unloading at runtime, making techniques that accelerate model loading and enable fast initial inference highly valuable.

To address these challenges, various model compression techniques have been developed. Among them, pruning [4,12,13] and quantization [14,15] reduce model size and computational cost by removing redundant parameters or lowering numerical precision. Another widely studied method is Knowledge Distillation (KD) [6], where a compact student model is trained to mimic the behavior of a larger, high-performing teacher model. By learning from the teacher's outputs, the student can achieve competitive accuracy while maintaining a smaller footprint.

KD has proven effective in real world applications, with models like MobileNet [16–18], TinyBERT [19], EfficientNet [20], and MobileBERT [21] demonstrating its impact in enabling efficient deep learning on edge devices. Initially, KD focused on matching the final outputs (logits) of the teacher and student networks [6]. However, recent research has extended this concept to hinted loss [8], which includes an intermediate feature alignment step. In this step, the student is guided to match the teacher's internal representations, leading to more robust and informative knowledge transfer. Methods such as layer-wise distillation [21,22] and attention transfer [23,24] exemplify this progression. Attention transfer proposes re-weighting feature maps with attention maps for loss construction [23]. ReviewKD [25] addresses the challenge of arbitrarily selecting specific layers for distillation by aggregating information across all teacher layers using trainable attention blocks. Neuron Selectivity Transfer [26] and Similarity Preserving KD [22] involve the construction of relational matrices based on batches and features; these matrices then serve as input for their distillation loss functions.

Despite these advancements, the primary objective of existing intermediate feature alignment techniques is to improve the standalone performance of the student model [9]. In contrast, our work introduces a novel perspective: training a student model whose layers can be seamlessly replaced by corresponding layers from the teacher model at inference time, without degrading performance. This approach enables Progressive Weight Loading (PWL)—a mechanism that supports fast initial inference and gradually upgrades the model toward full teacher level performance in a resource aware manner.

3 Design Proposal

3.1 Progressive Weight Loading Overview

PWL starts inference with a smaller, efficient student model and incrementally replaces its layers with those from a larger, more powerful teacher model. The objective of PWL is to progressively enhance performance from the baseline level of the student to the superior level of the teacher. Key benefits of PWL include (Fig. 2):

1. **Fast Initial Inference**: By initially deploying the smaller student model, PWL enables rapid model loading and inference, critical for latency-sensitive applications such as autonomous driving or interactive AI services.
2. **Memory Aware Performance Scaling**: PWL provides dynamic control over the memory performance trade-off, making it particularly suitable for mobile and resource-constrained environments. Unlike conventional deployments—which rely entirely on either a small student or a large teacher model, PWL supports partial loading of teacher layers according to the available system memory.

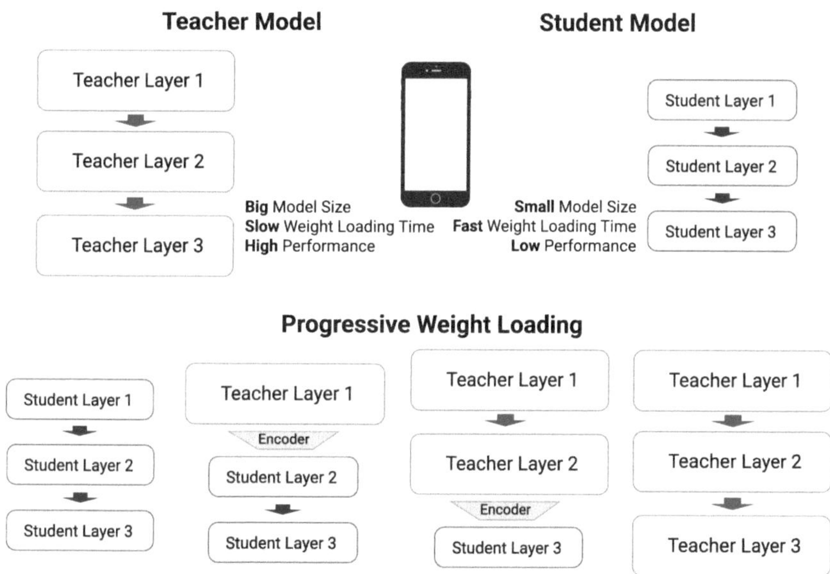

Fig. 2. Conceptual overview of Progressive Weight Loading (PWL). The student model is initially loaded, and its layers are progressively replaced by those of the teacher model, starting from the input layer. This approach enables a dynamic trade-off between model size and performance, making it well-suited to resource-constrained environments such as mobile and edge computing.

The primary goal of PWL is to achieve gradual and seamless performance improvement as student model's layers are incrementally replaced with corresponding layers from the teacher model. However, this approach poses several challenges:

- **Feature Alignment**: Differences in architecture between student and teacher models complicate the alignment of their internal feature representations. Therefore, a dedicated feature converter is required to map the student's features to the teacher's feature space and vice versa.
- **Training Strategy**: An effective training strategy must be developed to prevent performance degradation during progressive layer replacement. This strategy should facilitate the seamless alignment of student and teacher features, ensuring the student model effectively mimics both the logits and the intermediate representations of the teacher.

To address these challenges, we introduce two key components: the **Invertible Feature Converter** and the **Training Strategy for PWL**.

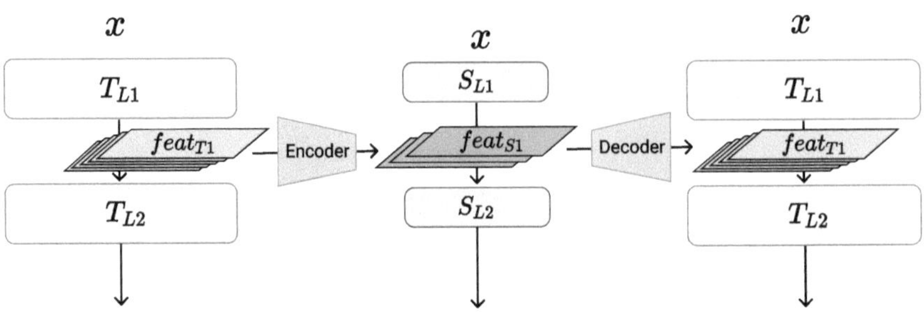

Fig. 3. Architecture of the feature converter. Since features from the teacher and student models often differ in dimensionality or channel size, they must be transformed to a common space for effective comparison. Our proposed solution employs a lightweight autoencoder-style converter, consisting of simple linear layers for both the encoder and decoder.

3.2 Invertible Feature Converter

One of the critical challenges we address is aligning different feature representations between student and teacher model layers. The goal is to ensure compatibility between features extracted from corresponding layers, enabling the progressive loading of teacher model layers into a student model (Fig. 3).

We define the features from the student and teacher models as follows 1:

$$\begin{aligned} \text{feat}_{Si} &= S_{Li} \circ S_{Li-1} \circ \cdots \circ S_{L1}(x), \\ \text{feat}_{Ti} &= T_{Li} \circ T_{Li-1} \circ \cdots \circ T_{L1}(x). \end{aligned} \tag{1}$$

where $f_{S_{1:i}}$ represents the output feature from layers 1 to i of the student model, and $f_{T_{1:i}}$ represents the corresponding feature from the teacher model.

For conventional CNN based architectures (e.g., VGG, ResNet), these features typically differ in the number of channels, given by 2:

$$\begin{aligned} \text{feat}_{Si} &\in \mathbb{R}^{C_s \times W \times H}, \\ \text{feat}_{Ti} &\in \mathbb{R}^{C_t \times W \times H}. \end{aligned} \tag{2}$$

where usually $C_s < C_t$.

In transformer-based models such as Vision Transformer (ViT), the features differ primarily in embedding dimensionality 3:

$$\begin{aligned} \text{feat}_{Si} &\in \mathbb{R}^{\text{num\_blocks} \times d_S}, \\ \text{feat}_{Ti} &\in \mathbb{R}^{\text{num\_blocks} \times d_T}. \end{aligned} \tag{3}$$

where typically $d_s < d_t$.

To convert teacher features to student features, we propose using a lightweight linear mapping. Specifically, we employ encoder decoder pairs for each layer 4, designed to map high dimensional teacher features to low dimensional student features and vice versa. For CNN based models, these mappings are implemented as 1×1 convolutional layers, whereas for transformer-based models, simple linear layers are used.

Crucially, this feature mapping must be invertible to enable flexible layer replacement. Suppose we replace a student layer S_{L2} with its teacher counterpart T_{L2}. First, the student feature feat_{S1} must be mapped to feat_{T1} before being processed by T_{L2}. Subsequently, the resulting teacher feature feat_{T2} needs to be mapped back to feat_{S2} to continue processing by the student layer S_{L3}. Thus, bidirectional mappings are essential:

$$\begin{aligned} \text{Encoder}_i(\text{feat}_{Ti}) &= \text{feat}_{Si}, \\ \text{Decoder}_i(\text{feat}_{Si}) &= \text{feat}_{Ti}. \end{aligned} \tag{4}$$

We propose an autoencoder-style [27] architecture for these encoder decoder feature converters, parameterized by learnable weights. These encoders and decoders are jointly optimized with the student model during the distillation training process, ensuring accurate and efficient feature alignment for Progressive Weight Loading (Fig. 4).

3.3 Training Strategy for PWL

The training strategy for PWL involves jointly optimizing the student model and the encoder decoder [27] feature converters through a distillation framework. The Teacher model guides the student model to learn from its logits and intermediate representations. During this process, the encoder decoder converters are simultaneously trained to minimize the discrepancy between corresponding student and teacher features.

Our training objective comprises 4 primary components:

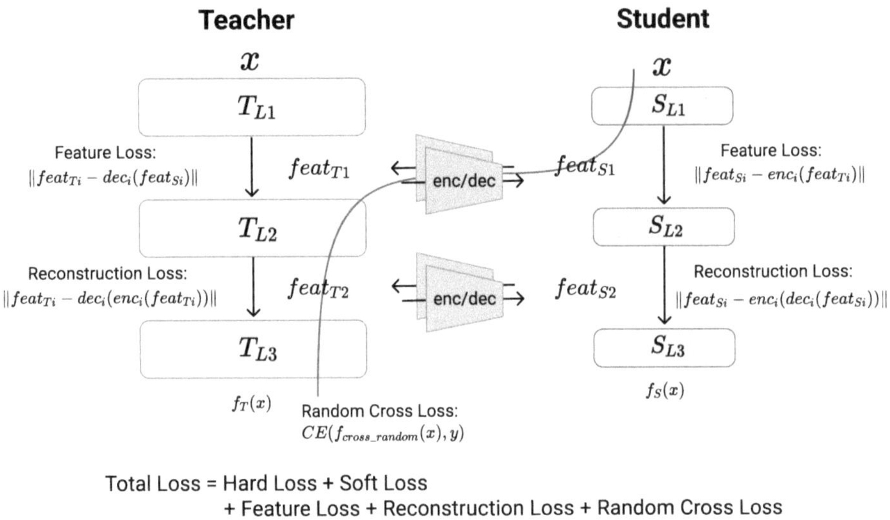

Fig. 4. Training strategy for PWL. The student model is optimized using a combination of five losses to support progressive layer replacement. Hard loss and soft loss supervise the student using ground-truth labels and teacher logits, respectively. Feature loss and reconstruction loss encourage alignment of intermediate representations between the student and teacher. Random cross loss mitigates performance degradation when individual student layers are replaced with corresponding teacher layers.

Distillation Loss 5: The distillation loss L_{distill} consists of two components a hard target loss that enforces correct predictions against ground truth labels, and a soft target loss that encourages the student model to mimic the teacher's output distribution [6].

$$L_{\text{distill}} = \alpha\, L_{\text{hard}} + (1 - \alpha)\, L_{\text{soft}} \tag{5}$$

where

$$L_{\text{hard}} = \text{CE}(p_s, y), \tag{6}$$

$$L_{\text{soft}} = T^2\, \text{KL}\big(\sigma(\frac{z_t}{T}) \,\|\, \sigma(\frac{z_s}{T})\big). \tag{7}$$

with z_t and z_s being the teacher and student logits respectively, σ denoting the softmax function, y the ground truth label, $T > 1$ the temperature parameter [28] used for softening logits, and $\alpha \in [0, 1]$ balancing the hard and soft losses.

Feature Loss 8: This loss ensures feature compatibility across corresponding layers by minimizing the L2 distance between converted features:

$$L_{feature} = \sum_i ||\text{Encoder}_i(\text{feat}_{Ti}) - \text{feat}_{Si}||^2 + ||\text{Decoder}_i(\text{feat}_{Si}) - \text{feat}_{Si}||^2 \tag{8}$$

Reconstruction Loss 9: We also introduce a reconstruction loss to encourage the encoder-decoder pairs to be near-invertible. This loss minimizes the discrepancy between the original teacher feature and its reconstruction after passing through the encoder and decoder:

$$L_{\text{recon}} = \sum_i \left|\left|\text{feat}_{Ti} - \text{Decoder}_i\big(\text{Encoder}_i(\text{feat}_{Ti})\big)\right|\right|^2 + \left|\left|\text{feat}_{Si} - \text{Encoder}_i\big(\text{Decoder}_i(\text{feat}_{Si})\big)\right|\right|^2 \tag{9}$$

Including this term helps the feature converters preserve essential information in the teacher features during mapping, ensuring smooth transitions when progressively replacing student layers with teacher layers. It acts as a regularizer [29] preventing the mappings from collapsing to trivial or lossy transformations and stabilizing training.

Random Cross Loss 12: To ensure consistent accuracy regardless of which student layers are replaced by corresponding teacher layers during progressive loading, we introduce a Random Cross Loss. In each training iteration, a random subset of student layers is replaced by the corresponding teacher layers, with encoder and decoder feature converters applied as needed.

Formally, let the full model consist of L layers, and let $\mathcal{R} \subseteq \{1, 2, \dots, L\}$ denote the random subset of layers replaced by teacher layers in a given iteration. The mixed model's output logits, denoted by z_{mix} 10, are defined as

$$z_{\text{mix}} = f\big(x; \{\tilde{L}_i\}_{i=1}^{L}\big) \tag{10}$$

where

$$\tilde{L}_i = \begin{cases} T_{L_i}(\cdot) & \text{if } i \in \mathcal{R} \text{ (teacher layer with encoder/decoder conversion)}, \\ S_{L_i}(\cdot) & \text{if } i \notin \mathcal{R} \text{ (student layer)}. \end{cases} \tag{11}$$

Here, S_{L_i} and T_{L_i} represent the student and teacher implementations of the i th layer, respectively, with feature conversion applied to teacher layers to ensure compatibility.

The Random Cross Loss is then computed as the cross entropy between the mixed model's output and the ground truth label y:

$$L_{\text{random-cross}} = \text{CE}\big(\sigma(z_{\text{mix}}), y\big) \tag{12}$$

where $\sigma(\cdot)$ denotes the softmax function.

This loss encourages the model to maintain stable and high performance across arbitrary combinations of student and teacher layers during progressive weight loading.

Total Loss 13: Combining these losses, the final training objective is:

$$L_{\text{total}} = L_{\text{distill}} + \lambda_1 L_{\text{feature}} + \lambda_2 L_{\text{recon}} + \lambda_3 L_{\text{random-cross}} \tag{13}$$

where λ_1, λ_2, and λ_3 are hyperparameters that balance the contributions of feature alignment loss, reconstruction loss, and Random Cross Loss respectively.

4 Implementation Details

All source code, including model definitions, training scripts, and evaluation utilities, is publicly available at: https://github.com/5yearsKim/ProgressiveWeightLoading.

4.1 Framework and Environment

All models and training routines are implemented in **PyTorch 2.7** using **Python 3.12**. Experiments are conducted on a system equipped with an **NVIDIA A100 GPU** and **CUDA 12.6**.

Model statistics, such as parameter counts and memory usage, are obtained using the `torchinfo` library.

4.2 Dataset and Preprocessing

We evaluate our method on two benchmark datasets: **CIFAR-10** and **CIFAR-100** [30]. For training, we apply standard data augmentation techniques commonly used for these datasets [31,32], including:

- `RandomCrop(32, padding=4)`
- `RandomHorizontalFlip(p=0.5)`
- `RandomRotation(15°)`

All images are normalized [31] using dataset-specific mean and standard deviation values prior to input into the model.

4.3 Model Architecture

We designed distinct architectures for teacher and student models across three standard architectures VGG [33], ResNet [34], and Vision Transformer (ViT) [35]—to rigorously evaluate Progressive Weight Loading (PWL). Each architecture is divided into four main blocks, allowing clear comparisons of intermediate representations and facilitating layer-wise progressive loading.

VGG Architecture. For the VGG model, the teacher follows the classical VGG16 style architecture [33] comprising four convolutional blocks followed by three fully connected (FC) layers. The student architecture significantly reduces complexity, adopting a VGG6 style model featuring only five convolutional layers distributed across four blocks and a single FC layer. Additionally, each convolutional block's channel size is halved compared to the teacher, except for the initial block.

ResNet Architecture. The ResNet teacher model adopts the widely recognized ResNet-50 architecture [34]. It consists of four convolutional blocks containing 3, 4, 6, and 3 residual layers, respectively. Each residual layer includes two 1×1 convolutional layers and one 3×3 convolutional layer, with channel dimensions selected as 64, 128, 256, and 512. Conversely, the student architecture simplifies to a ResNet-18 style model, featuring only a single residual layer per block with channel dimensions reduced by half, except for the first block.

ViT Architecture. For the Vision Transformer (ViT), the teacher model uses a ViT-tiny configuration [35] with 12 transformer layers evenly divided into four blocks (three layers per block), each with an embedding dimension of 192. The student variant simplifies this by allocating just one transformer layer per block, maintaining the same embedding dimension to facilitate feature mapping between corresponding layers.

Table 1 summarizes the specific architectural differences between teacher and student models, highlighting parameter reductions and resulting memory efficiencies for each architecture.

4.4 Experiment Setup

We adopt distinct training strategies for CNN based model(VGG and ResNet) and for transformer-based models(ViT), to reflect their architectural differences.

For CNN based distillation, we train the student models from scratch using standard supervised learning with an extended training schedule. Models are trained for 160 epochs on CIFAR-10 and CIFAR-100 using a cosine annealing learning rate schedule starting from 5e-2 and decaying to 1e-5. We use the SGD optimizer with a momentum of 0.9 and weight decay of 5e-4. This prolonged training stabilizes convergence and facilitates effective feature alignment with the teacher model.

For transformer-based architectures, we adopt a two stage training process. First, the student model is pretrained using intermediate representation (IR) matching and feature loss 8. Then, the student is finetuned on CIFAR-10 or CIFAR-100 for 5 epochs using the AdamW optimizer with a fixed learning rate of 5e-5.

Table 1. Comparison of teacher and student architectures for VGG, ResNet, and ViT. Each model is divided into four corresponding blocks of layers for structural alignment and progressive replacement.

Block	**Teacher (VGG16 style)**	**Student (VGG6 style)**
Block 1	2 Conv 3×3 (64) → 2 Conv 3×3 (128)	1 Conv 3×3 (64) → 1 Conv 3×3(128)
Block 2	3 Conv 3×3 (256)	1 Conv 3×3 (128)
Block 3	3 Conv 3×3 (512)	1 Conv 3×3 (256)
Block 4	3 Conv 3×3 (512)	1 Conv 3×3 (256)
Post blocks	3 FC	1 FC
#Params	14.7M	0.9M
Memory (MB)	64.1	5.1 (8.3%)

Block	**Teacher (ResNet-50 style)**	**Student (ResNet-18 style)**
Block 1	3 ResNet layers (64)	1 ResNet layer (32)
Block 2	4 ResNet layers (128)	1 ResNet layer (64)
Block 3	6 ResNet layers (256)	1 ResNet layer (128)
Block 4	3 ResNet layers (512)	1 ResNet layer (256)
Post blocks	Global Pooling + FC	Global Pooling + FC
#Params	10.6M	1.2M
Memory (MB)	61.2	8.9 (14.5%)

Block	**Teacher (ViT-tiny, 12 layers)**	**Student (ViT-tiny, 4 layers)**
Block 1	3 ViT layers (192 dim)	1 ViT layer (192 dim)
Block 2	3 ViT layers (192 dim)	1 ViT layer (192 dim)
Block 3	3 ViT layers (192 dim)	1 ViT layer (192 dim)
Block 4	3 ViT layers (192 dim)	1 ViT layer (192 dim)
Post blocks	FC	FC
#Params	5.5M	2.1M
Memory (MB)	62.8	22.7 (36.1%)

To enhance stability, we assign a smaller learning rate 1/10th of the base rate to the encoder and decoder layers used for feature conversion. This prevents overfitting of the converters and ensures consistent performance when student layers are progressively replaced by teacher layers.

For the loss formulation, we set the balancing coefficient α in distill loss (L_{distill}) 5 to 0.6, assigning a weight of 0.6 to the hard target loss (L_{hard}) 6 and 0.4 to the soft target loss (L_{soft}) 7. For the total loss 13, we configure the loss weights as follows: $\lambda_1 = 1.0$ and $\lambda_2 = 1.0$ for the feature loss (L_{feature}) 8 and reconstruction loss (L_{recon}) 9, respectively. The weight for the Random Cross Loss ($L_{\text{random-cross}}$) 12 is set to $\lambda_3 = 1.8$, reflecting its greater influence in stabilizing performance during progressive layer replacement.

5 Result and Analysis

Table 2. Comparison of distillation performance with and without PWL training. The student model trained with PWL shows no degradation in performance compared to standard distillation.

Model	CIFAR10			CIFAR100		
	VGG	ResNet	ViT	VGG	ResNet	ViT
Teacher	93.8	94.8	97.4	74.2	75.7	82.3
Student (w/o PWL training)	91.3	92.0	94.3	70.8	72.4	75.2
Student (w/ PWL training)	**91.7**	**92.9**	**94.1**	**71.1**	**72.1**	**74.6**

We evaluate the classification accuracy of student models trained with and without the proposed PWL loss. As shown in Table 2, the inclusion of PWL loss leads to negligible or minor performance changes across architectures. Specifically, VGG and ResNet show marginal improvements, while ViT experiences a slight decrease in accuracy. These results confirm that incorporating PWL training does not negatively impact the overall effectiveness of knowledge distillation. Importantly, it enables the capability of progressively loading teacher weights into the student model without degrading performance.

Table 3 presents the classification performance and memory usage as teacher layers are progressively loaded into the student model, block by block, from input to output. For all three architectures—VGG, ResNet, and ViT—we observe a clear upward trend in accuracy on both CIFAR-10 and CIFAR-100 datasets as more teacher layers are introduced. This confirms the effectiveness of Progressive Weight Loading (PWL) in bridging the performance gap between the student and teacher models.

Specifically, for VGG and ResNet, accuracy improves steadily while memory usage increases in proportion to the number of loaded teacher blocks. ViT

Table 3. Gradual performance improvements as teacher weights are progressively loaded from input to output layers in VGG, ResNet, and ViT models.

Layers Loaded	CIFAR10 (%)	CIFAR100 (%)	Memory Loaded(MB)
VGGNet			
Student ($S_{L1}S_{L2}S_{L3}S_{L4}$)	91.7	71.1	5.1
$T_{L1} \rightarrow S_{L2} \rightarrow S_{L3} \rightarrow S_{L4}$	92.1	70.7	8.3
$T_{L1} \rightarrow T_{L2} \rightarrow S_{L3} \rightarrow S_{L4}$	93.1	72.5	16.3
$T_{L1} \rightarrow T_{L2} \rightarrow T_{L3} \rightarrow S_{L4}$	92.7	73.9	39.3
Teacher ($T_{L1}T_{L2}T_{L3}T_{L4}$)	93.8	74.2	64.1
ResNet			
Student ($S_{L1}S_{L2}S_{L3}S_{L4}$)	92.3	71.2	8.9
$S_{L1} \rightarrow S_{L2} \rightarrow S_{L3} \rightarrow T_{L4}$	91.9	71.3	12.9
$S_{L1} \rightarrow S_{L2} \rightarrow T_{L3} \rightarrow T_{L4}$	92.9	73.0	26.6
$S_{L1} \rightarrow T_{L2} \rightarrow T_{L3} \rightarrow T_{L4}$	94.4	72.5	42.1
Teacher ($T_{L1}T_{L2}T_{L3}T_{L4}$)	94.8	73.4	61.2
ViT			
Student ($S_{L1}S_{L2}S_{L3}S_{L4}$)	94.3	74.6	22.7
$S_{L1} \rightarrow S_{L2} \rightarrow S_{L3} \rightarrow S_{L4}$	95.5	76.2	32.2
$S_{L1} \rightarrow S_{L2} \rightarrow S_{L3} \rightarrow S_{L4}$	96.4	79.8	43.3
$S_{L1} \rightarrow S_{L2} \rightarrow S_{L3} \rightarrow T_{L4}$	97.1	81.4	52.5
Teacher ($T_{L1}T_{L2}T_{L3}T_{L4}$)	97.8	82.3	62.8

exhibits a more pronounced performance gain, particularly on CIFAR-100, indicating that transformer-based architectures may benefit more from incremental upgrades. Notably, this progressive transition does not result in abrupt changes in performance, demonstrating the stability and smooth integration of teacher layers at each stage.

These results highlight that PWL enables flexible trade-offs between accuracy and resource usage, allowing systems to scale performance in response to available memory or computational constraints.

We evaluate the loading time of the model for VGG, ResNet and ViT. As shown in Fig. 5, because PWL first loads the entire student model, the time to first inference is identical to the total time required to load the student model itself. We then incrementally replaced each student layer with its teacher counterpart, while still allowing the unreplaced student layers to perform inference, and measured the time for each step. The total loading time of teacher layers with PWL exceeds the total loading time of the student model, but it has a benefit in that it can still inference with gradually improving performance during the loading time.

Figure 5 presents a comparison of loading times for the student model, the full teacher model, and the progressive layer by layer loading process using PWL

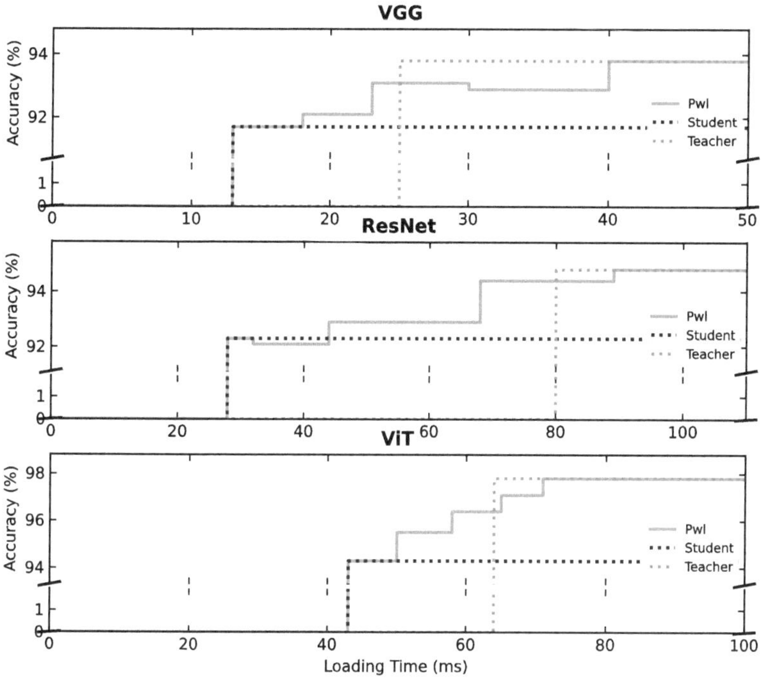

Fig. 5. Loading time vs. CIFAR-10 accuracy for student, PWL stages, and teacher models across VGG, ResNet, and ViT architectures. PWL delivers inference speed on par with the student model while steadily increasing accuracy as layers are replaced with teacher weights.

across VGG, ResNet, and ViT architectures. The "Student Total" row reflects the initial loading time required to load the entire student model, while the "Teacher Total" row shows the time needed to load the complete teacher model from scratch.

In the "Student → Teacher Replace" row, we measure the cumulative time taken as teacher layers are incrementally loaded on top of the already initialized student model. Although the total time for progressive loading exceeds the teacher model's loading time, PWL offers a critical advantage: inference can begin immediately with the student model and continue throughout the loading process with gradually improving performance. This incremental and non blocking behavior is especially valuable for latency sensitive scenarios, where maintaining continuous availability is more important than waiting for a full teacher model to load.

Table 4 summarizes the practical benefits of the proposed PWL method. For ResNet with CIFAR-10 dataset, PWL achieves the same maximum accuracy (94.8%) but with a significantly reduced initial inference time—comparable to that of the lightweight student model, compared to teacher model. Moreover, while the teacher model demands a fixed memory footprint of 61.2 MB, PWL

Table 4. System requirements for ResNet on CIFAR-10. PWL achieves fast initial inference comparable to the student model, while progressively reaching the maximum accuracy of the teacher model.

	Initial Inference Time	Maximum Accuracy	Memory Requirement
Student	**24.12 ms**	92.9%	8.9 MB
Teacher	65.36 ms	**94.8%**	61.2 MB
PWL	**24.3 ms**	**94.8%**	**8–62 MB (flexible)**

offers a flexible memory range (8–62 MB), allowing it to adapt to system constraints by progressively loading teacher layers. This adaptability enables efficient resource utilization and fast initial responses, making PWL particularly suitable for deployment in latency sensitive or memory constrained environments.

6 Ablation Study

Table 5 presents an ablation study evaluating the impact of different teacher layer loading orders on classification accuracy for VGG, ResNet, and ViT across CIFAR-10 and CIFAR-100. We tested three strategies: **prefix loading** (replacing layers from input to output), **suffix loading** (from output to input), and **contiguous block loading** (replacing a block of intermediate layers).

For VGG and ResNet, the accuracy was relatively stable regardless of loading order, though prefix loading consistently yielded slightly better results. In contrast, ViT exhibited a significant sensitivity to the loading strategy. Prefix loading led to smooth and progressive accuracy gains, whereas suffix and contiguous loading resulted in performance degradation.

These results highlight that for PWL to be effective especially in attention based architectures like ViT—progressive loading from early layers (prefix loading) is the most robust and optimal strategy.

Also, we assessed the individual effectiveness of each component in the proposed PWL training. Table 6 and Fig. 6 presents an ablation study evaluating the contribution of each component in the proposed loss function (Eq. 13) on the ResNet model trained with CIFAR-10. Two evaluation metrics are used: the classification accuracy of the final distilled student model, and the **Cross Accuracy**, which is defined as the mean accuracy across intermediate hybrid models where teacher layers progressively replace student layers. For example, with three blocks, Cross Accuracy includes the average of models like $T_{L1}S_{L2}S_{L3}$ and $T_{L1}T_{L2}S_{L3}$.

The results demonstrate that $L_{feature}$ plays a critical role in both student accuracy and cross accuracy. This indicates that aligning internal feature representations not only improves final performance but also enhances model stability during layer-wise replacement. On the other hand, L_{recon} and $L_{random-cross}$ do not significantly affect the distilled student's final accuracy but greatly improve

Table 5. Ablation study on the effectiveness of layer replacement order, conducted on VGG, ResNet, and ViT using CIFAR-10 and CIFAR-100. Results show that replacing layers in prefix loading—from input to output—yields the most stable and consistent performance improvement.

Loading Order	CIFAR10			CIFAR100		
	VGG	ResNet	ViT	VGG	ResNet	ViT
Prefix Loading						
Student($S_{L1}S_{L2}S_{L3}S_{L4}$)	91.7	92.3	94.3	71.1	72.1	74.6
$T_{L1} \rightarrow S_{L2} \rightarrow S_{L3} \rightarrow S_{L4}$	92.1	91.9	95.5	70.6	71.4	76.2
$T_{L1} \rightarrow T_{L2} \rightarrow S_{L3} \rightarrow S_{L4}$	93.1	92.9	96.4	72.5	72.8	79.8
$T_{L1} \rightarrow T_{L2} \rightarrow T_{L3} \rightarrow S_{L4}$	92.7	94.4	97.1	73.8	73.6	81.4
Teacher($T_{L1}T_{L2}T_{L3}T_{L4}$)	93.8	94.8	97.4	74.2	75.7	82.3
Suffix Loading						
Student($S_{L1}S_{L2}S_{L3}S_{L4}$)	91.7	92.3	94.3	71.1	72.1	74.6
$S_{L1} \rightarrow S_{L2} \rightarrow S_{L3} \rightarrow T_{L4}$	91.0	88.8	82.1	65.6	69.2	61.3
$S_{L1} \rightarrow S_{L2} \rightarrow T_{L3} \rightarrow T_{L4}$	90.3	93.4	84.2	67.6	73.7	64.7
$S_{L1} \rightarrow T_{L2} \rightarrow T_{L3} \rightarrow T_{L4}$	91.4	94.3	87.5	69.1	74.5	68.8
Teacher($T_{L1}T_{L2}T_{L3}T_{L4}$)	93.8	94.8	97.4	74.2	75.7	82.3
Contiguous Block Loading						
Student($S_{L1}S_{L2}S_{L3}S_{L4}$)	91.7	91.8	94.3	53.1	72.1	74.6
$S_{L1} \rightarrow T_{L2} \rightarrow S_{L3} \rightarrow S_{L4}$	86.1	88.1	84.5	59.4	65.2	62.1
$S_{L1} \rightarrow S_{L2} \rightarrow T_{L3} \rightarrow S_{L4}$	88.4	90.2	81.2	64.1	68.8	59.7
$S_{L1} \rightarrow T_{L2} \rightarrow T_{L3} \rightarrow S_{L4}$	89.8	89.1	78.2	65.8	71.0	58.3
Teacher($T_{L1}T_{L2}T_{L3}T_{L4}$)	93.8	94.2	97.4	56.1	75.7	82.3

Table 6. Ablation study on the effectiveness of each loss component for ResNet on CIFAR-10. We evaluate the impact of feature loss, reconstruction loss, and random cross loss, each of which contributes to improving either the final student accuracy or the cross-layer accuracy during progressive weight replacement.

Configuration	Student Acc (%)	Cross Acc (mean, %)
Normal	92.8	93.1
w/o L_{recon}	92.4	88.9 (↓)
w/o $L_{feature}$	88.4 (↓)	82.0 (↓)
w/o $L_{random-cross}$	92.3	44.2 (↓)

cross accuracy. Notably, removing $L_{random-cross}$ leads to a dramatic drop in cross accuracy (from 93.1% to 44.2%), confirming its essential role in ensuring seamless replacement between student and teacher layers during progressive loading. These findings support that each component of the proposed loss function contributes to different but complementary aspects of PWL effectiveness.

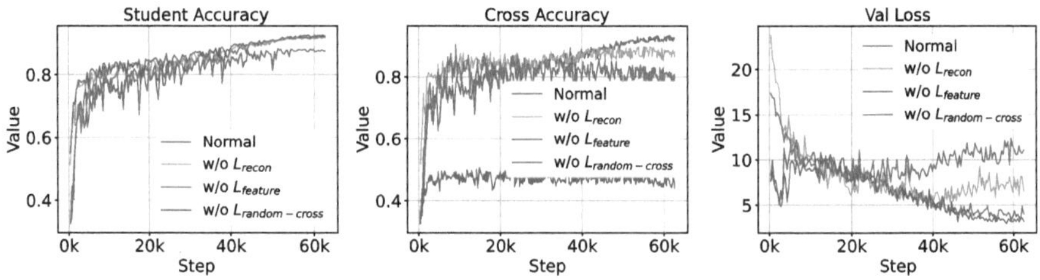

Fig. 6. Training metrics—student accuracy, cross accuracy, and validation loss—for ResNet on CIFAR-10, illustrating the impact of ablating feature loss, reconstruction loss, and random-cross loss.

7 Discussion and Future Work

7.1 Invertibility of the Feature Converter

An important point of discussion is whether the feature converter needs to be invertible. We conclude that invertibility is essential when enabling arbitrary layer replacement between the student and teacher models, rather than following a fixed, sequential order. Our ablation study Table 5 shows extensive examples of arbitrary layer replacement order sequence. Also, as shown in Table 6, the invertibility from reconstruction loss contributes to cross accuracy, indicating that preserving information through the converter is beneficial for seamless layer-wise replacement.

We also examined the possibility of enforcing strict invertibility using QR decomposition [36] or normalizing flow-based architectures [37–39]. However, to maintain simplicity and computational efficiency, we opted for an autoencoder-style feature converter.

7.2 Combining with Other Model Compression Methods

Model compression techniques such as quantization [14,15,40] and pruning [4,12,13] are essential for deploying deep learning models in resource-constrained environments like mobile devices. Progressive Weight Loading (PWL) is compatible with these techniques and can further enhance efficiency by enabling faster model loading and earlier inference.

Although integrating PWL with compression methods is beyond the scope of this study, it presents a promising direction for future research. Such a combination could lead to highly optimized deployments of deep learning models, particularly in latency-sensitive or memory-constrained applications.

7.3 Application to Other Domains

The need for deploying large-scale models extends beyond vision tasks to domains such as text-to-speech (TTS), natural language processing (NLP), and audio processing. In this work, we validate the PWL approach on image classification tasks as a proof of concept.

Given the effectiveness of PWL on transformer-based models like ViT, we anticipate its potential applicability to other domains, particularly in NLP and audio, where large transformer models are prevalent. Exploring these applications remains an important direction for future work.

8 Conclusion

We propose Progressive Weight Loading (PWL), a novel approach that enables fast initial inference and efficient performance-memory trade-offs by progressively replacing the student model's layers with those of a pre-trained teacher model. To support this, we introduced a training method that aligns intermediate feature representations between student and teacher layers, ensuring smooth and consistent performance gains as layers are incrementally upgraded.

Through extensive experiments across VGG, ResNet, and ViT architectures, we demonstrated that PWL not only maintains distillation performance but also allows for dynamic and flexible deployment, making it particularly suitable for latency-sensitive and memory-constrained environments. This study demonstrates that the PWL technique can be applied to domains where large scale Transformer models are pervasive such as natural language processing and speech and future work will focus on validating PWL in these settings and rigorously quantifying its benefits for model scalability and responsiveness.

Appendix

A Feature Converter Capacity Study

Table 7. Different size of feature converters.

	Tiny	Medium	Heavy
Architecture	Single Linear	Two-layer MLP with bottleneck	Three-layer MLP with non-linearities
#params	98k	163k	310k

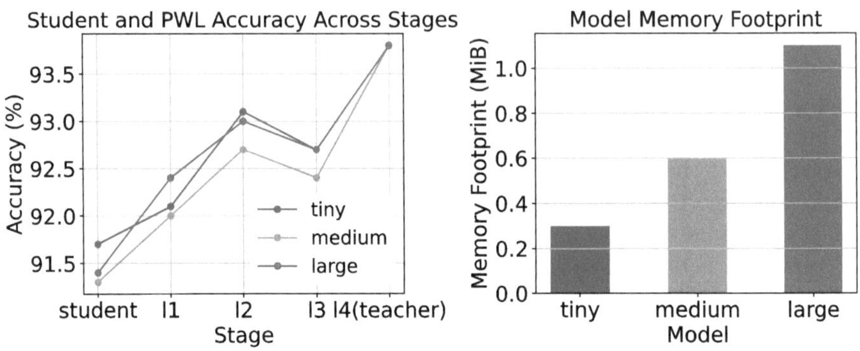

Fig. 7. Effect of feature converter capacity on ResNet accuracy for CIFAR-10.

We evaluate three feature converter architectures—Tiny, Medium, and Heavy—to understand how converter capacity affects both inference accuracy and memory footprint during progressive weight loading.

- **Tiny**: a single linear layer (equivalent to a 1x1 convolution).
- **Medium**: a two-layer MLP with a bottleneck.
- **Heavy**: a three-layer MLP with nonlinear activations.

We integrate each converter into a ResNet backbone trained on CIFAR-10 and measure (1) the student accuracy after each layer replacement (cross accuracy), and (2) the converter's parameter count. Table 7 and Fig. 7 summarize these results.

Despite a more than threefold increase in parameters—from 98 k (Tiny) to 310 k (Heavy)—all three converters achieve nearly identical final accuracy (within 0.3 %). This negligible performance gain, combined with the stricter memory constraints of mobile applications, motivates our choice of the Tiny converter for all subsequent experiments.

B Applying PWL to Extremely Small Student Model

Table 8. Applying PWL to a highly compact student network. LeNet-5 student model is replaced to VGG16 teacher model

Layers Loaded	CIFAR10 (%)	CIFAR100 (%)	Memory Loaded(MiB)
LeNet5 -> VGGNet			
Student ($S_{L1}S_{L2}S_{L3}S_{L4}$)	68.4	54.9	<1MiB
$T_{L1} \rightarrow S_{L2} \rightarrow S_{L3} \rightarrow S_{L4}$	76.1	58.7	6.3
$T_{L1} \rightarrow T_{L2} \rightarrow S_{L3} \rightarrow S_{L4}$	78.0	62.1	12.1
$T_{L1} \rightarrow T_{L2} \rightarrow T_{L3} \rightarrow S_{L4}$	82.1	65.7	31.8
Teacher ($T_{L1}T_{L2}T_{L3}T_{L4}$)	93.8	74.2	64.1

We investigated whether Progressive Weight Loading (PWL) can be effectively applied to extremely compact student models, particularly for scenarios where ultra-fast initial inference is prioritized over model accuracy—such as in real-time operating systems (RTOS) or resource-constrained embedded environments.

To this end, we adopted LeNet-5 [41] as the student model due to its minimal size (less than 1MiB) and experimented with distilling knowledge from a VGG16 teacher model. Our goal was to evaluate whether PWL could progressively enhance the student model's performance by incrementally replacing its layers with those of the teacher.

As shown in Table 8, we observe a clear performance improvement on both CIFAR-10 and CIFAR-100 as more layers are replaced. Starting from a baseline LeNet-5, performance improves steadily with each layer swapped, culminating in the full teacher model. This result highlights the potential of PWL even for extremely lightweight models, making it a promising strategy for systems where memory is scarce and rapid model activation is critical.

C Attention Map for ViT

Figure 8 presents the class-token attention overlaid on a CIFAR-10 image for both the student (with PWL) and teacher ViT models. For each transformer block, we extract the attention weights from the block's final layer and upsample them to the input resolution. The heat-maps reveal that, at every block boundary, the student model attends to essentially the similar image regions as the teacher. This strong correspondence in spatial focus demonstrates that PWL not only maintains predictive accuracy but also preserves the teacher's interpretability and feature-localization behavior throughout progressive weight replacement.

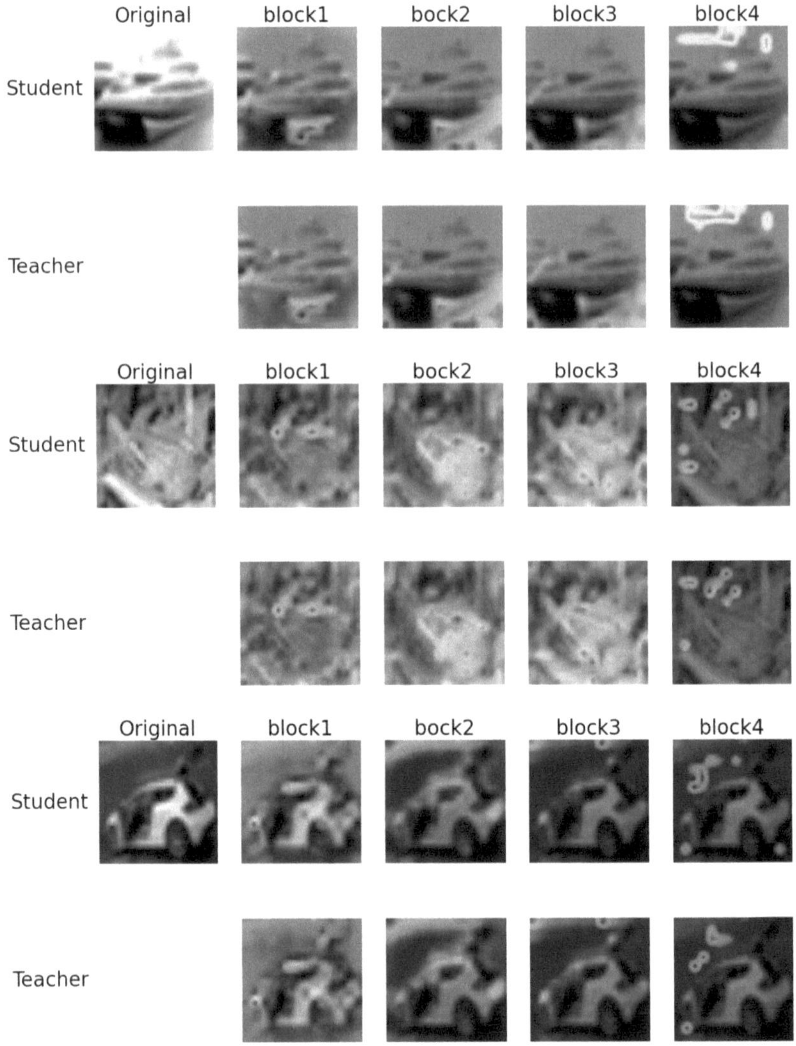

Fig. 8. Comparison of attention maps from the final layer of each block for both student and teacher models.

References

1. Kaplan, J., et al.: Scaling laws for neural language models. CoRR abs/2001.08361 (2020). https://arxiv.org/abs/2001.08361
2. Strubell, E., Ganesh, A., McCallum, A.: Energy and policy considerations for deep learning in NLP. CoRR abs/1906.02243 (2019). http://arxiv.org/abs/1906.02243
3. Patterson, D.A., et al.: Carbon emissions and large neural network training. CoRR abs/2104.10350 (2021). https://arxiv.org/abs/2104.10350

4. Han, S., Mao, H., Dally, W.J.: Deep compression: compressing deep neural networks with pruning, trained quantization and Huffman coding. arXiv preprint arXiv:1510.00149 (2015)
5. Han, X., et al.: Hermes: memory-efficient pipeline inference for large models on edge devices. In: Proceedings of the 42nd IEEE International Conference on Computer Design (ICCD), pp. 454–461. IEEE (2024). https://doi.org/10.1109/ICCD63220.2024.00076
6. Hinton, G., Vinyals, O., Dean, J.: Distilling the knowledge in a neural network. CoRR abs/1503.02531 (2015). http://arxiv.org/abs/1503.02531
7. Buciluă, C., Caruana, R., Niculescu-Mizil, A.: Model compression. In: Proceedings of the 12th ACM SIGKDD International Conference on Knowledge Discovery and Data Mining, pp. 535–541 (2006). https://doi.org/10.1145/1150402.1150464
8. Romero, A., Ballas, N., Kahou, S.E., Chassang, A., Gatta, C., Bengio, Y.: Fitnets: hints for thin deep nets. In: International Conference on Learning Representations (ICLR) (2015). http://arxiv.org/abs/1412.6550
9. Gou, J., Yu, B., Maybank, S.J., Tao, D.: Knowledge distillation: a survey. Int. J. Comput. Vision **129**(6), 1789–1819 (2021). https://doi.org/10.1007/s11263-021-01453-z
10. Chen, J., Ran, X.: Deep learning with edge computing: a review. Proc. IEEE **107**(8), 1655–1674 (2019). https://doi.org/10.1109/JPROC.2019.2921977
11. Shuvo, M.M.H., Islam, S.K., Cheng, J., Morshed, B.I.: Efficient acceleration of deep learning inference on resource-constrained edge devices: a review. Proc. IEEE **111**(1), 42–91 (2022). https://doi.org/10.1109/JPROC.2022.3226481
12. Molchanov, P., Tyree, S., Karras, T., Aila, T., Kautz, J.: Pruning convolutional neural networks for resource efficient inference. arXiv preprint arXiv:1611.06440 (2016). https://doi.org/10.48550/arXiv.1611.06440
13. Molchanov, D., Ashukha, A., Vetrov, D.: Variational dropout sparsifies deep neural networks. In: International Conference on Machine Learning, pp. 2498–2507. PMLR (2017). https://doi.org/10.48550/arXiv.1701.05369
14. Hubara, I., Courbariaux, M., Soudry, D., El-Yaniv, R., Bengio, Y.: Quantized neural networks: training neural networks with low precision weights and activations. J. Mach. Learn. Res. **18**(187), 1–30 (2018)
15. Frantar, E., Ashkboos, S., Hoefler, T., Alistarh, D.: GPTQ: accurate post-training quantization for generative pre-trained transformers. In: International Conference on Learning Representations (ICLR) (2023). https://arxiv.org/abs/2210.17323
16. Howard, A.G., et al.: Mobilenets: efficient convolutional neural networks for mobile vision applications. CoRR abs/1704.04861 (2017). http://arxiv.org/abs/1704.04861
17. Sandler, M., Howard, A., Zhu, M., Zhmoginov, A., Chen, L.C.: Mobilenetv2: inverted residuals and linear bottlenecks. In: Proceedings of the IEEE Conference on Computer Vision and Pattern Recognition, pp. 4510–4520 (2018)
18. Howard, A., et al.: Searching for mobilenetv3. In: Proceedings of the IEEE/CVF International Conference on Computer Vision, pp. 1314–1324 (2019). https://doi.org/10.1109/ICCV.2019.00140
19. Jiao, X., et al.: Tinybert: distilling BERT for natural language understanding. In: Findings of the Association for Computational Linguistics: EMNLP 2020, pp. 4163–4174 (2020). https://aclanthology.org/2020.findings-emnlp.372
20. Tan, M., Le, Q.: Efficientnet: rethinking model scaling for convolutional neural networks. In: International Conference on Machine Learning, pp. 6105–6114. PMLR (2019). https://doi.org/10.48550/arXiv.1905.11946

21. Sun, Z., Yu, H., Song, X., Liu, R., Yang, Y., Zhou, D.: Mobilebert: a compact task-agnostic BERT for resource-limited devices. In: Proceedings of the 58th Annual Meeting of the Association for Computational Linguistics (ACL), pp. 2158–2170 (2020). https://aclanthology.org/2020.acl-main.195
22. Tung, F., Mori, G.: Similarity-preserving knowledge distillation. In: Proceedings of the IEEE/CVF International Conference on Computer Vision, pp. 1365–1374 (2019)
23. Zagoruyko, S., Komodakis, N.: Paying more attention to attention: improving the performance of convolutional neural networks via attention transfer. In: International Conference on Learning Representations (ICLR) (2017). https://arxiv.org/abs/1612.03928
24. Ji, M., Heo, B., Park, S.: Show, attend and distill: knowledge distillation via attention-based feature matching. In: Proceedings of the AAAI Conference on Artificial Intelligence, vol. 35, pp. 7945–7952 (2021). https://doi.org/10.48550/arXiv.2102.02973
25. Chen, P., Liu, S., Zhao, H., Jia, J.: Distilling knowledge via knowledge review. In: Proceedings of the IEEE/CVF Conference on Computer Vision and Pattern Recognition, pp. 5008–5017 (2021). https://doi.org/10.1109/CVPR46437.2021.00497
26. Huang, Z., Wang, N.: Like what you like: knowledge distill via neuron selectivity transfer. CoRR abs/1707.01219 (2017). https://arxiv.org/abs/1707.01219
27. Hinton, G.E., Salakhutdinov, R.R.: Reducing the dimensionality of data with neural networks. Science **313**, 504–507 (2006). https://doi.org/10.1126/science.1127647
28. Guo, C., Pleiss, G., Sun, Y., Weinberger, K.Q.: On calibration of modern neural networks. In: International Conference on Machine Learning, pp. 1321–1330. PMLR (2017). https://doi.org/10.48550/arXiv.1706.04599
29. Vincent, P., Larochelle, H., Bengio, Y., Manzagol, P.A.: Extracting and composing robust features with denoising autoencoders. In: Proceedings of the 25th International Conference on Machine Learning, pp. 1096–1103 (2008). https://doi.org/10.1145/1390156.1390294
30. Krizhevsky, A., Hinton, G.E.: Learning multiple layers of features from tiny images. Technical report, Department of Computer Science, University of Toronto (2009)
31. Krizhevsky, A., Sutskever, I., Hinton, G.E.: Imagenet classification with deep convolutional neural networks. In: Advances in Neural Information Processing Systems 25, pp. 1106–1114 (2012). https://doi.org/10.1145/3065386
32. Szegedy, C., et al.: Going deeper with convolutions. In: Proceedings of the IEEE Conference on Computer Vision and Pattern Recognition, pp. 1–9 (2015). https://doi.org/10.1109/CVPR.2015.7298594
33. Simonyan, K., Zisserman, A.: Very deep convolutional networks for large-scale image recognition. In: International Conference on Learning Representations (ICLR) (2015). http://arxiv.org/abs/1409.1556
34. He, K., Zhang, X., Ren, S., Sun, J.: Deep residual learning for image recognition. In: Proceedings of the IEEE Conference on Computer Vision and Pattern Recognition, pp. 770–778 (2016). https://doi.org/10.1109/CVPR.2016.90
35. Dosovitskiy, A., et al.: An image is worth 16x16 words: transformers for image recognition at scale. In: International Conference on Learning Representations (ICLR) (2021). https://arxiv.org/abs/2010.11929
36. Francis, J.G.F.: The QR transformation–part 2. Comput. J. **4**(4), 332–345 (1962). https://doi.org/10.1093/comjnl/4.4.332

37. Papamakarios, G., Nalisnick, E., Rezende, D.J., Mohamed, S., Lakshminarayanan, B.: Normalizing flows for probabilistic modeling and inference. J. Mach. Learn. Res. **22**(57), 1–64 (2021)
38. Dinh, L., Sohl-Dickstein, J., Bengio, S.: Density estimation using real NVP. arXiv preprint arXiv:1605.08803 (2016)
39. Kingma, D.P., Dhariwal, P.: Glow: generative flow with invertible 1x1 convolutions. In: Advances in Neural Information Processing Systems 31, pp. 10236–10245 (2018). https://doi.org/10.48550/arXiv.1807.03039
40. Esser, S.K., McKinstry, J.L., Bablani, D., Appuswamy, R., Modha, D.S.: Learned step size quantization. In: International Conference on Learning Representations (ICLR) (2020). https://arxiv.org/abs/1902.08153
41. LeCun, Y., Bottou, L., Bengio, Y., Haffner, P.: Gradient-based learning applied to document recognition. Proc. IEEE **86**(11), 2278–2324 (2002). https://doi.org/10.1109/5.726791

Multi-task Skill Learning via Meta-policy Guided Fine-Tuning

Hang Ren[1(✉)], Lanlan Gong[2], and Fei Zhu[1]

[1] School of Computer Science and Technology, Soochow University, Suzhou 215006, China
20234227046@stu.suda.edu.cn, zhufei@suda.edu.cn
[2] Suzhou City University, Suzhou 215104, China
Gongll@szcu.edu.cn

Abstract. Although current meta-reinforcement learning methods have achieved promising progress in robot learning, they are mainly effective for short-horizon tasks with dense rewards and exhibit limited performance on complex, long-horizon tasks with sparse rewards that are prevalent in real-world applications. Recent advances leverage prior experience from offline datasets to improve skill acquisition in long-horizon tasks; however, these approaches still rely on substantial environment interaction. To address these challenges, we propose a novel algorithm called Meta-Policy Guided Skill Learning via Multi-Task Fine-Tuning (MSLMF). This method combines the strengths of meta-learning and multi-task learning by first extracting a meta-policy from offline datasets and then employing a dynamic multi-task sampling strategy for fine-tuning, enabling balanced training across tasks and rapid generalization to novel tasks. Experimental results demonstrate that, in challenging tasks such as maze navigation and kitchen manipulation with sparse rewards, MSLMF substantially improves exploration efficiency and convergence speed compared to baseline methods, thereby accelerating learning on previously unseen tasks.

Keywords: Reinforcement learning · Meta policy · Multi-task learning · Skill learning

1 Introduction

In recent years, despite the notable successes of reinforcement learning (RL) across various domains, its broader application remains limited due to low data efficiency and poor generalization of learned policies. Typically, RL agents require extensive trial-and-error exploration from scratch to acquire desired skills, contrasting sharply with human cognitive abilities that leverage knowledge transfer to achieve rapid learning. Meta-learning addresses this gap through a "learning to learn" paradigm, enabling models to adapt to new tasks based on prior experiences rapidly. Consequently, researchers have explored the deep integration of meta-learning and reinforcement learning, leading to the emergence of

L. Zhang and K.-K. R. Choo (Eds.): MobiQuitous 2025, LNICST 683, pp. 452–464, 2026.
https://doi.org/10.1007/978-3-032-22500-9_25

meta-reinforcement learning (Meta-RL). The core mechanism underlying Meta-RL is the rapid transfer of knowledge across tasks by encoding experiences, allowing agents to build reusable cognitive frameworks based on historical interactions.

Meta-reinforcement learning (Meta-RL), which combines the strengths of meta-learning and reinforcement learning, has achieved promising progress. Meta-RL approaches can be broadly categorized into gradient-based and context-based methods. The former explicitly adapts to new tasks by performing gradient updates on model parameters [16], typically involving a two-level optimization process (inner-loop adaptation for each task and outer-loop meta-optimization across tasks) [20]. In contrast, context-based methods implicitly adapt to novel tasks by inferring a task embedding through a context encoder, with the policy and value networks conditioned on this inferred representation [23]. To address sample efficiency concerns in the meta-training phase, researchers have explored leveraging offline datasets to enhance algorithm performance [10,17,27]. Certain studies have integrated task-level attention with contrastive objectives in offline meta-learning, improving the discriminability and robustness of task representations and demonstrating strong performance even under sparse rewards and distributional shifts [15]. The FOCAL algorithm combines offline reinforcement learning with online self-supervised learning to tackle performance degradation stemming from data distribution shifts when adapting to new tasks, a common issue in conventional offline Meta-RL frameworks [4].

Multi-task reinforcement learning (MTRL) enhances agent generalization and accelerates learning on target tasks by facilitating knowledge transfer across multiple related tasks through joint training. Compared to single-task reinforcement learning, MTRL leverages shared representations to extract standard features among tasks, thereby reducing redundant learning and improving sample efficiency [21,24].

To further improve agent learning efficiency in novel environments and unseen tasks, and to address the inefficiency caused by distribution mismatch between the meta-training set and the target tasks, this paper proposes a multi-task meta-policy fine-tuning framework with the following key components:

- A dynamic multi-task meta-learning sampling strategy is proposed, which adaptively adjusts the sampling probabilities of tasks according to their learning progress, prioritizing updates for tasks that are underperforming or have not yet converged. This approach accelerates the balancing of performance across tasks.
- A prioritized experience replay mechanism is introduced, where each sample is assigned a priority and those that contribute more significantly to the update are sampled more frequently, enabling faster correction of policy bias and accelerated convergence.
- An importance sampling-weighted loss correction is proposed, in which the loss of each sample is multiplied by its corresponding importance sampling weight, thereby enhancing the stability and robustness of exploration.

2 Related Work

2.1 Meta Reinforcement Learning

Meta-reinforcement learning (Meta-RL) aims to enable agents to rapidly adapt to novel tasks or changing environments with minimal interaction or samples by learning at the meta-task level [1,21]. In meta-RL, the ability to extract high-quality and discriminative contextual information is a key factor influencing adaptation performance. Fu et al. proposed a novel approach that incorporates contrastive learning into the context encoder and jointly optimizes it with meta-training in an end-to-end fashion, which significantly improves the task discriminability of meta-RL algorithms across different tasks [7]. Mitchell et al. introduced a new framework that leverages advantage-weighted filtering to select and amplify the contribution of high-quality data, thereby promoting rapid adaptation to previously unseen tasks [11]. Bing et al. equipped agents with flexible environment/task representations, adaptive memory mechanisms, and hierarchical multi-stage update strategies, enabling rapid adaptation and sustained performance following environmental changes [2].

Although meta-learning is designed to enhance a model's adaptability to new tasks, existing meta-reinforcement learning algorithms often struggle to maintain stable exploration and efficient learning when confronted with unknown tasks in long-term, complex environments.

2.2 Multi-task Reinforcement Learning

Multi-task reinforcement learning (MTRL) enables a single agent or a unified model architecture to learn multiple tasks either simultaneously or sequentially, thereby enhancing generalization, accelerating training, and reducing sample complexity [22,26]. Compared to conventional single-task reinforcement learning, MTRL leverages shared representations or policies to capture latent relationships across different tasks [18], which helps alleviate issues of data scarcity and overfitting commonly encountered in single-task learning.

Parameter sharing has been widely recognized as a fundamental mechanism for improving the efficiency of multi-task reinforcement learning (MTRL) [5,6]. On one hand, sharing the lower-level feature extraction networks across multiple related tasks reduces model redundancy and training costs; on the other hand, exploiting standard features among tasks promotes the generalization capability of representation learning [3,25]. A further critical challenge in MTRL is effectively exploring the state space for different tasks during training. Sodhani et al. proposed a context-based multi-task reinforcement learning approach, which leverages task meta-data to guide a hybrid encoder framework for the dynamic extraction and composition of state representations, thereby significantly enhancing sample efficiency [19].

Since multi-task learning inherently involves handling data from multiple tasks and potential instability resulting from task conflicts, ensuring the robustness of the policy and the ability to acquire transferable skills applicable to previously unseen tasks remain open research questions.

3 Preliminaries

3.1 Problem Formulation

Following prior work in reinforcement learning [14], we define a state-action trajectory dataset $D = s_t, a_t$.. Since this dataset comprises data collected from multiple tasks exhibiting diverse behaviors, but is not specific to any single task, we refer to it as a task-agnostic dataset. This dataset is used to train the meta-policy. Each meta-training task $T = \{\mathcal{T}_1, \ldots, \mathcal{T}_\mathcal{N}\}$ is formulated as a Markov Decision Process (MDP), i.e., a five-tuple $\{S, A, P, R, \gamma\}$ consisting of the state space, action space, transition function, reward function, and discount factor. Our objective is to leverage the offline dataset D and the meta-training tasks T to accelerate the training of a policy $\pi(a|s)$ for a target task $\mathcal{T}^*$, which is also modeled as an MDP. Notably, the offline dataset D does not contain solutions or expert demonstrations for the target task $\mathcal{T}^*$, and is thus referred to as a task-agnostic dataset.

Therefore, this work aims to develop an algorithm that leverages offline data, meta-training tasks, and multi-task fine-tuning to enable rapid adaptation to previously unseen target tasks by efficiently exploiting transferable skills.

3.2 Skill-Based Meta-training

A successful approach for accelerating the learning of unseen tasks using task-agnostic datasets is to facilitate the transfer of reusable skills—i.e., short-horizon behaviors that can be composed to solve long-horizon tasks. Previous work on skill-based reinforcement learning, such as Skill-Prior RL (SPiRL) [14], proposed a framework in which, during new task learning, the agent leverages a learned skill policy to make decisions in the space of skills rather than directly in the raw action space. The reinforcement learning objective for the target task is extended based on the popular offline RL algorithm Soft Actor-Critic (SAC) [9], where the learned skill prior is used to guide the high-level policy (Eq. 1).

$$\max_{\pi} E_{(s_t, z_t)\sim\rho^\pi} \left[r(s_t, z_t) - \alpha D_{KL}\big(\pi(z|s_t) \parallel p(z|s_t)\big)\right] \tag{1}$$

Nam et al. [12] extended SPiRL by integrating skill abstraction with meta-learning, thereby substantially reducing the exploration burden in novel tasks. Specifically, their framework augments conventional hierarchical skill learning with an additional meta-policy layer, wherein the optimization objective explicitly includes the log-probability of the skill prior. This formulation facilitates a structured search in the learned skill space, enabling the agent to rapidly adapt to unseen tasks by effectively composing previously acquired skills:

$$\max_{q,\pi} E_{z\sim q}\left[\sum_{t=0}^{K-1} \log \pi(a_t|s_t, z) - \beta D_{KL}\left(q(z|s_{0:K}, a_{0:K-1}), \mathcal{N}(0, \mathbf{I})\right)\right] \tag{2}$$

where D_{KL} denotes the Kullback-Leibler divergence between the policy and the skill prior, and α is a weighting coefficient.

4 Method

We propose a method called "Meta-policy Guided Skill Learning via Multi-task Fine-tuning" (MSLMF). MSLMF leverages offline datasets and a set of meta-training tasks to train a meta-policy, and further accelerates adaptation to unseen tasks via multi-task dynamic sampling for fine-tuning. Our approach consists of two stages: (1) Skill-based Meta-training Stage: Skills are extracted from offline datasets, and the meta-policy is trained; (2) Target Task learning: The meta-policy is fine-tuned with multi-task data to enable rapid adaptation to the target task. Figure 1 illustrates an overview of the proposed framework.

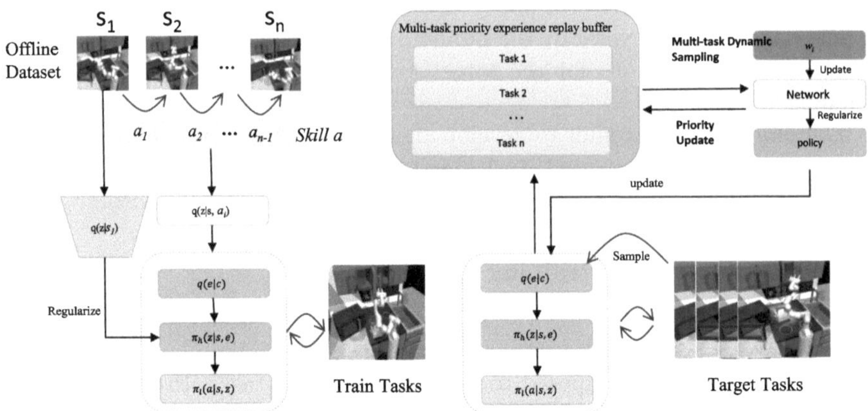

Fig. 1. Method frame diagram.

4.1 Skill-Based Meta-training

During the meta-training process, we obtain a meta-policy for task solving by extracting reusable skills from the offline dataset and performing meta-training. Specifically, we employ the skill extraction approach proposed by Pertsch et al. [13] to obtain a set of reusable skills from the offline dataset D, and regularize the output of the skill encoder with a Gaussian prior to yield smoother skill representations:

$$\log p(a_i) \geq E_q\Big[\log p(a_i|z) - \beta\big(\log q(z|a_i) - \log p(z)\big)\Big] \tag{3}$$

where β controls the strength of regularization.

Subsequently, the meta-policy is trained on a set of meta-training tasks to rapidly leverage the extracted skills for solving new tasks. We train a task encoder that outputs a task embedding e from data sampled from the offline dataset, enabling the high-level policy to make decisions in the learned skill space. Thus, the meta-policy only needs to learn how to compose the set of pretrained behaviors, allowing our approach to achieve rapid meta-training in complex, long-horizon tasks.

4.2 Target Task Learning

When faced with an unseen target task, it is essential to leverage the meta-policy acquired during the meta-training phase to enable rapid adaptation and maximize cumulative reward.

We first interact with the target task's environment using the meta-trained policy to collect task-specific conditional transition data $c*$, which is then encoded into a target task embedding $e*$. Subsequently, the meta-policy is fine-tuned via multi-task dynamic sampling, guiding the skill distribution to concentrate on the skills required for solving the target task.

The detailed fine-tuning procedure is outlined in Algorithm 1. We distinguish the data and priority arrays for each task using different task indices, with each task maintaining its own transition storage. For a given task, we initialize the policy and network parameters using the multi-task conditional network (incorporating both encoding conditions and task embeddings), and the collected data is stored in a multi-task replay buffer. In each training iteration, a batch of data is sampled from the buffer according to the current task label using a dynamic sampling strategy, where sampling probabilities and importance-sampling weights for each sample are calculated based on their priorities as in Eq. 4. The parameters and target Q-network are updated using weighted TD errors. Simultaneously, the policy network generates action distributions, and the KL divergence with the prior policy is computed; the policy loss is constructed by combining this divergence with the minimum Q-value from multiple Q-networks, and the policy network is updated accordingly. Finally, the priorities of samples in the replay buffer are updated according to the current TD errors. This enables the system to dynamically adjust data sampling and training update strategies in the multi-task setting, thereby achieving efficient and stable reinforcement learning training.

$$\text{loss} = \frac{1}{N} \sum_{i=1}^{N} w_i \left(q(s_i, a_i) - y_i\right)^2 \tag{4}$$

where w_i represents the importance sampling weight assigned to the i-th sample.

Algorithm 2 describes the process of multi-task dynamic sampling. A priority array is first extracted from valid transitions for the current task. Weighted random sampling is then performed based on these priorities to obtain sample indices. Importance sampling weights are subsequently computed according to the sampling probabilities and normalized. Finally, the corresponding transition data are retrieved to construct the batch for training. This procedure implements a dynamic sampling strategy across multiple tasks.

Algorithm 1. Multi-task Prioritized Experience Fine-tuning

Require: $q\_networks$, Weighting coefficient α
$(batch, indices, weights) \leftarrow$ multi-task dynamic sampling by Alg. 2
calculate target q $target\_q$
for network in $q\_networks$ **do**
  Predict $current\_q$
  $td\_error \leftarrow current\_q - target\_q$
  $qf\_loss \leftarrow qf\_loss + \text{avg}(td\_error^2 \times weights)$
end for
Update q networks
Sample actions from action distribution
KL $\leftarrow kl\_divergence()$
$min\_q = 1\text{e}9$
for action in actions **do**
  Compute q values
  $min\_q = \min(min\_q, q)$
end for
$policy\_loss \leftarrow \text{avg}(-min\_q + \alpha \times KL)$
Recompute new_q for state-action pair
$new\_priorities \leftarrow |target\_q - new\_q| + 1e^{-6}$
Update priorities

Algorithm 2. Multi-task Dynamic Sampling

Require: $task\_id$, sample size n, data storage $trans$, priority array $priorities$, valid data size, priority parameter γ
Ensure: $batch$, $indices$, $weights$
$task\_priorities \leftarrow priorities[task\_id]$
if $\sum task\_priorities = 0$ **then**
  $pb \leftarrow$ uniform distribution
else
  $pb \leftarrow task\_priorities * \gamma$
  $pb \leftarrow pb / \sum pb$
end if
Sample n indices $indices \sim pb$
$weights \leftarrow (1 \div (size \times pb[indices] \times \alpha))$
Retrieve $transitions \leftarrow trans[task\_id][indices]$
Build $batch$ from $transitions$

5 Experiment

5.1 Environments

We evaluate our approach in two challenging domains: a continuous-control maze navigation environment and a simulated robotic kitchen manipulation environment, as illustrated in Fig. 2. In both settings, agents are required to acquire skills by solving complex, long-horizon tasks with sparse rewards. Our method's performance is assessed based on the sparse rewards obtained in these two environments.

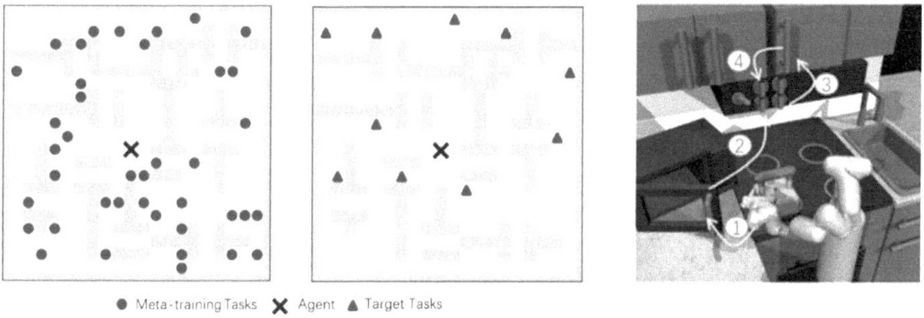

Fig. 2. Experimental environment: maze navigation (left), kitchen operation (right).

- **Maze Navigation**: In the maze navigation environment, agents must explore over hundreds of steps to successfully reach unknown goal locations. Upon reaching a goal, the agent receives a binary, sparse reward.
  The offline dataset is constructed by randomly sampling goal locations within the maze and generating trajectories to collect task-agnostic data. These trajectories are collected without access to any reward signals or task labels. During training, the agent always starts from the maze's center, and 20 randomly selected goals are used for meta-training. Subsequently, 10 additional random goals are designated as unseen target tasks, for which the meta-trained model is further adapted. Importantly, all meta-training and target tasks are evaluated using the same sparse reward formulation.
- **Kitchen Manipulation**The simulated kitchen environment is based on the Franka Kitchen scenario proposed by Gupta et al. [8]. This environment features a 7-DoF Franka robotic arm interacting with a kitchen scene. In each experiment, the agent is required to control the robot arm via continuous commands to complete various manipulation tasks, with the robot capable of performing seven different types of operations. Each task involves manipulating multiple distinct components, and the agent only receives a sparse reward upon successfully completing subtasks.
  We employ the manipulation sequence dataset provided by Gupta et al. for offline pretraining. In each trajectory, the robot executes a sequence of actions composed of four subtasks. For our experiments, we define 25 meta-training tasks and 10 target tasks, all requiring the agent to complete four subtasks sequentially. Notably, each task is comprised of a unique combination of subtasks, with no repetition of subtasks within a single task.

5.2 Baselines

We compare our method with prior skill-based, meta-reinforcement, and multi-task reinforcement learning approaches.

- **SiMRL** leverages prior experience from offline datasets to address long-horizon sparse reward tasks. However, it does not employ multi-task parameter sharing to improve learning efficiency. Our comparison demonstrates that multi-task parameter sharing in our method yields improved performance.
- **SPiRL** learns skills and skill priors from offline datasets to augment reinforcement learning, thereby reducing the exploration space and focusing on actions derived from past experience to enhance learning. Our results show that incorporating meta-training and multi-task mechanisms, as in our approach, leads to further performance gains.
- **MTRL** serves as a multi-task reinforcement learning baseline. In our comparative experiments, the multi-task RL algorithm uses a soft parameter sharing approach, where each task is learned via shared parameters to address task diversity and complexity. Each individual policy is trained with SPiRL using skills extracted from the offline dataset. Thus, MTRL, like our method, leverages both meta-training tasks and offline data, enabling a direct comparison with our approach.

5.3 Result

Figure 3 presents a comparison of our method and baseline approaches in two domains: the success rate within 500 exploration steps in the maze navigation environment, and the number of completed subtasks within 1000 exploration steps in the kitchen manipulation environment.

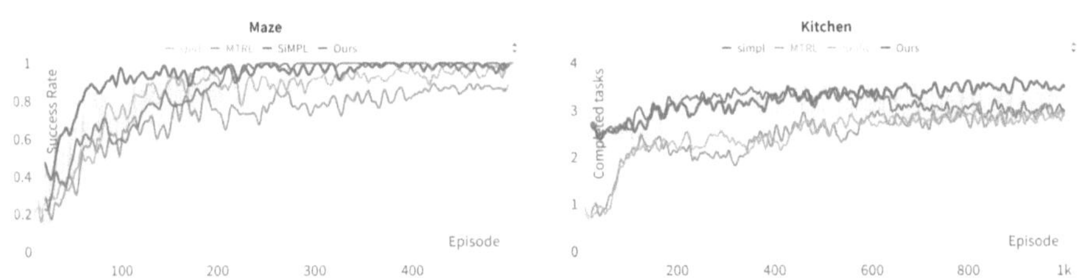

Fig. 3. Experimental results: Maze navigation success rate (left) Number of kitchen operations completed subtasks (right). Compared to other baseline approaches, our method, which combines the advantages of meta-learning and multi-task learning, demonstrates a superior learning effect in maze navigation and kitchen manipulation environments.

As observed, our proposed MSLMF algorithm demonstrates superior learning efficiency on previously unseen target tasks compared to all baselines. In the maze navigation environment, our method achieves a higher initial exploration performance, with the policy rapidly converging after only a few learning iterations. Similarly, in the kitchen manipulation environment, the policy quickly masters subtasks and exhibits better stability during the later stages of exploration. This rapid performance improvement and faster convergence indicate that, beyond leveraging offline data and meta-learning, the integration of meta-learning and multi-task learning in our approach significantly enhances both the learning efficiency and stability on target tasks.

Table 1 reports the mean and standard error of rewards achieved by our method and baselines across different environments. The results clearly show that, compared with baseline methods, our approach achieves higher and more stable sparse rewards in both environments.

Table 1. Experimental Results

Method	Maze Navigation (%)	Kitchen Manipulation
Ours	**97.43 ± 6.16**	**3.23 ± 0.39**
Simpl	96.47 ± 10.95	3.10 ± 0.37
SPiRL	81.42 ± 22.69	2.46 ± 0.59
MTRL	70.62 ± 20.98	2.44 ± 0.62

6 Analysis

6.1 Analysis of the Number of Meta-training Tasks

In this section, we aim to investigate the impact of the number of meta-training tasks on both the skill-based meta-training phase and the target task learning phase. Specifically, we conduct experiments and analyses in the maze navigation environment to assess how the diversity of tasks within the meta-training distribution affects learning on target tasks.

Our method is trained with both a smaller number of meta-training tasks (10, 20) and a larger number (40), followed by evaluation on the same set of ten target tasks, to systematically examine the influence of meta-training task quantity on overall performance.

As shown in Table 2, our approach consistently achieves higher average rewards and lower standard deviations compared to SiMPL, even under sparser meta-training task distributions (i.e., fewer meta-training tasks), thereby exhibiting superior sample efficiency. These results highlight the benefits of integrating meta-learning with multi-task learning as proposed in this paper, and further demonstrate that our method can deliver improved performance with reduced training resources.

6.2 Ablation

Dynamic sampling and prioritized experience replay (PER) are two critical components of our proposed method. To validate the effectiveness and contribution of each component, we conduct ablation experiments comparing the full method

Table 2. Experimental results of different meta training tasks

Meta-training Tasks	Ours (%)	SiMPL (%)
10 Meta-training Tasks	**94.17 ± 12.57**	90.56 ± 13.95
20 Meta-training Tasks	**96.30 ± 9.66**	92.99 ± 15.23
40 Meta-training Tasks	**97.43 ± 6.16**	96.47 ± 10.95

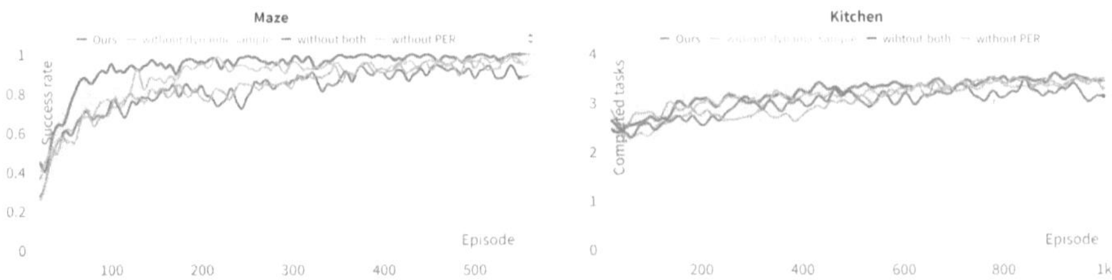

Fig. 4. Ablation Study: Impact of Dynamic Sampling and Prioritized Experience Replay Modules

against variants with either component removed or both components omitted. This enables us to explicitly assess the impact of each module on the overall performance. Specifically, we compare our complete method with versions that exclude the dynamic sampling strategy, the PER component, or both, in order to highlight the individual roles of these components.

As shown in Fig. 4, the removal of both key components results in the poorest performance on both the maze and kitchen environments. Incorporating PER leads to performance improvement, and similarly, the inclusion of the dynamic sampling strategy also enhances performance, clearly demonstrating the effectiveness of both components. Notably, the impact of the dynamic sampling strategy is more pronounced. We hypothesize that this is because dynamic sampling can directly regulate the allocation of training resources among different tasks, thus improving training balance and overall average performance. In contrast, PER mainly optimizes the sampling order within each task and cannot address the imbalance in training progress across tasks, resulting in a more limited overall performance gain.

7 Conclusion

We propose a skill learning framework guided by meta-policy multi-task fine-tuning, referred to as "Meta-Policy Guided Skill Learning via Multi-Task Fine-Tuning". This approach leverages prior experience from large-scale offline datasets, enabling meta-learning for long-horizon and complex tasks without requiring additional rewards or task annotations. By incorporating multi-task guided fine-tuning, the proposed method allows for rapid adaptation to unseen tasks and accelerates learning.

Specifically, our method first extracts and learns reusable skills from the offline dataset to train a meta-policy, and subsequently applies multi-task dynamic sampling to fine-tune the policy. This strategy balances performance across tasks and expedites the learning process for target tasks. Experimental results in both the maze navigation and kitchen manipulation environments demonstrate that our method outperforms baseline approaches in these long-horizon, complex task domains.

For future work, we plan to investigate the scalability of our approach in environments with imbalanced task distributions and novel scenarios, further extending the applicability of our method.

References

1. Beck, J., et al.: A survey of meta-reinforcement learning. arXiv preprint arXiv:2301.08028 (2023)
2. Bing, Z., Lerch, D., Huang, K., Knoll, A.: Meta-reinforcement learning in non-stationary and dynamic environments. IEEE Trans. Pattern Anal. Mach. Intell. **45**(3), 3476–3491 (2022)
3. Chen, J., Tamboli, D., Lan, T., Aggarwal, V.: Multi-task hierarchical adversarial inverse reinforcement learning. In: International Conference on Machine Learning, pp. 4895–4920. PMLR (2023)
4. Cho, M., Park, J., Lee, S., Sung, Y.: Hard tasks first: multi-task reinforcement learning through task scheduling. In: Forty-First International Conference on Machine Learning (2024)
5. D'Eramo, C., Tateo, D., Bonarini, A., Restelli, M., Peters, J.: Sharing knowledge in multi-task deep reinforcement learning. arXiv preprint arXiv:2401.09561 (2024)
6. Du, Y., et al.: Multi-task deep reinforcement learning for intelligent multi-zone residential HVAC control. Electric Power Syst. Res. **192**, 106959 (2021)
7. Fu, H., et al.: Towards effective context for meta-reinforcement learning: an approach based on contrastive learning. In: Proceedings of the AAAI Conference on Artificial Intelligence, vol. 35, pp. 7457–7465 (2021)
8. Gupta, A., Kumar, V., Lynch, C., Levine, S., Hausman, K.: Relay policy learning: solving long-horizon tasks via imitation and reinforcement learning. arXiv preprint arXiv:1910.11956 (2019)
9. Haarnoja, T., et al.: Soft actor-critic algorithms and applications. arXiv preprint arXiv:1812.05905 (2018)
10. Li, L., et al.: Towards an information theoretic framework of context-based offline meta-reinforcement learning. arXiv preprint arXiv:2402.02429 (2024)
11. Mitchell, E., Rafailov, R., Peng, X.B., Levine, S., Finn, C.: Offline meta-reinforcement learning with advantage weighting. In: International Conference on Machine Learning, pp. 7780–7791. PMLR (2021)
12. Nam, T., Sun, S.H., Pertsch, K., Hwang, S.J., Lim, J.J.: Skill-based meta-reinforcement learning. arXiv preprint arXiv:2204.11828 (2022)
13. Pertsch, K., Lee, Y., Lim, J.: Accelerating reinforcement learning with learned skill priors. In: Conference on Robot Learning, pp. 188–204. PMLR (2021)
14. Pertsch, K., Lee, Y., Wu, Y., Lim, J.J.: Guided reinforcement learning with learned skills. arXiv preprint arXiv:2107.10253 (2021)

15. Pong, V.H., Nair, A.V., Smith, L.M., Huang, C., Levine, S.: Offline meta-reinforcement learning with online self-supervision. In: International Conference on Machine Learning, pp. 17811–17829. PMLR (2022)
16. Rakelly, K., Zhou, A., Finn, C., Levine, S., Quillen, D.: Efficient off-policy meta-reinforcement learning via probabilistic context variables. In: International Conference on Machine Learning, pp. 5331–5340. PMLR (2019)
17. Rengarajan, D., Chaudhary, S., Kim, J., Kalathil, D., Shakkottai, S.: Enhanced meta reinforcement learning via demonstrations in sparse reward environments. Adv. Neural. Inf. Process. Syst. **35**, 2737–2749 (2022)
18. Ruiz, C., Alaiz, C.M., Dorronsoro, J.R.: A survey on kernel-based multi-task learning. Neurocomputing **577**, 127255 (2024)
19. Sodhani, S., Zhang, A., Pineau, J.: Multi-task reinforcement learning with context-based representations. In: International Conference on Machine Learning, pp. 9767–9779. PMLR (2021)
20. Tang, Y., Kozuno, T., Rowland, M., Munos, R., Valko, M.: Unifying gradient estimators for meta-reinforcement learning via off-policy evaluation. Adv. Neural. Inf. Process. Syst. **34**, 5303–5315 (2021)
21. Stooke, A., et al.: Open-ended learning leads to generally capable agents. arXiv preprint arXiv:2107.12808 (2021)
22. Vandenhende, S., Georgoulis, S., Van Gansbeke, W., Proesmans, M., Dai, D., Van Gool, L.: Multi-task learning for dense prediction tasks: a survey. IEEE Trans. Pattern Anal. Mach. Intell. **44**(7), 3614–3633 (2021)
23. Wang, H., Liu, Z., Hu, G., Wang, X., Han, Z.: Offline meta-reinforcement learning for active pantograph control in high-speed railways. IEEE Trans. Ind. Inform. (2024)
24. Yang, T., Cen, S., Wei, Y., Chen, Y., Chi, Y.: Federated natural policy gradient and actor critic methods for multi-task reinforcement learning. Adv. Neural. Inf. Process. Syst. **37**, 121304–121375 (2024)
25. Yu, T., Kumar, A., Chebotar, Y., Hausman, K., Levine, S., Finn, C.: Conservative data sharing for multi-task offline reinforcement learning. Adv. Neural. Inf. Process. Syst. **34**, 11501–11516 (2021)
26. Zhang, Y., Yang, Q.: A survey on multi-task learning. IEEE Trans. Knowl. Data Eng. **34**(12), 5586–5609 (2021)
27. Zhou, R., Gao, C.X., Zhang, Z., Yu, Y.: Generalizable task representation learning for offline meta-reinforcement learning with data limitations. In: Proceedings of the AAAI Conference on Artificial Intelligence, vol. 38, pp. 17132–17140 (2024)

A Trustworthy Task Offloading Scheme Based on Tournament and Elitist Genetic Algorithm for Vehicular Networks

Mingfeng Huang[1], Mingcong Bai[1], Xiaoyu Zhu[2(✉)], Hui Yin[2], and Rihui Wang[2]

[1] School of Computer, Changsha University of Science and Technology, Changsha 410114, China

[2] College of Computer Science and Engineering, Changsha University, Changsha 410083, China

zhuxiaoyu@ccsu.edu.cn

Abstract. Internet of Vehicles (IoV) has characteristics such as heterogeneous computing power, frequent switching, and rapid vehicle movement, which makes task offloading more challenging in this dynamic environment. On the one hand, massive nodes may initiate false or malicious tasks to seize resources, and on the other hand, the collaboration efficiency between vehicles and servers also needs to be strengthened. To this end, a Trustworthy task Offloading scheme based on Tournament and Elitist Genetic algorithm (TOTEG) is proposed. It first uses trust mechanisms to filter out malicious tasks, and evaluates tasks comprehensively from data sensitivity, source node request frequency, and offloading quality. Then, it utilizes the genetic algorithm to iteratively search for optimal offloading decisions. TOTEG redefines the fitness function and introduces an improved chromosome correction mechanism. By integrating elitism and tournament selection, it not only significantly accelerates the convergence speed, but also effectively mitigates the risk of converging to local optima. Finally, extensive experiments conducted on real-world datasets demonstrate that, compared with benchmark methods, TOTEG scheme significantly outperforms in offloading cost. It reduces the overhead by 18.04%, decreases the latency by 27.46%, and improves task success rate by 15.77%.

Keywords: Vehicular network · Task offloading · Trust evaluation · Gene algorithm

1 Introduction

With the rapid development of vehicular communication, cloud computing and edge computing, the transportation network is accelerating towards unmanned, intelligent and diversified directions [1, 2]. Against this background, the Internet of Vehicles (IoV) has emerged as an ideal solution to meet the emerging demands of the mobile network, covering multiple fields such as autonomous driving, intelligent transportation and safety warning [3]. According to the IDC's latest report, the compound annual growth rate of

L. Zhang and K.-K. R. Choo (Eds.): MobiQuitous 2025, LNICST 683, pp. 465–485, 2026.
https://doi.org/10.1007/978-3-032-22500-9_26

automobiles worldwide will reach 16.8% in the next five years [4], and it is estimated that by 2026, the number of autonomous vehicles is expected to reach 64.25 million [5]. As the scale of IoV network continues to climb, the requirements for computing power, storage, and energy consumption are becoming increasingly high. Due to limitations of on-board computing capabilities, how to support delay-sensitive and computation-intensive tasks become a huge challenge [6].

Mobile Edge Computing (MEC) provides an opportunity to solve above problems. It uses task offloading technology to offload tasks that are difficult for vehicles to handle to edge servers or the cloud [7, 8]. By leveraging the powerful storage and computing ability of cloud and the low delay advantages of edge servers, it compensates for the vehicle's deficiencies in energy and computing power [9].

In recent years, researchers have carried out some work on task offloading. For example, Tan et al. [10] propose a distributed task offloading method to minimize task response time. Kuang et al. [11] model partial offloading and resource allocation as non-convex mixed integer optimization problems and propose a two-stage alternating method. Liu et al. [12] propose a collaborative distributed offloading framework, which utilizes asynchronous deep reinforcement to find the optimal task scheduling strategy. However, most of these studies are applied in edge computing scenarios, while task offloading in IoV is more challenging. On the one hand, due to the frequent switching and rapid vehicle movement, more and more fake and malicious tasks are mixed in the offloading tasks [13]. In addition, the offloading process is vulnerable to the dynamic impact of channel quality, propagation loss, server availability, etc. Specifically, the limitations of existing research are reflected in the following aspects:

First, most research adopt the task computing mode with vehicle-edge-cloud collaboration, but lacks an evaluation on task reliability. As a collaborative network, the Internet of Vehicles involves numerous vehicles and server nodes. If there are false deception, free riding, selfishness, and other nodes in the requesting nodes, they may generate false or malicious tasks, seize and consume resources, resulting in some servers dying due to excessive resource consumption, leading to problems such as task accumulation, resource waste, and high failure rates. This risk increases linearly with the expansion of the network size.

Second, the existing solutions are inefficient in adapting to dynamic topology changes and complex offloading environment. The methods commonly used in IoV are reinforcement learning, game theory and heuristic methods. Reinforcement learning has a poor generalization ability in the face of huge states and action spaces, and need to collect all global information to make decisions, which will lead to more energy consumption. While game theory can characterize the competition and cooperation relationships in offloading, but they carry a heavy burden on information exchange and sometimes it is difficult to obtain Nash equilibrium. Heuristic methods, as a classic approach, have the characteristics of easy implementation and fast optimization speed, but the premise is to avoid falling into local optima due to environmental dynamism.

To address the aforementioned challenges, a trustworthy task offloading scheme is proposed in this paper, abbreviated as TOTEG. Unlike existing approaches, TOTEG first evaluates the credibility of tasks prior to offloading, thereby filtering out false or malicious tasks. Then, it further proposes a genetic algorithm based on tournament selection and elitism to avoid falling into local optima in the dynamic IoV. The main contributions of this paper are as follows:

- We conduct a comprehensive analysis of task credibility from perspectives of data sensitivity, source node request frequency, and offloading quality. Compared with existing methods, we effectively ensure task quality by utilizing trust mechanisms, which avoid resource preemption and task accumulation caused by malicious tasks.
- We propose a trustworthy task offloading scheme based on tournament selection and elitist genetic algorithm. In this scheme, we redesign the chromosome encoding and fitness function, embedding elitism and tournament ideas into selection, crossover, and mutation processes, and utilizing task priority for the chromosome correction. Compared with traditional genetic algorithms, it not only accelerates convergence speed, but also reduces the risk of falling into local optima in dynamic environments.
- We conduct extensive experiments based on real-world datasets. Performance analysis results demonstrate that, TOTEG achieves an 18.04% reduction in overhead and a 27.46% decrease in delay compared to benchmark methods, while simultaneously increasing the task success rate by 15.77%.

The rest of this paper is organized as follows. Section 2 reviews the related work. Section 3 outlines the system model. Section 4 elaborates on the proposed TOTEG scheme. Section 5 presents simulation results. Finally, Sect. 6 concludes the paper.

2 Related Work

2.1 Task Offloading in Vehicular Network

The vehicle-edge cloud collaborative offloading has become the research focus. For example, Lee et al. [13] introduce a task allocation and offloading ratio identification method. It addresses the min-max fractional optimization problem in wireless MEC networks. Zhao et al. [14] combine connectivity model, vehicle selection mechanism and deep reinforcement learning based on the A3C algorithm to propose a novel method to optimize delay. Wu et al. [15] propose an innovative algorithm based on multilayer deep reinforcement learning, optimizing task delay and energy consumption in vehicle networks. Gu et al. [16] introduce a task offloading model that integrates a digital twin, convolutional attention for environmental state representation, and a synchronous A2C network combined with an auction mechanism. Zeng et al. [17] solve the problem of minimizing data migration delay, and propose a collaborative caching strategy to optimize data storage and retrieval. Hu et al. [18] propose an edge-cloud collaborative offloading framework and a solution based on the hybrid DDPG-D3QN algorithm, which is used to optimize server selection, task partitioning and computing allocation. Ni et al. [19] propose an offloading scheduling scheme in biomedical data processing and analysis, which aims to maximize system utility by optimizing system parameters, thereby addressing the limitations of traditional edge computing in processing complex tasks. Binh et al. 8 introduce a task offloading approach, it uses Markov decision process and develops two reinforcement learning algorithms. Sohaib et al. [20] propose a general edge computing framework that integrates online-offline learning methods, demonstrating superior performance compared to traditional MEC and RL policies.

However, most of the aforementioned literature primarily focuses on delay and energy consumption, while neglecting the potential for offloading failures and ignoring factors like possible malicious attacks or false tasks in the environment.

2.2 Task Offloading with Trust

Recently, researchers focus on enhancing the reliability of offloading. For example, Min et al. [21] introduce an SDLPTO scheme that integrates differential privacy with deep Q-network. By employing a perturbed distance probability density function, it safeguards user location information against potential leaks. Ruan et al. [22] employ a trust degree to evaluate the credibility of node objects. Chen et al. [23] transforms task offloading into a trust-guided bipartite graph matching problem, solving the problems of trust, resource allocation and task completion in dynamic collaboration. Mao et al. [24] establish a task offloading model based on trusted RSU services, combining QoS trust and social trust, enhancing the detection rate of trust evaluation. Wang et al. [25] propose a decentralized distributed training framework based on trusted AIoT device collectives. Bai et al. [26] propose an innovative scheme called low-cost unmanned aerial vehicle task offloading scheme based on trustable and trackable data routing. By leveraging security trust to directly and indirectly infer the security level of RSUs, Cao et al. [27] proposes an evaluation mechanism based on security trust incentives.

Different from most existing studies that focus on the trust degree of nodes, this paper uses super nodes as an intermediate layer and evaluates the comprehensive trust of tasks by considering data sensitivity, source node request frequency, and offloading quality. In addition, we model the offloading problem as a joint optimization of delay and energy consumption, and use improved genetic algorithm to minimize overhead.

3 System Model

3.1 Network Model

In this paper, we consider a network composed of m vehicles, n MEC servers, z super nodes and 1 cloud server, as shown in Fig. 1. The main notations for this article are listed in Table 1. Among them, the set of vehicles is $\mathbb{N} = \{N_1, N_2, ..., N_m\}$, the set of MEC servers is $\mathbb{M} = \{MEC_1, MEC_2, ..., MEC_n\}$, the cloud node is $\mathbb{C}$, and $\mathbb{X} = \mathbb{N} \cup \mathbb{M} \cup \mathbb{C}$, representing the set of all task computing nodes x_i.

The cloud server consists of large data centers and has strong task processing capabilities as well as huge storage capacity. MEC servers are deployed near users, made up of small servers with certain computing and storage capabilities. They process tasks locally with a small delay. Super nodes are hardware between vehicles and MEC servers, responsible for evaluating tasks, and making offloading decisions. Vehicles generate various tasks. When local computing is not available, tasks are offloaded to MEC or cloud servers for execution.

This paper adopts a binary task offloading mode. Each task can only be executed completely as an independent entity on the vehicle, edge server, or cloud server and cannot be further divided. Suppose the set of tasks is $\mathbb{T} = \{T_1, T_2,...,T_i,...\}$, and the characteristics of each task T_i are represented by the tuple $\{d_i, c_i, t_i^{max}, a_i\}$, where d_i is the task data volume, c_i is the number of CPU cycles required for task computing, t_i^{max} is the maximum tolerable delay for task computing, and a_i is the task offloading decision. Consider any computing node $x_k = \{C_k, V_k\}, x_k \in \mathbb{X}$, where C_k represents the total computing power resources of the computing node, and V_k represents the total data capacity of the computing node. This paper uses $\mathbb{A}$ to represent the task offloading decision vector set, $\mathbb{A} = \{a_1, a_2, ..., a_i, ...\}$. Where $a_1 = 0$ indicates that the first task is executed locally, and $a_1 = j$ indicates that the task is offloaded to the *j-th* server node for execution, including edge nodes and cloud nodes.

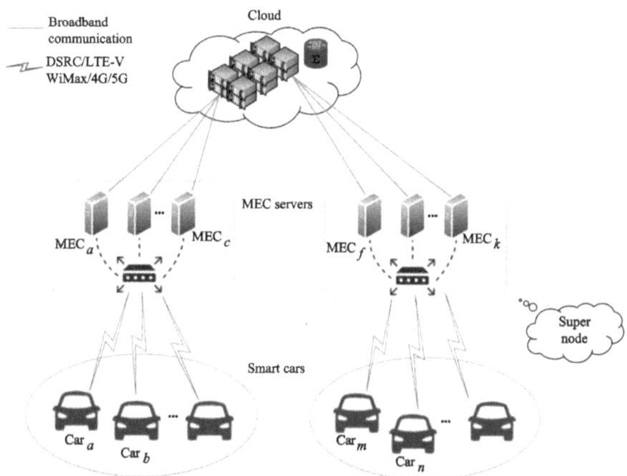

Fig. 1. Network Architecture

3.2 Communication Model

Due to the dynamic complexity of the vehicular environment, when constructing the communication model, we consider the mutual interference between different devices and model the transmission rate between nodes based on the hybrid channel model, which is specifically expressed as:

$$\varphi_{i,j} = Wlb\left(1 + \frac{P_{i,j}H_{i,j}}{\sigma^2 + \sum_{k \neq i, l \neq j} P_{k,l}H_{k,l}}\right) \tag{1}$$

Among them, W is the channel bandwidth, σ^2 is the power of white Gaussian noise, $P_{i,j}$ is the power consumption for transmission from vehicle N_i to MEC_j, $H_{i,j}$ is the channel gain between node N_i and MEC_j, and $\sum_{k \neq i, l \neq j} P_{k,l}H_{k,l}$ represents the mutual interference between different devices.

Considering the possible transmission loss, it is proposed to calculate the channel gain $H_{i,j}$ based on the free-space path loss model, which is as follows:

$$H_{i,j} = G\left(\omega \cdot \frac{3 \times 10^8}{4\pi F_c dis_{i,j}}\right) \tag{2}$$

Among them, G is the antenna gain, ω is the path loss coefficient, F_c is the carrier frequency, and $dis_{i,j}$ is the distance between N_i and the edge node MEC_j.

3.3 Computing Model

When the task is executed by the vehicle locally, assuming that the task computing capability of vehicle N_j is f_{N_j}, the task processing delay at this time is expressed as:

$$D_{i,j} = c_i / f_{N_j} \tag{3}$$

Drawing on the widely adopted energy consumption model $E = \mathcal{E}P^2D$, where $\mathcal{E}$ is the energy coefficient of the CPU chip, and P_{N_i} is the computing power of a single CPU cycle for the vehicle, the energy consumption of local computing is expressed as:

$$E_{i,j} = \mathcal{E}\left(P_{N_i}\right)^2 c_i \tag{4}$$

When the task is offloaded to the MEC server for execution, the task processing delay at this time is expressed as:

$$D_{i,MEC_k} = d_i / \varphi_{i,k} + c_i / f_{MEC_k} + d_i' / \varphi_{k,i} \tag{5}$$

Among them, d_i is the amount of task input data, $\varphi_{i,k}$ is the data transmission rate from the vehicle N_i generating the task to the MEC_k, $\varphi_{k,i}$ is the transmission rate during data return, d_i' is the amount of data returned for the task calculation result, and f_{MEC_k} is the task computing capability of the edge node.

At this stage, assuming that P_{MEC_k} is the computing power of a single CPU cycle of the MEC server and $P_{i,k}$ is transmission power consumption, the energy consumption of task processing can be expressed as follows:

$$E_{i,MEC_k} = \mathcal{E}\left(P_{MEC_k}\right)^2 c_i / f_{MEC_k} + P_{i,k}\left(d_i/\varphi_{i,k} + d_i'/\varphi_{k,i}\right) \tag{6}$$

When a task is offloaded to the cloud server for execution, the total task processing delay can be expressed as:

$$D_{i,Cloud} = d_i / \varphi_{i,k} + d_i / \varphi_{k,Cl} + c_i / f_{Cl} + d_i' / \varphi_{Cl,k} + d_i' / \varphi_{k,i} \tag{7}$$

Here, $\varphi_{k,Cl}$ represents the data transmission rate from MEC_k to the cloud server, $\varphi_{Cl,k}$ denotes the data transmission rate when the cloud server returns the result to the edge node, and f_{Cl} indicates the task computing capability of the cloud server.

At this time, assuming that the transmission power from the edge node MEC_k to the cloud server is $P_{K,Cl}$ and the transmission power for result feedback from the cloud server is $P_{Cl,k}$, the total energy consumption for task processing can be expressed as:

$$E_{i,Cloud} = \mathcal{E}(P_{Cl})^2 c_i / f_{Cl} + P_{i,k}\left(d_i / \varphi_{i,k} + d_i' / \varphi_{k,i}\right) + P_{k,Cl}\left(d_i / \varphi_{k,Cl} + d_i' / \varphi_{Cl,k}\right) \tag{8}$$

3.4 Problem Statement

This paper aims to design an efficient task offloading strategy based on trust evaluation. By formulating task offloading as a joint optimization problem of energy consumption and delay, the objective is to minimize the overall energy consumption and task delay in the system. The specific optimization goal is expressed as follows:

$$min \sum_{i=1}^{|\mathbb{T}|} \left(\lambda E_{i,j} + (1-\lambda) D_{i,j}\right)$$

$$C1 : D_i \leq t_i^{max}, \forall T_i \in \mathbb{T}$$

$$C2 : \sum_{i=1}^{|\mathbb{T}|} d_{i,j} \leq V_j, \forall x_j \in \mathbb{X}$$

$$C3 : \sum_{i=1}^{|\mathbb{T}|} c_{i,j} \leq C_j, \forall x_j \in \mathbb{X} \tag{9}$$

Among them, λ is a weight parameter that facilitates the dynamic trade-off between delay and energy consumption. For each task T_i, $E_{i,j}$ denotes the energy consumption incurred when the task is executed by computing node x_j, while $D_{i,j}$ represents the processing delay. Constraints $C1$-$C3$ are the conditions that the optimization objective must satisfy. Specifically, $C1$ ensures that the execution time of each task does not exceed its maximum tolerable delay. $C2$ and $C3$ guarantee that the computing node has adequate capacity and computational power to execute the task.

The parameters and definitions mainly involved in this article are given in Table 1.

Table 1. Main notation descriptions.

Notation	Description
$\mathbb{N}$	the vehicle node set
$\mathbb{M}$	the MEC node set
$\mathbb{C}$	the cloud node
$\mathbb{X}$	the set of all task computing nodes
$\mathbb{T}$	the task set
d_i	the task data volume
c_i	the number of CPU cycles required for task computing
t_i^{max}	the maximum tolerable delay for task computing
a_i	the task offloading decision
s_i	the data sensitivity

(continued)

Table 1. (*continued*)

Notation	Description
e_i	the source node offloading quality
F_j	the source node request frequency
S_i	the comprehensive trust score of task T_i
$\mathbb{C}$	the chromosome set
g_p	the chromosome population sizes

4 The Design of TOTEG

4.1 Overview

In this section, we introduce implementation of Trustworthy task Offloading scheme based on Tournament and Elitist Genetic algorithm (TOTEG), as shown in Fig. 2.

First, the super node conducts a trust evaluation on offloading tasks. This evaluation incorporates multiple factors such as task data sensitivity, the source vehicle node's success rate, and offloading request frequency to derive a comprehensive trust score. The comprehensive trust score is then compared against a predefined trust threshold. If the score falls below this threshold, the offloading task is immediately rejected. If it meets or exceeds the threshold, the task is added to the trusted task queue for further offloading decision. After completing the evaluation, the feature database is updated.

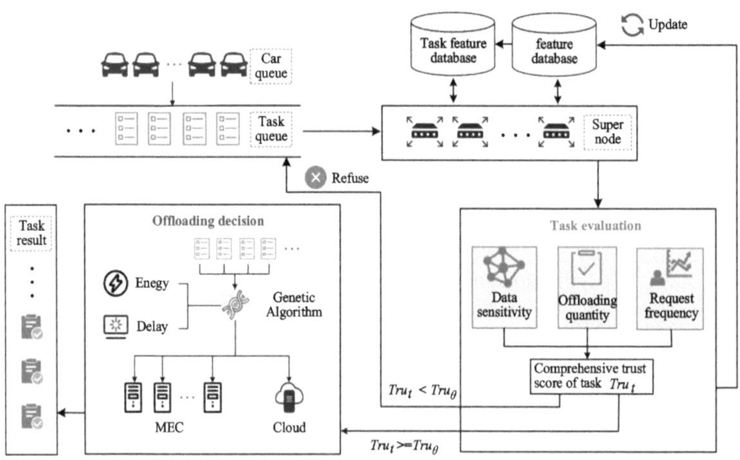

Fig. 2. Framework of the proposed TOTEG scheme

Then, the super node determines the offloading decision using a genetic algorithm. The initial population is generated by encoding the tasks from the trusted task queue into chromosomes. The validity of each chromosome is rigorously evaluated according to the remaining computing power and capacity of each computing node. The fitness of each chromosome is calculated, where a smaller fitness indicates a better solution. After multiple rounds of crossover and mutation, the optimal solution is obtained.

Finally, tasks are offloaded to MEC nodes or cloud server for execution. Once the execution is complete, the results are transmitted back to the vehicle. Following this, the data related to the offloading execution status is updated in the feature database.

4.2 Trust Evaluation of Task

The trust of each task T_i is calculated based on the following three criteria.

First, to better protect users' sensitive data, we propose a method to calculate the data sensitivity s_i of task T_i within the current time period:

$$s_i = 1 - d_i^{Sens} / d_i \tag{10}$$

Here, d_i^{Sens} represents the amount of sensitive data required for task T_i. A higher proportion of sensitive data in the task requirement results in a lower sensitivity value.

Then, to improve the quality of tasks executed by edge MEC nodes, we evaluate the offloading quality of the source vehicle node N_i by analyzing its historical offloading situation. Specifically, within the current time period, let q_i^{suc} and q_i^{fail} represent the number of successful and failed tasks of N_i has participated in offloading, respectively. The source node offloading quality of N_i is expressed as:

$$e_i = \frac{q_i^{suc} + 1}{q_i^{suc} + q_i^{fail} + 2} \tag{11}$$

When the node has no historical record, the q_i^{suc} and q_i^{fail} are set to 0, and the neutral value of e_i is assigned as 0.5.

To prevent the malicious occupation and wasteful use of computing resources at edge nodes by certain terminal nodes, we define the standard average number of offloading requests for all vehicles within any observation period as r_j^{avg}. We propose a method to calculate the source node offloading request frequency by analyzing the relationship between the actual offloading request frequency of the node and the standard average number of offloading requests. Let the number of offloading requests sent by node N_j within the current time period be r_j, and let the source node request frequency be denoted as F_j. The formula for calculating F_j is given by:

$$F_j = \frac{1}{1 + \varpi \times \left| r_j - r_j^{avg} \right|} \tag{12}$$

Here, ϖ represents the request frequency weight of the node, where $\varpi \in (0, 1]$.

Finally, based on the three evaluation indicators obtained through calculation, we determine the comprehensive trust of task S_i in the current time period as follows:

$$S_i = \mu F_j + \theta s_i + (1 - \mu - \theta) e_i \tag{13}$$

where μ and θ are weight parameters set by the system according to actual needs, reflecting the importance of data sensitivity and offloading quality. These parameters satisfy the conditions $\mu \in (0,1)$ and $\in (0,1 - \mu)$.

The obtained comprehensive trust score S_i is compared against the preset trust threshold S_{tr}. If S_i is less than S_{tr}, T_i is deemed untrustworthy, and the super node will refrain from allocating computing nodes to T_i. Conversely, T_i is identified as a trustworthy task. The super node will then add T_i to the trusted task queue and make offloading decisions for each task in the queue.

4.3 Task Offloading Based on Genetic Algorithm

To determine the optimal offloading decision, this paper employs a genetic algorithm that integrates tournament selection and elitism. For each task T_i, the super node follows these steps to make an offloading decision and execute the offloading process:

Chromosomes Initialization. The details of this part are illustrated in Algorithm 1. In this paper, the chromosome set is denoted as $\mathbb{C} = \{Ch_1, Ch_2, \ldots, Ch_i, \ldots\}$. As illustrated in the Fig. 3, the first gene is denoted as a_1 with a value of 4, indicating that the first task should be offloaded to the fourth edge node. During the initialization process, the number of genes within a chromosome corresponds to the number of tasks. The genes are generated by invoking a random function from a predefined library, with their values drawn from the set of computing nodes $\mathbb{X}$ Specifically, the initialization procedure involves iterating over the entire chromosome and generating the value for each gene using the random function. If the node corresponding to this value has sufficient capacity and computing power to execute the current task, the process proceeds to the next step; otherwise, the value is regenerated until it is valid.

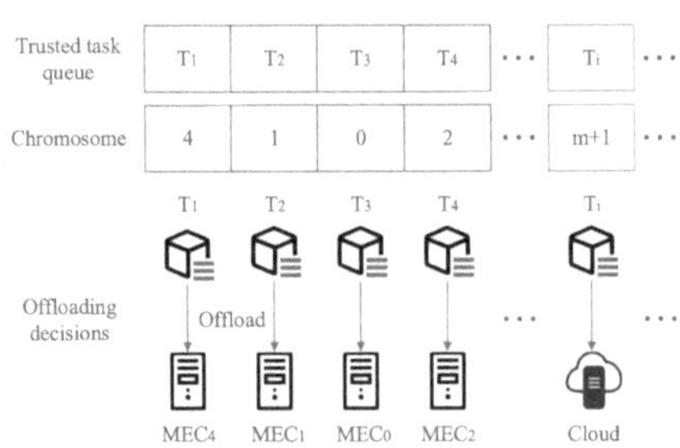

Fig. 3. Structure of chromosome

Algorithm 1 : Population generation algorithm

Input: Task set $\mathbb{T}$, computing node set $\mathbb{X}$, chromosome population sizes g_p
Output: chromosomal population $\mathbb{C}$
Initial: $\mathbb{P} = null$, $Chromosome = null$, $g_p = 40$
1.**For** i from 0 to g_p **Do**
2. **For** each $T \in \mathbb{T}$ **Do**
3. Randomly select a node x_r from $\mathbb{X}$
4. **If** $C_r - c > 0$ and $V_r - d > 0$ **Do**
5. $Ch_i \leftarrow Ch_i \cup x_r$
6. **Else** go to 3
7. **End For**
8. $\mathbb{C} \leftarrow \mathbb{C} \cup Ch_i$
9.**End For**
10.return $\mathbb{C}$

Fitness Evaluation. According to Eq. (9), to achieve the optimal task offloading sequence, it is essential to minimize the overall overhead of the system's task offloading process. Consequently, the fitness function is defined as follows:

$$\phi = \sum_{i=1}^{|\mathbb{T}|} \left(\lambda E_{i,j} + (1-\lambda) D_{i,j} \right) \tag{14}$$

A lower fitness value of a chromosome signifies a more optimal offloading sequence, consequently leading to a reduction in task offloading overhead. By rapidly sorting chromosomes in ascending order based on their fitness values, the elitist strategy can be implemented more efficiently.

Chromosomes Selection. The specific selection process is described in Algorithm 2. First, sort the chromosomes in ascending order based on their calculated fitness values. Before each iteration, apply an elitism strategy to retain the top $\beta\%$ of individuals from the current population with the lowest fitness values. This ensures that the best-performing individuals are preserved across iterations. Then, utilize the tournament selection method to randomly select n_t chromosomes from the population for comparison each time, retaining those with lower fitness values to generate the next generation. This process ensures that higher-quality chromosomes are selected in each iteration. Repeat this step until the size of the parent chromosome set for generating the next generation matches the original population size.

Algorithm 2 : Selection operation of the chromosomes

Input: Chromosomal population $\mathbb{C}$, elitism ratio β, tournament selection size $n_{\mathfrak{t}}$, tournament selection list $\mathfrak{t}$
Output: Selected chromosome set $\mathbb{C}_s$
Initial: $\mathbb{C}_s = null$, $\beta = 3\%$, $n_{\mathfrak{t}} = 3$, $\mathfrak{t} = null$
1.Sort $\mathbb{C}$ based on fitness in ascending order
2.$\mathbb{C}_s \leftarrow \mathbb{C}_s \cup$ {top β% individuals by fitness from $\mathbb{C}$}
3.**While** $|\mathbb{C}_s| < |\mathbb{C}|$ **Do**
4.   Randomly select $n_{\mathfrak{t}}$ individuals from $\mathbb{C}$ into $\mathfrak{t}$
5. $\mathbb{C} \leftarrow \mathbb{C} \cup$ {individual with the lowest fitness in $\mathfrak{t}$}
6.   Clear $\mathfrak{t}$
7.**End While**
8.Return $\mathbb{C}_s$

Chromosomes Crossover. The specific crossover process is shown in Algorithm 3. To achieve this, construct a recombination sequence of the same length as the chromosome by randomly selecting values of 0 or 1. Here, 0 indicates no crossover at the current position, while 1 signifies that a crossover should occur. Next, randomly select two parent chromosomes from the current population and perform recombination according to the generated sequence. The crossover process is illustrated in Fig. 4.

Algorithm 3 : Crossover operation of the chromosomes

Input: Set of selected chromosomes $\mathbb{C}_s$
Output: Population of offspring chromosomes $\mathbb{C}_c$
Initial: $\mathbb{C}_c = null$
1.**While** $|\mathbb{C}_c| < |\mathbb{C}|_s$ **Do**
2.   Randomly select two individuals Ch_x, Ch_y from $\mathbb{C}_s$
3.   **For** *i* from 0 to $|Ch_x|$ **Do**
4.   Randomly generate key using 0 or 1
5.   **If** key=1 **Do**
6.   Exchanging genes on two individuals
7.   **End If**
8.   **End For**
9. $\mathbb{C}_c \leftarrow \mathbb{C}_c \cup \{Ch_x, Ch_y\}$
10.**End While**
11.return $\mathbb{C}_c$

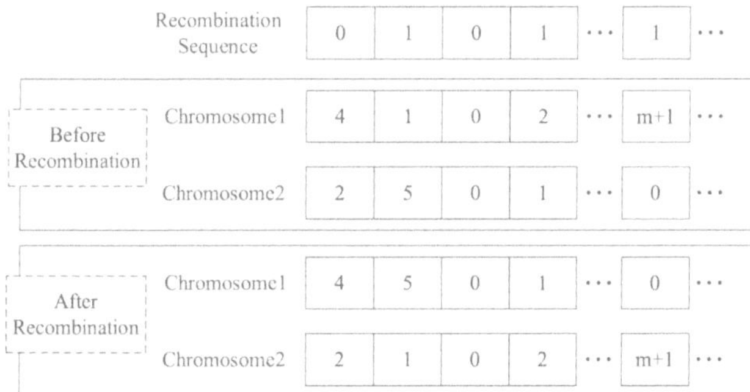

Fig. 4. Schematic illustration of chromosomal crossover

Chromosome Mutation. The details of this part are shown in Algorithm 4. First, randomly select a gene from one chromosome and alter its value to a new random value. The purpose of mutation is to escape local optima while preserving the integrity of previously discovered optimal solutions. The mutation probability should be set sufficiently low to ensure it does not negatively impact on the overall convergence of the algorithm.

Algorithm 4 : Mutation operation of the chromosomes

Input: Population of offspring chromosomes $\mathbb{C}_c$, Mutation probability p_m
Output: Population of chromosomes after mutation $\mathbb{C}_m$
Initial: $p_m = 0.1$
1. **For** each $Ch \in \mathbb{C}_c$ **Do**
2. Generate a random probability p_r
3. **If** $p_r < p_m$ **Do**
4. Randomly select a individual Ch_r and a task T_r
5. Randomly select a node x_r from $\mathbb{X}$
6. **If** $C_r - c_r > 0$ and $V_r - d_r > 0$ **Do**
7. $a_r \leftarrow x_r$
8. **Else** go to 5
9. **End If**
10. **End For**

Chromosome Repair. Due to the limited computing power and capacity resources of edge nodes, if illegal solutions arise after crossover and mutation, these solutions must be corrected. The specific process for this part is detailed in Algorithm 5. Assume that the priority of task T_i is Γ_i. Specifically, set the task with least resource requirement and the lowest tolerable delay to have the highest priority Γ. Suppose that under the current offloading strategy, a MEC node that cannot meet the constraint conditions is MEC_i, and the task set assigned to MEC_i is $\mathbb{T}_{MEC_i}$. Sort $\mathbb{T}_{MEC_i}$ according to the priority Γ. Modify the offloading strategy for the task with the lowest Γ in $\mathbb{T}_{MEC_i}$ by offloading it to the cloud server until MEC_i can complete all tasks within the constraint conditions. Apply this method iteratively to correct all edge nodes that do not meet the constraint conditions until all solutions are valid.

Finally, initialize various parameters and set the maximum number of iterations to ξ. Perform iterative loops according to the specified steps until the chromosome with the lowest fitness value is identified. To prevent the loss of the optimal individual during iterations, preserve this chromosome for subsequent iterations. If the iteration count reaches the predefined maximum, the algorithm terminates immediately. The sequence represented by the chromosome with the lowest fitness at termination is considered the optimal task offloading sequence.

Algorithm 5 : Correction algorithm

Input: Assigned task set $\mathbb{T}_{MEC_i}$

Output: Modified assigned task set $\mathbb{T}'_{MEC_i}$

Initial: $d_{MEC_i} = \sum_{j=0}^{|\mathbb{T}_{MEC_i}|} d_j$, $c_{MEC_i} = \sum_{j=0}^{|\mathbb{T}_{MEC_i}|} c_j$, $\mathbb{T}'_{MEC_i} = \mathbb{T}_{MEC_i}$

1.**For** each $T \in \mathbb{T}_{MEC_i}$ **Do**
2. Calculate Γ
3.**End For**
4.Sort $\mathbb{T}'_{MEC_i}$ by Γ
5.**While** $d_{MEC_i} > V_i$ or $c_{MEC_i} > C_i$ **Do**
6. Remove T with the smallest Γ from $\mathbb{T}'_{MEC_i}$
7. $a_{MEC_i} \leftarrow$ Cloud
8. Recalculate the value of d_{MEC_i} and c_{MEC_i}
9.**End While**
10.Return $\mathbb{T}'_{MEC_i}$

5 Experiment Results and Performance Analysis

In this section, we evaluate the performance of TOTEG through simulations. First, we detail the simulation settings, then, we conduct a comparative analysis from three perspectives: task offloading delay, energy consumption, and load balancing, to comprehensively assess the impact of the TOTEG algorithm on system overhead.

5.1 Experiment Setup

This paper establishes an experimental scenario comprising 200 vehicles, 50 MEC servers, and 1 cloud server. They are distributed within a 25-km radius centered at (116.41667, 39.91667). To more accurately simulate the communication and collaboration between vehicles and servers, we utilize the "parking places of Beijing" dataset to construct a realistic distribution of vehicle nodes and tasks [28], and the "T-drive" dataset to model the placement of MEC servers [29]. Each vehicle generates 3 to 5 computational tasks for processing. By default, 10% of the tasks are designated as malicious, introducing potential system interference. The specific parameter settings for the experiment are detailed in Table 2.

Table 2. Parameter for the simulation experiment

Parameter	value
The carrier frequency	2.4 GHz
The power of white Gaussian noise	−120 dBm
The power consumption for transmission from vehicle	32 dBm
The task data volume	$[100 \sim 900]$ KB
The number of CPU cycles required for task computing	$[0.2 \sim 1.2] \times 10^9$
The maximum tolerable delay for task computing	$[1 \sim 3]$ s
The task computing capability of vehicle	$[0.5 \sim 3]$ GHz
The task computing capability of the edge node	$[2 \sim 5]$ GHz
The computing power consumption of vehicle	0.5 W
The computing power consumption of edge server	0.5 W
The task computing capability of the cloud server	5 GHz

5.2 Methods of Comparison

For comparison, we select three baseline methods. Their implementation is as follows:

Greedy Offloading Algorithm (Greedy). This algorithm prioritizes high-priority tasks with the shortest tolerable delay to ensure the offloading time constraints are met.

Genetic Algorithm (GA). This approach employs a genetic algorithm without task reliability considerations. The optimization objectives are minimizing both the energy consumption and delay costs.

Discrete Bat Algorithm (DBA). As described in [30], this method does not account for task reliability. Each bat represents a potential offloading strategy. By adjusting the bat's position, which corresponds to selecting the appropriate node for task offloading, the algorithm explores the solution space to optimize system performance.

5.3 Impact of Population Size

First, we analysis the impact of population size. Because only heuristic algorithms include population and iteration concepts, so discussions on population size and iteration do not apply to greedy algorithms. Figure 5 illustrates its effects on the offloading delay and energy consumption of the GA, DBA, and TOTEG algorithms. For delay, when population size rose from 10 to 20, DBA-optimized delay first slightly increased then decreased; from 10 to 40, GA-optimized delay dropped by 26.11% and TOTEG's by 14.18%; beyond 40, all three methods' delay rose, indicating that an excessively large population may reduce optimization efficiency and potentially lead to suboptimal solutions. For the energy consumption, population size has minimal effect on DBA but substantial effect on TOTEG. When it rises from 10 to 40, TOTEG cuts energy consumption by 15.19%. GA and TOTEG reach optimal energy consumption at size 40; beyond that, optimization tends to converge to local optima, and population size affects energy consumption similarly to time. Thus, the heuristic algorithm's population size is set to 40 in subsequent experiments, and TOTEG consistently outperforms GA and DBA in optimizing delay and energy, with better stability and effectiveness.

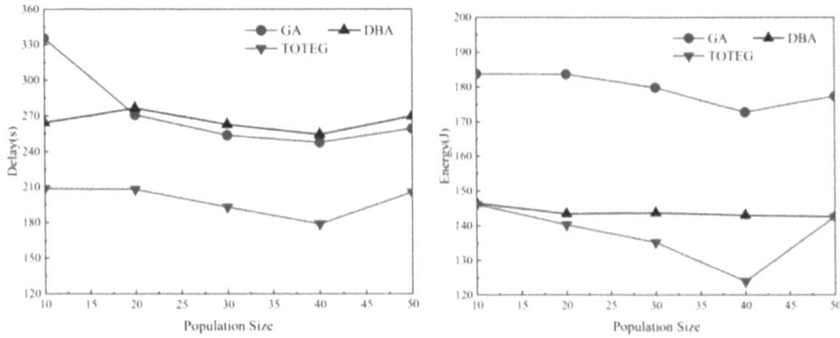

(a) (b)

Fig. 5. The impact of population size

5.4 Impact of Iteration Count

Figure 6 illustrates the system overhead trend of the GA, DBA, and TOTEG algorithms over 1000 consecutive iterations.

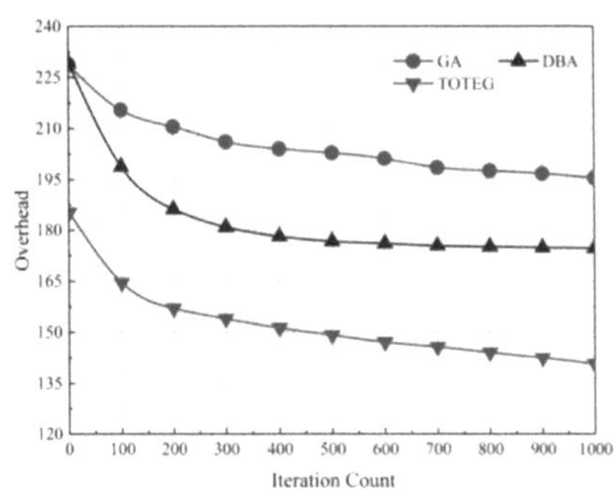

Fig. 6. The impact of iteration numbers on overhead

As the number of iterations increases, system overhead decreases progressively and eventually stabilizes. DBA outperforms GA in iteration outcomes and convergence speed. While TOTEG exhibits a convergence rate comparable to DBA, the overhead of GA and DBA, which lack task trust evaluation, are notably higher after 1000 iterations due to the presence of malicious task interference. Ultimately, TOTEG reduced overhead by an additional 14.99% compared to DBA. This shows that under malicious task interference, TOTEG can effectively filter out untrusted tasks to significantly enhance system offloading efficiency and reduce system overhead.

5.5 Impact of Single Task Size

Figure 7(a) illustrates the effect of task size on delay. When the task data volume is below 300 KB, the delays observed using the Greedy, GA, and DBA methods are comparable. As task size increases, the delay for all methods rises significantly. Specifically, the increase in delay for the Greedy method is the most substantial, followed by DBA. In large task environments, TOTEG demonstrates superior delay performance.

Figure 7(b) illustrates the energy consumption of each method with varying task sizes. When the task data volume is below 300 KB, the energy consumption of the Greedy, GA, and DBA methods remains largely comparable. However, as the task data size increases, a noticeable divergence in energy consumption becomes apparent. Notably, the energy consumption of GA escalates at a relatively rapid pace. For data volumes under 600 KB, TOTEG demonstrates significantly superior performance compared to Greedy and DBA, effectively reducing system energy consumption and showcasing a more pronounced optimization effect. Conversely, when the task data volume reaches or exceeds 600 KB, the performance of Greedy and DBA surpasses that of TOTEG. Therefore, for tasks of medium and small sizes, TOTEG outperforms the other three methods in terms of energy consumption optimization.

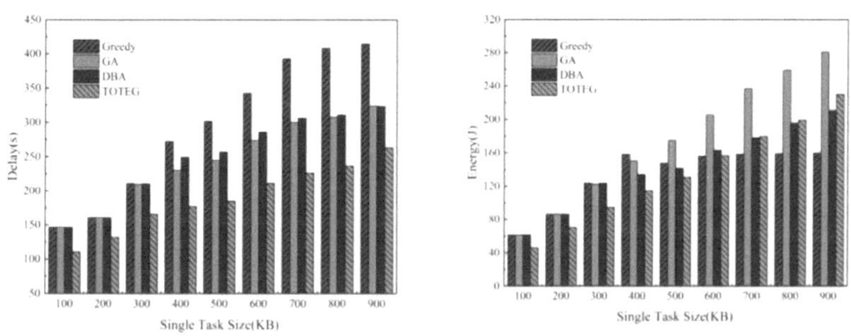

(a) (b)

Fig. 7. The impact of single task size

5.6 Impact of Task Quantity

Figure 8(a) illustrates the offloading delay for each method under varying task quantities. It is evident from the figure that as the task quantity increases, the overall offloading delay progressively increases. Specifically, the increase in offloading delay is most pronounced for the Greedy method, followed by DBA. While GA performs better than DBA, it still falls short compared to TOTEG. This disparity can be attributed primarily to the presence of malicious tasks, which consume resources and cause legitimate tasks to remain in a waiting state for extended periods. For TOTEG, as the comprehensive trust of malicious tasks will not exceed the trust threshold. Consequently, the increase in offloading delay remains relatively minimal. Specifically, when the number of tasks increased to 1000, the performance disparity between the greedy algorithm and TOTEG widened to 41.28%. This demonstrates that TOTEG exhibits superior stability and effectively mitigates the adverse impact of malicious tasks on offloading delay.

Figure 8(b) illustrates the impact of task quantity on energy consumption. As depicted, TOTEG exhibits superior performance compared to other methods. Conversely, the Greedy algorithm demonstrates the highest energy consumption, with the Genetic Algorithm following closely behind. While DBA performs better than both Greedy and Genetic Algorithm, it remains inferior to TOTEG. Notably, as the number of tasks surpasses 600, DBA's performance progressively converges towards that of TOTEG but does not surpass it. The findings suggest that within a task count of 600, TOTEG effectively mitigates malicious task interference, thereby avoiding resource occupation and achieving significant reductions in energy consumption.

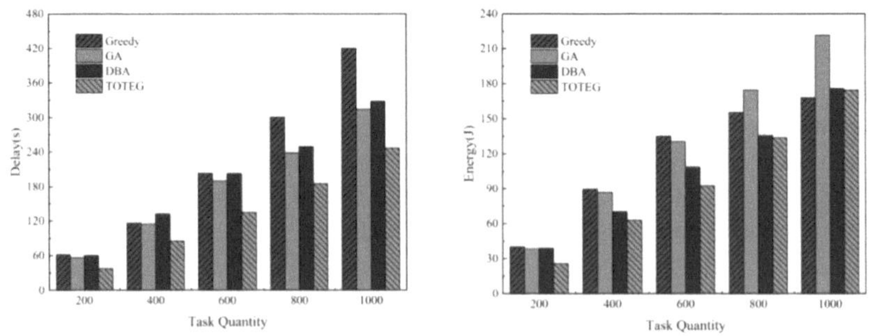

(a) (b)

Fig. 8. The impact of task quality

5.7 Impact of Malicious Task

Figure 9 illustrates the impact of proportions of malicious tasks on four key system metrics for the TOTEG, Greedy, DBA, and GA methods. These metrics are offloading success rate, system overhead, delay, and energy consumption.

The success rate is defined as the ratio of successfully completed tasks to the total number of tasks in a given network and task environment. Even when the proportion of malicious tasks is high, TOTEG maintains a relatively stable offloading success rate. When the proportion of malicious tasks reaches 50%, TOTEG's success rate is 46.3% higher than DBA's. In contrast, Greedy, DBA, and GA see significant drops in their success rates as the number of malicious tasks increases. TOTEG can do this because it conducts comprehensive trust evaluation on node behavior and tasks. This evaluation helps filter out unreliable false tasks and reject their offloading requests. It also ensures offloading tasks are allocated to the most suitable computing resources.

In terms of system overhead, Greedy, DBA, and GA have a steady increase in total overhead as the proportion of malicious tasks goes up. This is because malicious tasks disrupt normal offloading processes. But TOTEG filters out malicious tasks effectively. This leads to a gradual drop in its system overhead.

For the delay, Greedy, DBA, and GA do not have a trust evaluation strategy. Their offloading delay increases as malicious tasks become more common. The reason is that malicious tasks interfere with offloading, take over resources, and reduce performance.

TOTEG is different—it has an integrated trust evaluation mechanism. This mechanism filters out most malicious tasks, so TOTEG's total offloading delay tends to decrease.

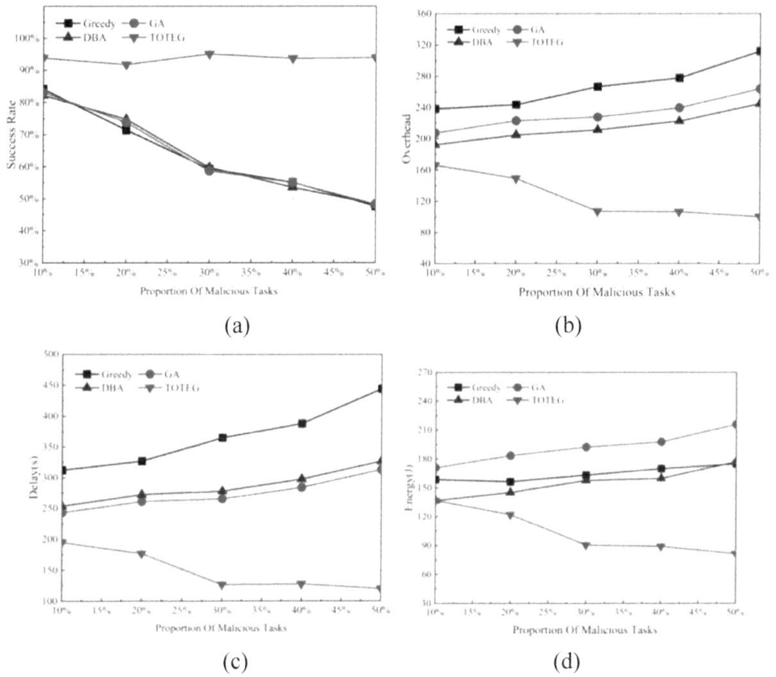

Fig. 9. The impact of the proportion of malicious tasks

Regarding energy consumption, the Greedy, DBA, and GA methods see rising energy consumption as the proportion of malicious tasks increases. Among them, Greedy is relatively less affected. GA and DBA are affected to a similar degree. TOTEG uses its trust evaluation mechanism to identify and filter out false tasks. So, its energy consumption goes down as the proportion of malicious tasks rises.

6 Conclusion

In this paper, we propose a trustworthy task offloading scheme based on tournament and elitist genetic algorithm with the vehicle-edge-cloud cooperation architecture. In this scheme, we consider malicious task interference, offloading overhead, delay and energy consumption. In order to achieve the optimal offloading decision, we use the trust mechanism to filter false and malicious tasks, and improve the genetic algorithm to obtain the offloading decision iteratively. The real-world simulation results prove that TOTEG outperforms the benchmark methods in many aspects. In the future work, we will discuss the decay trend of node and task trust over time, and incorporate it into the decision-making basis. In addition, we will further evaluate its applicability in increasingly complex scenarios.

Acknowledgements. This work was supported by National Natural Science Foundation of China under Grant 62402063, 62302062, 62372068 and 62372067, the Natural Science Foundation of Hunan Province under Grant 2024JJ6067, 2025JJ50371, 2025JJ50372, 2023JJ40081.

References

1. Deng, X., Wang, L., Gui, J., et al.: A review of 6G autonomous intelligent transportation systems: mechanisms, applications and challenges. J. Syst. Archit. 102929 (2023)
2. Sun, G., Wang, Z., Su, H., et al.: Profit maximization of independent task offloading in MEC-enabled 5G internet of vehicles. IEEE Trans. Intell. Transp. Syst. **25**(11), 16449–16461 (2024)
3. Wang, X., Alassafi, M.O., Alsaadi, F.E., et al.: Enabling efficient vehicle-road cooperation through AIoT: a deep learning approach to computational offloading. IEEE Internet Things J. **11**(22), 36127–36139 (2024)
4. Argote-Cabañero, J., Christofa, E., Skabardonis, A.: Connected vehicle penetration rate for estimation of arterial measures of effectiveness. Transp. Res. Part C Emerg. Technol. **60**, 298–312 (2015)
5. Aldhanhani, T., Abraham, A., Hamidouche, W., Shaaban, M.: Future trends in smart green IoV: vehicle-to-everything in the era of electric vehicles. IEEE Open J. Veh. Technol. **5**, 278–297 (2024)
6. Wu, M., Song, Q., Guo, L., et al.: Energy-efficient secure computation offloading in wireless powered mobile edge computing systems. IEEE Trans. Veh. Technol. **72**(5), 6907–6912 (2023)
7. Pang, S., Hou, L., Gui, H., et al.: Multi-mobile vehicles task offloading for vehicle-edge-cloud collaboration: a dependency-aware and deep reinforcement learning approach. Comput. Commun. **213**, 359–371 (2024)
8. Binh, T.H., Vo, H., Nguyen, B.M., et al.: Reinforcement learning for optimizing delay-sensitive task offloading in vehicular edge-cloud computing. IEEE Internet Things J. **11**(2), 2058–2069 (2023)
9. Fotia, L., Delicato, F., Fortino, G.: Trust in edge-based internet of things architectures: state of the art and research challenges. ACM Comput. Surv. **55**(9), 1–34 (2023)
10. Tan, L., Feng, L., Dán, G., Törngren, M.: Decentralized convex optimization for joint task offloading and resource allocation of vehicular edge computing systems. IEEE Trans. Veh. Technol. **71**(12), 13226–13241 (2022)
11. Kuang, Z., Li, L., Gao, J., Zhao, L., Liu, A.: Partial offloading scheduling and power allocation for mobile edge computing systems. IEEE Internet Things J. **6**(4), 6774–6785 (2019)
12. Liu, L., Feng, J., Mu, X., et al.: Asynchronous deep reinforcement learning for collaborative task computing and on-demand resource allocation in vehicular edge computing. IEEE Trans. Intell. Transp. Syst. **24**(12), 15513–15526 (2023)
13. Lee, H., Choi, S.I., Lee, S.H., et al.: Distributed task offloading in mobile edge computing with virtual machines. IEEE Internet Things J. **11**(13), 24083–24097 (2024)
14. Zhao, W., Cheng, Y., Liu, Z., et al.: Asynchronous DRL based multi-hop task offloading in RSU-assisted IoV networks. IEEE Trans. Cogn. Commun. Network. **11**(1), 546–555 (2024)
15. Wu, J., Tang, M., Jiang, C., et al.: Cloud-edge-end collaborative task offloading in vehicular edge networks: a multi-layer deep reinforcement learning approach. IEEE Internet Things J. **11**(22), 36272–36290 (2024)
16. Gu, L., Cui, M., Xu, L., et al.: Collaborative offloading method for digital twin empowered cloud edge computing on internet of vehicles. Tsinghua Sci. Technol. **28**(3), 433–451 (2022)

17. Zeng, F., Zhang, K., Wu, L., et al.: Efficient caching in vehicular edge computing based on edge-cloud collaboration. IEEE Trans. Veh. Technol. **72**(2), 2468–2481 (2022)
18. Hu, H., Wu, D., Zhou, F., et al.: Intelligent resource allocation for edge-cloud collaborative networks: a hybrid DDPG-D3QN approach. IEEE Trans. Veh. Technol. **72**(8), 10696–10709 (2023)
19. Ni, Z., Chen, H., Li, Z., et al.: MSCET: a multi-scenario offloading schedule for biomedical data processing and analysis in cloud-edge-terminal collaborative vehicular networks. IEEE/ACM Trans. Comput. Biol. Bioinf. **20**(4), 2376–2386 (2021)
20. Sohaib, M., Jeon, S.W., Yu, W.: Hybrid online–offline learning for task offloading in mobile edge computing systems. IEEE Trans. Wireless Commun. **23**(7), 6873–6888 (2023)
21. Min, M., Liu, Z., Duan, J., et al.: Safe-learning-based location-privacy-preserved task offloading in mobile edge computing. Electronics **13**(1), 89 (2023)
22. Ruan, Y., Durresi, A., Uslu, S.: Trust assessment for internet of things in multi-access edge computing. In: 2018 IEEE 32nd International conference on advanced information networking and applications (AINA), pp. 1155–1161. IEEE (2018)
23. Chen, J., Wang, X., Shen, X.: Goal-driven trusted collaborator selection and task offloading in dynamic collaborative systems. IEEE Internet Things J. **12**(7), 8537–8551 (2024)
24. Mao, M., Hu, T., Zhao, W.: Reliable task offloading mechanism based on trusted roadside unit service for internet of vehicles. Ad Hoc Netw. **139**, 103045 (2023)
25. Wang, Z., Liu, S., Guo, B., et al.: CrowdLearning: a decentralized distributed training framework based on collectives of trusted AIoT devices. IEEE Trans. Mob. Comput. **23**(12), 13420–13437 (2024)
26. Bai, J., Gui, J., Huang, G., et al.: A lowcost UAV task offloading scheme based on trustable and trackable data routing. IEEE Trans. Intell. Veh. **9**(9), 5797–5812 (2023)
27. Cao, T., Yi, J., Wang, X., et al.: Interaction trust-driven data distribution for vehicle social networks: a matching theory approach. IEEE Trans. Comput. Soc. Syst. **11**(3), 4071–4086 (2024)
28. Beijing City Lab, 2014, Data 30, Parking places of Beijing. http://www.beijingcitylab.org
29. Beijing City Lab, 2014, Data 4, T-Drive Taxi Trajectories. http://www.beijingcitylab.org
30. Chen, C., Zeng, Y., Li, H., et al.: A multihop task offloading decision model in MEC-enabled internet of vehicles. IEEE Internet Things J. **10**(4), 3215–3230 (2022)

Author Index

L. Zhang and K.-K. R. Choo (Eds.): MobiQuitous 2025, LNICST 683, pp. 487–488, 2026.
https://doi.org/10.1007/978-3-032-22500-9

MIX
Papier aus verantwortungsvollen Quellen
Paper from responsible sources
FSC® C105338

If you have any concerns about our products,
you can contact us on
ProductSafety@springernature.com

In case Publisher is established outside the EU,
the EU authorized representative is:
Springer Nature Customer Service Center GmbH
Europaplatz 3, 69115 Heidelberg, Germany

Printed by Libri Plureos GmbH
in Hamburg, Germany